THE
FEDERAL
ROLE
IN
URBAN MASS
TRANSPORTATION

THE
FEDERAL
ROLE
IN
URBAN MASS
TRANSPORTATION

George M. Smerk

*Indiana
University
Press*

BLOOMINGTON AND INDIANAPOLIS

The paper used in this publication meets the minimum requirements of American
National Standard for Information Sciences—Permanence of Paper for Printed
Library Materials, ANSI Z39.48-1984.

Manufactured in the United States of America

Library of Congress Cataloging-in-Publication Data

Smerk, George M.
The federal role in urban mass transportation / George M. Smerk.
p.   cm.
Includes bibliographical references (p.).
ISBN 0-253-35283-5 (alk. paper)
1. Local transit—Government policy—United States.   2. Urban
transportation policy—United States.   I. Title.
HE4461.S64   1991
388.4'068—dc20   90-34510
                                                                CIP

1 2 3 4 5   95 94 93 92 91

CONTENTS

Tables

Acknowledgments

My thanks to my many friends in the urban mass transportation community who shared their knowledge and insights with me over the years. Special thanks to my colleagues over the last twenty years at the Indiana University Institute for Urban Transportation who provided support, knowledge, experience, and an unbeatable can-do spirit. My deep appreciation and thanks to Anita Goldman and Cheryll Fifer-Brown who typed and word-processed this material in its countless versions.

My deepest and warmest thanks to my wife, Mary Ann, who read and commented and encouraged me in dealing with this book in all of its versions and variations over thirty years.

THE
FEDERAL
ROLE
IN
URBAN MASS
TRANSPORTATION

To Mary Ann
Super wife and super Editor-in-Chief

1.

Federal Mass Transportation Policy: Transit in Transition

Why is there a federal role in urban mass transportation in the United States? This is a simple question with a complex answer. As the following pages will relate in some detail, the federal transit program is a policy and an activity that arose in the 1960s as a result of a perceived crisis and at a time when the attitude of the nation, as expressed in federal action, was one of seeking equity not just in matters relating to urban transportation, but in many areas of concern.

As is often the case in governmental activity in a democracy, the federal transit policy developed during a time of profound change in cities and urban places; yet the change was not, and still is not, fully perceived and most certainly not fully understood. The world is moving toward an epoch of many large cities (perhaps this familiar term isn't really the most accurate word, because "city" summons up images that may not be valued at present, but it will suffice for now), urban places of a size and structure for which we have no real models from the past. The United States and what has happened here may well be surrogates for real knowledge and understanding of complicated urban events on a world-wide scale. In any event, in the 1960s there was finally a realization that urban changes were taking place and that there were problems in urban transportation. It was then that a federal mass transit policy arose to undertake to solve those problems.

At the hands of national administrations and Congresses generally committed to equity and a sense of even-handed treatment (a fair hope, of course, but never fully realized or even realizable) and to providing opportunities for citizens to participate in the economic, social, and cultural benefits of American society, the federal urban mass transportation program grew substantially in its scope of activities and in the dollars spent on transit by the federal government. From the 1960s until the 1980s, the program found increasing support in Congress and from the beneficiaries of programs on the local level. In the 1980s, the federal transit program faltered at the hands of a presidential administration less interested in equity than in promoting the growth of the private sector and in relying more strictly on the market mechanism unfettered by subsidies. There is no doubt that the temper of the times helped to create and shape the policies and the programs as they have evolved over the years. At a different period in American life the outcome would probably have been vastly different.

The late 1950s and early 1960s, then, were a very different period in government than later decades. The mass transportation program began its life during a period when the nation first began to focus on urban problems as features of a unique landscape of difficulties that were not amenable to mindsets or to solutions attempted or even adopted for other problems. When the federal transit aid program started, there had been virtually no thought given to public support of transit by state or local governments, except for a few large cities. In a very real sense, the federal action began before there was widespread, grass-roots pressure for a federal aid program for mass transportation.

Since 1960, support of mass transit and other support by state and local governments has risen greatly to become very large indeed in many cases. At times, the reason for this growth has been the withdrawal or slackening of federal support after federal leadership had initially pointed the way. In any event, coeval with the development of the federal role in transit, state and local government has come increasingly to deal with the complex and difficult problems of cities in an urbanized and industrialized society. In the 1980s, the private sector saw the opportunity and took up the challenge of cooperative transit ventures with government in urban areas in a way vital to urban well-being and simultaneously constructive and useful to all citizens. In many instances, competitive private enterprise is providing transit services at a cost to the public that is lower than transit service provided solely by publicly owned and operated agencies.

The great virtue of mass transit is that it has the capability to move large numbers of people using relatively little space. Because it is parsimonious in the use of space and capacious in carrying throngs of people, mass transportation is absolutely vital to the existence of large cities; without transit, really large, concentrated cities could not function without undergoing major restructuring and large expenditures of capital, which would substantially change the built environment. Mass transit is decidedly advantageous for cities of moderate size and can be vital to many of the inhabitants but it may not be absolutely essential to the functioning of urban life. Transit may be only marginally useful in small urban or non-urban places, where its value may be primarily for a very specialized clientele who, for many reasons, may not have ready access to other means of transportation.

The mass transportation program administered by the Urban Mass Transportation Administration (UMTA) is unique in that it is the only subdivision of the U.S. Department of Transportation that is justified by the Welfare Clause rather than by the Interstate Commerce Clause of the Constitution. (The Welfare Clause is not a justification for womb-to-tomb security for panhandlers and the undeserving poor; rather, it is the rationale for the activities of the national government that promote life, liberty, and the pursuit of happiness by the citizenry.) A result of this justification is that the benefits of transit are often obscure and hard to tie down objectively and precisely. Lamentably, there is little research on the values of transit that is reliable and comprehensive. It becomes a matter of political calculus rather than scientific measure.

Given the kind of complex and pluralistic society the U.S. has, transit may help in the achievement of many goals, but its effectiveness is muted and modified by politics and by the way that U.S. democracy and its attitudes and prejudices toward control affect strong action to reach certain objectives. Transit, given this disposition on all levels of American government (excepting in times of crisis), as well as the absence of supportive policies, programs and efforts, is not very effective in doing things and achieving ends other than moving people. While it incidentally may promote fuel savings, reductions in pollution, decongestion of cities, diminishing unemployment, and a host of other good works, it is not a particularly potent way of achieving much more by itself. Indeed, it appears that the only way the full potential of transit may be reached is through a level of planning and implementation of urban development that is foreign to American tastes. A necessary complement would be control of transportation demand by means of a program prohibiting auto use or adopting various schemes to diminish it, such as full-cost pricing of parking. This sort of action would be politically unpalatable in the extreme; at the least, it would be viewed as an infringement on personal freedom and perhaps would involve a substantial increase in the personal cost of driving a car.

The federal transit program, especially the federal investment in rail facilities, has been thoroughly condemned by many economists as not being cost-effective. Yet the programs are just as soundly lauded by politicians who perhaps see benefits to themselves and to the voters that may be obscure to the economists of today but may have been well understood by the political economists of times past. However intended, much of the criticism has been constructive in result, and a tendency toward more careful analysis of transit investments has developed.

The federal mass transit programs came into being and developed during a time when it was becoming necessary to redefine the city. The old, tightly built city of high density, with one central and highly vigorous focal point that had resulted from the implosion of population, economic, and industrial activity in the nineteenth century, had given way to the concept and reality of the new metropolitan area: large in size, thin in population density, often obscure in its lineaments, and containing a large number of major focal points instead of one dominating central business district. This has been perhaps the hardest of all the changes to deal with, because while it can be called a metropolitan area (or an "urbanized area" in the language of the U.S. Census Bureau), there is no governmental unit that fits the newly evolved body. The tight social, economic, and cultural ties that defined a city as much as did its political or physical borders have weakened, and it is still not clear if anything has replaced those bonds. This is a concern, not for reasons of civic boosterism or chauvinism, but because of the important identification of citizenship to residents of a nation or of a place within a national setting.

The great change in American cities has occurred mainly since the First World War and has been stimulated by personal devices for an ideal living environment and anointed by federal housing and highway policies. The "metropolitan area," "exurbs," and "techno-burbs" are names given to highly urban but relatively low-density places that, to the dismay of many residents and observers, lack the coherent form of past cities and from a transportation viewpoint appear to float on a sea of automobile traffic.

The piling up of large numbers of people in cities was a commonplace event, a product of the alteration in production that is most often called the Industrial Revolution. That revolution spawned major changes in transportation and population distribution. Cities of the early industrial age, in the nineteenth century, grew rapidly and were largely shaped by public transportation. As the cities expanded in population, that new population geared itself to public transportation. In the absence of widely available private transportation, the inhabitants gathered themselves close to the arteries of the streetcar system and, later, to the rapid transit lines in the largest cities. Even as the large industrial cities were gaining in population and economic vigor, there were the first stirrings of suburban development as a small number of middle-class and upper-middle-class people established permanent homes outside the city. With the post–Civil War development of commuter railroad service and with the late nineteenth-century construction of electric streetcars and interurban lines that pushed out beyond the densely populated central city, the suburbs became more democratic and attracted more citizens with limited financial resources. The commuter railroad and streetcar suburbs were established and flourished because of their connection with the central city by means of public transportation. Thus, people might have lived in the suburbs, but they were tied economically, as well as socially and culturally, to the central city and its central business district.

The move of population beyond the suburbs oriented to public transportation began in the 1920s. The arrival of the automobile permitted many people to live outside the range of public transportation. The Great Depression of the 1930s and the Second World War slowed down the population movement to this newly automobile-oriented suburb. Then, after the Second World War, America's urbanized population burst the bonds of the old public transportation-oriented suburbs to produce a new kind of urban place and society that was not umbilically connected to a central city. Residences and the entire spectrum of economic activity came to exist within the orbit of the old central city, but were free-floating rather than directly attached to it. Today, much of the travel within the larger metropolitan areas goes between these new urban places and is borne almost entirely by the private automobile, because the density for effective and efficient public transportation is lacking. Except in the most casual, fitful, or unusual instances, there may be but little personal relationship between the dwellers in much of the metropolitan area and the central city.

The changes in American cities in recent times were joined by major changes in the provision of urban mass transportation. Since 1945, the public transportation industry of the U.S. has changed from primarily a regulated private enterprise for profit to a public enterprise. This alteration in ownership at first was largely stimulated by infusions of federal money and eventually by significant contributions of state and local funds. The reason for the change was the lack of profitability of private transit firms and the real threat that there would be no public transportation available in urban places if the defection of passengers to the suburbs and their cars continued to escalate.

Despite the changes in ownership and the public dollars that have been spent, the transit industry remains troubled. There are a number of reasons for this, which include high labor and equipment costs, historic lack of investment, poor marketing, pork-barrel politics, heavy subsidies to the automobile owner, and erratic public policy. Additionally, a major part of the transit problem is ascribable to its inability to serve the new type of metropolitan living. By the 1980s, it was no longer indubitable that mass transportation was truly relevant and useful in urbanized areas. Not so many years ago, mass transportation was often viewed as an unalloyed solution to transportation congestion in urban areas. The 1980s saw the stirrings of doubt regarding this belief begin to arise.

The times of the transit program chronicled in these pages are probably unparalleled with regard to the combined private and public investment in America's cities and in the creation of spectacular and homely (in the true sense of that word) places of great vigor and excitement, as well as places of often breathtaking beauty with an ability to stir the emotions. Yet the times are also quite possibly unparalleled in the mounting squalor found in U.S. cities. American urban locales in the 1980s may be historically unmatched in this country as places of crime, substance addiction, meanness, filth and decay, and as harbors of the despondence of human beings who are deprived of hope, crushed by ignorance and despair, and preyed upon in all the urban ugliness by both human and inhuman vermin. America's cities can be both very good and very bad places to live in.

Policy is not formed in a vacuum; there are forces at work in the effort to find solutions to perceived problems, and there are ups and downs to be traced. Having followed these programs for several decades, this author has come to two conclusions: (1) the federal transit programs tenaciously cling to life; and (2) transit is a tool for a better urban life that has not heretofore been used effectively enough.

What follows is a study of the development of federal transit policy. It is also the story of an industry that has changed markedly since the beginnings of federal policy. What has been accomplished, the barriers to greater accomplishments, and the problems that remain will also be pointed out before this story ends.

Easy to condemn as a waste of tax money and easy to praise as a boon to urban life and development, transit and the programs promoting it on all levels of government generate both opposition and support contained in controversy. This book will make the best effort possible to understand the setting of the times in which the policy and programs in transit were formulated and carried out in the second half of the twentieth century.

2.

Urban Mass Transit in the Mid–1980s

INTRODUCTION: THE BLOOM IS OFF THE ROSE

The year 1985 is an opportune vantage point from which to view federal attitudes toward urban mass transportation. By that year, the federal programs in urban mass transportation were almost a quarter-century old. Since 1961, these programs had evolved into a broad spectrum of federal aid to urban mass transportation. Along the way, the federal efforts had stimulated substantial participation by state and local government in the process of continually improving and supporting urban mass transportation. The transit industry, in 1960 a sick and seriously declining business operating over-age equipment and suffering from rapidly waning patronage, had by 1985 become a growing industry once more. If not in ebullient health, patronage was rising after some recessionary downturns in the early 1980s, many new facilities were in operation, and billions of public dollars were being spent on transit each year.

Even so, the mid–1980s were a time of contraction for the federal transit program. One would expect that a 25-year-old federal program would be pretty well established and institutionalized within the federal government. Yet, there was the cliff-hanger element concerning the federal transit programs as the Reagan administration (1980-88) regularly attempted to make profound cuts in the federal budget for transit and even to move to eliminate the program completely. There was small comfort on the part of the staff within the agency responsible for the program, the Urban Mass Transportation Administration of the U.S. Department of Transportation, and morale was at an all-time low. It was also a time of tension in the relationship between the federal government and the mass transit programs of the client cities. It was, indeed, perhaps a watershed period in the evolution of policy and perhaps in the advanced stages of devolution of that policy.

The Reagan administration made it clear that it wanted to do away with what it deemed to be the "unseemly federal role in mass transportation." In his 1986 budget testimony before Congress, David Stockman, head of the Office of Management and Budget, was playing his role as the Reagan administration's Charon to conduct offensive federal programs to the underworld to which conservative doctrinal purity had condemned them; massive contraction of the program was proposed in the budget. Amtrak and the mass transit programs were high on the administration's hit list. This was not a new effort on Mr. Stockman's part, and although Tom Wicker of *The New York Times* reported that Stockman had thrown a tantrum in the hearings, he handled a difficult job well. Congress was not amused.[1]

Even higher in the federal establishment, President Reagan himself decided to pick on the newly opened and still incomplete Miami Metro Rail Rapid Transit System as an example of a bad choice for the use of federal dollars (indeed, in a State of the Union address). The anecdotal remark that it would have been cheaper to buy limousines for everyone than to build the Miami rapid transit line did not help build the confidence of the Metro Rail system's employees and proponents.[2] It was a far cry from Lyndon Johnson's participation in turning over the first spade of earth for the beginning of construction on the San Francisco Bay Area Rapid Transit District and the Washington Metro rapid transit line. Amtrak and mass transit, as it turned out, were, in the eyes of this administration, a litmus test; if such programs, which were billed as being the darlings of the big spenders, could be eliminated, there was in the minds of administration stalwarts, indeed, a hope of reducing the disastrously high federal deficit.

The administration's position regarding transit bore witness to the sad fact that the nation was faced with the monstrous issue of the stunning level of the federal deficit, which reached $200 billion of red ink in fiscal 1985. There were appeals to patriotism on the emotional level and more serious and rational calls to do something to bring the nation's budget more into balance. Clearly, cuts of such magnitude—Amtrak would have been eliminated at one fell swoop and the transit program would have been dispensed with over a short period of time— symbolized the perceived worthlessness of these programs. Beauty is in the eye of the beholder, however, for the transit programs had been supported by other administrations, and had been highly valued by Congress. Furthermore, mass transportation was seen as a bipartisan issue rather than as a special darling of the Democrats in Congress or in the White House. The strongest support for transit programs came in the administrations of Presidents Nixon and Ford, and the transit program had always enjoyed very solid support from Republicans in Congress.

SOME OBSERVATIONS OF THE TRANSIT SCENE

In contrast to the ill will of the Reagan administration toward the federal role in mass transit and toward mass transit in general, 1985 was a year of major positive transit happenings. While there were the usual more or less routine purchases of additional or replacement buses, as well as dedications of new maintenance and office facilities and downtown bus terminals, most of the big news focused on the rail transit openings. These were generally cheerful events, in marked contrast to the prevailing transit gloom at the Urban Mass Transportation Administration (UMTA) in Washington. For example, after many years of dithering about, and many years of careful planning, not to mention years of construction, Pittsburgh finally got its first downtown subway. The opening of this underground light rapid transit line was greeted with enthusiasm and artwork. The three underground stations were tastefully decorated with the deliberate intention to create civic beauty and a civilized atmosphere in the subway. The construction of this subway, which finally removed the streetcars from the congested downtown Pittsburgh streets, had strong support from the business community. Civic leaders in Pittsburgh are known less for giddy flights of fancy than for solid investments in the present and future of their city.[3]

Miami had some things to cheer about even though it was the target of public presidential disdain. The Miami system has operated relatively smoothly and has won acclaim for the attractiveness of its equipment and other facilities. The invective hurled by the Chief Executive was rather rare because it is unusual for a president to pick out a particular project in a particular city for attack. Admittedly, the Miami Metro Rail System was carrying far less than the number of people that had been predicted. The projections, however, had been made on the expectation of no additional parking space in downtown Miami, gasoline at $2.00 a gallon, fares at 50 cents, and the operation of the complete system, including the downtown "peoplemover" that links the elevated rapid transit line with the heart of the Miami central business district. A number of additional parking spaces (about 6,000) were added to downtown Miami; the price of gasoline went much lower than $2.00 per gallon, and the fare on the Metro was a dollar. Moreover, if the Miami system was moving only 17,000 riders a day at the time instead of the predicted 100,000 (not a statistic calculated to bring cheer to the supporters of rail transit) the fact that the system wasn't even finished yet might have given pause to the contempt thrust at it. While the first part of the Miami system opened in the spring of 1984, it was not until the spring of 1985 that the whole length of the first phase of the rapid transit line was open. The automated peoplemover system was not finished until 1986. To those who were knowledgeable about the situation, the comments about Miami's rapid transit system made by President Reagan seemed a cheap shot.[4]

In Boston, the long-awaited extension of the Massachusetts Bay Transportation Authority's Red Line subway through Cambridge and on to Alewife station in Somerville was cheered happily, and politicians beamed for the cameras as ribbons were cut. Engineering and architecture groups liked what they saw well enough to give MBTA an award for the distinction and engineering of the stations. Attractive stations in artwork and design were, as in Pittsburgh, examples of civic pride. Meanwhile, the more mundane process of rerailing large portions of the Red Line and Green Line subway were under way and were also the subject of celebration in the Hub City.[5]

In Philadelphia, the likewise long-awaited airport high speed line was finally opened in the spring of 1985. This airport commuter rail line was originally supposed to be ready for the 1976 bicentennial celebration. (It is not true that it was supposed to open for the 1876 centennial, the sarcastic remarks of spoil-sports to the contrary.) Despite the happiness, some observers wondered why the service was only operating on half-hourly headways. Perhaps it was a classic example of a procrustean bed; all the Philadelphia commuter lines are connected together and they run on half-hour headways throughout much of the day, ergo half-hour service to the airport. An even larger project in the Quaker City that opened at about the same time was the center-city commuter rail tunnel. This project linked the former Pennsylvania Railroad electric commuter rail lines with those of the Reading Company.[6]

Yet another long-awaited cheerful event took place in the mid–1980s at the east end of Lake Erie: the Buffalo light rapid transit subway and surface line opened in May 1985. Even though the line was not completely finished at the date of the opening—the two stations nearest the State University of New York at Buffalo were not completed in time—after two weeks of regular revenue service, approximately 13,000 to 15,000 daily riders were using the new light rail, and this level of ridership was realized even before the restructuring of the bus system to feed into the rail line. The subway stations were also decorated with artwork, far removed from the civic eyesores that typically characterize rapid transit stations in the U.S.[7]

There was, however, some bad transit news in 1985. For example, in Chicago, furious bus patrons were literally steaming because of windows that did not open. The Chicago Transit Authority (CTA) had thrown in the towel (no pun intended) and indicated that it was no longer able to maintain the air conditioners in the buses. Many of these vehicles had sealed windows and the heat was unbearable in hot summer conditions. A program to replace the sealed windows with windows that opened was running many months behind schedule. The newspapers were also quick to jump on the apparent replacement of competent professionals at the CTA by political hacks. But there was good news here as well; the O'Hare extension of the CTA rapid transit line saw its millionth passenger in May of 1985, about three months earlier than had been expected.[8]

If there was a great deal of activity in many cases, there was also general unhappiness within the transit community about the way the Urban Mass Transportation Administration had slowed down parceling out the federal transit money. The leadership at UMTA had apparently taken seriously the administration's proposed policies toward transit. The perception was that UMTA dragged its heels unmercifully on funding anything that was not in the budget that David Stockman had introduced. The Reagan administration was denying the need and the justification for the federal transit program and was taking the position that transit was the responsibility of state and local governments. Congress, however, had not acquiesced to this position and complained. Although the transit industry was increasing pressure on the lower levels of government to act, UMTA was not funding projects that had been approved earlier and for which there were funds available. A note of desperate interest was added to the hapless UMTA bureaucracy by the threat from on high to lay off a large number of UMTA employees even if Congress did give UMTA a full budget for fiscal 1986. Many of the best and most dedicated UMTA personnel were seeking jobs elsewhere. Spirits were at an all-time low, particularly in the ten regional UMTA offices that Stockman had proposed closing.

Again, 1985 was a year of vivid contrasts; if morale at UMTA was low, morale in Oregon was high, as the Portland light rail line moved ahead with construction along many parts of the route. San Diego, feeling strong and confident because of the success of the San Diego trolley, which had been in operation for about three years, pushed its eastward extension with vigor. In San Jose, the Guadalupe Corridor light rapid transit line through Silicon Valley was very well under way.[9]

If there was good news in Pittsburgh in the opening of the subway, there was also bad news financially. The Port Authority Transit threatened to shut down the whole of the service for part of June. An arrangement was finally made with the Pennsylvania Department of Transportation for an increase in state aid in return for a cut in operating aid through the elimination of some service.[10]

There was gloom in Detroit because the much-feted downtown peoplemover was faced with vast cost overruns and alleged mismanagement of construction. The construction got under way with enthusiasm, as the line circling through downtown Detroit was expected to play a role in helping to revive the partially derelict heart of the Motor City. A contract was signed with the U.S. branch of the Urban Transportation Development Corporation, a crown corporation of the Canadian Province of Ontario, to build the line and supply the rolling stock. However, construction fell behind schedule; there were reputed sloppy procedures and delays caused by a modification of the route and some stations, resulting in a significant cost escalation. The Detroit project was attacked by UMTA's administrator as an example of all that was wrong with the federal transit program.[11]

In April the *Wall Street Journal* published an article devoted to the subject of crowded highways, citing the appalling traffic jams of the time and predicting far worse to come in rapidly growing suburban areas.[12] What was particularly interesting about the article is that it could have been written 25 years earlier, in the late '50s or the very early '60s, at a time when the nation had not yet come to grips with urban problems in general or urban transportation problems in particular. Public officials were still in a total quandary, because the public apparently was unwilling to build more roads in the more built-up suburbs and because something had to be done to relieve the congestion. Had nothing really been learned in a quarter century?

Another contrast appeared, in the city most identified with the automobile as an essential part of life. In 1986, Los Angeles began to build a light rail transit line after years of study and analysis, paralysis by analysis, and the wonders of Proposition A. Proposition A supplied a 0.5 percent sales tax to help support mass transit. Los Angeles planned and intended to build an extensive light rail system with its own money. The first to be built was a line from downtown Los

Angeles to Long Beach, retracing the steps of the last rail service to be operated in Los Angeles. Another line, running east-west along the Century Freeway, would link together employment centers. A heavy rail line, with some hoped-for federal aid, was also expected to—and did—get under way in 1986. The return of rail transportation to what has been the quintessential auto-dominated city is and should be an eyebrow-raiser to those who seek clues as to what happens in a city that has just about reached the limits of highway transportation. The proposed heavy rapid transit line to be built (in the Wilshire corridor and then across the Hollywood Hills to North Hollywood and Van Nuys) was in some trouble; it depended on federal funding for construction, and UMTA was reluctant to provide the funds.[13]

In Texas, the Dallas Area Rapid Transit and the ambitious light rail system that was expected to eventually embrace over 200 miles of line, received a favorable vote in a referendum held in 1983. This project was locally financed. As with all things Texan, it was expected be a major venture, one that apparently was proceeding fairly smoothly after the citizens of Dallas agreed to tax themselves to carry out the project.[14] Subsequently, the steep downturn in the Texas oil-based economy and consequent quibbles and second thoughts delayed the construction. A referendum was held in June of 1988 on the issuance of bonds to get the money up front to move ahead rapidly on the rail line rather than pursue a pay-as-you-go method of financing. It was soundly rejected by voters.

If things were upbeat in Los Angeles and Dallas, two highly auto-oriented cities, the shelves and files were particularly well-filled in the mid–1980s with old and new tomes which suggested strongly that supporting mass transit did not make any sense any more—especially rail transit. Apparently, few city officials paid much attention.

Within all this, it is very clear that transit is a political issue as well as a transportation issue. Politicians on all levels of government see personal benefits as well as advantages to their constituents because of the very tangibility of transit, especially of rail transit. Emotions, understandably, tend to run high. Moreover, there are many facets of the political side of the issue. Indeed, there can be no one way to achieve an end—even if one knew what the end was—in a highly diverse, pluralistic democracy. The Reagan administration was providing strong encouragement for activity by the private sector in the mass transit field. Undoubtedly, the private sector could play a much larger role in providing mass transportation in the future than it has in the immediate past. At the same time, expecting too much of the private sector is probably either unwise or naive. The private sector abandoned transit, often at a profit, by selling out to public agencies. Many times there was no intent on the part of the private providers to continue to offer the service at a subsidy. This is not surprising, because public agencies seem to have trouble subsidizing private firms once the decision is made to provide public support. Even though Americans laud the private sector, in many cases they don't appear to support its subsidization to provide a needed service. Even so, the use of private-sector activity in public transportation is worth pushing if it helps reduce the cost of providing the service.[15]

Private-sector advocates take the position that competition would be good for urban mass transportation, and they cite the virtues of the generally healthy private sector of the economy. The administration's policy of thrusting transit and other activities back to state and local government was not necessarily a vote strictly in favor of private enterprise but rather one toward a different level of concern and control over transit investment. A contrast here is that the tax reform proposed by the president would not have provided a write-off of state and local taxes, so that local or state governments would have a decently reasonable political time in taking on the burden of programs turned over to them by the federal establishment. The argument was not that there should be no transit, but was over which level of government should supply the subsidy.[16]

When one turns from strictly contrasting issues to some general urban transportation considerations during the years around 1985, the situation becomes even muddier. One can even raise the question of whether or not the United States is interested in its cities. The waning interest of government on all levels and of scholars and other writers is apparent. There seem to be relatively few books written on urban issues and problems in the 1980s, whereas throughout the 1960s and 1970s there was a veritable torrent of urban-oriented writing. The books of the 1980s increasingly focus on suburban and exurban matters.

The lack of interest in urban affairs may bespeak a shrug of the shoulders; perhaps the problems of poverty, blight, crime, and ugliness are felt to be beyond control or solution. Perhaps it is just fatigue on the part of a body politic which is tired of books, newspapers, and radio and television telling of problems and mistakes, with victory for Americans as remote in the man-made jungles of many American cities as it was in the jungles of Viet Nam. Perhaps that war provides our analogy: When the precise purpose of an action is dim, or the solution apparently beyond grasping, and much treasure and manpower has been exhausted toward no real sense of victory, why not walk away from the nettlesome situation, leaving only the memory and the wreckage to show that we tried?

If there is some evidence of the U.S. walking away from difficulties, there is truly an abundance of vigor in many downtowns as more and more cities realize reinvestment in central locations. Public and private money in large quantities is going into cities as diverse as Baltimore and Indianapolis, Denver and Milwaukee. Perhaps somewhat late in the game of throwing away downtowns, people began to realize that the power of the built environment to move and attract people is large and that there is success for the investor who utilizes aged structures as an attractive and intriguing complement and counterpoint to new structures. If recent federal policy has a tone of being anti-city, there is evidence that the business community and the people realize cities are good business propositions. Often a transit investment has acted as a stimulating catalyst in hatching a revivifying downtown project.

Despite urban vigor of a traditional sort in a traditional urban setting, the patterns of significant growth are undeniably outside the urban centers. Public policy cannot ignore the conventional city; at the same time it cannot ignore the new types of urban-like growth in settings that are far from the norm. America is continuing to grow beyond sprawls in its old suburban context. Often called exurban, it is a growth pattern that sees a return to the small town and rural areas, which may be a development neither widely recognized nor appreciated as a trend to contend with. It promises to create challenges for which the nation as a whole and the subdivisions of government may not be prepared to face.

What is happening is not just a return to the small rural community of a romanticized past (as symbolized annually in Christmas cards) but an imposition of functions that are normally associated with the downtowns (or other parts) of cities. Office parks are sprouting in cornfields far removed from any major or even minor metropolitan center. Factories are increasingly footloose; they are no longer tied by necessity to rail service—although they may be served by rail—and increasingly the inbound and outbound goods are moved in the main by the ubiquitous truck on the ever-expanding network of highways. Substantial office developments are springing up in non-traditional places.

It is a clear trend that many of the best and the brightest Americans are increasingly spreading out to live in places beyond what is customarily considered to be urban or metropolitan in nature. Electronic communications assure these new frontiersmen that the links with metropolitan America are not severed. Therefore, they are able to pursue occupations that once were the sole province of metropolitan areas. People can live far apart and far afield and not be strangers to what is going on in society, but in so doing they can also choose not to be embroiled in the difficulties that are the focus of so many of the problems of traditional urban society.

The people who are choosing to live far away from cities and urban problems are most often well-educated and relatively well-off financially. They are choosing the small town or rural setting for a quality of life that apparently seems foreclosed to them in the older, traditional larger urbanized areas and the traditional suburb and metropolitan areas. In deserting the urban and metropolitan setting for a more rural dwelling place, this population still demands urban services, such as police and fire protection, water, sewage, and trash collection. This is a form of development that challenges traditional government and politics because the services are demanded in places without the means or organization to meet the needs easily. Escape from one set of problems into a new Arcadia is creating new problems that state and local governments may be hard pressed to meet.

Mass transit policy, federal or otherwise, is not terribly relevant to this type of development and what it may portend for the future of the nation. Nevertheless, there is still plenty of work for transit to do, because this more widespread dispersal of population has not solved the problems of urban mobility. There are still people to move into the customary urban and metropolitan settings, and there are still significant mobility impediments and related difficulties to be tackled. Urban mass transportation has a role to play in improving the quality of American life. Federal transit policy and programs, in partnership with state and local governments and the private sector, must work to solve urban transportation problems.[17]

THE PATH AHEAD

The start of federal programs in mass transit, under the Housing Act of 1961, was a significantly positive change in the attitude of government in the United States toward urban mass transportation. In the lexicon of those things that are thought of as private, transit was clearly *supposed* to be a private enterprise for profit. It had been so since 1830, when the first omnibuses ran in New York City. In the 1950s there were many opportunities for state and local governments to help arrest or modify the decline of privately owned urban mass transportation, particularly early in the game before the atrophy became serious. But in those days of largely inexperienced alternatives to private ownership, little was done. The attractiveness of the automobile as a means of urban transportation was a critical factor in weakening mass transit and its private provision. The consequences of allowing transit to disappear or those of dramatically cutting back on service were ignored in most places and by most people on the simple maxim that if the free market doesn't provide a good or service, it isn't needed. Unconsidered was the notion that as long ago as the 1920s, federal aid as well as aid from other levels of government to roads made it inevitable that transit would probably have to be a public venture. The eventual public ownership and operation of mass transit was not at all an ideological issue but a practical reaction to a practical problem—the local bus system was going out of business. The threat brought the action.

During the quarter-century of federal urban mass transportation programs, that effort has gone through a number of stages. It began as a small program in 1961, with insufficient support in Congress to warrant its being a bill all of its own; mass transit aid in the shape of a demonstration program and a low-interest loan program had to be put well within the Housing Act of 1961 in order to pass the Congress. The small program gathered momentum enough to warrant its own Act in 1964. In the 1970s, the federal transit program became a large, broad-scoped program supporting virtually every facet of mass transportation. In the 1980s, with the coming of the Reagan administration and its different attitude toward government, the urban mass transportation program was seriously threatened. Despite the conflict between the Congress and the White House, the transit program, even though the expenditures have been cut back, has persevered under difficult conditions.[18]

The intention of this work is to review the development of the federal transit program over time. Because it is difficult to imagine why something is done without knowing of the setting, there will be a review of the environment that affected the elements of policy. The question of how—and why—the program came together, and the focus that shaped it, will be addressed.

There will also be a review of some of the criticisms of the federal programs, not so much to critique the criticisms, but to provide perspective. There are good, legitimate arguments on the side of federal aid to mass transit and there are good, legitimate arguments on the opposing side. Is there good sense cloaked in conservative, Reagan-styled rhetoric, which is a mix of popular politics, legend, anecdote, feeling good about America, and hard reality? That part of the transit environment is hard to judge, and the common sense of the Reagan position is often overlooked in the fulsome public relations haze of welfare queen stories. The vital germ of the Reagan ideology and position is the incentive to make things work well virtually automatically—the market system—without the troubling, mind-crunching, and bureaucratic state of coma that generally numbs governmental programs in U.S. society and culture.

Transit remains a strange anomaly. It is both a local and a national issue. It is by itself neither the savior of the cities nor the singular solution to a host of problems related to transportation. What makes it a national program is that the majority of Americans live in urban areas, and as the nation approaches the 21st century and is well into its own third century of existence, there are some basic questions that affect everyone: Will there still be cities? What will they be like? Transportation is a part of the answer to these questions.

3.

The Environment of Transit Policy: Cities in an Age of Change

PUBLIC POLICY: TRANSIT AND CHANGE

It is hard to define policy. A look in the dictionary and personal experience will tell us that it is a way of assuring that some goal or objective is reached. Of course, if we're not sure of the goal or objective, we may be equally uncertain of our policy. We may do just what comes naturally and become beguiled by—and perhaps the prisoner of—the process that attaches to almost all human activity and which, in time, may become the excuse for the activity itself. That is what makes it difficult to write about urban mass transportation policy. Not to give the game away, there nevertheless is no precise definition or even a clear notion of what the goals and objectives for urban mass transportation are, and it is thus difficult to create an effective policy toward an unknown end.

The theme of the above paragraph is a worry to which we will return later in these pages. Some things seem like good ideas, and some things seem like bad ideas; for example, it is clearly a bad idea to try to learn how to roller skate while carrying a hot pizza in each hand. Policy is particularly difficult to formulate when the situation is changing rapidly. This is, of course, a truism because the world is always changing. But there are times when the change is so rapid that the bundle of ideas that we carry with us does not provide any sure knowledge of where to go and what to do. In times of rapid change, in times of fear of loss of control, when there are no stars to guide us, doing anything is risky and doing things that are farsighted or (we hope) helpful means falling back on what is—or what appears to be—common sense.

Policy is not formed in a vacuum. Be it strategy for a corporation, a family, a nation or a subdivision of a nation, policy arises because there is a need for it. On the local, state, and national levels, the policies that develop reflect what is happening in the society at hand. However poorly defined the goals and objectives of that society may be, the policy adopted will reflect its concerns and worries and high hopes. In retrospect, it may not have been a noble policy or one that achieved something of worth; indeed, perhaps it may not even be very interesting to later generations who have their own events and problems upon which to focus.[1]

Likewise, policy reflects the values of a society. As an example, the society of the United States values personal financial success; it doesn't guarantee everyone will win, but seems to agree that, as part of the American social contract, U.S. public policy in the main should work toward the benefit of the individual. Much of the efforts of the post–World War II era toward the elimination of discrimination (on the basis of age, sex, race, religion, sexual preference, or national origin) was argued for on the basis of eliminating barriers to financial success rather than on the moral issue of discrimination in a society covenanted to equality by the canonical documents of the nation's founding. Americans are more comfortable, perhaps, with sharing a degree of prosperity than with thinking of the metaphysics or philosophy of all men being created equal. It is easier to comprehend the poor in pocketbook than the poor in spirit.

A work concerned with urban transportation and mass transit policy risks being considered as highly specialized and arcane, beyond the interest of ordinary citizens. On the contrary, its relevance stems from the plain reality that most Americans live in urban or metropolitan areas, and the policies adopted toward transportation have helped form the cities of today and have given a quality of life to the residents that might have been significantly different had different policies been followed.

All of this has to do with the difficulties of knowing the right thing to do in almost any human effort. This chapter presents a broad-brush look at the forces at work on cities and urban transportation and gives the first inkling of the transportation policies for cities in contemporary times. This material should provide a foundation for subsequent chapters that will deal in detail with programs and policies that have been developed by the federal government, as well as, of course, by state and local governments, to deal with urban mass transportation.

The term "transit industry" will be used in this work in a specific way. Here, transit industry refers to firms, agencies, and institutions that are devoted to providing urban mass transit service. While closely related, the term "transit community" as used here includes not only the operators, but also suppliers, planners, and the users of urban or other public transportation. "Public transportation" means any for-hire transportation, such as American Airlines, local cab services, Amtrak, or Greyhound—ownership is not the point. "Publicly owned transport" refers to transportation service provided by some public body as at least the partial activity of a unit of government. As an example, the Massachusetts Bay Transportation Authority owns and operates the bus, streetcar, rapid transit, and commuter rail services in Boston. "Transit" is here used to denote local mass transportation service by bus, streetcar, or rapid transit and may also include local commuter railroad service.

AN AGE OF CITIES: AN AGE OF CHANGE

The reason for having urban mass transportation, in the first place, is the need for movement within urban places. Thus it is that the subject of urban mass transportation demands a knowledge of urban places, for they are the setting for the operation of mass transit service. Cities and urban places have been involved in profound change since their inception in the western world, and many of these changes have been wrenching because of the resulting problems. There have always been urban problems, some which are unique to urban places. Others take an urban focus, such as housing or poverty, because of the concentration of people and thus of the problem. Much of what appears as difficulty is either misunderstood change or inadequate solutions; oftentimes the solution to a problem of one age may be the original problem of another. The glacial pace of urban development following the fall of Rome had seen only a very slow evolution up until about 500 years ago. The pace of change has picked up since that time to one of quicksilver rapidity, and much of what happened in the past was as baffling to the people of the time as are the quandaries that face us today.[2]

The reason for the existence of cities lies in the advantages that people have in close access to one another. This access offers social and economic benefits. The economic benefit results because people working together in even a rough harmony are more productive than people working alone (as per Adam Smith's division of labor theory). Specialization in skill or operation, cooperation in effort, and a structure of organization to hold people together always results in greater output and sometimes in greater surplus. The larger this surplus, the higher the standard of living; the surplus of a product must be exchanged for the surplus of other products for a city to thrive.

Transportation is essential in moving surplus to places when it is needed or wanted. The transport function may be as simple as moving a piece of work from one workbench to another in the same room or it may involve moving wheat halfway around the world. Cities that flourish depend upon adequate means of transportation so that the population can gain access to its various parts with ease for work, social activities, or cultural purposes. If cities are to achieve larger sizes, it must be possible to move surplus longer distances so that exchange may take place. The city thus depends on both internal and external transportation.

Cities of olden times (with a few exceptions, such as ancient Rome), were relatively small affairs. The things that urban dwellers needed were close at hand. There was no need for transportation much beyond walking for ordinary purposes. Few urban places between the fall of Rome and the beginning of the industrial age were large enough to warrant, for the able-bodied, any sort of conveyance or animal to ride. Indeed, the design of many medieval cities was such that the use of wheeled vehicles, while not impossible, was difficult on their crooked, narrow streets. Europe in the wake of the fall of Rome contained only small and isolated urban places, because the anarchic conditions prohibited the production of surplus sufficient to support urban places of size and substance. Fear of murderers and marauding bands kept trade to a bare trickle. If necessity is the mother of invention, then prior to the industrial age there was no necessity to push for the development of various means of urban transportation.

As Europe progressed from the Dark Ages into the Middle Ages, cities and civilization began to rise again. Many urban places were sited around castles within whose fortified walls the residents retreated in times of danger. As the darkest of the Dark Ages passed and times of peace grew larger, surplus and trade and the castle-oriented urban places expanded. Soon the population would not all fit inside the castle walls as danger approached, and likewise, there was increasing reluctance to leave immobile businesses and dwellings unprotected outside the castle walls. City government emerged, in large part, to build new walls to circumscribe the growing cities with additional ramparts for protection. But these places were still small enough for walking to provide for necessary movement. The street pattern of these cities generally conformed to the local topography or followed animal paths. This is not to say that there was no planning; the mazelike street patterns were often designed as part of the defense for the city if the walls were breached by enemies. Most of the urban places were not at all geared to wheeled traffic; for this reason markets depending upon wheeled transport were located close to the city gates.

Ancient and primitive cities were organic. That is, they developed naturally as forces worked upon them and, once an urban place was begun, it could grow as long as it could support itself from its immediately reachable hinterland, which supplied foodstuffs, wood for fires, and other commodities. Water was a key factor; if the population outstripped the capabilities of the natural water supply, there was no choice but to get rid of some of the population one way or another. The handling of human wastes was a part of this problem. If nature could no longer remove these wastes by natural processes and bacteria got into the water supply, the population of the area might very well be regulated by death. The very early organic city or urban place was innocent of engineering works and other efforts—usually requiring much capital—necessary to support a population by the creation of the environment needed to live beyond the means of a natural setting. Much of the life of these early cities was probably marginal. When the Middle Ages provided sufficient peace and trade to stimulate urban growth once more, capital was found to do the necessary engineering and construction work to assure water and sanitation as well as walls for protection, thus helping to insure a higher quality of life for the residents. A larger population within the city then became feasible.

Urban places that are strictly natural cannot grow very much. To support a large population, an urban place needs what we today call infrastructure, not only in the form of capital to construct necessary water and sewage facilities, bridges, and roads, but in addition its society must possess the intellectual capital to handle certain difficult tasks. Governance is one of these difficult tasks. Marshaling the skill and the capital was no mean task in places emerging from times of darkness and small surplus. Capital was often seized in the form of confiscated labor, and it was not uncommon for residents in or around an expanding urban community to work off their "taxes" in labor or provision of supplies

A major factor in permitting city population and geographical area to expand was transportation. Enlarging the hinterland to provide food and supplies to support an increasing population was a major function of transportation. As transportation improved, cities could grow larger; more investment in transport capital and capital support gave the means to move more goods and to support a greater population. Improvements to provide necessary external transportation came very slowly. Miserable, muddy, rough roads made surface movement difficult and costly; small two-wheeled carts provided only modest carrying capacity, and travel was painfully slow if the ox was used as motive power.[3] Low capacity meant that it was expensive to move goods very far, and this thus constricted the hinterland and helped to keep cities small in size. Larger urban places were located on rivers or near lakes and oceans because water provided a means of moving cargo more easily and in greater quantities than did overland transport.

As cities began to grow immediately prior to the industrial age during the period called (in retrospect) the Renaissance, a new pattern of city layout was imposed upon the urban scene. Urban places now were often the location of a mighty prince or others of power who could see that these city-states (eventually national states) had sufficient concentration of booty to pay for the works needed to support a relatively large population. Cities came to be planned by the ruler and were symbols of the power of this ruler. Cities of this period were often a result of the fancy in design of an egomaniac who wanted a larger population to adore him in the urban setting he used as a vehicle for his own person and vanity. This, however, should not obscure the fact that enormous public improvements and great strides in public health took place in such a setting and under such rule. Power is needed to wring change in the urban fabric, be it the power of a duly elected democratic body with gumption or that of a despot with absolute rule. The plans often called for a wide, smooth thoroughfare focusing on the palace of the ruler or on some other symbol of the ruler's government. The wide, flat streets made it possible for the ruler to display his army effectively and thus helped to quell any ideas about overthrowing him. The public works, constructed for whatever reason, provided more light and air than the cobblestoned streets of the Middle Ages, and they permitted greater use of wheeled vehicles. By the sixteenth and seventeenth centuries, there was a substantial increase in the number of wheeled vehicles using the streets of the expanding, more formally planned cities.[4]

The age of industry that dawned in the middle of the eighteenth century demanded larger urban places for the manufacturing processes of the time. A concentration of workers was necessary in the new mills and factories, and the concentration of markets made sales of necessities to concentrated markets relatively easy under the improving (but still, in comparison with our own times, relatively difficult) transport conditions. Coeval with industrialization, major public works in the form of roads and canals graced England and Western Europe, as well as the northeastern United States, in order to move the supplies and products both needed and made by the new, industrial urban places.

Improved roads, often turnpikes imposing a toll, began in the seventeenth century in a marked way in England. The turnpike movement flourished in the mid-eighteenth century and began to fade with the coming of the railroads in the nineteenth century. Improved waterways and some artificial canal building started in the mid-eighteenth century. The canal movement was also strong until the coming of the railway—when the iron roads proved to be capable of moving large volumes of freight at a much lower capital cost, more often and with greater flexibility, than could canals. The railways provided a generally available, high-capacity, mechanical transportation system that moved freight and passengers with much greater speed than was possible on the typical canal, which required horses to pull the canal boats. (The use of steam-powered tugs to pull the boats on early canals was not feasible, because the greater speed caused wave motion that tended to destabilize or even wash away the banks of the canals and rivers.[5])

The development of mechanical transport systems to help supply cities with foodstuffs and material for manufacture, as well as to disperse their produce, was a mixed blessing. By the early part of the nineteenth century, larger populations teemed in more urban places than ever before in human history. Population probably also reached a higher density than ever before, and the Dickensian squalor of the industrial city was a symbol of both progress and decline.

The nineteenth century produced the classic slum of the type that Jacob Riis photographed and wrote about so eloquently; that is, the high density, tenement-type housing apparently so degrading to the spirit that only the toughest and most talented could possibly make it out alive. There was a limited expansion of dwellings and activity possible in a city that depended upon walking for most of its urban transportation.

Before the advent of steel frame construction and safe elevators, tall buildings were not feasible. Buildings had to be jammed tightly together, as is given witness by the row houses in the older parts of Philadelphia and Baltimore. The transit industry was born to meet the problems of urban growth and to enable people to live beyond normal walking distances. And so, with the push of an increasing demand for their products, industrial cities grew to an unprecedented size and number, giving fact to the idea that industrialization and sufficient ingenuity and capital could permit cities to grow in an unnatural or non-organic fashion.

The transit-oriented city was predictable to a large extent: population growth could take place only along the arteries of public transportation. Although density was relatively high, relief from enormous overcrowding was possible because of the high speeds attained by the electric street railway and rapid transit and commuter rail lines. Longer distances could be traveled on the electric railways in the same time as short distances on the animal-powered railways. Cities took on starfish shapes along the lines of public transit, which was truly a shaper of cities, particularly in the U.S. since many of its cities started and grew rapidly in the nineteenth century. In an age typified by an almost total lack of private transportation, the population perforce geared itself to public transportation. The transit companies were often in the real estate business; they would buy land outside the built-up portion of the city and extend a streetcar line into the undeveloped area. Soon houses would appear, and the transit company profited from both land and house sales, as well as from the fares collected from the new residents.

The age of transit as a dominant form of urban travel was not one that lasted very long. If transit was the principal means of transportation in cities from about the time of the U.S. Civil War up to the First World War, it was clearly in a sparring match with the private automobile in the United States and in some other places between the World Wars. The post–World War II period has clearly been the age of the automobile. Worldwide, the phenomenon takes place: cities are spreading out, moving away from the dense form and patterns of the past, a movement partially caused and certainly enabled by the use of the automobile as a principal means of transportation. This change in living patterns has implications for cities and for transportation.[6]

THE SUBURBAN IDEAL

For several hundred years there has been a clear preference for suburban locations among English-speaking people. Before the mid-eighteenth century the outer reaches of London suburbia were the haunts of the new nobility created by Henry VIII; fearing plots, the king forbade his new noblemen from having permanent dwellings in the capital city. Closer in, the suburbs of not only London, but of most cities, were the dwelling places of the poor, the desperate and often of those of the criminal element. The suburbs closest to the city were the location of slums, because property values and rents in the central portion of the city were too high for the poor. This began to change as the upper middle-class business and professional people began to locate their homes in the suburbs. This was a major modification because of the low repute in which the suburbs were held and because of the requirements of business.

Business demanded communication and face-to-face contact; a dwelling place and business placed close to the center of economic activity was essential to maintain communication links. Following the medieval pattern, the London businessman and his employees often lived in the same house, or the employees lived immediately adjacent to their employer in the mews and alleys behind the master's house. In addition, the business offices and warehouses were often in the same structure as the businessman's dwelling place. The relatively wealthy and the relatively poor were thus all jumbled together in a classless fashion within the noisy tangle of the center city. Moreover, at least until the mid-eighteenth century, it was quite normal for the entire family, women included, to be engaged in the business. Necessity demanded this participation; it helped control expenses, and it kept business secrets within the family.

The separation of the classes spatially and of family functions by sex began when some eighteenth-century London upper-middle-class businessmen, seeking partial relief from the city's pressures, purchased or built small weekend and holiday villas some miles outside the built-up parts of the city. To some extent, these middle-class quasi-expatriates from the city were aping the nobility but on a much reduced scale. With few exceptions, the place purchased or rented was not a working estate with vast lands to manage. At first, the family might actually live in the villa for a total of only a few weeks of the year. Spurred by the religious fervor of the Anglican reform movement advanced and encouraged by William Wilberforce (best known for his anti-slavery work), the middle class began to move permanently to the suburbs. Wilberforce and his followers made a strong argument that the family was a precious thing and that the women and children should not be exposed to the noise, dirt, and evils of the center city. It was not an unacceptable argument for the middle class, and the reformers went further to point out that the woman's job was the virtue of the family, as was cultivation of a strong religious sense in her husband and children. This could best be accomplished in the relative peace and purity of the suburb. The home was to be the cradle of protection for the family.

In what was to set a momentous precedent, the last half of the eighteenth century saw members of the upper middle class of London beginning to dwell permanently in the suburban villas, with the breadwinner commuting daily to the office or factory in his carriage. The expense of such travel foreclosed suburban living to those who could not afford horses and a carriage; the classes were effectively separated by this cost of transportation. The wife as mother, preserver of the moral standards of the family, and manager of the household, soon became the middle-class norm. In a relatively short span of time, the suburban ideal of London's middle-class, well-off businessman became the desired living pattern of those who were successful or who wished to be considered as such. By the beginning of the nineteenth century, the upper middle-class suburb became common in London and the idea was also adopted in the British provincial cities.

The popularity of suburban living caught on more slowly in the U.S., but by the end of the 1830s the suburbs were considered the ideal for successful persons and the best environment for an increasingly family-centered society. The U.S. suburbs became more reachable physically, as well as economically, as railroads radiated out of the cities, which meant that people could travel between work in the city and a home in the suburbs without the need to support a carriage and horses along with their substantial attendant expense. Many railroads encouraged such travel by cutting or commuting their fares for suburban dwellers. This was done for good, businesslike purposes. The railroads exploited their outlying property holdings by selling some of it for the homes of the new suburbanites; equally practical, the railroads hoped that good commuter rail service would influence satisfied business-oriented suburban dwellers to ship their freight on the railroad that served their daily travel needs.

Even with cut-rate fares, traveling on a commuter railroad was expensive because the fares were usually based on distance. Major democratization of the U.S. suburban areas came with the development and extension of the street railways out into undeveloped areas. Invented in 1832, it was not until the 1850s that the horsecar was needed or adopted for use outside of the very largest cities. As they were first built, such lines served the already built-up portions of the city and then, especially after the Civil War, began to push out into undeveloped territory. The street railway companies were often in the real estate business or worked in close association with land developers. The land beyond the city's built-up portion gained value immediately upon the extension of the streetcar, and soon houses were being built along the streetcar streets. The modest fares of the streetcar, rarely more than a flat charge of five cents, regardless of the distance traveled, opened up the suburbs to a broader income range of the middle class. There were many promoters of the virtues and values of the suburbs, and some of the newly popular magazines directed toward women went to great lengths to encourage them to press for a new home in the suburbs as a synonym for the good life. There were additional forces making the move out of the city easier. For example, pattern books to be used by local carpenters and precut houses made it relatively inexpensive to build a home that fit the suburban ideal of a little castle for the family on its own plot of ground.

The first outward population push of the nineteenth century was not really noted as a problem or as a diminution of size or draining of citizenry from the central cities because annexation was relatively easy and because many cities grew simply by annexing the built-up areas beyond their earlier civil boundaries. Nineteenth-century cities grew significantly in size, not just in population. In more recent times annexation became very difficult or virtually impossible, so the twentieth-century surge of population in the suburbs has been outside the city, hence the loss of center-city inhabitants both proportionately and absolutely.

The development of the electric streetcar and the interurban electric railroad in the last decade and a half of the nineteenth century substantially extended the range and area that public transportation might serve within a reasonable travel time; from the 1880s urbanized areas rapidly pushed outward along the lines of public transportation. It was the electric car with its average speed of ten miles per hour that really opened up the suburbs to the great bulk of the middle class. In so doing the suburban ideal became available to a broad range of the American population of various income levels. It was very much a middle-class journey to the outer parts of the urbanized area; the poor were left behind in the older parts of the cities where the housing stock was old and decaying and where many workplaces could be reached by walking.

In the years between 1890 and 1920, public transportation (both commuter rail and the streetcar) helped create the classic suburb: workplace and home were separated, a journey to work was required, but the suburbs were tied closely to the central city for the economic tasks of work and shopping. Virtually all social and cultural activity was city-oriented. The suburbs were almost entirely dwelling places, and they were not self-sufficient. Some retail and service establishments grew up along the streetcar lines and at the interurban and commuter rail stations, but downtown, where the transit lines focused, was the real heart of the urbanized setting, the true central business district of a truly central city.

The automobile was an element of the American scene by 1900, but it was not until about 1920 that affordable, reliable automobiles were available that were within the capacity of middle-class families to buy. Early cars were almost always expensive and prone to break down. This changed quickly, and by 1920 Henry Ford supplied good, reliable transportation for less than $400; used cars cost much less. In 1916 the federal government, responding to a rising clamor for better highways, began the federal-aid highway program, and states and cities began to patch and pave the execrable American roads. The suburban development that took place in the 1920s, however, was still largely along the lines of public transportation and the people living in those suburbs were not dependent on the motor car. The development of America's suburbs was interrupted by the Great Depression and the Second World War. When that war was over, a variety of forces would foster a suburban growth explosion.

The Depression created enormous unemployment, and joblessness was particularly acute in the construction trades. In order to stimulate home building and put people back to work, the Roosevelt administration inaugurated the policy of federally guaranteed mortgages. For a small down payment and a mortgage amortized over a twenty or thirty-year period, the suburban home was available to a huge proportion of the American population in the prosperous post–World War II era. Cars were inexpensive, and gas was plentiful and cheap, so the new suburbanites were not particularly bothered by the lack of public transportation. The stage was set for unprecedented suburban growth, growth which has continued without pause until the present.

Left behind in the central city were the poor. Federal policy helped to create and to perpetuate the urban slums. Many older parts of the cities were not deemed eligible for a mortgage guarantee if the property showed signs of deterioration or if there was a threat to the neighborhood that would lower property values. The presence of blacks or other ethnic groups defined as undesirable was enough to classify property as risky. Mortgage guarantees, however, were readily available in the white suburbs, and builders and lenders made sure that the new subdivisions would qualify for them. When the federal government began to supply funds for public housing, the decision on where to build was left up to the individual communities. No suburbs wanted large numbers of the poor dumped on their doorsteps, so the public housing was generally concentrated in the already-existing slums of central cities. Often built as high-rise buildings, these projects became almost instant vertical slums, often worse than the decayed housing they replaced.

The suburbs and the exurbs beyond the slums are thus places of class distinction; the white middle class lives out beyond the boundaries of the central city, while the poor, often black or Hispanic, occupy the central area. Many observers are deeply concerned, but those people who seek escape from central city problems work hard to keep this economic-cum-social segregation alive.

Those who manage mass transportation properties and those who are promoters of transit are faced with a serious problem in attempting to deal with suburbanization. In central cities, where transit functions well because of its ability to provide an effective and efficient service in densely populated areas, population is steadily falling and there has been a trend away from central city locations for industry since the 1940s. Downtowns are often troubled, but in general appear to have held on to banking, government, and other office functions where face-to-face contact is necessary. The strength of retailing in downtown is uncertain in many places, while generally the suburbs have won hands down. This is revealed primarily by the closing or downsizing of many downtown flagship department stores. There is a small trend of the middle class returning to downtown residential locations, often occupying and radically improving old slum areas of "interesting" yet deteriorated neighborhoods convenient to downtowns. The gentrification factor may become important in the future, but it is currently too small to halt the current movement outward.

Some cities, of course, have experienced a major renewal of their downtowns; Indianapolis and St. Louis are good examples. Even so, and despite the attractiveness of such places, which often combine revivification of old, interesting structures and exciting post-modern architecture, there appears to be no cessation of the outward tide.

Plainly, the suburban type of living and working is desired by the American people. The same trend is apparent around the world, particularly in English-speaking countries. This pattern of suburban development and population distribution is not amenable to successful transit service. Alternative forms of transit, or paratransit, and stress on carpooling and van pooling have much merit but are only of limited effectiveness. Movement in the suburbs is based on the private automobile, especially within and between suburban communities. Paradoxically, commuter rail and express bus service may be gaining large numbers of patrons for those trips to work that are focused on the downtown business district.

The extremely rapid push to the suburbs, while not totally surprising, came on with an unexpected rush in the 1970s and 1980s, far exceeding the expectations of planners. It was perhaps stimulated initially by the white flight inspired by school integration and improvements in communications that made center-city business locations less vital. After a while, the services available in suburb locations reached critical mass and, in large measure, the center city was no longer needed. The shift of so much activity to the outer sectors of metropolitan areas has caused what can best be termed appalling traffic congestion. Development of outlying centers of activity that include shopping, offices, residences, and manufacturing in places that once were rural, two-lane road territories only a decade before has created dramatic transportation problems.

Despite the congestion, the problem persists because all parts of the urbanized milieu are interested, often to the point of desperation, in new development and in the tax revenue such development brings. Lamentably, in all too many cases the costs of new development bring only more costs, costs which may exceed the expected benefits. Development attracts traffic that may soon make the highway system inadequate, and the pervasive nature of the development often produces a pattern of diffuse but heavy traffic. There may be no strong corridor of demand sufficient to justify some heroic highway or transit measure. Worse still is the question of where to place such major improvements. Suburban development may not be high density by the standards of the old central cities, but where the problems are heaviest, the land is usually fully developed and occupied. No one wants a widened highway in his front yard, or a superhighway in his backyard. In some cases, a rail or utility line or right-of-way may be available, but it may be of dubious value in an unfocused area because the rights-of-way may not really link together what needs to be joined. To build some major highway or transit facility that might offer some hope is political suicide in many places because too many property owners' toes would be stepped upon. Worse yet, a major highway improvement, be it widening a road or building a new one, simply spurs more development and stimulates more traffic and likewise more traffic congestion. The suburban dream is proclaimed by some to have turned into a nightmare. Perhaps the essence of the vision is unsullied, but all too often the transportation portion is indeed a bad dream.

The impact of the suburban trend has been largely negative for mass transit, as might be expected. The changing pattern of geographic dispersion of housing and jobs in urbanized areas, joined by rising incomes, higher levels of automobile ownership, and the greater mobility independence of women and the elderly have all diminished transit's attractiveness. Markets for transit that were once considered captive are no longer so. A result has been declining productivity of transit while costs have risen steadily, especially in expansion of transit service to the outer parts of a metropolitan area. Transit ridership has grown, however, after reaching a low point in 1972; by 1987 ridership was at a point just slightly below that of 1965. In addition, the 1980 census revealed that the proportion of urban work trips by transit had dropped from 13 percent in 1970 to 9 percent in 1980, and that the share of total urban trips had fallen from 3.6 percent in 1969 to 2.6 percent in 1983.[7]

THE CITY SPLITS OPEN

What has happened to cities in the period since the end of the Second World War is probably without precedent, due to the swiftness of change. Propelled by increased population and the startling mobility provided by the automobile, the tightly built-up city of the industrial age opened up and spread well beyond its former bounds as established by public transportation in the years between 1865 and 1920. The new reality is the thinly populated metropolitan area. The spreading out of population is both costly and beneficial and, looking toward the near future, gives rise to problems and questions, some probably not yet asked or even imagined. All over the world, in the more advanced nations the cities appear to be spreading out; as this happens the automobile is becoming more deeply entrenched as the only reasonable means of serving the transportation requirements of thinly populated yet still clearly urban places. Free-standing houses, fresh air, grass and flowers are the prizes sought and obtained. The prices are the greater cost of a spread-out infrastructure and the potential of severe automobile traffic congestion at economic activity centers in the multi-nucleated metropolitan areas discussed above.

There are clearly serious issues arising from the suburbanization, metro-politanization, technoburbanization, and fragmentation of American cities. These are grievous problems. The recognition of the expansion of the metropolitan area, the criticism of what has been happening, and the pervasive problem and the growing feeling that things should, somehow, be better, gives rise to some questions: Is there any one way a city should be structured in terms of shape and density and in the location and interrelationship of human and urban functions? Is there one right way a city should be? If there is, it is obvious that transportation as an integral part of the city will have a role to play in achieving what is most appropriate.

Clearly there are a number of factors to consider. An urban place must be a suitable setting for human beings. Historically—in the United States, at least—the planning and the policy of urban development were predominantly private in nature and limited to profit-making situations. "Ask not what you can do for your city, but what you can do for yourself," would have been the natural battle cry of urban developers ringing down through the ages of urban America. Only inciden-tally was any of this activity aimed at producing a good setting; if some develop-ment did produce one it was because it was necessary to do so in order to earn a profit.

It is possible for a place to be both real estate and home. One is always on dangerous ground when discussing the public good because it is such an elusive concept. Whatever the public good is, there is nothing wrong with businesses attempting to make a profit in their activities. It is not the task of business purposely to do those things that result in public good; that is the role of govern-ment. Assuming a reasonable democracy, government must forge the policy and take the necessary action to provide a decent setting for its people. And govern-ment is also responsible for creating an environment to encourage enterprise and to provide incentives for development. Clearly, there is a natural tension be-tween the public good and the private good, a tension often given vigorous expression in the urban setting.

As an urban nation, all levels of government have to be involved in the process of providing a good, livable city. If there is a vacuum, the public will eventually demand actions to create or foster either public or private means to achieve desired ends. What the means will be depends upon the values and precedents of the community or nation, and the knowledge and background of the people and their leaders. What happens in American cities is, over time, no accident, but merely the result of the public's will or of its inattentiveness.

CITIES ON THE WAY TO SOMETHING

Cities in the United States and in other parts of the world appear now to be caught somewhere between the old, highly concentrated urban places and the new, giant metropolitan or mega-urban areas. With changes in the form and structure of cities taking place rapidly, it is difficult to predict what even the next decade will bring, much less the next half-century. In all probability, there will be no point of equilibrium but rather a constant shift and change of urban areas. It seems likely that the closer-in suburban area will become more densely populated, a kind of thickening of the fabric, the extent of which may well depend upon the caliber of transportation access to places of economic activity, land use policy, and supporting utility infrastructure.

As the twentieth century comes to a close, the transit industry in the United States (here pointing out that most of the rest of the developed world is following the urban patterns of the United States) is perched on the edge of the city that was. Transit is an awkward inhabitant of the spreadout type of city that is. And transit is either a critical necessity or a total irrelevancy to the city that will be. In many places the changes in the urban area have been such that transit, as it has existed historically and has been operated in most places, does not really meet the needs of the area as a whole and only with difficulty satisfies the needs of particular groups of people. In a very real way it is as if a mature industry were once again pushed into the awkwardness of adolescence.

We know that transport is important to the quality of life in an urban place. Whatever its shape, form, or density, the city of the future and its quality of life will be affected in a substantial manner by transportation and the means of transport used. What mass transit does better than anything else is move large numbers of people in a space-saving manner; whether or not that will be an important function in the future is a matter of debate. Planners, policy makers, administrators, managers, and all the others involved in transit and urban transportation are often baffled about which is the proper path to take. The advice that such people give to legislators on all levels of government is therefore suspect. Everyone involved in considering the prospects of urban transportation brings past baggage, much of which, unfortunately, may be completely irrelevant to the present and future.

As is true of every generation, the current group of planners and policymakers know only what they have grown up with; it is virtually impossible to rise intellectually above the conventional wisdom of what has worked to solve problems within our experiences. We have the experience of using water to douse a bonfire; putting water on a chemical fire may make things worse, but the natural inclination is to use water rather than the proper fire extinguishing materials. Many of the people who are responsible for urban mass transit policy have tended to view urban transportation as a shaper of cities, a bringer of freedom, a concentrator, a means of mobility for the elderly and handicapped, the avenue to the good urban or suburban life, and the provider of access to decent jobs for the poor. Whether or not this is true today is a matter of conjecture, depending upon the other activities that lend support to transportation in achieving desirable ends. Making urban transportation policy, and mass transit policy, is a very difficult task.

The prognosis for dealing effectively with the new urban reality is not good. Given that we knew what we were getting into, and that legislators were emboldened enough to make supportive policy and to adopt supportive programs, there are many constraints to policymaking and political possibilities, of which lack of perfect knowledge is perhaps the least hampering. Perhaps the major compulsion in our political democracy is that whatever is done will take a safe course; there will be a compromise between what may appear to be extremes. In sizing up what course of action to take to work on a problem, the legislators will try not to alienate voters, be they motorists or transit users. However, because there are more motorists than transit users, it is not difficult to guess, in most cases, which voice will be heard the louder.

Always overriding American thought in the public sector is this: "Don't spend too much—keep taxes low!" The solution to urban transportation policy will, in all likelihood, carry with it the dictum "Don't plan too much," for planning is often viewed as socialistic or communistic and may even spoil private profit ventures. At the same time, despite emotional rejection of planning in many quarters, prudent use of public funds demands guidelines. Action too often depends upon urgent necessity as a motivating force, and yet many good public managers, by nature, abhor such crisis situations.[8]

In considering public policy relevant to today's urban condition and transportation reality, one of the key constraints on the actions that elected officials and appointed officials take is the ultimate point of political wisdom in the American democracy: "Don't take away what the voters already have." A close corollary to that is: "Don't spoil or alter expectations." Overall, the actions must not hurt private enterprise—or at least not too badly. The wise legislator also knows that actions have to be taken for which the political credit outweighs the political liabilities. There are few things that don't have opposite sides to them; there are few benefits that don't have costs. The politician, by all means, must work to do something that is understandable to the public that elected him. And whatever is done must also be proclaimed as being progress. Furthermore, actions in these sensitive times should not overtly or knowingly make the environment worse. In the new metropolitan areas, plagued with auto traffic, the apparently wise course would be to decrease that traffic somehow; the political reaction is to build more highways to solve the problem.[9]

The American system of government is not geared to radical change; the familiar checks and balances assure that. The chances are first-rate that whatever policy is eventually made will be conservative in nature, while cities move on to new forms and problems that neither existing policy nor the policy likely to develop in the next few years will help in any way. If past experience is any guide, the steps taken will be reactive.

Will the new cities (such as the mega-urb that we are fast approaching) and the services and infrastructures to make them function be profoundly different from the cities of the past? Will old cities (and city forms and functions) and old ways have to be destroyed in order to create the new? Will the present urban form and structures be absorbed by new forms and structures, or will the present be a useful and functioning part of the new cities, helping to keep their identity as a part of the varied nature of urban places, a valued reminder of what the city and its inhabitants once were, and from which both have moved on?

The broad movement which is discernible in the United States today toward the mega-urb is toward a spatially large, multi-nucleated city. The future edges or boundaries of such places are likely to be quite fuzzy, if the immediate past is any guide. There will, of course, be links holding the new form together, and these aspects and their limits may form the boundary points. They will be economic, social, and cultural ties and the provision of infrastructure and services. The latter presupposes some kind of governmental or intergovernmental arrangement to provide and maintain them.

PROBLEMS IN THE NEW CITIES

The idea and potential reality of the mega-urb has been around for at least a quarter of a century, ever since 1960. In the U.S. there have been efforts to deal with the future planning requirements, but it has not been a matter that has received really profound thought. It wasn't too worrisome back in the 1960s and 1970s because most American cities weren't yet at the point of the ultimate in explosive growth. Today, it is not unreasonable to ask what incentives will hold the residents in the new form. Will the spatially dispersed city of the future—a city form probably far more diffuse than the present cities we know—be able to provide, both socially and culturally, for its residents? Will it be planned well enough to reduce the need for enormous amounts of travel? Will there be any allegiance or pride in this gigantic creation? Will there be a feeling of at least some degree of personal control, so vital for the mental health and happiness of its citizens? Will the population of such a place feel that they are citizens or merely residents? Will this question be puzzling their minds: "I live here: Do I belong here?"

These are questions that have never really been posed before in a serious fashion by those involved in forging governmental policy. There is the possibility that policy may produce a kind of urban setting that is deleterious in the broadest sense to the health and happiness of individuals, as well as to society and the economy as a whole. Government must tread very carefully in what is most certainly an area of legitimate governmental concern. Shaping and giving form and substance to mega-urb, or whatever the city of the future might be, involves transportation of all types and that transport can act as a tool in the process of defining whatever is the urban future. Or, conversely, the transportation structure may forever be condemned to playing catch-up, and unable to handle the burdens imposed upon it.

THE DILEMMA OF GOVERNMENT

A major problem of all societies is how to uncover, understand, and meet the future. There is a legitimate concern over the urban future in the U.S. Can the type of city now evolving be successfully governed? There is no unit of government currently available to administer even present metropolitan areas in the United States; this is and has been a major problem. Because a metropolitan area embraces a multiplicity of separately incorporated cities, counties, and special units of government, it is often viewed very much as a special case. However, even small cities today embrace more than just the civil municipality in terms of the ties of culture, society, and economic factors that make a city.

It is probably safe to assume that Americans will, over time, freely put up with only what they feel they can control, that is, what is perceived to be manageable. Will the mega-urb be manageable? The problem of multiple jurisdictions is that of trying to fund and administer the necessary infrastructure, services, and land use. Unless a small civil war is desired, communities with developed areas abutting each other must have compatible land uses. Who will manage such an effort? As cities spread out to large size (including small urban places in the south and southwestern parts of the United States), there will be a need to create some new infrastructure which, in fact, will repeat the existing infrastructure in metropolitan areas in the older, already developed parts of the U.S. that are giving up population. Given the need for many things in U.S. society other than sewers, streets, water mains, and other major pieces of urban capital, is it a wise policy that allows some expensive facilities to fall into disuse while great expenditures are made elsewhere on the same things? This is a type of decision that has not been made before in the U.S.; it smacks of concern over limitation, and limits are not normally popular in U.S. society.

There apparently is no incentive, in a relatively wealthy society, for a city that is efficient. It is probably fair to say that the U.S. public feels it can afford to spread out somewhat. The payment on that spreading out may be deferred.

The portent for government suitable to the mega-urb challenge is not encouraging, nor is the development of a rational and reasonable policy to meet what may be a new reality. The recent trend has been away from an interest and exercise of creative concern for the U.S. urban future through governmental activity. The Reaganesque thinking of the 1980s made the population feel comfortable and even patriotic, with actions of doubtful sense. The promotion of the notion that government is evil in and of itself is not the stuff of a philosophical approach toward the better good for a larger number. The essence of the market system so strongly pushed by Reagan and his followers is that those involved should benefit themselves and not others. The market system, with all its benefits and strengths, must be contained within a framework of law and policy in order to avoid extremes and to benefit the public as a whole. Yet the popular drift of the administration of a highly popular president was toward a diminution of all government, not just the federal government. It was difficult for state and local government to take action; raising taxes to do the things the public wants was almost impossible in many places.

In reviewing the urban environment the idea of cutting back on government cannot be ignored. The Reagan administration as a whole has been very anti-government in tone with selected thinking about what part of the government to be "anti" about. To manage for oneself and to encourage self-reliance are ideas that have great merit, but they are a move away from any kind of social contract between various classes of society and various groups of people who may dwell within current cities and who will be dwellers of the mega-urb. This is worrisome to those who feel there must be some degree of reasonable harmony within a community if it is to work in a generally beneficial way for all involved.

It is probably a temporary phenomenon, but there are those who claim to see a withering of the public spirit and a withdrawal of interest on the part of residents. The wilting of public spirit may also be joined by a withdrawal of federal leadership that has proven to be so important in the last 50 or 60 years of American life. For all its faults, and the sluggishness and timidity of much of the effort, the prime leadership has come from the federal level of government. Despite these faults, the federal government nevertheless usually rises above the understandable parochialism of state and local government.

The role that mass transit might play in the new kind of cities is unknown. The lack of incentive for efficient use of space is bad news for transit. The virtue of transit is the ability to move a large number of people in a relatively small place. Transit is only marginally helpful in trying to achieve certain nontransport goals, such as mainstreaming the handicapped. Transit might play an important role in linking together the sub-centers that will make up the critical pieces of the multiple nuclei of the new urban form. There is no reason that transit cannot provide a useful service to a newer, larger urban setting, but a different approach may be needed. One can take the highly transit-oriented approach and demand that the outer perimeter of the city form around the public transportation system. That may not be realistic. Whatever the role of transit, it can only be defined within the context of what the policy for urban growth and development might be. The goals for the city will shape the goals of transit, assuming the development of the urban places is carried out with forethought rather than as a series of reactions.

Is there a federal role for urban transportation? There is no good evidence that the federal role has been effective in controlling the growth of cities. In some places it seems that the likelihood of better policies and control depends upon the public's perception of the need for such activity. The context of federal transit policy depends on the public's perception of it as helpful in providing something of value to the places served as individual entities and in offering a benefit nationally by accomplishing ends not achievable by other means. The federal presence is perhaps most useful when it helps to create an environment to encourage action by other levels of government and the private sector.

Out of the jumble of conflicting forces, the U.S. has evolved a program of aid toward urban mass transportation. Like all programs with fuzzy goals, the policy has become the child of the action. In the following pages we will trace the actions in urban transportation taken by the federal government and the circumstances that produced it.

4.

The Rise and Fall of Mass Transit

THE BEGINNINGS OF TRANSIT: 1830–1880

Transit is an old industry in the U.S., and like many other old industries, it has had its ups and downs. It began in New York City in 1830 with the introduction of omnibus service; rail transit followed quickly in 1832 with the installation of the first horsedrawn streetcars, running upon rails laid in the street. The narrow shape of Manhattan Island had much to do with the initiation of transit at such an early time; in the 1830s, New York City's business district was located near the Battery on the south end of the island. The growing population, pushing north along the narrow strip of land, was soon living at too great a distance to be able to walk to it conveniently. It was for this same reason that elevated railways were first built in New York, beginning in 1869. Thus, the spread of population was far away from the city's business core and there were only a few north-south streets to accommodate movement, streets that had soon become seriously over-crowded. Truly speedy transit had to move at a level other than that of the street.

The small size of the city and a lack of major physical barriers (such as the Hudson and North rivers in the case of Manhattan) that molded development in long, stretched-out patterns meant that most American urban places did not require transit service in the early part of the nineteenth century. Walking was a cheap and practical means of transportation, and in the great majority of U.S. cities, a half-hour's walk provided access to most of the city.

By the decade before the Civil War, however, the influx of population to cities in the early stages of industrialization demanded public transportation. Baltimore, Cincinnati, Philadelphia, and Pittsburgh, to name only a few, soon found that street railways were a practical means of offering service to meet the rising need to cover distances too great for walking. The rapid industrialization in northern cities during the Civil War stimulated even greater population growth, and with it the growth of transit service, primarily in the form of horsecar lines.

Entrepreneurs came forward with capital to build the street railways in hope of making a profit by providing transportation to America's burgeoning cities. Continued post–Civil War urban population growth, resulting from rural and foreign immigration into U.S. cities, forced the physical expansion of urban places and soon made the horsecar a ubiquitous feature of any urban locale that hoped to be counted among the ranks of cities of importance.

Population growth and the sheer physical size that a city needed to accommodate it soon made the horsecar too slow and too low in capacity to handle the growing urban population's needs. Two technical innovations came along to help solve the problem. The first of these, the cable car, was introduced in San Francisco in 1873 and was soon put to use in many other cities. Cable cars offered higher speed and much greater carrying capacity than horsecars. The cable railways were expensive to build because of their relatively complicated technology, and their use was limited to those places that had hills too steep for a horse-powered streetcar to surmount or passenger traffic sufficient to lure the necessary capital. San Francisco is an example of the cable car pressed into service because of steep hills, while Chicago street railway traffic was so heavy that it outstripped the passenger throughput capabilities of the animal-powered railways.

Even while the cable car was at the peak of its development, in 1888 the experiments of many inventors and innovators were finally pulled together into a highly practical design with the introduction of the electric streetcar in a form virtually like the modern one. During the remainder of the golden age of mass transit, the electric streetcar reigned supreme as the common man's magic carpet. It was the shaper of cities. Electric lines were much cheaper to build than cable lines and much less costly to operate than animal-powered railways. They were also tokens of progress for most cities, and as such, many lines were built that were uneconomic, merely to show that a city was progressive. Having an electric streetcar line in a small city or town was a symbol of truly being a part of the modern world, much as is the local airport today.[1]

THE TRANSIT AGE: 1880-1920

Probably the apogee of the concentrated city shaped by public transportation came roughly between 1880 and 1920, at least in the United States. In the first twenty years of this period, there was a substantial and rapid increase in population and the physical size of cities, as rural and foreign immigrants were lured by the economic, social, and cultural advantages of urban life. In the early stages of the forty-year period defined here, it was not possible to build structures up to any great height; the age was innocent of the steelframed skyscraper and high-rise apartment building. If one assumes that 30 minutes is an ideal maximum travel time to work or shop, then the city formed by the horsedrawn streetcar—average speed four miles per hour—was constrained to a radius of but two miles. The much faster electric cars, with an average speed of ten miles per hour, made it easily possible for the radius of the city to be pushed outward to five or six miles.

The initial pattern of mass transit development, in most cities, was for a number of competing transit firms to be established. In a city of consequence, it was not unusual to find a half dozen operators, and in really large cities there were some examples of a score or more of transit operators at one time. These separate firms began to merge and eventually succumbed to a virtually complete unification of local transit service in the majority of U.S. cities, beginning around 1880 and continuing into the first decade of the twentieth century. This was done for a number of reasons. One was profit, because trading in securities and merging always seems to leave someone with a margin of profit. Some mergers took place for the sake of urban improvement and because of pressure from city government for service changes and upgrading that could not be rendered very effectively by large numbers of unintegrated transit operators. Through mergers and unification of service a true system of public transportation could be created. Mergers were also carried out to make the transit properties more attractive for investment purposes. If several street railway properties could get together, the move toward a monopoly position—even if not totally attained—would render the properties more favorable for investment than the separate firms would have been. Another reason to merge was to prepare for the adoption of mechanical traction. Then it would be easier for a large company to borrow the money needed to switch to electric traction (when that form of motive power became practical in the late 1880s).

The transit industry has always been one faced with major changes in the way it does things. During the Civil War and immediately afterward, many independent horsecar lines in cities both large and small became involved with syndicates of street railway developers who helped finance system expansion and enjoyed the profits of promotion as well as operation. The syndicates were often behind the early merger movement. With electrification of the transit industry came yet another change; as the beginning of the twentieth century approached, the urban mass transit industry found itself closely allied with the electric utilities industry.

The tie between transit and the utilities industry is an important one, for it shaped thinking in the industry for many years. One of the interesting changes facing the transit industry was that of the challenge of successfully navigating the shoals of a major advance in technology. Going from animal power to cable and electric traction takes more than a slight leap of the imagination, for it requires different management techniques. The electrification of the formerly animal-powered and cable-powered lines, as well as the construction of wholly new electric lines, illustrates one of the earliest instances of the construction of electrical generating and transmission facilities and the use of that electricity. Often the street railway company was the first thing in town to use electricity, and it was not uncommon for such firms to sell their surplus to the city for street lighting and to individuals and businesses for home illumination or the operation of factory machinery.

Management in the transit industry changed dramatically with electrification, as it shifted from requiring the talents of those who knew how to oversee what amounted to a gigantic livery stable to one needing professional, skilled management trained in engineering (particularly electrical engineering). Eventually, a large proportion of the transit industry became subsidiaries of electric utilities, and the two fitted together well. When home lighting in the evening was the predominant use of electricity and generating capacity, the heavy daytime use of electric transit provided a good balance; the electric railway provided a means of making better use of the generating capacity that had to be geared to peak demand.[2]

At the turn of the century, urban mass transit was a centerpiece of urban life. It was almost the universal means of urban transportation in a time virtually devoid of private transportation. Persons from all walks of life used transit. Horses and buggies were too expensive for most ordinary folks to keep in an urban setting; livery stables rented rigs when the use of a carriage was necessary, and large cities offered cab service. Bicycles, while popular, were perceived more as a recreational vehicle than as a regular means of transportation, particularly in cities with a harsh climate or difficult topography. Walking or the use of the streetcar were, then, the primary means of transportation.

Few people today can understand just how much citizens once depended upon mass transit for transportation to work for the vital business of making a living. Transit was also the conveyance to church, school, shopping, and the vaudeville show. It provided a way of getting to the amusement park (often owned by the transit company) for recreation. Social and cultural events were reached by rides on the streetcar. Even death found the urban dwellers of many American cities firmly within the service offerings of the local transit system. Funeral trolleys were not at all unusual to move the deceased and mourners from the mortuary to the cemetery. In some cities, the street railways provided pickup and distribution of the U.S. mail. A few transit properties offered express package service and many transported newspapers to points outside the central business district for final distribution by various types of news vendors.[3]

In what was, in retrospect, the golden age of urban public transportation in the United States, the industry was able to overcome the peak demand problem that weighs so heavily on it in large cities at the present time. In addition to the traditional rush hours, there was heavy off-peak travel which made it possible to use the capacity of plant, equipment, and personnel more effectively and efficiently than would be possible today.

Transit and politics have always been intertwined. This is because transit (in its original state at least) was a sitting duck—sitting right in the middle of the city streets. The need to operate streetcars in the city streets was sensible because it would have cost far too much for the slender resources of early companies to have totally separate and private rights-of-way. Franchises were needed in order to operate in the public streets, which demanded the involvement of local government. Politicians, being human, were awake to the value of a dollar, and it wasn't long before bribery and other corruptive devices were being utilized to gain the valuable rights on important streets. Because it was so visible and universal a service, transit also made an easy target for politicians, either to criticize or to use for their own advancement. On this count, little has changed today. Over the years many mayors and councilmen have won elections because they kept their campaign promise to keep the fares low, despite the often desperate need for higher fares and more revenue for the sake of decent maintenance. Often, fares were forced to remain at unreasonably low levels, a factor in the process that led to the eventual demise of private ownership and management of mass transit, as well as the slow but certain process of depleting capital resources. So interrelated were the transit companies and the politicians that eventually the public came to distrust transit—they have always distrusted politicians—and in many places there was a strong disregard of the plight of transit by the public and even outright hostility to the providers of transit service.[4]

The policy of government at all levels toward mass transit developed in the nineteenth century, during a time of laissez-faire in which private enterprise triumphed. This is an interesting time in American history, in that the robber barons of the period often produced something of worth as opposed to mere take-overs of other industries. It was a time when the spirit of Jacksonian democracy was rampant in the United States. The thought and the policy was that the federal government—and usually other levels of government as well—should stay out of transportation in addition to a host of other typically private activities. According to this philosophy and ensuing policy, providing transportation investments or service was the responsibility of other levels of government or of private enterprise; the federal government should stay out of the picture. These persuasive material attitudes concerning ownership led to a sharp split in feelings regarding public and private enterprise. Private enterprise produced results in the shape of products and services that met the public's needs, and it created useful and highly productive jobs. If the public sector is supposed to be careful and ultra-prudent in spending the taxpayers' dollars, private enterprise may be bold and decisive, willing to take risks. In the U.S., society generally applauded entrepreneurs for taking risks; after all, it was their money.

Private enterprises are never hesitant to point out that the slow and bumbling government bureaucracy is both ineffective and inefficient and thus the very antithesis of vigorous private enterprise. Alas, bureaucracy is the way it is because the American public wants it to be that way; the public wants and expects government to be responsible. When one deals with the public's money, one must be careful. The public demands it. So government is typically slow and cautious, and it works in those areas where enterprises can find no profit or not enough profit to be worth the trouble of the private sector. Public ventures are often cursed for not being profitable or at least cheap to carry out. Frankly, it is tough to look good within the public sector of the U.S.[5]

Of course, transit in its private enterprise phase, from 1830 to 1970, had its share of irresponsibility. It also joined with much of the rest of private enterprise in glorifying the worst parts of the laissez-faire tradition. There is, however, a corrective process. When the arrogant misdeeds became too bad—in transit or other fields—they were eventually corrected by law. This action was not always necessarily in time to help whoever had been injured, but it bears out the fact that no monopoly or arrogant or irresponsible behavior in a competitive situation can last for very long, because the public will demand to be protected against it.

As noted above, general policy on the part of cities led to controls over the transit industry through franchises and ordinances. Some of this control was simple regulation afforded by the process of incorporation, because the limited liability business corporation—the typical device used in the transit industry—is and was very much a child of the states' ability to limit what a corporation might do. By the turn of the century, transit was generally considered to be a public utility, was treated as such, and was included in economic regulation by the states. This regulation embraced the entry into the field and the rates charged and gave a degree of control over the quality of service. It was the same kind of regulation as that imposed upon electrical utilities, which is not too surprising, as the utilities were the parents of many transit systems.

The initial development of the transit industry insofar as public policy toward transit was concerned had been to let the private sector develop it and then to let the public sector regulate it as a monopoly. In retrospect, this was not bad public policy. It produced more transit service on a widespread basis to urban places of all sizes and at generally reasonable rates to the public. Private enterprise was encouraged to invest in providing the service and to make rapid and revolutionary changes in motive power. Indeed, the investment in rapid electrification of the street railways was a major assistant in ushering in the age of extensive use of electricity. At the same time, there was a natural conflict between the public and transit, because it intruded so much in their lives as part of their daily need to get around.

Economic regulation had taken care of some of the worst abuses, but regulation and public policy were far from perfect, especially in those areas that were not generally visible to the public. Regulation, when it came, usually did not work effectively to prevent or overcome overcapitalization in transit. Much of the industry was overcapitalized and consequently, given certain economic conditions, was in very bad financial shape. This financial mismanagement would eventually lead to a considerable portion of the transit industry falling into bankruptcy during World War I.

The wise and scrupulous owners and managers of transit should not be forgotten; they gave the public value for their money and stockholders a reasonable return on their investment. They were often targets (as was all of transit) of stupid or venal politicians, and many were unfairly tarred with the brush of corruption that was certainly applicable to those traction barons who dealt unfairly and greedily with the public, sold watered securities, and sought only to grasp and not to give. The well-managed property earned the highest accolades for quality of service, exchanged value for money, and earned the respect of the community and the industry.

The Golden Age of Transit—if there was, indeed, such a time—began to wane during the First World War. Shortly after the war started in Europe in August of 1914, both belligerent sides began to purchase supplies from the U.S.

Demand soon grew to the point of stimulating a virulent inflation. As the U.S. approached and eventually crossed over into a wartime posture itself, the inflation grew worse as both peaceful and military production bid for resources and all prices shot up to unexpected heights. Transit companies were hit with sharply increased costs for their supplies and wages necessary to keep personnel. Defense industries wooed away transit employees by offering not only higher wages but more comfortable and predictable working hours as well. The transit properties enjoyed a huge increase in ridership, but the typical franchise limit of a five-cent fare in many instances did not cover the sharply increasing costs for labor and material. A major burden on those street railways that were not conservatively financed was the interest due on bonded debts. Particularly hard hit were properties where the outstanding securities far exceeded the asset value, and thus the ability to generate revenues to cover bond interest, bond sinking funds, and dividends on the equity shares. The transit industry was faced with the incredibly difficult problems of sharply rising costs of operation, franchise costs (street and bridge repair, snow removal, street sprinkling, and franchise taxes), and interest charges, concurrent with severe limits on its ability to charge sufficiently high fares to cover them. The ultimate irony of record-breaking ridership and bankruptcy faced the transit industry and by 1918 about half the street railway mileage in the U.S. was in bankruptcy.

So severe was the plight of the transit industry—which was, of course, vital to the war effort and to basic urban mobility—that President Wilson formed the Federal Electric Railways Commission (FERC) to investigate and make recommendations to help solve the problems. Much of what we know today about the problems of the transit industry at the time of its flowering and at the threshold of decline is a result of the extensive hearings held by this body. The FERC, not as a surprise, found that the electric railway industry was absolutely essential to the health and vitality of urban places and their population, and it made recommendations aplenty. As with most such investigations and reports, it did an adequate job of at least attempting to solve the problems of the past, but it did nothing to resolve the problems that lay immediately ahead. This is not to heap blame on the FERC; we are always oblivious to major trends and changes going on about us. In the eighteenth century, Gibbon chronicled the changed conditions within the empire to which the Romans were heedless, changes which brought about the fall of the empire and the beginning of the darkest of ages. Gibbon did not realize that steam and democracy were changing his world, too. The FERC was equally innocent of foreknowledge.[6]

TRANSIT VERSUS THE AUTOMOBILE AND SUBURBANIZATION

At the critical dawn of the automobile age, the transit industry faced a situation that would change it dramatically and would alter, perhaps forever, the decisive role it had played in the growth and life of cities in America and abroad. By 1920 the transit industry had been seriously weakened by the financial problems latent within it; overcapitalization had brought the industry to a sorry state even without the competition of the automobile. The franchise requirement costs continued, and in many places the franchise requirement of the five-cent fare, which could not produce sufficient revenues to cover costs or make a reasonable return on investment, was only reluctantly abandoned. Major political battles over fare levels and revenues were common in the 1920s. The transit industry was in a poor position to meet the enormous competition of the family car.[7]

Public ownership would not have been an unreasonable option at this point, but there was strong opposition both inside and outside the industry to what was often pictured as the rankest example of creeping socialism.[8] The industry, treated as a regulated public utility, was a monopoly—at least a monopoly of public transit—that was becoming increasingly irrelevant as the private automobile became dominant in both intercity and intracity passenger transportation. Still, the monopoly attitude of management continued, and the public continued to view transit as a monolithic creature. Public antagonism toward transit had never been unknown. It was hardly a surprising attitude toward a service that had been highly important in daily life and often in the hands of a powerful and distant syndicate or public utility holding company. As a necessary service that was widely used and exposed to the vicissitudes of street traffic, transit could never be perfect, and the imperfections were magnified, not only by the public's usual pleasure in griping, but also by the flames of unhappiness often stoked by politicians looking for an issue and by newspapers seeking headlines.

The inherent attractiveness of the automobile was abetted by advances made in cars themselves and in the willingness of government to aid in their use. The 1920s saw major improvements in automobile engines and drivetrain components, bodies became better, and General Motors began to produce enclosed cars at reasonable prices. It became practical to use automobiles throughout the year, even in harsh winter climates. The self-starter, introduced in 1912, had widened the use of cars beyond those who were strong enough to crank the engines. The self-starter also made possible higher compression engines with much more power than their predecessors, as well as concomitant improvements in performance, including the ability to move the new heavier, enclosed bodies. Gasoline was upgraded in purity and quality, and the addition of tetraethyl lead to gasoline prevented the higher compression engines from knocking. Tires improved greatly in quality and endurance between 1920 and 1925, and their price went down. The mass production of automobiles and their many components drove down the initial price of a car and the cost of operating it. For its part, government on all levels began to implement costly programs to improve highways. The federal government commenced its aid for intercity highways in 1916; state and local government, wisely counting the potential votes from millions of motorists, began to spend increasing sums of money on roads and streets. The 1920s were a great time to own an automobile, a vehicle that provided mobility, the pleasures and pride of ownership, and often lower costs for family trips.[9]

The transit industry as a whole remained profitable for many years after the severe competition from the automobile began in earnest in 1920; but the profits were often marginal, particularly during the Depression and again in the twenty years immediately after World War II. Deferred maintenance and a failure to spend the funds needed to replenish capital began in the 1920s as a result of the malaise that spread during World War I and because of the strong automobile competition thereafter. Major cost-cutting programs were undertaken during the First World War and in the 1920s. Lighter weight cars that used less electricity and were much easier on tracks and roadbeds had been introduced during the First World War and their use increased during the 1920s. Transit properties with large numbers of older, heavier cars that were in too good a condition to scrap sought to cut costs by doing away with the two-man operation of streetcars, a development that was fought by the unions and often made impossible in the short run by city ordinances requiring operation by both motorman and conductor, ostensibly for safety's sake. The new lightweight cars were often fitted with deadman controls and other devices to bring them to a safe stop even if the motorman became incapacitated.

The use of buses by transit systems, rare before the First World War, became important in the 1920s. The demand for transit service into the suburbs that developed in the 1920s was often met by the use of small buses, a much less costly alternative than laying track, stringing trolley wire, and building substations. In some cities marginal streetcar lines were replaced by buses, especially if the tracks were in need of renewal. A happy feature of buses was that from the very beginning they were one-man vehicles; there were a few exceptions in those cities operating double-decker buses that were designed for very large crowds and required a conductor. A severe financial pinch in some smaller cities often led to the replacement of streetcars entirely by buses as the auto-filled 1920s moved on. All over the transit industry there were service cuts to reduce operating costs, but this did little to reduce the fixed costs associated with track, the power distribution facilities, and the large amount of equipment needed to meet rush-hour demands.[10]

The transit industry also sought to boost revenues by fare increases that were reluctantly granted by the regulatory agencies, which were, at last, waking up to the plight of the industry. Many ingenious marketing ideas were also tried to boost ridership.[11] The desire to provide a better service with a better vehicle was also strong in the industry, and in the late 1920s, the Electric Railway Presidents' Conference Committee on equipment began to subscribe funds for the purpose of carrying out the basic engineering work to develop a new and better streetcar, one that would be competitive in comfort and swiftness with the private automobile. The deservedly famous and durable PCC car of the mid–1930s was the result of this effort.[12]

Urban expansion in the 1920s created a dilemma for the transit industry. Expanding service out into suburban areas meant heavy construction costs. Because of the pressure from politicians to keep fares low, it was difficult for a transit property to levy distance-based zone fares that reflected the higher costs of operating lengthier routes. Thus there was simply no profit potential in operating long routes at fares that might have been quite adequate for shorter trips in the more densely built-up portions of the city. Extending transit operation with buses did make sense, but this required many passengers to transfer on their way to and from the heart of the city. Moreover, buses were too small to carry the crowds using the streetcars in the central portion of the urban area. Eventually, of course, the problem solved itself; buses became larger and the number of patrons declined so that buses could handle the crowds.[13]

The Great Depression hurt the transit industry severely. Ridership fell as unemployment soared. The federal government, while not yet embarking upon an urban highway policy, did begin to spend money on urban highways as a part of its measures to help defeat the Depression. Automobiles crowded the streets, hindering streetcar operations, but the trackbound streetcars were often viewed as the problem and many urban officials made getting rid of streetcars a major goal. In smaller cities, attrition did the job. Many streetcar operations had begun in the first decade of the century, and many cars had been purchased in the period between 1910 and the First World War; the track and the equipment were nearing the end of their economic life and were simply scrapped in favor of continuing transit service with buses.

A major source of strength in the transit industry had been the close relationship of many of the properties with the utilities industry. The big utility companies helped to provide capital and management expertise to their transit subsidiaries. Sadly for the transit industry, the federal government, in the Holding Company Act of 1935, began to break up the utilities, forcing the power companies to begin to divest themselves of their transit subsidiaries.[14]

A greatly weakened transit industry took up the formidable challenge of handling the record crowds of World War II. Pressing every available piece of equipment into service, the industry did a magnificent job. Not only was almost everybody either in the armed services or working in defense in more peaceful industries, thus in need of transportation, but rationing of gasoline and tires and the unavailability of new automobiles between early 1942 and late 1945 forced large numbers of people onto the commuter railroads, rapid transit trains, buses, and streetcars. Lucky was the transit property that had received a fleet of PCC cars or new buses on the eve of the war.

TRANSIT AND CITIES IN THE 1950S

The 1950s were a crucial time in the U.S. for both cities and the transit systems that served them. Largely unobserved or unnoted, as is often the case, crises were developing and almost nothing was done to understand or even perceive these problems, much less to solve anything. It was a time of rapid change in transit, most of it for the worse in terms of the health of the industry, as a private enterprise or for the quality and quantity of service offered to its customers. There were dramatic declines in patronage. Ridership was 17.2 billion passengers in 1950, 11.5 billion in 1955, and 9.3 billion in 1960. The number of riders continued to fall through the 1960s; it was 8.2 billion in 1965 and 7.3 billion in 1970.[15]

As noted earlier, the major physical change for the cities was a rapid expansion to the suburbs, a population relocation of no mean size. The metropolitanization of the cities took place with a vengeance in the fifteen years following the end of the Second World War. There was, of course, a great pent-up demand for new housing that came on the heels of the years of the Depression and wartime stringency. Most of those houses constructed since the end of the war were built outside the political boundaries of the central cities. It was a good way to escape urban problems and the apparently inexorable rise in city taxes. The federal mortgage guarantees under both the Federal Housing Administration and Veterans Administration programs had standards for property that could not be met by much of the housing in central portions of an urban area. Housing entrepreneurs and speculators built in the suburbs, where such guarantees were available, where farmland could be assembled cheaply, and where there was sufficient room to build houses in a large enough number in one place to enjoy economies of scale. The automobile made it possible to move out of the city and far away from public transportation.[16]

Many transit properties found themselves cash rich at the end of the war. Foreseeing continued declines in patronage once wartime restrictions on new automobiles were lifted and gasoline and tires became plentiful again, most transit management correctly decided to retrench. For the most part, those cities that still had streetcar service planned to either abandon the electric cars as soon as possible or withdraw slowly from the use of rail vehicles, with only the heaviest routes remaining rail-served. Communities in the latter category were often those with relatively new fleets of PCC cars or batches of cars ready for delivery at the end of the war.

As part of the orderly withdrawal from the use of streetcars, many transit properties, wishing to get the last years of productive use out of electrical substations and power distribution facilities, switched to trolleybuses. Trolleybuses, while more expensive to buy than motor buses, had longer lives and generally lower operating costs; their flashing getaway meant that they could hold their own in traffic while their freedom from rails meant they could steer around minor obstructions that stalled the streetcars. Higher speed possibilities meant greater throughput with fewer vehicles than switching to diesel buses would require. As the fixed-power distribution facilities were due for replacement, the trolleybuses could be phased out and replaced by diesel buses. Management felt it could have many of the advantages of the streetcar without the large expense of track maintenance.

The manufacturers of motor buses reaped a large harvest of orders in the late 1940s and early 1950s as transit systems all over the nation sought to replace prewar buses as quickly as possible, to buy additional buses for streetcar replacement, and then to buy new equipment to replace those few buses that had been acquired during wartime. The manufacturers supplied the transit industry with much better buses than had been available before the war. Improvements in transmissions and diesel engines spelled the end of the stick-shift transit bus powered by a gasoline engine. By the mid–1950s the diesel-powered, rear-engine bus with automatic transmission became the standard. Two standard sizes were available by that time: thirty-five-foot-long buses seating forty-five passengers, and forty-foot buses seating fifty-one or fifty-three passengers. The diesel engine had enough power to move these large buses with reasonable speed and good performance even on troublesome terrain. The buses were large enough to replace streetcars on just about a one-for-one basis as transit patronage declined. The automatic transmission made every driver potentially a good, smooth driver with no gears to clash. In the mid–1950s air-suspension systems replaced metal springs on transit buses and afforded a greatly improved ride.

The declines in transit patronage came even quicker than had been expected and by the very early fifties many cities that had stuck with streetcars regretted the decision; in many cases even the heaviest routes had patronage that buses could handle easily. Within a relatively short time Cincinnati, Cleveland, Dallas, Detroit, Kansas City, and Louisville sold off their newest streetcars. Some of these places switched to trolleybuses, but most chose diesel buses, thus relieving themselves once and for all from the costly burdens of maintaining track, trolley wire, and a power distribution system.[17]

Transit patronage declined more rapidly than estimated immediately after the war for reasons that transit managers could not possibly have predicted. The move to the suburbs—expensive and difficult to serve with conventional transit service—occurred more quickly than had been foreseen. As the population surged outward to new and more remote locations, many transit properties did not really try to serve the more distant suburbs because it simply cost too much and the virtually universal flat fare did not make suburban expansion a profitable venture. The almost universal move in the U.S. to the forty-hour, five-day work week came on rapidly in the five years after the war. Before and during the Second World War, the typical transit-riding worker generally labored five and a half or six days a week, thus making six round trips by transit each work week; the forty-hour week reduced the number of round trips to five. Fewer work trips meant less efficient use of plant and equipment. Television kept people at home in the evening, first in the big cities and then, as it spread, to smaller places; the family trip on the bus downtown for a movie in the evening became a thing of the past. Shopping facilities moved with the population to the suburbs, and fewer people came downtown to shop; instead they got in the car and drove to the shopping center nearby. Fewer customers and less ridership at the off-peak hours of the day were the products of these changes.

Central cities suffered from as many changes as did the transit industry, most of them perhaps almost as unexpected in their speed and severity. The population shifted out of the central city in increasing numbers, bringing about the paradox of rising urbanized populations along with an increasing number living in suburban areas. For a time population stabilized in central cities, largely due to an influx of poor, often black, rural immigrants; however, during the 1950s the process of the wealthier and middle-class citizens deserting the old central city for the blandishments of the suburbs was a major trend. Many of those who left were a real loss to the central city, because they were often those with the greatest talents and the highest levels of education, achievement, and income. The new suburbanites were people who could take an active part in urban affairs, and their wealth meant that they did not depend heavily upon welfare and other aids aimed at the low-income resident. Worse yet, in addition to the loss of the cream of the citizen crop, the older cities were burdened with an infrastructure that had not seen much investment since the 1920s. The Depression and the war had put major improvement well on the back burners. In the 1950s replenishment of urban capital was needed, but a burden of less wealthy citizens who required more urban services meant that cities were often unable to secure the tax revenues to pay for the refurbishment of their infrastructure. The private sector was splitting its investments and capital replenishment between central cities and the suburbs, with the suburbs gradually getting an increasing share.[18]

Many urban issues were addressed in the 1950s, of course, but many were also ignored; they were certainly not considered on any national basis. The early part of the decade brought the heartbreak of another military conflict to the nation, this time the Korean War, which ended only in a bothersome stalemate after the expenditure of many lives and much treasure. There were other diversions. It was the time of the McCarthy Era with "witch-hunts" and serious concern about the Russians and the atom bomb. The sweet taste of the great victory of World War II had gone sour in less than a decade.

Even though most Americans were living in urban areas, attention was not focused there. Part of the reason was that the national leadership and much of the leadership on the state and local levels had been born in the last two decades of the nineteenth century. For many leaders in the U.S. in all levels of government, the critical youthful experiences that imprint upon a person what is proper and seemly had largely been rural experiences, and thus their world of ideas tended to be limited. Urban matters were foreign to such people, even if they had, in time, come to live in urbanized areas for many years. The urban infrastructure, so tired and dilapidated after the Depression and World War II years, received insufficient attention. The vision of the good life was suburban and borne on rubber tires. The major transportation problem then was congestion, and the deliverance from the problem was better roads that would provide the balm of relief. In the immediate aftermath of World War II, there was no leadership willing to push for new solutions to urban problems.

The U.S. may not have had an urban transportation policy, but it did have an urban highway program. In the Highway Act of 1944, the Congress authorized that federal money could be spent on urban highways for the first time; expenditures could commence six months after the cessation of hostilities in World War II. And why not an urban highway aid program by the federal government? Highways were considered an unmitigated good thing at the time. In peacetime the burgeoning suburbs needed improved and new roads to help the suburbanites reach jobs that were still focused on the central city. As the decade wore on and more economic activity began to take place outside the central city, there was a need for a cobweb of roads to meet the suburban needs. Little thought was given to other means of transportation.

But still there was urban and suburban highway congestion, apparently impervious to how many roads were built or existing highways improved. In 1956, Nirvana appeared at hand in the shape of the Interstate System of Defense Highways. The Interstate System roads were to be built to high standards, similar to or even higher than the toll roads that had been built by several of the states. The Interstate System was not a new issue; it had actually been planned in the 1930s. There was much debate in Congress as to how these roads were to be financed. It was finally decided that a highway trust fund would be established by the federal government into which all the federal tax receipts on fuel and truck tires and parts would go. All the federal highway expenditures would be drawn from this source, including the Interstate System. Cities and states were at first reluctant to go along with the idea of the Interstate System, because the standards were so high that these units of government felt that they could not afford to pay the usual 50 percent of the highway cost that had been the rule ever since the federal highway program got under way. To sweeten the deal, the federal government would pay 90 percent of the cost of an interstate highway; state or local government only had to find 10 percent of the money.

Virtually no thought was given to investment by government in transit; after all, except in a very few places, it was a private enterprise responsibility. The federal highway policy in urban places, on the other hand, was very much shaped by the thinking and the actions of Robert Moses, the building mogul of New York City. Moses had contempt for the poor and the common, those who depended upon public transportation. He was interested in the winners in society, those who could afford automobiles and needed better roads upon which to use them. As an example of his contempt for transit, Moses effectively kept buses off the impressive system of parkways which he built in New York City by making the bridges over those roads so low that buses would not fit beneath them.[19]

The transit industry was practically invisible at the time. There were no parades of shiny new streetcars, no majestic traction barons to damn as they wove their syndicates and collected hundreds of millions of nickels. Only Mike Quill, the feisty leader of the Transportation Workers Union, had national recognition, and this was of a largely negative nature. Moreover, the industry did keep going; there was no crisis, and without a crisis, the U.S. government is unlikely to act.

Even if a sharp and notable crisis was lacking, transit was not a happy place to be in the 1950s because of the constant erosion of ridership. Management's natural reaction was to enter a cycle of service cutbacks and fare increases which further discouraged riders and ridership. Eventually, the process came to feed on itself. Many smaller cities lost service entirely, and transit service was becoming lackluster in medium-sized cities. The problem went below the surface. Some streetcars and trolleybuses were purchased in the 1950s, as well as some new rapid transit and commuter cars, but there was not the sort of dramatic replacement of facilities and equipment necessary to keep service quality on a basis that was even modestly competitive with the automobile. Despite substantial improvement in bus design and features, nothing as notable as the PCC car came along to direct the public eye toward transit. Railroad commuter services were often provided by cars that had been built in the World War I era, or even earlier. The railroads could not be blamed because there was no profit to be found for the privately owned railroads that operated all the commuter roads. Few new bus garages were constructed; most transit properties made do with structures built to handle electric streetcars that were often originally constructed in the nineteenth century or in the first decades of the twentieth century. Many places had inadequate indoor storage for buses even where the climate was so brisk in winter that it was difficult to start diesel engines; as a result, on cold winter nights the engines were kept running, to the unhappiness of neighbors serenaded by the throbbing motors and the bouquet of diesel fumes.

But the transit industry as a whole stayed at least marginally profitable until the mid–1960s; it was a last hurrah, and probably specious at that. It is not an unfair statement to say that the "profits" of the transit industry, however marginal they may have been in some places, were due in part to a failure to maintain fixed plant and equipment adequately. Most transit properties bought a few new buses from time to time, often purchased with the sale of copper and other elements of abandoned trolleybuses or streetcar systems. The investment in trolleybuses, almost always as a replacement for streetcars, was brisk in the first eight years after the war; then it ceased, and the trolleybus operations were abandoned when replacement of their electrical systems was needed. The abandonment of the electric buses was often the source of the down payment on new diesel buses.

In retrospective terms of what would have been best for transit and its users, the early 1950s would have been the ideal time for public investment in transit. Ridership was still very high by the standards of the decades that followed. Good equipment and good service at reasonable prices might have helped to hold on to many riders so that, even if publicly owned, a significant portion of operating and capital costs could have been paid from the farebox. But the industry and the cities served were not interested in public ownership; the rubric of private enterprise prevailed. The market showed the way; if people did not use transit it was because it was not needed.

There were a few bright spots for the transit industry. For instance, Cleveland completed its rapid transit system in 1955. The rapid transit line had been planned and the right-of-way acquired in the 1920s when Cleveland was considered one of the most progressive cities in the nation. The completion had hung fire until after the Depression and the war were over. Chicago created a manmade canyon across the city by building the Congress Street Expressway (now the Eisenhower Expressway), but it had transit in the median strip as a way of getting maximum transportation impact and passenger throughput out of the space while conserving dollars. In San Francisco, moves were underway that would eventually lead to the creation of the Bay Area Rapid Transit system. Some planners in certain cities tried to interest the public and the politicians in transit, but their success was limited; in the 1950s Uncle Sam would help an urban place build highways but nothing was available for mass transit.

For the cause of better cities and better transit, the 1950s was a wasted decade. Urban problems were surging, but little thought was given to them; politicians have a short time horizon—until the next election—and the problems were long-term in development and solution. If anything was to be done, it would need a crisis to bring it about.

5.

The Advent of Federal Transit Policy

The problems of cities and the problems of urban mass transportation are inextricably linked together. They share their origins in the rapid pace of twentieth-century urbanization and in the resulting restructuring of the city from the densely populated core area typical of the nineteenth century to the growth of the more sprawling and thinly populated metropolitan area of the mid and late twentieth century. These movements foreshadow the development of the giant urban area which is dubbed "mega-urb" in this book. More and more Americans live in urban places, but an increasing proportion also live in the suburban areas or, more recently, in modestly sized cities. Earlier chapters have recounted the forces at work in the American milieu that produced the situation America faced in coping with this new kind of urban experience.

The 1950s offered the most dazzling display of urban growth Americans had ever seen, and to say that the institution of government was unprepared for it is a decided understatement. It was a period of serious transport problems, but the start of the decade saw a reawakening of concern over transportation, a concern that had been dormant throughout the years of the Great Depression and World War II. Out of the problems that arose, there was a reaction that led to the development of a federal mass transportation policy.

The urban transportation problem in the 1950s was seen in a simplistic way, almost exclusively as one of traffic congestion. As a result of this limited view, the early phases of development of federal mass transportation policy categorized transit as a way of helping to decrease traffic congestion or as a means to help handle increasing volumes of traffic in ways that were more efficient in their use of valuable urban space.

With twenty-twenty hindsight, it appears naive to view the urban transportation problem as merely one of congestion. It is and was much more complex. An important facet of the urban transportation problem was a lack of mobility for a good number of citizens; many Americans simply do not have regular access to transportation. The key words here are "regular access," because the failure to have a car ready to meet the slightest whim is not a problem if there is good public transportation close by or if the residential development is so well-planned and constructed that all important services and needs are within an easy walk.

Lack of mobility is not a small problem. Many Americans are too old or too young to regularly operate an automobile even if one were available. Others cannot afford to own a car in the first place, or they can't afford to keep the one they own in repair. In the absence of good public transportation or of good planning and development, these people suffer from lack of mobility. They are cut off from economic and social activity; in effect they are marooned. The pulse of motion may beat around them, but they may be helpless to participate.

Thwarted mobility is the second facet of the urban transportation problem that can be identified. It is the problem that arises out of the traffic jam and traffic congestion, as well as overcrowded transit facilities. The most vivid example of this, of course, is the jammed superhighway covered by a pall of exhaust fumes and smog. The cars do not move, or they crawl at a snail's pace, and the area transportation facilities and equipment are rendered impotent by overcrowding. An equal sign of the problem is congested public transportation, exemplified by jammed subway and commuter trains and overcrowded buses and streetcars. The sheer volume of traffic is such that the transportation resources cannot be used efficiently, and the effectiveness of the means of transportation is sorely limited. The problem is compounded by the sheer cost of expensive fuel, consumed by motorists fuming in a traffic jam, and by a rapid transit system with trains creeping through tunnels because traffic is so great that it cannot be handled with dispatch. The burden of thwarted mobility lies in the high marginal cost of both private and public transit at the peak hours.

Congestion robs a city of its vitality. It is costly in terms of the time, effort, and money which are stolen in the process of delay, and which are spent on traffic control devices, traffic engineering, policing, and the construction of roads, streets, transit facilities, and other parts of the necessary infrastructure. Congestion and impediments to smooth and easy flow are thieves. The overcrowded street exemplifies the problem. Abustle with traffic, it is a moat which is difficult to cross; such streets hinder both personal circulation on foot and free and easy access to the economic, cultural, and social advantages that lie within a congested area. The area becomes unattractive, and people look elsewhere for the things the congested area was supposed to supply. It was and is a problem of central cities; the 1970s saw the problem expand to include suburban arteries as well.

In discussing the steps taken to ward off thwarted mobility, we get to the third facet of the problem, which is mobility purchased at very high costs. Huge expenditures for highways and subways, parking facilities, and sophisticated traffic control devices are part of the pecuniary cost. The ugliness of so much of the transportation infrastructure and the overwhelming presence of transportation equipment—principally automobiles and trucks in large numbers—in our cities makes them less felicitous places in which to live. A king's ransom pales in comparison to the sums spent on urban transportation in what appear to be near-hopeless efforts to gain improvement.

Traffic problems are not new; the jam of horsedrawn vehicles in cities in the nineteenth century was almost as bad as that of the congestion of the 1970s and 1980s and certainly was a source of severe pollution. What is sad is that apparently no real progress has been made since then. In some places of extreme auto use, such as Los Angeles and Houston, the cities are clearly no Baghdad on the freeway. They are, rather, places where, for many, much of the zest of urban life and the pleasures of travel have been extracted and replaced mainly by tension, fatigue, and often a sense of desperation. The loss of vitality, amenity, pure air, and time means that cities (including many of their suburbs) have become simultaneously less attractive and more costly places in which to live or work. The central city had traditionally been the place which suffered most from such conditions. By the 1980s the problem had also spread to the inner suburbs so that the entire metropolitan area (or the mega-urb, to use the clumsy term), was becoming an increasingly congested and costly place in which to reside.

The urban transportation problem and its causes have been growing over the course of a century. A major factor behind the three-faceted problem was the distribution of population. Forces worked to move people from denser areas that could be ably served by a steadily improving technology in urban mass transportation to suburbs that were difficult to serve efficiently by any means of transportation other than the automobile (which, perforce, becomes a vehicle of necessity, not choice).

Another major factor was the virtual collapse of the urban mass transportation industry as an important part of life in most American cities. Much of the former batch of customers moved away to the suburbs. As noted earlier, the great drop-off in the use of public transportation—particularly during off-peak hours—led to higher fares and cutbacks in the amount of service offered, which pushed more and more Americans into cars. Particularly since 1945, the growth of cities has been in relatively thinly populated areas, in which the automobile is the only practical alternative for most residents.

The reaction of the transit industry to the geographic dispersion of its market in the 1950s and after was one that could be expected by an industry suffering from decline. The privately owned transit industry of the twenty years after the Second World War was not in a position to fight back effectively. Understandably, the discouragement of management with the situation meant that existing managers became more conservative (even reactive). Indeed, the plight of the transit industry was such that new blood did not easily find its way into the ranks of transit managers. The entire style of management became one of reaction rather than pro-action; most thoughts of actively marketing the service were abandoned, as was any investigation of the market itself. Indeed, buying decent new equipment on a regular basis became virtually impossible as the economic situation deteriorated.

One might think that this situation could have been headed off had wise urban planning been carried out to alert the public and civil servants to the threats to free and easy mobility that lay ahead. Unfortunately, for much of this century of population shifts, increased auto use, and transit decline, planners were ignored. Moreover, planning was not a particularly respected activity in the United States, especially after World War I. Even today, planning often lacks support from the community, despite the fact that it is absolutely essential to plan ahead and to implement rational undertakings.

For the most part, local public officials were fairly indifferent to mass transportation as an important part of the solution to problems of lack of mobility and thwarted mobility. Most of the cards were dealt to the highway people. Transit was given a back seat. Indeed, transportation problems were, one might say, in a state of limbo insofar as the thinking of local officials was concerned. Moreover, the inconvenient aspect of transportation problems is that they don't fit neatly within civil city boundaries. Transportation problems wash over an entire metropolitan area. Because all metropolitan areas are made up of a large number of separate political subdivisions and taxing authorities, it is virtually impossible for the varied units within a metropolitan area to work together to bring the full resources of that area to bear on the transportation situation. This lack of ability on the part of local government to do anything much to help itself meant that the door was wide open to activity either by state or by federal government. Because (until the 1960s) the states had done little to aid or abet improvements in urban places, a dearth of leadership existed. Nature and government both abhor a vacuum, and the gap was filled not by local or state action but by action taken by the federal government.[1]

THE 1950S AND CONVENTIONAL WISDOM

Each decade of the twentieth century appears to have been dominated by one problem or another that had a tendency to steal attention from the basics of public policy that deals with where we live—in the United States, that place is usually an urban setting. Fear and fatuousness appeared to rule much of the 1950s, a decade preoccupied with war and defense and threat and containment. We were edgy about the Soviet Union, and the Korean War confirmed our worst fears. It was followed in our list of concerns by the atom bomb in the hands of the Russians. Senator Joseph McCarthy and his witch-hunts distracted public attention from the important, day-to-day business of the cities. The public itself was for the most part enjoying an unparalleled prosperity, and was concerned with the important and time-consuming business of family formation. Most people are understandably preoccupied with their own problems, leaving little time for the broader concerns of the community. In short, from a public viewpoint, there was no great attention paid on the national scene to the implications of the great urban revolution that was taking place. Much of the tone of modern American urban life for the remainder of the twentieth century was established in the 1950s against a background of the nation's leadership, which largely ignored the issue. The major shifts in population, automobile use, urban decay, and sprawl were duly noted in the jeremiads of Lewis Mumford and other social-urban critics, but were remarkably uninvestigated; consideration of key issues was scotched by lack of interest and ignorance. With other problems seeming to loom larger, leadership did not lead.

If there was any thought at all about mass transportation, it was viewed—as it had been traditionally viewed—as a private business for profit, usually operating under a franchise on the public streets. Because it had always been private, there was little concern over transit as an activity for the government to take action about other than to keep fares low and to play some regulatory role. For the public and its leaders (outside of the largest cities: Boston, Chicago, New York, Philadelphia, and San Francisco), the world of ideas did not include much space for mass transit. Transit had been an issue of some importance in many cities for the first two or three decades of the century, but it had become of less importance to politicians as it declined in importance in urban life. Highways, roads, streets, and parking were the transportation issues of burning political concern in the 1950s, not transit.

Of course, there was no firm national grasp of general urban problems either. Congress represented largely rural interests, state legislatures were dominated by rural constituencies, and there was little government recognition that by 1950 two-thirds of the population was living in urban areas. Even colleges and universities—far from being in the forefront of knowledge and concern—as a whole ignored urban studies and urban issues. Only the most quixotic politician or scholar dared risk going outside the conventional; many areas of interest and importance remained unpondered and ignored because attention was simply unthinkable.[2]

Indeed, there was not even much of a context in which to consider urban transportation problems and policy because of the sorry state of general transportation policy. In sad fact, there was no coordinated national transportation policy (there still isn't!). In the 1950s, then, there was no one place in either state or federal government where all of transportation was represented. On the state level, transportation meant highways. The Bureau of Public Roads, then a part of the Department of Commerce, and the various transportation regulatory agencies were the only federal agencies dealing with transportation. Highways dominated the national interest as part of the rapid increase in the number of automobiles and, to many minds (not broad ones), balanced transportation meant 50 percent asphalt and 50 percent concrete. Virtually the only great transportation concern of U.S. government was highways. The same was true on the part of state governments. In the great majority of states there was a highway department, period. In certain instances, there might have been an airport commission and, perhaps, a small bureaucracy to serve that commission.

The last place to expect much progress in terms of development of public policy toward transportation was on the urban scene. Suburbanization became the ultimate reality of postwar urbanization and expansion. As the growth of the metropolitan area became a fact, the exodus of money and talent to the suburbs, the division into a multiplicity of small and often competing jurisdictions, and the financial incapacity of much of the metropolitan area to deal with metropolitan issues precluded any deep thought about national transportation policy. The problem that came to a head in the 1950s is that cities became increasingly and alarmingly incapable of solving their problems by themselves.

Out of the 1950s came a kind of conventional wisdom toward urban transportation:

1. Highways were wanted and needed.

2. Building highways was good—building enough of them in the right places would solve the urban transportation problem, which was viewed simply as congestion.

3. If transit lost money, it was because it wasn't needed—the market test was the yardstick to use.

4. From the viewpoint of conventional federal thinking in the Eisenhower administration, the opinion was that most problems should be solved locally—that the federal government should get out of most urban programs.

The federal government had no role; the Holding Company Act of 1935 had had an impact on the industry in that it largely divorced transit from electric utilities. The Sherman Act had been behind the anti-transit case brought against National City Lines. For their part, the states were involved through incorporation laws and economic regulation of transit as a public utility, the latter becoming increasingly irrelevant in the age of the automobile. Local government may or may not have had much say about the issues of economic regulation—entry, rates, and service. Almost without exception, local government would fight fare increases.

By the mid–1950s if there was any perception of transit—apart from the large cities—it was as a part of the expected street furniture at best, and at worst as a dying industry giving poor service to a dwindling clientele at higher fares. After all, the publicity for the Interstate Highway System told Americans they would soon be able to drive from coast to coast without stopping for a traffic signal. Who cared about transit outside the big cities?

If the urban transportation issue was poorly recognized and voiced, forces were at work that would soon elevate the matter to an issue of importance.

THE URBAN TRANSPORTATION CRISIS OF 1958

Federal mass transportation activity was the eventual product of a crisis situation that arose in 1958. The emergency was inadvertently created by a federal action intended to help the railroads. Oddly enough, the pressure for federal action began in one city that had already tried to help itself as urban transportation problems mounted in the 1950s.[3]

In the early 1950s in Philadelphia, where the Democrats had just been elected as a party of reform and reinvigoration, they began programs that would help bring the Quaker City into the twentieth century. One of the major items of concern was transportation. Philadelphia enjoyed an excellent infrastructure of

high capacity public transportation facilities, including extensive electrified commuter rail structures, rapid transit, streetcars, and light rail. Sadly, over the years
there had been little modernization of either the facilities or the equipment; the
visible elements of plant and equipment had grown shabby and patronage had
been slipping. By the 1950s, the lack of investment had become acutely obvious
and was particularly severe for the commuter railroads. Both the Reading and
Pennsylvania railroads were suffering from serious financial losses on their commuter service. Understandably, there was no incentive for them to invest in their
services or to make any changes other than taking cost-cutting steps or raising
fares. The carriers persisted in providing the service because of the strength of
the belief by regulators and society—as well as local politicians—in the common
carrier obligation according to which the carriers were expected to provide such
service, typically cross-subsidized internally from freight earnings. The two commuter rail carriers moved approximately 100,000 people daily within the Philadelphia region. Consequently, the loss of service and a shift of the patrons to
private automobiles would be a disaster in Philadelphia's network of deservedly
notorious narrow streets. Seeing the role of the commuter railroad slowly withering away, the political leadership of Philadelphia took what was, at the time, bold
action.

The first step was taken in 1953 by Mayor Joseph S. Clark when he created
the Urban Traffic and Transportation Board to investigate the city's transport
problems. Other urban issues were also under investigation, as part of the new
mayor's attempt to come to grips with the lack of action from previous city
administrations representing a complacent and corrupt political machine in the
last decades of its power. The board took its work seriously, and in late 1955
recommended a coordinated road and rail program, with emphasis on upgrading
the service on existing rail facilities as well as extending them more widely
throughout the Philadelphia area. This multimodal approach appeared more attractive than relying upon highways alone, particularly in light of the high cost
per mile for freeways and the difficult traffic and formidable parking problems
that would inevitably develop in Philadelphia's compact central city area if an
auto-dominant program were undertaken. The board estimated that the price tag
for transit improvements would be $25 million within the city and at least $65
million on a regional basis; these were alarming sums of money at the time. The
recommended program appeared to be a hopelessly expensive undertaking indeed, especially because the city of Philadelphia had neither the money nor the
jurisdiction to do the job. The suburban counties and communities were emotionally, politically, and financially unwilling to go along. The rural-dominated
Pennsylvania state legislature of the mid–1950s made help from that quarter out
of the question.[4]

Federal funds were in use in Philadelphia's urban renewal program, and
federal money was available for urban highways; why not federal aid for mass
transportation? Richardson Dilworth, who succeeded Clark as mayor, worked
with federal officials to see about the possibility of diverting some of the federal
highway money for Philadelphia's mass transportation purposes in 1956 and

1957. The mayor ran into strong opposition from highway groups. Dilworth then proposed an alternate plan in which highway funds would be used only for the planning and engineering work in designing mass transit systems. Dilworth suggested a federal lending agency modeled on the Federal National Mortgage Association to provide the capital funds needed for construction. The bill providing for such legislation was introduced in the U.S. House of Representatives by Congressman William Green of Philadelphia in 1957. The legislative proposal was well ahead of its time and the unprecedented bill was never permitted to reach the floor of the House; it expired quietly in committee without attracting much notice. Equally unsuccessful were additional efforts by Philadelphia to interest Congress and the U.S. Department of Commerce—where nonregulatory matters in transportation were housed up until the creation of the U.S. Department of Transportation in 1967—in aiding mass transportation.

Philadelphia was not the only American city with mass transit improvements on its mind. Constrained by nature to a very hilly peninsula, San Francisco was considering mass transportation as a tool to solve some of its problems in the 1950s. Rapid population growth and the automotive explosion after the Second World War made an already troublesome transport problem even more difficult, and it threatened to grow worse despite major investments in costly bridges and road improvements. The counties affected prevailed upon the California legislature to create the San Francisco Bay Area Rapid Transit Commission in 1951, and $750,000 was given by the state to study the city's transportation problem and the role that rapid transit might play in providing relief. In 1957, again at the request of the Bay Area counties, the state created the San Francisco Bay Area Rapid Transit District (BART) to carry out planning and development work. Even before the planning and analysis, it was expected that the BART project would be a major one.[5]

A few other cities had made sporadic attempts to cope with rising urban transportation problems; indeed, some had made notable efforts from the earliest days of the century. At that time, plans for better urban mobility called for bold and often extensive construction of rapid transit lines, including putting streetcars in subways in downtown areas. Pittsburgh and Chicago had developed such plans before the First World War, but these schemes for transit improvement had reached only partial fruition in Chicago, and no action was taken in Pittsburgh for over 60 years.

The 1950s did see the beginning of large scale urban planning projects, but, as explained earlier, this meant the generation of primarily highway-oriented plans. So-called transportation planning was carried out in the 1950s, but even the elaborate volumes of the Chicago Area Transportation Study and the Pittsburgh Area Transportation Study paid modest attention to mass transportation. Those conducting the studies can hardly be blamed; it was simply unimaginable that mass transportation could ever hope to find the money needed to make major improvements. The problems in transportation these studies addressed were mainly highway problems with highway solutions. In some ways, the assumptions of a future much like the past, upon which these and other transport studies of the 1950s and early 1960s were based, were similar to the assumptions of those at the Federal Electric Railway Commission in 1920. In the immediate post–World War I period, it was inconceivable that urban transportation in the future would not be based on the electric streetcar, as it was then. In the post–World War II era, few could imagine urban transportation progress in terms other than those of the private automobile operating upon publicly provided highways.[6]

A major cause of the limited outlook was the lack of a power or pressure group representing the mass transportation viewpoint. From the 1940s through the early 1960s, the American Transit Association, the trade organization for transit, was not really a lobbying organization and did not command a national presence or position outside the industry it represented; it was primarily a statistical and information agency. ATA was headquartered in New York, far from the halls of Congress, a sure sign that lobbying was not really a serious part of its job. In local government, most American cities had no position on what should be done about mass transportation, and their actions often did more to hinder effective mass transportation service than to help it.[7] Planners, downtown business interests, labor, civic interest groups, and academics who were interested in urban affairs were either ignorant, uninterested, or unable to take a position on transit. Virtually all transportation-related interest continued to focus on highways, a form of transportation for which there was great political, financial, and popular support. Among carriers, the railroads wanted to cut their passenger service losses through discontinuation of money-losing commuter services. The railroads had been anxious to find relief for their many problems stemming from government policy; however, even though they lobbied hard, the rail carriers could not claim any great success with Congress in the first half of the 1950s. On the national level, mass transit was not an issue. Likewise, urban transportation was not a matter of any note to the federal government. If there was any opinion on the matter in Washington, it was that urban mass transportation problems were strictly a local affair and should be handled on the local level.

THE TRANSPORTATION ACT OF 1958
AND ITS UNEXPECTED RESULTS

The power of limited thinking creates a world of limited options along with a fear of change and risky ventures to solve problems both evolutionary and incidental. Oftentimes, some outside force will cause an interruption in the pattern of life or operation and demands new consideration and thought. In 1958, there arose the kind of crisis that always appears necessary to force various groups together in order to gain action. Oddly enough, the whole process that eventually led to the development of a federal role in urban mass transportation got under way inadvertently, as Congress strove to provide some legislative relief for the nation's railroads. The law of unexpected consequences was at work almost before anyone noticed.

After a difficult time in the Depression and then a boom during World War

II, the American railroads entered the postwar period with a strong sense of optimism. Expectations appeared sanguine even for the railroad passenger business, which had been generally unprofitable since the mid–1920s, when the federally aided intercity highway system and increasingly easy availability of automobiles on credit began to siphon passenger traffic away from the rails. The advent of the streamlined, air-conditioned, often diesel-powered trains of the 1930s had won some increase in patronage. Wartime also saw trains both crowded and profitable. Even though it was soon clear that more federal money, as well as state and local funds, would be expended on highways, air traffic control systems, and airports, the railways invested heavily in new passenger equipment and made a bid for the expected expansion of travel in the postwar world of which they assumed a reasonable share would be on the rails.

It was not long before optimism gave way to disappointment. By the early 1950s, it was quite evident that the great rise in travel would not be by rail. Subsidized auto and air travel were tough competition for unsubsidized rail passenger trains, and subsidized waterways and highway trucks were likewise proving to be difficult competition for rail freight service. Increasing numbers of people traveled by automobile, and the air transportation business began an almost explosive period of growth, which became even stronger with the introduction of jet travel in the late 1950s. Freight transportation profits had always permitted the railways to maintain their passenger operations, even though the passenger service lost money, through the process of internal cross-subsidization. However, even freight revenues began to languish in the 1950s against the severe inroads of competing modes of transport, particularly highway trucks.

The railroads lost large categories of freight, such as perishables and cattle, to trucks. The economic ups and downs of the fifties also hurt rail earnings, because when business in general is bad, it is usually very bad for the railroads. The fitful behavior of the economy and the shrinking revenues and profits spurred the railroads to seek legislative relief in hope of gaining a more equal footing with their competition. A major area of relief needed, according to the railroads, was freedom from the obligation to carry passengers. In 1957 alone the railroads had considerable reason to grieve about passenger service. The losses from this service, according to the Interstate Commerce Commission (ICC), totaled $723.7 million.[8]

After a number of years of hearings and serious lobbying, Congress finally provided some relief for the railroads by means of the Transportation Act of 1958.[9] One part of the Act dealt with the problems of the railroads in attempting to relieve themselves of the burdens of unremunerative passenger transportation. Prior to the 1958 Act, the discontinuance of a single passenger train was a matter for the action of state regulatory commissions, whereas ICC jurisdiction involved only the complete abandonment of a line. Gaining permission to discontinue a passenger train from state bodies was typically a very drawn-out and expensive affair. Sections 13a (1) and (2) of the 1958 Act sought to remedy the situation. In its seventy-fifth Annual Report, the Interstate Commerce Commission explained this portion of the law as follows:

Under section 13a (1), enacted in 1958, railroads desiring to discontinue or change the operation or service of any train operating between points in two or more States, but whose right to do so is governed by State laws, may elect to file a notice with the Commission of their intent to make the discontinuance or change, and 30 days thereafter, put it into effect regardless of State laws or decisions to the contrary, unless, within that time, the Commission enters upon an investigation of the proposal. If it does so, it may order the operation or service continued for not exceeding 4 months, pending a decision in the investigation, at which time, provided it makes the required statutory findings, the Commission may require continuance (or restoration) of the service for not more than 1 year thereafter. If it decided not to enter upon an investigation, or if the Commission fails to decide the case within the 4-month period, the carrier may discontinue or change the service as proposed. Under section 13a (2), where the proposed discontinuance or change in service of a train wholly within a single state is prohibited by the Constitution or the statutes of that State, or where the State authority having jurisdiction had denied an application or petition or has not acted finally on such application or petition within 120 days from their presentation, the carrier may file an application with the Commission for authority to effect the discontinuance or change. The Commission may authorize it only after notice and hearing and upon prescribed findings.[10]

Under the terms of the new law, interstate passenger service could be withdrawn quickly after the proper notice was given, unless, of course, the ICC investigated and required that the service be continued. Even where there was some delay, eventual relief generally took only a few years. To discontinue passenger service of an intrastate nature required carriers to seek relief from state agencies first; after that course of action was exhausted, under the 1958 Act the Interstate Commerce Commission was petitioned by the carrier for relief. History shows that such relief was usually not long delayed. The 1958 Act was the first major step in moving railroads away from passenger service. The pace of discontinuation was modest at first, but it picked up speed when the postal service stopped moving the mail by train and shifted carriage of the post to air and truck transportation. The creation of Amtrak in 1971 brought virtually all intercity rail passenger service under public delivery.[11]

In the twentieth century, commuter railway service is among the prime contenders for the financial millstone title. In the troubled rail passenger service of the 1950s, discontinuation of commuter service was high on the list of priorities for the rail carriers concerned. All commuter service was, of course, vulnerable under the 1958 Act, most especially that of the New York City region, much of which was interstate by nature. The Transportation Act of 1958 was signed into law by President Eisenhower on August 12, 1958, and on that very day—almost before the ink was dry—the New York Central Railroad posted notices announcing that it would discontinue its West Shore Ferry Service (the ferry linked Manhattan with New York Central's commuter railway operation on the west side of the Hudson River). The Erie Railroad followed suit shortly afterward. The ICC did not investigate the action proposed by the New York Central, and thirty days later the ferry boats stopped running. West Shore passengers were forced to switch to buses for the final trip into Manhattan, and to add insult to injury, the trip took longer. West Shore commuters, needless to say, soon found other ways to get to New York. The New York Central was soon able to completely justify removing the rail passenger service because of the ensuing lack of patronage.

Throughout the autumn of 1958, with the New York Central example before it, the New York area commuter railroads made ominous noises and announced whopping deficits from hauling passengers. At the beginning of December the Lehigh Valley and the Delaware, Lackawanna & Western railroads announced plans for the abandonment of commuter service, and the Pennsylvania Railroad stated it would discontinue most off-peak commuter service to Manhattan. Railroads in Boston, Chicago, and Philadelphia made similar threats. Unexpectedly, legislation aimed at helping the railroads had become the vehicle for a major threat to the commuter rail portion of urban mass transportation. At least one of the consequences of the 1958 Act was unexpected—it sparked the advent of federal policy in urban mass transportation.[12]

The threat to commuter service created alarm and brought forth a reaction from older and larger cities. In the New York City area, attempts were made to join with New Jersey and Connecticut to find some way to retain commuter railway service. In Philadelphia, the city formed a nonprofit corporation, called the Passenger Service Improvement Corporation, to lease improved commuter rail service at reduced fares from the Reading and Pennsylvania railroads.[13]

Eventually it became clear to public officials in the cities threatened with cessation of railway commuter service that they must follow the same course of action with regard to their trains as had been taken to meet the critical difficulties of the Depression period of the 1930s. In the Great Depression, the cities had been unable to help themselves, and state governments had proved unable or unwilling to act effectively. As mentioned earlier, state government was frequently dominated by rural interests, even though rural residents were usually a minority. The scattering of urban resources through urban fragmentation was particularly troublesome in the cases of commuter service that typically crossed many political borders. The Passenger Service Improvement Corporation in Philadelphia was effective because it worked with the extensive commuter service within the boundaries of the City and County of Philadelphia. Not many other places with commuter rail service could offer an effective operation solely within the boundaries of a city.

The federal government, which had inadvertently touched off the urban transportation crisis, appeared now to be the best place to look for solutions. In the latter 1950s, it seemed obvious that getting succor from the federal government for urban transport, apart from highways, was not going to be easy, because there was hostility to any enlargement of federal functions in metropolitan areas. President Eisenhower wanted federal involvement in cities and local areas to be as low as possible, and mass transportation seemed particularly local in nature. The administration was fully committed to highways—indeed, it had initiated the

Interstate Highway System program—and the powerful highway interest groups were apt to take a dim view of any mass transit programs, especially if it appeared that highway money might be diverted for this purpose.[14] Philosophically, the Eisenhower administration and the whole of Washington were not opposed to positive action; indeed, to the consternation of the right-wing Republicans, the Eisenhower administration—and, in effect, much of the general thrust of mainstream Republican thinking—seemed bent on carrying out the philosophical thrust of the attitude of Republican elder statesman Thomas E. Dewey, which was to accept New Deal pro-action and problem solving but to make it work more efficiently. But transit was so palpably local! Given the spectrum of ideas and possibilities that were politically thinkable at the time, federal aid to transit was beyond the pale. It was not an issue with which the Eisenhower administration could be comfortable.

The position of the Eisenhower administration on urban transportation problems was perhaps most clearly set out in *Federal Transportation Policy and Program,* issued by the Commerce Department in March 1960:

> Metropolitan areas are increasingly congested with mass highway transportation, and are afflicted by rush-hour jams, parking area deficiencies and commuter and rapid transit losses.
>
> This is primarily a local problem but the Federal Government contributes toward the problem with its huge highway program. It also has a deep concern in the railroad system and upon the extent to which the Nation can secure the benefit of the railroads' capability for mass long-distance transport of freight. Ways and means must also be found to encourage tax relief by local and State jurisdictions in helping solve the problems of commuter or local passenger deficits.
>
> The Federal Government should encourage communities to make broad land-use plans with transportation as an essential part. It should consider as a long-run problem means by which such forward planning can be encouraged. It should also consider possible community charges on highway gateways and parking areas to help reduce the highway congestion and help finance the over-all transportation plan. Jointly with communities, the Federal authorities should consider the total urban transport situation so that Federal participation may contribute to the efficiency with which urban transport as a whole is performed.[15]

Beneath the "federalese" it is clear that the administration did not feel that the federal government should touch the urban transport problem directly, even with the admission that a large part of the commuter railway problem was due to federal highway policy. Some members of the staff who had performed the background work on the policy statement disagreed with the stated position of the administration on urban transportation. Ernest W. Williams, the director of the transportation study, and David W. Bluestone, a member of the staff, issued an appendix to the Commerce Department's policy statement to help set the record straight.[16] Their position on urban transportation is of considerable interest:

> Downtown areas were not designed to handle the traffic load which results from . . . [population] dispersion and the accompanying reliance upon the pri-

vate automobile. The two major past and continuing trends are the resulting decline in business activity in the heart of the central city, and a sharp reduction in the use of public transportation facilities.

From the standpoint of total cost, serious problems are raised by these trends. Mass transportation is clearly much less expensive per passenger mile than total costs of the private automobile with an average of less than two occupants. From the standpoint of efficiency, there is little doubt that per passenger . . . transit vehicles are far more efficient in terms of space occupied. . . . Rail lines are similarly much better space users.

The present highway program has provided substantial sums for improving access to our major metropolitan areas. However, the present program does not require any test to determine the most efficient use of these funds in terms of passenger movement. Merely adding highways which will attract more automobiles which will in turn require more highways is no solution to the problems of urban development.

Since our essential purpose is to move people rather than vehicles and since the objective of moving people is to facilitate the purchase and provision of services in our downtown areas, it is becoming increasingly apparent that a new look must be taken at long-range transportation planning in our cities.

In all cities, one thing is clear: while continued highway development is essential, it is being viewed increasingly as one part of the total transportation problem.

The conclusion is clear that urban planning must allow for increased use or at least maintenance of existing rail transit facilities. In the long run, it will be false economy for the nation to devote public funds exclusively to the highway program without encouraging the cities to develop long-range plans to ensure the most efficient use of money, material and manpower in the handling of urban transportation. As a minimum, the Federal Government must provide incentives to encourage such planning in our cities.

Our highway program should be re-examined with respect to urban transportation. The emphasis should be on appraising total transportation supply and requirements in our cities, in close coordination with other municipal planning. Highway expenditures should be based on integrated plans. Our cities must be encouraged to look at total economies as well.

This means that tax or other adjustments for private companies hauling passengers by rail or bus must be considered as alternatives to increased expenditures on widened streets or reduced taxables due to declining business activity in the central business district. The net cost to the area as a whole must be considered in arriving at sound transport solutions.

Some of the funds in the highway program and possibly in the urban renewal program may be usable in connection with such planning. Because the problem of commutation by rail is especially acute in some areas where service is rapidly being curtailed, Federal or State loans to municipalities or metropolitan authorities may need to be considered especially where localities may acquire commuter rail facilities and equipment and lease them to the carriers.[17]

As the Williams and Bluestone rationale revealed, there were persons and departments within the federal government that were becoming deeply concerned by the urban transportation situation. By 1958, a conference was held in the Sagamore Center at Syracuse University to focus on the need for regionwide, comprehensive planning of urban transportation, including mass transportation. Its report pushed for evaluation of the plans by a cost and benefit analysis of user and nonuser impacts. The recommendations were endorsed but progress was slow; only large urban areas were really doing the "right" kind of planning, as evidenced by the pioneering Chicago Area Transportation Study.[18]

Another early sign of the federal government's recognition of the gravity of urban transportation's plight was the joint effort by the Bureau of Public Roads (of the U.S. Department of Commerce) and the Housing and Home Finance Agency. The latter body had been created in 1947 as the agency responsible for the major housing programs of the federal government. In November of 1960, the two agencies announced that thereafter they would coordinate their joint efforts and provide for joint planning of both highways and urban development in U.S. metropolitan areas.[19]

There were two sources of funding for the joint program. The highway law of the time provided for 1.5 percent of program funds to be used for purposes of research and planning dealing with the federal highway system; the money was allocated to the states for their work with the federal highway system. The Housing and Home Finance Agency had been providing money for metropolitan planning and comprehensive planning work in connection with urban renewal for a number of years. An important joint policy statement was issued by the two agencies in November 1960, pointing to the federal interest in fostering sound urban and metropolitan growth. In it the enormous impact of the federal highway program was recognized:

> The Federal-aid highway program is the largest program of Federal aid for capital aid in urban areas and often constitutes the most crucial single factor in the community development. The impact upon the community of the highways constructed under this program is direct, widespread, and often of massive proportions.[20]

Despite these activities, the urban mass transportation situation had not been considered very deeply or thoughtfully, and full recognition of a need to take more decisive action was a latent factor in the federal establishment. A national transit-aid program was not apt to grow in soil of such barrenness.

With a potential crisis in urban commuter service facing the few major cities that had such services and an official administration position opposed to enlarging the federal role in urban affairs, the situation appeared bleak. Even given a more favorable attitude in the late 1950s, Washington was not set up to investigate or administer a program to aid mass transport for urban areas. Responsibility for both urban issues and transportation matters was quite unfocused and was scattered among various agencies and departments. Despite the reality of the majority of Americans dwelling in urban areas, there was no agency (albeit a few in the area of housing) that regularly focused on urban affairs. The federal government was poorly organized to handle the specific problems of urban transportation through formulation of policies and programs. Indeed, at that time the federal level of government was not even very well arranged to formulate objectives and policies for transportation in general. Highway policy, air transportation policy, and rail, water, and pipeline policy were each formulated with little consideration for the interrelated nature of transportation.

Perhaps the greatest difficulty in gaining support in Washington was that mass transportation problems, particularly when narrowly viewed in 1958 as mainly a commuter railway problem, had small appeal in Congress. Commuter rail service on a substantial scale existed only in Boston, Chicago, New York, Philadelphia, and San Francisco. There appeared to be little political mileage in a problem that appeared to affect only a few large cities. If anything was to be done, it would have to be made a broader issue. Perhaps even more striking, except for the concern of a few big city mayors, this seemed not to be a city issue; American cities were neither doing much of anything locally to help transit nor even giving much consideration to it.[21]

REACTION TO THE CRISIS

Work was begun in the fall of 1958 to counter the potential problems created by the threat of discontinuation of commuter rail service. The support for action which eventually led to federal legislative programs in mass transportation came initially from the mayors of a few large central cities; they were joined by the presidents of the railroads that provided commuter rail service in these cities. There was no support initially from the transit industry or from transit labor, neither of which were in a position organizationally, emotionally, or intellectually to deal with the notion of a federal role in urban transportation. Indeed, because the transit industry was largely in private hands, most transit property owners or managers would have opposed federal transit aid; it was not within their world of ideas. The railroad managers, increasingly desperate for relief from commuter rail losses, were more amenable to some kind of aid from government. They saw it as a way of preserving the integrity of the privately owned railroad companies.

There was a lack of support at the time from the bulk of suburban areas, which may seem strange because suburban areas were direct beneficiaries of commuter rail services. However, in the world of suburban ideas, highway transportation was practically the only consideration. There was naturally serious concern and interest in the suburban areas served by rail commuter service. The threat to discontinue or cut back on that service focused attention on the issue. Suburban residents and leaders would eventually come to be major advocates of federal, state, and local support of commuter rail and transit service.

This is not to say that the support of the suburbs for transit programs that would have metropolitan impact was easily forthcoming. The dominant forces for federal transit programs were the central cities, which is not surprising. The suburban areas rimming the central city tend to be preoccupied with local problems; such communities are rarely equipped even to consider cooperative action with other adjacent or nearby political jurisdictions. They tend to be suspicious because of the fear of threatened loss of autonomy that cooperation might bring. Moreover, in a metropolitan joint effort the possible need to spend local funds without direct and visible benefits for the cost involved was unpopular. Even today, the reaction to any proposal to band together with other suburban or central city governmental bodies is almost universally one of hostility. In the late 1950s such an action would have been virtually impossible. As for dealing with the federal government, suburban efforts have tended to be sporadic, quite limited, and usually crisis-stimulated. The rather narrow suburban viewpoint, usually tinged with relief at escape from problems of the central city, makes it difficult for suburbanites to see the whole of a problem that might affect an entire metropolitan area. Almost invariably, what is sought are short-run solutions to very local aspects of a problem. Particularly in the late 1950s, outcries from suburban areas in danger of losing their commuter service were limited to pleas for the salvation of service on their particular line.

In Washington, pressures from suburban communities have often been relatively weak. The local congressman may be the only real voice a suburb has in the nation's capital, and the disparity of pleas, plans, and programs the representative may be called upon to support are often contradictory, especially if the district covers all or part of the central city as well as the suburban area. As suburbs grew to embrace larger populations than the central city, as did occur in the 1960s and 1970s, a congressman would naturally become more attuned to suburban issues. This would not make the task easier, because of conflicting goals of suburbs and cities. Because most federal initiatives must have broad benefits in order to gain congressional support and legislative success, the wise congressman is forced to serve his constituents by doing nothing on many issues and picking and choosing support for efforts that will benefit the majority of those who elect him.

However, on some issues that seem likely to affect all suburban communities in the same way—such as a federal policy of enforcing open housing or some federal program that is visualized as resulting in a power grab by central cities—there may be sufficient separate pressures of a similar nature put on congressmen throughout the country to have the same effect as would a single powerful pressure group. Over time, suburban support for transit became about as strong as support from central cities.

The attitude of the states with regard to expanded federal programs in urban areas was oftentimes negative, especially in the late 1950s. Rural elements in state legislatures harbored resentment and antipathy for the cities within the state.[22] While it is less true perhaps today than in the 1950s, there is an often considerable fear that any sort of regional authority or federally sponsored regional action may be harmful to state prestige and sovereignty, which may cause the state government to become financially entangled. Direct links between the city and the federal government are also resisted by state governments, because they reflect upon the ability of the states to care for their own, damage a state's status, and render the states open to the threat of melting even further into the background on many of the vital issues which concern an urbanized society. This attitude was prevalent in the period under discussion because of the perceived threat of being bypassed as a level of government that does nothing useful in a given area or for a given problem. Paradoxically, lack of state action—for whatever reason—has had a strong tendency to push the cities even closer to the federal level of government, exactly the opposite of what the states wished to happen.

It should be noted that, for transit as well as other matters, over the years state government became much more energetic in playing a pro-active as well as a reactive role in working toward solutions to problems. More effective lobbying on the state level is one reason for this. Moreover, an increasing number of federal programs involve partnership with the states, or with state and local government. A less selfless reason is that it is always pleasant for members of a state general assembly to finally understand that a federal program can create the best of all possible worlds for them. The state legislator can rail against an overly large federal government and the level of federal taxes, while the area he or she represents enjoys the benefits of federal money through various programs. Congress gets the blame for taxes, while the state and local politicians get the credit for having brought dollars into their venue. It is for this same reason that local government officials are tempted by (and usually fall for) the allure of accepting state and federal dollars and blaming the upper levels of government for high taxes.

It has been the central cities, therefore, with their burdens of slums, crime, eroding tax bases, massive intrusions of highways, the upper-class diaspora, and the lower class in-migration that carried the message on key urban and metropolitan issues to Washington to ward off or mitigate certain problems (mass transit is a good example). When realization of the crisis came, they carried the day.

The big cities in particular enjoyed the support of prominent, powerful, and practical leaders in politics and business. They were helped by lobbying groups, such as the American Municipal Association (now called the National League of Cities) and the United States Conference of Mayors. These large, well-financed trade and lobbying groups were skillful at providing the information and arguing the case for cities.

In the years after the Second World War, the major cities carried on a sustained effort to interest the federal government in broadening its responsibilities in the urban sphere. As urban problems developed in the post-war period an alliance of interest groups formed. At first, because most of the larger American cities were generally governed by the Democratic party, it consisted of Democratic politicians allied with downtown economic interests and some of the large metropolitan newspapers. Over time this group was joined by civic groups with a regional interest, some parts of organized labor, planners, and even college professors who saw the light outside of their towers. Concerning the urban transportation problem, the alliance was joined first by the commuter railroads, and in the mid–1960s, by the transit industry.[23]

At the beginning of the development of a federal urban mass transportation policy, the primary champion of the cause was Richardson Dilworth, Democratic mayor of Philadelphia. Dilworth was seriously concerned over the threat of cessation of commuter rail services, especially given the dense development and narrow streets of his downtown. He was joined in his efforts most actively by Mayor Robert Wagner of New York and Mayor Richard J. Daley of Chicago. Wagner and Daley were also worried about the serious impact that cuts or the elimination of commuter rail service would have on their cities' vitality and continued economic strength.

Despite the failure to gain federal aid through the legislation introduced by Congressman Green, Mayors Dilworth, Wagner, Daley, and representatives of other cities and the railroads met in Chicago in January 1959, determined to find a course of action in the wake of the Transportation Act of 1958. At the meeting were representatives of Allentown (Pennsylvania), Baltimore, Boston, Chicago, Cleveland, Detroit, Kansas City, Milwaukee, New York, Philadelphia, St. Louis, and Washington. The city representatives were joined by a delegation of railroad executives, representing the Baltimore & Ohio, Boston & Maine, Burlington, Chicago & North Western, Erie-Lackawanna, Jersey Central, Long Island, Milwaukee Road, Missouri Pacific, New Haven, New York Central, Pennsylvania, Reading, Rock Island, and Southern Pacific. Only the Missouri Pacific was not involved in commuter service.

A consensus was developed between the city representatives and the commuter line roads from the east coast: the federal government had a role to play in preserving and improving commuter rail service. The western commuter roads, especially those serving Chicago, were in less desperate financial shape than were the eastern lines and were more reluctant to support federal intervention. There was concern that any sort of federal aid would lead eventually to a federal takeover of the railroads. The western railroads were especially concerned that they would eventually become socialized. A smaller working group headed by Dilworth was a product of the meeting; its purpose was to devise a plan or program that all the interested could rally behind.[24]

The Dilworth group met in Philadelphia in March 1959. It chose to conduct a study in order to gain more time for agreement and to gather information to help provide a factual basis for their argument for federal aid. The research work was done by the Philadelphia contingent. The result was a study entitled *The Collapse of Commuter Service,* issued by the American Municipal Association late in 1959. The study examined five cities with commuter rail or rapid transit systems: Boston, Chicago, Cleveland, New York, and Philadelphia. The report sought to attract attention to the national nature of the urban transportation problem. While the primary focus of the study was on commuter railroads, it did take on a broader, mass transportation context. The study stated:

> The vast importance of the problem of mass transportation is indicated by the fact that more than 60% of the total U.S. population is contained in the Standard Metropolitan Areas, and by the end of the next decade, almost 80% of the U.S. population will be located in these areas.

The study discussed the very basic issue of costs:

> If only twenty-five percent of those now riding mass transportation lines were to be forced onto the highways . . . it would cost these five cities $4.4 billion to

provide the highway capacity to move a comparable number of people. . . . If the commuter lines were to suspend operations completely, it would cost $17.4 billion to build highways to serve a comparable number of people in these five cities. This does not include the additional costs of constructing parking facilities, the loss in taxes or the cost of traffic engineering. . . .[25]

The report included a recommendation that a federal lending agency (not unlike the Reconstruction Finance Corporation) be established to provide funds for urban transportation programs.[26]

The Collapse of Commuter Service marked the start of a vigorous public campaign for federal transit aid. Strong pressure from Mayor Dilworth and the commuter rail group found success at the American Municipal Association congress held in Denver in December 1959. The AMA adopted a resolution calling on Congress to establish a policy that would promote a means of transport in addition to highways. Because capital was badly needed for often threadbare urban rail operations, Congress was also urged to provide long-term, low-interest loans to help cities buy new equipment and replace or refurbish outmoded facilities. Federal transit grants were not called for in the report, but it was recommended that such a program should be the subject of further study.[27]

Despite the AMA resolution, there was not a great deal of enthusiasm within the AMA for a program that was narrowly focused on rail commuter and rapid transit problems. Only a handful of U.S. cities had rail transit or commuter rail facilities and service; thus the direct concern was limited. Nevertheless, the point had been made and an influential pressure group had had its attention drawn to the issue of a potential federal role in urban transportation. What had been unthinkable and unconsidered had been introduced to the AMA's world of ideas.[28]

A firmer coalition between the commuter rail oriented central cities and the railroads was a major plan arising from the efforts of 1959. Some of the railroads still viewed federal participation with suspicion. In retrospect, this seems both naive and refreshing. The railroads wanted to go it alone in the best fashion of private enterprise—despite the drubbing they were taking on all sides from subsidized competition—rather than accept subsidies themselves. Dilworth worked closely with James Symes, president of the Pennsylvania Railroad, to put together draft legislation to be presented to Congress under the auspices of the American Municipal Association. What Dilworth and Symes aimed at was a program designed to provide help to meet immediate needs and yet one that could evolve into a longer term legislative program agreeable to both the AMA and the railroads. Unfortunately, the legislation was not much more than a rehash of the ill-fated Green Bill of 1958. In its essential elements it was similar to the approach of the Reconstruction Finance Corporation. It called for low-interest loans to be made by the Department of Commerce to states, local governments, and authorities for the acquisition, maintenance, and improvement of mass transport equipment and facilities.

It was realistically expected that the proposed legislation would get a cold, reception from the Eisenhower administration and the 86th Congress. The railroad input avoided the usual legislative mistakes of the railroad industry (which usually sought to help itself by denying the benefits of government aid to other modes) by the simple expedient of getting benefits for themselves.[29] The legislative proposal was made more attractive to cities without rail transportation by calling for aid to mass transportation in general rather than big-city commuter railroads and rapid transit in particular; that, it was hoped, would gain support from traffic-beleaguered cities throughout the country. The proponents of the legislation did not deceive themselves that the legislation would pass the first time around. They realized that time would be needed to convince a reluctant Congress. Therefore, the first push would be to help educate the lawmakers. Passage of the act was hoped for in the next session of Congress.

Putting the administration of the proposed bill in the hands of the highway-oriented U.S. Department of Commerce was, in retrospect, a strategic error. It was understandable in that there seemed no other logical place within the federal government to put such a program. However, the Department of Commerce reflected the policy of the Eisenhower administration in opposing more federal programs for cities. There was an added reason: support of transit-oriented legislation might possibly raise some doubts about the wisdom of the federal highway program. This program was administered by the Department of Commerce through the Bureau of Public Roads and had just recently been enlarged by the creation of the Interstate Highway program in 1956.

February 1960 saw a delegation of mayors and railroad representatives in Washington. They presented the case for the proposed transit legislation before the Secretary of Commerce, representatives of the Budget Bureau, congressional leaders, and representatives of the congressional committees that would consider the measure. As no surprise, the legislation received a noncommittal if not chilly reception. But there was an important achievement in pledges of support for the proposed legislation from both Senate Majority Leader Lyndon Johnson and House Speaker Sam Rayburn.[30] Even so, the future of federal mass transportation policy was not encouraging until Harrison Williams entered the scene.

If there is one place in the United States where commuter rail service and mass transportation are important issues, it is New Jersey, sandwiched as it is between the great metropolitan areas of New York and Philadelphia. Cities and mass transportation interests found a champion in Congress in Senator Harrison Williams of New Jersey. Williams was an ambitious man, a freshman in the Senate in 1960, and he was seeking an issue or role that he could play that would be important to his New Jersey constituents and still possess relatively broad national interest. Williams found his issue in mass transportation.

As a senator, Williams was in an excellent position to get action on transit legislation even though he had little seniority. The six-year term of a senator permits more effort to be directed to important matters of legislation, as opposed to representatives who, it seems, are always running for re-election. A senator also has more resources for vital staff work. The statewide constituency means that a senator must have a wider viewpoint and gain skills in dealing with complex, varied, and often contradictory legislation. Better yet for someone wanting to initiate a transit program, a senator can deal with metropolitan issues in a way a representative cannot, because a member of the House of Representatives from a metropolitan area can usually afford and reflect only a sub-regional outlook. Moreover, the Senate traditionally has been far more interested in needed innovations in government and more intent upon the federal government exercising its leadership function than the House. In the late 1950s and into the 1960s, the Senate was probably far more representative of the changing needs of the increasingly urbanized American society than was the House.

Williams and his staff went to work on a new strategy for the transit legislation, and they made alterations to the Dilworth and Symes legislative proposal. The first strategic move was to shift the bill from the venue of the Department of Commerce by offering the legislation as a measure for urban areas rather than as a transportation program. That way, the legislation would fall under the jurisdiction of the Housing and Home Finance Agency, which in 1960 was the nearest thing to a Department of Urban Affairs within the federal government. The legislation would then be under the jurisdiction of the Senate Commission on Banking and Currency, of which Williams was a member. It was expected by Williams that this committee—liberal and urban oriented—would be friendlier to the legislation than the Commerce Committee, which would have handled the legislation as it was originally drafted by Dilworth and Symes. To be more acceptable to Congress, the original proposal for $500 million in loan authorizations was cut to $100 million. The revised legislation was written to emphasize that it was intended to deal with urban mass transportation problems in general, rather than as a commuter railway oriented bill designed to counteract the potential impact of the Transportation Act of 1958 on rail commuter service. Backed by the American Municipal Association and the commuter railroad interests, the transit bill was introduced into the Senate on March 24, 1960.[31] So the transit legislation was on its way—the committee jurisdiction was comfortable and the potential of the program falling under the aegis of HHFA was happy news for Dilworth and other mayors who were familiar with that agency and interested in working with it.

The Senate was friendly to the legislation, and the Williams bill, S.3278, was passed on June 27, 1960. However, Williams's best efforts and strong lobbying by urban interests represented by the AMA and the railroads were not enough to win the day. In the House of Representatives, the bill never got out of committee. Support in the House was not expected to be strong, so what happened was not a surprise. It was expected that the 1960 election might alter attitudes in the House. Indeed, the election changed the White House. In so doing, the election broadened the world of ideas and enlarged the choices to be considered in urban transportation.

The Democrats did not make a grand sweep of Congress in the 1960 election, but by a narrow margin they elected a president who had made a strong point in his campaign of the importance of urban issues. John F. Kennedy saw a need for the federal government to play an increased role in helping U.S. cities deal with their problems.

His opponent, Richard Nixon, virtually ignored the urban issue; in this Nixon followed a practice standard in earlier politics. Whether Kennedy's urban stance was vital to his winning the close election is debatable. It probably had only marginal influence, but Kennedy's stand on the problems of urban areas was certain and it included support for urban transportation.

The election of John Kennedy shifted the attitude of the national government toward urban problems and the relationship between the levels of governments. The tone was struck by Kennedy in 1959 (when he was running for the nomination to the Presidency) in a speech to the 1959 American Municipal Congress in Denver:

> Our national defense posture, our federal budget, our schools, highways, interest rates, race relations, reclamation, juvenile delinquency and the steel strike will be great issues in the 1960 election. But I would like to stress perhaps the greatest issue in a sense but the issue which is going to be talked about probably the least based on my own experience of traveling around the United States in the past year. I am asked what I think on the subject of birth control for India and what we should do in outer space, but hardly ever am I asked what we should do about the cities of the United States. I would say this is the greatest unspoken issue in the 1960 election and I think therefore we should address ourselves to it.[32]

FEDERAL URBAN TRANSPORT POLICY: GENESIS TIME

When the Kennedy administration took office in 1961, the way seemed fairly clear for federal participation in urban mass transportation programs. The original rationale for a federal role in transit was born of the reaction to the threat to commuter train service embodied in the passenger train discontinuation provisions of the Transportation Act of 1958. The anxiety of cities about commuter rail service was that loss of that service would add greatly to congestion. Congestion was the one universal element that was meaningful to all parties concerned about cities. However, although the legislation introduced by Senator Williams had moved thoughts about urban mass transportation from the limited commuter railroad issue to mass transportation as a whole, no substantial pressure came from any major segment of the public. Even in Harrison Williams's home state of New Jersey, there was little outcry for federal transit aid. Support for federal transit action was narrow. Over the next decade, perhaps the main difficulty faced by the supporters of federal programs for transit would be to broaden the base of support beyond that of big cities.

If there was no broad support in Congress, it could have been much worse. The issue appeared so remote that no major opposition group outside the Congress had formed. A coalition of highway interests—including automobile and tire manufacturers, petroleum companies, highway construction firms, and other interests who saw themselves threatened by an attack on highway programs—might have created a formidable opposition group. In league with the American Automobile Association and other associations of automobile users, all of which were major forces behind the Interstate Highway System, any organized opposition could probably have thoroughly undermined any effort to find and develop federal support for urban mass transportation. Because the period between 1958 and 1961 produced not much more than a ground swell, it appeared that the highway interests were unworried about the several proposed programs for urban mass transportation. Dilworth, Williams, and other supporters of mass transportation legislation were careful to avoid an either-or approach, so that the mass transport legislation was wisely promoted by Williams and his colleagues in terms of both highways *and* mass transport.[33]

The opposition which did develop against the program came from those who disputed growth in federal programs or who were particularly antagonistic to increased federal activity on the local level. As an issue with no grassroots public support in 1961, transit had virtually no political appeal save for representatives of large urban areas highly dependent upon transit and commuter rail transportation. In contrast with the push for civil rights legislation, an issue freighted with deep moral as well as political implications, urban mass transportation legislation seemed a picayune matter indeed. Because transit was no longer the critical player in local urban life it once had been, it was not an issue to stir the senses. It was not a well-understood issue and in its context of urban quality of life, a subject that was relatively unexamined in America at the time, transit as a federal activity was apt to elicit a yawn. Even to many persons in Washington who were not adverse to federal action, it still seemed as if urban mass transportation was a local issue to be handled on the local level.

The world is not static, and Washington was in the process of re-evaluating the federal approach to many urban problems. Even prior to the election of John Kennedy, there had been a rising concern about these kinds of problems. Much of the concern was not yet very well articulated, but thoughtful people were beginning to join with long-time observers of the urban scene, such as Lewis Mumford, in a growing sense of dismay over what was happening to U.S. cities, which had become the setting of the lives of most Americans. Congestion and its associated costs to urban life were very real factors of concern to citizens and political leaders alike. Despite spending vast sums of money on highways, congestion did not go away—it just got moved around in some places. If there was a transportation problem in the cities, most Americans would have said that it was congestion.

The Kennedy administration showed evidence of an overall concern for the urban situation. This was understandable because of the strong base of support for the Democratic party in urban places; most large cities had Democratic mayors and common councils as the norm. Housing, civil rights, education, redevelopment, and race relations were matters of vital interest, and frankly, they were also items that attracted much greater and more public and administration interest than did urban mass transportation.

The federal government began a direct role in urban affairs during the early days of the New Deal through the exercise of its legitimate, but largely unused, welfare powers. In an earlier time, such interference would have been condemned as exceeding the constitutional and traditional role of the federal government, but the emergency conditions of the Great Depression permitted the federal government to take action hitherto undreamed of. This is an expression of the American penchant for governmental innovation in tough situations. The standard, laissez-faire approaches to combat the Depression had not worked; government should have a go at fixing what had broken down.[34]

The initial broad programs undertaken in the first Roosevelt administration were knocked down with monotonous regularity by a conservative Supreme Court that reflected a Jeffersonian bias in its conception of the proper role of the federal government. Moreover, it was a sign of the deep American distrust of centralization of power, be it in government, business, or organized labor. With caution bred of desperation, from the late 1930s on, the federal government had usually taken on the roles of leader and provider of funds, but had typically left the day-to-day operations of federal programs to state and local officials or to private enterprise.[35] The caution fostered by early New Deal setbacks had frequently been translated into unimaginative programs with modest payoff. This, along with a healthy fear of risk by administrators on all levels of government, had almost guaranteed that federal urban programs and federal programs in general would be less than satisfactory. Animated by this spirit of caution, whatever action the federal government chose to take in mass transportation was unlikely to be revolutionary in nature or scope. This conventional, understandably cautious approach meant that all dimensions and possibilities of a program or policy were unlikely to be explored. Program response based on legislation was most apt to attempt a solution to an obvious problem—for example, a mass transportation provider, such as a commuter railroad, going out of business—rather than to explore the full possibilities of what something like mass transportation, coordinated with other means of transportation, could do to make more substantive improvements in urban life. There was no philosophy, no ideal, and no model of what cities should or might be that was generally understood or accepted by the public or by those charged with oversight and management of cities. It is not a setting that leads to much that is exciting or potentially very useful. From the outset, the usefulness of federal transit policy and programs would be limited by the failure to understand—or care—if American cities could be much different than they were. Only a vivid and widespread and well-understood crisis could lead to a major change in approach.

The failure of many federal programs since the 1930s to really improve urban areas and urban life throughout the nation has resulted in part from suburban attitudes. Many suburban political officials, probably supported by most suburban dwellers, regard the central city as something to be milked, not fed. This attitude stems from the fear of becoming entangled—financially if not otherwise—in some of the awful and apparently unsolvable problems that plagued the big cities. Most people had moved to the suburbs in pursuit of the American suburban ideal, which from its beginning in mid-eighteenth century England had sought escape and relief from real and perceived urban problems. There also arose a genuine fear of the minority groups—usually non-white—that were taking over increasing proportions of central city areas.

The first twenty years of the post–World War II era in America often found whatever political strength the suburban areas had—and it was often unformed—in Washington, generally allied with the strategically powerful Southern conservative group and various big business pressure groups to achieve certain ends through the process of political compromise. Thus it was assured that whatever action taken in urban areas by the federal government would definitely benefit private interests and the suburbs, although it would not necessarily meet any of the higher ends for which programs had been initiated.

Lack of follow-through can be devastating to one's game of golf; the same holds true for governmental programs. Legislation for various kinds of federal or other governmental action may have enthusiastic support in the time leading up to its consideration by Congress or another legislative body; however, when the legislation becomes law, the enthusiasm dies and careful evaluation of the programs is abandoned until some great problem or crisis is recognized. To many members of the public, the problem is solved when a bill is passed. The vital implementation phase is largely anticlimactic, and the public usually shows little interest in making sure a law accomplishes its stated goals until a considerable time has passed. Then what has or has not happened is viewed with alarm, and solutions are sought which may be too little or far too late.

Moreover, a statement of an overall strategy and workable goals for a program are usually omitted. As a consequence, there are no clear and workable objectives established to use as benchmarks on performance. Usually, there is money provided for given purposes, such as capital to buy transit equipment or build transit facilities, with only the vaguest of workable goals at hand. Under these circumstances, it is difficult to prove success—and it may be equally difficult to prove failure in a rational way.

Even though many federal programs had been aimed at helping cities, honest men could say in 1961 and afterward that federal programs actually aided in the devitalization of the cities. The Federal Housing Administration and Veterans Administration loan programs had mainly aided suburban development, not the central cities. Urban renewal projects often displaced low-income groups, forcing them to double up in already overcrowded neighborhoods, while the renewal project itself provided housing for medium and upper income groups. Public housing projects, especially the huge, high-rise variety, often turned a bad horizontal slum into an even worse, more highly concentrated, vertical jungle of violence, fear, and despair. The highway program did not relieve congestion; it often did relocate the congestion—severe congestion appears to have moved further out into the suburbs in the 1980s than it was in the 1960s—and indeed, the federal highway program probably made congestion worse by encouraging greater use of the automobile in the sprawling suburbs that federal housing policy had done so much to spawn.[36]

In short, many of the problems of the cities are the result of federal programs. Paradoxically, the very failure, or perceived failure, of a governmental program may provide a major rationale for other programs to correct the problems and to provide equity for those injured by the first program. With justice, one may argue that the federal highway program and other federal activities had a devastating impact on the mass transit industry; equity is served by aiding the injured industry. Typically, the program or policy that caused the mischief in the first place is not ended, although it may be altered, because to do so would upset those who had come to expect it and depend upon it. Thus, the federal highway and transit programs continue side by side, often with one usually canceling out many of the potential benefits of the other.[37]

THE AIMS OF FEDERAL POLICY

It is not out of order to state that federal mass transportation policy is innocent of workable goals in the sense of a goal as a long-term, ideal situation. This does not mean that initially (as well as over the years) there have not been a variety of goals and purposes. The initial aims of federal urban transportation policy were shaped by both the shorter-run needs of big cities which were fearful of losing vital commuter railway and mass transit services, as well as by the longer-run needs of providing for less chaotic development in rapidly growing metropolitan areas. The big-city mayors had sought federal help because metropolitan areas could not help themselves and the states were unwilling or unable to provide aid. The mayors and the American Municipal Association wanted help to preserve existing transportation services as reasonable alternatives for the private automobile. The initial policy of the federal government was to treat mass transport as an integral part of urban development. Over the years, as other problem areas arose on the urban scene, such as air pollution, economic development, energy conservation, and mainstreaming the handicapped, mass transportation was expected to play a role.

The federal policy aims for mass transportation were perhaps most clearly stated in President Kennedy's transportation message of 1962:

> To conserve and enhance values in existing urban areas is essential. But at least as important are steps to promote economic efficiency and livability in areas of future development. In less than 20 years we can expect well over half of our expanded population to be living in 40 great urban complexes. Many smaller places will also experience phenomenal growth. The ways that people and goods can be moved in these areas will have a major influence on their structure, on the efficiency of their economy, and on the availability for social and cultural opportunities they can offer their citizens. Our national welfare therefore requires the provision of good urban transportation, with the properly balanced use of private vehicles and modern mass transport to help shape as well as serve urban growth.[38]

According to Kennedy's message, there were three broad goals: (1) to preserve and enhance urban values; (2) to serve the population at the lowest cost; and (3) to help shape cities. This was to be accomplished in a coordinated manner which would achieve a balance between the use of private and public vehicles. In the context of the president's message, the goals treat the urban mass transportation issue in a far broader perspective than had hitherto been the case. The idea of saving the commuter trains is embraced within these three objectives, but there is also a much broader ideal expressed, particularly the need to establish a livable future for American cities. That said, the message is not very hopeful in charting a course of action; somebody, most likely an executive agency, would have to translate the goals into objectives and action plans. At the time of the message, there was no Department of Transportation, no Urban Mass Transportation Administration, and no highly organized lobbying group (such as APTA). There was only the Housing and Home Finance Agency's tiny branch that carried out the mass transit programs that had been established in 1961. In short, there was no other part of the federal establishment to carry the ball.

In any case, behind the goal of preservation and enhancement of urban values, looking into the Kennedy message one sees an understanding that American central cities were in deep trouble, growing financially weaker yet becoming increasingly overburdened by social problems. Unattractive either for visits or investments, the old central city core area—the time-honored CBD and its immediate environs—had become for many Americans a place to work in and then get away from.

Preservation of the city was not a completely unselfish motive, because continued deterioration endangered property values. Federal programs seen as preserving value were most appealing. Retail establishments also recognized that improved access to downtown shopping districts would boost sales. Social interests and needs could also to be met by the urban mass transportation program, especially if it reduced congestion and enhanced mobility to help life become more interesting and vital. From the perspective of the 1980s, the attitudes of the late 1950s and early 1960s show a lack of concern over the social and economic costs of automobile accidents, reduced air pollution, and energy conservation, and the improved urban aesthetics that might be aided through greater use of mass transportation.

In having the shaping of cities as a goal for mass transportation policy, one can even see an attempt to regain some of the lost opportunities of the New Deal 1930s. Then, failure of effective control and bold action by the federal government—which, frankly, had other priorities and a top leadership that was not attuned to urban issues or comfortable with them—had encouraged sprawling metropolitan development and its resultant fragmentation. Indeed, as strange as it may seem in the gridlocked 1980s, urban highway building in the 1930s and for several more decades was seen as a form of social and economic therapy.[39] There was an obvious need for shaping, reshaping, and rationalizing development on the urban scene, and properly geared mass transportation policy could help in such programs. But all of this was to be made incredibly more difficult because of the restructuring of America, by plan or default, into an automobile-oriented society. Without deep thought, the nation had come to a point where a strong and vigorous role for transit in urban places would be enormously difficult and expensive to create. In the early 1960s few observers realized what a tremendously problem-filled job it would be and that with neither a clear mission nor firm, specific objectives, the task might be well-nigh impossible and amount to not much more than a huge expenditure of funds by all levels of government with little to show for the effort.

The goal of providing mobility to urban populations at the lowest possible cost was very attractive. Relatively modest mass transit investments might make large highway investment unnecessary. Moreover, it could help deflect rapidly growing metropolitan areas from a course of large population growth with people almost entirely dependent upon the automobile. To many observers of the urban scene that would be unthinkable; there would be too many people, too many cars, and too little room.

THE HOUSING ACT OF 1961

When the Kennedy administration took office in early 1961, it seemed to bring an almost immediate promise of fulfillment of the aims of Senator Williams, the AMA, and central city-railroad interests for a federal role in urban mass transportation. Expanding the balloon of hope were two reports which took a favorable view of federal aid to mass transportation. Former Harvard Law School Dean James Landis, in his report on the federal regulatory agencies, recommended to the president that the federal government guarantee loans for the commuter railroads.[40] Another bit of encouragement came from the Doyle Report, a study conducted for the Senate Commerce Committee. Under the leadership of General John Doyle, a group of researchers concerned itself with transportation in general and railroads in particular. The Doyle Report had its roots in the senatorial investigations of 1958 which led up to the passage of the Transportation Act of 1958. The eastern commuter railroads had requested that a section on urban mass transportation be included in the report. The study took note of the advanced age of much of the U.S. commuter rail fleet and the dilapidation of its facilities. To solve the commuter rail problem, the Doyle Report recommended a loan program to be administered by the Interstate Commerce Commission.[41] In retrospect it does not appear to be a very bold suggestion; however, it was well within the conventional wisdom and the spectrum of ideas at the time.

Senator Williams's urban mass transportation bill in 1961, introduced shortly before the Kennedy inauguration, included a loan program similar to that recommended by the Doyle Report and a demonstration grant program (real life, practical experimentation) that Williams and his chief legislative assistant, ArDee Ames, had developed as a way of "kicking off" the federal mass transit program. It appeared to have the makings of a modest but solid beginning.

To the dismay of Senator Williams and the coalition of transit supporters, the new Kennedy administration did not welcome the legislation. There were a number of reasons for its attitude. Early in the Kennedy administration came the Bay of Pigs fiasco, a fumbled attempt to invade Cuba made by Cuban exiles and aided by the U.S., for which the new president took responsibility.[42] This failure badly strained the credibility of the new administration and would clearly make it difficult to get its legislative programs through Congress. In order to build the needed legislative momentum the president was advised to advance a program of legislation that was generally supported by Congress. A transit bill, or other legislation for which there was little support, would be apt to fail and thus interrupt the flow and passage of what the administration felt to be more important legislation in advancing its plans to improve the economy, uphold civil rights, and take bold steps into the future.

A good part of the reluctance of the administration stemmed from the desire of key officials to wait until a comprehensive study was completed to provide information on just how much need there was in urban mass transportation; there was fear on the part of the Bureau of the Budget that to move ahead on a new program in urban mass transportation without some idea of the dollars involved would be unwise. HHFA Administrator Robert C. Weaver was concerned that the transit program, if placed in his agency, would eat up too many of the dollars that were consigned to the housing program. He also thought it was premature to move without a comprehensive study of the transit issue.

There was also a jurisdictional battle. Secretary of Commerce Luther Hodges wanted the transit program in his department, taking the position that there were other transportation functions in Commerce (most notably the Bureau of Public Roads), and that it would be a mistake to scatter transportation into various parts of the federal government. Williams was dead set against lodging the transit programs in Commerce because the committee jurisdiction in the Senate would fall to Senator George Smathers's subcommittee on surface transportation. The legislation would thus be taken out of Williams's hands and, because he had decided to make a reputation on the transit question, steal his issue. Williams was also afraid that the transit legislation would die in the Smathers subcommittee.

The tendency in the White House was to wait for the comprehensive study to be finished, which would take at least a year; Williams did not want the delay. He mounted hearings to remind the White House of the strong support for the bill. The coalition of the AMA and the commuter railroads was joined by endorsements from central city business and civic interests. Organized labor belatedly gave its support, and there was also backing from three governors in the hearings. Governor David Lawrence of Pennsylvania gave strong support, reflecting upon the experience he had as mayor of Pittsburgh. Governor John Volpe of Massachusetts (well-known as a major highway contractor) and later President Nixon's first Secretary of Transportation, cited the need for transit aid to provide balance in transportation. Very important, because it brought the western cities into the picture, was the support of Governor Edmund Brown of California. Sadly for Williams, the governors of New York and his own New Jersey did not support the legislation, on the grounds that it did nothing to ameliorate the fragmentation of transportation systems in urban areas—an obvious factor in transportation in the New York City metropolitan area. The suburban areas of the country were silent.

There seemed to be little hope of a bill on the single issue of transit getting through Congress, but the administration and Williams felt that by making transit a part of the omnibus housing act, a bill that enjoyed wide support in the Congress, the transit legislation would stand a fair chance. Even so, the administration proposed a transit-only bill. To the disappointment of Williams and the transit coalition, the housing bill went to Congress without the transit portion. Taking initiative, Williams introduced his transit legislation as an amendment to the $6 billion housing bill. Continuing pressure from Williams's coalition convinced the White House in May that a transit act of some sort would have to be passed in 1961. A series of compromises took place between the White House and the Senate and within the Senate itself. After much hard work by Williams the Senate passed the housing bill on June 12, 1961. It contained $150 million for mass transit planning, demonstrations, and loans.

Now, what would the House do? It was known to be less supportive of transit and lacked a champion for the issues. The situation brightened on June 19, when President Kennedy sent his transit bill to the House along with a policy statement supporting transit and recommending placing it within the HHFA. But the financial recommendation was only for a $10 million emergency loan program. By June 26, more compromise had led to the White House accepting the idea of a $75 million transit program.

On June 28, after more compromise and negotiation, a measure was adopted by the conference of the House and Senate and a $5.6 billion housing bill was reported out containing a transit program, and the president signed it on June 30, 1961. The federal mass transit programs had gotten under way.[43]

There were three urban mass transportation provisions in the Housing Act of 1961. First of all, $25 million was authorized for mass transportation demonstration projects. As it turned out, in the very early stages of the federal program and policy development, the demonstration proved to be perhaps the most notable and important part of the act. Second, mass transportation planning was included as an integral part of comprehensive urban planning under the Section 701 program of planning grants. The planning effort was to help prepare studies to solve problems of congestion, improve mobility, and cut transport needs.

Third, loans for capital improvement purposes were authorized under the Act of 1961. Noting that it was difficult for many mass transport undertakings to raise money at reasonable interest rates, the Housing and Home Finance Agency was authorized to loan funds at low interest in circumstances where repayment was reasonably certain.[44] A total of $50 million was authorized for the loans. As it turned out, this portion of the Act and subsequent loan programs included in mass transport legislation remained largely unused. In the early 1960s potential applicants were reluctant to seek loans; one reason was that many cities were at their borrowing limit. Another, perhaps more practical reason was the hope of eventually getting federal transit grants that would not need to be repaid. The idea that many transit operations (predominantly in private ownership at this time) would be able to pay off a loan was an overly optimistic one.

Several precedents were set in the new legislation. The federal transit funds could not go directly to a private company, and most of the transit industry was privately owned at the time; the federal money had to be channeled through a government or governmental agency. This is not an uncommon feature of federal programs of aid and it was felt to be a way of assuring coordination between local transportation programs. Furthermore, because HHFA was in the practice of dealing directly with cities and largely bypassing the states, the transit program was handled in the same way. Had the program been lodged in the Department of Commerce, the practice of the Bureau of Public Roads of dealing with states might have been adopted. This would have greatly reduced the number of clients with which those administering the transit act would have had to deal. It might also have encouraged earlier and more substantial financial contributions to transit from state government.

The mass transit portion of the Housing Act of 1961 was a modest start for the federal transit program, especially when compared with the high hopes of the coalition that had worked so hard to get the program enacted. The dollars were small: despite the $75 million authorization, only $42.5 million was appropriated to pay for the demonstrations and the loans. Even so, it was a start, a foundation to build upon. Even if the new law did not provide grants of capital and money to help pay operating expenses for financially troubled transit properties, the 1961 Act offered eventual hope for more favorable action in the future.

The demonstrations were of critical importance at this time because they had the potential to attract attention. The same amount of money spent at the same time on the development of some modest capital projects would have been virtually invisible to local public officials, the media, and members of Congress. In terms of what the small demonstration grant program of the time helped to engender, there was probably no other way the money could have been spent that would have been so productive in arousing nationwide transit interest.

The Act of 1961 in and of itself did not do much to help the sagging fortunes of urban commuter railways or mass transit systems. However, to some extent it did help answer the question of whether or not people would ride transit if it was improved. Mayor Richardson Dilworth, at the 1962 hearings on mass transportation legislation before the Congress, could point with great pride to the success of Philadelphia's Passenger Service Improvement Corporation and its city-sponsored commuter railroad experiments within Philadelphia, which showed that patrons could be wooed back to mass transportation.[45] Moreover, successful results from a number of demonstration studies would be powerful ammunition in getting the federal government to play a greater role in solving urban mass transportation problems. Successful demonstrations would ward off the inevitable criticism—leveled again a quarter century later during the Reagan administration—that investing funds in mass transportation was pouring money down a rat hole. Such criticism was bound to arise when urban transport interests again approached Congress for an expanded program of federal aid. The demonstrations initiated by the 1961 Housing Act provided a hedge for congressional and other supporters; it gave time for lobbying and didn't cost much. A capital program by its very nature would perforce not only require considerable money but also considerable time to carry out the capital improvements. Demonstrations had faster payoff.

HIGHWAY ACT OF 1962

For whatever reasons, and in whatever way the U.S. was moving toward an urban transportation policy that embraced both highways and transit, it is only logical that a means be found to understand urban places better. The Highway Act of 1961 was a vital and logical part of the package of legislation necessary for an intelligent approach to the urban transportation problem. No one had to be a genius to see that the highway programs of the federal government had been a mixed blessing; highways brought both benefits and costs in their wake. That point was made most strongly as the Interstate Highway System began to impinge on cities, where the impact of the superhighways was not always a happy one. A fault in the program was that the highway-planning process was rather narrow in its scope and focus; it concentrated almost entirely on the engineering issues of highway construction. The spillover costs and benefits were virtually ignored. As a result of narrow planning, there were too many unexpected results, such as the blight and disfigurement of the urban fabric created by the presence of a giant engineering work occupied by scores of thousands of noisy, fume-spewing vehicles, located smack in the middle of often heavily urbanized places. The Kennedy administration was alert to the proposition that building only highways in urban places was not enough and that consideration should also be given to alternatives to highways. The key was to broaden the scope of planning. The Highway Act of 1962 and its planning provision is an example of belated federal effort to rationalize past programs which had inadvertently gone astray and produced unforeseen developments. It was also an early effort to consider factors later embraced within the environmental movement.

Tying strings to federal highway money was one way of producing better planning. Under the terms of Section 9 of the Highway Act of 1962, in any urban area with a population of 50,000 or more there would be no federal highway money made available unless the proposed highway projects were based on a comprehensive and continuing planning process, carried on in cooperation with the state and local levels of government. This new planning requirement took effect July 1, 1965.[46] In requiring comprehensive and continuing planning, the Highway Act of 1962 guaranteed that urban areas will at least have given consideration to transport alternatives other than highways.[47]

However imperfect, the comprehensive planning requirement of the Highway Act of 1962 made it possible to resolve the mistakes occurring through misinterpretation of model planning legislation of the late 1920s. Secretary of Commerce Herbert Hoover appointed a nine-man committee to prepare the Standard City Planning Enabling Act of 1928. Hoover's aim was to insure more orderly urban development, and the 1928 Act became the model for the urban planning process adopted by most municipalities throughout the United States. "The 1928 Act specifies as the principal duty of the City Planning Commission the preparation, adoption, and maintenance of a long-range comprehensive, general plan for the physical development of a city."[48] The aim of the legislation was laudable; the weakness came in the interpretation of the Act.

As the 1928 Act was interpreted, planning commissions might adopt the urban general plan as a whole or in pieces. The plans turned out were often anything but comprehensive and too often were piecemeal efforts. Planning and planners became bogged down to the point of quibbling over zoning and other micro-aspects of city planning, rather than devoting time and talent to overall comprehensive planning. The apparent failure of cities to understand just how highways could carve up a city, or the proper role for urban mass transportation, or how urban sprawl and suburban blight could be prevented is understandable, albeit lamentable.[49]

If the urban general plan was poorly handled, transportation planning was apt to be even more clumsily handled in the 1920s and 1930s. Because of its almost inescapable involvement in politics because of the need for and value of franchise, transit was tainted in many cities. The hearings of the Federal Electric Railways Commission (discussed in earlier pages) had drawn attention to the often sleazy relationships between politicians and street railways. Compared to transit, the professional highway engineers appeared to be smart, young, apolitical, and free from the stigma of old boodling politics. The planning of the 1920s, and for forty years thereafter, more often met the needs of those who controlled the planning process than the need of the public. The commercial and financial groups that had business interests in the city center and saw value in concentration would have their say, as would the highway interests that saw a bigger market for their products and services in the process of decentralizing residential, industrial, and commercial areas.[50]

Section 9 of the Highway Act of 1962 offered an opportunity to mend some of the damage created during the New Deal years of the 1930s in the urban planning process and in the role of mass transportation in that planning. So great was the economic distress caused by the Great Depression that there was an understandable tendency for quick fixes. Rural and regional projects received the large-scale physical planning efforts sponsored by the federal government, and little effort was devoted to the needs of central cities and mass transit. Action was necessary to solve the grim problems of people living in that era of severe economic distress, with the consequence that so little thought was given to transit, it fell between the proverbial cracks. No leader pleaded its cause on a national level. As to a leader setting the tone for far-sighted urban action, it was noted earlier that President Franklin Roosevelt was much more interested in international and rural issues and was not overly fond of cities. The General Motors futurama exhibit at the 1939 New York World's Fair probably had more influence on urban transportation planning than did any political leader.

If the planning efforts were pragmatic during the New Deal, it does not mean that the efforts were well-informed or broad in scope. Moreover, there was a lamentable, if understandable, lack of trust between planners and politicians during the difficult times that faced the nation and its cities. Both planners and politicians were innocent of the professional background that we have come to expect of such persons today. Unfortunately, many planners did not see any great need for solid and broad-based professional training in planning in the 1920s, 1930s, and much later in the time under discussion. The U.S. is still paying for the shortcomings in planning. There was nothing of the boldness of the plan of a Daniel Burnham; Frank Lloyd Wright was often construed as a flack for suburban developers and as increasingly narcissistic in his work.[51]

Thinking small is a formidable force when it comes to eliminating broad and constructive consideration about a truly creative and balanced means of providing mobility in American cities. There is no telling the damage done to urban transportation nationwide by the works of Robert Moses and his arrogant approach to New York City's transportation situation by concentrating on highways only. Moses's enormous power in New York, as well as his influence on the federal highway and transportation programs, are a part of the legacy that all U.S. cities share. Most awful of the products of Moses's genius was the never-ending cycle of building first-rate highways that attracted cars, became congested, and then must be supplemented by still more highways.[52]

Regardless of the problems and lost opportunities of times past, the pragmatic and intellectual groundwork for a more ambitious federal role in urban transportation had been laid by the early 1960s. The work of the big city mayors, Senator Williams and his staff, and some of the more thoughtful people in the U.S. Department of Commerce was about to bear fruit. As a nation, Americans try not to be dogmatic; the United States has usually eschewed blind faith in doctrine, other than to grasp after a more complete democracy. However flawed in execution, American policy generally seeks an understanding of the problems of the people and their institutions and makes an effort to solve those problems through debate, discussions, lobbying, compromise, and pursuit of what is possible at a given time. Pragmatism—what works—has been a keystone of the American governmental process. It was that pragmatic approach that was to prevail in the formulation of federal mass transit policy.

Let's pause for an intellectual retrospective of the thought behind an emerging urban transportation policy in the 1960s. The initial factors which conditioned federal urban transport policies were, first of all, a growing understanding of the need for a broad attack on urban problems. After the early 1960s a key element in this attack was urban mass transportation, even in instances in which transit by itself was a relatively deficient means of achieving a desired end. Second was the matter of equity. That meant the policy should seek to redress at least some of the urban transportation imbalances caused by the highways-only program under the Highway Act of 1944—a policy which had continued unabated from war's end until 1961—by providing reasonable alternatives to the use of the private automobile. Unfortunately, no crystal ball revealed a future in which, despite the efforts to improve and expand mass transit and make it an attractive alternative, the automotive traffic congestion would grow far worse and more widespread than it was.

A third point is that the urban transportation problem was seen mainly as congestion because of its visible nature and the vocal complaints of the public increasingly stuck in traffic jams. There were strong signs of a broader view, but to most people in the 1960s (as well as in the 1980s), the federal transit programs were mainly aimed at relieving traffic congestion.

A shift in attitude at the Bureau of the Budget in the 1960s and 1970s had a large role in shaping federal policy in urban transportation. (Under President Nixon, the Bureau of the Budget became the Office of Management and Budget.) During this period the Bureau of the Budget was increasingly unwilling to concentrate the federal government's financial power behind any one program in a given field, usually seeking a mix of alternatives. To date, the Budget Bureau has not publicly questioned the sanctity of road building in the United States, although under the Reagan administration a more conservatively doctrinaire Office of Management and Budget has most certainly questioned federal expenditures for transit. During the Nixon administration the wisdom of trust funds (such as the Highway Trust Fund) was questioned. Money which was so inflexibly committed served to hamper administration efforts to dampen the rise of inflation or to use alternative spending policies to provide a boost for the economy when needed.

As the 1960s wore on, it was increasingly clear that the policy of highway construction was no longer to have a monopoly on federal funds in urban transportation. Despite this change in policy by the federal government, it has not been an easy time for the cause of transit, either inside or outside of the federal government. Policies and programs change, the fondest hopes are thwarted by reality and the fickleness of events (the petroleum situation is an example) along with rising costs and the wilderness of rules, regulations, and pork-barrel politics.

6.

A Program Develops: The Urban Mass Transportation Act of 1964 and the 1966 Amendments

The transit industry was still marginally profitable on an industry-wide basis in 1964. Even so, the industry was not healthy and help was needed if service was to continue on a generally available basis at reasonable fares. The legislation that would become the major foundation of the federal transit program moved from a program of planning loans and demonstrations to one that included capital grants. Given the deteriorating state of the equipment and physical plant, capital funds were needed to provide a financial transfusion for urban mass transportation. Capital funds were available through the loan provisions of the 1961 Act, but this approach was usually foreclosed to the most needy cases, those which could not hope to pay back the money borrowed.

The Housing Act of 1961 was really temporary legislation; it did not deal in a realistic fashion with the capital needs of the transit industry. The 1961 Act had been most specific in stating that demonstration grant money could not be used for capital projects.[1] This point was noted by John C. Kohl, the Housing and Home Finance Agency (HHFA) assistant administrator in charge of the Office of Transportation:

> . . . the prohibition of the use of demonstration grants for "major long-term capital improvement" has been conscientiously applied because the principal and sometimes sole objective of some proposals was the construction of a permanent transit facility for which regular financing had proved impossible. Rentals and other recognized charges for the use of capital equipment or facilities during the term of a demonstration was, however, recognized as a proper use of funds insofar as the particular items could be shown to be essential for the attainment of project objectives. Provision for crediting the project with any remaining capital value at its conclusion has been a mandatory requirement in these cases.[2]

Passage of the legislation was not easy. The main congressional hurdle was the House of Representatives. The House—with its strong rural, non-urban, conservative predilections—was the main factor impeding progress in the development of the urban mass transportation program in the three years after 1961, even though there was growing support for a federal transit program on the part of smaller cities and suburban areas.[3] House opposition, plus the lack of apparent strong grass-roots support from the public and the absence of strong and continuous pressure on Congress from a well-organized power group, enabled opponents of the program to prevent passage.

There had been some reason to believe that action would come much earlier. In the early months of 1962, it appeared as if new and far more comprehensive mass transportation legislation would soon be forthcoming, because President Kennedy had devoted a large portion of his transportation message of April 1962 to urban mass transportation. In the urban section of his transportation message, President Kennedy recommended

> . . . that the Congress authorize the first installment of a long-range program of Federal aid to our urban regions for the revitalization and needed expansion of public mass transportation [through] a capital grant authorization of $500 million to be made available over a three-year period, with $100 million to be made available in fiscal 1963. . . .[4]

The program the president recommended called for continuation of the demonstration and loan provision of the Act of 1961 and for comprehensive planning. The planning recommendations became a part of the Highway Act of 1962, as discussed in the previous chapter. Through his message, the president had given a boost to improved land-use planning and had urged a far stronger and larger capital grant program than supporters of mass transportation had hoped.[5]

Immediately following the president's message, Senator Williams introduced legislation containing a capital grant program. Hearings were soon held in both the House and the Senate. These hearings were generally successful in pointing out the need for federal aid and gave evidence of support for the measure from various urban interest groups.

The support was not as broad or deep from urban political leaders as might have been expected, save for the coalition of big-city mayors mentioned previously. At the time of these early hearings on a relatively comprehensive transit program, the great majority of transit was still provided by unsubsidized private firms. To political leaders in most American cities transit embodied at best a troublesome fight on fare increases; in some places it was a continual succession of owners as properties changed hands in an effort on the part of some owners to get out of the transit business in the best financial shape possible. In contemplating more federal action in transit, Congress was actually ahead of most city leaders who were, if possible, in the main less than indifferent to the plight of transit and the thought of providing financial aid. As David Jones has noted, in most urban places, federal concern was in advance of local concern.[6] In addition, there was no strong, well-organized antagonism; the strongest opposition came from the Chamber of Commerce of the United States and the American Farm Bureau Federation. Both of these groups possessed deep philosophical reservations about federal programs on the local level (the same position taken by Ronald Reagan in his successful presidential campaigns of 1980 and 1984). The opponents recited the litany of free enterprise and no enlargement of government spending. Labor gave cautious support to the proposed transit legislation but expressed a short-sighted concern over the possible loss of jobs that might result from improved and more efficient transport systems. The loss of the right to strike was a concern if the program encouraged an increase in municipal ownership of transit companies. Automotive interests also gave cautious approval, taking care to point out that mass transportation and the private automobile were complementary to one another and that there was a laudable and necessary—though limited—role for mass transportation. They were, however, firm in resisting any diversion of highway user fees for the support of mass transportation programs.[7]

The House and Senate Banking Committees both reported favorably on the proposed legislation. In the process of developing the new law, Senator Frank J. Lausche (D-Ohio), a major foe of the mass transportation program, insisted that because some commuter trips were interstate in nature the Senate Commerce Committee should hold a hearing on the legislation. In September, Senator Lausche held a one-day hearing that was generally hostile in tone; it was not a matter of wonder that the Commerce Committee reported the bill without recommendation.[8] Favorable action was expected in the Senate, but the House Rules Committee kept the bill from reaching the House floor. The Urban Mass Transportation Act of 1962 died a lingering death as the 87th Congress passed into history. Despite this setback, Congress did pass a bill extending the 1961 Act for six months beyond its scheduled expiration date.[9]

The defeat of the 1962 Urban Mass Transportation bill in the supposedly liberal House Rules Committee was a surprise to supporters of a federal role in transit, particularly after President Kennedy's strong support for a program of greater aid to urban transit and the eloquent arguments in favor of transit aid in the president's transportation message. Undaunted, Senator Harrison Williams submitted a 1963 Urban Mass Transportation bill on January 9, 1963, early in the first session of the 88th Congress. Again, opposition developed from Senator Lausche and others on the surface transportation subcommittee. In spite of this, the Williams bill, largely intact, passed the Senate by a 52-41 vote on April 4.[10] In the House there was trouble; southern representatives, in an effort to retaliate against the Kennedy administration's civil rights program, took on an anti-urban stance. It was felt that there was a good chance the House version of the bill would never get out of committee.

The impatient had much to be fidgety about. The House version of the bill remained in committee for more than a year, but in real fact the House Rules Committee was not responsible for the delay. The bill was held in the Rules Committee because House Speaker John McCormack felt that if the bill did come up for a vote on the floor of the House, it stood a good chance of being defeated.

There were two good strategic reasons for the speaker's reluctance; one was the need, for the transit bill's sake, to wait for a propitious moment. The second was political wisdom on the part of McCormack regarding more important legislation in the eyes of the Johnson administration.[11]

After President Kennedy's assassination, President Johnson had supported the Kennedy programs, including the mass transportation legislation, and called for passage of the program of legislation that President Kennedy had worked for as a memorial to the deceased. Thus, first on the Johnson administration's list of priority legislation was civil rights. Speaker McCormack was fearful he would jeopardize the Johnson administration's reputation for legislative success by bringing the urban mass transportation bill to the floor of the House prematurely. The speaker did not wish to break the momentum that the Johnson administration was developing for the difficult passage of the civil rights legislation, legislation that was intended to be its crowning achievement. The dynamism of success would, it was expected, carry Johnson to his own term as president in the upcoming 1964 election.

For this reason, despite the best efforts of transit proponents, by April of 1964 the mass transportation bill had not been included on the White House list of "must" legislation. This set into motion an unusual train of events. To fully appreciate what happened, one must go back to 1963. At that time there was a proposal before the House of Representatives for the construction of a rapid transit system in the District of Columbia. Labor lobbyists in Washington, in a virtual explosion of short-sightedness, were persuaded to bring pressure against Congress to defeat the bill as an anti-labor measure. It was an old refrain: organized labor was worried about the loss of bargaining rights of employees of a publicly owned and operated subway system. Labor was also concerned that the proposed subway system would put bus drivers out of work. Too late, labor leaders realized their mistake in thinking small; defeat of the bill would actually reduce job opportunities, because federal aid to transit on a national basis would strengthen the tottering transit industry and create more job opportunities. By the time labor saw its error, it was too late to make its change of heart known to Congress and the bill was defeated in the House. Out of this defeat, however, transit supporters saw what was needed. To get desired action, particularly in the House of Representatives where support was shaky, a strong and coordinated lobbying approach was necessary.

Transit proponents then formed a pressure group to push the transit bill using the time-honored process of unflagging lobbying. The lobbying vehicle was called the Urban Passenger Transportation Association (UPTA), which represented the central city interests, the transit industry, the railroads, and organized labor (which was now firmly in the camp of transit as long as there was a *quid pro quo* in the legislation that protected jobs). Labor's active interest and membership in this group was made known to President Johnson, and between April and May of 1964 the mass transportation bill now found itself on the White House priority list of legislation.[12]

With the UPTA group successful in impressing the White House, the problem then became one of persuading enough congressmen to vote in favor of it to assure passage. As in all things political, success means having enough votes. The speaker had to be shown that there were sufficient Republican votes from northern urban centers to offset the predicted loss of Southern Democrats opposed to the transit bill because of their fear of more (after civil rights legislation) federal incursions into local matters. In early May, the UPTA reported that 35 to 40 Republicans would vote for the bill. McCormack finally moved the transit bill out of committee, but remained unwilling to schedule it for a House vote. The speaker, yearning to keep the momentum of legislative success rolling on, could hardly be blamed for his foot-dragging, because late in May the House Republican Policy Committee took a firm party stand of direct and unalterable opposition to the mass transit bill. The Republican Policy Committee rarely digs in its heels when it fears defections from G.O.P. ranks, but UPTA had been busy lining up Republican support and the transit lobbyists felt they had enough votes to get the transit bill passed.

The action of Representative William Widnall of New Jersey, a most effective supporter of mass transit legislation, was a key factor in getting the bill onto the floor of the House. Widnall threatened to embarrass both Speaker McCormack and the White House; he promised to call a press conference to indicate that there was Republican support sufficient to pass the bill and at the same time denounce the speaker and the White House for obstruction of legislative procedures. Unable to put it off any longer, McCormack set the vote on the transit legislation for June 25, and the House passed the bill 212-189. The Senate accepted the House changes in a roll-call (47-36) vote on June 30, and on July 9, 1964, President Johnson signed into law the Urban Mass Transportation Act of 1964.[13]

Senator Mike Mansfield (D-Montana) is reported to have called the Urban Mass Transportation Act of 1964 a "legislative miracle." Never in memory had so many Republicans deserted the party line set by the Republican Policy Committee. The Act of 1964 was a major step forward in the development of a federal program of mass transportation encouragement and support.

Miracle or not, the original Act had its shortcomings in that it did not call for the achievement of definite workable goals and objectives. This is not unique; few laws establishing programs such as the federal mass transit aid effort are very specific about what is to be achieved and when it is expected to come to fruition. What the Urban Mass Transportation Act of 1964 did do was begin federal support of a program that would help repair the nation's mass transit system. On another important score, the original mass transit act bore no overt relationship with other policies that, upon reflection, would have appeared to be intimately related.

In an undertaking of ideal wisdom, the issue of public policy in urban transportation would not exist in a vacuum but would be developed in coordination with urban policy. Unfortunately in 1964, as today, there is no national urban policy. Mass transit is ideally suited to meet the passenger transportation needs of the classic, densely populated city of the nineteenth century and the classic, public-transport oriented suburbs that are closely bound by economic, social, and cultural ties to the central city. Even in 1964 the harbinger of the mega-urb was visible as American cities were exploding into metropolitan areas of relatively thinly populated suburbs that were virtually impossible to serve with conventional transit. There was no urban policy that would press development to a form and density that mass transit and other public services could serve effectively and efficiently. Federal housing policy could have been molded to help shape metropolitan areas to be less dependent upon the automobile and less hungry for highway expenditure. This has not been done. The transit legislation promoted a form of transportation that was increasingly anomalous to much of metropolitan growth in the decades to come. This does not mean that revivification of transit was useless. It simply means that its beneficial impact would be muted and the benefits it could have provided lay unrealized, while the area of fastest growth lay awash in automobiles.

Moreover, ideally—perhaps it's an academic ideal—urban transportation policy should also be made in conjunction with energy policy, environmental policy, economic policy, and defense policy. In 1964, the failure to make such connections is understandable; energy was not a matter for concern then, nor was the environment a cause for worry or national policy. Other than a general policy of helping to stimulate economic growth and employment, there was no relationship with economic policy. Defense-policy relationships were missing. To have expected such far-sighted relationships and considerations, however rational they may seem, is not practical in the method by which public policy is forged in the U.S.[14]

The 1964 Act, in any event, is the cornerstone of the federal transit program. Its aim is to provide aid for the improvement and development of mass transportation and to encourage the planning and establishment of areawide coordinated transport. Along with the planning provision of the Highway Act of 1962, the intention was to offer incentives to plan and develop a rational and integrated urban transport system combining both the private automobile and mass transportation. The 1964 transit legislation was also expected to produce a kind of equity. A major reason for the decline of transit was the federal role in the provision of urban highways, so it was only fair to now help the transit industry and its clients, both of which had been negatively affected by highway programs.[15]

Foreshadowing the calls of the Reagan administration in the 1980s for a greater private role in transit, amendments to the 1964 Act at the time of its passage sought to continue a strong role for the private sector (95 percent of the transit industry was privately owned in 1964), and federal aid was to be barred from use in the acquisition of private transit systems unless it was essential to the development of a coordinated mass transit system. In practice, many private firms, only too eager to unload a losing enterprise, were anxious to sell out to the public sector.[16] As noted earlier, the notion of subsidizing a private, for-profit firm with public funds is not a popular one in the U.S.

With knowledge of arguments that surfaced in the 1980s about whether or not a federal role in urban mass transportation was proper, the passage of the original Urban Mass Transportation Act used the rationale that the transit problem was national in scope. The reasoning behind the legislation noted that it was indeed a local issue only in that certain national problems had more impact in some places than in others. Moreover, attempting to solve some problems greatly outstripped the ability of a number of states and localities within states. Continued vitality and growth of urban areas was deemed to be very much in the national interest as a part of national economic policy, especially in recognition of the highly urban nature of the U.S. and, as noted earlier, for the sake of equity. The fact that many local transportation problems were really interstate in nature was another major consideration; it was pointed out that 53 of the some 200 metropolitan areas of 1964 either bordered on or crossed state lines. Also stressed in the justification for a federal role in urban transportation was the severe cost burden caused by the heavy use of automobiles in American cities. The problems of smog, rising insurance rates (due to an increasing toll of accidents), and rising costs of police needed to handle congestion and parking problems were a part of the burden of the automobile that balanced some of the many benefits. The sheer waste of man-hours in traffic congestion was also part of the justification.[17] The enormous cost and impossibility of building enough highways to meet the constantly increasing auto demand were factors of importance. The subsidy to transit was given because it was expected to be a cheaper alternative than meeting mobility needs exclusively with the automobile. Another way to view this is that transit provided more carrying capacity in a corridor without the need for large amounts of precious and expensive urban space.

The objections to the legislation centered on the point that transit was a purely local issue and that spending the money would only increase the federal deficit. The opponents predicted (correctly) that it would be an expensive program over time, and they noted the vast expenditures needed in New York City alone and the large-scale effort to get underway in San Francisco. There were also concerns that fares of local transit might be set by the federal government, that the legislation would encourage public ownership of transit, and that it would have a negative effect on labor.

There was legitimacy to the concerns over cost. In making up for years of deferred maintenance and lack of investment in transit, the money needed for capital improvements would be a large sum. No one could have foreseen the sharp inflation that would hit the U.S. (as a result of the war in Vietnam) or the sharply rising cost of petroleum that would boost prices still further, as a consequence of the OPEC embargo of the early 1970s and the Iranian Revolution of the late 1970s. The significant inflation made catching up on transit capital improvements even more expensive than could possibly have been imagined in 1964. Unfounded were the fears of federal fare-setting, and the labor protection clause in the 1964 legislation (Section 13c) assured no negative impact on labor.

The 1964 Act had three major parts. First, the demonstration program originating under the Housing Act of 1961 was continued. One change under the 1964 legislation was that the HHFA administrator (a position equivalent in later years to administrator of the Urban Mass Transportation Administration) was given authority to initiate demonstrations independently upon finding a need as well as to support locally initiated demonstrations. Local matching funds were not mandatory, but the assumption was that as a matter of policy the two-thirds federal, one-third local contributions followed under the 1961 Act would be continued. In practice, the federal share in demonstration projects has often been more than two-thirds. In time, the demonstration program moved away from being primarily one of local initiation to one proposed largely by the Urban Mass Transportation Administration as part of a research, development, and demonstration program.

Second, the program of low interest-rate loans begun under the 1961 Act was also part of the 1964 legislation. It had not been used much and would be used even less in the future.

Third, the major new element in the act was the capital grants: a long-run program of aid and a short-run, or emergency, program. Under the long-run program, if a city satisfied the requirement that "the facilities and equipment for which the assistance is sought are needed for carrying out a program . . . for a unified or officially coordinated urban transportation system as a part of a comprehensive and continuing program of planned development, capital will be made available up to two-thirds of the net project cost of a capital project."[18] The federal money could be used for almost any transit-related capital project except the construction of public highways.

The short-run program was designed to keep a troubled transit property from ceasing operation. If the planning for the development of a unified or coordinated transport system was underway, but not yet completed, a federal grant of up to 50 percent of the net project cost could be made. However, if the planning process was completed within three years of the execution of the grant agreement, the federal contribution would be increased to the full two-thirds of the net project cost. The act realistically encouraged planning and yet allowed operations to continue and for the provision of capital aid to serve the public.[19]

The Urban Mass Transportation Act of 1964 contained other important provisions. Persons displaced by federal capital improvement projects could receive payments of up to $200 for purposes of relocation, and displaced business firms could receive up to $3,000. In recognition of the role of labor in gaining passage of the Act, job protection was provided, including continuation of the rights of collective bargaining, wage security, and retraining of adversely affected personnel when necessary. While all grants or loans were to be made to public bodies, private enterprise received encouragement to participate in conjunction with and through public agencies. Finally, in an effort to make sure that New York or other large cities did not capture all the funds, no one state could receive more than 12.5 percent of the total funds disbursed in any given year.

In time, the labor protection clause (Section 13c) came to be one of the most controversial sections of the Act—it was always a topic to rouse the ire of transit managers. Essentially, grants of capital (and later, operating aid) would require the approval of the local transit labor unions. This was handled in a

somewhat convoluted fashion via the U.S. Department of Labor. Transit management typically views 13c as a club over its head; labor sees it as protection.
During the Reagan administration the issue of the role of the private sector also
became controversial, and great stress was given to private participation.

By later standards in an age ripe with inflation, the amount of federal money
was petty. The 1964 Act authorized the expenditure of $75 million for the fiscal
year of 1965, and $150 million each year for the fiscal years 1966 and 1967. Up
to $10 million of this sum was to be available for demonstration grants the first
year of the Act; this was to be increased to $20 million on July 2, 1966.[20]

AMENDMENTS OF 1966

Few new federal programs are allowed to remain unchanged for very long.
Supporters and opponents seek alterations, and urban mass transportation legislation was no exception. The addition of the capital grant program and the
associated planning requirements of the Urban Mass Transportation Act of 1964
had changed the transit program profoundly. The Act had made the program a
"real and permanent" program in a way not possible as long as the transit
program was only a part of the Housing Act. The 1964 Act provided a federal
program of aid and encouragement to mass transport that was well beyond the
inchoate transit program of the Housing Act of 1961.

As part of the evolutionary process involved in developing the federal policies and programs for mass transit, the organization within the federal government for managing transit programs changed as well. In December of 1966 the
HHFA was merged into the newly formed Department of Housing and Urban
Development (HUD). The location of the program was a continuing sign that the
federal mass transit program was viewed more as an urban program than as a
transportation program.

There were gaps in the federal transit program, and one of the most conspicuous of these was money. Despite the importance of the Urban Mass Transportation Act of 1964 as a legislative milestone, the programs were modest indeed
compared with other federal expenditures for transportation. From the passage of
the Housing Act of 1961, up to the last quarter of 1966, the federal government
spent $375 million for programs under the Acts of 1961 and 1964; during the
same time period federal expenditures were about $24 *billion* for highways, air-
ways, and waterways.[21] A small amount of progress had been made in awakening
public interest and in attracting the attention of elected and appointed public
officials on all governmental levels. Any approach to transit improvement had to
be accompanied by the realization of the magnitude of the job. Relatively little
capital had been invested in public transportation since the 1920s. A realist,
appraising the world of mass transportation in the U.S., would have concluded
that a great deal of the work had to be done and large investments had to be put
in full play before any substantial improvement in urban mass transport quality
and quantity would be realized. Until the amount of federal and other sources of
funds was increased, there was scarcely any hope that mass transit could contribute positive improvements to the quality of urban life.

For example, in 1966, only Boston, Chicago, Cleveland, New York, and Philadelphia had rapid transit systems. All of those systems were planning improvements or expansion or were in relatively advanced stages of planning or construction. Also, San Francisco was in the process of building a rapid transit system and there was strong interest in the construction of rapid transit systems in Atlanta, Baltimore, Buffalo, Los Angeles, and Miami. It was only a matter of time before strong interest would become solid plans and plans would become concrete proposals for constructing such facilities with federal aid.

Beyond the upgrading and expansion of facilities and equipment for rapid transit, the commuter railway operations serving Boston, New York, and Philadelphia were in need of considerable renovation. Many of the cars were well past their economic life and in some cases passenger facilities were primitive. There was a strong possibility in the mid-1960s that additional cities would find commuter rail service desirable in the near future, thus requiring additional capital funds.[22]

In addition to improvement or expansion of rapid transit and commuter railway services, there was a need for more modest, but still expensive, projects. Replacing aging bus fleets would require large expenditures, as would the construction of new garages, maintenance facilities, and terminal and passenger support facilities. Furthermore, it was a time when the U.S., still confident of its technology and technological superiority, possessed some enthusiasm for technological innovation in transit. Some cities expressed interest in constructing systems based upon transport modes not currently in vogue, particularly where demand was expected to be too great for buses to handle readily and yet not large enough to warrant full-scale rapid transit.[23] To any clear-eyed, knowledgeable observer in the aftermath of the passage of the Act of 1964, much money had to be spent to make mass transport a reasonably competitive alternative to the private automobile.[24]

The magnitude of the task of revivifying mass transportation was large, and in many cities capital expenditures alone would not do the job. Transit systems both large and small had trouble covering operating costs. Service levels were poor in many places and expansion of service to rapidly developing outlying areas was not possible. Under the provision of the 1964 Act, there was no federally supported solution to that problem. Some cities and transit properties were in such bad financial shape that they could not match federal grants for demonstration or capital purposes, even after projects were approved by the Department of Housing and Urban Development.[25]

The need to provide plans and develop cost estimates in order to qualify for a capital grant was another problem. This was not too serious for a modest bus-oriented project, but planning for a rail commuter service or rapid transit facility was an expensive matter. There was no federal aid available for such purposes under the 1964 Act, and local money was in short supply.

Meanwhile, as a background to the picture developing in transit, the problems of cities were beginning to be re-discovered. Crime, filth, poverty, decay, dilapidation, a starving need in many places for a major rehabilitation of physical capital, and the defection of the middle class to the suburbs were not unique to the 1960s. By that time, however, the difficulties and their sheer magnitude had found their way into the popular news media. There, all the troubles were distilled into one of money and the lack thereof. Local financial problems pointed out the organizational difficulties of local government springing from governmental fragmentation on the local level, particularly in the larger metropolitan areas. The Act of 1964 and the Highway Act of 1962 did encourage coordinated transportation efforts on the local level, but the incentives were not sufficient at the time to strongly encourage metropolitan-wide merging of effort and financial capabilities.[26]

There was also a need for more mass transportation research in the mid-1960s. As an industry in decline for many years, transit had not enjoyed the advantages of research. Apart from the development of the PCC streetcar in the 1930s and the deliberately paced improvements to buses (air-bag suspension and factory air conditioning were innovations of the mid- and late 1950s), the development of transit technology had been stagnant for forty years. The demonstration program was providing a valuable boost in knowledge about mass transport, although by its nature at the time it was not a systematic research program. In the early years, most of the demonstrations were not technical in nature.

Developing new means of urban public transportation seemed imperative, including improved, fume-free propulsion systems. There was also a need to investigate and understand more about the economic, psychological, and sociological factors behind the demand for various modes of transport. As far as data on mass transportation was concerned, the only statistics were those published regularly by the American Transit Association. Moreover, there was but little knowledge of mass transportation methods and research carried on abroad, except for work in Canada, and that too was largely the result of the meetings held by the American Transit Association. In summary, there was not much solid information except the ATA data, which was supplied on a voluntary and confidential basis by ATA members and was available publicly only in aggregate form.

At about that time a painful shortcoming in the American transport system became plain. What was and is often called the "American transportation system" was found to be a hodgepodge of competing and uncoordinated private and public carriers. The development of U.S. transportation was a product of competition and speculation over a long period of time by entrepreneurs who had little incentive to coordinate transportation service in any systematic fashion. Making a trip or shipping freight by more than one mode of transportation was often difficult in the extreme. Bus and rail stations were often far apart in the downtowns of major cities; lugging luggage and a cab ride was needed to change from one mode to another. Neither rail nor intercity bus service offered access to airports out in the suburbs. Worse still, the coordination between the intra-urban and interurban public transport systems was either totally inadequate or nonexistent. In many cases, so difficult was it to get to and utilize public transport that the traveler had no rational choice other than to either stay home or to make the trip by private automobile.[27]

Another problem was the management of transit systems. The need to really sell mass transit service to the public was vital. This was a difficult task at best because of the subsidies provided to the motorists; charges for the use of highways did not cover highway costs, municipally owned parking facilities often subsidized parking, and many employers offered free parking for employees as a perquisite of employment that was especially attractive in crowded cities where daily parking costs were high. Lamentably, the transit industry was neither consumer- nor marketing-oriented. If mass transportation was to play a larger role in urban areas, the service offered would have to be effectively sold to the public, and most transit managers knew little about marketing. In decline since 1945, the transit industry was not attractive to talented and experienced business managers or to bright young college graduates. Genuinely professional management, equipped with the broad base of skills needed to operate a business successfully in the mid–twentieth century, was sorely lacking in transit. Many of the larger transit properties had strong core groups of engineers—often electrical—who held management positions, but they rarely were versed in managerial skills needed to understand the market and successfully sell mass transport services in the face of severe automotive competition.

Looking toward the future of the transit industry, some means was needed to upgrade the proficiency of those currently involved in transit management. A way was also needed to encourage young people of talent to find their way into transit management and related fields. More and better managers were absolutely essential if the new and improved transit properties were to function smoothly.

The year for mending the perceived gaps in the federal mass transit program was 1966, when the authorization of funds under the Act of 1964 ran out. Several urban transportation issues had stirred interest early in the second session of the 89th Congress. One of these would be a matter of prime interest to the transit industry—federal operating aid. To address it, on January 20, 1965, Senator Harrison Williams introduced S.2804, a bill to amend the Urban Mass Transportation Act of 1964 to authorize certain grants to assure adequate commuter service in urban areas. The proposed legislation was aimed at providing federal funds to defray 50 percent of the cost of mass transportation deficits. Senator Williams also introduced S.2805, a bill to amend section 13a of the Interstate Commerce Act, relating to the discontinuance or change of certain operations or services of common carriers by rail in order to require the Interstate Commerce Commission to give full consideration to all financial assistance available before permitting any such discontinuance or change. These particular bills were of special interest to the senator's home state of New Jersey. The privately provided, deficit-ridden commuter railways in the New York metropolitan area of the Garden State were growing increasingly morbid and were making it clear to public officials that the near future held either severe cuts in service or complete discontinuation of the service. As it turned out, the notion of covering operating deficits with federal aid was put aside for a time, but it would re-emerge later and become one of the most controversial federal transit issues.

Transit legislation introduced by Senator Joseph Tydings (D-Maryland) focused on the need for more research and development work. The substance of his legislative proposal was that

> the Administrator [at the time the bill was introduced, the administrator of HHFA—upon the formation of a new Cabinet level department for urban affairs it was to be the Secretary of the Department of Housing and Urban Development] shall undertake a program of research designed to achieve a technological breakthrough in the development of new kinds of public intraurban transportation systems which can transport persons in metropolitan areas from place to place within such areas quickly, safely, and economically, without polluting the air, and in such a way as to meet the real needs of the people and at the same time contribute to good city planning.[28]

The bill would have authorized $10 million annually from the federal coffers to develop new urban transport technology.

The major changes finally adopted in 1966 were introduced by Senator Williams and reported out of the Committee on Banking and Currency on August 8, 1966, as S.3700; the committee recommended passage. The bill called for an increase in the transit authorization each year from $150 million to $225 million. It also called for aid for the planning, engineering, and designing of urban mass transport systems, the training programs to help upgrade transport management, and grants to college and other non-profit institutions for research purposes. The Secretary of Housing and Urban Development was directed to conduct research to develop new mass transit systems. Killed in committee was a measure introduced by Senator Williams to allow the federal government to cover up to 50 percent of the operating deficits of transport agencies.[29]

The House Committee on Banking and Currency reported favorably on H.R. 14810, a bill similar to S.3700. It differed in that it had no provisions for management training programs and authorized only $175 million annually for mass transportation.[30]

There was an important distinction between the House and Senate bills. The House version provided that beginning with fiscal 1968, $175 million would be authorized "for each fiscal year thereafter," thus making the federal mass transportation activity a permanently funded program of the federal government.[31] The provision offered certainty of continuation of the federal mass transport assistance program. It would add substantiality to the efforts of the Department of Housing and Urban Development and would relieve HUD of the need to return periodically to Congress to justify the continuance of the program. The provisions would also "give assurance that a locality starting on . . . expensive, long-term commitments for new or improved transit' systems can count on continuing Federal assistance."[32]

In committee, Representative Fino (D-New York) had fought vainly for a provision that would allow federal funds to be used to pay the interest on local bond issues sold for the purchase of mass transport equipment or the construction of facilities. Representative Fino also tried to delete the provision of the

1964 Act that limited any given state to no more than 12.5 percent of the annual allotment of funds. In an effort to keep pace with the provisions for federal aid to Interstate Highways, he attempted to change the matching ratio for capital grants to a minimum of two-thirds and a maximum of 90 percent from the federal side.

Fino represented a highly urbanized state and one that contained many transit-dependent people; he understood the mass transportation problem and its needs. In reflection of this, he appended an individual statement to the committee report from the House; he spoke up in behalf of his defeated amendments and worried over the lilliputian scale of fund authorizations in light of the enormous task that lay ahead in urban transportation:

> These amendments would be a great boon to mass transit in cities like New York, Philadelphia, Chicago, Los Angeles, and so forth. The present mass transportation program is not of sufficient scale to have a meaningful impact on the mass transit needs of the developed core areas of the megalopolis. Because of the 12 1/2 percent limitation on the share of the yearly mass transit program outlay that can go to any one State, New York City is not going to get much benefit even from the new enlarged, permanent program embodied in this legislation. Assuming a $175 million a year program, 12 1/2 percent of this— and that is the maximum New York State share, not New York City's share—is less than $22 million. The New York City subway operating deficit last year was almost four times this figure. Sliced any way you will, the Mass Transportation Act program is still "small potatoes."
>
> I especially regret the noninclusion of my proposal that Mass Transportation Act funds be made available for the payment of interest costs on local bond issues floated to pay for transportation projects which are of a type that would qualify for regular Mass Transportation Act grants. Instead of subjecting the city of New York to the slow dole of funds mandated by the 12 1/2 percent of $175 million (statewide) limitation, payment of interest costs would enable the city to float a quarter of a billion dollar bond issue and pay the interest costs with the Federal aid. On a 25-year bond issue carrying 4 percent interest, the interest costs would equal the principal to be amortized and paid off, so that in effect the Federal grant share would be one-half. Of course, it would be one-half at the beginning, enabling the marshaling of a large sum of money, instead of a slow dole which does not encourage any large-scale local financial undertaking. Federal payment of interest costs would stimulate local borrowing on a large scale, whereas the slow dole, subject to the overall dollar and State percentage limitation, will never mobilize any large-scale change in mass transit patterns.[33]

As the years passed and the federal, state, and local contributions flowed and ebbed, Representative Fino's words were to prove prophetic.

There was extreme debate on the legislation which in both houses of Congress was fairly extensive, but it centered around the amount of money to be spent, rather than on the issue of whether or not the federal government had a role to play in urban transportation. This change in attitude was important to the federal mass transportation program and would have major implications in the development of the federal role in the years following 1966.

In the Senate, Senator John Tower (R-Texas) was a strong advocate of economy and introduced an amendment to cut authorized spending from the $225 million per annum recommended by the Committee on Banking and Currency to $150 million per annum. As justification for cutting back, Tower and his alliance cited the cost of the war in Vietnam and the urging of President Johnson that government keep its spending down.[34] Not surprisingly, Senator Lausche of Ohio, playing the role of the "Grinch Who Stole Christmas" and missing the point entirely, voiced disapproval of the complete aid program, saying:

> I respectfully submit to the committee that all of the demands for increased money come from the profligate management of the railway systems on the east coast—New York, New Jersey—and in that area in which they are trying to run a railroad system by charging practically nothing at all for the carriage of passengers.[35]

Several senators rebutted Lausche. Senator Jacob Javits (R-New York) spoke up for recognition of the great importance of cities in American life and stressed the vital need for ease of movement in urban places. He said at one point:

> The cities are fighting. This exemplifies the fact that they are fighting for a place in the sun which will recognize what they amount to, because they are, today, what the country was a hundred years ago; namely, they are the repository of the essential population of this country. Nothing typifies it more than mass transit.[36]

The Senate voted in favor of the transit bill, 47-34. Senator Tower won the day for the economy-minded, however, and the authorization for expenditures was reduced to $150 million per annum for the next two fiscal years, thus continuing the practice of very low budgets for mass transportation. Otherwise the bill went through unscathed.

There was little opposition in the debate on the House version of the bill. Although Representative Fino was unsuccessful in getting all the federal funds he wanted to pay interest on bonds, or in getting relaxation of the 12.5 percent limit on funds to any given state, there was ample support from many representatives. The big defeat came in the period for which funds would be authorized for the program. Instead of authorizing $175 million on an annual basis, the bill was amended to provide $175 million for one year only. The amended bill passed the House by a vote of 235-127 and was sent on to a joint Senate-House conference committee.[37] The Senate agreed to the conference report on August 25, the House concurred on August 26, and President Johnson signed the measure into law on September 8, 1966 as Public Law 89-562.

The first amendments to the Urban Mass Transportation Act of 1964 authorized $150 million for each of the fiscal years 1967, 1968, and 1969. Increased sums of money were to be devoted to the demonstration grant program: $40 million for the fiscal year commencing July 1, 1967, and $50 million for the fiscal year beginning July 1, 1968.

An important addition to the federal transit program came in what was then Section 9 (later Section 8) of the Urban Mass Transportation Act of 1964. As amended, funds were made available for the planning, engineering, and designing of urban mass transportation projects. Dubbed technical studies grants, this part of the federal mass transportation program was one of its most flexible and useful elements. Section 9 read, in part, as follows:

> Activities assisted under this section may include: (1) studies related to management, operations, capital requirements, and economic feasibility; (2) preparation of engineering and architectural surveys, plans, and specifications; and (3) other similar or related activities preliminary and in preparation for the construction, acquisition, or improved operation of mass transportation system facilities, and equipment.[38]

The new Section 10 authorized funds of up to $1,500,000 per year for management training purposes. This money was to be awarded in a maximum of 100 fellowships annually, not exceeding $12,000 each. Like so many of the mass transport programs, management training was a much-needed undertaking, but the sum of money involved was not in line with the need.

The university research program was established under Section 11, whereby $3,000,000 a year was made available in grants to public and private non-profit institutions of higher learning to conduct comprehensive research involving the problems of urban transportation. Moreover, under this section persons could also be trained for further research and managerial activities at operating properties. Section 11 was seen as a way of getting university faculty and students interested in transit issues and problems, and it would help to develop transit planners and managers. Here was a way of developing the transit managers of the future.

A final provision of the 1966 amendments directed the Secretary of Housing and Urban Development—HUD administered the urban mass transportation program at that time—to consult with the Secretary of Commerce and thereafter undertake a project to study, prepare, develop, and demonstrate new systems of urban transportation. This section encouraged investigation of the more exotic forms of transportation. Thus was the New Systems Research Program born, a perfect example of America's belief then in technological solutions to problems as well as a strong belief in the nation's technical prowess.

The New Systems program was the brainchild of Representative Henry Reuss (D-Wisconsin). Reuss felt that the demonstration grants provided for in the Housing Act of 1961 and the 1964 Act did not really address the technical needs of the urban transportation problem. Although he felt that the demonstrations had been useful, he did not believe they had fully considered the possibilities of technical solutions to urban transit difficulties.[39] The Johnson administration was neutral about such a program of research—representatives of urban transportation interest groups did not at first see any need for federal leadership in encouraging research of a more sophisticated nature.[40] Congressman Reuss introduced the New Systems idea as an amendment to the administration's transportation bill while the bill was under consideration in an executive session of the House Banking and Currency Committee. The Reuss amendment gained support and was included in the final version of the bill as it emerged from committee. In the Senate, Senator Joseph Tydings and nine other senators introduced similar legislation.[41]

As it turned out, HUD was not at all prepared to take on the New Systems Research Program; it had almost no staff to devote to the activity. Because HUD knew of the program only three months before the bill passed, it had made no plans as to how to carry out the work. When the transit bill became law it fell to HUD Assistant Secretary for Metropolitan Development Charles Haar to find a method and a means to conduct the study.

> Haar's philosophy on how to affect innovation was to acquire a good number of bright people, give each of them a problem to solve, keep them isolated from each other, and then evaluate the many forthcoming solutions.[42]

HUD tried to create a think-tank atmosphere, which was probably the only way to tackle the job given the constraints and the temper of the time. Despite the limited time and preparation possible in the situation, it was not a frivolous effort. Haar felt that aerospace, engineering, and consulting firms had the proper expertise to conduct the work. Requests for proposals were sent to interested industrial firms, universities, research institutes, consultants, and other potential performers, and seventeen contractors were finally selected early in 1967.[43] Because of Haar's personal bias, most of the firms chosen had a definite hardware orientation. Nevertheless, many of the contractors, in their final reports, fully recognized the formidable institutional problems involved in approaching the challenge of improving urban mass transportation.[44]

The New Systems program made 1967 an eventful year for mass transportation. For the first time, the Urban Transportation Administration (UTA) undertook research projects of a future-oriented nature for the purpose of determining what sort of urban mass transportation systems were either possible or needed. The research focused on three time periods: the immediate future—that is, up to three years; the more distant future—15 to 20 years in the future; and, finally, the period up to the turn of the century.[45]

The caliber of research work was very high in some cases and much of it was highly imaginative. A large portion of research is oriented to the future, especially in circumstances where the investigators are involved in aerospace, which in the 1960s was strongly affected by the U.S. space program and the landing of Americans on the moon in 1969. High technology and adequate funding were common coin in aerospace and the closely related defense programs. Some transit observers, including planners, managers, and local public officials, were impressed by the work, not because of its quality, but because of its lack of relevance to the real world. The immediate problem of most of the hard-pressed cities was, plain and simple, money. The anemic state of the budget for mass transit provided little encouragement for much in the way of technical innovation. The transit community was struggling to provide a decent and dependable service with elderly buses and antique railcars operating out of and upon facilities constructed before World War I; it appeared as if the cart had been set before the horse. It seemed pointless to study future systems when there wasn't enough money to provide a decent level of aid for existing systems.[46]

Looking back, in addition to not being the right relevant work, performed at the correct and relevant time, the New Systems project was a policy failure. Its long-range purpose was to help establish a comprehensive urban transport research program, but it ran afoul of impediments blocking the way into the system that develops policy. That system was unresponsive to the New Systems report, in large part because it gave little mandate for legislation. Assistant Secretary Haar had desired and anticipated rather exotic and visible hardware solutions to urban problems; he was disappointed that the recommendations were only partially hardware-oriented. Apparently, despite the best efforts of all the contract researchers, no technological gimmick appeared to solve the mass transportation problem.

In part because of Haar's disillusionment with the New System program, the findings and recommendations of the New Systems contractors and the report *Tomorrow's Transportation: New Systems for the Urban Future* did not find their way into the Johnson administration's legislative program. In any case it was too late: the Johnson administration was a lame duck by mid-1968, and the shift of the mass transportation program from HUD to the Department of Transportation was a certainty. Despite all the work, there was simply no one around who was willing to take action.[47]

Another event of 1967 had more potential importance for the future of mass transportation programs. As originally developed by the coalition of the big city mayors, the American Municipal Association, the commuter railroads, and Senator Harrison Williams, the federal urban mass transportation program was seen as more urban than transportation. As an urban program under the jurisdiction of the Housing and Home Finance Agency, then later under the Department of Housing and Urban Development, Senator Williams had control of the legislation because the transit bills were handled by the Committee on Banking and Currency, which oversaw urban legislation. Nothing stays the same, however.

On April 1, 1967, the new Department of Transportation (DOT) became a Cabinet-level agency of the federal government. When the Act establishing the Department of Transportation (Public Law 89-670) was passed, Congress ordered the secretaries of HUD and DOT to study the question of whether or not the mass transportation program should be moved into DOT. It took most of the remainder of 1967 to get the new department organized, but by early 1968 it became evident that DOT was interested in taking the urban mass transportation programs under its roof. Those who had a stake in transit questioned whether the urban mass transportation programs were, indeed, more urban than they were transportation and whether or not the transit program's constituency would be best served by a switch in departments.

Within the federal establishment, there was some disillusionment with HUD's handling of the mass transportation program. The Bureau of the Budget was apparently disappointed in the relatively slow progress that was being made, not only in carrying out substantial improvements in mass transportation, but also in working deftly and diplomatically with the Congress to gain more funds for the mass transportation program.[48] Mass transportation advocates, especially those from larger cities, were not pleased by the lack of progress in getting Congress to authorize and appropriate more money for transit capital improvements. Part of the problem was undoubtedly that HUD was closely identified with the Great Society programs of the Johnson administration, and the Great Society had fallen on hard times as the Johnson administration became enmeshed in the coils of the increasingly unpopular war in Vietnam. The mass transit programs could hardly avoid being tarred with the same Great Society brush as the rest of HUD, despite the fact that the origin and development of the federal urban mass transportation program was totally separate from the philosophy of the Great Society. In a marketing sense, the mass transit programs were poorly positioned for success.

One good reason for the apparent lack of progress in the mass transit program as housed in the HUD organization was that it lay rather deeply buried within the structure of that department, coming under the Office of Metropolitan Development. High-level administrators in HUD appeared far more interested in the larger problems of that particular section of the agency—that is, metropolitan development—rather than in the mass transit element. Another problem was that Charles Haar, the head of the metropolitan-development section in HUD, had trouble building and maintaining a strong and sound relationship with Congress. Such a relationship was essential in getting Congress to provide a level of funding that was realistic in reflecting the needs of the transit industry. Haar was accused, perhaps unjustly, of offending some key congressmen. Whatever the real problem with the relationship, the Urban Transportation Administration of HUD was poorly funded and seriously understaffed. For example, there was no travel money available for the UTA staff administering the demonstration program; it ran out in January 1968, six months before the new fiscal year would bring in more administrative funds. For six months, then, the surveillance of programs and projects could be carried out only by letter or telephone. The staff consisted of only two people to administer several millions of dollars of demonstrations.

From a strategic viewpoint in the process of getting more federal money for transit, the new Department of Transportation was not in any political hot water regarding Great Society programs or the general political debacle of the latter part of the Johnson administration. At the time of its start-up, and for a year or so thereafter, DOT was in a honeymoon period; experimentation and flexibility were still possible and much of the DOT bureaucracy had not yet fallen victim to the inevitable solidification and hardening of the innovative arteries that befalls all organizations as they age. This was not true of HUD, which in its formation had inherited many agencies which had been in existence for a long time and had acquired the bureaucratic barnacles of red tape. Worse, although it was a new department, HUD had lost much of its appeal to a Congress that was becoming increasingly cynical about the effectiveness of the HUD programs. The Department of Transportation was an extraordinary amalgamation of strange bedfellows that included old agencies—some with new names—and some brand-new agencies established to solve newly recognized problems or possibilities. DOT embraced many established pieces of federal activity, such as the Alaska Railroad and the U.S. Coast Guard; the Bureau of Public Roads (with its name changed to the Federal Highway Administration); and new elements, such as the Federal Railway Administration.

Alan Boyd, the first Secretary of DOT, testified to a House committee on the matter of the relatively low organizational level of the transit programs within HUD. Boyd promised that if the transit programs were shifted to DOT, the urban transportation agency would be placed on an equal footing with the Federal Highway Administration, the Federal Railway Administration, and the Federal Aviation Administration. Within the Johnson administration, the stage was set for change.

With little fanfare, President Johnson announced in early 1968 that unless there were objections, the Urban Transportation Administration would be switched out of HUD into DOT.[49] Shortly thereafter, the report of the study mandated by Congress, conducted by the secretaries of HUD and DOT, on the proper location of the mass transit programs in the government practically clinched the matter. The report of the secretaries stated:

> We therefore recommend that there be transferred to the Secretary of Transportation such functions and authorities as he may need to provide effective leadership in urban transportation matters. We also recommend that the Department of Housing and Urban Development intensify its efforts in promoting comprehensive planning, including comprehensive transportation planning, and that the two Departments work closely together in developing the standards, criteria, rules, regulations, or procedures that are needed to assure that transportation will be fully related to urban development goals.[50]

The Senate did not even hold hearings on the departmental change for the federal transit program. In the House hearings, Alan Boyd and HUD representatives assured the representatives that the two departments would work very closely together. They gave honest recognition to the difficulties of coordinating efforts between two federal departments.[51] A major question of the House committee was whether or not DOT would give full care to the role that transportation plays in urban development. Because of its particular mandate, HUD could reasonably be expected to be far more sensitive to the issues of urban development than would DOT.

Some strong lobbying went on behind the scenes within the administration; as a result key senators and congressmen were convinced that DOT was a better place for the mass transportation programs than HUD. Strangely enough, the results might have been different had HUD lobbied more strongly; despite its interest in retaining the transit programs, HUD simply did not apply enough effective lobbying muscle to keep the transit program. What is most peculiar is that in the continuing power battle in Washington, a federal department's status and power is a reflection of the money it spends. Although the State Department is an obvious exception, it is otherwise plain, for example, that its huge expenditures make the Department of Defense the top dog. The mass transit program· was bound to grow, and it would have been very rational in the Washington sense for HUD to have mounted an all-out campaign to retain the program. For whatever reason, HUD let the transit program go to DOT.

Rather nebulous assurances were given, both at the hearings and in a memorandum of agreement between the Secretary of Transportation and Secretary of Housing and Urban Development, that the two departments would work together. There was another element that was important to the future of the mass transit program. It was patent that interested and influential members of Congress intended to protect the transit program and that the mass transportation program would not be overwhelmed by the large DOT highway bureaucracy (the Federal Highway Administration had about 6,000 employees; at the time it was melded into DOT, the Urban Mass Transportation Administration had a total staff of 58). At the time, HUD was expected to continue to be involved in some parts of some transit programs—particularly the research and demonstration programs. The capital grant program was to move over completely to DOT, but the approval of the required comprehensive planning remained in the hands of HUD.[52]

At the end of 1968, HUD went quietly out of the transit business, and the Urban Transportation Administration moved over to DOT to become the Urban Mass Transportation Administration (UMTA). For a time HUD retained oversight of a few projects which had been started under its jurisdiction. However, by 1972, UMTA had its own in-house planning review staff, and the active role of HUD in the transit programs became virtually nil and has continued to be so.

Through most of 1968, because of the uncertainty of the departmental location of the mass transportation programs, those programs drifted uncertainly. Administrators were reluctant to make important decisions until the switchover was accomplished. Perhaps a better reason for *ennui* in the bureaucracy was the announcement by President Johnson that he would not run for office in 1968. The fact of a new president, whether Democrat or Republican, raised the spectre of major change in all levels of the federal establishment. This might be highly upsetting, and perhaps embarrassing, in regard to decisions which might be made in the interim. Added to the upset was the actual physical move of UMTA (and afterward of parts of DOT) into the new Department of Transportation building, which was finally ready for occupancy in September 1968. Filing cabinets loaded with work were carted about while staff tried to make do without the paperwork needed for the job. Finally, the election of Richard Nixon made lame ducks of the remnants of the Johnson administration and, under the circumstances, no major action was taken. As it turned out, 1968 was a period of slowdown and almost total stoppage of the federal transit program while the people involved tried to understand what was going to happen to them and to the program with which they worked.

7.

Major Growth in the Mass Transit Program: The Acts of 1970 and 1973

THE ACT OF 1970

Whatever else it might have been later, the Nixon administration came to office equipped with the baggage of the Republicanism of Thomas E. Dewey. Remembered as the candidate defeated without surprise by Franklin D. Roosevelt, and almost as a shock by Harry S. Truman, Dewey gave shape and form to pragmatic approaches for the Republican party. Dewey reasoned that the essential features of the New Deal were a sensible approach to the complex urbanized and industrialized America of the mid-twentieth century; the important thing was to make the New Deal work more efficiently and more effectively. To Thomas Dewey, this could be easier accomplished by Republicans than by the Democrats, who were hopelessly within the embrace of the interest groups that had helped to form the policies and establish the programs. Dewey's thinking persuaded the Eisenhower administration, which very definitely did not dismantle the New Deal but in many ways tried to make it work better. Despite some differences, Richard Nixon had picked up the mantle of Dewey when entering the White House.

Within a few months of taking office, the Nixon administration had a chance to evaluate what it had inherited. In the area of transportation, little had been done in the way of setting national transportation goals. It was also obvious that UMTA was conspicuously too undermanned to carry out any sort of major effort in mass transportation. UMTA was on the same organizational level in the Department of Transportation as the Federal Aeronautics Administration (FAA), which had 40,000 employees, whereas UMTA had a few more than 50 on its staff. That staff was highly dedicated and hardworking, but there were just not enough people to go around to administer UMTA's programs and projects effectively. While the expenditures by UMTA were not high compared to other federal agencies, on a per-employee basis it averaged out to one of the highest ratios of money to manpower in the federal government. The ordinary routine paper shuffling and overseeing of projects already in hand made it difficult for UMTA to evaluate new proposals.

Transit advocates were worried in early 1969. The attitude of the new administration toward mass transportation was unknown, and President Nixon was considered to be a conservative moderate. The program, regardless of party platform or campaign promises, might be gutted. There was another, related worry: the lack of a lobbying voice for the mass transportation program strong enough to move the program beyond its current status. The main constituency of the UMTA programs, the urban transportation industry, was relatively amateurish and seemed ineffective at the time in lobbying Congress. Also troubling was a dichotomy within the industry. As the 1950s had waxed and waned, those operating rail commuter or rapid transit operations had relatively little to do with the "bus transportation" people, who made up the majority of the members of the American Transit Association (ATA). In part this was because the bulk of the rail properties were publicly owned, whereas the remainder of the industry was in private hands. Many private transit people were very suspicious of government aid because of the inescapable strings attached to it. As a matter of principle, many ATA stalwarts were opposed to government aid—even though government aid to the competition was a major part of the reason for the decline of mass transit in the U.S.

The ATA had been founded in 1882, originally as the American Street Railway Association, to provide the services of a typical trade organization. With changes in name over time to reflect changes in the transit industry, ATA and its predecessors had provided a forum for the exchange of information and statistics. In one of the major engineering development projects of the 1930s, ATA had been behind the creation of the PCC car. At least until the very late 1960s, the ATA was unfamiliar with and did not participate strongly in lobbying for government aid, mainly because of its majority of private members.

Due to concern in the late 1950s that the ATA did not fully meet the needs of the major cities that were served by rail mass transportation, the railroads and the rail transit group formed the Institute for Rapid Transit (IRT); the rail transit properties usually maintained membership in both IRT and ATA. IRT was much more of a lobbying organization than was the ATA. From the start, the IRT membership understood the need for large sums of public money to revitalize and expand their properties. Many rail systems had suffered from decades of deferred maintenance; their leaders knew that local and state dollars were limited and that expanding the federal program in scope and in dollars appropriated was key to the success and survival of a reasonable quality of rail transit service.

Within the IRT itself, some of the commuter railroad members felt little community of interest with rapid transit operators; the railroads preferred to work through the Association of American Railroads (AAR). During the 1960s, the ATA, IRT, and AAR all attempted to carry out some lobbying activities, but they were less effective working separately than would have been a singular association. There was also some discomfort on the part of city officials who had become accustomed to working with the U.S. Department of Housing and Urban Development (HUD) and its predecessor agencies over the years on a variety of urban problems. Cities had to learn to work with the U.S. DOT, and it was difficult at the start.

Some of the concern was eased just after the changeover in administrations when President Nixon took a most encouraging position on the mass transportation issue. Both the President and Secretary of Transportation John Volpe took a strong stand on giving priority treatment to urban mass transportation issues and problems in the first session of Congress under the new administration. The transit industry and the coalition that supported it took great cheer because the mass transportation program was typically seen as a child of the Democratic party. The promise of support from a Republican president and his secretary of transportation gave transit supporters hope for increased bipartisan effort on behalf of the federal transit program.

Mass transportation advocates faced some inherent difficulties in getting increased congressional support. In the minds of many legislators, particularly Republicans and more conservative Democrats, the federal mass transportation program was a particularly bad example of the failure of the tarnished Great Society program. Moreover, while some key transit legislation had passed in the 1960s, the money appropriated was minuscule compared to the need. This was good evidence that through that decade, the federal mass transportation programs had never been wildly popular in Congress. As the new session of Congress began early in 1969, the transit program lacked glamour. There were pluses, but federal transit programs had not provided the sort of nationwide example of success and general acceptability that would have allowed almost any legislator to back them without suffering within his own constituency.

An observer in early 1969 would have been accurate in stating that mass transit was a really "safe" issue only for a senator from a state with one or more major urban centers or for a representative from a congressional district in a large urban area. Log-rolling had been effective in permitting senators and representatives from transit constituencies to gain support from colleagues from electorates where transit seemed unimportant, but in the best back-scratching practice of Congress, a senator from a rural, agricultural state would back the transit program in return for support from a senator from an urban state for an agriculture measure. What was apparently lacking to boost transit was grass roots support; the federal mass transit program was seen by many as a program beneficial almost exclusively to large cities. Non-urban legislators would simply not give overwhelming support to transit legislation and the money it required unless the matter was one that promised broad, national benefits.

Counteracting the image of mass transit as primarily a big-city concern was the slow but steady failures of private mass transit firms in all parts of the U.S. and in cities of all sizes. The industry in the aggregate ceased to be profitable in the mid-1960s for a variety of reasons. The growing inflation of the late 1960s was a serious blow to an industry that was fairly labor intensive. The cost of living was rising, and transit labor costs rose sharply as new contracts with transit workers' unions were hammered out. The cost of equipment and supplies also began to go up substantially, likewise due to inflation. If service was to be maintained, there was a limit to how much fares could be boosted and service cut. The aging fleet of transit vehicles grew inevitably older and more expensive to maintain, and there was little or no money in the transit property coffers for new equipment that was less costly to maintain. Marginal private operators all over the nation began to go out of business. An increasing number of cities—large, medium, and small—found that they would have to get into the transit business themselves if service was to continue. Slowly, pressure began to mount on Congress to augment the mass transit programs. The lobbying groups for cities began to take note of the transit problems expressed by their members.

One serious problem for cities was that the federal funding of the mass transportation program was uncertain, making intelligent planning difficult. Long-term capital projects, in particular, had a difficult time on the local level because there was no certainty that Congress would appropriate funds for capital grants in the future—or that the funds would be sufficient in magnitude even if granted. The latter factor was noteworthy, given the small sums appropriated for transit up to that time. Consequently, it was very difficult for a city to consider a major transit capital project or issue bonds without some certainty that the federal portion of the money would be there when it was needed for construction purposes. The transit situation was much different from that of the federal highway program; the federal Highway Trust Fund provided a steady and relatively predictable source of money. Moreover, a number of states also had trust-funded highway programs. Even if the federal highway money did not always move with the alacrity that state and local officials might wish, it had the beauty of certainty and it was possible to plan for highways in an effective and efficient fashion that was impossible for transit.

By 1969, a number of urban places that had received technical-studies grants in order to carry out more detailed planning of mass transportation systems had fulfilled their own needs and the requirements for federal capital grants. They were ready to give serious consideration to the construction and extension of rapid transit systems or to major improvements in their bus transit systems. Even so, without the future certainty of the capital grants—particularly for the rapid transit systems, which involved long lead times—it was impossible to move ahead. In Washington, as winter turned to spring, a process was beginning that would give the federal transit program a major boost.

Bills introduced into Congress in mid-February and early March of 1969 sought to remedy the problem of long-range funding. The Senate bill was introduced by Senator Harrison Williams, and bills in the House were put forth by Representatives Barrett, Koch, Moorhead, and Patman.[1] Due to the educational and lobbying effort that was going on, there was a remarkable similarity in the proposed legislation. All of the bills called for the use of trust fund financing, similar to the Highway Trust Fund, in order to provide sustained support for transit programs. To any program advocate, the trust fund approach was highly desirable because Congress does not have to make annual appropriations; the money flows in regularly and may be doled out just as regularly with no need for the Congress to tap the general fund for appropriations. With a trust fund arrangement, Congress does establish apportionments setting out the limits of money for the various programs falling under the program for which the trust fund was established. Transit supporters suggested the excise tax on new automobiles as a source of transit trust-fund money. This money did not go into the Highway Trust Fund, and utilizing it did not seem likely to generate opposition from the highway interests who fiercely guarded the Highway Trust Fund against diversion to other than highway purposes. The automobile excise tax was attractive to legislators because it would not entail imposing a new tax. Proceeds were merely earmarked for a specific purpose rather than letting it go into the general fund of the U.S. Treasury.

Transportation Secretary Volpe proved to be a vigorous advocate of increased money for the federal transit program. In his speeches and in much of his commentary on mass transportation in the spring and early summer of 1969, Secretary Volpe seemed to feel that he was voicing the position of the Nixon administration as he discussed and supported the use of a trust fund for transit. Highway interests greeted the secretary's advocacy with some dismay at first. Volpe's talk of using the excise tax on automobiles, however, rather than tapping the money of the Highway Trust Fund, calmed the fears of the highway lobby. With the secretary of transportation giving strong support for transit, the future began to look rosy for a greatly expanded federal mass transportation program.

The idea of a transit trust fund came to grief in August 1969 when President Nixon proposed a ten-billion-dollar program in mass transportation to extend over a twelve-year period. To Secretary Volpe's apparent surprise, and to the consternation of the transit support coalition, the president made clear that he had no intention of having the transit programs financed by means of a trust fund. This was consistent with the position of the Bureau of the Budget, which resisted trust funds because it felt they limited the flexibility of government to react to changing situations, needs, and problems.[2]

If the spring of 1969 had seen hope rise because of support for transit on the part of Secretary Volpe, there was other, less overt activity taking place that would have a major impact on transit. In early 1969, a coalition of interest groups began to form. A truly professional, consistent, and strong lobbying for transit had its genesis. The linchpin was the combination of the U.S. Conference of Mayors (or USCM, the new name of the American Municipal Association) and the National League of Cities (NLC). The Mayors' Conference and the League of Cities began to assemble a new mass transportation coalition, with Fred Burke, a highly skilled and effective lobbyist, employed to guide the work on the transit legislative program.[3] The initial coalition included the NLC/USCM, the Institute for Rapid Transit, the American Transit Association, and the railroads working with IRT and the Association of American Railroads.

Animated by the need to establish as broad a lobbying force as possible, in the early fall of 1969 the urban transportation interest group made it very clear to the highway interests that they, too, had an important stake in supporting a well-financed transit program. The critical point of attraction for the highway interests was the fact that the Highway Trust Fund was to come up for reevaluation and reauthorization by Congress in 1972. Big-city mayors working through NLC/ USCM made it known that they would not support continuation of both the Highway Trust Fund in its existing form and the steady flow of money to the highway interests unless the highway interests backed the mass transportation program. Faced with the handwriting on the wall, and assured that the Highway Trust Fund would not be tampered with for transit purposes, the highway interests agreed to support an enlarged federal transit program.

The highway interests saw wisdom in giving a little to get support in the future. Many mayors and public officials had become disillusioned with the highway program, which appeared to have shifted traffic problems rather than solved them. Citizens of urban areas were increasingly outraged at the practice of ramming highways through residential areas and places of historic interest. San Francisco was perhaps the first city to stage a "freeway revolt," but as highway construction advanced, public outcry rose in fervor, and voters took vengeance at the polls. The Bureau of the Budget felt that the Highway Trust Fund should be abolished or at least altered to allow the funds collected to be used more broadly. This attitude was shared by some members of Congress who were unhappy at the relative loss of control over money. In short, seeing a fight ahead on the extension of their trust fund, the highway people felt it wise to support the transit constituency of the NLC/USCM.[4]

The difficult problem of finding some sort of guaranteed funding for transit remained, even though it was apparent that general support for mass transit was building. The Nixon program called for an initial authorization of $3.1 billion, but Congress would still have to make annual appropriations. The long-range projects would continue to suffer from the uncertainty connected with the annual appropriations.[5]

The breakthrough came when Senator Harrison Williams introduced an amendment that was inspired by Fred Burke in his lobbying efforts for the growing transit coalition. The amendment was a classic compromise; it provided a means to overcome the objections to the short-term nature of the annual appropriations process and yet not depart too far from the administration's program.[6]

The gist of the Williams amendment was an authorization to the secretary of transportation to obligate grants not to exceed $3.1 billion. There were "not-to-exceed" provisions setting out specific sums to be available for obligation by July 1 of the years 1971 through 1974. Congress would assure that the funds would be available but would continue the normal practice of appropriating the money each year. The device was called "contract authority," and with it cities had the assurance that money would be available in the near future for capital projects in a fashion similar to a trust fund. But a trust fund would not be actually established.[7]

There was much work remaining to retain the support of the Nixon administration and to get Congress to pass the new transit legislation, but the Williams amendment provided an important breakthrough in thinking. After that, it was a matter of strengthening the coalition, carefully dealing with key senators and congressmen, and developing effective testimony to offer to the committees which would hold hearings on the transit bill.

While the prognosis for a new transit bill appeared favorable, some difficulty arose in the fall and winter of 1969, when the committee jurisdiction of the bills was questioned. As originally developed, the federal mass transportation program was viewed as essentially an urban issue rather than a transportation matter. It was natural for transit legislation to be considered by the House and Senate committees that deal with banking and currency, which are the committees that had traditionally treated urban or HUD matters. Even though the mass transportation programs had been shifted over to DOT, the banking and currency committees maintained that they still had jurisdiction; however, the House Interstate and Foreign Commerce Committee and the Senate Commerce Committee— which have jurisdiction on DOT legislation—insisted that they should handle the transit programs. This caused some worry on the part of mass transport advocates, because both banking and currency committees had many members who were firm supporters of transit legislation, while members of the DOT jurisdiction committees were largely unknown quantities. To the relief of the transit coalition, the committee jurisdiction was not changed at that time. Later on, in early 1973, an urban mass transportation subcommittee was formed as part of the House Banking and Currency Committee. Subsequently, the major jurisdiction in the House has shifted to the Committee on Public Works and Transportation.[8]

The coalition built by the NLC/USMC was doing its work and addressing the issue of broadening support for the federal mass transportation program. A major complaint about the federal transit program was that it did not really have broad, fundamental support but that it was primarily a program for big cities. This matter was addressed at the NLC Congress of Cities in San Diego in December of 1969. Fred Burke noted that the panel discussion sessions on mass transportation were crowded with mayors and other local public officials representing cities of all sizes from all parts of the nation. Most of them had just inherited (or expected to inherit) a transit system forced on them by the failure of a private transit firm. For many of these officials, the public takeover of traditionally privately owned transit had finally opened their eyes to the transit issue and the federal mass transportation program. The mayors wanted to help; Burke saw the opportunity to get a sizable choir of grass-roots political voices to sing a song of transit support to the Congress. Burke suggested strongly at several gatherings that the local officials contact their congressmen to let the House members know just how important the transit legislation was back home. A flood of letters, telephone calls, and personal visits from a broad constituency deluged Capitol Hill. Here was the nationwide support for mass transit that was so badly needed to carry the day in the Congress, and it was a major breakthrough in developing broad acceptance of the transit issue. Members of the House and Senate are often moved to take serious notice of issues brought before them by other elected persons. The testimony of transit managers may be construed as a "save my job" plea, whereas an elected official saying "help my constituents" is a different matter altogether. The grass roots were making their presence known to Congress, and the message hit home.[9]

The broad-spectrum political effort of the NLC/USCM coalition was enormously effective. It began to pull aboard even very conservative legislators without big-city constituencies. The NLC/USCM, both in its lobbying efforts and committee testimony, kept reiterating the point that the federal mass transportation programs benefited not only a few large cities but also the small towns and cities in states with large non-urban populations. To back up this point, there was strong evidence available from UMTA of the wide dispersion of funds through the capital grant program. Up to that time, the demonstration grants that were so important in getting the federal transit activity started tended to be concentrated in the larger cities on the east and west coasts. However, the capital grants and technical-study grants had been well distributed around the country to cities of all sizes, which was a point in favor of broad recognition of the value of the program.

It was during the lobbying effort at this time that the transit program came to be seen as not only generally beneficial in terms of providing mobility but also as a program which rather neatly filled certain welfare needs. For instance, a congressman could claim to one part of his electorate that by backing the mass transportation programs, he was taking important steps to relieve highway congestion so that his constituents with automobiles could drive more easily. On the other hand, he could also claim to low-income and minority groups in his district that improvements in mass transportation would be highly beneficial to them by providing access to jobs, medical care, and so on. The apparent failure of much of the Great Society effort to provide quick solutions to difficult problems had made many outright welfare programs decidedly unpopular, but a program that provided access to opportunities and that helped to create an environment in which positive things could happen was a different matter. In a very real sense, backing transit could be construed as being all things to all people.[10]

The work of the grass-roots coalition paid off. The Senate overwhelmingly passed the Williams bill by an 83 to 4 vote on February 3, 1970. The efforts of the transit lobby and its coalition was then directed toward the House. This was a more difficult chore, and the spring and summer of 1970 saw a concerted drive on the House of Representatives. On September 29, 1970, the House passed the transit bill by a vote of 327 to 16. President Nixon signed the transit aid bill into law on October 15, 1970. As a result of Fred Burke's leadership and the development of a strong coalition, a major victory had been achieved for the cause of urban mass transportation. The overwhelmingly favorable votes in both houses of Congress was not lost on transit's supporters.[11]

The federal mass transit program had certainly become a more respectable one in the eyes of Congress, thanks not only to the apparent merits of the program but also to the masterly job of lobbying that had been carried out. Some of the speeches made in the House on the occasion of the passage of the bill reflect the attitudes of Congress and the support that had developed, as well as the rationale for transit support by the federal government that has persisted through the years.

Representative Wright Patman, D-Texas: The transit industry has been the victim of the American desire for the automobile so that public transportation has not received much new capital and is now operating with old equipment, old ideas, and, all too often, uninspired management operating on the premise that their primary goal is to minimize losses. . . .

In view of the apparent local nature of the problem, some people might wonder why the Federal Government should undertake the vast responsibility of assisting communities in the development of their public transportation service. The first and most significant reason is the Federal interest in keeping the cities of this country healthy . . . it is not only fair but essential that we assist the cities in financing needed public transportation service.

A second and perhaps less obvious reason is the fundamental federal interest in building up this local transportation link which will enable other transportation modes to work more effectively. . . .[12]

Representative William B. Widnall, R-New Jersey: The urban Mass Transportation Assistance Act of 1970 . . . has been reported favorably and unanimously by the Banking and Currency Committee. A very similar bill, S.3154, passed the Senate by the overwhelming majority of 83 to 4.

I think these actions, and the degree of unanimity with which they were undertaken are significant barometers of a sense of urgency, not only within the House and the other body, but in the hearts and minds of the public in every part of our nation. The problems of mobility within our urban and metropolitan areas, not only for the affluent who can afford cars but also for the poor, the young, the old and the physically handicapped, must be solved—now. The problems of strangulation of our cities' streets and the wasteful use of valuable urban land for freeways and parking facilities by an ever increasing flood of automobiles, trucks, and buses must be solved—now. The problems of pollution of the very air we breathe by the exhaust emissions from millions upon millions of internal combustion engines must be solved—now.[13]

Representative Gerald Ford, R-Michigan, House minority leader, said: "I endorse the Urban Mass Transportation Assistance Act of 1970 as recommended by President Nixon. The need for this legislation is beyond question."[14]

It was one of the strange twists of politics that helped mass transportation to become a safe issue. Supporting transit helped the poor and the not-so-poor in cities large and small. Plain people and influential people around the country, carrying all shades of political opinion and in both political parties, had come to recognize the importance of aid to mass transportation in the urban, twentieth-century United States. The highway interests allied themselves with transit in an act that revealed political understanding of a high order. City officials made it plain that they wanted aid for transit as well as highways and that the support of urban, local politicians was necessary if the highway trust fund was to be renewed in 1972.

After almost ten years, the federal mass transportation programs of the United States government finally received major funding; however, even with the substantial increase in federal funding, the sums involved were still small in light of the magnitude of the task. The work of the coalition was far from over. The sheer size of the task ahead was daunting and the direction given the mass transit programs was still unclear, as it would remain. Nevertheless, the first major victory was sweet.

THE HIGHWAY ACT OF 1973

There were two goals for the intense lobbying effort that was mounted by the mass transportation coalition beginning in 1971. The first aim was to gain support for legislation that would provide federal operating subsidies for mass transportation. The idea of operating aid was not a new one, but until the support for transit was strong, there appeared to be little chance of passage. Operating aid was strongly opposed by the Nixon administration, which held that operating subsidies were financially unsound and lacked the necessary incentives for transit management to do a better job of serving the public without massive, bureaucratic involvement by the Urban Mass Transportation Administration on the local level. The principal, but unspoken, reason for the Nixon administration's opposition was a real concern that organized labor in the transit industry would make off with the lion's share of the subsidy through demands for high wages.

The second goal, the campaign for which was launched in early 1972, was to split off some of the Highway Trust Fund money for mass transportation purposes. The position of the White House was positive on this issue and the Nixon administration gave it very strong support. Both Secretary Volpe and his successor Secretary Claude Brinegar spoke out in support of this issue at every opportunity, as did the president.[15]

The issue of the renewal of the Trust Fund was a difficult one, so much so that the Congress was unable to pass a highway bill at all in 1972. The pro-highway and pro-transit lobbies were about equally balanced, and it was a tender issue in an election year. There were also some hard feelings on the part of the highway interests because of the proposed intrusion of transit into the then sacrosanct Highway Trust Fund. The highway people felt that they had been supportive of transit's cause—or at least had not blocked it—and felt betrayed. This was an understandable feeling, but it would be only fair to note that diversion of money from the Highway Trust Fund was not solely an idea of transit advocates. The Highway Trust Fund was seen as a rich source of money. Moreover, many local officials appeared to think that highway construction was part of the problem and not part of the solution.

With the start of the first session of the 93rd Congress, intense efforts were once again made to enact legislation that would open up the Highway Trust Fund to transit.[16] The Senate was first to pass such legislation. The House bill, although similar in many ways to the Senate bill, did not open up the Trust Fund for transit use.[17] There was an element of desperation in passing the reauthorization of the Highway Act that prodded Congress on. Many states were almost out of federal highway money as the midpoint of 1973 was reached—and passed. The highway lobby was stymied because the mass transit lobby was strong enough to block passage of a highway act. Compromise was necessary to get the federal highway funds rolling again, even if it meant opening the Highway Trust Fund to mass transportation purposes. In the heat of the summer of 1973, a conference committee of both houses worked to hammer out an accord. The conference committees were successful in reaching a compromise on July 20, 1973, and the Senate quickly ratified the much-amended legislation.[18]

With pressure mounting to get the highway money rolling once again, on August 3, 1973 the House voted 382 to 34 in favor of the conference report on the 1973 Federal Aid Highway Act. The president signed the act into law on August 13, as Public Law 93-87. The transit coalition had worked hard and had again been successful. Most interesting, however, the act revealed that the urban transportation priorities of the federal government had shifted materially away from the exclusive highway orientation that marked the period after the Second World War. Indeed, some observers noted at the time of the bill's passage that mass transit aid was the fastest growing of all federal programs; this rapid growth was to continue throughout the 1970s.

The passage of the Highway Act of 1973 was a powerful indication of the strong federal support for mass transportation improvement that had developed in the United States. The victory for transit was such that it might be said that the partnership between the federal government and the transit community was definitely confirmed by this federal action. It was not just a highway act in the sense of providing passenger transportation by means of the private automobile; it was really a transportation act because of its broad mobility implications in both rural and urban areas. The act gave local levels of government much more of a say in determining what sort of transportation system they really wished to have; no longer would local government have to opt for a major highway effort simply because highway funds were available. A desirable mass transit option could be chosen without depriving a city of funds. Prior to the 1973 Act, a city that chose not to carry through a highway project lost the money, but now it could switch the revenue to a transit project.

The Act was seen to have vital implications for transport improvements. President Nixon voiced the hopes for the law in the signing ceremony:

> This Act is not only a highway act. One of its most significant features is that it allows the Highway Trust Fund to be used for mass transit capital improvements. Under this Act, for the first time, states and localities will have the flexibility they need to set their own transportation priorities. The law will enable them to relieve congestion and pollution problems by developing more balanced transportation systems where that is appropriate rather than locking them into new highway expenditures which can sometimes make such problems even worse.[19]

The law was very much in tune with the Nixon administration's dislike of dedicated trust funds. Here was a trust fund that could be used for the general purpose of urban mobility.

In hard fact, the Highway Act of 1973 did not really begin the use of highway trust fund money for transit purposes. The 1970 Highway Act contained a modest provision that allowed money in the Interstate, Urban System, and Urban Extension funds to be used in the construction of transit support facilities. The

1970 Act covered such capital items as exclusive or preferential bus lanes, traffic control devices, bus passenger loading areas and facilities, shelters, and fringe area parking. Transportation corridor parking could be built to serve bus and other public transportation passengers. There is less to this than meets the eye, because the funds expended for mass transportation purposes could not exceed those that would have been spent in conventionally providing highway capacity. Under the 1973 Act this restriction was dropped, and all apportioned highway funds for the various systems could be used for the transit related purposes outlined above, even if the cost exceeded that of a conventional highway.

The financial status for transit was significantly raised. In addition to opening the Highway Trust Fund, the 1973 Act provided for an additional $3 billion in contract authority for mass transportation purposes than was available under the provisions of the 1970 Act. The 1973 Act increased the proportion of federal aid from two-thirds of the net project cost of a mass transportation capital grant project up to a mandatory 80 percent, which covered all projects administratively reserved after July 1, 1973. Furthermore, at the direction of the secretary of transportation, technical-studies grants for transit planning could receive up to 100 percent federal funding.

The gradual opening of the Highway Trust Fund for transit use was the obvious product of compromise. Compromise always creates strange conditions in law. Under the 1973 Act, there was a transition period in the use of the Highway Trust Fund money; in fiscal year 1974 cities could choose to use their share of the Highway Trust Fund's $800 million Urban Systems road apportionment for the construction of fixed mass transit facilities or for the purchase of buses and equipment for rail transit. In fiscal 1974, the money was to come from the general fund of the United States, and an offsetting amount would be kept in the Highway Trust Fund for highway use. For example, if local officials chose to invest in a mass transit improvement in place of a highway project, after approval of the secretary of transportation, 70 percent of the cost of the transit project would be paid from federal general funds. Urban System highway funds apportioned to the particular state would be reduced by an amount equal to the federal expenditure on the transit project.

In fiscal year 1975, up to $200 million—one quarter of the amount of the Trust Fund money earmarked for urban highway systems—could be used for mass transit purposes; however, the money could be used in fiscal 1975 only for bus-related projects. In fiscal year 1976, cities were given the freedom to tap the Trust Fund for the whole of the $800 million Urban Systems fund for mass transportation purposes, including rail as well as bus-related capital projects.

The decision to use Highway Trust Fund money for mass transportation was placed in the hands of local officials. They could use money as they chose within certain broad limits. The 1973 Act does not require that expenditures be made for mass transportation purposes; it merely permits the action. The experience over the years since 1973 has not seen an enormous use of Urban Systems money for transit. Many highway projects were and are years in the planning and execution and are often both highly desired and desirable improvements. It is not surprising that the uptake in the use of this money for transit is and will be limited. Even so, the flexibility offered by this portion of the law is beneficial.

Despite the general outcry for more transportation facilities, the public usually likes the concept more than it approves of the hard reality. In some cities, the construction of massive Interstate Highway projects were especially unpopular because of the large amount of urban destruction caused by highway building. Because 90 percent of Interstate Highway construction was federally funded, the engineers were usually not bashful in designing very large highways that swallowed up much land. In the 1950s and into the 1960s this did not seem to bring too much complaint from outlying areas. Outcry was muted at first even in the heart of the city, where massive highways were often built in the slums and, frankly, no one cared what the slum dwellers thought at the time. In some places, citizens rallied to stop urban Interstate construction, some even going so far as to chain themselves to bulldozers or to link arms and sit down in front of the earthmoving equipment.

In reaction to this, the 1973 Act had an Interstate switchover provision. This allowed cities, working together with their state governments, to trade money that was earmarked from the Highway Trust Fund for construction of Interstate Highway System segments in urban areas for an equal amount of general fund money to be used for mass transit or other highway purposes. In order to accomplish this switch, the governor of a state and local government officials must make a joint request to the secretary of transportation for approval of the deletion of the Interstate project. The secretary can withdraw his approval of a portion of the Interstate, if the segment is not to be replaced by a toll road in the same corridor or if the segment is not essential to the integrity of the overall Interstate system. Local officials may then give notice to the state highway department that local needs require, in place of the Interstate segment, construction of a fixed transit facility, a rail transit line, the purchase of bus or rail equipment, or a non-Interstate highway improvement. If the state highway department agrees that the transit or other project fits in with the comprehensive transportation plan for the urban area, it goes back to the U.S. DOT secretary for approval; this approval obligates the federal government to pay to the local area a sum not to exceed the expected cost of the withdrawn Interstate Highway segment. The federal share for the transit project will be a maximum of 80 percent of the net project cost. To preserve the integrity of the Interstate System, no segment could be removed that would leave the system incomplete. The mileage withdrawn from an urban segment of the Interstate in one state may then be applied to modification of the Interstate System in any other state. Interstate funds equal to the amount apportioned for the withdrawn segment are deducted from the withdrawing state's apportionment of Interstate Highway money.

The amount of money for transit is not calculated at the level earmarked for the highway when the Interstate segment is withdrawn. Instead, the rate of inflation is taken into consideration and the amount of money for transit-capital purposes reflects this higher sum. The money at a given time equals what it would have cost to build the Interstate segment at that time. Cities need not use all of the money from an Interstate withdrawal at one time but may use it gradually over time, with the money increased by the inflation factor.

The 1973 Act contained other elements that strengthened the role of the cities in dealing with urban transportation. Under the law, states are required to allocate a portion of their Urban Systems highway funds among urban areas with a population of 200,000 or more. All of the larger cities are thus assured of receiving some of the money. Previously, each state government had total discretion regarding the allocation of road money within its boarders. Also under the 1973 law, the federal government may allocate highway funds directly to metropolitan planning agencies for transportation-planning purposes without going through the state. These funds are in addition to the planning and research funds already available to cities before the passage of the 1973 Act.

As in all products of compromise, many interests were taken care of in the Highway Act of 1973. For example, rural areas and intercity transportation needs were not ignored; the Act assured $12 billion in the 1974-1976 period for the Interstate System and rural primary and secondary roads. Funds apportioned for the urban and rural Primary Systems and the Urban Systems could be used to construct bicycle paths and pedestrian walkways. Up to $40 million a year could be used under the 1973 law.

The Highway Act of 1973 took action to begin the process of improving rural mobility beyond merely providing roadways. This was a first step toward a more expansive program of aid for non-urban areas. Eventually it would become vital in generating broad support for the whole federal transit program to insure its continuation in extremely difficult times. Rural transit demonstration programs were encouraged to enhance the mobility of rural persons without access to automobiles. Funds amounting to $30 million in fiscal 1975 and $20 million in fiscal 1976 were to be taken from the Highway Trust Fund for the purpose of highway transit service demonstrations in rural areas. Funds were also available for capital improvements associated with these demonstrations.

The Act required that all equipment purchased for capital or other project purposes had to meet emissions and noise standards under the Clean Air Act and the Noise Control Act. Furthermore, in an early step to protect the private sector against competition from the public sector, transit properties had to agree not to compete for charter service outside the normal transit service area. Local public transit agencies also had to agree not to operate school bus service in competition with private school bus operators unless private operators were unable to offer adequate, safe transportation of schoolchildren at a reasonable cost. Schoolchildren may, of course, be carried as a part of regular transit operation, either at regular or special reduced fares. Transit properties lost their eligibility to get federal funds if the charter and school transportation rules were violated. The regulations did not bind transit properties operating charter or school service in the twelve months before the 1973 Act was passed. In the 1980s there was further restriction that transit agencies claimed virtually prohibited them from offering charter or special school services.

The 1973 Act began the process of providing for the needs of the elderly and handicapped. Under the law of 1973, if federal assistance is requested for mass transit, the secretary of transportation must be assured that transit projects receiving federal financial aid can be effectively used by elderly or handicapped persons. Meeting the needs of the elderly and handicapped was made concrete in requiring the rapid transit system under construction in Washington, D.C. to provide handicapped access to all Washington Metro rapid transit stations—this meant that elevators must be included in all rapid transit stations. Under the provisions of the Highway Act, the federal share of this installation was $65 million.

Despite the opening of the Highway Trust Fund for transit use, the notion of a transit trust fund did not die with the passage of the Act of 1973. The Act instructed the secretary of transportation to cooperate with the governor of each state, as well as with local officials, in making an evaluation of the mass transit element of the 1972 National Transportation Report based on the Transportation Needs Study of 1971. The mass transport requirements were to be reviewed carefully and a program developed to meet the transit needs existing in each urban area. The capital investment requirements and the operating and maintenance costs for the mass transit system programs were to be determined along with an appraisal of the financial resources available for transit at all levels of government.

The secretary of transportation was then required to study various revenue mechanisms, such as a tax on fuels used in mass transit service or an additional gasoline tax imposed in urban areas that might be used to finance mass transportation activities. A variety of potential sources of user tax revenues was to be investigated, along with the rates at which such taxes could be levied, the various mechanisms for collection of taxes, and the potential impact on transit usage caused by such taxes. The DOT secretary was to give a report to Congress no later than 180 days after enactment of the Highway Act. This meant that a recommendation for a transit trust fund or at least some other major source of revenue for public mass transportation was likely in 1974.[20]

The authorizations under the 1973 Highway Act· from which the various sums for mass transportation as well as highway related purposes were withdrawn are shown in Table 7.1.[21]

The UMTA contract authority for fiscal years 1974 to 1976 was $3 billion. The Department of Transportation appropriations bill for fiscal year 1974 included almost a billion dollars for mass transportation. The breakdown was as follows: Capital Facilities grants, $872,000,000; Technical Studies, $37,600,000; Research, Development and Demonstrations, $68,950,000; Administrative Expense, $7,000,000; total $985,500,000.[22]

The important features of the 1973 Act for transit were the increase in the amount of money for the federal transit program and that the Highway Trust Fund was no longer treated as a sacred cow. The mechanism that inevitably assured highway construction, whether or not it was the most desirable approach to the solution of mobility problems, had been changed, although this most certainly did not mean that America's zest for highways and highway construc-

Table 7.1
Authorizations—1973 Highway Act
($ in millions)

	FY '74	FY '75	FY '76
Federal Aid Highway			
Interstate	2,650	3,050	3,050
Rural Primary	697	715	715
Rural Secondary	390	400	400
Urban System	780	800	800
Urban Extensions	290	300	300
Subtotal	4,807	5,265	5,265
Other DOT Programs	466	493.5	613.5
Safety—Title II	461	763	801.5
Other Agency Programs	315	330	330
Total	6,049	6,851.5	7,010

tion was ended. More responsibility for the use of the funds was thrust upon the cities, since it was at their option—given the cooperation of the states—that money might be diverted from highway use to transit purposes. This did not produce a widespread shift of highway money for transit purposes but, as noted earlier, it did increase local flexibility in finding solutions to urban transportation problems. It was not a pot of gold for transit or a catastrophe for highway interests—no transportation revolution took place.

What was particularly significant was the cohesion of the transit lobby: its organization, the quality of its program of information and persuasion, and the receptivity of Congress. The support of the White House in opening the Highway Trust Fund was another critical factor. Fred Burke had been right about what was possible with a well-organized lobbying effort.

The Highway Act contained no provision for federal mass transit operating subsidies. Ever since the issue of operating aid was raised, both DOT and UMTA were firm in their opposition to such a program. However, with the energy shortage of the winter of 1973-1974, the Nixon administration reevaluated its position and began a push for what amounted to an urban transportation revenue sharing program that would give cities an option on spending block grants of federal money for capital or operating purposes. The 1973 Act was a major departure from previous transit funding as was the use of highway money. More changes were on the way, because the Nixon administration became more receptive to the idea of federal operating aid for transit.[23]

8.

The National Mass Transportation Assistance Act of 1974

The strong support for increased federal aid for mass transportation that was evidenced in the passage of the National Mass Transportation Assistance Act of 1974 contrasted sharply with the support for efforts of a decade earlier. The members of Congress in 1964 may have had reasonable doubts about the wisdom of a federal role in transit. There may have been doubts held even by those who voted for the legislation, but Congress had found a program it liked by 1974. The small size of the 1964 program, in dollar terms, was not sufficient to discourage those members of Congress whose support might have been more in the tradition of logrolling ("I'll vote for your program, you vote for mine") than absolute commitment. By 1974, however, it was fair to say that congressional support was both broad and deep and that transit expenditures by the federal government would grow larger and serve more purposes through expanded aid packages.[1]

Congressional support was partially animated by raising the concern and understanding of the problems of American cities. The 1960s had been a painful time of reevaluation of American life and of serious questioning of the status quo and right and wrong, in large part brought about by the Civil Rights movement and the protests against U.S. policy in Vietnam. Heightened sensibilities meant that solutions were being sought for a variety of ills: poverty, poor housing, air and other forms of pollution, general protection of the environment, safety, and energy; and mass transit, rightly or wrongly, was seen as a means of achieving at least a partial solution to the problems. Transit was identified with the past growth of relatively large and prosperous cities; as cities began to weaken and lose their attractiveness, transit was seen as a way of helping stay the decline or even pumping life into older cities.

The lobbying by the supporters of transit continued to follow the strategy that Fred Burke and other key supporters had devised. The planning and organization were taken seriously as the supporters of transit sought to complement their legislative victory of 1973 with operating aid. Advocacy of transit legislation by the U.S. Conference of Mayors and the National League of Cities remained, but it was the transit industry itself that gained the strength and skill to become the leader of the charge. A major step was the merger of the Institute for Rapid Transit, which represented the transit properties operating rail transit, and the American Transit Association. The merged lobbying and trade association was named the American Public Transit Association (APTA), and its aim from the beginning was to professionalize its efforts to offer better services to members and to become a real presence and influence on Capitol Hill.[2]

Casting a cloud over much of the time involved in forwarding the transit legislation in 1974 was the Watergate Affair. Watergate eroded public confidence in the office of the President of the United States and brought public respect for politicians (never particularly high) to what may have been an all-time low in modern American history. The White House spent much time and effort trying to protect President Nixon, even while attempting to exercise leadership and maintain an attitude of business as usual. Had the president and the executive sector of the federal government not been otherwise involved, the legislation for transit in 1974 might not have been passed and would probably have been in different form.

Other factors were on the minds of the public and public officials in the gestation period of the 1974 legislation, which had its earliest roots in the efforts leading up to the passage of the 1970 legislation. There was serious concern over inflation, which had been produced in part by the Vietnam War and in part by the price of energy, which was beginning to rise sharply as a result of the embargo of crude oil by the Organization of Petroleum Exporting Countries (OPEC). Egypt and Syria, smarting from their defeat in the 1973 Yom Kippur War with Israel, sought, along with other Arabian OPEC members, to punish Israel's supporters in the West. The OPEC nations also at last realized that the energy-wasteful West was a proverbial sitting duck, depending heavily upon OPEC for basic energy. Thus, it was a suitable target for increased prices in fuel. The sudden national concern over the availability and price of petroleum-based fuels caused people in all walks of life to think about the vulnerability of transportation. Alternatives to the growth in the use of the private car were seriously considered, and interest and support for transit grew because it offered a means of potentially less wasteful transportation in urban places.[3]

THE LONG ROAD TO A TRANSIT ACT

By 1974, the proponents of mass transit had succeeded in achieving a substantial increase in the amount of federal money available for capital purposes in particular, as well as for planning, research, and demonstration efforts. The capital assistance program was of the largest scale because of the need to make up for a half-century of sparse investment in mass transportation. The progress of the federal transit program had been encouraging to transit proponents. One thing that had not been accomplished, however, was a change in federal policy to provide operating subsidies for mass transportation.

In the fall of 1974, transit proponents were successful in finally getting a program of operating aid. The National Transportation Assistance Act of 1974, as it came to be called, was the final product of a long and complex series of events. An extended discussion of the process by which the 1974 Act came into being will be instructive, not only in revealing a legislative tug-of-war (with compromise as the rope), but also in understanding the milieu in which future transit legislation was forged and how the program continued despite some intense opposition.

Federal operating assistance was high on the list of items transit proponents were seeking in the early part of 1973. S.386 was the bill that was designed to provide what transit interests wanted. This bill was originally introduced by Senator Harrison Williams of New Jersey in the first session of the 93rd Congress on January 16, 1973. Senator Williams was joined in the bi-partisan effort by Senators Case, Cranston, Javits, Percy, Randolph, and Stevenson. The main thrust of the bill, as initially introduced, was an attempt to increase the federal share of capital grants to 90 percent from the two-thirds federal capital share then prevailing. (As the reader will recall, the Highway Act of 1973, passed subsequent to the introduction of S.386, raised the federal capital share to 80 percent.) However, in Section 3 of S.386 there was a stipulation for operating subsidies. Under the provisions of the bill as initially put forward, a federal subsidy could be supplied if the secretary of transportation found: (1) that a subsidy was needed to help provide the service necessary to carry out a mass transit development program; (2) that the applicant had a comprehensive plan for capital or service improvement that would provide more efficient, economical, and convenient transit service; and (3) that the service was efficiently operated. The subsidy was not to exceed twice the amount of financial assistance provided from state or local sources for operating purposes. The bill would provide $400 million per year for two years.[4]

S.386 thus gave recognition to the plight of transit firms which, while ravaged by the virulent inflation related to the Vietnam War and the hike in crude oil prices by the Organization of Petroleum Exporting Countries, also wished to maintain (or even lower) fares, in order to help increase ridership. It should also be noted that, despite a decade of federal transit assistance programs, transit patronage had continued to decrease. In many cities, fares had risen to relatively high levels (by historical standards) with the usual effect of merely driving away patrons. Despite the growing operating deficit, it was clearly unwise for transit agencies to continue to boost fares, chase away passengers, and perhaps end up with a larger deficit than before. On the other hand, the transit industry was wise enough to see that an increase in patronage would be an easily understood indication that the federal transit programs were beginning to have a positive impact on the transit industry. Federal subsidies were a way of taking some of the burden of operating deficits off the backs of often fiscally strapped local government.[5]

Subsequently, on March 14, 1973, Senator Williams offered an amendment to the then-proposed 1973 Highway Act, that, among other things, would have made the key operating subsidy provision of S.386 a part of the highway bill. The amendment was accepted with support from Senator Lloyd Bentsen, a Democrat from Texas, the chairman of the subcommittee on transportation within the Public Works Committee.

On April 2, 1973, Representative Joseph G. Minish, a Democrat from New Jersey and chairman of the House Banking and Currency Committee's subcommittee on mass transportation, introduced an operating subsidies bill as H.R. 6452. The bill was reported by the House Banking Committee on April 16, 1973. Meanwhile, on April 10, the House Public Works Committee had reported a highway bill with $3 billion for UMTA capital projects that allocated nothing for operating subsidies. In the debate on the House floor over the highway bill, an effort was made to include operating subsidy money. Representative Jim Wright (D-Texas), the floor manager, opposed the effort to amend on the grounds that President Nixon would veto the whole Highway Act if it included any operating subsidies. Consequently, on May 2, 1973, the Minish bill was withdrawn from the calendar. The aim was to at least assure the passage of the highway bill and then work later on the operating assistance measures. Over in the Senate, its version of the Highway Act already included the operating subsidy measure introduced by Williams. However, when the House and Senate conference committees were involved in their marathon session on the Highway Act of 1973, the operating subsidy measure was dropped so that any White House opposition would be avoided.

The Highway Act of 1973, safely signed into law on August 13 as Public Law 93-87, marked the beginning of a renewed effort by transit interest groups to gain federal operating subsidies. Already, on July 31, the Williams operating subsidy bill was reported by the Senate Banking, Housing, and Urban Affairs Committee.[6] The Minish bill was scheduled for House action on September 10, 1973, but was delayed because of anticipated opposition. Speaker of the House Carl Albert worked carefully with the bill and its scheduling so that it could be passed. On October 3, 1973, the Minish bill (H.R. 6452) was passed 219-195 by the House, and an effort to amend the bill and remove the operating subsidy element was narrowly put down by a 205-210 vote. The House then put the Williams bill number, S.386, on the Minish bill, and the Minish-Williams bill, as it came to be called, became the operating subsidy measure of Congress.

Differences between the House and Senate versions of S.386 were resolved in conference committee action on December 19, 1973. However, the conference committee, fearing a pocket veto by President Nixon over the holidays at the end of the year, delayed a formal report on the measure.[7]

While all of the above was going on, the forces concerned with mass transit down at the grass-roots level (big and small city politicians and transit operators) were not resting on their victory laurels earned by passage of the Highway Act of 1973. As the energy crisis of the winter of 1973-74 was attracting the attention and annoyance of the American people, the transit lobby began its work, pointing out the importance of mass transit in countering the devastating effect on mobility that a prolonged shortage of gasoline could have.[8] Even the Nixon administration began to waffle slightly on its position of opposition to operating subsidies. In late November 1973, Governor Nelson Rockefeller of New York, Mayor-Elect Abraham Beame of New York City, and Nassau County (also of New York) Executive Ralph G. Casco came to Washington to confer with Secretary of Transportation Claude Brinegar. These officials were particularly interested in aid to help preserve the 35-cent New York City transit fare. Brinegar made the first peep of support from the administration for something other than capital subsidies, stating: "The time has come, I think, to take a broader look at how to build and run mass transit systems by giving localities funds to distribute themselves."[9]

Other, more liberal noises concerning possible operating subsidies emerged from the Nixon administration as 1974 dawned. The president's State of the Union Message on January 30, 1984, outlined a new approach to urban transportation whereby a single fund would be made available for either highways or mass transport. This was followed up in more detail by a radio speech made by the president on February 9, 1974. On February 13, Secretary Brinegar presented the Unified Transportation Assistance Program (UTAP) at the White House, and on February 19 the administration proposal was introduced as H.R. 12859 by Representative John Blatnik, Democrat of Minnesota. Soon afterward, on February 21, Senator Jennings Randolph (D-Virginia) introduced an administration bill into the Senate as S.3035.[10]

With the publication of the federal budget for 1975, the Nixon administration's intent with the UTAP program was officially revealed; it called for $2.3 billion in spending authority for capital projects, operating assistance, city streets, and roads. The great difference between this and other legislation that was introduced—and the factor that perhaps had the most wrenching impact on congressional thought—was that UTAP sought to combine the existing urban transit and urban highway programs. Under the terms of the UTAP program, beginning in July 1974 (the beginning of fiscal year 1975), $1.4 billion would have been made available for transit. One-half of this sum would have been allocated to states on the basis of population. Cities receiving funds under UTAP would have the option to use the funds for either capital or operating purposes. The other half of the money—$700 million—would be used for the "regular" UMTA mass transit discretionary grant programs. The so-called "formula funds" would not have stayed at the same $700 million level as the years went by; $800 million was to be provided in fiscal 1976, $900 million in 1977, and $2 billion per annum in 1978, 1979, and 1980. The discretionary funds under the control of the secretary of transportation would remain at $700 million over the entire time period.[11] Capital funds were to be available on an 80-20 basis under the UTAP program.

In putting forth the UTAP bill the administration was attempting to make a major change in policy, because it would mean a basic alteration in the law as it involved the highway program. What the administration wanted and proposed was, in essence, a six-year $15.9 billion program of modified, specialized revenue sharing. This thrust was a follow-up of the philosophy of the regular federal revenue sharing program, which had proved to be popular. Moreover, revenue sharing was viewed as removing much of the burden of decision-making from the shoulders of the federal bureaucracy. The onus for poor decisions on how the money was spent would rest on the local level of government. As a more substantial change in the status quo, three years after its passage, UTAP would combine the existing mass transit and urban highway programs into one unified urban transportation program.

Because it dealt with highway matters, the UTAP legislation was referred to the Public Works committees of both the House and the Senate committees that had jurisdiction over highway programs. Up to this time mass transit programs had always come under the jurisdiction of the House and Senate committees on Banking and Currency; the dealings with the Minish-Williams bill, S.386, had been in the hands of those committees. The feeling on the part of the administration was, apparently, that the going would be much easier if the bill were placed in the care of the Public Works committees. Eventually, this step was to arouse much ill will in the House.

Opposition to UTAP was mounted on two bases. First of all, transit officials and other transit supporters held that UTAP really did not provide any new money for transit and that there would still be too little available to meet needs. On the other side of the coin, state highway officials and the interests involved in highway construction were most fearful that the transformations wrought in the Highway Trust Fund—already eroded by the passage of the Highway Act of 1973—would seriously cut into the money available for highways. This was especially worrisome as the sharp rise in inflation at the time caused construction and maintenance costs to rise even more than expected. There was also concern that the revenues accruing to the Highway Trust Fund might be diminished by various fuel-saving steps taken in reaction to the energy situation. The highway interests did not object to earmarking funds for mass transportation, but they were seriously and genuinely concerned with the possibility that there would not be enough money to go around for highways in an atmosphere of sharply rising costs and stable or falling Trust Fund income. Moreover, still smarting from the opening of the Highway Trust Fund by the 1973 Act, highway interests feared the long-run danger of perhaps the total demolition of the Trust Fund or a major diminishment of the sums available for roadbuilding. In short, neither the transit interests nor the highway interests thought there was enough money available under UTAP for either mass transportation or highway needs.[12] UTAP was legislation that did not make any of the potentially affected parties overjoyed.

On February 20, 1974, the backers of Minish-Williams from the House and Senate and the members of the conference committee assigned to iron out the differences in the bills attempted to modify S.386 in order to make it more acceptable to the administration so that the threat of a presidential veto might be avoided. The conferees compromised by amending S.386 to permit local transit agencies to use allocated funds for either capital subsidies or operating subsidies at their discretion.[13] But, as a consequence, conflict arose in the House over the point that the conference committee had, in essence, rewritten S.386, because neither the Williams nor Minish Bills, as originally passed by their respective houses of the Congress, had involved capital-improvement provisions. The supporters of Minish-Williams requested the House Rules Committee to waive the point of order that would have been inevitable, because the bill from conference committee included matters of substance not passed in the original legislative action. The Rules Committee overwhelmingly moved on March 6 not to grant the rule that would let the Minish-Williams bill move on.[14] Instead, the Rules Committee wished the House Public Works Committee to move ahead with the UTAP legislation.

The Rules Committee was spurred in its move by an unsuccessful effort in the House to strip S.386 of its capital provisions. The margin was so narrow (205-210) that supporters of S.386 felt that they would have little chance to marshal the support necessary to override a presidential veto of any legislation that included the operating-aid element. Moreover, there was growing opposition in Congress to the formula by which the money that was to be made available under S.386 would be allocated. Indeed, since the provision of S.386 gave as much emphasis to transit ridership and vehicle mileage as it did to population, there was a feeling that the bill was weighted too much in favor of large cities with very large transit operations, most especially New York City. The Minish-Williams bill, as a result of the conference committee's attempt to make it compatible with UTAP, as well as with the original Minish bill passed by the House, had provided that the money made available would be based on a formula that worked as follows: 50 percent on the basis of the population of urbanized areas, 25 percent on the basis of the number of revenue passengers carried, and 25 percent on the basis of total revenue vehicle miles.[15]

While matters were churning about on Capitol Hill, some UMTA officials, recognizing the ravages of inflation on the transit industry, were prone to support the Minish-Williams bill as a good emergency measure that would help tide the transit industry over until some longer-range program could be worked out by the administration and Congress. For its part, UMTA was not unfavorably disposed because, in its view, the S.386 provisions were really not unlike the provisions of UTAP in that they allowed for a local option on the use of funds for either capital or operating purposes. UMTA support was squelched by higher echelons in the administration; apparently the White House felt it could get a better deal out of UTAP, handled by the Public Works committees, than was possible with the Minish-Williams bill that had been a product of the Banking and Currency committees. The Department of Transportation, closely reflecting administration policy, eventually went so far as to speak with the staff and members of the Rules Committee in order to state its staunch disapproval of S.386. Indeed, Secretary Brinegar went on record in opposition to S.386 and urged that the president veto it.[16]

Brinegar was particularly afraid that UTAP would be set back if S.386 became law, and DOT was hopeful that UTAP would provide the basis for a true long-range approach to federal transit policy and urban transportation programs. Brinegar also took the position that UTAP would give the cities more money for transit purposes, although Representative Minish countered that UTAP was nothing more than new dressing for old money, whereas S.386 was all new money. Secretary Brinegar was also opposed on the grounds that S.386 would be difficult to administer and, furthermore, that the UTAP population formula was the most fair. Finally, Brinegar was unhappy with the Minish-Williams provision that would have given the money directly to transit officials rather than work through the states as UTAP proposed. Minish-Williams supporters countered with the point that, under the terms of S.386, before local transit officials could receive funds they had to be designated by local elected officials and approved by the secretary of transportation.[17]

Behind the scenes, there were other, less visible reasons for the administration's proposal and support of the UTAP program. Richard Nixon was in deep trouble in the early months of 1974 as a result of the growing public knowledge of his involvement in the Watergate Affair and the subsequent cover-up. Charges were flying that the president's efforts to defend himself against the strong possibility of impeachment proceedings had seriously weakened him as an effective chief executive. UTAP was supposed to be evidence—along with other programs in other areas—of strong, farsighted leadership on the part of the president. The Nixon administration tried to sell the UTAP program as a true long-range measure that would help satisfy the national needs in the area of mass transportation. If successful in getting the Congress to pass UTAP instead of the Minish-Williams bill, the possibility of a serious conflict with Congress over a certain presidential veto of Minish-Williams could be avoided at a time when the Congress was likely to hold the fate of the Nixon presidency in its hands.

Beyond the strategic ends sought by the White House, there were other reasons for the strong administration support of an approach to transit along the lines of UTAP. One of the most important was the result of a DOT review of UMTA, which revealed the disturbing fact that in 1973-74 there would apparently be more applications for UMTA money than UMTA had money to give out. This was cause for agitation. Up to that time, UMTA's problems in dealing with its constituents were mostly involved with the bureaucratic functions of seeing that applications were in proper form, that guidelines and rules were followed, and that all of the "i's" were dotted and "t's" crossed, according to standard operating procedure.[18] With a shortfall of funds and the threat that the money situation would grow worse in years to come, UMTA would face the bureaucratic nightmare of having to choose among applications. This meant that UMTA would have to develop rankings and priorities in order to select winners among competing projects; the implementation of such a policy would, at worst, inevitably lead to monumental snafus and, at best, kindle the ire of members of Congress who saw mass transportation projects for their districts languish because of lack of funds.

The shortage of money for mass transportation had grown sufficiently serious for the Office of Management and Budget (OMB) to institute a moratorium on new projects involving railways in September of 1973. Not unlike what would happen in the 1980s, the DOT secretary and the UMTA administrator, seemingly on cue, went about the country pouring cold water on rail projects; and in light of the money problems, telling such places as Los Angeles that, if it wanted a rail rapid transit system, it should not expect money on an 80-20 basis. In a move guaranteed to make rail advocates justifiably unhappy, the Office of Management and Budget deleted all UMTA-requested money for rail projects in the fiscal year of 1975.[19]

In any event, it was expected that the problem of decision-making could be avoided if funds were distributed according to a formula. Thus UTAP took on an added measure of attractiveness to those in the federal establishment charged with managing the mass transit programs, because real decision-making and the choice among projects was placed in the hands of local officials.[20]

And while decision-making was being localized, it made sense to include the option of using formula-distributed money for operating purposes as well as for capital. This move would help overcome a problem that had been gnawing at UMTA—namely, that cities had been forced to use capital-intensive approaches to transit problems because capital was what was available. There was speculation that equipment procured with UMTA money was being under-maintained and otherwise handled inefficiently because federal money could be had to replace it but not to repair it. Maintenance was an operating cost, but a cost that had to be paid strictly from local funds. The provision of operating subsidies was seen as a way of encouraging local officials to move toward more efficiently run, less capital-intensive transit systems.[21]

There was also concern that federal operating subsidies might not act to improve transit. On one hand, there was fear that the federal operating money would be appropriated by organized labor in the transit industry. On the other hand, there was concern that local officials would not maintain the level of local subsidy but would merely replace local expenditures with federal operating subsidies. This seemed hardly the way to achieve the improvements in transit that transit advocates, UMTA, and DOT were all hoping for; perhaps the most important thing that could happen would be a boost in transit ridership to show that the federal transit programs were clearly achieving a measure of success.

While the Public Works committees of both houses of Congress held hearings on the UTAP proposals and while S.386 appeared to be a dormant issue, there was no lack of effort in bringing forth new bills. The transit industry and transit proponents had been busy making their case, and Congress had been dutifully working on alternative pieces of legislation. The House mass transportation subcommittee (of the Committee on Banking and Currency) was developing a long-range program that would provide about $3.5 billion per year for transit purposes, or about $21-25 billion over a six-year period. What the subcommittee was aiming at was a program that was far better than UTAP. One of the troubles with UTAP, as introduced, was that it would only authorize $15.9 billion over six years and only $6.6 billion of that sum could be spent for either highways or transit. It was expected that the bulk of the optional highway-transit funds would go for highways, because there was no denying that there was usually substantial local support for highway improvement.

The details for the mass transportation subcommittee bill were revealed in the first week of June 1974. The aid package in the bill was divided into four categories. Category one would provide funds for cities already having fixed rail systems or those in which the planning or construction of such systems was at an advanced stage. Atlanta, Baltimore, Boston, Chicago, Cleveland, New York, Philadelphia, Pittsburgh, and San Francisco would qualify. Category two would make funds available for the rest of the country; it was proposed that federal funds would be distributed to the states on the basis of population. Category three would provide discretionary funds controlled by the secretary of transportation for areas having special transportation needs that could not be covered under the first two categories. Category four would provide both capital and operating support for rural transit services. All of the funds called for in the bill would come from the general fund; none would be taken from the Highway Trust Fund. In fund distribution, capital projects would receive federal aid on a 75-25 basis, while operating subsidy money would be made available on a 50-50 basis. The proposed legislation, dubbed the Federal Mass Transportation Act of 1974, would also change the name of UMTA to Federal Mass Transportation Administration.[22]

Democratic Senator Lloyd Bentsen of Texas was the father of another transit bill. This was S.3601, the Urban Public Transportation Assistance Act of 1974. It also involved a categorization of funding. Category one would apply to all urban areas with a population over 750,000; 70 percent of the funding of $17.5 billion over five years would be allocated to these cities. Up to one-half of the funds available for federal operating aid would be on a fifty-fifty basis and capital grants would be on an eighty-twenty basis. Category two would involve the use of 20 percent of the funds and would be made available to cities with populations ranging from 50,000 to 750,000. The money would go to the states; however, areas with over 200,000 people would receive earmarked funds based on the ratio of their population to the total population of all urbanized areas in the state; the same ratios of aid would apply as in Category one. Category three, in an effort to provide incentive to cities to improve transit, set aside 10 percent of the total funds as discretionary money for the secretary of transportation to use in areas showing increases in usage of mass transit.[23]

In late June 1974, Senator Williams introduced his version of a long-range transit measure. This was the National Mass Transportation Assistance Act, S.3719, proposing an expenditure of $18 billion over five years. Of that sum, $12.5 billion (or $2.5 billion annually) was to go for capital grants on an eighty-twenty basis. Another $5 billion was to be parceled out at the rate of $1 billion per year for either operating aid or minor capital improvements, depending upon local option. The $1 billion in annual optional funds would be distributed as follows: one-half of the funds would be prorated on the ratio of population of a given area to the total U.S. population, one-fourth would be prorated on the ratio of work trips traveled on mass transit in a given area to the total of work trips in all such areas throughout the country, and the final one-fourth would be based upon the ratio of mass transportation vehicle-miles in a given area to those traveled in all urbanized areas of the country. The capital funds would be available on an eighty-twenty basis. An additional $100 million annually would be distributed on a population basis for non-urban mass transit. In order to qualify for funds, all recipients would have to provide half fares for the elderly in the off-peak hours of the day.[24]

Representative William S. Moorhead (D-Pennsylvania), chairman of the urban affairs subcommittee of the Joint Economic Committee, also presented an urban mass transit assistance act to the House. Like Senator Williams's S.3719, it called for $18 billion to be spent over a five-year period. Of that sum, $2.5 billion was to be expended in the first year, rising to $4.1 billion by the fifth year. The grants under the Moorhead bill would be available for either capital or operating purposes, at local option. Initially, the distribution of funds would be carried out on a basis similar to the Williams bill. Within two years, however, the work trips part of the formula would be replaced by a market share formula that would reflect the percentage of total trips carried by public transportation in a given urbanized area. A $1 billion supplemental fund would be made available at the discretion of the secretary of transportation for help with capital projects for those places in which particular and unique needs could not be met by the formula grant program. This portion of the funds could also be used to help those areas that had committed themselves to major capital-intensive transportation systems.

As an interesting wrinkle, the Moorhead bill would go on to establish a Mass Transportation Performance Incentive Fund. This would be distributed by the DOT secretary to encourage efficiency by rewarding those transit properties under which system operating costs and efficiency compared favorably with national average operating cost. This would, of course, require a uniform data and financial reporting system, not only for implementation of the efficiency program, but also to put the market share formula in place. The bill also provided for demonstration grants to test the practicality of fare-free transportation coupons for elderly, poor, and handicapped persons.[25]

After a long series of hearings over the late spring and early summer, the House Public Works Committee finally reported out a transit bill on July 25, 1974; it was a revised and amended version of H.R. 12859.[26] Like other bills discussed above, this called for several categories of fund distribution to handle the $20 billion total called for in the bill. Category A embraced $10.9 billion that would provide funds by application for operating and capital purposes in urbanized areas that already had fixed guideway systems—Boston, Chicago, Cleveland, New York, Philadelphia, and San Francisco. Other cities could join in Category A whenever voters or local public officials adopted an areawide transportation plan, approved by the secretary of transportation, that called for a fixed facility. In addition, the local area had to adopt a means of assuring funding for 25 percent of the costs from local and state funds. The actual amount to be received would be at the secretary's discretion; in making up his mind, the secretary was to use guidelines that included transit usage, population of the urban area, previously approved projects, and the commitment of local funds.

Category B involved the use of $2.8 billion; this money was to be apportioned to the states using a population formula. The funds to urbanized areas or incorporated municipalities of over 1,000,000 people would be earmarked; the remainder would be handled on a project-by-project basis.

Category C called for $5.4 billion in discretionary funds, distributed by the secretary for capital projects only, in those urbanized areas not included in Category A. Finally, the $920 million in Category D would be apportioned to the states using a population formula for areas of 50,000 or less. Within their jurisdictions, Category D money was to be apportioned by the states on a project-by-project basis. Under the terms of the bill, capital facilities and equipment would be funded on a seventy-five–twenty-five basis, and operating assistance would be available on a fifty-fifty basis. All projects in all categories would have to be approved by elected public officials of general-purpose local governments (not specific transit agencies) affected by transit projects. The government in question would have to be the one that contained the majority of the population that would be served by the project. The legislation, in a move to cover all transit problems, also called for the lifting of the restriction on charter work with buses purchased with UMTA funds under H.R. 12859. However, buses purchased under the provision of the Highway Act of 1973 would still be under the ban.[27]

In the flurry of legislative proposals, all relatively similar, one was led to ask: what of the Minish-Williams bill S.386 that had been stuck in legislative limbo while the long-range transit proposals had occupied center stage? On July 30, five days after the House reported H.R. 12859, the House voted (221-181) to send the Minish-Williams bill back to conference.[28] Without doubt, S.386 looked as if it was consigned to the legislative bone pile; as events developed, however, there was a lot of life left in it.

As the dog days of summer approached, the Watergate Affair closed in on the president with impeachment and trial inevitable. The president decided to call it quits. Upon the resignation of Richard Nixon on August 9, 1974, mass transportation matters seemed uncertain for a time, because the new president, Gerald Ford, was not known as a great friend of transit, despite his support of the 1970 Act. The new president made it clear that he would not support a transit measure in the $20 billion range because he felt that amount would be inflationary. President Ford felt his first responsibility was to fight against the inflation that had been ravaging the country. However, by the middle of August, the president gave word that he would support a transit measure calling for $11.8 billion.[29]

More than that, the new president pledged his support for a program of operating aid, with the decision of whether to use federal funds for capital or for operating purposes to be left to officials on the local level.[30] In the meantime, on Capitol Hill, the House had passed the Public Works Committee Bill, H.R. 12859, after considerable compromise. In making up its mind, the House had cut the money involved from $20.4 billion to $11.8 billion, in line with President Ford's demands that the amount of spending be cut. Furthermore, in the compromise version, the federal operating-aid portion was cut to involve only one-third federal money.[31]

The distribution of funds under the compromise bill provided 54 percent of the money for Category A that would embrace the rail cities—Boston, Chicago, Cleveland, New York, Philadelphia, and San Francisco. Atlanta, Baltimore, and Pittsburgh were also included in Category A. Category A cities could use the money for either operating aid or for capital purposes, but not more than 50 percent of the total could be employed to cover operating costs in any given year. Under Category B, 15 percent of the funds would be allocated to the 260 urban areas in the United States with a population of over 50,000 and could be used for either operating or capital subsidies. In Category C, 26 percent of the funds could be distributed to the same areas as in Category B; however, the money could be used for capital projects only. Finally, 4.5 percent was provided in Category D for rural areas or for either capital or operating subsidies in urban areas of less than 50,000 people.[32]

If the House had passed H.R. 12859, there was no sign that the Senate was going to pass its version of what came to be called the "long-run" transit aid package. Indeed, doubt ran high on the passage of any bill in the late summer of 1974. In the House Public Works Committee there were some thorny problems that had to be settled. One of the most difficult was the issue of how to divide whatever money was made available among the large metropolitan areas and the rest of the urban areas of the U.S. Several formulas to achieve this end are outlined in the discussion above, but there were felt to be problems with all of them. There were also difficulties associated with the role of state and local governments in carrying out transit projects. The question of whether or not to extend the Federal Aid Highway program through fiscal 1980 was another issue that was difficult to resolve, because the Public Works Committee was faced with the fact that the highway programs would otherwise end in fiscal 1977.[33]

Moreover, there were some serious objections on the part of mass transit supporters both in and out of Congress regarding the provisions of H.R. 12859. The bill would amend U.S. Code Title 23, the Federal Highway Act, and cause major changes for both highway and transit interests, changes that were very upsetting to both groups. The bill would also completely abolish the UMTA programs. The whole of the mass transit aid program would be subject to the procedures of the federal highway program. Supporters of transit were fearful of what would happen to mass transit if it was left to the mercies of state highway departments. Moreover, both President Nixon and Secretary of Transportation Brinegar had objected to the operating-aid provision. There was fear that, to use political rhetoric, it would become a bottomless pit or a rathole down which to squander taxpayers' dollars.[34] It became clear that the Senate was not about to go along with H.R. 12859 and that it would not come up with a long-range bill of its own and go through what promised to be a difficult conference process before the end of the 93rd Congress. Overriding all legislative considerations in the first two months of the summer of 1974 was the strong likelihood that the House would be involved in the impeachment, and the Senate in the trial, of President Nixon during the fall and early winter.

Like Lazarus, S.386 (the Minish-Williams bill) emerged into life once again, once it became almost certain that no other measure was likely to pass before adjournment. The resignation of President Nixon at least removed the threat of his promised veto of the Minish-Williams bill. Then, in an almost unprecedented action, the conferees on S.386 decided to hold another day of hearings on September 25, 1974. It was an indication of good lobbying on the part of what was now a coalition led by the American Public Transit Association, because as hope for a long-range transit bill faded, the tense financial position of many transit properties did not improve. It was essential that some emergency measure be passed to provide the relief needed. The transit industry rose to support S.386 as a compromise. Strong support came from the U.S. Conference of Mayors. Indeed, the president of the U.S. Conference of Mayors, Mayor Joseph L. Alioto of San Francisco, accompanied by Mayor Richard Daley of Chicago and Mayor Abraham Beame of New York, met with President Ford at the White House to urge his support for the Minish-Williams bill. As a result of this meeting, President Ford agreed to confer with Senator Williams. At the same time, the president was hopeful that a long-term bill would pass Congress, and he asked the mayors to help him hold congressional feet to the fire so that a transit bill would be passed before Congress adjourned.[35]

Even as the eventual flow of events was becoming clear and as it was increasingly apparent that no long-range bill that smacked of H.R. 12859 was going to get through the Senate, DOT and UMTA officials were still taking a position of opposition to S.386 and maintaining that DOT would recommend a presidential veto of that bill. It was, to say the least, a prime example of a federal department being out of touch with political reality.

By the latter part of September 1979, the Minish-Williams bill shaped up as providing $200 million in operating aid for fiscal 1975 and $400 million for fiscal 1976. This money was to be distributed by means of a formula that a compromise had structured, which was to be based 50 percent on population and 50 percent on population density, with operating subsidies placed on a fifty-fifty basis. Capital aid under the formula provisions was to be on an eighty-twenty basis.[36]

The climax came in November. The Mayors' Conference, APTA and other transit interests, and organized labor prodded Congress to pass S.386. President Ford added his voice, so that pressure was being applied to Congress from both ends of Pennsylvania Avenue. On the Hill, Senator Williams, joined by Senator John Tower of Texas (the same coalition of a liberal Democrat from the Northeast and a conservative Republican from the Southwest that had proved to be so effective in the passage of the 1970 legislation) sent a joint letter to their colleagues strongly urging passage of S.386. However, matters were stalled in the House because the Rules Committee had to exercise its prerogative to grant the rule that would bring the Minish-Williams bill to the floor. The members of the House Public Works Committee were unhappy about the whole matter for, in effect, what they thought was going to be a new role in transit for them was about to be yanked away.

Pressures from the transit lobby and the White House were laid on Congressman Ray Madden (D-Indiana), chairman of the Rules Committee, to grant the rule. The strategy adopted by transit proponents was to add to the pressure by first passing the bill in the Senate by a substantial majority.

As time came for action, the bill that the Congress would consider authorized a total of $11.8 billion in expenditures over six years. Of that sum, $7.8 billion would be for capital purposes and $3.9 billion in formula grants would be available for either capital or operating aid, depending upon local option. Five hundred million dollars was also to be made available through the states to small cities and rural areas.[37]

According to plan, the Senate passed S.386 (voting 64-17) on November 19 after only thirty minutes of discussion. The House Rules Committee got the message, and the Minish-Williams bill came to the floor of the House on November 21. In the House the voices raised in opposition were not so much against the bill itself but rather against the way in which it had been pushed through. The Public Works Committee members were especially angry, with Chairman John A. Blatnik (D-Minnesota) stating: "It violates every rule and every step of orderly procedure." Another member, William H. Harsha (R-Ohio), declared it to be "the product of a handful of members working alone in haste" and held S.386 to be "the most outrageous violation of the rules and precedents of the house." This venom concerned the point that the bill had been rewritten in conference committee.

The arguments of opponents to the Minish-Williams bill on the matter of procedure had little impact. The debate in the House included the reading of a telegram from President Ford strongly urging passage of S.386. Mr. Ford stressed the importance of the bill and stated that "it represents a responsible step in our efforts to reduce energy consumption and control inflation." Representative John B. Anderson (R-Illinois) summed up the position about the energy crisis: "If you want to fight inflation, this is the only bill before us. We want a bill and we're not going to get a bill unless we adopt this conference report." The Minish-Williams bill, S.386, passed the House of Representatives by a large margin vote (288-109).[38] President Ford signed Public Law 93-503, the National Mass Transportation Assistance Act of 1974, into law on November 26, 1974.[39]

PROVISIONS OF THE 1974 ACT

The new mass transit bill was finally signed into law, but just what had been produced? To begin with, in any reading of the bill, it is apparent that it is the product of considerable compromise. As a result, it fell far short of solving all transit problems. In the process of legislative evaluation, a number of changes were made in the bills as initially passed by both the House and the Senate in 1973—which is what upset the Rules Committee—in an effort to meet the needs of the transit industry and the pressures of the cities, along with a nod or two in the direction of the Nixon administration, its wishes, and its threats to veto. This is evidenced, for example, by the new requirements in the 1974 Act for comprehensive transportation planning on a statewide basis. Federal transit legislation, prior to the 1974 Act, required regional comprehensive planning in and around metropolitan areas, but such planning was not necessarily coordinated with state planning. Under the terms of Section 102 of the 1974 Act, no project was to be approved after July 1, 1976, unless the DOT secretary—that is, UMTA—found that there was a continuing comprehensive planning process being carried out on a statewide level. Moreover, the U.S. DOT was to cooperate with the states in order to help develop long-range state programs and plans which were "properly coordinated with plans for improvements in other affected forms of transportation and which are formulated with due consideration to their probable effect on future development of urban areas of more than fifty thousand population."[40]

Additional compromise is found in the derivation of the formula in Section 5 (or formula grant portion of the program) and in the amount of funds to be made available for the formula grants. The formula funds were spread over six fiscal years, as follows: 1975, $300,000,000; 1976, $500,000,000; 1977, $650,000,000; 1978, $775,000,000; 1979, $850,000,000; and 1980, $900,000,000. The original distribution formula contained in S.386 was to be based in part on revenue passengers and in part on vehicle miles. There was well-taken criticism from administration sources that definitive information on these two factors was not obtainable and, moreover, would be subject to manipulation. The conference committee, therefore, decided to utilize the factors of population and population density based on the 1970 census. In so doing, the committee on S.386 followed the recommendations of the administration.[41]

Moreover, in the distribution of the funds, the states were involved in keeping with the philosophy of the Nixon administration regarding increased involvement of state government in the federal transit programs. Under the new law, in urbanized areas of 200,000 people or more, a designated recipient for funds would be selected by the governor, local officials, and officials of the transportation authority. Where a state agency was directly responsible for financing, construction, and operation of transit service, the secretary would designate the state agency as the recipient. Perhaps the most important state rule was for those urban areas of less than 200,000 people, in which case the governor of the state was to be the recipient of the funds. The governor was to distribute the funds as he saw fit. At the end of the six-year term of the Act, however, each of the urbanized areas was to receive the same total amount it would have received had the formula-distribution method of direct allocation been utilized.

Before an urbanized area could get any money under the formula-distribution provisions, it had to submit a program of projects annually to both UMTA and the state governor. The governor had 30 days to comment upon the program of projects. After UMTA approved the program of projects, each urbanized area had to submit individual applications to UMTA for each project.

The 1974 Act by no means gave the key to the U.S. Treasury to the transit industry. For those who thought that the 1974 law would allow local deficits to be pared down dramatically at federal expense, in order to qualify for federal funds the existing level of local support had to be maintained for all practical purposes. The operating subsidy money was, in essence, for "new" deficits. As the conference report noted:

To be eligible for grants under this provision, the recipient must continue to maintain State and local operating and capital funds, and the transit system must maintain other revenues, such as advertising, concessions, and property leases. This maintenance of effort provision is to be on a two-year average of the total of State and local funds used to finance operating costs and other non-farebox income. The State and local revenues and other incomes can be used as local matching share but that [sic] revenues gained by farebox shall not be eligible.[42]

Those using the Section 5 formula-grant provision, as noted earlier, may receive from the federal government eighty percent of the cost of a capital improvement. Under the appropriate conditions, fifty percent of the operating loss could be derived from the federal formula funds. The law also provided that transit properties receiving aid under this provision had to charge half fares to handicapped and elderly riders during off-peak hours.

It should be noted that the operating-subsidy provisions did not apply to cities of under 50,000 people. Such cities could use the funds, distributed in the sum of $100 million per annum, only for the purpose of capital improvements.[43]

Moreover, in order to be eligible for funds under the Section 5 formula program, the beneficiaries of governors' designated recipients had to adopt a uniform reporting system. Under the 1974 Act, the secretary of transportation was mandated to devise such a system by January 10, 1977. After July 1, 1978, all beneficiaries of grants had to be participants in the uniform accounting system.[44]

Harking back to concern for the private sector, those receiving aid under Section 5 of the 1974 Act could not engage in school bus operations in competition with private transit properties. Those firms that were engaged in school bus operations more than twelve months prior to the passage of the Act were permitted to continue to offer such service.[45]

The Act also empowered the secretary of transportation to investigate safety hazards created by the use of funds provided by the Act. Moreover, the secretary might require the state or local public body in question to develop and submit a plan to correct any safety hazards. Financial assistance could be withheld until such a plan was approved or implemented.[46]

The Act also attempted to encourage experimentation on fare-free mass transportation by encouraging demonstrations of such programs. Authorization for $20 million per year for fiscal 1975 and 1976 was given for this purpose. The federal share of such demonstrations was 80 percent of the operating cost, plus the authorization of capital costs for any fiscal year in which such a demonstration project was in operation. In selecting the cities for such demonstration projects, the secretary was to attempt to choose a broad cross-section of types and conditions. In addition, the impact of reduced fares on the following factors was to be determined:

1. The effects of such systems on (i) vehicle traffic and attendant air pollution, congestion, and noise; (ii) the mobility of urban residents; and (iii) the economic viability of central city business

2. The mode of mass transportation that can best meet the desired objectives

3. The extent to which frivolous ridership increases as a result of reduced fare or fare-free systems

4. The extent to which the need for urban highways might be reduced as a result of reduced fare or fare-free systems; and

5. The best means of financing reduced fare or fare-free transportation on a continuing basis[47]

Naturally, the passage of the Act brought considerable euphoria to its supporters. The fact that another major step had been taken in fleshing out a more complete program of federal aid to mass transit made the bill important in the development of the federal role in urban mass transportation. It should be carefully noted that the bill was not intended to be the final word on federal mass transit programs. The Act of 1974 was intended to be a short-run measure for the purpose of keeping mass transit viable until longer-range measures could be enacted.

The provisions of the new Act caused some headaches. More red tape was involved, not just on the federal level but also on the state levels, by involving governors and state agencies in the federal grant procedures. In some places this added state involvement moved along rather smoothly; such was the case in states that already had a mature and functioning department of transportation or a mass transportation agency. In states without such institutions, the situation was chaotic for a while.

The requirement that there be a uniform system of accounts for the transit industry was a wise step and one that should have been taken some time earlier. At the time the law was passed, UMTA support had helped in the development of the so-called F.A.R.E. system of accounting and information collection for transit.[48] This eventually became the heart of the Section 15 reporting mechanism.

After all the bills and compromises, the transit industry not only had new legislation that provided operating aid, but it also had a clearer mission from Congress, which was: to keep fares stable, expand service, and increase ridership. This the industry proceeded to do during the remainder of the seventies.

9.

The Surface Transportation Act of 1978

On November 24, 1974, amendments to the Urban Mass Transportation Act of 1964 provided formula grants under Section 5 of the Urban Mass Transportation Act and by doing so changed the nature of the federal mass transit program. The monies allocated to urbanized areas under this portion of the Act could be utilized, at local option, for either capital or operating purposes.[1] Not really appreciated fully at first, these amendments changed the federal mass transportation program from one that was purely discretionary to one in which about one-third of the money was distributed according to a formula. This altered the outlook and expectations of transit management, along with the perspectives of local public officials who came to realize that, if their municipality qualified for Section 5 aid, they were entitled to a sum of federal money for transit purposes. Federal mass transportation policy changes had produced what was partially an entitlement program.

For a time after the passage of the 1974 Act, relatively little action occurred on new legislation for mass transportation. This was a period in which the transit industry and the Urban Mass Transportation Administration (UMTA) worked with the new program and sought to understand its impact. It would take some time for any results in the form of stable transit fares, improved service, and increased ridership (all were goals of the 1974 Act) to become evident. This hiatus was expected to end in 1977 when, after a period of learning from the application of the 1974 Act, new legislation could be promulgated and enacted to close bothersome gaps and increase the level and scope of transit aid.

The period between 1974 and the time when the new legislative effort for transit would be made is of importance in understanding what happened later. The departure of Richard Nixon from the presidency had placed his successor, Gerald Ford, in the position of being the nation's first unelected president. The word of the press and the eye of television had been directed toward the Watergate Affair for two years, pushing other news out of the upper rank of public interest. The debacle of the Nixon presidency had caused a rising trend of questioning the activities of government and its officials. If Watergate helped to focus attention on government, this was probably more a continuation of the lack of trust in government that has always been present in some measure in American democracy. However, the questioning and distrust were strengthened by the war in Vietnam and the less-than-candid reporting of that conflict by the national government.

At the same time, there were rising national concerns over the quality of life, and government action was taken to deal with what was perceived as a serious decline in or threat to the environment. With no indication that an outbreak of common sense based on self-preservation would guide public and corporate America to act responsibly, laws were passed. Local, state, and federal programs to solve environmental, housing, poverty, and other problems joined earlier programs of government. Americans, as befits members of a great democracy, are possibly more aware of the actions of their government than are many other nationalities because they have more to say about what government does. By the mid-1970s, government was looming larger in the lives of the U.S. public, and not always positively. Coming especially close in a complex world to being particularly both-ersome were the rules and regulations and the general government presence concerning automobiles and the use of energy. Motorists were faced with a national speed limit of 55 miles per hour and, in reaction to laws establishing miles-per-gallon targets for automobiles, auto manufacturers began to downsize automobiles. The great American chariot got smaller and had to go slower.

Although government was playing a larger role in the lives of Americans, it was not always scoring high marks for its efforts. Indeed, unhappiness with government seemed to be one of the more galling irritations in American life during the 1970s, and it spread to the public's view of politicians. Despite hoopla and election promises, the individuals elected to office seemed to offer much less than promised, and the great machinery of the government, lubricated and fueled with huge sums of tax money, seemed incapable of achieving even the most simple task. As a symbol of disenchantment with government and politicians, the general disappointment with his pardoning of Richard Nixon probably cost Gerald Ford re-election to the presidency in his own right in 1976. In the 1970s, as at no time before in memory, candidates found it profitable to run against the government—to be opposed to Washington. One of those who came from outside the national government, and by background and instinct made a point of his distance from Washington and his opposition to many of its ways, was Jimmy Carter, the former governor of Georgia.

Nominated by his party as the 1976 Democratic presidential candidate, Carter faced Gerald Ford and won. Those backing the federal transit programs could take cheer from both candidates. President Ford had been most supportive; in addition, the transit program had fared well under the previous eight years of Republicans in the White House. Mr. Carter's victory was seen as good news for transit. Indeed, during the election process, a feeling emerged that the first year of the Carter administration would be a good one for transit. In his campaign, Mr. Carter had expressed support for mass transportation. For example, he informed the Democratic National Convention's Platform Committee that ". . . arresting this deterioration [of existing transit programs] and completing needed work on new urban transit systems must become the nation's first transportation priority."[2] In remarks to the U.S. Conference of Mayors, Mr. Carter called for a substantial increase in the amount of money available for mass transportation from the Highway Trust Fund, a larger operating subsidy, and a study of the feasibility of utilizing the trust fund device to finance all transportation modes.

After the election, the transit industry was also generally enthusiastic about the selection of former Congressman Brock Adams (D-Washington) as secretary of transportation. On Capital Hill, Adams was a strong supporter of public transit. In 1973, Congressman Adams had voted to open up the Highway Trust Fund for mass transportation; in 1973-74, he backed legislative efforts which eventually found their way into the operating provisions of the 1974 amendments to the Urban Mass Transportation Act of 1964.

The industry was also pleased that the slow but apparently steady growth in transit ridership continued in 1975, despite the sharp downturn in the economy. This was seen as evidence that the rising federal expenditure on transit was bearing some fruit.[3] The federal programs, moreover, had stimulated increased support and material aid from state and local government. The requirement that federal grants be matched by local or state funds was instrumental in the passage of favorable laws. This was true even in states not thought to be so urbanized that transit would be a major interest or force. For example, in 1967 Indiana provided enlightened legislation enabling cities to create public transportation corporations with taxing authority and jurisdiction extending beyond civil city boundaries. In 1975 Indiana began to provide state matching funds for federal grants; in 1980 this program gained a regular source of funding through dedication of a percentage of the state's gross sales tax revenue.

On the basis of Mr. Carter's statements before he became president, plus the attitude of Brock Adams and the performance of the industry, transit proponents and observers of the transit field were fairly confident that 1977 could and would mark the beginning of a new and better era for mass transit. This sanguine attitude of transit proponents was soon dashed by the events of 1977.

THE LEGISLATIVE PROGRAM OF APTA

In its role as the principal lobbying lead for mass transportation on the federal level, the American Public Transit Association (APTA) laid out its 1977 program of legislation, which contained three principal goals. The first was to increase the level of the major capital investment program in mass transportation to an average of $4.5 billion yearly over the next five years. The second goal was continued funding of the Section 5 formula grant program which was to end, under the existing law, in 1980. The APTA program called for $1.1 billion in Section 5 formula grant money in 1981 and approximately $1.25 billion for 1982. The third element in the program was for an effective urban street program as authorized under the Federal Aid Highway Act of 1973.

The $800 million annually set aside for urban highway or transit purposes had not been working effectively. Approximately $2.6 billion had been apportioned to states, yet less than half that amount had actually been assigned to approved projects. Local governments were spending $5 to $6 billion of their own money for maintenance purposes; the transit industry's position was that money should be authorized from general revenues and allocated to urban areas in a fashion similar to the Section 5 formula grant program. The money was to be used for street maintenance and improvement.[4] The transit industry, recognizing the road and transit problems of cities, took a position that was sympathetic. In so doing, APTA sought to continue the development of a peaceful and constructive alliance with highway interests which had been in the process of growth for several years.

Adding to these positive feelings, the transit industry perceived the new 95th Congress to have generally liberal tendencies and to be very much an urban Congress. For example, the House of Representatives had 250 members who represented areas interested in urban mass transportation. In terms of composition, then, it appeared that Congress would continue to be favorably disposed toward transit improvements.

The APTA legislative program sought $15 billion for transit; of this, $11.8 billion would be new money and $3.3 billion would be funds as yet unspent under provisions of the 1974 Act. Annually, half a billion dollars would be made available for routine bus replacements, and an additional hundred million would be for downtown peoplemovers. The additional money was directed at maintaining what amounted to a straight line of funding growth in the face of expected continuing inflationary pressures.[5] It was obvious that it was not the aim of this financial program to strike out in new directions or to make enormous additions of real dollars—it was a relatively conservative approach compared to the programs sought and won in 1973 and 1974.

A bill reflecting the APTA program was introduced by Senator Harrison A. Williams, Jr., on January 12, 1977. As S.208, the proposed legislation would authorize a five-year capital grant program of rising amounts averaging $2.28 billion each year. At the time legislation was introduced, the obligation levels at the Urban Mass Transportation Administration (UMTA) were about $1.2 billion annually. S.208 also included a discretionary fund of $250 million per year for five years. The formula grant program was to be continued from 1978 to 1982, a special fund of a half billion dollars per year, for the purchase of new bus equipment, was included, and there were provisions to make transportation services more accessible to the elderly, the handicapped, and residents of rural areas.[6]

As a major break for non-urbanized areas (cities of less than 50,000 people), the $500 million already set aside for capital improvements in non-urbanized areas was to be made available for operating as well as capital assistance purposes in much the same fashion as the formula grant program for urbanized areas. For those interested in increasing the scale of the program of management upgrading and improvement, the restrictions on the number of fellowships under Section 10 of the Urban Mass Transportation Act (which had been set at 100 per year in the 1966 amendments to the Act) would be eliminated. This would increase the number of persons who could participate in and benefit from management training and renewal programs. It was expected that the changes would probably increase the number of such programs as well.[7]

S.208 would also expand the definition of construction under Sections 3 and 5 (respectively, the capital improvement and formula grant programs) of the Urban Mass Transportation Act to include preliminary engineering. Under Section 16 of the Act, which involved the elderly and the handicapped, service was to be provided by either accessible, regular fixed-route services or by substitute special services. The secretary of transportation could mandate the purchase of accessible equipment in order to insure mobility. The bill would also require local advisory committees of elderly and handicapped people to insure adequate planning and service; a national advisory council on transportation for the elderly and handicapped was to be established.[8]

The transit industry, working through APTA, testified on behalf of S.208 on February 24, 1977. Appearing before the Senate Banking Committee, the APTA spokesman, while supporting S.208, recommended that some additions be made to the National Mass Transportation Assistance Act of 1977 (as S.208 had been dubbed). It was suggested that Section 5 money be specifically directed to all urbanized areas. Under the existing law, the formula grant funds were provided directly only to urbanized areas of more than 200,000 people. The money for urbanized areas between 50,000 and 200,000 people was made available to the governor of the state in a lump sum, an amount equal to what the smaller urbanized areas would get individually under the Section 5 formula. At the discretion of the governor, the funds might be parceled out in any one year by means other than the federal formula, provided that at the end of the life of the formula grant program financial authorizations (that is, by 1980), the actual division of the funds would assure that each urbanized area had received money equal to adherence to the federal statutory formula based 50 percent on population and 50 percent on population density.

APTA also recommended that Section 3 capital grant money be used to increase the federal share (which was 70 percent) of federal aid urban system, non-highway public transportation project money to the 80 percent level of regular Section 3 projects. It was believed that this would encourage local government to opt to use more highway money for mass transit purposes.

Also, APTA called for 1 percent of the additional Section 5 funds provided each year to be set aside for hardware and policy research. More money for non-urbanized areas was also requested. It was felt that separate section authorization was needed on a statutory basis to make sure the monies would flow to non-urbanized areas, which were beginning to awaken to the needs of residents who, for various reasons, did not have private transportation available. Smaller cities were also interested in transit as a symbol of their status as true urban places.

The transit industry also pushed for relief from the labor protection clauses under Sections 13c and 3e(4) of the Act for demonstrations and innovative projects to be carried out under the proposed language in Section 5c(1)c.[9] Such projects were to be in the nature of new, exemplary, innovative undertakings in specialized transit service.

Legislation of a similar nature was also introduced in the House by Representatives James J. Howard (D-New Jersey) and Bob Edgar (D-Pennsylvania). The Howard bill would have required that half of the buses bought by a transit system with the next federal grant be made fully accessible to the handicapped. The remainder of the buses would have to be capable of being made accessible. Studies would then be made of the transportation needs of elderly and handicapped citizens within a given system's service area; no further grants could be made during this study period. Results of the study would be given to the secretary of transportation, who would then determine the proportion of buses purchased in future orders which would have to be totally accessible. The aim of this legislation was to end the debate and controversy over the question of total accessibility for elderly and handicapped citizens and whether or not all vehicles should be equipped with wheelchair ramps, lifts, and other devices.

Representative Edgar's bill called for an annual set-aside of $350 million to purchase buses and vans. A similar amount of money would be made available for rail or fixed guideway equipment. Operating aid provisions of the law would be changed; a supplemental fund would be distributed under a special formula, taking into account an urbanized area's share of total passenger miles of service. The secretary of transportation could withhold operating aid if it were discovered that state and local governments were making no substantive progress toward stable and predictable sources of state or local aid.[10]

UNEXPECTED TROUBLE ALONG THE WAY TO A TRANSIT BILL

As the winter snows of 1977 melted away, so did the expectations of the transit industry for relatively easy sledding for the mass transit legislation that was moving through Congress. The first serious blow was the position taken by Secretary of Transportation Brock Adams in his testimony at the hearings on S.208. Appearing before the subcommittee on housing and urban affairs of the Senate Committee on Banking on February 25, 1977, Adams told the group that the new administration wished to look at all issues and concerns insofar as transportation was concerned. The secretary made it clear that the administration did not wish to foreclose any options open to it in the future and that passage of S.208 would do so. He also dropped a bombshell when he said: "Fortunately, there is no urgent need to provide additional or extended program authorizations for the mass transit program. . . ."[11] In other words, there was already enough money for urban mass transportation. This was not the message that presidential candidate Jimmy Carter had given regarding transit.

The secretary also indicated that there was no need to be upset about the contract authority provisions of the Urban Mass Transportation Act, which was estimated to be about $1 billion in deficit by the Ford administration. Under Ford, the principle of not letting the outstanding program commitments exceed the total contract authority had been followed. Adams suggested that attention be paid to the annual funding requirements and that as some projects reached completion and needed less money, other projects could be begun. Under this philosophy, it would no longer be necessary to set aside or freeze available contract authority to cover all existing future year commitments.[12]

Secretary Adams also testified in a similar fashion before the subcommittee on surface transportation of the House Committee on Public Works and Transportation. From the testimony given by the secretary and the heart of the news release issued by the Department of Transportation on his testimony, it was clear that there was a strong desire on the part of the new administration to balance the federal budget by 1980 and, as the secretary had testified, to keep open as many options as possible in transportation.[13]

Passage of S.208 in 1977 or 1978 would commit the Carter administration to a mass transit program that would extend beyond its already elected term of office and well into a possible second term. Admittedly, there was a need for a close examination of transportation policy in the U.S., along with a review of related policy issues, such as urban affairs, energy, environment, and economic development. To many in the transit field, however, the promise of something or another in a year or so was not very satisfying.

The transit industry was quick to express disappointment and concern over Secretary Adams's testimony. APTA immediately pointed out that the testimonies delivered by transit operators, mayors, labor union officials, and other spokesmen for American cities were markedly different from that of the secretary. Moreover, the secretary had candidly admitted that because of inflation, his approach to funding would drive up construction costs drastically because it would postpone new rail starts until 1980. The transit industry, talking on some of the key issues and concerns of the day, took the position that this delay would dissipate transit's potential for conserving energy, cutting traffic congestion, and reducing air pollution.[14]

Other observers thought that the secretary's approach was another way of promoting a consolidated transportation account and elimination of the principle and practice of tying certain funds to given purposes, such as federal fuel tax receipts paid into the Highway Trust Fund. The secretary took the position that such an account would enable the federal government to shift the national investments in transportation as national needs changed over time, rather than simply adding up the interests of each concerned group and finding one way or another to pay for the transport facilities provided. If the Williams bill S.208 were passed, pressure would be taken off the transit industry to compete for funds from a consolidated source of federal funding for transportation.[15]

If there was gloom in the transit industry arising from Secretary Adams's position on S.208, it was nothing compared to the industry's reaction to the handwritten memo of March 21, 1977, from President Carter to Secretary Adams. The memo read:

> To Brock Adams: I suspect that many of the rapid transit systems are grossly over-designed. We should insist on: a) off-street parking, b) one-way

streets, c) special bus lanes, d) surface rail/bus as preferable alternatives to subways. In urban areas, no construction at all would be needed if a, b, and c are required. Signed: J. Carter.[16]

To say the least, supporters of transit, especially rail transit, were dismayed. It was hard to believe that this President Carter was the same man as candidate Carter who had called for more funds for transit. From anyone else the memo would not have been much of a problem; but as a writing of the President of the United States it was extremely bad news for transit proponents. In the aftermath of the memo, charges were leveled that the Carter administration was looking more toward holding down the budget than doing anything particularly creative in dealing with the problems of energy, the environment, or the transportation realities of metropolitan areas. For his part, Secretary Adams viewed the president's memo as doing nothing more than supporting the UMTA policy of examining alternatives before giving large grants for rail systems.

Meanwhile, in line with what came to be recognized as President Carter's fiscal conservatism, the administration brought pressure on Senator Williams to pare down the dollar amount called for in S.208. A compromise was reached that would have whittled the $11.4 billion mass transit funding called for in S.208 to $5.7 billion.[17]

The only positive note from the administration was an advertising campaign to be conducted with the cooperation of the White House. It provided for car cards and other ads to be carried on transit vehicles quoting Jimmy Carter as saying, "Thanks for taking the bus and saving energy."[18] This was pretty meager stuff from the candidate from whom so much had been expected, and in the minds of those supporting transit it was not much of a counteragent to the memo to Secretary Adams.

The gloom over the president's attitude mounted when the Carter position on energy and the Carter energy program were presented to the public. Conspicuous by its absence was any mention of urban mass transportation's part in an energy program. The transit industry had taken a position on energy in a policy statement from APTA that was aimed at: (1) reducing gasoline consumption, (2) increasing the productivity of the urban transportation systems with respect to energy, and (3) correlating federal urban policies and programs to channel urban growth into energy efficient patterns.[19]

The Carter energy policy was focused mainly on the demand side. It called for a number of taxes that would help discourage the use of energy. It was a program that was not terribly popular, despite the slowly growing public concern over energy and the palpable power of OPEC to control energy prices in a world heavily dependent on the crude petroleum produced by the OPEC nations. The policy was faulted in some quarters for being too much on the side of conservation and not enough on the side of new exploration or development of new sources of energy. The policy was also criticized because of its potential inflationary impact and lack of sufficient disincentives to really cut down on the utilization of energy.[20]

Although President Carter had called the nation's efforts on the energy issue the moral equivalent of war, many persons felt it to be the moral equivalent of nothing. Many critics thought the policy had not been well thought out and that it lacked form and content that would have made it easily sellable in Congress. Moreover, a study by the General Accounting Office revealed that the plan, even if fully approved by Congress, would fall short of its goals.[21] Criticism of the president's position on mass transit was widespread in certain quarters. Much of the criticism was leveled at other portions of this proposed program, but there was clear puzzlement over the glaring omission of transit.[22]

The *Washington Post* even suggested brazenly that one of the best ways to conserve energy and create a good example would be by getting rid of the government parking subsidy for the cars of certain federal employees. At the time, there were 41,000 parking spaces in Washington, D.C. and the surrounding area available to privileged federal employees. Three-fourths of these spaces were free; the remainder cost from $5 to $20 per month, which was appreciably less than the commercial rates on such parking.[23]

Whether or not it was proper to consider transit as a separate issue from energy, or as one to be solved as part of an overall program in transportation to be presented by Secretary Adams to Congress in the spring of 1978, misses the point. It is obvious that the Carter administration did not feel that the transit situation was serious enough to warrant more money. Nor was transit considered vital as an ingredient in the program laid out to help attack the looming shortage of petroleum-based sources of energy.

For his part, Secretary Adams attempted to get the extra gas-tax money that would be derived from new levies aimed at discouraging use of gasoline utilized for transit purposes. According to Adams's proposal, two cents of the proposed nickel-per-gallon hike in the gasoline tax would go into a consolidated transportation account and be directed to mass transit programs. An additional two cents of the tax would be devoted to energy-related research in transportation. The remaining penny of the added tax would be used to provide transportation grants to states. The secretary spoke for himself, while the White House took the position that the administration would prefer to see the tax money rebated to the taxpayers.[24] For a variety of reasons, most patently his lack of enthusiasm for airline deregulation, Secretary Adams was not a favorite in the innermost circles of the Carter administration.[25]

As 1977 moved on, there was a strong feeling growing in the transit industry that the Carter administration was very definitely anti-transit, primarily because it had ignored transit in the energy message and because it had fought Secretary Adams's attempts to utilize some of the gas taxes for transit purposes. Part of the problem might have been the difference in priorities between the Carter administration and the president himself, as it appeared to people concerned with the transit issue. For example, Vernon Jordan of the Urban League and Jimmy Carter were obviously on different timetables when it came to various social and civil rights issues, even though both apparently agreed on the goals to be sought.[26]

How a president views an issue is, in part, a direct result of the perceptions of those who advise him. Obviously, no president can be an expert on all issues, because there are just too many of them. On the energy question, Mr. Carter apparently listened mainly to James Schlesinger, secretary of the new Department of Energy. Secretary of Transportation Adams was one of the cabinet officers excluded from the drafting sessions on energy policy. It was hardly a revelation, then, that the administration's policy proposal on energy was virtually silent on mass transportation.[27]

At the end of June, the Senate finally passed legislation authorizing $5.3 billion in new federal funds for mass transit. This was the compromise Williams Bill, S.208. The bill authorized $4.75 billion for capital programs; $500 million in operating aid to non-urbanized areas was made available, utilizing funds already set aside for capital improvements in non-urbanized areas. Special aid was also provided to large cities and commuter railroads not operated by Conrail. The $125 million of Section 5 funds that had been "borrowed" for the 1977 transition quarter from fiscal year 1980 money was put back into the funds to be used in 1980.

When the formula grant program was made a part of the federal transit program in 1974, it was clear that it would need tinkering. Large transit properties (especially in older, transit-oriented cities) were irked by the distribution of the Section 5 money under the formula based 50 percent on population and 50 percent on population density; they felt the formula gave them too little money and gave too much to large but non-transit-oriented cities in the South and West. Many transit properties in cities of smaller size could not use all of the Section 5 money allocated to them by the formula, which was a bitter pill to swallow for some desperate and impecunious large properties. Reflecting the concern of the larger cities, the Williams bill created a second "tier" of $295 million to aid transit in the nation's largest cities. The money was to be distributed under a formula to be devised by the secretary of transportation. It would be based on the share of the national total of revenue passengers, vehicle miles, and population, and it would be weighted by population density. The funds for this would come from recycling $145 million in unused Section 5 operating funds that would otherwise be returned to the Treasury; in addition there would be new authorizations of $50 million annually for 1978 through 1980.[28]

As happened so often in developing transit legislation, there were alarms and discursions. While the transit bill was being debated in the Senate, Senator Hayakawa of California introduced an amendment to withhold assistance under the Urban Mass Transportation Act from any locality which maintained or enforced any restriction or requirement relating to the operation of the taxicab business, except for certain restrictions having to do with licensing, insurance, and safety. Senator Hayakawa's objective was to increase job opportunities.

The Hayakawa amendment promised to be the proverbial can of worms if it were enacted into law, because it provided something to upset both the taxi industry and the transit industry. Without regulation, the taxi industry, in many cases essentially a local oligopoly or monopoly, would be faced with significant competition. Because the taxi industry was far from robust, it was expected to fight the amendment. Transit operators, on the other hand, might feel that they would be subjected to the same sort of unregulated competition once visited upon them by the jitneys and so would also be likely to fight the Hayakawa amendment.

Senator Hayakawa withdrew his amendment at the time of debate on the Senate floor on June 23, 1977, on the promise that hearings would be held on the matter in the future.[29]

At the very end of 1977, Secretary Adams presented an administration transit bill proposal. He had requested the House not to act on its version of S.208 until he had presented his program, and the House had complied. The proposed legislation would meld the highway and transit programs together.

On the transit side, the funding patterns would be changed so that two-thirds of the money would be distributed by formula for capital and operating purposes, and one-third would be discretionary money for major capital projects (primarily rail). All routine replacement of equipment would be supported by the formula funds rather than discretionary funds. It was proposed in early statements regarding the legislation that only one-third of operating costs would be covered by formula funds. This would be a serious problem to those transit properties that covered less than one-third of their operating costs out of the farebox.[30]

The transit industry clearly did not get what it wanted in 1977. Just as obvious was the low priority assigned to transit by the Carter administration, and it was necessary for the transit industry to fight hard for what it did gain. Support at the time appeared firm in Congress, and APTA and other favorably disposed lobbying groups strove to maintain that support. Looking back, it was good basic training for the battles that would face the transit industry in the 1980s.[31]

THE TRANSIT PROGRAM OF 1978

The year 1978 was to be a trying one for the transit industry. Throughout the year, the main message from the Carter administration was for fiscal conservation, the concept of a single transportation fund for highways and transit, and a single agency to administer the program, with all the potential problems that such a move would bring to the transit operators. The president also attacked the federal transit program. On April 11, 1978, for example, Mr. Carter included the transit program as one of five federal programs that were especially responsible for the sharp rise in federal expenditures; he pledged to fight growth in the transit program.[32]

The year also presented other problems to the transit industry. Section 504 of the Rehabilitation Act of 1973 (under the jurisdiction of the Department of Health, Education, and Welfare, or HEW) was the source of major concern. The draft regulations published in the Federal Register on June 8 called for implementation of the Act in line with guidelines issued by HEW in January 1978. In essence, the proposed rules required that handicapped persons not be denied the opportunity to use or benefit from federally assisted programs. For transit agencies receiving federal aid, it meant that all vehicles would have to serve the handicapped, as would all stations and other facilities.[33]

This was the beginning of the transit industry's dilemma over the potential cost impact of the implementation of Section 504. Unless there was a significant increase in the amount of dollars available, it would be very difficult to observe the rule. Sharp increases in federal funding seemed unlikely, not only because of the anti-spending attitude of the Carter administration toward transit, but also because of the tax-cutting attitudes on the state and local levels, animated in large part by the success of property-tax-cutting Proposition 13 in California. Transit was expected to do more, but the money available was apparently diminishing.

The threat of increased costs to implement full accessibility to transit (expenditures viewed as of doubtful usefulness by a probable majority of the transit industry), as well as a cheeseparing attitude on the part of local government and perhaps state government, made passage of a well-funded federal mass transit bill essential. As it turned out, getting a transit bill passed was to be more difficult than anyone suspected in early 1978.

Secretary Adams proposed an administration bill in January 1978 (introduced in Congress as S.2441) that a combined transportation program be enacted to bring together transit and highway funding in a single account. The aim was to set up a means by which, eventually, all transportation programs in the president's budget would be separated into a single, functional classification.[34] The key elements of Secretary Adams's proposed program would have brought about some major changes for transit. All routine bus and rail modernization and rail rolling stock grants would be shifted away from the discretionary program of Section 3 of the Act and be placed in the formula grant program of Section 5. The formula grant program was proposed for a two-year extension, with a funding level of $1.9 billion in fiscal 1979 and $1.95 billion in fiscal 1980.

At local initiative, up to half of the formula funds could be used for highway projects. Total authorizations would be based on a formula embracing population, population density, and commuter rail mileage, so that the sums would be equal to the amounts then available under the existing law in Sections 5, 17, and 18. Remaining funds would be allocated on the basis of rapid transit route miles, the number of buses over twelve years of age, and bus seat miles. No more than 50 percent of the formula funds could be used for operating assistance, and operating assistance projects would be limited to one-third of total operating expenses. This latter feature would replace the maintenance of effort and local share requirements of the existing Section 5 program.

The secretary proposed that discretionary funds for capital improvements under Section 3 of the Mass Transit Act be limited to new systems, major extensions of existing transit systems, and very large bus projects. The Section 3 program was to be authorized for a five-year period, beginning at $1.65 billion in fiscal 1979 and rising to $1.85 billion by fiscal 1983. The authorization for Section 3 would include $775 million each year for Interstate substitution projects, with the federal share for the substitution increased to 90 percent (from 70 percent under the existing law).

Under the secretary's recommendations, the small urban and rural areas would not be forgotten. A formula-based transit capital and operating assistance program was to be created for non-urbanized areas, with assistance for operating aid limited to one-third of costs.

Turning to highways, the secretary proposed that for the Federal Aid Urban Systems funds, the federal share be raised to 80 percent. Governors and local officials would jointly designate recipients in areas of over one million people. The DOT secretary could waive local share requirements for a two-year period in certain distressed cities. For the Interstate System, all Interstate transfer projects would be at a 90 percent federal share. The states were to be required to complete the environmental impact statement process for Interstate segments or request withdrawal of all Interstate projects by September 30, 1982.

As for planning, UMTA and Federal Highway Administration planning assistance programs were to be consolidated in a single grant at an 80 percent federal share. Planning funds were to go directly to designated recipients in areas of over one million, with those plans to be certified by the secretary.[35]

The transit industry's reaction was negative toward both the proposed legislation and the proposed budget for mass transportation. Whereas APTA had hoped for $4.5 billion for transit in fiscal year 1979, the Carter budget allowed only $2.86 billion for transit; this was down sharply from the $3.154 billion contained in the fiscal 1978 budget. APTA pointed out that the proposed increase in operating funds was less than the predicted rate of inflation, meaning a real cutback in federal operating aid.[36]

The money levels in the transit bill introduced as H.R. 11733 by Representative James Howard (D-New Jersey), chairman of the House Surface Transportation Subcommittee, were of greater appeal to transit advocates. The bill, known as the Surface Transportation Assistance Act of 1978, called for more than $4.4 billion in funding for transit. It also included the highway provisions discussed in the proposals of Secretary Adams.

The Howard bill, in its original form, called for advanced authorization of approximately $4.5 billion a year through fiscal 1988. The Section 3 capital aid program of discretionary funds allotted $1.8 billion divided into specific categories: $200 million for bus purchases; $350 million for rail rolling stock; $650 million for rail modernization; and $600 million for new rapid transit starts. For rural areas, $150 million was provided, to be used for either capital or operating purposes. As a new wrinkle, half of the rural fund was earmarked for private intercity bus operating aid.

The Section 5 formula grant program would be extended beyond 1980, to 1982, with $900 million in each of the last two fiscal years. Representative Howard's legislative proposal sought to meet the needs claimed by the larger transit properties that had not been met by the original Section 5 program of 1974. A second tier of Section 5 money was to be provided for operating aid and to create a special fund for bus purchases. The second tier funds would total $250 million per year for four years, with 85 percent to go to the twenty-five U.S. cities with more than one million people; the remaining 15 percent would be distributed to cities of less than one million people. In both cases the formula would be based half on population and half on population density. The formula grant program would include $400 million for bus purchases in addition to the $200 million already earmarked for that purpose under Section 3.

Aid for commuter railroads was to be restructured with the abolition of Section 17, which legislated reimbursement of the Consolidated Rail Corporation (Conrail) and Amtrak, and other possible operators of commuter rail service. All non-Amtrak rail aid was to be centered in Section 18. The level would be $100 million per annum for either capital or operating purposes; a minimum of $500,000 and a maximum of 30 percent of the total funds would be made available to any city with commuter rail service.

The Howard bill did not permit use of mass transit formula funds for highway purposes. However, $600 million per year of the Interstate System funds could be shifted to mass transit capital projects. Planning money under Section 9 was to total $60 million per year. Sections 6, 10, and 11 would receive $150 million per year.[37] Another $50 million was to be provided for intercity bus terminals and shelters, which would be funded at an 80 percent federal share.[38]

If transit proponents were disappointed over the sparse funding in the administration bill and cheered by the higher level of funding in the Howard bill, they were also realistic enough to be worried by the threat of a veto by President Carter of a transit bill that would increase transit spending above the levels set out in the administration bill. APTA testified before the Howard subcommittee on surface transportation that $4.4 billion was needed in fiscal 1979.[39]

In the Senate, the Banking, Housing, and Urban Affairs Committee considered the administration bill, S.2441, in early May, 1978. At that time, Senator Harrison Williams offered amendments to the legislative proposal. He sought to make the bill more realistic in terms of the needs of the transit industry by increasing the amount of federal funds and by eliminating some of the administration provisions that had brought strong negative reactions from the transit community. Williams called for approximately $15.1 billion to be authorized through fiscal 1982 with approximately $3.53 billion available in fiscal 1979, rising to $3.9 billion in fiscal 1982. The Williams amendments would allow use of Interstate transfer funds as needed, rather than include them in the total spending budget for transit as called for in S.2441. Unlike the Howard bill, the Williams amendments did not earmark or set ceilings or provide set-asides for particular types of capital improvements. Nevertheless, the monetary authorizations would be about the same. To determine the second tier of money for the nation's largest cities, the Williams amendments called for a complex formula based on population, population density, fixed guideway route miles, commuter rail train miles, and bus seat miles. Commuter rail would be funded through the Section 5 program, and Sections 17 and 18 would be abolished. A new Section 18 for non-urbanized areas was also proposed.[40]

During the summer of 1978, the Howard bill and the amended version of S.2441 moved sluggishly through Congress. There was, of course, some continued tinkering with the bills.[41] The pace was slowed by concern over the funding levels in the combined transit and highway bills and by the illnesses of Congressman Howard and other key persons in the House during the summer.

Some delay was also caused by the combination of the highway and transit elements into one bill and by the fiscally conservative noises coming out of the White House, as the administration savored public thoughts and feelings on inflation and taxation. As an example, the Carter administration asked for $47 billion over a four-year period with a renewal of the Highway Trust Fund for four years; the House Public Works and Transportation Committee approved a bill for $66.5 billion that also extended the Highway Trust Fund for six years. Such discrepancies raised the obvious concern over a presidential veto at worst, and long sessions of a conference committee to iron out differences at best.[42]

A factor that was both good and bad for transit was its decision to combine forces with the highway interests to get a joint bill through Congress. The transit industry did not wish to compete with the highway interests because of the danger of losing in any serious confrontation. The argument that had successfully led to the opening of the Highway Trust Fund to transit use in 1973 was no longer valid. Thanks to inflation, the unexpectedly rapid deterioration of the Interstate Highways, and a growing problem with highway bridges, there was not enough money in the trust fund or in its future expected revenues to handle the job of rehabilitating the nation's road system, much less to provide a significant source of money for transit.

The national philosophy toward transportation was and is in the process of change. The emphasis that began to surface in 1978, and which continued, was no longer on building new facilities, but on the maintenance and reconstruction of existing ones. Thanks to inflation and the damage wrought by weather, road de-icing agents, and heavy trucks, the cost of mending the highways promised to be even more costly than their initial construction. With highway dollars promising to be scarce, the transit forces did not wish to do battle over the same pool of money, feeling they would probably lose.[43]

As the fall of 1978 approached, it was clear that there was going to be a cliff-hanging element in the transit legislation. The House did not take up the legislation until September. The White House threatened a veto if too much money was involved and, because 1978 was an election year, Congress wanted to adjourn before the middle of October so that members could go home to campaign.

Late in September, neither H.R. 11733 nor S.2441 had passed their respective houses; both Congressman Howard and Senator Williams amended the bills, not only to win the favor of their colleagues but also to fit in with what the White House claimed was its limit. Senator Williams made public a letter from Secretary Adams on September 25, stating that the Carter administration would support the $14.45 billion (plus $2.8 billion in Interstate Transfer Funds) through 1983 as the ceiling within the time frame.[44] On October 3, the Senate approved S.2441.[45]

The fate of the transit legislation was uncertain until the very last minute. Congress was to adjourn on Saturday, October 14. As it had been shaped by compromise, the much-amended Surface Transportation Assistance Act of 1978

Table 9.1
Status of Federal Transit Assistance
(Numbers in Millions of Dollars)

	Actual Appropriations H.R.				11733 as Passed by Congress		
	FY 1977	FY 1978	FY 1979	FY 1980	FY 1981	FY 1982	FY 1983
Discretionary	1455	1250	1375	1410	1515	1600	1580
Capital	1400	1225	1299.4	1332.4	1431.7	1512	—
Planning and Innovative Techniques	55[1]	25[2]	75.6[4]	77.6[4]	83.3[4]	88[4]	—
Formula	820	1402.5	1515	1580	1665	1765	—
Basic	775	850	850	900	900	900	—
Second Tier	—	150	250	250	250	250	—
Bus Capital	—	300	300	300	370	455	—
Rail	45	75	115	130	145	160	—
Planning	—	28.5	—	—	—	—	—
Small Urban and Rural	—	76.5	90	100	110	120	—
Miscellaneous	90	81.6	90	95	100	105	—
Bus Terminal	—	—	40	40	40	40	—
Intercity Bus Operating	—	—	30	30	30	30	—
Transportation Institutes	—	—	10	10	10	10	—
Waterborne Demo.	—	—	20	5	—	—	—
TOTAL	2365	2811.6	3270	3270	3470	3670	1580
Interstate Substitution	789[3]	400			such sums as are necessary		

[1]For planning.

[2]For planning; total is 55; 25 from Section 3, 28.5 from Section 5, and 1.5 from Small Urban and Rural.

[3]Includes approximately 140 for highway projects.

[4]Set aside of 5.5 percent for planning grants and grants for innovative methods and techniques.

Source: Estimates of the American Public Transit Association, October 18, 1978.

had a price tag of $53.8 billion for highways and mass transit over a four-year-plus period; the House Senate Conference Committee on the Surface Transportation Act of 1978 had whittled down the cost of the bill well below the $66.5 billion sum in the version originally approved by Congressman Howard's subcommittee on surface transportation.

There was still serious concern over whether or not the president would sign the bill, because he was being advised by the Office of Management and Budget that the bill was too costly. On the other hand, the president was being advised by Secretary Adams and several White House aides to sign the bill. The threat of a presidential veto was still very strong, and on October 13, the U.S. Conference of Mayors got word to its constituent cities to lobby the White House vigorously for presidential approval.

As night fell on the Capitol, it was clear that Congress would have to run a marathon all-night session on October 14 in order to complete the necessary work on tax cuts and energy legislation.

The energy legislation was of particular interest and importance to President Carter, who had stated repeatedly that it was his highest-priority measure. Unfortunately for the president, the energy legislation package was in deep trouble in the House; a procedural vote on October 13 had given the administration a victory of only one vote (207-206) on the energy bill. That note and President Carter's interest in the energy legislation proved to be the key to passage of the Surface Transportation Act.

As the long night of October 14 moved on, White House aides stationed in an anteroom next to the House floor were buttonholing House members, trying to lobby support for the Carter energy bill. Congressman Howard was approached and he made it clear that, although he was considered a supporter of the energy legislation, he would vote against it and get three other New Jersey Democrats in the House to do likewise. That is, Howard would vote against it unless the president would support the $53.8 billion highway and transit bill, with $15 billion for transit. The threatening word was transmitted to the White House by Speaker Thomas P. O'Neill; that night a reluctant President Carter indicated that he would sign the transportation bill. With that assurance, the Surface Transportation Act of 1978 was passed by Congress early on the morning of October 15. Hardball political logrolling had scored another victory.[46]

THE SURFACE TRANSPORTATION ACT OF 1978

The new transit act contained more money for mass transportation than had been authorized in the past and made some very basic changes in the mass transit program. The transit portion of the joint highway transit bill totaled $15.16 billion divided over the fiscal years as follows: 1979, $3.17 billion; 1980, $3.27 billion; 1981, $3.47 billion; 1982, $3.67 billion; and 1983, $1.58 billion for capital purposes.[47] The breakdown in the use of the funds is shown in Table 9.1.

The 1978 law authorized $6.525 billion for formula grants under Section 5 over four fiscal years and $7.48 billion in discretionary capital improvement funds under Section 3. The Section 3 programs continued all the existing uses but also allowed use of the funds for alternatives analysis, introduction of new technology, joint development projects, and intermodal coordination. The interstate transfer program continued, but with a federal proportion of 85 percent. It was expected that the transfers would amount to about $2.8 billion over the four fiscal years in which the Act was authorized, but no limit was set on the total amount of money that could be switched.[48]

Section 3 discretionary capital assistance funds could not be used for projects until Section 5 or Section 18 (the new small urban and rural assistance program) allocations were expended. In happy contrast to the perceived anti-rail attitude in the inchoate stages of developing the legislation, under the 1978 Act at least $350 million had to be spent each year on rail modernization projects; $200 million was available each year for intermodal terminals and transit-related urban development projects.

There were major changes in the Section 5 formula grant program. A basic level of Section 5 aid used the existing formula based half on population and half on population density. In addition, a second tier of Section 5 funds was added, amounting to $150 million for fiscal 1979 and $250 million for each of the next four years; 85 percent of the money in this tier was to go to cities of a population of 750,000 or more and the remainder was directed to other urbanized areas.

A bus capital improvement fund was included within the amended Section 5; $300 million was set aside for fiscal 1979 and 1980, with $370 million for 1981 and $455 million for 1982. The bus replacement fund was to be allocated according to the existing population–population density formula for the first two years; after that the DOT secretary was requested to develop a need-based formula by January 1, 1980.

Rail funds were earmarked in the revised Section 5 to be used only for operating or capital projects involving commuter rail or fixed guideway transit systems. A third of this rail money was to be distributed on the basis of fixed guideway route miles, with a limit of 30 percent of the total to any one state's portion of fixed guideway miles. The remaining two-thirds of the money was to be distributed on the basis of commuter rail train miles and commuter rail route miles. This was limited to 30 percent of any single state's portion of an urbanized area. A minimum of one-half of one percent was to go to any eligible state portion of a rail system.

A new approach to maintenance of effort requirements—the local-fund input—liberalized that part of the program. Substitution of increased fare revenue for local public funds was permitted. Moreover, if the local maintenance of effort was reduced, the federal funds were to be decreased on a pro-rata basis rather than being withdrawn completely, as was the case under the legislation up to that time. The provision on maintenance of effort was eliminated after fiscal 1981.

Some major changes were made in the planning sections of the Act. The former Sections 8 and 9 were repealed, and a new Section 8 contained all planning requirements and planning and technical study authorization. Planning grants were tied to the capital grant program in that the planning grants were to total 5.5 percent of the annual Section 3 appropriation.

The new program of aid for non-urbanized and rural areas was one of the major changes brought about by the Act. It provided a formula grant program for small cities and rural areas, similar to that initiated in 1974 for the urbanized areas. Under the new Section 18, each state was entitled to an amount equal to the total amount appropriated by Congress, multiplied by the ratio of the population of the state in non-urban areas compared to the total non-urban population in the U.S. For example, if a state contained 2.4 percent of the non-urbanized population of the U.S., that state would receive 2.4 percent of the Section 18 money.

In the past, non-urbanized areas were eligible for capital grants but not operating aid. The new program under Section 18 provided funds that could also be used for operating purposes. As with the Section 5 program, the federal share for Section 18 was 50 percent of operating expenses and 80 percent of capital projects. Federal funds would be available for projects included in the annual program of projects submitted by each state to the DOT secretary. Up to 15 percent of the apportionment could be used by the states for planning, administration and coordination, and technical assistance. Section 13c, the labor protection clause, applied to Section 18 aid, but it could be waived by the secretary of labor.

The money allocated under Section 18 was given to the state in what amounted to a block grant. The state program had to provide for a fair and equitable distribution of the funds within the state, which meant that states had to provide a mechanism—probably their own formula based on the federal formula—that assured such distribution of the money. The eligible recipients of Section 18 money through the states included public bodies, nonprofit agencies, and operators of services. Private providers of service were eligible for Section 18 money by means of purchase of service agreements with local public bodies.

In addition, under Section 21 of the Urban Mass Transportation Act of 1964, as amended, intercity bus and intermodal terminals could be built or acquired. Private bus operators had to develop an equitable arrangement to use the facilities. Section 22 authorized operating grants to states and local public bodies in order to pay half of the direct costs of purchase of service agreements with private intercity bus operators for provision of service in non-urbanized areas.

There were many other changes made by the 1978 Act. Section 10, which provided grants for management training programs for those already involved in mass transportation management or supervision, was amended to remove the former limitation of 100 fellowships a year. This provided greater flexibility in the program and would permit more transit personnel to upgrade their managerial skills. The aid authorized in the 1978 Act was the lesser of either $24,000 or 75 percent of the sum of tuition, additional training costs, or the regular salary of the grant recipient.

Section 11 of the Act, which provided funds for university research and training programs, was amended to provide for the establishment and operation of transportation centers at nonprofit educational institutions. A sum of $10 million was authorized for this program; for each institution, the state had to provide a match from other than federal funds equal to the amount of the federal grant. The transportation institutes were expected to carry out research and service in transportation. As it turned out, it took many years before this provision of the Surface Transportation Act was implemented.

Other parts of the Act authorized a demonstration of waterborne public transit with $20 million in fiscal 1979 and $5 million in fiscal 1980. Certain loans made under Section 3 prior to 1970 were converted into grants. Recognizing the substantial inroads made by foreign equipment manufacturers and domestic manufacturers, a "Buy American" provision was included; it required substantial manufacture in the United States for all capital projects of more than $500,000; waivers by the DOT secretary were possible. The secretary could also make grants or contracts for alleviating national and local problems that called for human resource needs—such undertakings as those involved with employee training manpower and training research, programs to increase minority and female employee opportunities, and assistance for minority business organizations.

The 1978 Act also required that a public hearing be held prior to the time that a transit operating agency implemented general fare increases or major service changes. Environmental and economic impacts had to be considered before such changes were made. Easing the problems of equipment purchase, the secretary was authorized to use performance, standardization, life cycle costs, and other factors for the acquisition of rolling stock in addition to initial cost.[49]

The highway portion of the Surface Transportation Act was called the Federal Highway Act of 1978. Very briefly, it extended the Highway Trust Fund for four more years. Construction authorizations of $13.45 billion were allocated for the Interstate System; any excess funds could be used for other purposes. Interstate System resurfacing was made a permanent part of the program, with $900 million allocated. The federal share for such work was reduced to 75 percent of the cost rather than 90 percent. For the Primary Highway System, $7.9 billion was authorized, with the federal share of money increased to 75 percent; 20 percent of the funds were to be used for the rehabilitation of existing highways. An authorization of $2.45 billion was made for the secondary highway system, with the federal share increased to 75 percent and 20 percent dedicated to rehabilitation of existing highways. The Urban System allocation remained at $3.2 billion, but the federal share was increased to 75 percent.[50]

THE PROPOSED SURFACE TRANSPORTATION ADMINISTRATION

Passage of the 1978 Act was followed almost immediately by Secretary Adams's official proposal for a Surface Transportation Administration. The storminess and delay over passage of the Surface Transportation Act had delayed the proposal to merge the Urban Mass Transportation Administration and the Federal Highway Administration (FHWA).

A prime argument for such an action was that, because of the federal hiring freeze imposed by President Carter to help cut down federal spending, it would be impossible to hire the additional personnel needed by UMTA to supervise the mass transportation program properly, as well as speed up delivery of federal transit funds. The proposal for joining the two agencies asserted that major efficiencies would be gained and that the delivery process would be accelerated.

With the federal highway-construction program winding down, the FHWA was assumed to have excess personnel. By merging the FHWA and UMTA, it was expected that there would be sufficient personnel to handle both jobs. Moreover, the FHWA's delivery mechanism, with an office in each state, would be helpful in delivering transit funds.[51] The mechanism would involve the Washington head-quarters, ten regional offices, and fifty-two divisional offices mainly located in state capitals.

Speaking for the transit industry (and indirectly for much of the UMTA staff), APTA pointed out that transit would benefit poorly from such an arrangement. Thanks to the regionalization carried out in UMTA in the early part of 1978, most UMTA grants were approved in the regional offices, with Washington involved only in major projects. Under the proposed dispensation, transit capital grants would have had to be approved in the district office, the regional office, and the Washington office. Moreover, major transit expenditures would still require an extensive alternatives analysis. Highway expenditures would need only the approval of the district office. Despite protestations from the DOT secretary's office that the Surface Transportation Administration would somehow improve the situation for transit, there was no real proof given in the proposal.[52]

As proposed, the Surface Transportation Administration (STA) was an excellent example of bureaucratic thinking: personnel were viewed as interchangeable blocks, with the expectation that arranging them in "neat stacks" would produce "neat results." Such naive thinking entirely disregarded the delicate relationships that have to be developed between the staffs of bureaucracies on the local, state, and federal levels in order to make any program involving the three levels of government truly work effectively and efficiently.

Over the years mutual understanding and respect have been developed by both FHWA and UMTA and their clients. To change the relationships would not seem to be useful, especially if done in an abrupt, ill-conceived manner. Worse yet for mass transit, FHWA personnel outnumbered UMTA personnel about eight to one (at the time FHWA had about 4,900 employees, UMTA about 600), and many of the FHWA staff were very senior in federal service. This meant that, in any given office of the Surface Transportation Administration, the preponderance of the personnel would be former FHWA staff and the senior STA staff would be dominated by FHWA. It was no secret in 1978, or later, that knowledge of FHWA personnel about transit was very limited, and their handling of transit matters would almost certainly reflect that void for a substantial period of time.[53]

APTA set up a special task force on the reorganization plan and met with Secretary Adams shortly after the promulgation of the STA proposal. APTA's task force expressed the concern of the transit community over the vagueness of key policy and implementation issues relative to STA—especially how it would do many things, including simplification of the grant process. DOT was requested to provide flow diagrams that would show how the actual decisions would be made.

The task force also requested that the proposed reorganization take place through the legislative route, rather than through a presidential organization order, in order to ensure full discussion of all the issues. The task force was also worried because there would be no guaranteed funding source for major transit projects. Another cause for anxiety was that all major capital grants under Section 3 would have to be approved in Washington rather than allowing at least some projects to be approved by UMTA regional offices.

The task force suggested that major highway projects should be subjected to the same alternatives analysis required for transit projects. The task force made suggestions for a slow phase-in of the changes without the quick melding of FHWA and UMTA. Serious concern was expressed about UMTA personnel being overwhelmed by FHWA personnel.[54]

THOUGHTS ON TRANSIT POLICY

Both the STA proposal and the approach that the Carter administration took on the transit bill that it introduced early in 1978 evidenced muddled thinking toward mass transportation. This was probably reflective, in part, of the Carter administration's well-known lack of familiarity with certain finer points of the ways in which federal programs are formed and carried out, including matters such as the need to work with client parties. The administration missed opportunities in 1977 and 1978 either to look beyond the immediate interests and short-run problems of the transit community or to pursue policies consistent with a greater recognition of transit's potential usefulness as a vital tool for improving the quality of urban life and for contributing toward other objectives, such as energy conservation and environmental improvement. Transit's tie-ins with these objectives seem obvious, but had been largely unrecognized or disregarded by the administration, as exemplified by the Carter energy program.

The Carter administration apparently failed to recognize that it arrived on the national scene at what was a watershed point for mass transit. After years of declining patronage, transit use began to move slowly upward in the early 1970s. Funds that had been invested in transit over the course of a decade by federal, state, and local governments were apparently beginning to pay off. While the oil embargo of 1973-74 occurred at approximately the same time (and is often given as the main reason for the positive patronage trend), the continued increase in transit use throughout the decade was not the result of any widespread, strongly held feeling that the nation faced a shortage of petroleum-based sources of energy. The most probable explanation is that modest but steady growth in the quantity and quality (not always separate factors in transit) of transit service was the principal cause of the post-1970 increases in transit use.

If the Carter administration had recognized what was happening in urban mass transportation and had understood mass transit's possibilities for continued development, it might have been moved to build upon the foundation of progress made during the late 1960s and early 1970s. It might have taken new policy actions designed to place mass transit more firmly within the overall structure of transportation and the fabric of urban areas. More careful approaches to planning and the use of various federal carrots and sticks might have led to a more rational form of urban and suburban development. It may have been a last opportunity to contain the sprawl of development; the opportunity was not taken.

In addition to increasing the effectiveness of already existing provisions in the transit program, the administration could have taken action in the areas that the transit industry itself has not always fully recognized as being vital to the continuing supply of effective, high-quality transit service. For example, the administration could have sought means for: (1) the strengthening of transit managerial expertise through policies designed to improve the industry's ability and incentive to engage in adequate levels of managerial recruitment, training, and development; and (2) achieving greater "institutionalization" of transit through actions designed to build transit into the value structures of urban areas and the nation as a whole. The latter effort would have helped strengthen support for transit and its participation on local and state levels.

However, instead of pursuing these and other creative possibilities—and providing the nation with coherent policies toward particular forms of transit aid, levels of funding, and general directions for transit—the administration sought to do nothing more than cut budgets and engage in what appeared to be a poorly thought out bureaucratic "neatening" process. Of course, if the transit industry thought the Carter administration was not particularly supportive of transit, it could not yet imagine the hostility toward transit that would emerge during the succeeding two Reagan administrations.

The Congress, for its part, had (as in the past) made policy through enactment of the Surface Transportation Act of 1978 on the basis of ad hoc compromise rather than by following a plan of action clearly linked with long-term goals. Nevertheless, congressional efforts produced funding levels for the 1978 Act that appeared reasonably adequate in the short run, barring unexpected surges in inflation. Most welcome in many places was the extension of assistance for coverage of operating costs of public passenger services in less densely populated areas.

The 1978 Act carried the transit programs on for four years. Ideally, this should have give the transit industry and the local, state, and federal governments time to: (1) recall and rethink the ways in which transit could contribute toward the achievement of various vital national objectives; and (2) move toward the development of coherent long-term goals for urban mass transit policies and programs. As it turned out, it was instead to be a period of conflict and uncertainty.

10.

A Troubled Coalition:
The Transit Act That Never Was

PERSPECTIVE

The passage and signing of a new federal mass transit bill in 1980 was to be the culmination of two years of strenuous effort, conflict, and compromise. It was to cap a decade of extensive development of federal policy and programs in urban mass transportation. Although the federal mass transit programs were initiated in 1961, the reader will recall that it was not until late 1970 that major funding was available for mass transit purposes. As the 1970s moved on, the federal mass transportation program expanded in scope and in the amount of federal dollars devoted to it, largely due to the unity of effort in lobbying Congress for increased federal activity. Congress embraced the program, and urban mass transportation was viewed as a "safe" bipartisan issue. Lobbying activity also involved state and local governments, and programs of aid to transit grew on those levels as well. Also giving a boost to transit support were public interest and concern about the environment, such as the fight against pollution, urban renewal and the problems of energy. Transit seemed to offer something to almost every interest. It could help provide mobility for the poor and enhance the value of downtown business property for the wealthy. Mass transit could also haul the janitor to his job in a downtown office building while commuter trains moved the executive to his suite.

The 1970s saw the virtual completion of the transit industry's transition from private to public ownership at almost all of the major transit properties in the nation. Practically all the ridership, all the equipment, and all the employees in the mass transit field had moved to the public sector.[1] The transit industry came to be viewed mainly as a social service rather than as a commercial enterprise, even though it continued to operate with many private enterprise concepts (many quite valid, some only excess baggage). As a result, transit was expected to bear certain burdens and carry out public policy roles not necessarily expected of the private sector.

The Surface Transportation Act of 1978 had expanded the level of federal transit funding and continued it until the early 1980s; it also made formula aid available to non-urbanized areas. As the 1970s ended, the transit community made an effort to have additional legislation enacted, mainly to increase the amount of federal money available. This chapter traces that legislative effort.

ENVIRONMENT OF THE LEGISLATIVE EFFORT

As always, the efforts of the transit industry were played out against a background and an environment that helped to shape both the struggle and the reaction to it. Inflation was probably the most serious economic factor in this period of legislative effort; it was rampant in the United States in 1979 and 1980. Much of the sharp rise in prices in 1979 was due to the rising cost of petroleum-based energy that was triggered by a revolution in Iran and the continuing strength of the cartel of the Organization of Petroleum Exporting Countries (OPEC). Such energy costs permeated the entire American economy. To an additional degree, the inflationary policies of the federal government and its deficit spending for many years were also to blame for some of the elements of inflation. In any event, inflation had grown so much (reaching an annual rate of about 18 percent in early 1980) that some observers proclaimed that an inflation mentality had developed in the United States and that people were spending their money as fast as they could in order to buy goods and enjoy services before the prices went up again.

Inflation put severe pressure on the transit industry as the cost of supplies, equipment, and labor shot up dramatically. Federal operating aid had helped transit properties to maintain relative stability in fares in the 1970s, and the proportion of costs covered by the farebox had declined. For example, in 1975 the transit industry had covered 58 percent of its costs from operating revenue; by 1981 (the low point) this figure had fallen to 37.8 percent.[2] The need for more money was clear as transit properties faced the sad reality of potentially large unfunded deficits.

The economy was sorely troubled as the decade of the 1970s became the 1980s. At the point when the prime interest rate reached 20 percent and inflation was at 18 percent, the federal government adopted restrictive credit policies; that action, coupled with the restrictive policies of the Federal Reserve System initiated in the fall of 1979, triggered a recession in the first half of 1980 which hit sharply during the second quarter of 1980. Some gloomier observers proclaimed a collapse in the economy for, indeed, the drop-offs in the economic indicators were dramatic. The construction industry was severely damaged by high interest rates and high mortgage rates. The automobile industry suffered its most serious decline since the Great Depression of the 1930s. It was not so much that demand for cars diminished as that American automobile manufacturers lamentably had somewhere lost their great skill at marketing cars successfully by giving the public what it wanted. American manufacturers simply could not supply the high-mileage, small cars that the American public wanted as a counteragent to high gasoline prices. Over a quarter of a million U.S. auto workers were laid off as a result of the distress in the automobile industry. Congress, the administration, and candidates for political office took note of the situation. The transit industry was not immune to the economic drop. One impact on transit was a decline in patronage in cities hit hard by the recession.

The dismal energy situation was a leading factor in the background of transit and other legislative and governmental activities; it had been a matter of conjecture and debate since the oil embargo of 1973-74. Before 1979, many Americans seemed not to believe that there was a potential oil shortage or that the United States was going to suffer much from the fact that it was importing more than half its oil. The revolutionary upheavals in Iran and the cutbacks in Iranian production of oil early in 1979 brought home to the American public that there was, indeed, an energy problem. In the second quarter of 1979, gasoline scarcity was beginning on the east and west coasts of the United States, and motorists formed long lines to fill their tanks. Transit use increased sharply in the cities where there were shortages of fuel. Prices of gasoline began to rise sharply, reaching more than a dollar a gallon by the beginning of 1980. As the price of gasoline went up, the sale of large American cars went down. There was also a severe impact on transit costs as the price of diesel fuel rose to levels that were unimaginable just a few years earlier.[3] Many transit managers had, understandably, far underestimated fuel costs and unfunded deficits caused worries.

An important background factor closely related to transit was the Section 504 imbroglio. Section 504 of the Rehabilitation Act of 1973 mandated that public transit facilities be accessible to all, regardless of handicaps. Under the Carter administration, the U.S. Department of Transportation adopted rules and regulations concerning the implementation of the Rehabilitation Act of 1973 and created a major furor among transit operators by requiring that equipment purchased with federal funds should be made fully accessible. Full accessibility meant that all new buses had to be equipped with lifts or other means of allowing wheelchairs to board; older buses in a fleet would have to be at least partially retrofitted so that 50 percent of peak hour equipment would be fully accessible within three years, or an interim service that was accessible would have to be provided. All communities had to meet the 50 percent standard by 1989. Existing rail systems were given a longer time to meet these requirements, but there would eventually have to be full accessibility at all major stations. All new rapid transit systems had to be fully accessible when built. The reaction of the transit industry was mainly negative, because the requirements were expected to be costly in terms of both capital and operating expense, and yet there was no more money made available to cover these costs.[4]

Closely related to the Section 504 issue in the early part of 1979 was a unique transit environmental issue called the Transbus. The Transbus was to be the standard transit bus, the product of a federal research and development effort to come up with a safer, more comfortable, and fully accessible vehicle. It had been discussed for several years but had not aroused much support or favor from the transit industry. Transbus became a major part of the issue of Section 504 because of its accessibility, and handicapped-rights groups strongly supported it. However, there were many transit observers who felt that the proposed date for delivery of the Transbus had been set much too soon and that considerable development of component parts was necessary before construction of such a vehicle was practical. When a consortium of transit properties in Los Angeles, Philadelphia, and Miami sought bids on the Transbus, no manufacturer responded. In short, none of the American or foreign manufacturers chose to attempt to meet the specifications that had been established within the time frame set.[5]

Meanwhile, there were many, including members of Congress, who investigated the potential impact on capital and operating costs related to fully accessible transit. It was a growing concern that not only would there be great increases in capital costs to meet the Section 504 requirements, but that operating costs would also rise. Moreover, many operators genuinely felt that accessibility and mobility were not the same thing and that to have every bus accessible would not meet the actual needs of the handicapped community. Transit systems would have to operate special services to provide this mobility, as well as operate fully accessible vehicles in regular route service. The debate on this issue continued throughout 1979 and 1980, as will be seen later.[6]

The transit industry was strong in its opposition to the Section 504 requirements, and the American Public Transit Association brought suit against the federal government on this issue. The court decided that the federal government had every right to impose such rules and regulations but did demand that UMTA provide an environmental impact statement on the implementation of Section 504.[7]

An important part of the background affecting transit legislation was the Carter administration. It was perceived as one of the major stumbling blocks that transit faced in 1979-80. The first two years of the administration made it clear—at least to people involved in public transportation—that there was an anti-transit bias in the administration. It was also rather obvious that the administration's lack of interest in transit seemed at odds with its clear interest and efforts concerning energy.

If transit was a low priority matter, a thing that did have high priority in the eyes of President Carter was a balanced budget, which he had promised by fiscal year 1981 during his election campaign in 1976. Efforts were made to cut back the size of the federal budget deficit, and items unpopular at the White House were clearly not going to be favored with much support.

Remarkably, a major change occurred in the White House in the wake of the gas shortages and skyrocketing gasoline prices in the spring and summer of 1979. As a reaction to fuel problems, the Carter administration began to change its tune and give support to transit as an alternative to the automobile. The administration requested a $2.8 billion transit budget for fiscal year 1980 and a $1.35 billion advance appropriation for capital funds for fiscal 1981.[8]

The major turnabout in the attitude of the administration was symbolized when President Carter appeared at the APTA annual convention in New York and pledged strong support for mass transportation. He called the transit industry to rally behind him in passing the windfall profits tax on the high prices of decontrolled oil. The president strove to have a portion of the revenue from the windfall profits tax set aside for mass transit uses.[9] This was really a remarkable position change, made all the more drastic because no president had ever addressed an APTA annual meeting before. Jimmy Carter had become a born-again transit advocate.

The window of opportunity opened by the Carter administration, as evidenced by the president's address to APTA, did not remain open for long as other highly visible and disturbing factors intervened. As inflation waxed and new records in interest rates and inflation rates were set, the balanced budget returned in early 1980 as a major factor in fighting inflation. Indeed, the president submitted a reduced budget to the Congress only a short time after delivering his original budget. There were overall program-level reductions in the Department of Transportation of $1.9 billion for fiscal year 1980 and $600 million in fiscal year 1981; the latter was a cut of 9.1 percent. With regard to mass transportation, the major share of transit cuts would be absorbed by Section 3 capital money, Interstate transfer funds, and transportation energy initiatives; a total of $681 million was the proposed reduction for fiscal years 1980 and 1981. In addition, UMTA research and development programs were proposed for an $8 million reduction in 1980 and an $11 million cut in fiscal 1981. The urban initiatives program for 1981 was proposed for an $80 million reduction. The fiscal 1980 supplemental request, which had been originally pegged at $1.3 billion, was to be cut back to $675 million.[10]

On Capitol Hill, noting it was an election year, Congress jumped on the anti-inflation, balanced-budget bandwagon carrying bags full of budget cuts. Included in the cutting process was mass transit. Later, as 1980 wore on and in partial response to the call of Republican presidential candidate Ronald Reagan for a tax cut, and again alert to the reality of an election year, Congress hastily adopted a tax-cutting posture.[11]

It is fair to say that in early 1980 political chaos reigned in Washington, both at the White House and on Capitol Hill; the various players dashed madly back and forth slashing budgets and proposing to cut taxes. Meanwhile, the deep recession that saw the economy plunge in the second quarter of 1980 gave promise that the fiscal 1981 budget would, indeed, be out of balance. It all bore out a point made by one observer of the Washington scene: ". . . even though $300 billion (close to one fifth of GNP) is spent each year in this country on transportation, the federal government has no logical, unified, comprehensive, and equitable policy on the matter, but pursues instead a fragmented, willy-nilly, counterproductive approach to the whole subject."[12]

The reader will recall that the transit industry had a number of reasons for unhappiness in early 1979; a major concern was the idea of the Surface Transportation Administration. Creating the STA (neither the first nor the last time the notion would surface) was part of Secretary of Transportation Brock Adams's position that the Urban Transportation Administration and the Federal Highway

Administration should be merged. As a program it seemed to have academic promise, but not much more, because it neither reckoned with constituencies that had already developed nor did it figure out how to make the several programs work satisfactorily. Fear of the UMTA bureaucracy being swallowed by the FHWA bureaucracy was a factor; furthermore, both highway and transit proponents felt they would hurt by the change. Change was a terrible thought to all participants in the programs.

The downfall of Brock Adams in the summer of 1979, when President Carter cleaned house in his Cabinet, brought an end to any serious push for an STA. There was some concern over the fact that part of the reason for Adams's leaving had to do with his criticism of the Carter administration for its lack of support of public transportation. The transit industry generally felt better about the naming of Neil Goldschmidt to the office of secretary. Goldschmidt had been mayor of Portland, Oregon, and had been a strong advocate of public transportation.[13]

An agreeable factor was that public opinion toward transit seemed to be more favorable in 1979 and 1980 than had hitherto been the case. The proof was in the riding, as transit patronage had been rising ever since the early 1970s. The pace of increase quickened in the summer of 1979 as petroleum shortages developed and a combination of the Iranian revolution and the opportunism of OPEC caused the price of a barrel of imported crude oil to rise sharply. Even more, it is generally fair to say that a good portion of the American public was probably willing to have some of their tax dollars spent on mass transit even if they did not use it themselves.[14]

Even so, the industry did suffer some black eyes. There were articles by academics and others casting doubt on the worth of mass transit as a major saver of energy or much of anything else.[15] Another development that did not help to build public confidence was that New York, San Francisco, and Chicago all had transit strikes in 1979 or 1980 that brought enormous inconvenience to many citizens of the affected cities. Certain transit properties, such as the Southeastern Pennsylvania Transportation Authority in Philadelphia (SEPTA) and the Massachusetts Bay Transportation Authority in Boston, had major difficulties that attracted national attention in the press. SEPTA was also the unhappy star of some scathing articles in the Wall Street Journal.[16] The Boston Globe won a Pulitzer prize for its expose of the mismanagement of the MBTA. Bad press for transit was nothing new, and it would continue.

A more serious problem than bad press was the conflict that developed within the transit industry over the division of money in the Section 5 formula funds. This conflict involved the very largest systems pitted against the rest of the transit industry. Some of the ways most favored by Congress for dividing the Section 5 formula money would have greatly diminished the amount of money available to transit in every place in the nation save New York and a few other very large cities. Yet the largest cities were facing great difficulties in making ends meet. New York estimated that it would run an unfunded transit deficit of almost $400 million in 1981—certainly a situation that called for tough work to find the money. Had there been a good likelihood of a substantial increase in federal funding, there would have been little problem, because all transit properties would have received more aid regardless of the formula. But the expectation through much of 1980 was that there would be little, if any, real increase. Thus, there was an unseemly scramble over a piece of a shrinking pie.[17]

There were problems of a different sort in the non-urbanized areas that received funding under Section 18 of the Urban Mass Transportation Act of 1978. When the Act was passed, Congress decided that UMTA did not have sufficient personnel to take care of the job and therefore turned the administration of the Section 18 program over to the Federal Highway Administration. To some extent, FHWA continued the philosophy—one that probably made sense in highway construction programs—of spreading the money very precisely to existing transit properties in smaller cities.[18] The FHWA was therefore responding to the rural initiatives program of the White House, which, to be frank, was one of the ploys used by the Carter administration to help get President Carter re-elected by making him popular in rural areas. Moreover, FHWA, probably as a result of treading carefully in a new area, was extremely cautious in letting the Section 18 money be released (the money was to be spent in an undefined fair and equitable manner). The program was administered with great punctiliousness and was viewed by many hopeful recipients as a papershuffler's dream. For a variety of reasons, the Section 18 money was slow to be committed, leading some congressmen (especially Robert Duncan, chairman of the transportation appropriations subcommittee in the House) to call for cutbacks in the appropriations.[19]

The relatively poor quality of much small-city transit service remained a fact of life, and small-city transit also remained almost a separate industry, not quite really a part of the rest of the transit industry in medium and large cities. In the early stages of federal support, small transit properties were not usually participants in APTA or in state bodies, although over time many small properties became more active. At first, the management of such properties was often totally unprofessional. Usually organized as city departments, transit was used in many places for political purposes as much as for mobility. No great breakthroughs in service quality or managerial prowess were observed, especially in the early days, although much useful transportation service was delivered. Without the certainty of a continuing federal commitment, there was some doubt about the usefulness of the program as viewed from the small-city perspective, as well as reluctance in some small cities to either initiate or upgrade service. Uncertainty about federal support was made real in the Reagan administration, leading many small transit operations to ally themselves with larger transit properties in lobbying efforts on the state level. This bred an increase in state aid programs for transit; again, as on the federal level, broad grass-roots support had a powerful impact on legislative bodies as well as on the executive branches of government.

Management was also a problem throughout the industry, as it was noted that about 70 percent of the top management personnel in the industry would be retired by the mid-1980s and that there was an insufficient supply of people to take their places. Little had really been done by the industry or by UMTA to get more people properly trained and into the mainstream of transit management, which was hardly a wonder given the scramble for capital and operating funds. Indeed, in its budget-cutting melee, Congress cut the budget for UMTA's Section 11 University Research and Training Program in half, to a sum of only $1 million. While this program was mainly directed toward research, it did encourage faculty members to work in the transit area and to teach transit-oriented courses that could encourage young people to choose transit management or planning as a career area.

The industries supplying equipment to public transportation were also having a difficult time. Boeing-Vertol, upon losing an order for 300 rapid transit cars for Chicago to the Budd Company, dropped out of the carbuilding business. This left only the Budd Company as an American carbuilder, and Budd was a subsidiary of a German firm.[20] During the time period under discussion, foreign equipment manufacturers won orders in Atlanta, Cleveland, Boston, and some other cities. This became a matter for concern as the 1980 recession ground on, and there was criticism from Congress and other quarters about public transit money being spent abroad.

The bus industry also had its difficulties: Grumman-Flxible and GMC were involved with many teething problems with the new ADB (Advanced Design Bus) equipment that was being turned out. Difficulties with earlier rail cars, particularly the light rapid transit vehicles built by Boeing-Vertol for Boston, had cast doubt upon America's ability to build streetcars. Private studies showed some serious design and mechanical difficulties with the new Advanced Design Buses. The ADBs were so plagued with problems that many transit properties—the Chicago Transit Authority is a notable case—refused to buy them.[21] In December 1980 and January 1981, cracks were discovered in the frames of Grumman-Flxible ADBs. All such buses were pulled off the streets of New York—totaling over 600 vehicles—and older buses leased from Washington, D.C., had to be used to maintain service.[22]

Finally, UMTA was being accused of indulging in excessive bureaucratic procedures—i.e., red tape. Indeed, the UMTA administrator admitted in a speech at the APTA Eastern Conference in Kansas City in May 1980 that more of his time was spent on regulatory matters than on policy or seeing that the programs worked the way that they were supposed to.[23]

Reviewing the environment faced by the transit industry in 1979 and 1980, any reasonable observer would have to admit that it was a troubled scene and one ripe for mischief. From the viewpoint of those seeking quick ratification of a favorable piece of transit legislation, there were many factors threatening to delay passage.

DEVELOPMENT OF THE LEGISLATION

Soon after the passage of the 1978 Surface Transportation Act, the transit community gathered its forces to begin the lobbying effort aimed at meeting the problems that continued to exist. Many of the perceived problems were financial in nature. An appropriations hearing in April 1979 resulted in strong indications of serious underfunding of the transit program. Those testifying cited the increasing age of bus fleets (the first generation of buses purchased with federal aid were approaching the end of their economic life) and the need for more federal capital money under Section 3 of the Urban Mass Transportation Act to speed up the replacement. It was obvious that the bus replacement money in the Section 5 formula grant program was insufficient. There was also a feeling that the Urban Initiatives Program, strongly supported by the Carter administration, would drain off money from other types of mass transit investments. Several mayors and governors testified of their concerns about the underfunding of transit, a serious shortfall if public transportation was to play a role in solving or counterattacking the menacing energy situation that was then unfolding.[24]

Taking to heart some of the opinions generated in the early part of the year, the House Appropriations Committee approved transit funds for fiscal year 1980 at a level higher than the Carter administration had called for, but the amount was still less than the 1978 Act authorized.[25] Even so, in mid-1979 Congress was becoming aware of the nation's serious problems related to energy. The international ripple effect of the cutback in petroleum from Iran had already caused fuel shortages in some areas of the country, and newspapers and television news programs offered their readers and viewers pictures of long gas lines formed to buy the precious fuel. While the actual shortages of fuel were short-lived, the price of gasoline, heating fuel, and diesel fuel began to rise quickly. Use of mass transportation began to mount. The attitude that transit was a part of the solution to urban mobility problems in the face of expensive gasoline was growing.

By midsummer the impact of the gasoline shortage and price rise was sufficient to cause Democratic Congressman James Howard of New Jersey, chairman of the House Committee on Public Works and Transportation, to call a hearing in which the energy situation was discussed in some detail. A windfall profits tax on the oil companies, with some of the receipts to be used for mass transit purposes, was also discussed. It was an idea that was gathering more support as the major oil companies began to announce substantial profits for the previous year. This attitude continued into the fall of 1979 with the profitable quarterly reports of the oil companies adding momentum. The transit trust fund idea resurfaced, this time using the windfall profits tax to supply the money. The busy Howard hearings also deliberated the potential of public transit to conserve energy, the precise impact of the gas shortage on transit, the areas in which federal transit funding might be more quickly and effectively used to conserve energy and alleviate problems of the gasoline shortage, and the proportion of the windfall profits tax to be devoted to transit purposes.[26]

The fall of 1979 was earlier noted as a period that offered a window of opportunity, as a time before high inflation and high interest rates caused a budget-cutting frenzy in early 1980. October saw the introduction by Congressmen H. T. Johnson, William Harsha, and Bud Shuster of H.R. 5375, which was entitled "The Transportation Systems Efficiency Act of 1979." The proposed legislation included a section that would establish a public transportation trust fund. In the bill, ten-year authorizations estimated at $45.5 billion would be derived, according to Title III of the bill, from utilizing 25 percent of the windfall profits taxes.

There was also an attempt to make adjustments in the formula for distribution of Section 5 formula grant aid, an issue that was to crop up again. The bill called for the secretary of transportation on October 1 of each fiscal year to authorize appropriation of the following: three-fourths of the money in the ratio which population in urban areas in each state bears to the total population in urban areas in all states, and one-fourth in accordance with the apportionment formula for the federal-aid primary system of highways established in Section 104 (b)(1). Title 23 of the United States Code was to be amended to permit grants for energy conservation measures on non-toll public roads, including preferential treatment for mass transit and other high-occupancy vehicles, with the federal share of the costs to be 90 percent.[27]

On November 1, 1979, the Senate passed H.R. 4440, the department of transportation's appropriation bill for 1980. The bill included no money to help pay for the controversial improvements that were mandated under Section 504, intended to provide accessibility to the handicapped. The transit industry, as expected, reacted negatively. In counterpoint, groups representing the handicapped, treating the issue as a civil-rights matter, began to press vigorously for transit accessibility. The report of the appropriations committee included a discussion of life-cycle costing of transit rolling stock and the use of funds for intercity buses. The final appropriation made on November 8, 1979 called for $1.37 billion in Section 3 discretionary capital funds, $1.405 billion in Section 5 formula money, $85 million in Section 18 money for non-urbanized areas, $69.3 million in funds for research and development, demonstrations, and university research and training, and $10 million for waterborne demonstrations. There was an extra $15 million in Section 5 over the original Senate level that was intended for the second tier of money made available for larger transit properties.[28]

Early in 1980 several major bills were introduced in Congress. H.R. 6417, offered by Representative Howard, was officially entitled "The Surface Transportation Act of 1980." The bill called for a number of changes in the federal transit program that would serve to ameliorate the division that was starting to grow between the large city and small city and rural transit systems. For example, the proposed funding for new starts, automated guideway transit, and extensions to rail systems would be separated within the Section 3 discretionary funding authorizations. Five percent of the Section 3 money had to be spent in areas with a population of less than 200,000. Advance Section 5 appropriations could be made in an appropriations act. Valid Medicare cards would be acceptable identification for half-fare rates for the elderly and the handicapped. Prior notification of issuance of letters of intent by UMTA for Section 3 funding had to be given to the Senate and House authorizing committees.

In other proposed changes, where the Surface Transportation Act of 1978 had called for the ending of maintenance-of-effort requirements for Section 5 aid on October 1, 1981, maintenance of effort (to make sure that local support did not diminish below the average of the previous two years) would be continued under the Howard bill. That bill also modified the definition of fixed guideways to include streetcar lines running in the city streets and the overhead wire systems used in support of trolleybus operations. Continuation of commuter trains was to be funded, and there was to be authorization of a waterborne demonstration project near Portland, Oregon.[29]

The Carter administration also sent to Capitol Hill a bill which was officially named "The Transportation Improvement and Development Act of 1980." Under this proposal, UMTA was to be given the authority to purchase and stockpile buses, which would help to even out the demand for vehicles (to aid manufacturers) and permit faster deliveries (to help transit properties). Like the Howard bill, the administration bill called for funding for new starts, automated guideway transit, and rail extensions to be separated within Section 3 discretionary funding authorizations. In a similar vein, funding for the research, development and demonstration programs, and the managerial training program would be separated from administrative expenses where they had been lumped together in the past. The administration bill provided for two percent of Section 3 funds to be devoted to the Section 20 human resources program; this was a program guaranteeing bonding and venture capital funds for minority and female firms.

The administration bill also proposed that the formula for apportionment of Section 5 bus capital funds should no longer be based on population–population density but on fleet size or vehicle miles. Moreover, interest expense incurred in advancing capital projects under Section 5 would be eligible for reimbursement.

The matter of federal operating aid for transit was always upsetting to the fiscally conservative, even if they were supporters of the notion of federal transit aid. It was viewed as a bottomless pit into which endless streams of money would be poured with no apparent impact on filling the hole. Following up on an idea which had been percolating for several years, the administration proposed that a cap be placed on operating assistance at 25 percent of total operating expenses, with a hold-harmless provision for transit properties that would be damaged. As in the Howard bill, the definition of fixed guideway would be modified to include trolley lines that operated in city streets. Looking toward potential energy-related problems, the secretary of transportation was given the authority to reprogram funds and waive legislative and administrative requirements in a declared emergency. The administration proposed that DOT be given the authority to establish transit safety criteria and require safety plans from grant recipients at the expense of having funds withheld for non-compliance. It was also proposed that the use of 1980 census figures for apportionment of funds would be delayed until a study was completed to determine the impact of such a change. Eligibility for use of Interstate transfer funds would be expanded to all types of transit projects. The federal share for Interstate transfer projects would be increased from 85 to 90 percent, and the Interstate substitute-highway projects would be funded from the Highway Trust Fund rather than the general fund of the Treasury.[30]

Senator Harrison Williams introduced his transit legislation as S.2296, the Federal Public Transportation Act of 1980. This bill was generally similar to the other proposed legislation. In its original version, the Williams bill required DOT to prepare both an interim and a final plan for allocating rail modernization funds. As with the administration bill, DOT would be given the authority to purchase and stockpile buses. Prior notification of issuance of letters of intent for Section 3 funding had to be given to the House and Senate authorizing committees. The Williams bill would also permit advance Section 5 appropriations to be made in an appropriations act. The formula for apportionment of Section 5 bus capital funds would be based not on population–population density but on bus-revenue vehicle miles, which would be beneficial to the larger transit properties. As in both the Howard and the administration bills, the definition of fixed guideways was modified to include trolley lines that ran in city streets. DOT would also be given authority to establish transit safety criteria and require safety plans. Finally, a formula factor, involving commuter trains, would be phased into the UMTA program starting in fiscal year 1981.[31]

As Congress began to consider the legislation, the ideas contained in the legislative proposals began to be somewhat modified. For example, Secretary of Transportation Goldschmidt testified that the money should go where transit service was actually being provided, rather than continuing to use formulas based on population and population density that were geared more to providing equitable distribution of money across the whole spectrum of urbanized areas. He pushed for a service basis for the allocation of formula funds. The secretary also indicated that the Carter administration would propose greatly increased federal financial support for mass transit from 1980 to 1985. The Section 3 discretionary capital program and the Section 18 program for non-urbanized areas were proposed for significant expansion.

Testifying on an issue that would become paramount in the fortunes of the 1980 transit legislative proposals, Goldschmidt said:

> The money ought to go where the service is. The current formula bears little relationship to transit service in an area. It delivers an ambiguous signal about local responsibility and offers no reward where exceptional effort is made. We want to change this to provide a clear signal of what the federal role is, so that local transit authorities can plan and develop their own level of financial assistance.

He went on to describe the administration's proposal to change the basic Section 5 formula to one based 50 percent on population and 50 percent on the number of revenue miles traveled by transit vehicles.[32]

While the new legislation was being considered in March of 1980, the economic plight of the nation began to share the national spotlight with both the American hostages that had been taken by the revolutionary government of Iran and the coming presidential election. Sensing the need to at least attempt to control what was controllable, the push began in Congress and the administration for a balanced budget; the 18 percent annual inflation rate and a prime interest rate of 20 percent precipitated a major governmental reaction. In March the Carter administration began to promote a tightening of credit and, as noted earlier, the president actually submitted a second budget. Meanwhile, efforts to enact a windfall profits tax, a portion of which would have gone for mass transportation, waned.[33]

In April of 1980 the ax fell on transit programs in the general flurry of budget cutting that was rampant in Congress at the time. The Senate Budget Committee was particularly active and made extensive cuts in the transit program. Gone was the use of windfall profits tax energy initiatives for 1980 and 1981. The removal of transit as a beneficiary of the windfall profits tax was a particularly bitter pill to swallow for the transit industry and for UMTA. The administration also received a slap in the face, because this amounted to a general reneging on the promise made by President Carter to the transit people in return for their support of the windfall profits tax—whatever golden view the transit community might have enjoyed for sharp increases in funding in the 1981 budget was abruptly dimmed. Perhaps the industry was a bit spoiled by its excellent record of success in funding in the 1970s. Nonetheless, it was deeply concerned about the serious impact inflation was having on transit operating and capital expenses. Transit forces attempted to strike back by encouraging a letter-writing campaign to congressmen and senators to get them to provide more money for mass transportation.[34]

Animated by the likelihood of less funds available for mass transportation for fiscal 1981, the larger cities went to work both through APTA and individually on a major lobbying effort. As a result of vigorous efforts by the industry, the transit authorizing legislation reported out by the Senate Committee on Banking, Housing, and Urban Affairs made substantial revisions in the Section 5 formulas that would have favored large cities. Under the proposed provision, 80 percent of the formula money would have been based on the relative share of revenue rail and bus vehicle miles, with a 45 percent cap placed on the use of rail as a factor in the distribution of funds. Twenty percent of the formula would be based on the relative share of a given urbanized area of revenue vehicle miles. Local option was provided to meet the provisions of Section 504, under which each community could decide how it would meet the requirement of accessibility for the handicapped.[35]

A sharp division appeared in transit ranks in April. The money was growing short everywhere because of inflation, and the legislation that was making its way through Congress appeared to be tilted toward large cities by using service provided as a factor for divvying up the money. Smaller transit properties would indeed receive much less under the new formula. For example, New York City would go from $273,048,000 in 1980 to $496,925,000 in 1985, progressing each year from $273,048,000 to $305,010,000 in 1981, $422,094,000 in 1982, $450,156,000 in 1983, and $473,541,000 in 1984. Phoenix, on the other hand, would receive the following: 1980, $7,490,000; 1981, $8,474,000; 1982, $4,414,000; 1983, $4,707,000; 1984, $4,951,000; and 1985, $5,196,000. Other examples are striking. Indianapolis would fall from $7,955,000 under the old formula in 1981 to only $5,160,000 in 1982; Peoria would fall from

$2,150,000 in 1981 to $1,521,000 in 1982. The bag was a mixed one, however. Tucson would benefit under the revised formula that was proposed, rising from $2,764,000 to $3,000,000 between 1981 and 1982. Charlotte, N.C., would rise from $2,561,000 to $2,857,000 between 1981 and 1982.

The review of the funding changes wrought by alterations in the formula brought dissatisfaction and division to the transit industry. In essence, it was a problem of appropriation. Had the amount of federal money been sufficiently large to give everyone additional funds regardless of the change in proportion, there would have been no problems. As it was, the transit operators in smaller cities, their expectations sorely abused, felt that they were being sacrificed to help pay the bills of big city transit.[36]

Meanwhile, the conferees on the House and Senate Budget committees continued to struggle to balance the budget. Never forgetting it was an election year and that the electorate was smarting under sharply increased gasoline prices, the gasoline tax of ten cents per gallon proposed by President Carter was struck down, which further threatened a balanced budget. Savings of some $900 million expected from cuts in food stamps evaporated when the committees found that such cuts could not be made. As Congress deliberated, the fortunes of transit, which had seemed so bright and assured only six months before, began to have serious ups and downs. There was, for example, tentative agreement by Budget Committee conferees in May that there would be no supplemental budget for UMTA in fiscal year 1980.[37] It appeared that transit was not keeping its support. A part of the reason was the dichotomy between large and small systems that was growing as the year moved deeper into the lawmaking season.

The final result of the House and Senate Budget committees' working back and forth was that, for fiscal 1981, the budget proposals for transit would amount to only $3.1 billion from the Senate and $5 billion from the House. Added to the veneer of gloom covering the industry was the result of the National Personal Transportation Study issued in early May. The study showed the relatively small use made of public transportation—a fact that, if anyone paid attention to it, made it more difficult to argue for increases in transit expenditures. The transit authorization bills were reported by the House Committee on Public Works and Transportation as H.R. 6417; the Senate Committee on Banking, Housing, and Urban Affairs reported on the Williams bill, S.2296.[38] There was finally some good news for transit, because the Senate committee also reported S.2004, which increased the fiscal year 1980 Section 3 money authorizations by $450 million.

On May 21, 1980, the House and Senate budget conferees once again acted to slash domestic spending in order to achieve a balanced budget. The final result of the conference committee was a total transportation function budget authority approved for $22 billion. Spending authority was set at $18.65 billion. There was also agreement given to a $400 million fiscal year 1980 energy-initiative supplemental appropriation approved by the House.[39]

Opposition to the 1981 budget grew. At the end of May, President Carter and others criticized Congress' apparent willingness to spend too much for defense. The full House rejected the conference committee budget, which could have led to cuts from fiscal year 1980 levels in Section 5 funding despite rising transit patronage and continuing inflation that reduced the value of the dollar.[40] The magic in the case for transit was apparently not working, and the industry was faced with a highly upsetting burst of inflation and budgets thrown awry by the sharp and steady increase in fuel prices.

By early June, the situation was still gloomy. There was almost a $2 billion difference in the bills being considered in the House and the Senate. The most serious deficiencies were found in the Section 5 program. APTA tried, through various and vigorous lobbying efforts, to boost the levels of appropriations for Section 5. As noted earlier, a major bone of contention was the Section 5 formula, an increasingly important factor in the progress of the legislative package. In the Senate version, 80 percent of the total would be distributed on the basis of each urbanized area's share of bus and rail vehicle miles; 20 percent of the total, for bus and bus-facility capital projects, would be allocated on the basis of each urbanized area's bus-revenue vehicle miles. In this proposal the operating formula provided less money for small properties. To reiterate a point, had the overall level of funds been high enough so that everyone would win, there would have been no problem. The split in the industry that had emerged earlier in the year grew wider as the year progressed, making it extremely difficult for APTA to carry out its lobbying efforts. The most difficult issue was the service-based formula; this matter eventually killed the 1980 transit legislative effort.

Some words of background and a reminder on the Section 5 formula are in order at this point and key to why trouble emerged from a previously peaceful and cooperative process. As readers of earlier chapters will recall, between 1971 and 1974, in an effort to develop an operating assistance program, the legislative promoters had originally favored a performance formula, but no compromise could be reached on what the components of such a formula should be. Therefore, when the formula grant program was finally initiated in the Act of 1974, a population–population density formula basis was utilized as a compromise.

The formula was relatively objective; the Census Bureau calculated the population and population density of each urbanized area from the results of the decennial census. The fact elements for each urbanized area were thus available and easy to use in dividing up the funds appropriated. The amount of money was simply cranked into the computer and the formula neatly churned out the allocation of money for each urbanized area. The formula roughly reflected need on the assumption that big cities operated more transit than did smaller urban places. The formula was not unfair, but it was deemed irrelevant by some transit properties. On the other hand, service-based formulas were more difficult to work with. For example, if revenue vehicle miles were used as a factor, there would have to be a mechanism for auditing the actual number of miles operated. The difficulties are obvious.

Equity notwithstanding, the simple problem was that the larger cities did not receive sufficient money. The 1978 Act modified the original 1974 formula program by creating several tiers as a compromise to get more money to the transit-intensive areas of the county.[41] The end result of the multiple-tier approach was to give larger city transit properties several chances to get at the available part of money. While the attempt was a good one, it was thwarted in its delivery by budget and appropriations reductions. Even though the issue of service-based formula was being vigorously discussed, the House, in Representative Howard's bill, H.R. 6417, retained the existing population–population density formula; but the authorizing levels included by the House revealed concern for targeting expenditures in areas deemed necessary.

Originally, Senator Williams had favored retention of the population–population density formula. He changed his mind, however, under pressure from such groups as the U.S. Conference of Mayors, the National League of Cities, and the National Association of Counties, all of which were in favor of a service-based formula. APTA supported the service-based formula, but recommended putting off the implementation of such an idea until the impact of the change could be studied and better understood. Senator Williams became such a devout advocate of the change in formulas that he opposed extension of the Section 5 program beyond fiscal 1981 unless the service-based formula was used. His reason for opposition was that the population–population density formula lacked a coherent rationale other than the fact that it was straightforward and, in its way, objective. He also felt that the current formula did not move scarce financial resources to the areas providing transit service and that because the current operating assistance program lacked support in Congress, its continuation and growth were threatened without a service-based formula. The senator noted that transit interests had called for a service-based formula since 1971 and also had the support of the U.S. Conference of Mayors and other groups.[42]

The APTA government affairs steering committee was sensitive to the problems of the smaller cities that would generally lose federal operating money if a service-based formula was used; it voted to recommend changes to the executive committee of APTA, changes which would inspire an APTA push for a modified service-based formula. Under these modifications, all urbanized areas with a population under 250,000 (this would embrace 197 areas) would not be subject to the new formula but would continue to receive funds on the basis of the population–population density formula. The funding levels would be set at amounts that would be received by these areas under the existing Tier 1 and Tier 2 distribution of the UMTA money.[43]

The APTA proposals were really a compromise; they called for all areas with a population over 250,000 to enjoy the distribution of funds as in the Senate service-based formula proposal. However, instead of using bus-revenue vehicle miles, the formula would include a factor based 75 percent on bus-revenue vehicle miles and 25 percent on population, weighted by density. APTA also pushed for a formula modification in each population area over 740,000, in which the formula attributable to any rail-revenue vehicle miles would be subject to a minimum of one-half percent and a maximum of 45 percent. This proposal was designed to soften the impact of New York's huge rail mileage on all other rail operations.

On Capitol Hill the Senate and House conferees agreed (on June 11) on a

1981 budget of $613.3 billion. The transportation appropriation called for was $18.75 billion, with authorization for fiscal year 1981 up to $22.1 billion. As an additional bit of cheer for transit proponents, an ABC-Harris poll found that 54 percent of those queried did not approve of transit budget cuts.[44]

On June 12, 1980, the transportation subcommittee of the House Committee on Appropriations marked up the DOT appropriation bill for fiscal 1981 as follows: in Section 3, $600 million for bus purchases, $980 million for rail modernization, $435 million for new starts, $35 million for peoplemovers, and $25 million for innovative technology, for a total of $2.22 billion. In Section 5, $850 million was allocated for Tier 1; $200 million for Tier 2; $100 million for Tier 3; and $350 million for Tier 4, for a total of $1.5 billion. The markup included only $65 million for Section 18 aid to non-urbanized areas. Congressman Duncan, who was chairman of the subcommittee on transportation at the time, noted that the Section 18 money was not being spent up to the amount appropriated; he felt that if the money was not being used up to the level of appropriations, the appropriations should be cut back.[45]

While the House was still considering the new transit legislation, the Senate passed S.2296, the Williams bill. It called for an authorization of $24.8 billion, which added $12.7 billion to the existing authorization under the 1978 Act that was scheduled to expire in fiscal year 1982. Senator Williams amended his original bill to establish bus vehicle miles as the formula for distribution of the Section 5 bus capital funds in fiscal year 1981 for cities with a population over 200,000. Population and population density would be used for areas of 50,000 to 200,000 inhabitants. An amendment was passed that provided that a minimum of one percent of Section 18 funds be apportioned to each state and that the set-aside for eligible Section 18 administrative funds be reduced from 15 percent to 10 percent. An amendment to allow local option in meeting the Section 504 requirements was adopted. A new and stricter "Buy American" provision was included in the Act, which specified that at least 70 percent of the materials and supplies in transit equipment must be from the United States. The amendments clearly reflected the perceived needs of the transit community; in particular, the "Buy American" provision reflected the understandable growing concern over foreign competition in equipment supply.

Complex formulas abounded in amendments aimed at dividing what appeared to be a shrinking financial resource base. As an example, Senator John Tower (R-Texas) amended the Section 5 formula by proposing as its basis the following percentages of the Section 5 authorization, beginning in fiscal year 1982: for the group of urbanized areas with a population over 200,000, 68.8 percent of the Section 5 authorization would be based on bus- and rail-revenue vehicle miles; 17.2 percent would be based on bus-revenue vehicle miles for capital purposes only. For cities with a population between 50,000 and 200,000, 7.2 percent of the Section 5 authorization would be based on population and population density or, at the choice of the state, the revenue-vehicle-mile formula. A similar formula would be used to distribute 1.8 percent of the Section 5 authorization for capital purposes only. Finally, 5 percent of the Section 5 authorization would go to areas with a population under 50,000 and would be based on population only. Twenty-five percent of the funds for areas with a population of 50,000 to 200,000 could be transferred to either of the other population groups.[46]

A ray of sunshine broke through when, in early July, a supplemental compromise was reached and a total supplement of $330 million was added in the fiscal year 1980 UMTA budget. Of this sum, $150 million was for bus and bus facilities; $110 million was for rail modernization; and $70 million was for new rail starts.[47]

The amendments and counter-amendments were fair evidence of the diverse points of view held by various parts of the transit community and the efforts of the Congress to meet the needs of its various constituencies. Some of the problems could not be solved on a realistic basis with the available resources.

THE SUMMER OF DISCONTENT

As the summer of 1980 passed its midpoint, much action was needed on the transit scene in Washington. There remained the vital issue of a budget for the federal mass transit programs for fiscal year 1981. The House still had to pass a transit authorization bill and, of course, there had to be concurrence between the House and the Senate on the legislation that would authorize the changes. By mid-July, time was already running out. The national election was, of course, to be held in early November, and the senators and congressmen were eager to get back to their districts and states to politic for re-election; there would be pressure to recess Congress as early as possible in September. There was some hope that the transit bill might be passed by Congress and sent to the White House before the congressional election-campaign recess began, but that did not happen. In retrospect, the delay proved to be highly unfortunate for transit interests.

Within the transit community keen attention was, very naturally, drawn to the presidential election and to the positions of the candidates on mass transit. The Democratic candidate was President Jimmy Carter, who had not been enthusiastic about transit in the early days of his administration. But as a born-again transit advocate during the gasoline shortage and price rise of 1979, he had become supportive. There was strong evidence that the Carter administration, if put back into office, would be a relatively strong advocate of mass transit, although, considering Carter's earlier attitude toward mass transportation, there was some skepticism about his adherence to the Democratic platform pledge to strengthen the mass transit systems of the nation. Even so, the administration was pushing for major increases in transit funding to be paid for out of the windfall profits tax. From APTA's soundings on the issue and the actions of a Congress controlled by Democrats for the entire span of the federal mass transportation program, it was clear that the Democrats saw a strong federal role in mass transportation as a very desirable thing.[48]

The precise position of Republican candidate Ronald Reagan was more difficult to assess. An interview published in the *New York Times* on January 2, 1980, quoted Reagan as stating that the ideal situation would be for local authorities to provide all of their own public transit funding. As a second choice, Reagan would continue federal aid, but in the form of block grants to cities to spend on whatever programs they wished. Such a program would mean that transit would have to compete with sewers and police cars for the use of federal•dollars. On the other hand, as governor of California, Reagan had taken a moderately progressive stance on mass transit. Even more positive in tone, when Reagan's vice-presidential running mate, George Bush, had been seeking the Republican nomination for president himself, he had indicated that, if president, he would give transit high priority. He favored spending federal dollars in a fashion that would attract the maximum number of riders.[49]

The Republican platform noted the need for mass transit systems of reasonable quality and affordability to meet public needs. The platform also noted that the main responsibility for transit rested on local governments and that they should be given latitude to design the systems that best met their requirements. The federal role should be one of providing aid through surface transportation block grants; that meant competition between highways and transit for the same pot of money. The platform also contained a statement endorsing the personal freedom of Americans to use their automobiles whenever and wherever they wished, regardless of energy emergencies. The platform further called for the repeal of most of the windfall profits tax and rejected the notion of gasoline and other energy taxes.[50] There weren't a lot of laughs in the Republican platform for transit, which reflected the old-time conservative religion on federal programs aimed at cities—which, incidentally, were usually presided over by Democrats.

In June, the Republican National Committee's advisory council on transportation issued a report calling for a twenty-year trust fund for transit and ride-sharing capital investment. The trust fund might be based on the windfall profits tax, fuel taxes, and user taxes. Private transportation systems were to be encouraged by federal action. The advisory council also urged federal stimulation of the idea of light rapid transit.[51] The position of the advisory council reflected what may be called the Thomas E. Dewey School of Republicanism, which sought to take a thoughtful, good-management approach to government. In any case, the Republican position on mass transit was, with the exception of the proposals offered by the advisory council on transportation, much less supportive of federal mass transit programs than that taken by Democrats.

Independent candidate John B. Anderson had a consistently strong record of support for mass transit in his twenty years in the House of Representatives. Anderson supported the windfall profits tax as a source of transit money. He also spoke out for an $8 billion annual program to aid mass transit, urban roads, and sewers, and he was generally very sensitive to the problems of the American infrastructure and the potential mischief to the nation that ignoring the infrastructure could cause. He called for major investments in transit improvements.[52]

As the campaign moved from the late summer into the fall, Congress got back to the subject of mass transit. APTA sought to stimulate its members to contact their representatives by letter and personally, if possible, to help move the House to adopt favorable legislation. In particular, APTA members were urged to find support for an amendment to the proposed House legislation, introduced by Representative James Cleveland, Republican of Vermont,[53] that would provide for local options in meeting the Section 504 accessibility requirements.

Concern over the change in the Section 5 formula continued into the fall as well. UMTA calculated what would happen under the various formulas so that all could see the impact that would result from the proposed changes, and the UMTA administrator pledged that there would be a new formula.[54] There were moves within APTA to soothe the feelings of members who saw their level of federal funding threatened by the formula change. "Need" and "equity" were key words in discussions of the transit industry. The upsetting situation apparently made some members of the industry forget the need for unity. APTA was, in a real sense, caught in the middle.

While the House was unable to make progress on its bill for new transit legislation because of its provisions dealing with elderly and handicapped persons (particularly the Section 504 modifications), the Senate moved ahead with its approval of appropriations for fiscal year 1981. On September 24, the House and Senate concurred on the 1981 appropriation for transit.[55] The head of the Senate subcommittee on transportation appropriations was Birch Bayh of Indiana. Bayh was facing a tough challenge in his re-election campaign; his Republican adversary styled Bayh as a big spender. Bayh walked a tightrope and held the appropriation down from the approximately $5 billion requested by the Carter administration for transit purposes. Finally, the UMTA budget for 1981 was set at $4.615 billion. The breakdown in funding is shown in Table 10.1.

The controversy over living with the requirements of Section 504 reared its head again in September when the New York Metropolitan Transportation Authority (MTA) refused to file a transition plan on accessibility as required in UMTA/DOT regulations. The refusal to file the plan meant that New York might lose all federal transit aid, which totaled about $375 million a year at that time. The decision was made by New York because the cost of providing accessibility was estimated to be $1.5 billion; an estimated $100 million in additional annual operating cost was another factor. The New York MTA felt that the money could be better spent on rehabilitating the system rather than fitting it out for accessibility to serve only a relatively few patrons.[56] The move dramatized the plight of the transit industry, which was being required to do something expensive in the face of inflation and a level of federal aid that promised to be less than was hoped.

No transit legislation would be passed as long as there was hope on the part of at least some components of the transit industry that complying with Section 504 would be made less burdensome. Anticipation of more federal money for transit, and some relief from the speed with which accessibility had to be provided, would probably have produced great lobbying pressure for passage of legislation by the early fall of 1980. That expectation did not exist and the pressure to pass the legislation was largely absent.

When Congress went into recess for the 1980 election, it was plain that if

Table 10.1
FY 1981 Transit Budget
Conference Committee Report
(billions of dollars)

Section 3

Discretionary Grants		$2.190
Bus & Bus Facilities	.580	
Rail Modernization	.945	
New Starts	.435	
Downtown Peoplemovers	.050	
Urban Initiatives	.090	
Planning	.065	
Innovative Techniques	.015	
Technology Introduction	.010	

Section 5

Formula Grants		1.455
Basic	.850	
Second Tier	.165	
Commuter	.090	
Bus Capital	.350	

Research and Development	.0655
Administration	.022
Small Urban and Rural	.0725
Interstate Transfer	.800
Waterborne Demonstration	.010
Program Total	$4.615

there was to be transit legislation it would have to be passed in the lame-duck session after the election. No one realized just how lame the duck would be. The Republicans won a smashing victory, with Ronald Reagan totally overpowering Jimmy Carter in the presidential election. Moreover, the Republicans gained control of the Senate, the first time that party had controlled either house of the Congress in over a quarter of a century. Birch Bayh, Democrat of Indiana, lost his bid for a fourth term and, of course, his position as chairman of the subcommittee on transportation appropriations of the Senate Appropriations Committee. Senator Harrison Williams of New Jersey, the major proponent of transit legislation in the Senate, was not up for election, but he lost his position as chairman of the subcommittee on housing and urban affairs of the Committee on Banking, Housing and Urban Affairs. Williams's place was taken by Republican Senator Richard Lugar of Indiana.[57] As a result, Lugar became responsible for the authorizing legislation for transit.

Congress reconvened soon after the election and work began on the House mass transit bill. Congressman James Howard of New Jersey was scheduled to present an amendment on the floor to bring the proposed House bill closer to the legislation already passed in the Senate. This was done to help speed up passage of the bill. Work started in the House on November 21; by December 3 the House had handily passed a bill by vote of 346 to 33. The bill authorized approximately $20 billion for transit through fiscal year 1985; it included $1.5 billion to be used between 1985 and 1990 for new rail starts, extensions of rail systems, downtown peoplemovers, and automated fixed-guideway systems. A version of the Cleveland amendment for local option on Section 504 accessibility was also included. A compromise Section 5 formula, to take effect in fiscal year 1982, would be based on a combination of the existing population–population density formula and a new service-based formula.[58] The House bill was generally considered to be quite favorable to transit and, given the environment in which it passed, about as good a piece of legislation as transit interests could hope for.

The bill went to the Senate. There it was killed by a filibuster by Senator Richard Lugar. Senator Lugar took the position that there was no need for new transit legislation because the existing legislation carried the mass transit programs through fiscal year 1982. He also contended that the changes in the aid formula would help only larger, older cities with established transit systems. He thought that the new administration and the new Congress should have the opportunity to formulate a new mass transit policy, a policy that in large part was expected to be written by Senator Lugar as chairman of the subcommittee on housing and urban affairs.[59]

To make matters even more gloomy for the transit industry and the transit community, on the heels of the Reagan victory and during the period of consideration of the House bill and the eventual defeat of the 1980 legislation, chilling trial balloons were launched by the Reagan transition team and affiliated groups regarding policy changes that might affect transit. Among these were various "statements" and "reports" of groups that called for substantial cutbacks in federal support for transit and other subsidized transportation ventures (such as Amtrak), along with philosophical comments reiterating the typical Republican position regarding subsidies as unwholesome. Unfortunately, the subsidies, particularly operating subsidies, loomed large in virtually all discussion of transit and of Amtrak. All modes of transportation, save pipelines, are the beneficiary of some degree of subsidization, but this fact was not particularly blatant or well-recognized. Another report, this one by a group established in 1979 by President Carter, indicated that the older cities in the Northeast and Midwest that were already in a state of decline should be allowed to continue that descent with no help from the federal government. Instead, it was felt that federal help should go to the cities of the South and Southwest that were growing rapidly. This was very bad news to those responsible for the operation of the major mass transit services of the U.S. As 1981 began, there was a strong aura of uncertainty about the future shape and scope of the federal mass transit programs.[60]

RETROSPECTIVE

A good question to ask is: Why did the proposed transit legislation of 1980 go down to such an apparently unseemly end? As the reader will remember, the situation looked bright only a year before the 1980 legislation was filibustered away. In retrospect, probably the best time in recent years to have passed some legislation favorable to mass transit—favorable in the sense of a healthy increase in authorizations—was in the last three months of 1979. The gasoline shortage and price rise of the spring and summer of 1979 had stimulated great interest in transit as a part of the solution to energy-related problems, and both Congress and the Carter administration were most favorably disposed. Indeed, the support pledged by President Carter in his speech to the 1979 APTA annual meeting was probably the high point of support by the federal government in recent years. Unfortunately, the moment was to be but a fleeting one.

Obviously it takes time to pass legislation, but the 1980 transit legislation was seriously delayed and became a victim of a lame-duck Congress. The two major stumbling blocks to quick passage of a favorable piece of transit legislation were the Section 504 requirements and the proposed change in the formula for distribution of Section 5 funds.

The key factor was the expected large increase in capital and operating cost of full accessibility for the handicapped on regular-route scheduled service and the apparent unwillingness of the federal government to pick up the expenses that would result from the effort to achieve it. Given the lack of use by the handicapped of what little accessible, regular-route transit service was already offered, transit operators foresaw that, even with full accessibility to regular transit service, special transit services would also have to be offered to provide the mobility that the handicapped needed to participate fully in community life. Representatives of the handicapped argued from a civil-rights standpoint that their constituents had a right in simple justice and equity to be able to use the facilities and services that had been paid for in part by their taxes. They also stressed the wish of the handicapped to be part of the mainstream of life in the community and not solely dependent upon special services that bore the stigma of being "special" and therefore apart from the mainstream. Congress and the Carter administration could easily be caught in the middle of such an argument, one that grew even more difficult to deal with in an election year.

The wrangling over the Section 5 formula served to divide the transit industry at a time when concerted effort was needed, especially after the Carter administration and Congress were diverted by the passion for a balanced budget and other election-year exhibitions of fiscal restraint in the face of record inflation and interest rates. With twenty-twenty hindsight, what the industry should have sought to do was to work together, both large cities and small, to increase the Section 5 authorization and appropriation so that, regardless of how the formula was changed, no one place or size grouping of cities would be a loser. The bigger transit operations cannot be accused of wanting more money to meet their needs, but the smaller ones cannot be blamed for their legitimate concern over absolute losses in aid, losses of sometimes large magnitude. It should come as no surprise, therefore, that Senator Lugar of Indiana, whose filibuster killed the 1980 legislation, was from a state in which there would be major losses (to Indianapolis, South Bend, and Fort Wayne) under a service-based formula. In seeking to find a compromise position, there were inevitable delays. The delays resulting from Section 5 and Section 504 held back the passage of legislation unduly.

Senator Lugar's call for a review of policy, and perhaps the writing of new policy during the Reagan administration, was not an unexpected action, considering that a major change of political power had taken place, but it is a more difficult task than may appear on the face of it. From the beginning of federal programs in transit, there has been a parceling out of money for what were thought to be worthy purposes. Lamentably, as the reader will recall, there have never really been clear-cut goals or concrete objectives for the policy. Elusive purposes for programs are no stranger to government in the United States on all levels; most often the situation is one of a problem that is met by passing a law, and perhaps by providing some money to pay for one sort of program or another.[61] However, programs inescapably take on a life of their own as they are shaped to meet the needs of client groups. To question the programs may be wise, but to make sweeping changes, to take away something that has been in place for a while, is difficult and often politically and administratively inexpedient.

Establishing a new urban transportation policy, or perhaps merely restructuring the mass transit programs, are not simple affairs. Urban transportation policy does not exist in a vacuum; it must be developed in relation to inter-city transportation policy, economic policy, energy policy, urban policy, and environmental policy. There was no evidence that the new administration was prepared to undertake such a major rethinking of key areas of federal responsibility in a coordinated and integrated fashion, particularly because what existed in all these closely related areas had been established in a piecemeal fashion over a long period of time. Even if the Reagan administration chose to do so, the task would have been enormously difficult and complex. Because of the many groups affected, the political pressures brought by a large number of interests would probably substantially delay any solid effort. It would also require that both houses of Congress and the administration be strongly committed to a creative, integrated policy development. At the moment of their great election triumph, the Republicans still did not control the House. Even if they had, party discipline withered away in the 1970s, and there was no assurance that the kind of policy approach that was really needed to ponder a truly enlightened and far-reaching program of policy development could be achieved before the next national election in 1982 or before the authorization for transit ran out in the same year.

So the future was cloudy for mass transit legislation and policy in the early 1980s. A brief and probably bright opportunity for a significant increase in federal transit aid slipped by in late 1979. Whether the hoped-for improvement in the lot of the transit-consuming public would have been achieved cannot be known. More chilling, the highly negative trial balloons concerning massive cuts or elimination of the federal transit program were a solid warning to the transit community of what lay ahead.[62]

11.

Federal Mass Transit Policy in the Age of Reagan, 1981-1982

Just before Christmas 1982 the U.S. Senate passed H.R. 6211, after long and arduous labor. Compromises and filibusters had aided and plagued the process of legislating a reauthorization of federal mass transit policy. It was a hectic process, and transit interests faced the most determined opposition to the program in twenty years. The finale was a surprisingly progressive piece of legislation. What were the key factors in the political environment and national transit milieus that affected creation and passage of this legislation?

The development of federal policy toward mass transportation in 1981 had as its immediate background a failure to advance policy or funding in 1979 and 1980. The transit industry had spent much of that time seeking new authorizing legislation. As the reader will recall, the purposes of this proposed legislation were an increase in the level of federal funding (particularly of operating aid), and a change in the formula by which operating aid was dispersed. Internecine warfare had broken out in the transit industry between the large and small transit systems. When a compromise was finally reached, it was too late to get the bill passed in Congress before the national presidential election. The legislation proposal was filibustered and failed to pass the lame duck session of Congress after the 1980 election.[1]

The new president, Ronald Reagan, was clearly unhappy with the vast structure and bureaucracy of the federal government, particularly the social programs and the amount of money spent on them. For years, many observers as well as elected and appointed federal officials had felt that, perhaps, the federal government had bitten off more than could be properly chewed, so concern with the size of the federal government was not new with President Reagan or his administration. What was new was the intensity with which the new administration sought to cut back or eliminate programs thought to be unworthy or out of context with the new philosophy of government that swept into Washington with the inauguration of Ronald Reagan.[2]

As a corollary to the administration's wish to cut the scale of the federal government, there was to be a much stronger reliance upon market forces than in the past. There was to be a cutback on bothersome rules and regulations and the elimination of as much federal red tape as possible on federal programs that the administration wanted to continue. Consistent with this was a determination on the part of the Reagan administration to return as many federal programs to state and local government hands as possible.[3] What became dubbed the "New Federalism" had been discussed for many years by Ronald Reagan before he became president. The idea was given more formal status as the centerpiece of President Reagan's State of the Union message to Congress and the public, via television, on January 26, 1982.

This new relationship of the federal government to state and local government was to be achieved through a system of block grants, wherein federal money would be provided to state and local governments, but it would be up to the lower levels of government to decide how it would be expended. This would mean an end to many of the New Deal and Great Society categorical grant programs. There were also proposals in the State of the Union speech to create a trust fund to help the states in the long transition of current federal programs back to the states. Ronald Reagan was announcing a major change in the way all levels of government did their jobs.

As for transportation policy, the main tenets of the overall economic policy were to hold forth, especially the part about cutting back on the growth of federal spending. Some observers contended that this was not a policy at all—only a budget process to achieve the goal of a balanced federal budget by the end of the first Reagan administration. In order to reduce the budget deficit, major cuts were to be made in federal transportation-related programs, such as mass transit, Amtrak, and federal contributions to maintain operation of Conrail. The deregulation of air, rail, and trucking that started under the Carter administration was to be encouraged as a means of letting market forces prevail.[4]

THE REAGAN ADMINISTRATION'S PROPOSALS FOR TRANSIT

The Carter administration had proposed a budget for 1981 and, as required by law, for several years beyond that; the Carter budget had shown a deficit of over $40 billion for fiscal 1982. In the federal process, the administration budget is prepared for five years at a time; the budget for the next fiscal year is, of course, developed in much greater detail than the projections farther in the future. One purpose of this exercise is to reveal trends in income and expense. The Reagan administration, through the director of the Office of Management and Budget, David Stockman, sought to reduce the rate of increase in federal expenditures by making substantial cutbacks in many programs. The only real government expansion policy of the Reagan administration was to increase military spending. The huge Social Security program—always a political hot potato—was to be left pretty much untouched. This approach was very bad news for those affected by programs other than the military or Social Security because it left only about 17 percent of the budget really subject to any great change by

Congress or the administration. In other words, by the reorganization of several sacred cows, the cuts in the rate of overall federal spending increase would have to be made in less than one-fifth of the budget—and the federal mass transit program was in this part of the budget.

David Stockman's "black book" on the budget proposals of the Reagan administration became famous and even notorious in the press early in 1981, as he used it in testimony before Congress to back up his arguments for diminished federal spending. As far as transit was concerned, this called for the elimination of operating aid under Section 5 of the Urban Mass Transportation Act, which was to be carried out in stages with operating subsidies phased out by the 1984 federal fiscal year. Spending for capital and other programs would be roughly stabilized at the 1981 level of spending; there would be no escalator for inflation. Neither would there be federal capital funds for new rail transit starts, and the completion of rail systems already under construction would be stretched out over more years. A continuing role for the federal government in research and development, training, and information dissemination was recognized, although at a diminished level of support.

On a more positive note, there was to be an elimination of bothersome rules and regulations; gratifying to many in the transit industry was the proposed move toward local option in fulfilling the requirements of Section 504 of the Rehabilitation Act of 1973. Under the Carter administration, rules had been promulgated that would require the installation of lifts on all new buses, and other economically heroic measures to help make transit fully accessible to those in wheelchairs or otherwise seriously handicapped. For those worried about the proposed cutbacks in federal transit spending, Stockman and others in the administration pointed to significant savings stemming from the relaxation in rules. Yet many in the transit community failed to find cheer in the loss of millions of dollars of federal aid in return for paltry relief from red tape.

As an example of the change in the amount of dollars to be provided by the federal government, Table 11.1 shows the Carter administration proposals as the current base expenditures for transit capital programs, in comparison with the Reagan proposals. Table 11.2 reveals the Carter proposals as the base for federal operating aid for transit and the changes proposed by Stockman for the Reagan administration, including the phase-out of such aid in fiscal year 1985.

The administration's rationale for the changes in federal expenditures for transit capital improvements was that the primary responsibility for mass transit should remain with state and local governments. Given the economic situation, federal emphasis, it was felt, should be on maintaining existing transit systems that had proven effective and essential. The reductions were also based on the thought that the steadily increasing federal transit funding had helped to increase the cost of new transit systems. Part of the rationale was the assertion that "transit system energy savings are nonexistent or small in the short run and too speculative in the long run to justify major Federal investments on energy efficiency grounds."[5]

With the abiding rationale that "there is no reason for someone in Sioux

Table 11.1
Federal Funds for Mass Transit Capital Purposes,
Fiscal 1981-1986

	(in millions of dollars)					
	1981	1982	1983	1984	1985	1986
Current base:						
Budget authority	3.340	3.650	3.762	4.070	4.368	4.647
Outlays	2.744	2.800	3.010	3.337	3.669	3.996
Policy reduction:						
Budget authority	−210	−950	−1.047	−1.220	−1.368	1.497
Outlays	−31	−270	−545	−975	−1.284	−1.480
Proposed budget:						
Budget authority	3.130	2.700	2.715	2.850	3.000	3.150
Outlays	2.713	2.530	2.465	2.362	2.385	2.516

Table 11.2
Federal Funds for Mass Transit Operating Purposes,
Fiscal 1981-1986

	(in millions of dollars)					
	1981	1982	1983	1984	1985	1986
Current base:						
Budget authority	1.105	1.208	1.316	1.424	1.528	1.626
Outlays	750	876	1.053	1.168	1.284	1.398
Policy reduction:						
Budget authority	—	−103	−581	−1.059	−1.528	1.626
Outlays	—	−96	−256	−600	−1.083	−1.356
Proposed budget:						
Budget authority	1.105	1.105	735	365	—	—
Outlays	750	780	797	568	201	42

Source: Office of Management and Budget, *America's New Beginning: A Program for Economic Recovery*, p. 5–4. Reproduced by the American Association of State Highway and Transportation Officials, Standing Committee on Public Transportation (Hereafter referred to as AASHTO), February 19, 1981.

Falls to pay federal taxes so that someone in Los Angeles can get to work on time by public transportation,'' the Reagan administration proposed the reduction and phasing out of federal operating aid to transit. (Nothing was said, however, on whether or not someone in Los Angeles should pay federal taxes so that someone in Sioux Falls can get to work on time by highway.) In arguing against federal operating subsidies, it was pointed out that such money was supporting marginally effective conventional transit services and preventing the implementation of more cost-effective and innovative alternatives such as carpools, vanpools, subscription buses, and jitney services. The sharp increases in the transit deficit compared to fare increases were pointed out: from 1973 to 1978 costs increased an average of 13.2 percent per annum while fares rose an average of 3.5 percent per year. Also expressed was the thought that transit operating subsidies were not an especially efficient way to assist particular disadvantaged groups, such as the elderly, the poor, minorities, and youth.[6]

The position of the Reagan administration toward transit, to sum up, was to let state and local government pick up the operating cost of transit and to impose higher fares on transit users; the federal government would withdraw completely from transit operating subsidies. In the Reagan view, the federal role in mass transportation was a very limited one indeed. Anyone who had listened carefully to the speeches by candidate Reagan would not be surprised by this position, because this was what he had called for.[7] The Reagan position marked a 180-degree change from the position toward transit developed by the federal government from 1961 up to Reagan's election.

Coming into power in early 1981 meant that the Reagan administration had to deal with a soft economy plagued with high inflation, interest rates, and unemployment, as well as the challenge of formulating the federal budget for fiscal year 1982. Putting the Reagan economic recovery program into effect was a part of the budgetary process. As it turned out, developing the 1982 budget became a long, drawn-out affair. The president received considerable support, even from the Democrat-controlled House of Representatives, for substantial reductions in federal spending not only in transit but also in many other fields.[8] While it was not quite as enthusiastic, the president also received strong support from both houses of Congress for the tax cut program that was initiated in the summer of 1981 as part of the Reagan plan for restoring vitality to the economy. What finally happened was a forecast of what was to come in the future. There were cutbacks for transit funding in the 1982 budget, not only from the target expenditures proposed in the Carter budget, but also in absolute amount from the 1981 total. This was bad news for the transit community, because for the first time since 1964 there was a diminution of federal transit aid. It was, it turned out, something to which transit providers had to become accustomed.

Even with negotiation between Congress and the White House, there was no 1982 budget in place at the end of fiscal year 1981.[9] At the beginning of the 1982 fiscal year, a continuing budget resolution was passed by Congress that kept the government running from October 1 until November 20. Meanwhile, there was more bad news in store for transit and other programs when the federal budget deficit for 1982 was projected to be larger than had been expected; in September the president called for substantially higher budget cuts for 1982 on top of those made earlier; the second round of cuts was to chop another 12 percent off federal spending. The Congress, after its August recess and a return to the hustings to take the pulse of the electorate, was much less happy at giving the president the additional cuts he wanted.[10] Pain, and in particular the promise of pain, was being felt by the public.[11]

There was to be more budget trouble. When the budget resolution adopted before the November 20 termination of the continuing resolution was still too high, President Reagan refused to go along with it, which forced Congress to pass another continuing resolution in order to keep the federal government in business. Before the December 15 deadline of the second continuing resolution, Congress had agreed to a 1982 budget resolution that was acceptable to the president and had begun to turn out separate budget bills for the various pieces of the federal government. The transportation budget was sent to the president for his signature just before Christmas of 1981. The final 1982 budget figure for transit was a substantial reduction from what had been expected only a year earlier.[12] The bad news for transit trumpeted by David Stockman was coming true. Perhaps the transit industry was spoiled by the almost incredible success it had achieved in the 1970s in gaining steadily increasing federal support. The attitude of the top presidential appointees at UMTA was generally less positive than that of their predecessors; indeed, the threat from the administration to terminate the program was very real.

THE PROBLEMS AND VULNERABILITY OF TRANSIT

Perspective on what happened to the federal mass transportation programs and why, and the general and specific milieus of transit in relation to the Reagan administration, is instructive. Even before Ronald Reagan was sworn in as president, a cloud of gloom had begun to form over the transit industry as if in awful anticipation. At the end of 1980, an editorial in the *Louisville Courier Journal* expressed the hopes and fears for transit under the Reagan administration:

> The Reagan transportation advisors . . . have produced a report that is an almost pure dose of bad news to the city halls across the country. True, their recommendation that the last 1,547 miles of the 42,500 mile interstate highway system not be completed will bring sighs of relief in some urban areas where planned freeway projects are highly unpopular. But that doesn't begin to offset the damage that would be done to municipal coffers—and the nation's energy conservation efforts—by curtailing federal transit subsidies. Those subsidies have enabled cities to take over failing private transit systems . . . to buy new equipment, and to pay a portion of operating costs. Without them, transit fares or local taxes, or both, would have to be raised. Occasional fare increases . . . are justified. But a sharp increase to compensate for lost federal funds could discourage ridership at a time when the nation should be doing everything it can to persuade commuters to leave their cars at home. Local tax increases for transit sound plausible—in theory. But in many of the Northern cities that rely heavily on transit, local taxes already are so high that industries are leaving . . . the Reagan team's transit proposals aren't even a good starting point for debate. One hopes they will be quietly ignored after Mr. Reagan takes office.[13]

Under the new administration, transit was clearly vulnerable to major reductions in the amount and kind of funding that would be available. There was certainly nothing wrong with the move to reduce the size of the federal government and the enormous amount of money it took to operate. Many sober politicians and observers had felt for some time that federal spending was exceeding the ability of the nation to support it. The national debt approached one trillion dollars in 1981, making many persons uneasy. Indeed, the interest on the debt alone was a fairly significant cause of the budget deficit.[14] Some felt that a reduction in transit funding was not unreasonable if all parts of the federal establishment were to be treated on a relatively even-handed basis. Whether or not this was to be true was a matter for conjecture; obviously, it was administration policy that there was to be a major increase in defense spending and the Social Security programs were to be left relatively unscathed. The vocal opposition of the president to a tax increase, and the 1981 tax cuts, made unequivocal the president's desire for less government with less tax money to fuel it—except, of course, for ballooning defense expenditures. Defense spending had been down in the 1970s; Reagan aimed to change that situation by pouring money into defense.

As noted in previous pages, part of the problems of the federal transit aid program in the eyes of many observers was that the programs were linked with the Great Society agendum, even though they were not really parts of Great Society programs. It is these programs, forged at the apogee of the Johnson administration, that appeared to be the particular target of the new Republican administration. The all too common perception that transit use was almost exclusively an activity of the poor did not help with this administration, which confessed its belief in taking steps to benefit the middle and upper classes—the perceived taxpayers and investors of the society—and to lower the tax burden on those classes of society. Whatever the rationale, immediately after the inauguration, David A. Stockman, director of the Office of Management and Budget, circulated proposals that, among other cuts in transportation, proposed reducing funds for mass transit by $448 million in 1982, $1.1 billion in 1983, $1.4 billion in 1984, and $1.6 billion in 1985.[15]

To those unimpressed by transit as a federal program, transit appeared to be very much a local problem. This difficulty was present 20 years earlier when the first transit legislation was in the process of being passed. Transit became a national problem because of the widespread nature of the malady of collapsing transit systems. With privately owned transit systems threatening to go out of business—or actually leaving the scene—the inability of local and state governments to do anything about it, or their unwillingness to act, helped to push the federal government onto the scene. As was the case with many federal programs since the 1930s, the national government acted to fill a vacuum seen to exist on the state and local levels of government. Another reason for the federal transit program was the subsidized highway system that created extraordinarily competitive problems for even the best-run transit systems. Moreover, because highways were subsidized, it was not possible over the long run for transit to charge fares that reflected full cost. As the reader will recall from earlier chapters, federal policy to aid only highways in the first twenty years after World War II led to massive investments of federal, state, and local money in urban roads and virtually nothing invested in mass transit. An additional reason for transit aid was the belief that providing passenger capacity in urban corridors with transit was a cheaper alternative in many cases than building roads.[16]

As a fundamental truth, despite protestations otherwise from state and local governments, there is always a natural willingness to let someone else do the taxing. A standard governmental policy in the U.S. is almost always to push the burden of levying a tax and starting an aid program to a higher level of government and to let it be the villain in the eyes of the more localized taxpayers. State and local interest and wherewithal aside, human and political nature is such that it often prefers to let others—the federal government in this case—take the heat while letting the beneficial light shine on state and local government, both of which are usually delighted to take some of the credit in landing a federal grant. In any case, doubts about the propriety of federal aid can easily be generated if transit is claimed to be a purely local issue. One might hold that almost all benefits of all programs are local in impact and that there should be almost no federal role in any activity.

Despite two decades of federal activity in transit and increasing activity and aid by state and local government, the failure across the transit industry (almost without exception) to institutionalize transit as a vital part of the community was a major problem. If transit is institutionalized, it becomes an important part of the value structure of the community it serves. Transit becomes entwined within the essential fabric of the community and by so doing, through responsive interaction with important elements of community life, comes to have a claim on the resources of the community for its support.[17] It is probably rare in the U.S., outside of major cities where public transportation is typically viewed as absolutely essential (even if it is unloved), for transit to have such support that it is unthinkable to deny it reasonable community largesse for its continuation and growth.

Another important factor was the propriety of public ownership. With the exception of a few large cities where public ownership had been in place for many years—Chicago, Cleveland, Detroit, New York, and San Francisco, to name a few—it is probably fair to say that, nationally, the United States was still not comfortable with the idea of publicly owned transit service. Transit, for far too many years and far too recently, had been a private enterprise operated for profit. Much of the nomenclature of the private enterprise days still hangs over transit—such as the use of the term deficit, which makes it appear that transit management is often doing something wrong if it doesn't make a profit. Otherwise, even though transit is considered by many to be a public service as are libraries, streets, sewers, garbage collection, and police and fire protection, it is still often viewed and treated as a somehow unwholesome and failed enterprise if it doesn't make money. It may be a matter of semantics, but it is still a tender issue and the term "deficit" is often devastating. Worse yet, operating subsidies for transit are in plain view in the federal budget; subsidies for the other modes are more coyly presented.[18]

The failure to build a strong transit consumer constituency or business constituency was another major area of vulnerability. Rather than enlisting its rather substantial ridership as part of the lobbying force, the transit industry has too often viewed its users as the enemy—as an unruly problem—or at the least, as a cross to bear. The real outreach style of community relations programs are still rare in transit. The motto adopted by the transit industry and the American Public Transit Association (APTA) in 1981, "Transit Means Business," is a good one and is certainly true.[19] In reality, it probably should have been claimed years ago. Clearly, the business community must be convinced that transit is worthwhile or else its valuable support will not be forthcoming. This appeared to be particularly important during the Reagan administration, when business was given all possible encouragement and attention. However worthy APTA's effort, it may be a good example of too little done too late.

Some of the fault in failing to build strong ties with the local community lies directly in the hands of transit managers. It is understandable, if not forgivable, because many other things occupy management's attention, and the industry has traditionally been undermanaged and usually badly understaffed as well. The monetary cutbacks—both threatened and real—under the Reagan administration strongly focused managerial time and effort on fiscal survival, often to the exclusion of virtually everything else. Basics in transit—dependable service, in clean vehicles, operated by skilled and courteous personnel, that takes people where they wish to go quickly—are often sacrificed because of the worry about money. There has also been a strong tendency in many places for transit policy makers and management to merely do the best job with what was already there; to make capital improvements but not really to restructure the entire service to meet the needs of its constituents as those needs have changed over the years. As one example, many cities are today polycentric, with a central business district (CBD) plus other major places of economic and social activity, such as huge regional shopping centers and office complexes. However, most transit systems remain centrally focused and the CBD is often the only place really well served within the community.[20]

The failure of the federal government to develop a coherent transit policy was another major sector of vulnerability for the transit industry. There were no workable goals and objectives for transit. Such a failure in specificity is not unusual behavior for Congress or for various administrations; when a problem is perceived, and there is sufficient support, a law is passed to solve the problem. It is rare, indeed, that a program has a clearcut, long-range aim with measurable objectives. Even though it may be a normal way of life in Congress and in the federal government, it is deleterious to the cause of mass transit; with nothing in particular to aim for over the years, it is difficult to prove that transit really achieved much because what was to be achieved was vague at best.[21]

Paradoxically, the goal of the operating aid program that was seriously jeopardized by the Reagan administration's cutbacks was probably one of the clearer aims that federal transit policy has had in its twenty years of existence. The aims of the 1974 legislation that created the formula grant programs, from which some of the funds may be used for operating aid, were to do three things: (1) maintain fare levels; (2) increase service; and (3) increase ridership. Transit statistics since 1974 show rather clearly that fare levels were maintained at about their 1974-75 levels throughout the 1970s, that there was a substantial increase in the amount of service available, and that ridership did, indeed, increase.[22]

Particularly tough to show, however, are victories other than those of increasing ridership, either nationally or on the local scene. Although transit proponents often claim many great virtues, it is difficult to prove that there has been success in many areas.[23] One might argue that transit can help to achieve goals other than transportation only if a concerted interplay of many forces are involved in producing economic development, environmental enhancement, energy savings, and increased opportunity and mobility for citizens.

Because the Reagan administration apparently had no real transportation policy (save for reliance on competitive private enterprise—which is a means, not an end), one was left with only a budget containing some figures in it for transportation; it is difficult for transit to argue its case under such circumstances. Also, the failure of the administration to endorse an energy policy, other than the play of market forces, diluted transit's ability to advance one of its major arguments—that is, that transit would be a good standby if gasoline for automobiles became short in supply or if the OPEC nations again raised their prices for crude oil to astronomical levels. The continuation of the federal capital programs proposed in the Reagan approach to transit was additional evidence that the federal and state levels of government were relatively comfortable with capital expenditures. Such expenditures are often viewed as proper in the sense that they are perceived to have a broad, stimulative effect on the economy. On the other hand, operating aid from either state or federal government is often viewed as throwing money down a rathole.

The difficulty here is in knowing just what roles various forms of transportation are supposed to play. As Alan Altshuler has pointed out so well, if we have had any sort of national transportation policy at all, it has been to provide alternatives. Traditionally, there has not been an effort in the United States by the federal or other governments to choose between competing claims of different types or forms of transportation—auto and transit—on the local level; the policy has been to help both and to allow both to be subsidized. Consumers can then exercise choice. Yet, that this may not be a particularly cost-effective course to take is obvious.

Again, in the perception of transit critics, the fact that transit doesn't appear to live up to many of the claims that have been made for it is an argument against continuing federal expenditures. Studies carried out over a number of years indicate that the role of transit in reducing the demand for energy, improving the environment, or helping central cities to grow has won it no Oscars.[24]

If government is not going to develop a rational policy for transit—and there is not much evidence that the situation will change—perhaps the transit industry should do so. One speculates that the members of the industry did not have the time, instinct, or desire to carry out the difficult job of policy formulation themselves. A coherent and systematic policy, defining the role of transit and naming goals and objectives, is necessary, and the vision of the transit industry—yet to be forged—of what should be done may be helpful to Congress and to the administration in power. Whatever that might be, a comprehensive and useful plan tied in with economic development, defense, the environment, energy, and urban and overall transportation policies would be desirable. In an ideal situation, components of the transit industry should develop a strategic plan for achieving their goals and then work together to sell the plan to their various constituencies.

Speaking of constituencies, as the 1980s began there was both a real and a future problem with the constituencies for transit in Congress due to the shift of population to the Sunbelt states. Most of the cities south of the Mason-Dixon Line and in the southwestern part of the nation were not as transit-oriented as were the older cities of the North, which had been served and substantially shaped by transit over a considerable portion of their histories. Representatives from the Sunbelt may legitimately have relatively small interest in transit, believing it to be an unimportant issue to the citizens who elect them. Moreover, Sunbelt cities, even if they are interested in improving mass transit, are difficult to serve well with conventional transit because of their thinly distributed, spread-out, and highly automobile-oriented nature. Transit in the South has, traditionally, served the relatively small and specialized market of the transit dependent. As Congress shifted its orientation away from areas with a strong history and background of transit, it may have made it harder to sell the programs. Regardless of where they hail from, those who make the laws regarding mass transit— and everything else—are, for the most part, not transit users themselves.[25] Lamentably, lawmakers certainly drive cars and use airlines; they may even use Amtrak, which is certainly a transportation presence with at least a touch of glamour. Mass transit is not glamorous. Longtime support of mass transit by certain legislators was weakened in the early part of 1982. Senator Harrison Williams of New Jersey was forced to resign from the Senate after having been convicted of receiving bribes and selling influence in the so-called Abscam Affair. His place as the Senate's major proponent of transit was taken by Senator Alfonse M. D'Amato (R-New York) and Senator Mark Andrews (R-North Dakota). Representative James Howard (D-New Jersey) continued his important role in the House.

1981: A BAD-NEWS YEAR FOR TRANSIT

The year 1981 was not a good one for the psyche of the transit industry. The Reagan proposals for cutbacks in the federal transit budget and the elimination of operating aid were probably the worst tidings,[26] but there was a lot of other bad news to go around. The General Accounting Office (GAO) prepared a report entitled *Soaring Transit Subsidies Must Be Controlled.* The report indicated that growing demands for transit subsidies were caused, in part, by a lack of improvement in productivity in the industry. For example, the cost per vehicle mile, eliminating the effects of inflation, had increased 17 percent, from $1.31 per mile in 1973 to $1.53 per mile in 1978. The report realistically pointed out that productivity improvements were difficult because of the peaked nature of transit demand and that labor agreements limited managerial flexibility in cutting labor costs.

The GAO report also directed attention to problems with maintenance. It found that many transit properties were not properly recruiting, training, and promoting their mechanics, did not have adequate preventive maintenance programs, did not properly control spare-parts inventories, and had restrictive work rules that forestalled efficient use of maintenance personnel. The General Accounting Office also found that transit fares were unrealistic and that by keeping fares low and simple (flat fares), transit operating agencies were not realizing as much revenue as was possible. Inequities in fares, as a result of the flat fares charged in most U.S. cities, typically caused the short, non-peak inner-city trip to cost more per mile than the longer work trip of the suburban rider.

Perhaps the most newsworthy part of the study was its estimate of the size of the future subsidy that would be required for transit. It found that $2.2 billion in subsidies was received by transit in 1978 from federal, state, and local sources. It was estimated that the subsidy needed by 1985 would be over $6 billion. The report urged Congress to rethink its 1974 policy of maintaining low transit fares and recommended that UMTA develop policies to help transit operators contain costs and increase revenues by various means. The size of the necessary subsidy was shocking to many people.[27]

There was also concern that the hard-won momentum that had been built in support of transit would flag as a result of the proposed cuts and thus set back by many years the development of reasonably good transit service in U.S. cities. Larger cities were particularly disturbed by David Stockman's pronouncements relative to rapid transit projects that were under construction. Stockman stated that a rail project "90 percent complete should probably be completed, one 50 percent complete may or may not be completed, and one only 10 percent complete should probably not be completed."[28]

There was bad news for transit riders across the nation as fares surged upward for the first time since the operating aid provisions had been written into the Urban Mass Transportation Act in 1974. Much of the fare increase experienced nationally was not due to any proposals of the Reagan administration but was the product of the stunning inflation experienced in 1979 and 1980. For example, for 1981, fares rose from 60 cents to 80 cents in Chicago, from 60 cents to 75 cents in Miami, from 50 cents to 65 cents in Milwaukee, from 60 cents to 75 cents in Pittsburgh and from 35 cents to 50 cents in Toledo. On a percentage basis these were substantial increases, especially in consideration of the total vehicle miles of transit service operated. Total vehicle miles rose from 2.0283 billion in 1978 to 2.1337 billion in 1981; miles declined to 2.1169 billion in 1983.[29]

In addition to the Reagan administration's threatened cuts in federal transit funding, there were other problems in transit across the nation that made news. Labor strife in a number of large cities had resulted in disruptive strikes. The physical deterioration of transit facilities in New York and Philadelphia, to name just two cities, had reached alarming proportions. There was a threat of major cuts in transit service in Chicago as the city and its state squabbled over transportation aid. New buses in New York developed cracks in the engine mountings. To the woe of the transit industry, the cloud just kept getting darker, with no silver lining in sight.[30]

Perhaps the most concentrated picture of the position of the transit industry in 1981, and of attitudes toward it, is found in the hearings held by the oversight subcommittee of the House Committee on Public Works and Transportation during the summer and fall. These hearings brought into focus many of the issues with regard to public transit in the U.S. and the role of the federal government.[31] The tone of the hearings was set by Oversight Subcommittee Chairman Elliott H. Levitas in his opening remarks:

> . . . The question is not whether we shall continue to operate transit systems . . . the question is under what conditions and circumstances they shall operate, and who shall pay the bill.
>
> The task before us is to help public transportation more successfully identify and carry out its very special but very vital role. But the past cannot necessarily delineate the future. Would the fortunes of public transportation improve if more federal dollars were made available, even if that were possible? Frankly, speaking for myself, I doubt it. The problems are more fundamental than that. In fact, it must be pointed out that transit has slipped into its present economic coma without any of the cutbacks that have been proposed by the Reagan Administration.[32]

The subcommittee hearings then ran the gamut of issues from the requirement for clear objectives for public transportation, the potential for transit in helping to save energy, the severe need for capital after many decades of capital malnutrition, to ways of bringing costs under control. Comments on why transit had not performed well, labor problems, and the difficulties of increasing productivity were themes heard over and over again in the testimony.[33]

A summary of all the hearings, reports, statements, positions, news items, and pronouncements covers a 180-degree course. Public financial support of transit—regardless of the level of government—was expensive, productivity had been falling, and transit had not achieved many of the things hoped for. Yet transit was essential—or at least essential enough to warrant federal capital expenditures. Transit had not achieved many of the things hoped for—downtown rejuvenation and control of pollution and fuel use, or increased safety—either because it was passe and couldn't achieve much under the best of conditions or because there had been insufficient money spent on it; which position is taken depends upon the eye and attitude of the beholder. Transit management existed in a goldfish-bowl atmosphere and was either good and doing the best it could under the circumstances, or it lacked the professionalism to do the job and consisted largely of political hacks. Labor was either overpaid and lazy, capturing the top dollar for little work, or it was struggling under difficult conditions to do its job without the resources needed. The position taken again depends upon one's vantage point.

To reiterate some earlier thoughts, it should be obvious that transit could not attain many of its hoped-for results because there was no government policy offering rational, long-range goals or objectives integrated with other policies affecting the urban fabric and urban life. The lack of real direction was true on the federal, state, and local levels. Regardless of how much was spent on transit, if there was no direction for the policy, and no supportive policy and programs in related fields, the results would always be less than satisfactory. As for the forlorn hope of achieving worthy purposes, how could transit halt suburban sprawl, for instance, in a community innocent of a firm policy to halt sprawl?

Much of the debate and discussion regarding transit since 1980 revolved around the operating aid program under Sections 5 and 9 of the Urban Mass Transportation Act. Opinions differed. On one hand, operating aid either sapped the initiative of management to control costs or egged labor on to demands that were easily met from the governmental trough; the moral fiber of all parties had been hopelessly rotted by evil subsidies. On the other hand, operating aid was absolutely necessary to reap the fruits of the investment in transit. Otherwise cities would collapse from traffic congestion and smog, the poor would get poorer, and the ranks of the unemployed and underemployed would grow. In all honesty, operating aid to transit, particularly in the face of the notably missing goals and objectives for a policy integrated with other related aspects of the urban fabric, can be just as rationally or irrationally justified or vilified as can a weapons system, a park, a convention center, a program to aid science education, or whatever.[34]

To sum up, what the U.S. witnessed concerning transit in the 1980s was a battle of assertions. There were positive assertions that good things would happen because of a certain policy, program, grant, or action, and there were negative assertions that nothing would happen because of a certain policy, program, grant, or action. Again, whether the results were good or bad or moving in the right or wrong direction was often more a matter in the subjective sense of the opinion-holder than one that could be objectively and positively stated. Like religion, the work of government relies upon faith.

THE CHORE FOR 1982

Reauthorizing legislation for mass transit was needed in 1982; the last authorizing legislation was passed in 1978 and ran through fiscal year 1982. Senator Richard Lugar (R-Indiana) made an effort in 1981 to write a reauthorizing bill that was, in essence, a modified administration bill—he was not successful. Congressman James Howard of New Jersey, chairman of the House Committee on Public Works and Transportation, was opposed to the 1981 reauthorization. It was Congressman Howard's strategy to hold off any work on reauthorization of mass transit until 1982, which was an election year; the general feeling of transit supporters in and out of Congress was that it would be easier to get transit legislation through on the most favorable terms during an election year. Congressman Howard also aimed at combining transit and highway legislation into another surface transportation act, such as the one passed in 1978. There was hope of developing a combined highway and transit effort, because both modes would be dependent upon the same piece of legislation and both would work for its passage. Without such a combination, supporters felt that the transit programs would be extremely vulnerable.[35]

To give some perspective to the 1982 legislative battle, there were some serious concerns affecting transit and other legislation in 1982. A major factor was the sad plight of the U.S. economy which, despite the high hopes of the Reagan administration, continued to worsen in 1981 and through the middle of 1982. Unemployment replaced inflation as a matter of national concern as industrial production slowed down and hundreds of thousands of workers were laid off.[36]

Also causing anxiety were the towering federal deficits projected because of the slowdown in the economy, which reduced the revenue from taxes, and the massive tax cuts which the administration and Congress had put through in the summer of 1981. Military spending was increased by the Reagan administration in the face of these projected reductions in income, and it was estimated in the first part of 1982 that the federal deficit for fiscal 1982 would be well in excess of $100 billion.[37]

Interest rates remained relatively high in 1981, falling only very slowly beginning in August. This reflected the business community's concern over the inflationary impact of increased defense spending as well as the expected borrowing by the U.S. Treasury to finance the biggest federal deficit in history. The business community also fretted about the deterioration of the U.S. infrastructure and the negative impact that it would eventually have on U.S. productivity. Many people shared enormous distress over declines in the basic services that government provides (e.g. water supply, sewers, garbage collection, and transit) and upon which the private sector of the economy depends.[38]

An imponderable in the proposed reduction in federal transit aid was the role of state and local government. Absorbing federal cutbacks in transit and other programs would not be easy for these levels of government under the best conditions. Worse luck, in many cases state and local coffers were being drained by some of the federal cutbacks and by the decline in their economies. Tax revenues were falling significantly in some jurisdictions because of the rise in unemployment. Worrisome to state and local government (and to any citizen with a sense of economic history) was that for the first time in fifty years the federal government would not undertake counter-cyclical action to help overcome the recession that grew increasingly serious toward the end of 1981 and at the beginning of 1982. From another viewpoint, one could hold that the massive federal deficits supported by borrowing were the Reagan administration's version of the supposed Democratic dictum of "tax and spend." Both policies have Keynesian implications.

As a result, transit advocates questioned just how much support would be given by state and local government to transit. If, as noted earlier, transit was still not seen as a vital service to many communities, particularly smaller ones, the support was apt to be sparse. Because most states had no particular goals or objectives for transit, when transit aid was provided it was generally a match to federal programs. In many places there was little institutionalization of transit and in smaller communities there was little understanding of the role that transit might play in improving the quality of life. None of this was a sign that in places other than the largest cities, or in states with large urban concentrations, there would be transit support matching the losses from the federal cutbacks.[39]

Transit was also plagued with the need to overcome its image of decline. The long, secular decrease in transit ridership that started in 1923 finally reversed itself in 1972-73 and ridership had generally increased modestly but steadily in the years since it bottomed out. But ridership totals were down rather seriously in 1981. This should not have amazed anyone; fares were increased substantially in many places, both as a reaction to the threat of substantial cuts in federal funding and in recognition of the continuing burden of inflation. Unemployment was also a factor. Work-related trips were the backbone of transit patronage, and where there was massive unemployment many people had nowhere to ride to.

Publicly and politically, the drop-off in transit ridership was more serious than it at first appeared. Ridership is the one sure and universally understandable sign of success or failure in public transit. Without continuing increases in ridership going for it, critics of transit are given the ammunition to shoot down transit aid with the argument that declining patronage is evidence that transit is not needed.

The spring of 1982 was the season for the introduction of new legislation for transit. All parties were keeping in mind that the transit authorization ran out at the end of September and that the Reagan administration was pledged not only to reduce the amount of federal money spent on transit but also to eliminate operating aid. The transit industry, represented by the American Public Transit Association, obviously wanted to retain a large measure of the then-existing Urban Mass Transportation Act of 1964, as amended. However, the APTA position remained flexible enough to salvage as much as possible in the compromise that it felt and hoped would eventually be struck. Speaking for the industry, APTA president Leonard Ronis testified to the transportation subcommittee of the House Appropriations Committee that federal operating assistance should be retained, that the discretionary capital grant program be continued, that Secretary of Transportation Lewis's five-cent increase in the federal gas tax should be approved (Lewis had proposed that one cent of the increased user charge might go to transit; this would yield about $1.1 billion), and that the safe harbor leasing provision for transit be continued.[40]

April saw the introduction of the first of several pieces of transit legislation. Senator Lugar introduced the Transit Assistance Act of 1982, S.2367, on April 12 for the administration; this was a modification of draft legislation that had been circulated in February. In the bill, a new Section 9 was prepared to take the place of Section 5 and would provide the formulatory basis for distributing UMTA capital funds by means of block grants. The proposed legislation called for the elimination of operating aid for transit and a new capital formula (with 75 percent federal and 25 percent local funding) allocating funds for urbanized areas in sums equal to an urbanized area's share of the total national nonfederal mass transportation revenues. The local funds embraced in the measure included: income from passenger fares; general transportation revenues from sources such as special fares, school bus services, charter service, freight movement, and auxiliary transportation revenues; non-transportation revenues; direct taxes levied for transit; state and local cash grants and reimbursements; special fare assistance provided by state and local governments; and subsidies from other sources of revenue.

Under the administration bill, operating aid would be cut 38 percent in fiscal years 1983 and 1984 and totally eliminated in fiscal 1985. Fifty percent of the Section 5 formula funds (from which operating aid could be derived) was to be distributed on the basis of the 1970 census figures for population and population density; the remainder of the money would be distributed on the basis of the 1980 census. In both cases population and population density were to be the factors used. The Section 18 program that had provided formula aid to small cities (population under 50,000) and nonurbanized areas would be supplanted by a new Section 21 that would authorize $300 million in funds for capital purposes only from fiscal 1983 through fiscal 1986; no operating aid was to be available for small cities or nonurbanized areas. Other features of the legislative proposal were the elimination of the federal requirement for half fare during off-peak hours for elderly and handicapped persons, curtailed public hearing requirements when Section 5 recipients planned service changes. It also allowed the secretary of transportation to establish a benchmark price for buses that would represent the maximum federal share for bus purchases.[41]

Also under the administration proposal, money under Section 9 would be available for planning, acquisition, construction, deployment of innovative demonstration results, and improvement of facilities and equipment, including the direct cost of spare parts in some situations. There would be no money available under Section 9 for new rail transit starts or extensions of existing systems.[42]

Many Republicans, especially those with constituencies in states with large urban populations, were not in total agreement with the proposals of the Reagan administration. On April 15, Senator Alfonse D'Amato of New York introduced S.2377, which called for continuation of operating aid. The Section 3 capital portion of the Urban Mass Transportation Act of 1964, as amended, would be divided into both a discretionary program (which had been the way all Section 3 money had been handled since 1964) and a capital formula grant program for urbanized areas of population over 200,000. The D'Amato proposal was intended to distribute authorized funds on the basis of 25.5 percent for discretionary grants; 68 percent for the new Section 3 formula program; 5 percent for a new Section 3 formula grant program for urbanized areas with population less than 200,000, and 2.5 percent for the Section 18 rural and small urban program.[43]

The Section 3 formula program for large-city bus grants would take 65 percent of the money distributed, using a formula based 50 percent on bus revenue miles and 50 percent on population and population density. Rail grants would get the remaining 35 percent of the money and the funds would be distributed on a formula based 30 percent on rail route miles and 70 percent on rail revenue vehicle miles.

The formula grant portion of Section 9 would fund capital on an 80 percent federal–20 percent local basis, and operating aid on a fifty-fifty basis, with no transit property receiving more than was allocated by UMTA in fiscal year 1982. The Section 3 capital discretionary funding would split the money on a 70 percent federal and 30 percent local basis.[44]

Legislative activity was not confined to the Senate. The surface transportation subcommittee of the House Public Works and Transportation Committee drafted H.R. 6211, the "Federal Public Transportation Act of 1982," which was Title III of the "Surface Transportation Assistance Act of 1982." This was made public, but not introduced, on April 23. The committee's chairman, Congressman James Howard of New Jersey, had kept his promise of 1981 to join the highway and transit legislation together in one bill, a move that was eventually to prove highly beneficial to the progress of the transit legislation. At the same time, the proposal of Secretary of Transportation Lewis for an addition to the federal gas tax was making the rounds in Washington; a portion of the proceeds (one penny) of this new money was to be set aside—it was assumed that the penny would yield about $1 billion annually for transit. The House legislative draft for H.R. 6211 assumed that there would be a five-cent per gallon increase in the federal gas tax to help fund both the highway and transit portions of the Surface Transportation Act of 1982.

The House bill also contained a discretionary Section 3 element. It called for continuing federal funding of 80 percent of the project, but it proposed considerably more money than the other bills introduced at the time. All of the bills contained a four-year authorization, with the administration bill S.2367 set at a total of $827 million; the D'Amato bill S.2377 at $3.639 billion; and the House bill H.R. 6211 at $4.024 billion.

The urban formula grants in H.R. 6211, as in the administration bill, would be included in a new Section 9, with funds earmarked each fiscal year for areas above and below the 200,000 population mark. Considerably higher levels of funding than in either the administration's or the D'Amato bill were to be authorized in the House proposal. A complex formula, including such elements as population and population density, bus revenue vehicle miles, fixed guideway revenue vehicle miles, fixed guideway route miles, and an element involving operating costs as a part of the formula, was to be used to distribute funds to places with population over 200,000. Money for areas with populations from 50,000 to 200,000 was to be distributed half on the basis of population and half on the basis of population density; this money was to be used either for construction or operating assistance, with a spending cap imposed based on the fiscal 1982 apportionment for operating assistance. The Section 18 nonurbanized area formula program was to continue with funding increasing gradually from $82 million to $96 million over four fiscal years; this was slightly less than the D'Amato proposal and a fair amount more than was proposed by the administration. The House bill changed the definition of fixed guideway to include streetcar and trolleybus; there was no provision on this point in the administration bill, while the D'Amato proposal added catenary (overhead wire) systems and systems usable by other forms of transportation.[45]

The Senate and House subcommittees overseeing transit legislation began their hearings at the end of April. These events were an ideal way to float ideas and to send up some trial balloons. At one of the hearings, Secretary Lewis commented that he could not support any legislative compromise that provided operating assistance at a level higher than that proposed in the administration bill; the major reason for Lewis's position was an expected veto by President Reagan of such legislation. In the House, UMTA Administrator Teele spoke in favor of the block grant provision under the proposed new Section 9 that would be the mechanism to distribute most of the capital funds in one grant to each urbanized area rather than project-by-project grants. However, Mr. Teele did not think the cap on operating assistance, with strict guidelines to use the funds for maintenance purposes only, would gain presidential approval. At the same time, Republican Senator D'Amato and Republican Congressman Bud Shuster of Pennsylvania debated the wisdom of the administration's desired phasing out of operating assistance.[46]

On May 6, another transit authorization bill was introduced into the Senate. Senator Alan J. Dixon of Illinois, stating that "I believe there is a continuing need, therefore, for substantial Federal funding unless we want to return to the pre-1964 era of deterioration, of bankruptcy, of failure," introduced S.2502, the "Federal Public Transportation Act of 1982." Senator Dixon proposed higher levels of federal funding than did the administration bill or that of Senator D'Amato but not as high as the House bill. S.2502, like the D'Amato and House bills, continued operating aid, retaining the Section 5 designation. The fiscal 1982 funding for operating aid was proposed as a cap; however, for new urbanized areas only 50 percent of the apportionment could be used for operating purposes. For the Section 18 nonurbanized area formula program, the funds were to be made available for two years after the fiscal year in which they were apportioned.[47]

With all the legislative proposals afloat to occupy time and thought, other issues also occupied the attention of the transit industry as it busied itself presenting its case before the various relevant committees and subcommittees of Congress. For example, an oil import fee was considered by the Senate Budget Committee; with a fee of five dollars per barrel on imported crude oil, the tax could yield $15 billion per year in revenues to help offset the expected federal budget deficit, but it was considered inflationary—and inflation remained a serious concern at the time—because it would raise the price at the fuel pump by 10 to 12 cents per gallon. The Senate Finance Committee and the House Ways and Means Committee were considering modification of the safe harbor leasing provisions of the 1981 tax law, which permitted transit authorities to sell depreciation rights on the locally funded share of transit vehicles. Another issue that surfaced was highway spending, to help create jobs at a time of the highest percentage of unemployment since the Great Depression.[48]

On May 17, the House Committee on Public Works and Transportation issued its report on the Surface Transportation Assistance Act of 1982, H.R. 6211. The report stressed the importance of the five-cent per gallon increase in the federal fuel tax as a means of supplying funds for both transit and highways, with one cent per gallon dedicated to transit through a public transportation trust fund. The federal transit program authorization would be extended for four years, and the block grant concept would be introduced. Twenty-five percent of each year's authorization would be available under the new public transportation trust fund on the basis of a contract authority provision to fund discretionary capital projects; the remaining 75 percent, available for both capital and operation costs, would be subject to the regular appropriation process.

A compromise yielded a mark for the distribution of the money as follows: 88.34 percent to communities of population over 200,000; 8.73 percent to communities with 50,000 to 200,000; and 2.93 percent to nonurbanized areas and communities under 50,000. The Section 9 block grant provision was touted as providing the benefits of greater simplicity, enhanced predictability in funding, and greater flexibility for state and local government. Reflecting the report of the oversight subcommittee and others, the committee report also stressed the need for maintenance and included language giving the secretary of transportation the power to review the maintenance capability of transit authorities before approving discretionary capital grants. Incentive was given to Section 9 recipients to use operating funds for capital expenses. Construction projects paid for with the funds available for maintenance and operating purposes ranged from 80 to 95 percent federal money. Ninety percent federal funding with Section 3 capital money would be available if all operating and maintenance funds were used for construction purposes. If, in any fiscal year, more than half but less than the total amount of money available for maintenance and operating expenses was used for construction, the federal share of Section 9 money for capital purposes would be increased to 85 percent.[49]

Ever since coming to office, the position of the Reagan administration in the area of transit had been to support continued federal funding for capital improvements; to oppose new rail starts (at least until after the economy had become buoyant again); and to phase out operating aid. Of the four bills that were up for consideration in May, only the administration's own bill fit the desired goals. The D'Amato and Dixon bills in the Senate and the House bill all favored much higher levels of funding than the administration bill, and the other three all provided for continuation of operating aid in one form or another. Sensing correctly that there was little sympathy in Congress for eliminating operating aid for transit, the Reagan administration showed some flexibility on the issue of operating aid, as revealed in an address by UMTA Administrator Arthur Teele. Speaking to the Eastern Conference of the American Public Transit Association in Nashville, Tennessee (in mid-May), Teele made it clear that compromise on the operating aid issue was possible; the main point was that some move in the direction of reducing operating aid, however nominal the reduction, would be acceptable to the administration.[50]

The May 15 deadline for the first concurrent budget resolution—as required by the Congressional Budget Act—was reached with mixed results for the pending transit legislation. The House reported H.R. 6211 on May 12. A key factor in this bill was the adoption of Representative Bud Shuster's amendments to increase the percentage of Section 9 block grant money to communities with population between 50,000 and 200,000 and a cut in the percentage to those places above 200,000. For example, for fiscal year 1983, the committee draft had specified $2.458 billion for large urban areas and $243 million for smaller ones. However, the transit industry's point that small urban places were more dependent upon operating aid than were large urban places had clearly made an impression on the members of the House Committee on Public Works and Transportation. The Senate Committee on Banking, Housing, and Urban Affairs reported an authorization bill with $1.449 billion for Section 3 discretionary capital, $1.365 billion for Section 5 urban formula money, $68.5 million for Section 18 nonurbanized formula funds, and $51.6 million for Section 6 research funds. The Senate committee could not resolve the differences between the administration bill (S.2367), the D'Amato bill (S.2377), and the Dixon bill (S.2505).[51]

At the time of the first budget resolution, then, the Senate and House had a level of $22.3 billion for all transportation purposes and $3.726 billion for transit. The level of transit funding for fiscal year 1983 in H.R. 6211 was $3.71 billion.[52]

Sensing that it was a good time for action, at this point the American Public Transit Association advised its members to meet with their senators and representatives during the Memorial Day recess of Congress and urge that there be no cuts in transit aid below the 1982 fiscal year levels; that there be an adequate discretionary capital grant program; and that federal operating assistance continue. Even though President Reagan was still opposed to Secretary Lewis's proposal for a five-cent gas tax, with one cent of that for transit, APTA urged its members to push for increased user fees for highways. The latter point made it clear that the transit-highway coalition was still working together to get a bill, essentially H.R. 6211, successfully passed.[53]

At the same time, APTA reminded members of Congress of the capital needs for the coming ten years in the transit industry, based on an APTA survey. The average annual needs were estimated as follows: new bus purchases, $846 million; modernization or replacement of bus facilities, $245 million; modernization of fixed-rail facilities, $1.35 billion; modernization and replacement of rail rolling stock, $513 million; planned rail extensions, $428 million; completion of new rail systems, $835 million; and new rail starts and automated guideway transit systems, $895 million. The total capital need for the decade was pegged at $50 billion. The gap between the industry projections and federal funding was significant. The projected need in 1982 for capital was $5.3 billion, but federal funding was set at $3.1 billion. For fiscal year 1983 the industry estimated capital needs at $5.6 billion, but the legislative proposals ranged from only $2.5 billion in the administration bill (S.2367) to $3.6 billion in the House bill (H.R. 6211).[54]

Despite pressure from the transit industry, by June 1982 the legislative process appeared to be on hold. Congress, anxious to get the budgets passed for fiscal year 1983 and doubly anxious to get out of Washington to campaign in the 1982 election (which, as in any federal election, would involve one-third of the Senate members, and all members of the House), directed its attention away from transit legislation and other legislative activities that appeared to be deadlocked. For the remainder of the summer months there were predictions from various observers of the transit scene that the best that could be expected was a one-year authorization bill for transit with a continuation of the fiscal 1982 federal funding levels. To this end, Senator Jake Garn (R-Utah) had introduced S.2606, which would authorize a one-year extension of the transit programs that would keep spending at the 1982 levels. As June went on, speculation increased that there would be no new transit authorization (the authorization ran out September 30) and that continued transit funding would be provided by an appropriations act. Another real possibility was that there would be no new authorization or appropriations legislation; funding for transit would be provided through a continuing resolution mechanism.[55]

In July, citing the congressional recesses coming up (Labor Day and the election), APTA predicted the likelihood for a lame-duck session of Congress after the election. APTA continued to urge its members to press for four-year authorizing legislation, with an increase in highway user fees to help pay for it. Stress was also put on the continuation of operating assistance and the use of the distribution scheme forwarded in the D'Amato bill (S.2377) and the House bill (H.R. 6211), with no cuts in transit funding below that of fiscal 1982. In the subcommittee on transportation of the House Appropriations Committee, the Department of Transportation Appropriations Bill was marked up, with $3.4 billion for transit.[56]

The possibility of a four-year transit bill waned as August proceeded. As a case in point, the House Public Works and Transportation Committee approved a one-year extension of the transit and highway programs because it believed a four-year extension was simply not feasible. The bill, H.R. 6965, was essentially an amendment to H.R. 6211. It proposed that no transit agency receive less Section 5 formula grant money in fiscal 1983 than it had in fiscal 1982. The funding level was set at $3.145 billion.[57]

Congress was in recess from August 10 until September 7. This month-long Labor Day recess gave members of the House an opportunity to run for re-election and, most importantly, to get important feedback from their constituents. Considering the level of unemployment in the country and the bad news about the economy in general, it can be assumed that members of Congress got an earful of comment. Senators, whether up for election or not, were similarly exposed to the electorate. One thing was clear: unemployment was a serious issue in the nation, and members of Congress were highly sensitized to this fact in late summer 1982. Highway and transit construction projects, even though it would take years for the projects to get underway, would give the electorate signs that Congress was doing something. Yet the future of the combined highway transit legislation remained bleak, as there was less than a month remaining in the authorization for either transit or highway funding as the lawmakers returned to Capitol Hill.

The legislative timetable after the Labor Day recess was a tight one. The one-year version of H.R. 6211 was to go to the floor of the House on September 13, contingent upon the Ways and Means Committee recommending an extension of the Highway Trust Fund. The transportation appropriations bill, H.R. 7019, was ready for House action in the second week of September, with $3.64 billion for transit. Congress had passed H.R. 4961, the $98.3 billion tax increase law, before the recess, and the president signed it; this provided for a special extension of the safe harbor leasing for mass transit as long as the vehicles were in service by January 1, 1988. On the sad side of events, Congressman Adam Benjamin, Jr., of the first district of Indiana, chairman of the critical transportation appropriation subcommittee and a good friend of transit, died suddenly of a heart attack over the Labor Day weekend. This was definitely both sad and bad news for the transit industry.[58]

As the deadline of September 30 neared for the end of the authorization for transit legislation, the House Rules Committee declined permission to let the House vote on H.R. 6211, thus killing all chances for new authorizing legislation within the stipulated time period. On the appropriations side, the Senate Appropriations Committee approved $3.45 billion for transit in fiscal 1983, or $192 million less than the House proposal. As noted earlier, both the House and Senate levels were higher than desired by the administration. With portent of things to come, on September 22, the House passed the continuing resolution bill, H.J. Res. 599, to provide funds from October 1 until December 15—or until specific appropriations bills had been passed. This action assured a lame-duck session after the November election. Under the continuing resolution, the level of funding for transit would be at the fiscal 1982 level or that of the House or Senate appropriations bills for 1983, whichever was lowest. The House and Senate over-rode President Reagan's veto of the fiscal 1982 supplemental appropriation (H.R. 6863), which included $46 million extra for transit.[59]

There was little activity on the congressional transit front between the end of September and the election of November 2. That election, while certainly not an outright repudiation of the policies of the Reagan administration, gave the president little to cheer about. The American public liked Ronald Reagan but did not like all of the things he wanted government to do or not do. With unemployment at an all time post-war high, the country faced somber times ahead as winter approached. Jobs, and things that government could do to help provide jobs, became the issue as Congress reconvened after the election for the lame-duck session.

In the meantime, there was some action within the administration. Secretary of Transportation Lewis redoubled his efforts to gain the five-cent gasoline tax increase. He took his case to President Reagan once again and this time was successful in gaining the president's support. Reagan had consistently opposed a gasoline tax increase as he had opposed all tax increases; just as consistently the president was in favor of user charges; therefore, Ronald Reagan could support the legislation. The language was interesting; although not initially mooted as a piece of legislation that would increase jobs, it was now discussed by the president as a jobs bill, and the five-cent fuel tax increase was dubbed a user charge, not a tax increase.[60]

Congress reconvened on November 29 for the lame-duck session. The Senate had to act on its transportation appropriations bill (S.2914); the House had passed its bill (H.R. 7019) on September 21. There was a strong chance of a presidential veto because the bills, and presumably what would emerge from the conference committee, bore higher price tags than the president wanted, but his support for the five-cent gas tax revived hope in the possibility of a four-year authorization bill, H.R. 6211.[61]

Congress swung into lame-duck action. On November 29, as the session took up, Senator Howard Baker, the majority leader, introduced the gas tax legislation. To help move the process along, on December 1 Senators Richard Lugar and Alfonse D'Amato offered an amendment to the gas tax bill. The Lugar-D'Amato bill (S.3072) had a base funding level for transit of $3.13 billion per year for three years as compared with the administration's bill, which was a little over $2 billion. The Lugar-D'Amato bill called for a one-year reduction in operating aid that only affected fiscal year 1983; it contained a 20 percent cut for systems serving populations of 1 million; a 10 percent cut for places with populations between 200,000 and 1 million; and a 5 percent reduction for cities of less than 200,000. Moreover, the bill would permit new rail starts using the money derived from the gas tax. A funding formula was included based on a revenue match, which would give more federal aid to properties that increased their fares.[62]

As far as the appropriation for transportation and transit was concerned, the activity on that front was somewhat obscured by the dramatics associated with the passage of H.R. 6211. In the late-night December 17 session, Congress approved the transportation appropriation bill, which contained $3.2 billion for transit commencing on October 1, 1982. President Reagan signed the appropriations bill on December 18. In the appropriation, $1.606 billion was approved for the discretionary Section 3 account, and $1.2 billion for Section 5 formula grants. Allocating the money was accomplished by a compromise in which 75 percent of the 1980 population and 25 percent of the 1970 population was to be used as the basis for Section 5 distribution. For the Section 18 non-urbanized area appropriation, the Congress agreed on $68.5 million. For administration, research, and development purposes, $86 million was appropriated.[63]

At 1:00 A.M. on December 17, 1982, the House passed H.R. 6211 and later on the same day passed the five-cent gas tax legislation—but a threat arose. The progress on the highway and transit bill was slowed in the Senate by a filibuster launched against the gas tax by Senators Jesse Helms and John East of North Carolina, Gordon Humphrey of New Hampshire, and Don Nickles of Oklahoma. Under the leadership of Majority Leader Howard Baker, the filibuster was broken and the Senate passed its version of the bill on December 20. With the bright promise of Christmas ahead, the results of the conference committee compromise of the House and Senate bills was passed by the House on December 21. Another filibuster by the same four senators delayed action by the Senate on the bill on December 21 and 22; a cloture vote of 81-5 put an end to the filibuster on the morning of December 23. The Senate then adopted final passage of H.R. 6211 on December 23 and, after a long, hard legislative road, a new transit authorization was finally in place.[64] It was a fine Christmas gift for the transit industry.

WHAT HAD CONGRESS WROUGHT?

The complex new transit legislation of Christmastide 1982 made major changes in the federal program of aid. The authorization was for four years. For fiscal year 1983 the Urban Mass Transportation Act of 1964, as amended, was funded under the fiscal 1983 DOT Appropriations Act. Beginning at the start of the 1984 fiscal year, on October 1, 1983, the new Section 9 block grant formula program was implemented. Both capital and operating aid were eligible expenses under Section 9, although operating aid was cut by about 16 percent from what prevailed prior to the new legislation. The funding source for the Section 3 discretionary funds was the extra one cent on the gas tax for transit, which was expected at the time to yield approximately $1.1 billion a year. In fiscal 1983 only, the gas tax money, which would not be flowing in until the additional nickel tax went into effect on April 1, 1983, was expected to be about $779 million; the money was to be distributed on a slightly modified version of the new Section 9 formula for capital projects.

Under the new law, the funding of the Section 3 projects continued under the terms of the 1983 fiscal year DOT Appropriations Act. Effective at the date of enactment of the new law, the federal share of capital aid dropped from 80 percent to 75 percent. The federal share for existing letters of intent and full-funding contracts remained the same. With an eye toward improving maintenance of federally aided capital projects, the recipients had to certify that they had the capability to maintain equipment; this clause was also effective on the date of enactment. With an eye toward the job-creating potential of transit capital projects, labor-intensive projects that could be started quickly were to be emphasized.

Section 5 formula programs would continue through fiscal 1983 under the terms of the DOT Appropriations Act, but there were to be no new Section 5 authorizations. Money under Section 5, including the fiscal 1983 sums, would remain available under the terms of Section 5 until September 30, 1985; after that time any unobligated funds were to be added to the Section 9 funds. In the effort to reduce the amount of federal money used for operating purposes, a cap was placed on operating aid. Urbanized areas with a population over one million could apply an amount equal to 80 percent of the fiscal 1982 appropriation to operating assistance. Urbanized areas between 200,000 and one million in population could apply 90 percent of the fiscal 1982 appropriation to operating assistance. Urbanized areas ranging in size from 50,000 to 200,000 were able to apply an amount equal to 95 percent of the fiscal 1982 appropriation to operating aid. Urbanized areas could also use part of their Tier IV (bus replacement funds under Section 5) to bring operating assistance up to the levels indicated above. Whenever a fund recipient transferred capital account money to operating aid, two-thirds of the amount transferred would go to the recipient and one-third was to be available to the secretary of transportation to make discretionary grants; in short, it was a three-for-two trade. This was expected to be useful to many small and medium transit properties that would find themselves with more federal capital money than they could hope to use intelligently; it turned out to be a popular option.

The Section 9 block grant program was the major innovation in the 1982 act. Of the money available for Section 9, 88.43 percent was earmarked for population areas with over 200,000; 8.64 percent to areas of 50,000 to 200,000 (on a distribution formula based one-half on population and one-half on population density); and 2.93 percent was to go to the nonurbanized areas covered under Section 18.

As might be expected from the compromise, the formula for dividing the money to population areas over 200,000 is complex. Essentially, two-thirds was for the bus tier, which was based one-half on bus revenue vehicle miles, one-quarter on population, and one-quarter on population density; and one-third went to the rail tier, based 60 percent on revenue vehicle miles and 40 percent on route miles.

Beginning with fiscal year 1984, there was an incentive tier affecting both bus and rail and based on vehicle and passenger miles per dollar of operating cost. The federal share of Section 9 money was 80 percent for capital projects and 50 percent for operating projects. As it was under Section 5, the Section 9 money went directly to designated recipients in urbanized areas with a population over 200,000 and to the governors of states having places with populations under 200,000. The Section 9 money was available for three years following the year of initial apportionment and was then available for reapportionment. Along the same lines as the discussion of Section 5 above, Section 9 expenditures were limited to a percentage of fiscal 1982 appropriation; this sum was 80 percent for places with population over one million, 90 percent for places between 200,000 and one million, and 95 percent for places under 200,000.

For those places affected by the Section 18 program, 2.93 percent of the Mass Transit Account funds (that is, the money yielded by the one cent for transit that was part of the five-cent increase in the fuel tax) was available for Section 18 in addition to the amounts in the fiscal 1983 DOT Appropriations Act. This shifted in fiscal years 1984 to 1986, when 2.93 percent per year of the Section 9 authorization was available for nonurbanized places. The Section 18 money was available for only two years after apportionment (instead of three years as was previously the case), after which time the Section 18 money apportioned to a state was to be reapportioned among the other states. This was an effort to cope with the problem in which some states fully obligate the Section 18 funds quickly while others dawdle. Governors are given additional flexibility under the new law: Section 18 funds may be transferred to urbanized areas with populations under 200,000 and vice versa. Governors may also transfer Section 9 money from urbanized areas with populations under 200,000 to areas of 300,000 or less, after consultation with the area from which the money is transferred. Designated recipients in urbanized areas of over 200,000 may transfer all or a portion of the apportionment they receive to the governor, who may distribute it to any urbanized area regardless of size.

Recognizing the concern over foreign competition, a new "Buy American" provision was included in the law. With four exceptions, 100 percent of the steel, cement, and manufactured products were required to be American-made. The exceptions were: non-availability from American sources, public-interest waivers, and a 25 percent price differentiation for everything except rolling stock, where the differential was 10 percent. The fourth exception involved rolling stock, which included train control, communications, and transit power equipment; up to 50 percent of these may be foreign with final assembly in the U.S.[65]

PERSPECTIVE

What perspective did the 1982 Act, and the events that led up to it, provide for better understanding of the status of federal mass transit policy in the Age of Reagan? In retrospect, the 1970s were truly heady days for the federal transit programs, when each amendment to the Urban Mass Transportation Act of 1964 added to the scope of the program and also usually added substantial amounts of federal money to transit coffers. In broad terms, the best the transit industry might have looked forward to at that point in the 1980s was a holding action in terms of federal funds and programs. The final two years leading to the Surface Transportation Act of 1982 were really a down-to-the-wire effort to preserve at least some of the gains of the past, including the retention of the operating-aid provisions in the face of an administration hostile to the program. The federal transit money available for fiscal 1983 was $2 billion less than the sums discussed for the federal transit program in the last year of the Carter administration.

The 1982 Act authorized $779 million from the Mass Transit Account of the Highway Trust Fund for fiscal 1983 to be added to the $3.2 billion from the general fund. For fiscal 1984, $1.25 billion was authorized from the Mass Transit Account and $2.75 billion from the general fund; in fiscal 1985, $1.1 billion from the Mass Transit Account and $2.95 billion from the general fund; and in fiscal 1986 the authorization called for $1.1 billion from the Mass Transit Account and $3.05 billion from the general fund. This meant essentially flat funding authorized for four years.[66]

The Reagan administration was clearly successful in cutting down on the amount of money and ending the increase in federal funds going to transit, at least compared to past trends and the Carter administration proposals. However, the amount of federal transit funds was at least $1 billion higher each year of the four-year authorization under the 1982 Act than under the administration's original proposals. Considering what else the administration cut, the transit industry was probably lucky. Although diminished significantly, the transit interests managed to retain operating aid, and the new Section 9 block grant provision was expected to make the whole process work more smoothly.

The Mass Transit Account of the Highway Trust Fund finally established the long-coveted guaranteed source of money for transit, going all the way back to the efforts of Secretary of Transportation John Volpe in the late 1960s and early 1970s. The guaranteed source of funding was a major victory for the transit industry. New rail starts, which the administration wanted eliminated until the economy recovered, continued. This provided a pleasing prospect for cities that were innocent of rail transit but seriously intent on such construction.

Notwithstanding the five-cent increase in the fuel tax and the Mass Transit Account in the Highway Trust Fund, the amounts of money for capital purposes were woefully small when recollecting the transit industry's estimate of capital needs of about $5 billion per year. Likewise, the extra money for highways, although certainly useful, was a pittance. Despite the strong efforts of the Reagan administration, Congress continued to support transit. Given the expected budget deficit for the remaining years of the Reagan administration, not much more could reasonably be expected.

The 1982 Act had created a major change in federal policy. Before its passage, about two-thirds of federal transit money was discretionary and one-third was non-discretionary. The transit legislation of 1982 shifted this proportion so that two-thirds of the federal money was apportioned by formula and only one-third was discretionary. This was very helpful, because in theory it meant that federal aid would be much more reliable than it had been in the past. It was easier for transit properties to plan ahead because of the certainty of funding. In practice, there was much delay in the release of the federal money, and the industry was highly frustrated in trying to get what was promised. Moreover, it was extremely difficult to get the Section 3 discretionary funds approved and released.

The federal mass transit program was actually no closer to attaining solid, workable, long-term goals and objectives with the passage of the 1982 Act than it had been before. As with all past legislation, the new Act was nothing more than a compromise—only this time the compromise was more complex than usual. Because the federal transit programs lacked discernible purpose, a real measure of success remained elusive.[67]

The 1982 transit legislation was far better than any observer of transit or anyone in the transit industry had a right to expect, given the opposition of the president and of the Office of Management and Budget to providing aid to transit. Transit may have not reached the heavenly gates, but it did not fall from grace, a fall that had seemed in the cards at the start of 1982.

The reason for transit's success was the lobbying effort for the transit bill and the breadth of that lobbying effort. The transit industry worked very hard to get the word out to its members on when to contact members of the House and Senate, and transit lobbyists were very active on Capitol Hill.

One interesting idea that was overcome by the final vote was the notion that there were only 18 senators who would strongly support mass transportation. This was based on the assumption that there were only nine states in which transit was really of vital importance. The importance of the Section 18 program in spreading transit benefits broadly out to the grass roots meant that there were transit supporters among the constituents of virtually every senator. The support in the Senate was very solid throughout and it became clear that senators were more thoughtful about transit issues and lent their support, whether or not there was a large transit constituency within the border of their states.

It is also quite clear that by linking transit and highways a strong coalition was formed; this is particularly true in the passage of the five-cent gasoline tax. The support of senators and representatives from areas in which transit was important was needed to pass the fuel tax, the benefits of which would sift down to places of all sizes in all of the states. From the transit perspective, Congressman Howard did the right thing in marrying the highway and transit bills. It was probably also a stroke of wisdom on his part to hold off on an authorization bill until 1982, when everyone's feet could be held to the fire.

Secretary of Transportation Drew Lewis deserves much credit in awakening the public interest to the issue of America's decaying infrastructure, of which highways and transit played a large part. He is to be conceded good marks for his work in convincing President Reagan that the highway gas tax and the other aspects of the user charge increase were really necessary to begin to rebuild the nation's highways and transit systems.

The new legislation bought some time for the transit industry. Continuation of programs deemed important by the industry provided the opportunity to work with state and local governments to gain more support from those levels of government.[68]

12.

The Urban Mass Transportation Act at 20

There was little celebrating over the twentieth anniversary of the Urban Mass Transportation Act of 1964—perhaps the reason was that there was not much over which to shout huzzahs. The transit community had hoped that 1984 would be a year for some modest tinkering and improvement in the program of federal aid. Instead, much of what was felt to be essential was maintained by Congress through a continuing resolution; possibly the worst thing to happen was the loss of the flexibility under a provision of the 1982 transit legislation that allowed a transit property to trade three dollars of capital aid for two dollars of operating aid.

As with all anniversaries, there were grim reminders of mortality. As 1984 ended, the federal mass transit program was once more under the threat of being totally eliminated. That it did not have much to show after twenty years was one conclusion that might have been drawn; another was that the transit community had been fortunate to retain the majority of its past gains in the face of the determination of the Reagan administration to gut the program. The Reagan administration worked against a bigger and better federal transit aid program. Despite a letter from UMTA of fulsome "we did it together"[1] praise for transit improvements as a joint effort between the federal government and local transit agencies, the industry had the melancholy burden of living with an administration hostile to transit.

After passage of the 1982 legislation, the transit industry was busy working to make sure that the gains that it had made through the 1964 Act and its subsequent amendments were not too seriously eroded by the hostile attacks of the administration. Those with long memories felt the irony of having made substantial progress from the difficult period of the late 1950s, to becoming the fastest-growing federal program of the 1970s, to being disparaged and slated for elimination in the 1980s. The transit industry never lacked for critics during this time; considering that national and local transportation politics had greatly favored the automobile for many years, the industry's performance, if not a wonder of the age, was better than could have been expected.[2]

From the time beginning in fiscal year 1965, the federal mass transportation program had provided more than $30 billion through over 7,000 capital and operating assistance grants. Approximately $24.5 billion was provided during the period in capital grants for vehicles and about $7 billion had been expended in operating aid. Federal funds helped purchase over 54,000 buses and almost 6,500 rail vehicles, along with 18 ferry boats, 35 peoplemover vehicles, and about 13,500 vans for transportation for the elderly and handicapped. More than $7.5 billion had been spent to modernize older rail systems of the U.S., of which about $3.2 billion was for commuter rail systems.[3]

Despite the administration's opposition, the transit industry was successful in getting favorable legislation passed with the Surface Transportation Act of 1982 (sometimes called the Surface Transportation Assistance Act) but sought to fine-tune the legislation in 1984, in particular to protect the program from threats arising from the Reagan administration's opposition to the operating-aid portion of the program. To understand what happened, it is first necessary to appreciate the background against which the transit industry worked.

THE ENVIRONMENT FOR FORGING TRANSIT LEGISLATION

The major factor affecting transit in the first four years of the 1980s was the Reagan administration and what came to be called the Reagan experiment, or the Reagan revolution. When President Ronald Reagan took office in January of 1981, he faced a nation that was plagued with high inflation, sluggish economic growth, rapidly rising federal expenditures, and a defense budget that was deemed inadequate by many observers. The nation was apparently looking for strong leadership. One might correctly speculate that the public was also looking for a successful presidency after many failed administrations in the 1960s and 1970s. In response to this situation, the new president boldly moved toward a comprehensive plan that was designed to stimulate the nation's economy, build up its defenses, and reduce the role of the federal government in the lives of Americans. To implement this plan, there were major recommendations to Congress and the public for shifts in federal regulations, tax, and budget policies. Many of the responsibilities that had been picked up by the federal government over the years were to be eliminated, reduced, or transferred to state and local governments and to the private sector.[4]

The president's philosophy and that of his advisors and his unofficial "kitchen cabinet" was very clearly one of social and economic Darwinism; this is one of the most fundamentally conservative social philosophies concerning the responsibilities of the federal government—or any other thing—for the plight of the unfortunate in American history. It reached its greatest vogue a century ago, egged on by the pronouncements of the Englishman Herbert Spencer and the American savant William Graham Sumner. The major counter to criticism on this point and the substantial cutbacks in social programs proposed by the new president was that the administration wanted to be judged not on its philosophical points but on its economic results. Eventually, it was probably the linking of

cutbacks in social service expenditure, with a promised improvement in economic performance, that sold the Reagan programs to Congress and a large
portion of the American people.[5] Certainly, President Reagan's 1984 re-election
followed in large part from the upbeat performance of the U.S. economy that
year. The American public, on an emotional level, was probably disillusioned
with a variety of federal programs that were aimed at solving problems but did
not seem to actually do so. Many of the Great Society programs of President
Lyndon Johnson suffered from this reproach.

At the heart of the Reagan program were sharp cuts in both the federal
income tax and expenditures on social programs, while at the same time outlays
for defense rose markedly. The president moved in the sincere hope that the tax
policy would significantly affect work, savings, and investment in order to improve the American economy's potential for long-term growth. It was prayed that
economic growth would be so stimulated by the tax cuts, and by the removal of
much of the regulation that increased the cost of doing business, that the deficit
would be eliminated and the increase in military spending would be easily
affordable.

Unfortunately, the main impact of the Reagan experiment had not only been
a return to a degree of prosperity and growth—especially in the later part of
1983 and through 1984—but also enormous federal deficits each year that many
economists and others felt would be a potential disaster for the United States.[6]
Despite efforts to cut federal spending for non-defense purposes, and a short rise
in the performance of the economy, the growth in the deficit became—or remained—the principal economic problem in the U.S. during the mid-1980s.

The administration took an original view on why there were problems at the
local level. It contended that the dependence of state and local governments and
organizations on the federal government for aid removed vitality from those
organizations and thus effectively hamstrung them. The Reagan administration
also contended that the federal role in various programs had distorted the priorities of local government, lessened administrative accountability, and crushed the
creative and healthy growth of institutions that were closer to the citizens than
was the distant federal establishment in Washington.[7] The word was that the
federal government would withdraw from programs and allow fewer rules and
regulations and more "freedom" to make up for the cutbacks in federal funds.
Ignored in all this was the fact that the economic resources and the problems of
the country are distributed unevenly among the states and the cities; for many
years the federal government has played an important role as a leveler. A major
function of any national government is cross-subsidization to relieve the worst
disparities of man and nature. It probably makes sense to share in the resources
of a country called the United States.

The transit program, along with many of the so-called social programs, was
potentially threatened as 1984 melded into 1985 by the steps the administration
might have eventually taken to cut the alarming deficits. In his re-election campaign, the president contended—to wild cheers—that taxes would not be raised
and, whether it was election-time fluff or not, the president steadfastly refused to

even consider a raise in taxes; in fact, the 1984 Republican platform called for passage of a balanced budget amendment to the Constitution and a return to the gold standard. In the election campaign Mr. Reagan's position was that the budget balance was supposed to be struck by the increase in federal tax receipts from real economic growth and by some cutbacks in federal spending. After the election, with the deficit continuing to balloon, the position of the administration was for sharp cuts in domestic spending. Some observers felt that, eventually, the social and economic costs of the Reagan experiment might prove to be higher than the nation wanted to pay, but there was no evidence of that in 1984.[8]

Looking more directly at the transit policy issue, by mid-1984 the guiding principles of President Reagan's policies as far as transportation was concerned may be summarized as follows:

1. Federal transportation expenditures would be financed through user charges. Only in situations where there were significant external benefits would non-users be expected to pick up a portion of the cost.
2. Transportation functions that were not national in nature should be returned to the states and to local governments.
3. The provision of transportation services by the private sector should be increased by returning transportation functions to private operators and by reducing federal regulations.
4. Federal regulations should be modified or eliminated where their costs exceed the benefits, where they restrict competition, or where they are not needed to accomplish national goals.
5. Federal transportation investments should be subjected to rigorous cost-benefit analysis in order to insure that benefits exceed costs. In the absence of a market or allocation mechanism in the private sector, the public must base its decision on this investment policy, and the analysis must include the full range of alternatives. Only the most cost-effective alternatives should be undertaken and only if the benefits exceed the costs.[9]

To this statement of philosophy adopted for transportation should be added the budget levels for highways and urban transit in the 1982-85 period as compared with those authorized by the Surface Transportation Assistance Act of 1982 (STAA 1982). The monies budgeted were considerably below those targeted by the STAA 1982,[10] and are fair evidence of the Reagan philosophy in action (see Table 12.1).[11]

It was partially as a defense against cutbacks in the money actually available in the federal transit program that the transit industry and its supporters sought new legislation in 1984. There was also serious concern over what might have been a complete shift in the federal attitude and approach, not only toward mass transportation but also toward many other activities that had become embedded in the role of the federal government in U.S. life since the New Deal days of the 1930s. Because the federal role in urban transportation, particularly in transit, had stimulated more activity by state and local government, a diminution in

Table 12.1
Comparison of Authorization and Budget for Highways
And Mass Transit

Surface Transportation Act of 1982 Authorization fixed by Fiscal Year				Federal Budget Level ($ million)			
1983	1984	1985	1986	1982 Actual	1983 Actual	1984 Estimate	1985 Estimate
Highway Program 12,714.0	13,857.2	14,595.8	15,376.1	8,532.7	13,465.5	13,509.5	14,114.0
Urban Transit Program 1,230.3	4,471.0	4,540.0	4,650.0	3,352.0	4,237.9	4,018.2	3,815.8
Total 13,944.3	18,328.2	18,135.8	20,026.1	12,064.7	17,703.4	17,527.7	17,920.

federal participation might have had a disastrous impact on transit in the long run by removing the leadership that federal funds had helped to provide. Another concern in larger urban areas was that a renaissance of the policy of one-sided federal aid to highways would only return urban areas to the unbalanced transportation plight that prevailed prior to the passage of the Urban Mass Transportation Act of 1964.[12]

The activities of the transit industry in seeking additional legislation only two years after the Surface Transportation Assistance Act of 1982 was passed took place in an environment that was very different from that of 1981 and 1982. In contrast to the nose-diving U.S. economy of 1981 and 1982, 1982-84 was a period of national economic recovery, with the economy booming along in a fashion not seen in many years. Even so, historically high unemployment levels stood in contrast to the thriving economy; unemployment, while falling dramatically from the better than 10 percent it had reached earlier in the downturn, did not move below 7 percent during 1984.[13] Interest rates were extremely high, particularly in real terms since the inflation rate was relatively low. The federal deficit was awesome: guesstimates for fiscal 1985 ranged from $160 billion in red ink to better than $200 billion.

The future appeared sunny for at least some of the participants in the economy. Expected changes in the demographics of U.S. society in the near future augured for low unemployment and gains in real wages. It was also felt that with an older labor force in place, thanks to fewer new entries because of the end of the great post-World War II baby boom, people would become more experienced and thus more skilled, and there would be a revival of U.S. productivity. In addition, newly developed machines, a product of the buoyant investment climate during a time of positive economic surge, would yield gains in productivity.

This generally positive economic expectation led many people in the transit field to speculate that there would be a need for additional capital investment in transit to meet the requirements of steady if not spectacular economic and population growth in urbanized areas. Indeed, the Railway Progress Institute postulated that $9.5 billion per year would be needed through the 1980s and 1990s to meet transit capital needs; some of this money was for the capital replenishment of existing transit capacity while other money was necessary for new investments and added capacity, particularly investments in rail facilities.[14]

There were also attempts to divine the future of transit and an effort to ascertain clearly what business transit was in and what business it should be in, what services it should provide, and how to pay for them. The question of positioning transit for the future was also raised; this was a point rarely considered by transit managers and policymakers on all levels, who usually took it as a given that transit must inescapably serve the tatty downside of the economy. Only modest consideration was typically given to the potential shaping force or other positive impacts transit might have on improving urban life and in helping to make the urban highway system work. This limited role notion was not surprising because Urban Mass Transportation Administration pronouncements usually did not sustain the idea that mass transit is for those who can afford much better, and during the Reagan days one heard little of the possible proactive role of transit in city development. However, in several conferences there was a thoughtful spelling out of federal shortcomings and managerial problems during the 1982-1984 period and an effort to understand what needed to be done and how to do it.[15]

Nationally, the economic recovery of 1983 and 1984 had been extremely helpful, and the once painfully strained finances of state and local government were in much better condition in 1984 than they had been two years previously during the transit industry's struggle for the Surface Transportation Act of 1982. The upsurge in the economy was helped by low oil prices, the improvement in Detroit's fortunes as sales of American cars (including the big cars that yielded a high profit) were going quite well, and the agreements on wages and working conditions and work rules with the unions (which had been quite favorable) to keep costs in line.[16]

THE ENVIRONMENT: LOCAL PROBLEMS

There were, of course, local transit problems around the nation. There were urban places—usually of modest scale—in which transit was an almost invisible issue; only accidents, defalcation, or other disasters were reported. Events in a few large cities were not so obscure and often drew national attention both from the trade press as well as the national media. In many cases the transit properties looked bad in the press—and looking bad is not difficult in the transit business. The litany of distress became familiar. In some large cities the unions seemed to be running the show and appeared to possess more power than did management. In a noteworthy situation, the advanced state of decay of the fixed assets of the New York City subway system at the time became a matter of national notice and comment and, because of New York's great visibility, provided a public black eye to the hapless NYCTA management and to the whole transit community. In addition, faulty equipment in New York was also drawn to public notice by the news media. All this was a sign of the fragile relationships that existed for transit on the local level in both political terms and in politics' close relative, financial capability.[17]

A case in point was the Chicago Area Regional Transportation Authority (RTA), which suffered, as did many activities in the Chicago area, from the upstate-downstate political conflict (Chicago versus other parts of the state) of Illinois. In 1981, the RTA was on the brink of insolvency and was forced to raise fares substantially and cut service—which caused massive losses in patronage. The RTA had to have help from the state, and the state demanded, among other things, that the RTA be restructured. The politics of it all were a long and difficult process. As it ended up, the RTA board was a holding company for the CTA board, PACE (the suburban bus service board), and METRA (the commuter rail-road board). All of this was played out in the headlines, and the reader got an impression that transit was the province of venal, short-sighted politicians and bumbling incompetents. By the time of this writing (in 1990), the reconstituted RTA was working quite well.[18]

In another part of the nation, one of the difficulties facing transit in both Philadelphia and Pittsburgh was the lack of any secure and regular source of funding on the state and local level. Each year the cities of the Keystone State must pray to its general assembly for state funds. The results are not good. To focus just on the Quaker City, the Southeastern Pennsylvania Transportation Authority (SEPTA) in the Philadelphia area suffered from severe deterioration of some of its lines over the years since its formation. Most notably awful by the early 1980s were the Broad Street Subway, decrepit PCC streetcars and ancient buses, and most of the physical plant of the north-side streetcar lines; all were in need of major capital replenishment. In addition, when Conrail had to spin off all of its commuter operations in the east, Philadelphia chose not to let the special commuter subsidiary of Amtrak (which Congress had established precisely for this purpose) take over SEPTA rail commuter operations. Instead, SEPTA chose to do the job itself and at the same time reduce the wages of the commuter rail employees to a level comparable to the pay of SEPTA's regular transit employees. A long labor strike in 1983 was the result; in reaction a huge chunk of the commuter rail ridership upon Philadelphia's extensive electric, multiple-unit commuter rail network was lost, and passengers returned slowly.[19] More recently, under determined management, significant improvements were made to SEPTA's Broad Street Subway, which was completely re-equipped with new rolling stock, had its stations renewed and refurbished, and became a showcase of transit in Philadelphia. However, by the end of 1984 ridership on the commuter rail network had not yet fully recovered.

In Washington, D.C., the Washington Metropolitan Area Transit Authority was chided about its procurement of railcars and there was also unhappiness pertaining to the problem on the bus side of the operation. Particularly visible and annoying were air-conditioners that did not work.

Without doubt, other cities' problems seemed minuscule in comparison with New York's, where severe deterioration of the subway system alone called for massive infusions of replenishment capital. One relatively conservative estimate was that New York City needed about $14-$15 billion just to bring the subway system up to an adequate standard; decades of deferred maintenance—partially the result of the politically inspired nickel fare that hung on for so long—assured that fixed facilities would suffer. A new management team in New York came on board in 1983 and worked hard to improve the situation.[20] An $8 billion capital replenishment program made progress. By 1988 most rapid transit cars were free of graffiti, stations were being cleaned and refurbished, service was being increased, and ridership was up.

THE ENVIRONMENT: UPBEAT FACTORS

Despite some difficult problems in some localities, 1983 and 1984 saw several reasons for good spirits in the transit industry. One factor behind the upbeat feeling was the Surface Transportation Act of 1982; it had turned out to be far better than anyone could have expected when the process toward the final legislation got under way early in 1982. Moreover, by the end of 1983, patronage on the nation's transit systems was once again increasing as the economy recovered, and this universally understood positive factor was helpful in many places.

The bus manufacturing business also appeared to be headed toward improvement. Only about 3,000 transit buses a year were sold since 1979, but there was a strong feeling in the industry that the bus market would boom, because the average bus was getting older and replacement had been held off during the trying years of the recession. The manufacturers felt that, with the economy and tax receipts brightening, cities and states would be able to provide the matches to federal grants and purchase new buses. There was clearly a strong interest on the part of the manufacturers for continued federal support. The picture was a bit mixed because of the intense competition facing domestic manufacturers from foreign bus manufacturing companies that were locating plants in the United States.[21] Indeed, in 1984 only 784 buses were ordered in the first six months, even though the industry had the capacity to produce almost 15,000 buses per year. The major reason given for the small number of vehicles ordered as prosperity returned was inordinate delay on the part of UMTA in approving capital grants.[22]

Behind the ebullience as prosperity returned was the concern of many cities over the need for reconstruction and renovation of key areas. There was an increased interest in downtown renewal in the nation, partly as a result of the well-publicized successes of the renewal programs in Boston, Baltimore, Toledo, and Philadelphia and the equally well-publicized ghastliness of Houston's monumental traffic congestion. While city officials were delighted at the promise of increasing downtown economic activity which could bring with it urban vitality—and choking automobile traffic—the dilemma facing the cities was that there was little hope that the funds or the support could be found for the insertion of new, much bigger highways into the already straining urban fabric.[23] To take advantage of the potential urban prosperity, consideration had to be given to transit and other means of making better use of the existing, limited urban space.

Also growing in the U.S. was an enormous enthusiasm for rail transit and the opening of several new rail operations around the nation spurred even more interest. Probably the most unexpected rail victory was the favorable referendum in Dallas, Texas, in which the voters voted "yes" on August 13, 1983, for an $8.7 billion transit project that was proposed to double the size of the Dallas Transit System bus operations within a two-year period. Dallas would then go on to build a lengthy rail system that would, after 30 years of construction, give Dallas a rail service of well over 100 route miles.

So great was the zest for rail transportation that a study by UMTA revealed 53 new-start projects proposed or in process, with a total price tag of around $19 billion. These included dedicated busways as well as light and heavy rail projects. UMTA's reaction to the demand for funding was not one of delight. UMTA Administrator Ralph Stanley made it clear that there was no way he felt his agency could ever come up with enough money to help pay the authorized federal share for all of the proposed new rail starts. Indeed, at the time the new-start money in UMTA's coffers was a pittance of about $400 million a year, derived from the Mass Transit Account of the Highway Trust Fund.[24] The dilemma of more demand for funds than money available gave added incentive to UMTA to develop what it called a new starts policy for rail transit.

There was also some reason to be cheerful about the federal transit appropriation for fiscal year 1984. Even though mass transit was funded below the level that had been authorized in the Surface Transportation Assistance Act of 1982, it was, even so, $540 million above what President Reagan's budget request had been. The U.S. DOT appropriations bill, H.R. 3329, provided $1.225 billion in contract authority under the Mass Transit Account of the Highway Trust Fund, which was for Section 3 discretionary grants. The Act made $2.389 billion available for Sections 9 and 18 formula grants for capital and operating assistance, and the three-for-two capital swap for operating assistance was continued for fiscal 1984.[25] Nevertheless, despite the relatively favorable funding for fiscal 1984, there were clouds on the horizon. The Reagan administration was slowly but quite surely cutting down on the real federal dollars going to mass transit.

ATTEMPTED CUTS IN TRANSIT FUNDING BY THE REAGAN ADMINISTRATION

President Reagan's signature was hardly dry on the Surface Transportation Assistance Act of 1982 when he and his administration began efforts to change the sunshiny world of transit promised by the hard-won legislation. With victory only recently in hand for the transit industry, the Reagan administration began to slash the 1984 budget proposals substantially below those authorized in the Surface Transportation Act and supported by the Congress.[26]

The transit industry was clearly shaken by the proposals of the administration for a 70 percent reduction in the mass transit operating assistance levels from those authorized in the STAA 1982. The administration did not give up its efforts to do away with the federal urban mass transportation program; it called for transit funds to be reduced from the authorized total of $4.77 billion to $4.71 billion. A 74 percent decrease in operating aid was proposed for fiscal year 1984 and elimination of all operating aid by fiscal year 1985. Operating assistance had been authorized at a level of $872.6 million by the STAA 1982; the 1984 Reagan administration budget allocated $283.4 million, for a cut of $589.2 million in operating aid. Operating aid was not the only thing touched—the Reagan administration reduced the formula capital funding from an authorized total of $1.88 billion to $1.69 billion. Subsidies for transit had retained their unpopularity at the White House.[27]

Perhaps there was a more subtle aspect to the lack of support for urban transit on the part of many people. It was particularly obvious during the presidential election year of 1984; no great interest or love of cities was expressed by the exceedingly popular Republican incumbent. The image of a "shining city upon a hill" was invoked by the president, a biblical metaphor that conjured up a sense of longing for an ideal for the whole society, certainly a worthy vision. However, there was little solid discussion from the president in his creation of images and metaphors that had an urban ring to them. All politicians wrap themselves in the flag and want to stand before large capital projects to cut ribbons, wear incongruous hard hats, and cultivate interest groups; all try to create negative images of what the other fellow is up to and what they would do given the chance—but there was no serious urban application in the president's messages with their images of happy suburbs and sublime farmlands. In light of the support the president received at the polls, this might have been considered evidence that America's concern for its urban places was fading.

For its part, however, the Reagan campaign aimed carefully at the individual and at making the individual as well as people in general feel good. It's pleasant, in any political discussion, to invoke happy pictures of happy people and to brush problems aside. Unfortunately, American cities have extraordinary difficulties, but the president did not want to talk about difficulties. Very much the same scenario was followed by Vice President George Bush in his successful campaign for the presidency in 1988; major issues were not really discussed.

What was thorny about cities for image-makers who were trying to give people good news and paint rosy pictures was that not only are the successes of American society concentrated in urban or metropolitan places, but so are its failures. It was this concentration factor, the massiveness of the success measured against the massiveness of the obstacles, that made urban issues the unspoken problem of the 1980s.[28]

The reaction to the position of the administration on cutting federal transit aid in 1983 was not long in coming. Members of Congress from both parties made strong comments that the provisions of the Surface Transportation Act would be carried out as Congress intended. Regardless of their political affiliation, several members of Congress were affronted by the terrible whack the administration took at the transit money in its budget bill, thus paying small heed to the will of Congress set forth in the Surface Transportation Assistance Act of 1982.[29]

Particularly disturbing to transit supporters was the fast shuffle on the use of the gas tax. One proposal of the Reagan administration was not only that the budget should be cut for mass transit but also that the money collected from the penny-on-the-gallon Mass Transit Account of the Highway Trust Fund should be used to replace general fund money earmarked for transit; transit would end up with less than before if such a plan was carried out. The transit industry had worked hard to get funding up to the authorized levels, and early in 1983 transit interests were particularly worried about the defalcation by the administration of gas tax money.[30]

THE FIGHT FOR FULL FUNDING: 1983-1984

The fight for full funding of the federal mass transit program occupied much of the spring and summer rhetorical and lobbying effort of the transit community in 1983 and again in 1984. APTA's position was that the administration was at least consistent in its opposition to transit aid. APTA noted that, while the administration had worked for and helped set up a block grant program under Section 9, the removal of the option of operating aid would take away the local control that block grants are supposed to provide. Indeed, the administration was strong in its support of as much local control as possible. On the issue of the ability of cities and states to pick up the slack, there was some considerable doubt on that point—particularly in 1983 when the most dire effects of the deep recession were still hanging on.

Key arguments in the administration's opposition to operating aid was that operating assistance leads inevitably to excesses in labor contracts, and that cities and states were quite able to provide funding. The point about excesses in labor contracts was held up as patently false by APTA Executive Vice President Jack Gilstrap. He cited U.S. Department of Commerce figures showing that the wages of transit operators actually lagged in comparison with other U.S. workers. Gilstrap stated that "during the years 1976 and 1982, transit wages increased 67 percent; all other industry wages grew by 75 percent; in transportation and other public utilities worker wages went up by 79 percent." Gilstrap also noted that twenty-two states projected deficits in 1983, forty-four states were raising taxes, and of 310 cities surveyed by the National League of Cities, 60 percent had deficits in 1982 and 75 percent were laying off workers. According to Gilstrap, the administration was inconsistent in its philosophical opposition to operating subsidies; he pointed out that the highway program was subsidized, that agricultural price supports are subsidies, and the Federal Aviation Administration provided a subsidy of $6.03 for each air passenger for each trip. The federal subsidy per transit rider at the time was 11 cents per trip.[31]

The uneven treatment of transit relative to other activities was also noted by the Congressional Budget Office. In reviewing the fiscal year 1984 budget, the CBO observed that about 30 percent of the discretionary spending in the budget was devoted to infrastructure—which included transportation systems, parks, water, mineral, and other natural resource programs and community development projects, etc. The CBO noted significant spending cuts in this area since 1981; the 1983 levels of spending would be a real reduction of about 15 percent. Two major areas would enjoy an increase in spending of about two percent per year between 1983 and 1988: the Federal Aid Highway Program and the Federal Aviation Administration operations. Outlays of federal grants to states under the Federal Aid Highway Program were estimated to rise from $8.4 billion in 1983 to $14.2 billion by 1988. Money spent on FAA was proposed to rise from $3.6 billion in 1983 to $5.4 billion by 1988. All other infrastructure spending would decline, and taking it on the chin worst of all, with the largest reduction relative to the base-line expenditures (the base-line incorporated the spending levels of the STAA 1981), was the Urban Mass Transportation Administration, with cuts of about $5 billion between 1983 and 1985, reflecting the proposed cut and then elimination of operating subsidies. One of the major image problems of transit was and is the overt nature of its federal subsidies; the highway and air subsidies are camouflaged.[32]

After all the sound and fury, a transportation budget for fiscal 1984 was finally passed. The Urban Mass Transportation Administration budget was $477 million higher in fiscal 1984 than the administration had recommended. The House of Representatives had wished for an even higher level but had finally compromised with the Senate so that the UMTA funding bill was about $185 million lower in the final bill than it had been in the House proposed legislation. An important factor for supporters of transit was the victory in the appropriations bill maintaining the level of transit operating assistance at $873 million and the new rail starts money included at around the $400 million mark.[33]

The same game was played in 1984 with the fiscal 1985 budget. Again the administration cast great doubt on rail transit systems as well as on urban transportation support as a federal activity. The Reagan administration proposed a 38 percent cut in UMTA operating assistance, and the proposal for the total UMTA budget was $4.1 billion, which was about $500 million less than the administration prepared for fiscal 1985 under the STAA 1982. The transit industry noted once again that the public transit proposal was at odds with the spirit of the STAA 1982. Cities, paying little attention to the solemn federal words that rail transit systems were not good, continued to push for rail systems.[34]

The Congressional Budget Office studied the president's fiscal 1985 transportation budget and noted that federal aid highway outlays would be $.1 billion below the base line in 1985, and over the 1985 to 1989 period, it would be down $3.7 billion. Transit funding would be cut $.2 billion below the 1984 level and the formula grants would be held at the 1984 level of $2.4 billion through 1989; operating assistance grants would be generally phased out. Capital grants were spent more slowly than operating funds, and the CBO determined that mass transit outlays in the 1985-89 period would be $7.2 billion below the base line.[35]

THE NEW STARTS POLICY

As the effort of the transit industry and its supporters to achieve a favorable level of transit funding proceeded in the spring of 1984, UMTA announced the "new starts" policy. The agency had developed a rating system for the allocation of federal discretionary capital assistance to ensure that federal funds for major investments in transit were directed toward the best projects. Under the proposal, projects were to be compared with one another in order to pick out those that had the highest relative merit. The intention and approach was different from one that would have evaluated each project in isolation and attempted to identify the absolute merits of each project or whether its benefits exceeded its costs.

The rating system was based on five factors. They were:

1. Federal *objectives* in urban transportation
2. *Criteria* to measure performance in each objective
3. *Indices* that measured combined performance on all objectives
4. *Ratings* that indicated UMTA's overall assessment of the project
5. *Funding decisions* that optimized the allocation of available funds

According to UMTA, the rating system was based on a specific statement of UMTA's objectives which supposedly had evolved over the years and were developed as a part of the dialogue between the executive branch—U.S. DOT and UMTA—and Congress.[36]

To determine whether or not a proposal for a major capital project met UMTA's objectives, UMTA identified for each objective the criteria to measure project performance. The intent of these criteria was to assure the reflection of all the benefits generated by each proposed project and also to avoid any bias toward a particular type of project or any geographic area of the country. To boil things down to a small number of indicators of investment worthiness, UMTA's method computed two indices that compared the trade-offs between the costs and the benefits from two different perspectives. One index was representative of the federal perspective and compared benefits against the required federal investment; the other represented society's perspective and compared benefits against the total cost of the project.

There were several threshold tests aimed at screening out clearly unattractive proposals. UMTA assigned each project a rating to represent its overall merit. Where different projects received the same rating, they were put in priority order on a judgmental basis with a reference to the performance on all criteria and emphasis on the magnitude, stability, and reliability of local financial commitments. With the project ratings and the estimated balance of UMTA's authorization that were not covered by letters of intent, UMTA would then recommend funding of the most highly rated projects that had completed preliminary engineering and a final environmental impact statement.[37]

Considering the issue of objectives, UMTA felt that the two primary purposes of the program were (1) to assist in the development of improved mass transportation facilities, equipment, techniques, and methods; and (2) to encourage the planning and establishment of area-wide urban mass transportation systems needed for economical and desirable urban development.[38]

The criteria were an essential part of the rating system. They included:

1. Cost-effectiveness
2. Local fiscal effort, including the stability and reliability of local funding sources
3. Private sector participation
4. The results of alternatives analysis
5. Participation of disadvantaged business enterprises
6. Support by local governments and the community

These criteria were incorporated into the rating system. Indices were computed from the first four criteria that provided an objective basis on which to compare investment proposals. The criterion of participation by disadvantaged business enterprises was applied as a minimum standard that all capital proposals must meet in order to be eligible for federal funding. The final criterion of local support was closely related to local fiscal effort and private sector participation.[39]

A key factor, of course, was cost-effectiveness, which UMTA viewed as the extent to which a project returned benefits relative to its cost. To make this operational, the cost-effectiveness of a proposed major investment was to be measured in terms of its added benefits and costs when compared to some other option of lower cost. Here what UMTA proposed to use was the transportation system management (TSM) alternative that was included in all alternatives analyses. The TSM possibilities are low capital cost means of making better use of already existing facilities.[40]

The benefit items that UMTA scrutinized most carefully in the policy included the attraction of new transit riders, improvement in service (reduction in travel times) for existing riders, and reductions in operating and maintenance costs for the transit operators.[41]

A very important part of the judgment on new starts was the local fiscal effort. To UMTA's way of thinking, this was defined as including the capital contributions from local and state government and from transportation and other agencies but did not include money from UMTA's Section 9 programs or the Interstate Highway Transfer Program. Local fiscal effort, according to UMTA, had three roles to play in determining the merit of the project. To begin with, if the match from the local level was above the statutory minimum, it would allow UMTA to provide aid to a much wider range of capital projects within the limits of its capital budget. Second, local fiscal effort was also an excellent indicator of the commitment on the local level to transit in general and to the particular capital improvement project at issue. Finally, a stable and reliable source of funding for the long-term operation of a local transit system removed from jeopardy the usefulness of the capital investment in a new transit facility. The local match and overmatch were treated by UMTA as credits against the cost of a project that made the federal investment more productive. Although a lack of local financing beyond the statutory minimum was not to be a penalty on the project, a significant local fiscal effort can work to make the project more attractive for the federal funds.[42]

The private-sector contributions were given important weight because such aid helped to reduce the federal costs and was yet another indicator of strong local support for transit investment. The alternative analysis showed up as a penalty if there was a more cost-effective alternative to achieve the same end, which meant that the proposal in question was a less productive use of federal money. As noted earlier, the participation of disadvantaged business enterprises was a statutory requirement. Support by local governments and the community was important because "UMTA considers other local actions to improve the effectiveness of the proposed investment, including the adoption of supportive land use in transportation policies (zoning and parking management, for example). The level of community support, as evidenced by endorsements by local officials, civic groups, and private citizens is also considered in UMTA's over-all evaluation of a project, but is secondary to the strength of financial commitments and adoption of supporting actions."[43]

The new starts position of UMTA did not create a tidal wave of joy in the transit industry. The policy was expected to favor cities in the Sun Belt that were often somewhat wealthier than northern urban centers. While there was tremendous variation in the amount of local share that a particular community could put up, there was a strong feeling among transit observers and members of the industry that the rapidly growing cities of the Sun Belt were better able to provide more substantial amounts of support than their more senior and less rapidly growing mid-western and northeastern cousins.[44] There was no doubt that the demand for funds for major capital improvements far outdistanced UMTA's ability to cover all the costs.[45]

There was also some debate over whether or not cost effectiveness was the best standard by which to judge a program's success. Floating over it all, of course, was the lack of established workable goals and objectives for the federal urban mass transportation program. Perhaps the greatest weakness of the new starts proposal was that by having it based on the supposed UMTA objectives, the decision policy factors were in reality not based on anything that was workable; it was football without a goal line, as had been the case from the start of the program of federal transit aid. In any event, Congress was unhappy with the proposed policy, as was APTA; the Senate Committee on Appropriations directed that UMTA postpone any final action on the new starts policy until Congress had an opportunity to review the matter and hold hearings.[46]

All in all, it was rather difficult to figure out just exactly how the Urban Mass Transportation Administration was to carry out whatever it was supposed to. Probably this unease was expressed best by the Senate Appropriations Committee when it stated:

The committee is concerned that in developing the new start policy UMTA has, by developing a single composite index, excluded other factors from consideration. The authorizing and appropriating committees of Congress must be assured that the reliance on a single composite index does not reduce to a mathematical formula certain factors which cannot be so precisely measured. Factors such as local economic development and the ability to recapture that development through special assessment districts should not be overlooked.[47]

SPRING 1984: INTRODUCTION OF LEGISLATION

The legislative process for new mass transit legislation began in the early part of February, 1984.[48] On February 7, the House Committee on Public Works and Transportation held three days of hearings on both the highway and transit programs. UMTA Administrator Ralph Stanley testified; under questioning he said that he did not recommend any increase in the authorization of the money to be spent from the Mass Transit Account of the Highway Trust Fund, even though the sum of money raised by the penny on the gallon of fuel user charge was expected to exceed earlier expectations. Stanley recommended that any change in authorization wait until the actual revenues were accumulated in the account. Stanley also discussed the new starts criteria and also indicated that he, speaking for UMTA, did not support a continuation of the $3 in capital for $2 in operating aid trade-in option under the Section 9 program.[49]

The Highway Users Federation also testified; it called for the "transit penny" from the Mass Transit Account to be freed up for use by states to fund highway projects if transit requirements within the state were being covered adequately in some other way. The federation also recommended elimination of transit use of the federal-aid urban system funds, which since 1973 could be used at local discretion for transit capital improvement purposes. Playing a much different tune, the American Public Transit Association and the National League of Cities, accompanied by representatives of a number of large transit systems, provided testimony that showed there was a five-year capital need in transit of over $36 billion.[50]

Interest in lawmaking picked up in March, particularly for legislation dealing with the budget; this was because the Budget Control Act required the authorizing and appropriating committees of Congress to submit their views and estimates of funding for programs to the respective budget committees in each house by the fifteenth of March of each year. The House Committee on Public Works and Transportation recommended full funding for transit up to the authorized levels of Section 9 operating and capital assistance and of the discretionary capital program under Section 3 of the Urban Mass Transportation Act. The House also pushed for authorization of Section 3 to the full level of the revenue produced by the Mass Transit Account of the Highway Trust Fund. The authorized level set by the Surface Transportation Assistance Act of 1982 was $1.1 billion, based on the expected yield from the "transit penny" on the federal gasoline tax. But collection had gone better than expected; the Congressional Budget Office estimated that the yield would be about $1.5 billion annually through fiscal 1987. In the Senate, the Committee on Banking, Housing and Urban Affairs took the position that the Surface Transportation Assistance Act of 1982 should provide adequate authorization for transit discretionary capital spending and so told the Budget Committee.[51]

As March of 1984 moved on, APTA's board of directors adopted a resolution setting forth the aims of the transit industry for the legislative session. The list of desires included funding of Section 9 to the full authorized level for both operating and capital purposes and extension of the authorizations through fiscal year 1987, with an extension of the three-for-two capital for operating assistance trade-in provisions for the whole of the authorization period. APTA further wanted authorization levels for the Section 3 discretionary program to be commensurate with the amount of money generated by the Mass Transit Account of the Highway Trust Fund. Also, APTA took a stand against the Reagan administration's expected end run to substitute the increases in Section 3 authorization for full funding of the Section 9 program from the general fund of the treasury. On distribution of Section 3 funds, the industry position was that for fiscal 1985, 43 percent should be for rail modernization, 38 percent for new start system development, 10 percent for extraordinary bus capital needs, and 9 percent for general capital needs. For fiscal 1986 and beyond, APTA's resolution called for the Section 3 money to be distributed on the basis of 40 percent for rail modernization, 40 percent for new starts, 10 percent for extraordinary bus capital needs, and 10 percent for general capital needs. Finally, the industry called for parity between new and formerly designated urbanized areas and continued funding authorized for the Interstate Transfer program at the existing levels.[52]

The hope of transit supporters that it would be possible to have a new combined highway and transit bill introduced and marked up by the subcommittee on surface transportation of the House Committee on Public Works and Transportation prior to the 1984 congressional Easter recess was doomed to disappointment. The situation became clouded. In the Senate, Senator Alfonse D'Amato introduced a bill on April 11, 1984, S.2554, which was dubbed the Public Transit Improvement Act of 1984. The Senate Committee on Banking, Housing and Urban Affairs did not have any scheduled hearings nor had it taken action for transit legislation when the Senate adjourned for the Easter recess. Meanwhile, the House had approved its version of the first concurrent budget resolution in H.Com.Res. 280; it had a total target of $29.1 billion for transportation programs but did not provide any breakdown of the amount for individual programs, such as transit. The Senate Budget Committee had also moved ahead and had approved a budget resolution with $29.8 billion for transportation programs.[53]

Senator D'Amato's bill would have increased the authorization levels for the Section 3 program to $1.3 billion in fiscal 1985 and to $1.4 billion in fiscal 1986, as compared with the $1.1 billion authorized over the whole period in the Surface Transportation Assistance Act of 1982. The proposed authorizations extended the Section 3 program through fiscal year 1987 at a level of $1.5 billion. In addition, the bill also provided for the extension of the three-for-two trade-in provisions through fiscal year 1986.[54]

On April 25, 1984, a highway and transit authorization bill was introduced in the House as H.R. 5504 by Congressmen Glenn Anderson (California), James Howard (New Jersey), Gene Snyder (Kentucky), and Bud Shuster (Pennsylvania). There was a degree of similarity between the House Bill and Senator D'Amato's proposed legislation.[55] The proposed legislation would establish multi-year contract authority for long-term projects; the UMTA letter of intent concept would be deleted and replaced by a multi-year contract concept. The significance of this proposal was that the secretary of transportation would be able to enter into binding multi-year contracts obligating funds from future year authorizations. Another provision would allow advanced construction approval authority by the secretary under Sections 3 and 9 of the Mass Transit Act.

To cut down on the process of Congress earmarking what were supposed to be discretionary funds, H.R. 5504 provided that in selecting projects under Section 3 of the Act, the secretary should not take into consideration statements of members of Congress or the reference to a project in any report of any committee of Congress. H.R. 5504 also called for the development of criteria for approval of new fixed guideway projects; provided for $10 million for a new university transportation center idea; and authorized necessary funding for the Interstate Transfer transit projects in fiscal years 1985 and 1986. The bill would also increase and extend through fiscal 1987 the Mass Transit Account of the Highway Trust Fund authorizations as follows: fiscal year 1985, $1.525 billion; fiscal year 1986, $1.5 billion; and fiscal year 1987, $1.5 billion. The definition of construction was amended to include bus remanufacturing projects that extend bus life by eight or more years.[56]

Mark-up on H.R. 5504, which was called the Surface Transportation and Uniform Relocation Assistance Act of 1984, was completed on May 2, 1984, by the subcommittee on surface transportation of the House Committee on Public Works on Transportation.[57] Nine amendments were adopted in the process. A matter of concern was the original language in the bill that would prevent Republican and Democratic administrations from using Section 3 for political purposes. As a result of this practice, Congress had earmarked more and more of the Section 3 funds over the preceding several years, particularly for new rail starts—mainly rapid transit. As it stood, H.R. 5504 would completely cut Congress out of the process of allocating these funds; the president and executive branch would have complete control. H.R. 5504 also expressed concern over the new starts policy that was being developed in the Reagan administration.[58]

The House passed H.R. 5504 on June 7, 1984, despite the protestations over several parts of the legislation by Congressman William Lehman, chairman of the House appropriations subcommittee on transportation.[59] However, transit legislation was getting nowhere in the Senate. Much controversy was raised by a proposal by Senator Symms of Idaho for an amendment to S.2527, the Federal-Aid Highway Act of 1984. His aim was to provide a minimum of one-half of one percent of the Section 3 transit discretionary capital money to each state. Symms's so-called "Fair Share Amendment" would permit the governor of each state to use the guaranteed one-half percent for highway purposes, if the secretary of transportation agreed that the transit funding in the state was already adequate and that the alternative use for highways would be more beneficial to the community in question. Symms argued that over the years the transit money had been concentrated in just a few large cities in a few states and that every state should receive some benefit from money (the penny for transit on the highway user charge) that was generated in all states.[60]

The reaction of the transit community was quick in coming, with letters of objection and lobbying efforts from the American Public Transit Association and the National League of Cities. On the other hand, the Highway Users Federation found the Symms Amendment to its liking. Others favorably disposed to the Idaho senator's idea, even if they did not agree with the precise letter of the Symms Amendment, were those leaders in certain cities and in state departments of transportation who felt that use of the "transit penny" was not really just because it was expected that most of this discretionary money would go to the rail projects of a few large cities.[61]

In mid-May APTA could report to its U.S. members that it had word of generous funding levels for transit from the House Appropriations subcommittee on transportation. The subcommittee had pegged the federal transit budget at a level $255 million above what the Reagan administration had requested. The word was that the Section 3 discretionary program was set at $1.125 billion, that there was a $2.55 billion allocation for Section 9 (with $875 million for operating assistance), and that Interstate transfer funding was set at $320 million. Moreover, the reaction of APTA to the approval of H.R. 5504 by the Public Works and Transportation Committee was favorable because it embraced many of the things called for in APTA's resolution of two months before.[62]

By the time the 1984 Fourth of July recess rolled around, Congress had moved but little on the Senate side toward formulating new transit authorizing legislation. The Senate Committee on Environment and Public Works reported a highway bill as S.2727. Senator D'Amato was expected to offer his transit bill, S.2554, as an amendment to S.2727. As noted, Senator Symms was planning to amend S.2527, the Federal Aid Highway Act of 1984.

Where the Senate, save for Senators Symms and D'Amato, was languid, the House pressed on and passed H.R. 5504. The transit industry had cause to be pleased because the bill called for an increase in the authorization of Section 3 up to $1.5 billion and extension of the program through fiscal year 1987. The Act provided for multi-year contract authority for certain long-term projects subject to congressional approval and established criteria for new starts. The three-for-two capital operating assistance trade-in option was included and restricted access to Section 3 funds for systems that used the option. Parity was established for new urbanized areas so that they would be on the same footing as established urbanized areas in the use of operating money. The Reagan administration promised to veto the bill.[63]

On the matter of appropriations for transportation, there was a major tizzy in the House when Representative James Howard, chairman of the Committee on Public Works and Transportation, objected to H.R. 5921, the Department of Transportation's Appropriations bill for fiscal 1985. The House Appropriations

Committee, according to Representative Howard, had legislated in an appropriations bill.[64] The Senate Appropriations Committee approved its version of H.R. 5921.

The summer of 1984 was a slow one for legislation, not only because of the customary recesses of Congress for the Fourth of July and Labor Day returns to the hustings, but also because of lengthy recesses for the Democratic and Republican National Conventions, respectively held in July and August. It was only the dust-ups concerning congressional etiquette, amendments, and proposed amendments that broke the soporific haze. As time went by, for example, Senator Symms's proposed amendment gathered no moss; it was opposed by no less than the American Public Transit Association, the U.S. Conference of Mayors, the National League of Cities, the transit labor unions, the National Association of Counties, and the Reagan administration.[65]

The pique of Representative James Howard with regard to the House Appropriations Committee found voice in a letter to his fellow House members. It is worth quoting:

> H.R. 5921 contains a significant number of provisions which constitute legislation in an appropriations bill, and therefore, intrudes on the jurisdiction of the Committee on Public Works and Transportation. In fact, this bill would not only dismantle much of what Congress accomplished when it enacted the 5-cent gas tax increase in the Surface Transportation Assistance Act of 1982, but is so egregious that it had to be considered *twice* by the Rules Committee.
>
> The provisions at issue were included either without consultation with our committee or over our strong objections. We, therefore, intend to oppose the previous question on the rule or the rule itself since it provides for numerous waivers of Rule XXI—*legislation in an Appropriation Bill*—many of which relate to matters under our Committee's jurisdiction.
>
> However, the real issue involved goes far beyond the proposed rule, the transportation appropriation bill, or the interests of a single committee. It goes to the very integrity and credibility of the legislative process; more specifically, it goes to the basic committee system which has proved so effective since the beginning of our nation.[66]

With very little working time left for the Congress because of all the recesses and because many senators and all congress members wanted to recess early in October to run for re-election, no transit legislation or appropriation bill was passed by the end of the 1984 fiscal year—September 30, 1984. Authorization and appropriations remained firmly blocked because, while the House had passed H.R. 5504, the highway and transit authorization bill, the conflict between Representative Howard's Committee on Public Works and Transportation and the House Appropriations Committee assured that there would be no action on the appropriation. For its part, the Senate had taken no action on a transit authorization bill, although the highway bill (S.2527) could have been the vehicle for a transit authorization. Internal wrangling over highways and a failure to consider transit in hearings produced no legislation. The upshot was that a continuing resolution was used to provide the appropriation to continue the Department of Transportation programs.[67] The continuing resolution, H.J. Res. 648, provided $4.15 billion for fiscal year 1985. No action was taken to extend the three-for-two trade option of capital assistance for operating assistance, and this provision of the 1982 Surface Transportation Act lapsed despite the pressure from the transit industry to have it continued.[68]

WHAT HAPPENED?

And so the governmental elephant labored and gave birth to nothing, not even a mouse. The transit program of the federal government chugged on, *sans* the three-for-two program, but not otherwise changed. The fate of transit legislation was in part a product of congressional infighting, but it was also due to the lack of a crisis. There was none facing transit or the highway program, and so no heroic measures were needed or taken.[69]

The presidential election took everybody's attention away from other issues, even if it did not take their minds off them. The election that returned Ronald Reagan to the White House with an overwhelming majority was really not about important issues that faced the nation; it seemed to be about not much of anything other than feeling good. The Democratic candidate, Walter Mondale, made noises and tried to raise key issues, such as the staggering size of the deficit, but no one paid much attention. He was deservedly defeated at the polls for trying to be a party pooper. President Reagan ran against Jimmy Carter again, made everybody feel good, basked in the prosperity of the economy, and was handsomely re-elected.[70]

After the cheering stopped, the second Reagan administration looked at the fruits of its victory and figured that something had to be done about the deficit that the hapless Mondale had bored everybody with. Even before Thanksgiving, rumors and trial balloons began to form a veritable barrage over Washington. With the aim of chopping federal spending, the so-called "domestic programs," such as transit, were proposed for axing or substantial cutbacks, along with such agencies as the Small Business Administration, the program for black-lung relief, federal revenue sharing, and other programs. It was a formidable hit list. Some persons, not cynical but wise in the ways of the U.S. government, made the point that the president had repeatedly said during the election campaign that he would not raise taxes to overcome the deficit unless it was absolutely necessary. All of the programs and agencies targeted for cutbacks had strong and vocal lobbying groups that would not give up easily. Many of the programs were dear to the hearts of the middle class, the group that pays the bulk of the taxes and does the bulk of the voting. Congress got an earful from these groups; enormous pressures were brought on the lawmakers to keep cuts to a minimum and to preserve certain programs.[71]

What about transit in all this? Despite the lack of a clear, long-run mission, the federal program of transit aid was popular. It pleased its urban political constituents and was warmly supported by Congress on a bipartisan basis. The "feel good" election of 1984, really an issueless affair in many ways, was no mandate to Ronald Reagan to dismantle the mass transportation programs or anything else. The administration's great crusade to gut the federal programs got little support from the middle class and even less from mayors and other local officials, many of whom were in the part of America that was most supportive of Ronald Reagan and Republicans. Despite reasonable concern about doing battle with a popular president, supporters of transit came to realize that the program was not going to go away. The main task of the transit community was to be ever vigilant and protect their position. But the dramatics of yet another fight with the White House loomed ahead when the authorization for the transit and highway programs ran out in 1986.[72]

13.

The Federal Mass Transit Programs, 1984-1987

If it is true that difficulty builds character, then the period between 1984 and 1987 was a time of great character development in the transit industry and community. Opposition to the federal mass transportation program by the Reagan administration was now an accepted feature of life, as was the continued strong backing of Congress. Despite expected roadblocks, 1986 was supposed to see the reauthorization of the federal transit programs. Before reauthorization became law, the transit industry was involved in a dramatic confrontation between the White House and Capitol Hill the likes of which had not been seen in many years.[1]

If the administration was not successful in eliminating the program, it did put up a good fight, and in the battle there were positive factors that emerged, such as the push for more competition to lower costs and greater support on the state and local levels.[2] For good reason, the transit industry appreciated the many strong transit supporters in Congress who acted as a shield against the negative aspirations of the administration.

There were other reasons for the transit industry, and others at odds with the administration, to take heart that the worst of their battles with the Reagan forces might be over. Revelations broke in November 1986 about secret arms dealing by the Reagan administration with Iran and the use of profits from the arms sales to help fund the civil war in Nicaragua. The Iran-Contra Affair caused a serious temporary decline in the president's popularity, and sharp questioning of Reagan and his policies on many issues got underway. Even more important, the Republicans lost control of the Senate in the 1986 election. The transit community had enjoyed support from the Republican-controlled Senate and expected even warmer support from a Democratic Senate.

A few examples of congressional support on key matters are instructive. The administration pushed what it called privatization as a means of containing transit cost. Privatization—a truly hideous word—really stood for the allowing of competition between private sector firms to help reduce the costs of some transit services. The idea is a good one, and even under public ownership, the transit industry had been bidding out some services (such as operating paratransit service, bus cleaning, and snowplowing and grounds maintenance) for many years. Privatization was a useful tool to help boost efficiency, but it was not a cure for the problems of non-farebox transit funding. Congress headed off efforts of the administration to make certain levels of private participation mandatory; the legislators regarded such a mandate as counterproductive.

Despite the administration's continued vocal opposition to rail transit projects, especially the so-called new starts, Congress made sure the money for completion or start-up did, indeed, go to rail projects. In the years between 1981 and 1987, to note just a few, Pittsburgh opened its new subway; Buffalo opened up its new light rail line, including a subway; there was expansion of the San Diego Trolley system; the Washington Metro Rail Rapid Transit System opened several major extensions and continued to build planned extensions; Miami opened its entire First Phase rapid transit system and downtown peoplemover feeder to the rapid transit line; Portland opened up its light rail transit line to the eastern suburbs; San Jose and Sacramento commenced construction during the period, and Sacramento began revenue operations in the spring of 1987; Seattle began a downtown tunnel for trolleybuses; money was earmarked for preliminary work on a light rail line in St. Louis; and Los Angeles started to build a major subway system.[3]

The reason for the interest of Congress is proof of the dictum of long-time Speaker of the House Thomas P. "Tip" O'Neill that all politics is local politics. As stated earlier, the simple and straightforward fact is that the federal mass transit program touches virtually every congressional district and at least some of the constituents of every senator. Even if that senator's state contained no urban places of any great size, the Section 18 program of federal support to nonurbanized and rural areas assured a transit constituency.

The Reagan administration was deeply frustrated on this issue by early 1987; it had not privatized transit as much as it had hoped and, apparently, had failed in its attempts—as many transit supporters saw it—to eliminate the transit program and taint it with obloquy.[4]

FACTORS AFFECTING TRANSIT POLICY

Between 1984 and 1987 many issues and factors had an impact upon federal transit policy. These elements were sometimes subtle or appeared unimportant but had a real influence on the program, the administrative style of the bureaucracy, the zeal of proponents, the arrogance of persons in power, and the strength of opposition. All of these factors—and more—had a role in what an administration or bureaucracy or Congress chose or feared to do. The factors, both real and imagined, may greatly affect the boldness and resolve of groups vying for attention, legislation, change in legislation, or reauthorization. Among the most important of these factors was the 1984 election, which returned President Reagan to the White House with an almost-complete majority of votes, having won all but Minnesota and the District of Columbia. The landslide was interpreted by the most zealous of Reagan supporters as a mandate for the president or his lieutenants to do anything he or they wanted. The victory emboldened the administration to push hard for transit aid cuts, as well as cuts in other out-of-favor programs. In retrospect, such actions stirred the resolve and braced the initiative of those opposed to Reagan administration positions.

The enormous federal deficit of the Reagan years continued to be a major issue. Although the deficit was downplayed by Reagan in the 1984 election campaign, immediately afterward the deficit and efforts to do something about it became major aims of discussion, debate, and criticism between the administration and Congress. The controversial Gramm-Rudman-Hollings debt reduction act was passed in 1985 as a supposed means of forcing Congress and the federal government to be fiscally responsible; much time was spent by Congress debating and eventually passing the legislation. Many concerned persons felt that the cutbacks needed in order to reach the Gramm-Rudman-Hollings deficit reduction targets would be substantial over time and perhaps harmful to many programs and the people they served.[5]

A sleeper at first, but a factor that grew very large indeed, was tax reform; when first mentioned as a major goal for the administration by President Reagan it was viewed as irrelevant in comparison with the deficit problem. As a real surprise to virtually everyone, 1986 saw major changes in the federal tax laws. The tax reform issue pushed other matters aside while Congress spent much time in debate over this major piece of legislation.[6]

Another time-consuming factor was the 1986 election. It was important for Republicans to do well if they wished to retain control of the U.S. Senate. They were under great stress because of the large number of G.O.P. Senate seats up for re-election. Worse yet for the freshmen and others whose senatorial campaigns were aided in 1980 by the presidential campaign of Ronald Reagan, 1986 was not a presidential year, and there were no Reagan coattails to ride. President Reagan lent his enormous prestige and popularity to the Republican cause during the election and stumped vigorously for Republican senatorial candidates. Even so, the Republicans lost control of the Senate, which they had held since 1981.[7]

Coming in on the heels of the 1986 election defeat was the Iran-contra scandal, which was directly connected to the White House and to close advisors of the president at the National Security Council. It burdened the administration and diverted its thinking away from much of anything else. For its part, the Congress spent much time rightfully viewing the Iran-contra issue with alarm, and as 1986 moved into 1987, began the process of investigating what had happened.[8]

The result of these and many other factors of lesser note was that transit during this period was not seen as an important issue. Indeed, it appeared in 1986 that even marrying the transit and highway legislation in a single act was no guarantee of raising its visibility or of guaranteeing its passage. Attention was diverted almost wholly from virtually all urban issues, nothing unusual since the election of Ronald Reagan. On a local level, however, transit often loomed as large and important. Thanks to the federal programs continuing over more than two decades, transit was more clearly understood by local politicians as a vital issue, and they worked hard to boost state and local support.[9] From the practical viewpoint of local politics, federal and other governmental funds for transit was a means of letting contracts, creating jobs, and hiring people.

In the bustle of activities in a dynamic society, some things get glossed over, and some aspects of transit did not get much attention. For example, where mass transit ridership in 1986 was relatively soft in places, extremely low fuel prices were given as the cause. Fuel prices had modified somewhat in 1984-85 but they tumbled significantly in 1986 and only began to rise once again early in 1987. Low gas prices might be considered a fool's paradise because the nation's reliance on imported fuel was higher in 1986 than it had been before the OPEC oil embargo in the early 1970s and subsequent years. Transit ridership fell in absolute numbers in some places. There was a little talk in general terms about the vulnerability of the nation in importing such a large portion of its fuel, but it was not a major issue in the election of 1986. It was certainly not a topic discussed by the Reagan administration.

One of the great paradoxes of American life was that the traffic jams that the federal highway and transit programs were supposed to eliminate grew much worse in the 1980s. After more than two decades of federal urban transit aid and more than four decades of federal highway aid to urban places, the grail of easily flowing traffic was as elusive as ever. Traffic congestion was a particularly serious problem in new and fast-growing suburbs. As the reader will recall, this growth in activity and traffic was part of the evolution of American cities as they spread out, and the need to travel and go greater distances steadily increased. Rising congestion was also evidence of the national failure to plan development in a fashion that would not make problems worse and to consider what transit might do to improve the urban mobility situation and its use as a tool for the improvement of urban life.

The prescription of the administration vis-a-vis public transportation was to eliminate federal support; the preoccupation of the transit industry was to preserve the federal programs. What that form of transportation could do to benefit the public was lost in the shuffle. In fact, the proportion of people using transit to go to work fell between 1970 and 1980, even though the absolute numbers were up nationally in that time period; the trend did not look encouraging. What was discouraging was that the nightmare of gridlocked suburbs was close to reality around all major U.S. cities. The confusing factor was that neither highway nor transit solutions proved practical from an economic viewpoint. Figuratively, in their development pattern, the suburbs had painted themselves into a corner; their relatively thin development did not often produce a few high-demand corridors that could justify the sizable expenditure for superior highways or transit in those corridors. Even worse, when corridors were clear-cut and obvious, it was often impossible to find the room or the money to undertake a needed project. All levels of government had failed to control highway demand, eliminate parking subsidies, encourage greater densities through zoning, or otherwise encourage transit use and discourage auto use. The problem of traffic, as many observers noted, was a self-inflicted wound.[10]

The failure to pass an authorization of the highway and transit acts in 1986 can be laid to such things as the deficit situation, Gramm-Rudman-Hollings, tax reform, the 1986 election, and perhaps the Iran-contra scandal. All of these factors diverted the attention and took the time of the Congress as well as the administration, but the 99th Congress was the key factor in what failed to occur. The 99th Congress was also the key to the dramatic events behind the passage of transit reauthorization legislation by the 100th Congress.

The failure to reauthorize during the 99th Congress was not the result of lack of effort. The first soundings on a new transit authorization developed in July of 1985 when Senator Frank R. Lautenberg (D-New Jersey) introduced legislation to reauthorize the Federal Mass Transit Program through 1989. The proposed legislation would have increased transit funding and changed the distribution of mass transit money. An interesting point, and an indication that at least a majority of Congress actively ignored the Reagan administration's push to eliminate the federal mass transit program, occurred in a Senate debate on June 25, 1985. When Senator Lautenberg introduced the legislation, he made it clear that it was intended to be a direct rejection of the administration's proposed massive retrenchment of the federal government in mass transportation.[11]

A short time later, on July 31, 1985, the House Public Works and Transportation Committee introduced legislation to reauthorize the highway and transit programs. The House bill called for annual authorizations for distribution of the mass transit funds collected by the penny per gallon devoted to transit out of the nine-cent federal gas tax, the receipts of which had run well in excess of what had been projected in the 1982 authorizing legislation. The bill also called for these funds to be distributed on the following basis: 40 percent on new starts, 40 percent for rail modernization, 10 percent for buses, and 10 percent at the discretion of the secretary of transportation. The legislation proposed permitting UMTA to enter into multi-year contracts to fund construction of mass transit systems rather than continue to rely on the traditional annual appropriations process. A new process for distribution of funds in the Mass Transit Account of the Highway Trust Fund was to be joined with the establishment of criteria to be used in funding new starts. The bill, H.R. 3129, was entitled the Surface Transportation and Relocation Assistance Act of 1985. As in the reauthorization of 1982, the transit legislation was coupled with the highway reauthorization in order to stimulate interest and support. In the past this strategy had been effective; this time troubles on the highway side were a major reason for the failure to pass the bill.[12]

While there was no big push on the legislation in the summer of 1985, it did not seem really necessary to rush, because the then current reauthorization continued through 1986. Congressman James Howard, chairman of the House Public Works and Transportation Committee, and the Senate supporters of mass transit had provided plenty of time to get the legislation enacted. Even so, there was little progress made, in part because the fall of 1985 found Congress preoccupied with the Gramm-Rudman-Hollings deficit reduction legislation. A non-urgent piece of legislation (and with a year to go on the existing authorization of the highway and transit programs, it was clearly not urgent) would not be pursued vigorously at that time. There was also some delay on the part of the House committee when the mark-up was postponed because of questions raised by the U.S. Treasury and the Congressional Budget Office concerning the revenue projections made in the bill for the highway and transit trust funds.

The transit industry was lobbying in the meantime for some solution to the excessive costs of liability insurance that faced both transit and local government. There was testimony by the American Public Transit Association (APTA) and others before Congress on this troubling issue. The concern over the Fair Labor Standards Act application to the transit industry also occupied the time of APTA and other pro-transit bodies.[13]

On a transit-related issue, Congressman Howard and the Public Works and Transportation Committee held a number of regional committee hearings for public input and discussion of what the members of the committee saw as the major problem between the mid–1980s and the turn of the century: the decay of the infrastructure in the U.S. Concerned persons were coming to realize that there were significant difficulties ahead because of the lack of infrastructure investment. Capital replenishment of the older, fixed facility transit properties—such as the New York subways and the Chicago elevated railways—was part of the concern of Congress. The aim was to develop a longer-run strategy than was typical in the U.S.[14]

On the administration side, the Transportation Department brought back an old refrain in beginning discussion of the desirability of merging the federal highway and transit aid to cities into an urban mobility block grant program. Under this idea, a block grant of funds would be provided by formula; the funds could be freely used for either highway or transit purposes. This was to become an important part of the administration's legislative proposals.[15]

PRELIMINARIES OF THE 1986 REAUTHORIZATION

After the 1985 Christmas break, the beginning of the 1986 push to reauthorize the Urban Mass Transportation Act was clouded by the return to Washington of Congress in the aftershock of the Gramm-Rudman-Hollings (GRH) passage, an action taken not long before the end of 1985. The GRH cuts were expected to affect transit to the tune of about 4.3 percent, or $157.8 million, during the final seven months of fiscal 1986. If that was bad news, there was better news for the transit industry when UMTA Administrator Ralph Stanley spoke at an APTA legislative committee meeting and announced an expedited grant approval procedure. As much as anything else, in addition to being a better grants management technique, this was to help quash the rising tide of complaints from throughout the transit industry about the administration's obstruction and delaying tactics in moving the transit money authorized and appropriated by Congress to the properties where it was needed and expected. Some transit people charged—correctly, one assumes, because it was a practice honored by tradition—that the administration was slowing down the outlays to make the budget deficit appear to be a little less than was the fact.[16]

APTA was a bit apprehensive as the year 1986 began, because it fully expected to see the Reagan administration set the federal highway and transit programs against one another in a battle for a smaller amount of funds by pushing for the use of a block grant that could be used for either highways or transit. The transit industry was pretty well convinced—and probably rightly so—that in many urban places, when the chips were down, the money would go for highways rather than transit.

The cloud of Gramm-Rudman-Hollings and the enormous size of the federal deficit promised to divert most of the attention of Congress in 1986. As almost a small voice in the wilderness, Senator Pete Domenici (R-New Mexico), chairman of the Senate Budget Committee, was frustrated in trying to work out some kind of compromise between defense and domestic program cuts and by the reality of the need for additional tax revenues to stop the growth of the deficit and help balance the federal budget. Domenici realized there were definite political limits to how much spending could be cut and that a rise in revenue was the only hope of approaching a balanced budget. He was constantly thwarted and discouraged by the White House.

The administration's legislative proposals were introduced in the Surface Transportation Reauthorization Act of 1986. The majority of the legislative package dealt with the highway programs. It was a four-year authorization to run from fiscal 1987 through fiscal 1990; under it the Highway Trust Fund and the user fees that financed it were extended for a four-year period through fiscal 1992. The proposed legislation authorized $14.1 billion each year from the Highway Trust Fund: highways and bridges, $10.57 billion; highway safety, $.16 billion; and a proposed highway and transit block grant, $3.32 billion. The program significantly increased what was called flexibility on the part of state and local government in the use of federal highway and transit funds by consolidating the highway and transit programs. Through APTA, the transit industry fought the highway transit block grant idea in order to stave off major confrontation between highway and transit interests on the local level.

Under the administration's bill, in addition to the block grant idea, the transit discretionary grant program would be discontinued. The transit operators who received federal funds would not be allowed to engage in any charter bus operations, and stimulation was to be given to private sector participation and competitive services. In what appeared to be an intrusion, transit agencies would be required to have private transportation company representatives on the policy board. To provide strong encouragement for the private sector, urban places that used the proposed block grant funds for transit would have to provide a rising scale of competitively developed transit services based on a percentage of total transit operating costs in a particular place. A proposed requirement would be 5 percent in 1987, which was to rise to 20 percent by 1990. To cut down on federal requirements, urbanized areas with a population of 50,000 to 200,000 would not have to follow federal transportation planning requirements but could continue to do so if they wished.[17]

The budget request that went along with the administration's proposal eliminated all general revenue for mass transit; the UMTA program would be funded entirely from the Mass Transit Account of the federal Highway Trust Fund. The fiscal 1987 proposal was for $1.2 billion for transit; $1.1 billion from this was to be placed in the highway transit block grant programs, which could be used by urban areas for either highway or transit projects. The administration also wanted a rescission of $521 million in discretionary funding for extensions of existing systems for fiscal year 1986; an exception would be where full funding contracts already existed. There was no funding proposed in fiscal 1987 for the Washington D.C. rapid transit system which, despite rising tides of riders, was consistently branded by the Reagan administration as a failure.

The transit industry viewed this proposed legislation as a serious threat. The cutbacks did not jibe with the growing, non-partisan concern in Congress and elsewhere that, despite the deficit problems, there were strong needs for federal infrastructure investment in the nation. Indeed, knowledgeable people in and out of Congress predicted that the infrastructure would be the major concern of the 1990s. The administration's proposals were considered unrealistic and in direct conflict with what many in Congress saw as a valid need for future investment.

As a counterpoint to considerations of extending the authorization there were also appropriation bills to consider, and attention had to be paid to the budget. The House Budget Committee, by late March 1986, had failed to find a consensus but there was general support from Budget Committee Chairman William Gray that domestic programs, such as transit, should be protected from severe cuts under Gramm-Rudman-Hollings. The fiscal 1987 spending plan of the Senate Budget Committee had slashed $25 billion from the defense increases, included fewer domestic reductions and assumed higher federal revenues of $19 billion due to some tax increases. For the transit side the situation was not so bright; a 20 percent reduction in operating assistance from the then-current levels along with a freeze in other funding was incorporated into the Senate budget proposal.

In a proposed money matter that appeared to add insult to injury, Secretary of Transportation Elizabeth Dole planned to take back from the larger cities $94 million in transit operating assistance to spend on Coast Guard and aviation programs. This cheeky effort was soundly rejected by the House Appropriations Committee.

Mid-April 1986 saw hearings in the Senate and the beginnings of a small effort by APTA to promote the idea of a dedicated source of funding for the entire federal transit program. To this end, APTA was floating the notion of increasing the federal gas tax by several more cents. The added revenue would be used to finance the entire transit program and, perhaps, a cent or two would also be added for highway purposes. This strategy would remove transit from the annual appropriations process and would transfer the transit funding from dependence on the general fund of the U.S. Treasury onto the safer ground of a trust fund.

More money for highways was a realistic and politic notion—realistically, the money was needed for maintenance of rapidly deteriorating highways and road bridges; politically, for highway interests had never been known to reject additional money.

The subcommittee on housing and urban affairs of the Senate Committee on Banking, Housing, and Urban Affairs received testimony beginning with UMTA Administrator Ralph Stanley defending the administration's legislative proposal. In opposition to that testimony, Francis B. Francois, the executive director of the American Association of State Highway and Transportation Officials, noted that any further cuts in federal mass transportation expenditures would cause serious harm to transit and the nation. He also pointed out that the proposed highway and transit block grant program would be a force leading toward instability at a time when stability was needed. In championing the administration position, Stanley took the tack that the combined highway-transit block grant program would increase stability and would mean that transportation decisions on the local level could be made on a basis of real need rather than simply trying to maximize the availability of highway and transit money.[18]

In other activity in the Senate, Senator Alfonse D'Amato introduced S.1931, requiring the preparation of construction management plans for major transit projects. This bill was a reaction to some strung out and costly capital projects that appeared to be badly managed, producing delays, poor workmanship, and costs well beyond budget. The administration supported the bill.[19]

The transit industry's goal of freezing federal mass transit expenditures was disturbed in mid-May by the budget resolution of the Senate that assumed a freeze on transit funding, except for a 20 percent reduction in federal operating assistance. The House resolution (H. Con. Res. 337) recommended a 10 percent cut in operating assistance and a similar reduction in Section 3 capital discretionary grants. At the same time Senators D'Amato and John Heinz (Republican of Pennsylvania) were circulating a discussion draft of a proposed piece of legislation entitled the "Federal Mass Transit Improvement Act of 1986." This was a four-year bill to extend the transit program pretty much along the lines of the existing law.

In the meantime, Congress rejected the Reagan administration's attempt in mid–1986 to cancel all new rail start funds for fiscal 1986 as well as some $224 million in selected projects from fiscal 1984 and 1985. With this action Congress had soundly rejected the Reagan administration's attempts to cut new starts on three different occasions. In this instance, if the White House had not allowed funds to flow, there would have been the threat of Congress bringing impoundment charges against the administration.[20]

Senator Symms of Idaho introduced S.2405 that would, in Section 129, make transit funds usable for highway projects. Under Senator Symms's proposal, Section 3 transit capital grants would be reconfigured so that each state would be guaranteed to receive not less than 85 percent of what its citizens paid in gasoline taxes that went into the Mass Transit Account. The funds would not only be available for transit spending but also for highway construction projects on any public roads. This dismayed the transit industry because it would totally gut the flexibility and availability of the money from the penny on the gas tax; under the Symms proposal it would have been impossible to marshal sufficient money to undertake any major transit capital project.

Senator Symms's effort raised an issue that troubled senators from states of small populations that would probably never need a rail transit project or any kind of major transit capital investment; their constituents paid the penny on the gas tax that went to fund the Section 3 programs of aid for major projects, but none of the funds would ever come back to the states to benefit those constituents. There was not much political mileage in the logical argument that, in an integrated national economy such as that of the U.S., money spent in Boston or New Orleans would benefit indirectly the people of Idaho, Montana, or Wyoming. True as that argument might be (and, truth to tell, much of the federal transit and highway program was for the purpose of generating external benefits), it was not a popular issue.

As it turned out, H.R. 3129 was to be the key piece of legislation. As the reader will recall, H.R. 3129 was introduced in August of 1985, but action on the bill was postponed because of disagreement over the estimates of the Highway Trust Fund revenues as well as the direction congressional action on the federal budget deficit would take. A revised version of the bill was prepared, based on additional information, and was scheduled for mark-up on June 19 of 1986.[21]

On June 25 the House Public Works and Transportation Committee approved a five-year reauthorization of $19.5 billion in transit assistance. The revised piece of legislation contained provisions that permitted multi-year contracting by Congress for major capital investment projects; the bill would establish an annual process for congressional review and approval of discretionary grant allocations. It also gave Congress the right to authorize advanced construction in transit projects. These provisions were to assert very definitely that Congress wanted a substantial voice in how transit money was to be spent. Statutory criteria were established on new rail starts and the bill called for the elimination of the annual ceiling on funding of Interstate Transfer transit projects. An old friend of the transit industry returned in the form of a proposal to reinstate the three-for-two trade-in of capital dollars for operating dollars. A set-aside of funds for construction management oversight of major capital projects was to be authorized, and public transit authorities were restricted from operating special or charter service in interstate commerce.

This latter element was the fruit of about a decade of lobbying by the privately owned intercity and charter bus industry. Again showing its lack of respect for the position of the White House, in approving H.R. 3129 the surface transportation subcommittee showed that administration efforts to slash transit funds and merge transit funds with some highway program funds into a surface transportation block grant program had not impressed Congress. Shortly thereafter Congressman Howard appeared before the House Ways and Means Committee to request a five-year extension of the Highway Trust Fund.[22]

While some of the news in the proposed legislation was good for transit, not so good was the substantial difference between the House and Senate bills. While this would become a problem subsequently, the transit industry was greatly encouraged when the House of Representatives voted on August 15 to approve H.R. 3129. As passed, this would continue federal mass transit programs from October 1, 1986 through September 30, 1991. There was regrettably little movement on the part of the Senate in contrast to the vigor shown in the House by Congressman Howard and his allies. Indeed, with the end of both the fiscal year and the authorization of the transit bill approaching, the Senate Committee on Banking, Housing and Urban Affairs had not yet reached consensus on the size and shape of a mass transit reauthorization bill.[23]

In point of fact the Senate version of transit funding was similar to H.R. 3129, but it did have some significant differences. It called for a 4.3 percent increase in Sections 9 and 18 formula funds for fiscal 1987. In subsequent years the funding was supposed to inch upward at a rate equal to the inflation rate. Consistent with the understanding of the high degree of dependence small transit properties had on federal operating aid, operating assistance was to be frozen except in small urban areas of between 50,000 and 200,000 people. For those medium-sized cities, the cap on operating aid imposed by the 1982 transit act would be lifted. The Senate bill called for a discretionary capital improvement fund of $1.75 billion. About a third of the Section 3 increase was set aside for areas of over a million in population for discretionary bus grants in what was called a balanced investment fund. The remainder of the revenue would be split, with 40 percent for new starts, 40 percent for rail modernization projects, 10 percent for major bus needs, and 10 percent for unspecified needs.

While not discussing the administration's notion of increased private participation in public transit as a means of increasing efficiency, both the House and Senate bills contained language to prohibit the secretary of transportation from conditioning mass transit grants on some level of private sector participation or prescribing a mode of operation of a mass transit system. This threw out the strict privatization measure of the administration bill and was another sign that Congress was ignoring most of the main points of the administration's legislative proposal.

If there was a lack of consensus on the Surface Transportation bills in the House and Senate, there was also a lack of time and consensus on the delicate issue of appropriations to keep the federal government operating. The issue was finally settled by the passage of an omnibus continuing resolution that totaled a half trillion dollars; this replaced thirteen separate appropriations bills that simply could not be passed in time. The president was rightfully critical of Congress's inability to do its job of appropriating money the way the Constitution intended.

Because of the sluggishness in the Senate, things looked bad for reauthorization of the transit bill as the summer of 1986 waned. By the week after Labor Day of 1986 there had been no sign of consensus reached. Indeed, Senator D'Amato's S.2543 had not yet been considered by the Senate Banking, Housing and Urban Affairs Committee. Adding to the problem of finding agreement, Senator Alan

Dixon of Illinois pushed an alternate bill that contained some basic differences in the way that transit funds would be distributed.[24]

By the very end of September the Senate managed to pass its version of H.R. 3129. Again, there were significant differences between the two houses' versions. The House bill called for a comprehensive five-year mass transit extension at funding levels above the then current law, while the Senate wanted a simple four-year extension at frozen expenditure levels. This was sufficient to cause difficulty, but from what might be called left field came a major stumbling block: the Senate wished to allow the states to raise the 55 mph speed limit to 65 mph on rural sections of the Interstate Highway Systems. It was proposed by senators from western states and reflected their constituents' fretfulness over the 55 mph limit in areas of low population and long distances. That was a policy change that Congressman James Howard, a strong supporter of the 55 mph speed limit, could not live with. Worse yet, for purposes of finding consensus, the House bill contained a billion dollars of so-called demonstration highway projects. These were viewed as pet projects of certain congressmen and were to be funded 100 percent by the federal government. The Senate was dismayed and generally viewed the projects as pork-barrel stuff, mainly aimed at getting a representative re-elected to his seat in the House rather than being important from a transportation point of view. House members stated firmly that the projects were important but had typically been long-delayed. Opponents of the demonstrations noted that one of the projects, a new tunnel under Boston Harbor, was "a going-away present" for retiring Speaker of the House O'Neill.[25]

To keep the government running for a while, with understandable and vocal reluctance President Reagan signed the continuing resolution, which extended the expenditure possibilities of the federal government for 45 days of fiscal year 1987.

Final adjournment of Congress came on October 8. Congress passed, and President Reagan signed, legislation (PL.99-500) continuing funds in fiscal year 1987 for the formula grant portion of the federal mass transit program. Because the lawmakers were deadlocked on H.R. 3129, the reauthorization of the transit and highway programs did not take place in the 99th Congress. Working from different versions, the conference of the House and Senate was unable to resolve its differences over the highway issues. Without consensus on the highway issues, the conferees agreed that a compromise extension of the transit program was not possible.[26]

A POLITICAL SOAP OPERA:
THE HUNDREDTH CONGRESS AT WORK

In the very first day of the 100th Congress, Representative Glenn M. Anderson (D-California), chairman of the surface transportation subcommittee of the House Committee on Public Works and Transportation, introduced the Highway and Transit Bill as H.R. 2. The House set January 21, 1987, for its action on the measure. In the Senate, now under control of the Democrats after the November election, the jurisdiction for the reauthorization was split; highways were under the Committee on Environment and Public Works, whereas transit was handled by the Banking Committee. Public Works carried the ball on the upper house's version of the reauthorization, S.184, and it intended to mark up its bill coeval with the House action on January 21. The Banking Committee was to work on the transit part of the bill, agree, and then offer it as an amendment to the highway bill on the Senate floor.[27]

The battleground issues were exactly the same as they had been in the 99th Congress with H.R. 3129. On the Senate side, the highway demonstrations inserted by the House stuck in the solons' craws. On the House side, with Congressman Howard being particularly vehement on this issue, the desire of the Senate to raise the 55 mph speed limit to 65 mph on rural portions of the Interstate System was also a matter that was strongly opposed.

If politics in Congress focused on legislation that was conceded to be something everyone wanted and was badly needed, with the differences arising from two very disparate issues, the problem with the White House was much different. Indeed, the White House did not really address the situation in January or February, as the president, badly weakened by the Iran-contra imbroglio, continued to focus inward and to a large extent avoid much of the public's eye. The Reagan administration did go through its annual effort to cut the federal transit program budget in drastic fashion, eliminate Amtrak, and do other wonderful things in transportation for which there was little or no interest or support. The White House proposal of January 5 called for a 56 percent cut in the federal budget funds for transit from $3.45 billion to $1.5 billion.[28]

In addition to the political fallout over selling arms to Iran, President Reagan underwent a prostate gland operation in early January that, under any conditions, would have slowed a man down. As February blended into March the problems of the White House grew more serious. The worst thing for the administration was the conception given shape by the media, and echoed on the part of the public in a variety of polls, that the presidency was badly weakened, that Ronald Reagan was detached and uninterested in the details of the presidency, and that the Reagan administration was coming apart.

The image of poor management techniques was heightened on February 26 by the Tower Commission report. Appointed by President Reagan and chaired by former Senator John Tower (R-Texas), the commission reported that the Reagan White House was not a place of order and dispatch but one in which the National Security Council staff worked out of control in violation of at least the spirit of the law. The president got his lumps because of his detached style and his lack of curiosity concerning important foreign policy issues. According to the Tower Commission, Ronald Reagan did not know what was going on in important issues; it was a disturbing picture of an enfeebled and increasingly ineffective administration.

The politics picked up again when, with much pressure from Mrs. Reagan, Donald Regan was replaced as White House chief of staff by former Senator Howard H. Baker. The naming of Senator Baker, who had been senate majority leader from 1981 to 1984, was viewed as something very good for the country and for Ronald Reagan. Indeed, so badly damaged was the president by the Tower Commission report that there were those who said that the role of Howard Baker would really be more that of a prime minister. Some jokesters quipped that the remainder of the Reagan administration would really be the first two years of the Baker administration.

Mr. Reagan's fading away was badly overestimated. Within a month it was clear that Howard Baker had been enormously helpful to the White House and had reorganized the staff and apparently reorganized Ronald Reagan. The president became more active, more visible, more confident, and was clearly looking for opportunities to prove that the old prowess was there. Indeed, the combined highway and transit bill was seized upon by Reagan as an opportunity to boost the presidential image.[29]

Meanwhile, as the legislation embodied in H.R. 2 moved through the congressional process, the issue of the highway speed limit arose once again and lost none of its controversial nature. In carrying out its work the House held two votes on H.R. 2; one of them was a special vote on the speed limit. Seeking consensus on legislation it was under enormous pressure to pass, the House voted to accept the Senate's wish to enable states to move to a higher speed limit on rural interstates if the states so wished. While this might have been a bitter pill for the House to swallow, the highway demonstrations inserted in H.R. 2 by the House were equally bitter medicine for the Senate. At the end of March, after both houses had choked down the compromise, the passage of the highway-transit bill was overwhelmingly supported. Only seventeen members of the Senate and seventeen members of the House had voted against the bill. But the final emergence of the transit legislation was not to be so easy; Ronald Reagan decided to make it a cliff-hanger.[30]

Searching for something with which to project a take-charge, macho image, the president decided, despite the advice of Howard Baker and other counselors, to veto the highway-transit bill, dubbing it a "budget-buster." It was most certainly not one of Ronald Reagan's best ideas. The legislation was popular and the support for it was strong in all quarters. The states were particularly anxious for H.R. 2 to pass because most had long since run out of federal highway money. Supporters of the legislation both inside Congress and out pointed to the fact (whether totally accurate or not is beside the point) that 700,000 to 800,000 jobs depended upon passage of the act in a timely fashion so that the 1987 construction season could be seized. To the minds of many in Congress and their constituents, H.R. 2 was a jobs-creating—or continuing—measure that also would help to build and repair highways and transit systems.

The president was strong in his support of raising the speed limit to 65 mph. He opposed the portions of H.R. 2 having to do with highway demonstrations, and it is true that there were a good many who agreed with him that the demonstrations offered some blatant examples of wallowing in the public trough. The president also opposed the public transit funding levels, which were considerably above the parsimonious levels of the Reagan budget proposals.

Whether or not H.R. 2 was a budget buster was debatable, and the question was certainly argued vigorously in and out of Congress. The five-year authorizing legislation of almost $88 billion was made up primarily of money from the Highway Trust Fund and its Mass Transit Account. Only a small portion of the total was money from the general fund of the Treasury. The Highway Trust Fund money could only be spent for highways and certain mass transit purposes, and it was already being collected. Indeed, millions mounted up daily from the collection of user charges, none of which could be spent on anything in the absence of the reauthorization in H.R. 2. The mass transit money, which came to about $18 billion of the $88 billion, encompassed approximately $11 billion of money from the general fund.

Despite warnings from his advisors and friends and foes in Congress, President Reagan vetoed H.R. 2 on Friday, March 27, 1987. Over the weekend the lobbying force for an override of the veto built momentum. On Tuesday, March 31, the House overwhelmingly voted to override the president's veto. Attention then turned to the Senate, where the situation would inescapably seem to be much closer because the proportion of Republicans to Democrats was much closer. The two-thirds vote necessary to override a presidential veto was missed when the Senate voted on April 1. All the Democrats, save for freshman Senator Terry Sanford of North Carolina, voted to override, along with thirteen Republicans. Senate Majority Leader Robert Byrd of West Virginia immediately changed his vote and voted against the override in a brilliant display of senatorial procedures. As a senator voting on the prevailing side, Byrd exercised his rights and asked that another vote be taken on the issue at a later time. Pressure was put on Sanford, and on the afternoon of April 1 he indicated that he would change his vote to support the override. Minority Leader Robert Dole delayed proceedings to give the Republicans time to persuade one or more of the Republican senators who had voted with the Democrats to override to switch their votes to support the president. Attention was turned to another override vote in the Senate on April 2.

The drama heightened when Ronald Reagan decided to go to the Capitol to push for support of his veto. On the morning of April 2, 1987, in the old Senate chamber, the president met with all the Republican senators, asking to stand firm those who had voted with him. Taking aside the 13 senators who had voted with the Democrats to override the veto, Ronald Reagan begged them to switch their votes in his behalf. It was a high-risk action in a game of hardball politics, and the president lost. Later that morning, the Senate voted 67-33 to override the president's veto, and H.R. 2 became law. That afternoon, anxious New Mexico state highway crews began to hang up 65 mph speed limit signs.[31]

Republican senators and congressmen had not supported Ronald Reagan for a very good reason; there was enormous pressure from back home to get the roads repaired, and in a match between the president and potholes, the potholes won. It was the essence of Tip O'Neill's opinion that all politics are local politics. In the minds of many senators and congressmen was the thought, "Ronald Reagan is not going to run again in 1988, but I am." The issue was practical, not really doctrinaire, and apparently no one really believed the legislation was a budget buster.

The transit matter was big in some local constituencies—the money for the Los Angeles subway was an important issue there—but it did not dominate public discussion as did the highway matter. One good reason was that the transit money that affected most communities continued to flow during the time of debate and setback; only the Section 3 capital grant program, funded completely from the Mass Transit Account of the Highway Trust Fund, was affected by the lack of reauthorization. Because Section 3 is only for large-scale or unusual programs, such as the subway in Los Angeles, it affects relatively few places. The money for the more ordinary capital expenditures, as well as operating aid (those programs falling under Section 9 of the Urban Mass Transportation Act) is from the general fund of the Treasury, with authorization for the expenditure arising from the aforementioned continuing resolution.

WHAT THE LAW INVOLVES

After the flurry of activity, emotion, and drama revolving around the override of the presidential veto, what was the transit content of H.R. 2? The legislation, prior to the veto, had been overwhelmingly supported in both houses of Congress: 407-17 in the House of Representatives and 79-17 in the Senate. This support was the fruit of a large-scale lobbying campaign, and the content of the transit legislation was shaped by that effort.

The new Federal Mass Transportation Act of 1987 was Public Law 100-17 and continued the authorization of federal transit programs for five years; the authorization was for $17.8 billion over fiscal years 1987 through 1991. On a positive note for transit supporters, the law authorized an increase in the amount of federal aid for fiscal 1988 by an amount 2.8 percent higher than the appropriations for fiscal 1987.[32]

The legislation faced up to the problem of the attitude of legislators from states with transit systems unlikely to benefit from the Section 3 capital grant program. This part of the Urban Mass Transportation Act was changed in the 1982 reauthorization to be used exclusively for large and costly or otherwise special capital projects that could not be handled by the funds routinely meted out under the formula of the Section 9 block grant program.

Transit supporters were fearful of legislation such as that introduced by Senator Symms of Idaho, which would have mandated that 85 percent of the Mass Transit Account money from each state had to be used only in the state in which it originated. As noted earlier, this would have virtually undermined the program of federal support for major investments in transit. Animated by this threat to the Section 3 program, a compromise called "blending" was introduced in the legislative process. Blending was introduced in a new Section 9(B) formula program. Under Section 9(B) a portion of the funds from the Mass Transit Account would be blended into both the Section 9 and Section 18 programs, thus making the monies available more broadly than by use for Section 3 grants only.

The source of the blending funds is one-half of all the Mass Transit Account funds in excess of $1 billion annually. The money from blending represented contract authority and was to be available for four years, inclusive of the year in which apportioned. If not used by that time, the blended funds would be put back into the formula program to be reapportioned by the regular formula process. The blended amounts could reach a healthy figure, because of the growth in income to the Mass Transit Account ever since the program was enacted. Assuming that the fully authorized amount of Mass Transit Account funds was available each year the law was in effect, the amount to be blended in the formula program would be $100 million in FY 1988, $125 million in FY 1989, $150 million in FY 1990, and $200 million in FY 1991.

The Mass Transit Account funds that could be used rose from $1.1 billion, under the provisions of the 1982 law, to $1.4 billion by fiscal year 1991, under the terms of the 1987 legislation. The Mass Transit Account was the source of funds for a number of the mass transit programs in addition to capital projects. The Section 8 planning grants would receive about $45 million each year; Section 16(b)(2) program of capital aid for private, non-profit providers of human service transportation (often dubbed the elderly and handicapped program) and Section 4(i) innovative techniques grants program would share a total of $35 million earmarked for them; university research centers (a new program establishing university centers in each of the ten federal administrative regions) would have $5 million earmarked annually. Finally, $3.2 million in start-up money would be used in FY 1987-88 for a new bus testing facility in the vicinity of Altoona, Pennsylvania. The residue and great bulk of the Mass Transit Account money was to be spent generally on the basis of 40 percent for new starts and extensions, 40 percent for rail modernization project grants, 10 percent for major bus projects, and the remaining 10 percent at the discretion of the secretary of transportation.[33]

With the beginning of fiscal year 1988, the Section 9 formula or block grants were authorized at $2.1 billion, or 5 percent above the previous level. The Section 18 grants for non-urbanized and rural areas were reauthorized at 2.9 percent of the formula funds total, which included the dollars blended in under Section 9(B).

Bundled together in a $50 million annual authorization were funds for the cost of administering UMTA, along with money for research, training, and human resources grants; $5 million was provided in an annual set-aside for a new Rural Transit Assistance Program (RTAP). In cases where federal Interstate Highway dollars were traded in for transit capital purposes under the Interstate Transfer provision of the Urban Mass Transportation Act, the authorization was set at $200 million each year; additionally, $100 million was added to the "cost-to-complete" estimate of residual Interstate Transfer projects.[34]

The 1982 reauthorizing legislation placed a cap on the amount of operating aid that could be used by cities of various size ranges. The new Act contained some good news for smaller urban areas in the 50,000 to 200,000 population range. In fiscal 1988 there would be a one-time, 32.3 percent increase in the cap on such aid to make up for inflation. Beginning in FY 1987, an area that had become urbanized since 1980 could use up to two-thirds of its Section 9 apportionment for operating purposes. This was a boon to smaller places, which had traditionally been much more dependent upon federal operating aid under Section 9 programs than had been larger cities. The federal share of capital projects under Section 9 stipulated previously that it not exceed 80 percent; the legislation of 1987 modified that to read "shall be 80 percent."[35]

New starts, generally meaning a new rail start, were strongly fought by the Reagan administration as being too costly for the value received. The 1987 law required that the U.S. DOT issue new start criteria. The new start had to be based upon the results of an alternatives analysis and a preliminary engineering study; the project must be considered to be cost-effective and should be supported by what is considered an acceptable proportion of local funding. New start projects under full-funding contracts or letters of intent by April 2 were exempted from the above provisions, as were projects for preliminary engineering, final design, or construction as of January 1, 1987.

The law also required a more careful approach to transit improvements. The local planning process had to include a long-term financial plan that enumerated the various sources of revenue; in short, a strategic financial plan was required for transit improvements to make sure that there were sufficient state, local, federal, and farebox revenues to complete a project and to operate it when it was completed.[36]

The new federal transit law was long and complex and contained many provisions to meet the needs of the industry, simple equity, general political logrolling, the requirements of administration, and the limits of money available. Among other things, it contained requirements for the oversight of the construction of major projects (tantalizingly, the law did not define a major project but left that up to UMTA); the oversight cost was covered 100 percent by the federal government, and the grant recipient must prepare and implement a project management plan. The "Buy American" requirement for transit rolling stock was changed to 55 percent from 50 percent for contracts made after fiscal year 1989; the proportion rises to 60 percent after fiscal 1991. There were also the expected provisions aiming money at given projects, such as money for the construction of the rapid transit system in Los Angeles, extra operating funds for the urbanized areas to help support rail commuter services in the Fort Lauderdale-Miami region, a study of the streetcar lines in Philadelphia, a study of the mass transit needs of the Virgin Islands, and the transfer of unused formula funds from Nevada to Santa Clara County in California.[37]

One of the more interesting provisions was the requirement that new bus models or existing bus models with major changes could not be purchased with federal money without first being tested for performance and safety at a new facility that Congress recommended be constructed in Altoona, Pennsylvania. The requirement was to go into effect in fiscal year 1989. It was mentioned earlier that the Mass Transit Account would be tapped for $3.2 million in start-up costs for the bus-testing facility; after the initial period there would be fees

charged for the testing. There could also be tests for rail cars. The testing provision was obviously a reaction to the problem suffered in the late 1970s and early
1980s by buses that were far less than perfect. Whether or not this would help
produce better buses was a matter of conjecture; it might cause manufacturers
extreme reluctance in introducing new models or in making significant innovations in existing models. Perhaps the only good to come of it would be money
pumped into the depressed economy of Altoona.[38]

THE MEANING OF IT ALL

Out of the throb of activity that produced the 1987 legislation concerning
the federal role in urban mass transportation, some expectations were revealed.
The federal mass transit program was decidedly a part of the federal establishment and a favored part of the package of programs attractive to members of
Congress and their constituents. As the nation had witnessed since 1981, the
White House might storm about the transit program and try in various ways to
dismantle it, but the federal transit program would apparently continue for the
foreseeable future much in its present form. The 1987 legislation gave the authorization for this program to continue for an unusually long time—five years—so
supporters of transit had adequate time to do their homework and maintain the
support always needed. The trend to move the bulk of the federal transit program
to a formula basis rather than a discretionary basis continued.

The change in the mass transportation program really amounted to fine-
tuning, not a radical departure from previous practices. Some of this was the
well-recognized reaction to a problem. For example, the "Buy American" clause
was an effort to pump more life into domestic transit equipment business, understandably chafed by the inroads of foreign competition often perceived as unfair.
The new long-term financial planning requirement was an example of an effort
to assure that local transit officials had thought through what was needed to
maintain and operate the capital resources provided with the help of the federal
transit program. Again, the blending technique was a response to a perceived
equity problem that created a political difficulty in certain states. Fine-tuning
would probably continue as experience showed problems or shortcomings.

Looking at mass transit programs from 1990, one may conclude that the
only major bit of change in the future may be to support them through a trust
fund in order to remove them from the threats of a hostile White House or the
rigors of sharp budget and appropriations cuts as the nation eventually begins to
deal with the enormous budget deficit. What happens in the next few years with
regard to the economy as a whole will determine the source of support; more
pennies on the gas tax for transit along with more pennies for highways is a good
guess, at least as a starting point.

Concern over the falling proportion of transit use out of total trips taken is
only partially real and may be bogus. As U.S. urban areas continue to spread out
and metropolitan areas become multi-nucleated, the transit patterns of the past
will have to change if transit is to play a useful role in the urban future. The count

of total person trips is subject to debate; the figures used may not be at all accurate.

Mass transit in the United States has not realized its full potential and probably will not as long as there are few incentives in many urban places to use transit, or if communities continue to be so laid out that the automobile is the only practical means of mobility. Management of demand is the possible answer to better movement of people in the urban setting; so far that does not seem to be a politically attractive solution. When the situation becomes bad enough, or there is not enough money to overcome mobility problems by the current means, the approach may change. It will not be easy.

Mass transit is a possible solution to urban mobility problems. It is not the last word, but it is a resource, a method to help solve mobility difficulties. It should not be rejected without thought. As the nation approaches the third millennium, perhaps a target for many great programs and efforts to solve difficult problems, transit may take its appropriate role as a tool for assuring all citizens ease of movement and access to economic, social, and cultural advantages that are the unique advantages of urban life.

The last chapter will explore some of the problems that plague the urban transportation scene and what may be done or not done to solve them.

14.

The Once and Future Program of Federal Mass Transit Policy

The U.S. federal mass transit policy and program is mature and many-faceted. It started in a small way in 1961, and the basic, broader program had its beginning in law in 1964. In its first stage, the federal transit program began as an unexpected reaction to problems that were suddenly thrust upon large cities fearing the loss of commuter rail service.

To the thoughtful makers of federal policy in the early 1960s, the federal mass transit program was a means of expanding the options available to cities in order to provide mobility for their citizens beyond just a federal highway approach. The first phase of federal transit policy was largely justified by the growing problem of congestion. Only a little later was recognition given to the lack of mobility suffered by many Americans and to the enormous social and economic cost of various programs and efforts to provide improved transportation and mobility in urban areas by means of federal highway programs alone.

The second stage of policy and program development was mainly a product of the 1970s, when the federal money available expanded greatly. In keeping with the issues of the day, mass transportation aid was also touted as a way to reduce pollution and cut down on fuel use. However, because transit use was not great enough in most places to have any real impact on pollution or energy conservation, it became obvious that it was difficult to justify transit on such a basis.

The third and current (as of 1990) stage of the federal transit policy and program has been largely a holding action. Transit supporters battled the Reagan administration for eight years to keep the program from obliteration. The program survived, although it fell victim to major cutbacks in federal funding and suffered a substantial loss in the purchasing power of the federal dollars that remained. State and local governments made up a significant portion of the lost federal funds. Supporters succeeded in keeping the federal transit program alive with help from strong congressional backing. The current mass transit program of the federal government is, quite plainly, a child of Congress. It's not difficult to see why: the federal mass transit program has impact on the local level in states and in congressional districts. By the end of the sixties, members of Congress came to realize that federal aid to mass transit was a pragmatic response to local needs initiated at a time when the privately owned transit industry was failing and when the financial means of cities and states to pick up the ball and operate mass transit as a public venture were seriously limited. The federal role filled a policy and program vacuum. American cities, for the most part, had no experience in—and no budget for—transit.

The federal transit program was initiated by pressure from big cities, and it is still viewed by some as a big-city program. However, the federal transit program was continued with increasing strength in the 1970s and to a large extent preserved against the onslaughts of the Reagan administration, thanks to support and pressure from smaller cities. It was recognized that the problems of mass transportation were not a singular big-city plague; they had impact in both large and small places across the United States.

Part of the attraction of the transit program is that it offers something for everyone. It enjoys broad, bipartisan support from big-city Democrats and suburban Republicans in Congress, and rurally based legislators are also interested, because federally supported programs provide mobility in smaller cities and the rural areas of the nation. For those interested in social improvement, it offers a social program providing mobility for jobs, access for elderly and handicapped people to various kinds of economic, social, and cultural activities, and is intended to help improve access without the need to own an automobile. On the other hand, it is also an economic development program. Transit is very much a part of the infrastructure upon which the private sector depends. Not only are many federal dollars spent that help boost the local economy in various places, but the presence of improved mass transit also enhances property values and makes certain areas of a city attractive for renovation, refurbishment, and large private investment. Put another way, even though the largest cities get the largest sums of federal transit money in both proportional and absolute terms, the federal transit program spreads money on a relatively broad basis, whether for purposes of income redistribution or economic stimulation.

The federal transit program has been skillfully handled and guided through the lawmaking process over the years. Congressman James Howard's wedding of transit and highway legislation on several occasions is a good example of a well-considered maneuver aimed at getting the transit program fully continued and supported to the maximum extent financially possible. Earlier, the efforts of Senator Harrison Williams were of extreme importance. The continuing strong support of the U.S. Conference of Mayors and National League of Cities was, and is, essential. The shrewd strategy established by Fred Burke working with and through the American Public Transit Association (APTA) also exemplifies very skillful and successful handling of the program, even in the difficult years of the Reagan administration. The lobbying force at APTA worked diligently to shape and gain support for the program in the time of growth, and APTA labored constantly to resist opposing efforts during the 1980s that threatened to destroy the program. The acid test of such success and of the popularity of the program with Congress is that the federal mass transit program has survived the forceful and continued opposition of a highly popular president.

White House support has been mixed over the years. The philosophy that the federal government has a broad role to play in a number of spheres was held fundamentally by Presidents Kennedy, Johnson, Nixon, and Ford. The administrations of Presidents Carter and Reagan reflected their philosophy that the federal government's presence should be basically limited in a number of areas. Another element at work in the Reagan administration was the question of why a Republican administration should spend federal money to help the opposition. The fact that most large cities are governed by Democrats and the perception that the mass transit program was aimed mainly at large cities, cooled off any interest the Reagan administration might have had in the program, despite the strong support for the transit program from congressional Republicans. Moreover, transit was perceived by members of the Reagan administration as a kind of welfare program, and welfare programs found relatively barren ground under their aegis. Also, the erroneous notion that the automobile is not subsidized seemed to have been held by President Reagan and some of his advisors.

Another reason that there was relatively lackluster support of transit from any one of the administrations is that it was not an important presidential issue, except peripherally during the 1970s fuel crisis. Transit was not and is not an issue that generates presidential concern in the same way as do issues involving the economy or national security. Transit is a national issue, but with a tightly focused sphere of impact because the delivery of the program is so local in nature. This local impact naturally aroused strong interest and support from representatives and senators whose constituents were affected by the quantity and quality of transit service.

The federal mass transit programs were responsible for rebuilding the transit industry. Though far from perfect, the transit industry by the mid–1980s was probably in the best physical shape it had enjoyed in many years. Most of the smaller and medium-sized systems that were served by bus received relatively new fleets of equipment, new facilities in which to store and maintain it, and new supporting equipment such as bus shelters and transfer facilities. Exceptions to the good condition of the U.S. transit systems can be found in some of the big-city rail systems, such as New York, Philadelphia, and Chicago, which, due to decades of deferred maintenance, still require substantial infusions of capital for infrastructure replenishment purposes. The need for capital, always great, has delayed some new starts in rail and other fixed facility development. But overall, looking back to the tired and undernourished situation in rail transit that existed in the early sixties, there have been some interesting and potentially valuable new rail systems put in place, and some older ones substantially upgraded.

The federal mass transit programs stimulated financial support from both state and local government. Initially, this was a result of the matching requirements that the federal program demanded. The program gave incentives to cities and states to levy specialized taxes or to appropriate general fund money for mass transit. The lure of federal money stimulated local transit people to lobby for support on the state and local levels so that they could take advantage of the federal programs. With sufficient practice, transit interests in some states became very proficient in getting state and local transit funds. Some state and local governments provide aid beyond that necessary just to match federal funds. As a result, the cutbacks in federal aid in the 1980s have been in large part countered by increased support from other levels of government.[1]

Another result of the federal programs was the more positive attitude of public officials toward mass transportation. Over the years, public officials at state and local government levels got accustomed to the idea of aid for mass transit as being a worthwhile effort. Something of the notion of "every real city needs a transit system" is not too farfetched a description of the way many states viewed mass transportation, and local officials in many places adopted the same attitude.

Even so, one real worry on the part of officials in all levels of government was the constant increase in the cost of providing transit service. Despite the money available, transit has led a fragile, hand-to-mouth existence in several places. Many mayors and transit managers have most certainly felt that way during the cutbacks of the Reagan administration as they scurried to find transit money closer to home. Animated by the Reagan administration threats, many of the state and local governments put together very decent programs with relatively high levels of support. Most importantly, it has become more and more "thinkable" for state and local governments to support transit strongly.[2]

THE MORE THINGS CHANGE, THE MORE THEY STAY THE SAME

In the early 1960s the development of the federal mass transportation policy heralded a real change in American urban life; it was hoped that the policy would have a substantial beneficial impact. That impact has been modest, at best, because whereas federal policy toward transit changed, other urban policies remained the same. The urban highway policy, housing, and civil-rights policies that encouraged suburbanization of the middle class and center-city ghettos for the poor and minorities stayed the same; these were forces working to tear the American city and metropolitan area apart. Transit may help build density—if given the opportunity. It certainly works best in places with a high density of population and economic development. The limited effect of transit on American cities since 1961 is due to the enormous power of other forces at work that create spread-out metropolitan areas that transit cannot serve very well.

The federal urban highway program continued virtually unabated; the relatively modest transit programs were carried out in tandem with highway development. It was, after all, the conventional wisdom. It was unthinkable that the federal highway program would be changed in any great way. By the end of the 1960s it was quite acceptable for subsidized mass transit to be offered, but at the same time, it was inconceivable not to continue the momentum of the urban highway program and, in reality, to keep highways as the dominant form of mobility. Expectations for transit and for the general improvement of mobility situations were broadened, but existing highway prospects were not really disappointed. Best of all, from a political standpoint the voters in their automobiles were not inconvenienced; they could enjoy the status quo. The end result was that transit really did not replace highways in almost any instance but was largely viewed as a way of adding some capacity to a given corridor. The possible impact of transit was, of course, lessened. Most persons involved either did not see the policy conflict or believed that the politics of the situation had little to do with policy consistency.

Those who thought that they would see transit play a role in shaping the development of metropolitan areas were disappointed. With the exception of a few rail systems, the shaping effect did not occur. The Bay Area Rapid Transit District in the San Francisco area, the Washington Metropolitan Area Transit Authority's Metrorail system, and the Metropolitan Atlanta Rapid Transit Authority show evidence of having had some effect on the way growth took place; but because of coeval highway programs there was no lack of growth away from the mass transit systems. Transit's impact was muted.

It is no surprise that the transit share of the urban travel market did not increase and, indeed, receded as sprawl largely induced by personal preference and congruent federal policy scattered development even more widely. The dashed hopes that transit would help cut pollution and contain the use of energy were a result of an increasing amount of the population moving out of transit's effective theater of operations. In most urbanized areas it would have taken great shifts of drivers from their automobiles to bus or rail service in order to have any conservational or environmental impact. Critics note that transit succeeded mainly in boosting the number of its employees; in this there was achievement.

A disappointing aspect of the transit picture is that it carried a smaller proportion of trips in the late 1980s than when the program started. The absolute number of patrons was higher than it had been in a number of years, but proportionately it slipped rather badly. For example, in 1969, public transit carried 3.4 percent of total person trips; this fell to 2.7 percent in 1977 and 2.6 percent in 1983. In the main this was due to population growth in urban places, combined with a massive shift in the distribution of population away from the central city where mass transportation functions with relative effectiveness and efficiency. Ridership remained relatively stable after 1980—between 8 billion and 8.4 billion annual trips. There was an increase in transit use proportionally in large urbanized areas, and a decrease in smaller urbanized areas.[3]

Transit has become irrelevant to the lives of most Americans who reside in parts of metropolitan areas outside of central cities. It doesn't provide a reasonable alternative to the automobile for the great majority of trips taken in many metropolitan areas. Sprawl and population distribution make increasing portions of metropolitan areas absolutely unservable with anything resembling conventional public transportation. Suburb-to-suburb transit is difficult at best and nonexistent in most places. Transit does not meet the orbital travel patterns of a large proportion of metropolitan dwellers. However, the situation is not totally negative; improvements in transit systems that serve central business districts have been significant enough in some cases to cause an increase in the proportion of downtown employees who use transit.

Transit is identified as the transportation of the poor, the black, and the Hispanic. Transit is not part of the American dream; it is not viewed as the transportation for the upwardly mobile. Commuter rail transportation is an exception to the foregoing point. Riding a commuter train has positive connotations because commuter service is usually associated with managers, professionals, and other high-income people living in relatively expensive places. The fact that commuter rail service is also a much better alternative than the automobile for long trips doesn't hurt either. Indeed, the 1980s saw what appeared to be an upsurge in commuter rail patronage.

A final factor is that mass transit, and transportation in general, are very expensive to provide. Good transit systems and good highways are not cheap. Regardless of the effectiveness of the expenditure, a great deal of money must be spent to achieve decent roads and transit service. What is troublesome in federal programs is that transit's operating subsidy is obvious in the federal budget. Federal highway money for maintenance, which is essentially an operating subsidy, is not so clearly set forth. As a result, it is often contended that there is no real subsidy to highways.

The realistic goals for transit have been fuzzy at best at all levels of government, and the commitment to use it as an effective tool has been weak. The unabated sprawl of population and the continued heavy expenditures for highways have, in truth, left transit to service primarily its traditionally captive market in larger metropolitan areas.

THE RESULTS OF THE FEDERAL TRANSIT PROGRAM

The federal mass transit program has produced a number of solid results, even if it has not had a dramatic impact on most cities. Perhaps the most important result is in improving the physical capital of the transit industry. Thousands of new buses and railcars have been placed into service since the conception of the federal mass transit program. For most transit properties in the U.S., it means that they are not operating equipment that could best be described as fugitives from the Smithsonian.[4] According to the records of the Urban Mass Transportation Administration, a grand total of $52,768,198,092 has been spent on the federal programs through fiscal 1987. Among other things, this money purchased 66,927 buses and 6,896 rail transit cars and locomotives (for rail commuter service). New starts assisted by UMTA and completed extensions total 322 miles; another 80 miles is under consideration. See Tables 14.1, 14.2, 14.3, and 14.4.

There has also been a major capital replenishment or total replacement of fixed facilities. With a few exceptions, bus facilities around the nation today are generally in good shape. Most bus maintenance facilities in use up until the 1960s had been originally built as streetcar barns and were constructed in the period from around 1900 through the 1920s. From then until the 1960s, the

Table 14.1
UMTA GRANT FUNDING SOURCES
INCLUDES LOAN AUTHORITY, UNRESTRICTED AUTHORITY, CONTRACT AUTHORITY AND APPROPRIATIONS

	SECTION 3	SECTION 8 (PLANNING)	SECTION 16(b)(2) (E&H)	INNOV. TECH. INTRO	SECTION 17	SECTION 5	SECTIONS 9/9A/9B	SECTIONS 18 & RTAP	SECTIONS 6/10/11/20/32	INTERSTATE TRANSFER	STARK-HARRIS	TOTAL	ADMINISTRATION	GRAND TOTAL
1961	17,500,000	0	0	0	0	0	0	0	25,000,000	0	0	42,500,000	0	42,500,000
1962	0	0	0	0	0	0	0	0	0	0	0	0	0	0
1963	0	0	0	0	0	0	0	0	0	0	0	0	0	0
1964	3,000,000	0	0	0	0	0	0	0	4,805,000	0	0	7,805,000	195,000	8,000,000
1965	65,000,000	0	0	0	0	0	0	0	0	0	0	65,000,000	300,000	65,300,000
1966	135,000,000	0	0	0	0	0	0	0	0	0	0	135,000,000	455,000	135,455,000
1967	130,000,000	0	0	0	0	0	0	0	0	0	0	130,000,000	735,000	130,735,000
1968	125,000,000	0	0	0	0	0	0	0	0	0	0	125,000,000	690,000	125,690,000
1969	169,147,000	5,000,000	0	0	0	0	0	0	0	0	0	174,147,000	853,000	175,000,000
1970	137,000,000	8,000,000	0	0	0	0	0	0	30,000,000	0	0	175,000,000	1,600,000	176,600,000
1971	555,475,000	15,000,000	0	0	0	0	0	0	26,200,000	0	0	596,675,000	3,325,000	600,000,000
1972	803,700,000	25,000,000	0	0	0	0	0	0	65,000,000	0	0	893,700,000	6,300,000	900,000,000
1973	863,708,000	33,500,000	0	0	0	0	0	0	96,250,000	0	0	993,458,000	6,542,000	1,000,000,000
1974	872,050,000	37,600,000	0	0	0	0	0	0	35,000,000	61,000,000	0	1,005,650,000	5,000,000	1,010,650,000
1975	1,330,110,000	36,610,000	19,900,000	0	0	300,000,000	0	0	45,050,000	65,700,000	0	1,797,370,000	5,960,000	1,803,330,000
1976	1,078,000,000	38,700,000	22,000,000	0	25,000,000	500,000,000	0	0	54,000,000	632,000,000	0	2,349,700,000	10,300,000	2,360,000,000
TQ	246,500,000	9,200,000	0	0	0	125,000,000	0	0	11,500,000	0	0	392,200,000	2,900,000	395,100,000
1977	1,228,000,000	43,200,000	22,000,000	0	55,000,000	650,000,000	0	0	61,200,000	570,072,080	0	2,629,472,080	12,600,000	2,642,072,080
1978	1,375,000,000	55,000,000	25,000,000	0	45,000,000	775,000,000	0	0	70,000,000	662,760,493	0	3,007,760,493	20,000,000	3,027,760,493
1979	1,175,000,000	55,000,000	20,000,000	0	0	1,403,500,000	0	76,500,000	68,500,000	623,765,105	0	3,422,265,105	16,849,000	3,439,114,105
1980	1,625,075,000	55,000,000	20,000,000	0	0	1,405,000,000	0	85,000,000	70,300,000	425,000,000	0	3,685,375,000	17,884,000	3,703,259,000
1981	2,095,000,000	45,000,000	25,000,000	25,000,000	0	1,455,000,000	0	72,500,000	56,840,000	615,032,414	0	4,389,372,414	22,200,000	4,411,572,414
1982	1,377,500,000	55,000,000	25,000,000	7,000,000	0	1,365,250,000	0	68,500,000	49,600,000	560,000,000	0	3,507,850,000	24,388,000	3,532,238,000
1983	1,606,650,000	50,000,000	25,000,000	10,000,000	0	1,200,000,000	756,175,000	91,325,000	58,250,000	412,000,000	240,000,000	4,449,400,000	28,407,000	4,477,807,000
1984	1,138,900,000	50,000,000	26,100,000	10,000,000	0	0	2,318,606,000	69,986,000	54,800,000	295,400,000	250,000,000	4,213,792,000	29,400,000	4,243,192,000
1985	1,018,800,000	50,000,000	26,200,000	5,000,000	0	0	2,377,729,650	71,770,350	51,000,000	250,000,000	250,000,000	4,100,500,000	31,000,000	4,131,500,000
1986	970,565,000	47,850,000	29,500,000	4,785,000	0	0	1,997,263,785	60,286,215	16,652,000	191,400,000	217,239,000	3,535,541,000	28,710,000	3,564,251,000*
1987	915,000,000	45,000,000	35,000,000	7,500,000	0	0	1,924,995,000	75,005,000	17,400,000	200,000,000	201,120,000	3,421,020,000	31,000,000	3,452,020,000
1988	1,050,500,000	45,000,000	35,000,000	0	0	0	1,667,064,000	69,389,000	12,217,000	123,500,000	180,500,000	3,183,170,000	31,882,000	3,215,052,000
TOTAL	22,107,330,000	804,660,000	355,700,000	69,285,000	125,000,000	9,178,750,000	11,041,833,435	740,261,565	979,414,000	5,687,630,092	1,338,859,000	52,428,723,092	339,475,000	52,768,198,092

* After Sequestration

1) The Interstate Transfer Substituion program appropriations in FY 1977 through FY 1981 included transit and highway funds. This column includes only the transit funds. The total approriations for these years are as follows: FY 1977-$575,000,000; FY 1978-$789,000,000; FY 1979-$700,000,000; FY 1980-$700,000,000; and FY 1981-$865,000,000.

2) Includes $5,000,000 for RTAP

NOTE: Breakdown of Loan Authority, Unrestricted Authority, and Contract Authority is provided in the next table.

Source: Jo Tucci (UGM-11), 1987 Urban Mass Transportation Administration Grants Assistance Programs Statistical Summaries (Washington, D.C.: Urban Mass Transportation Administration, August 31, 1988) Table B.

Table 14.2
FUNDING AUTHORITIES FOR FISCAL YEARS 1961–1988

FISCAL YEAR	LOAN AUTHORITY	UNRESTRICTED AUTHORITY	CONTRACT AUTHORITY	TOTAL
1961	42,500,000	0	0	42,500,000
1962	0	0	0	0
1963	0	0	0	0
1964	3,000,000	0	0	3,000,000
1965	5,000,000	60,000,000	0	65,000,000
1966	5,000,000	130,000,000	0	135,000,000
1967	0	130,000,000	0	130,000,000
1968	0	125,000,000	0	125,000,000
1969	0	175,000,000	0	175,000,000
1970	0	145,000,000	0	145,000,000
1971	0	194,000,000	376,675,000	570,675,000
1972	0	0	828,700,000	828,700,000
1973	0	(35,000,000)*	897,208,000	862,208,000
1974	0	0	909,600,000	909,600,000
1975	0	0	1,686,620,000	1,686,620,000
1976	0	0	2,082,700,000	2,082,700,000
TQ	0	0	380,700,000	380,700,000
1977	0	0	2,118,200,000	2,118,200,000
1978	0	0	2,580,000,000	2,580,000,000
1979	0	0	1,150,000,000	1,150,000,000
1980	0	0	0	0
1981	0	0	0	0
1982	0	0	0	0
1983	0	0	779,000,000	779,000,000
1984	0	0	1,225,000,000	1,225,000,000
1985	0	0	1,100,000,000	1,100,000,000
1986	0	0	1,052,700,000	1,052,700,000
1987	0	0	1,002,500,000	1,002,500,000
1988	0	0	1,130,500,000	1,130,500,000
TOTAL	55,500,000	924,000,000	19,300,103,000	20,279,603,000

* Transfer from UMTA appropriations to "Interim Operating Assistance" account, administered by the Office of the Secretary of Transportation to implement the Regional Rail Reorganization Act of 1973 pursuant to the Foreign Assistance and Related Programs Appropriation Act, 1974.

Source: Joe Tucci (UGM-11), *1987 Urban Mass Transportation Administration Grants Assistance Program Statistical Summaries* (Washington, D.C.: Urban Mass Transportation Administration, August 31, 1988) Table B-2.

Depression and the decline in the transit industry had precluded expenditures for building many facilities really geared to the maintenance and servicing of buses. This has changed since the mid–1960s, thanks to the federal transit program. It was typical for the first grant of transit capital from the federal government to

Table 14.3
NEW BUS COMMITMENTS
BY YEAR OF APPROVAL
(Does not include Sec. 16(b)(2) or Sec. 18)

	BY PROGRAM						BY VEHICLE				
FY	TOTAL	Sec.3	Sec.5	Sec.9A	Sec.9	FAUS	Int Transf	40'-35' Stand.	30' or Less	Vans	Articu- lated	Trolley*
65	358	358	0	0	0	0	0	266	92	0	0	0
66	1110	1110	0	0	0	0	0	951	159	0	0	0
67	311	311	0	0	0	0	0	216	95	0	0	0
68	637	637	0	0	0	0	0	525	112	0	0	0
69	501	501	0	0	0	0	0	416	85	0	0	0
70	1487	1487	0	0	0	0	0	1435	52	0	0	0
71	2521	2521	0	0	0	0	0	2296	225	0	0	0
72	3502	3502	0	0	0	0	0	3235	267	0	0	0
73	4072	4072	0	0	0	0	0	3599	473	0	0	0
74	5816	5378	0	0	0	438	0	5026	634	6	150	0
75	4426	4307	99	0	0	20	0	3755	586	25	60	0
76	3318	2867	391	0	0	60	0	2926	181	73	138	0
TQ	359	312	47	0	0	0	0	264	81	14	0	0
77	3798	3200	472	0	0	126	0	3264	410	74	50	0
78	3992	3620	331	0	0	41	0	3408	423	141	20	0
79	2939	1020	1611	0	0	99	209	2168	399	323	49	0
80	4223	1773	2191	0	0	78	181	3230	492	236	265	0
81	4611	2790	1647	0	0	45	129	3406	399	290	516	0
82	3250	1912	1290	0	0	11	37	2490	500	63	197	0
83	2863	1714	575	559	0	12	3	2131	254	248	230	0
84	2475	174	588	292	1371	17	33	1609	434	343	89	0
85	3051	83	449	134	2302	10	73	2139	485	306	97	24
86	3666	245	338	269	2788	4	22	2560	595	426	11	74
87	3641	236	0	0	3282	49	74	2673	395	439	76	58
TOTAL	66927	44130	10029	1254	9743	1010	761	53988	7828	3007	1948	156

*Prior to 1985 included with Standard Buses

Source: Jo Tucci (UGM-11), *1987 Urban Mass Transportation Administration Grants Assistance Program Statistical Summaries* (Washington, D.C.: Urban Mass Transportation Administration, August 31, 1988) Table 22.

include purchase of a private transit property, new buses, and a new mainte-nance and office facility. Even so, in some of the larger properties, with many deferred maintenance claims, old car barns are still being used to service buses. Availability of capital funds and local priorities have been the deciding factors.

The upgrading of rail facilities has typically been dependent upon the avail-ability of local matching funds and skilled lobbying at all levels to line up money and get it moving. This is often a function of the strength and organization of the local transit authority. Boston, which is probably unmatched among U.S. cities in its acquisition of federal transit funds relative to its size, has largely rebuilt its very old rail transit and commuter rail facilities. The re-railing, re-signaling, and re-powering of the lines have moved on steadily since the 1970s. Commuter rail

Table 14.4
NEW RAIL CARS BY TYPE AND FISCAL YEAR

FY	RAPID TRANSIT	LIGHT RAIL	COMMUTER ELECTRIC	COMMUTER DIESEL	DIESEL* LOCO	TOTAL
65	64	0	0	0	0	64
66	400	0	0	0	0	400
67	0	0	35	0	0	35
68	226	0	144	0	0	370
69	260	0	123	0	0	383
70	0	0	309	0	0	309
71	0	80	237	0	0	317
72	420	0	64	25	0	509
73	650	150	15	36	13	864
74	200	45	170	5	2	422
75	140	0	160	20	0	320
76	0	0	58	50	22	130
TQ	71	0	0	0	8	79
77	320	48	50	2	9	429
78	125	141	0	90	23	379
79	326	0	0	91	19	436
80	16	26	36	0	0	78
81	204	26	0	80	7	317
82	414	55	8	48	24	549
83	50	26	0	15	0	91
84	128	50	0	0	22	200
85	76	0	0	0	0	76
86	63	0	0	37	6	106
87	0	26	0	0	7	33
TOTAL	4,153	673	1409	499	162	6,896

* INCLUDED IN FY 84 ARE 4 ELECTRIC LOCOMOTIVES

Source: Jo Tucci (UGM-11), *1987 Urban Mass Transportation Grants Assistance Program Statistical Summaries* (Washington, D.C.: Urban Mass Transportation Administration, August 31, 1988) Table 23.

lines have attracted attention nationwide and there have also been, of course, extensions of existing lines and construction of new rail rapid transit lines. Instead of rehabilitation in one major case, Boston's Massachusetts Bay Transportation Authority has shifted a large portion of its Orange Line rapid transit system south of downtown to a completely new right-of-way shared with Amtrak, about a half-mile west of its original location. This massive undertaking allowed the very tired, 1902 vintage Washington Street elevated railway structure to be dismantled.

Philadelphia is like Boston in that it possesses a very old and very large rail transit infrastructure. Unfortunately, Philadelphia and its transit property, Southeastern Pennsylvania Transportation Authority (SEPTA), have been unable to get their act together sufficiently to find the local money or to deal effectively with the federal government to attract dollars necessary to upgrade its rail system. For the SEPTA commuter rail lines, the situation was not cheerful; bridges, the track structure itself, the signaling system, and the electric power supply system all needed major rehabilitation to make the railroad function properly and reliably. Instead of capital replenishment, in the 1970s Philadelphia chose to build a tunnel linking together the two separate electric commuter rail systems formerly operated by the Pennsylvania Railroad and the Reading Company. Whether or not this was a wise investment of dollars is still to be seen, but the money spent for that purpose was money that was not used to upgrade the existing facilities. Philadelphia did carry out a major rehabilitation of its north-south rapid transit line, the Broad Street Subway, the former Red Arrow trolley lines in the western suburbs, and the subway surface car lines operating out of the Market Street subway into West Philadelphia. At the time of this writing, rehabilitation work is going ahead slowly on the Frankford Elevated rapid transit line in the northeast section of the city. Almost all surface streetcar lines, except for the subway-surface lines serving West Philadelphia, are in relatively wretched physical condition. The city of Philadelphia seems to be generally interested in rehabilitation of its streetcar service while SEPTA remains reluctant. The lack of a dedicated source of funding is a major problem in the city, along with a governing board that is dominated by the suburbs and thus is often caught in conflict. The way to the bank eludes Philadelphia; this is ironic because Philadelphia was among the very first cities to work actively to improve mass transportation.

Thanks to federal funds, Cleveland has totally rehabilitated its light rail services and has made major improvements in its heavy rail rapid transit lines. Newark's light rail line has been rehabilitated and its forty-year-old PCC cars rebuilt. Chicago's elevated lines are almost a century old in some cases, and while substantial rehabilitation has taken place, the capital replenishment needs far outdistance the capital available. The trolleybus systems in Boston, Dayton, Philadelphia, San Francisco, and Seattle have all enjoyed major upgrading of fixed facilities and rolling stock due to federal funds, and the systems in Seattle and San Francisco have been expanded. Seattle is busy building a trolleybus tunnel to relieve congestion. Ferry boats and their facilities have been replaced or upgraded in New York, San Francisco, and Seattle.

New York is, as usual, a special case among American cities. The fixed facility infrastructure is so huge that it is not really comparable with anything else in the U.S. Political pressure kept the fares unrealistically low for many years and played a big role in building up a large backlog of deferred maintenance. Poor management in the past and a lack of funds over the years, coupled with union domination of the property, had crippled the ability of the New York City Transit Authority to work effectively. A new management team that was employed in the early 1980s moved to change this situation, and remarkable progress has been made on rehabilitation of rolling stock and the track structure, as well as in purchasing new cars and in some cosmetic improvement of stations. Even so, the job is so large that the complete rehabilitation of tunnels, trackage, signaling systems, power distribution systems, and other parts of the infrastructure will take a long time. The commuter railroads in the New York area were generally not allowed to decline to quite such serious depths as the subway system. The federal and state dollars have had a generally positive effect on upgrading the commuter rail service in the city area.

The expansion of transit service was one of the goals of the federal mass transit program. Bus service in the United States generally covers a much larger urbanized service area in each metropolitan region than it did before the federal programs. This matches the development of the suburban areas. Unfortunately, one of the reasons for the escalating transit deficit was the expansion of bus service into thinly populated areas where the costs greatly exceeded the revenues. There have also been some new services and intensified services in central cities along with some limited rethinking of the routing and service patterns.[5]

The expansion of rail rapid transit services was almost unimaginable before the federal mass transit program. Rapid transit service has been augmented in Boston, Philadelphia, and Chicago; some of the extensions and improvements of the Bay Area Rapid Transit District in San Francisco have utilized federal funding. The new rapid transit systems in Washington D.C., Miami, Atlanta, and Baltimore have all been supported with federal funds. The upgrading of light rapid transit has taken place in Pittsburgh and Philadelphia. Pittsburgh upgraded a part of its streetcar system to light rapid transit standards and built a new downtown light rail subway. New light rail lines have been constructed in Portland, Sacramento, the San Jose area in California, and portions of the San Diego system have been expanded with federal funds. Buffalo has constructed a light rail line that is part of a major downtown rejuvenation effort; it too includes a subway.

There have been improvements in commuter rail service in the New York and Boston areas, and relatively substantial expansion of the small commuter rail service in the Baltimore-Washington area. Chicago has also enjoyed a substantial upgrading of its commuter rail service, as has the San Francisco-to-San Jose commuter rail line. Detroit lost its small service to Pontiac. Pittsburgh lost its one commuter rail service in 1989. Both cutbacks are mainly due to the pinch of local finance.

Newfangled transportation in the form of so-called peoplemovers have been put into service in Detroit, Miami, and Jacksonville, Florida. The Miami and Jacksonville peoplemovers—automated transit cars on an elevated guideway—are proposed for expansion. The Detroit line was to be part of the distribution service for a light rapid transit system that was never built. The pioneer peoplemover, in Morgantown, West Virginia, continues to serve the University of West Virginia and the town as it has since the early 1970s.

Transit became an option for controversial highways in a few urban areas, such as Interstate 95 through Boston and the Crosstown Expressway in Chicago. Even so, it is most unusual for transit to be an alternative for a major highway. In a number of instances the availability of federal funds and eventually of state matching funds encouraged communities that had never had it to provide transit service. The Section 18 and Section 16(b)(2) programs have encouraged service in small cities and rural areas. For example, in 1977 there were 1,034 transit systems; this had risen to an estimated 2,361 by 1985.[6]

Interest in transit has also been generated among the general public. Some people who are not in any way connected with the transit industry or the transit community have become strong supporters of improved public transportation for their cities or metropolitan areas. These supporters see transit as an important part of the basic service of their communities. This enthusiasm ranges from a kind of boosterism to a more sober view of the range of urban services needed to benefit all members of the community. Oddly enough, the transit industry has not really used the traveling public, who are the users of its service, as part of the strong lobbying and support effort generally mounted to champion the federal programs. Popular participation in lobbying for transit does happen on a local basis, but apparently the difficulty of organizing transit users has precluded this grass roots type of support for transit on a national basis.

The federal programs stimulated local and state governments to take a look at urban mass transportation, an urban service that most cities were reluctant to become involved with prior to the advent of the federal mass transit program. To a certain extent, the Jones thesis that the federal programs actually began before there was any local support developed is probably true. This change in the conventional wisdom and a broadening of the world of ideas on the state and local level to embrace support of transit was very much a product of federal transit policy.[7]

THE FEDERAL MASS TRANSIT PROGRAM IN THE LATE 1980S

The federal mass transit program is becoming increasingly formula based. At the beginning it was a discretionary program, but starting in 1974 with the Section 5 formula grant program, an increasing amount of federal money has been allocated according to a formula. This is apparently a good idea, for managers on local levels have the advantage of knowing what the amount of funding will be, although they must still face the vicissitudes of the annual congressional appropriations process that decides the precise amount that will be available each year. This formula program breaks down when there are constant threats from the administration, as has been true in the Reagan years. Even a frozen level of funding is acceptable if it is at least predictable. A by-product of the federal approach has been an increasing use of formula-based means of distributing state funds.

The block grant idea has attractions. Ideally, a given sum of money arrived at by a formula would be allocated to a given place and could be spent for a broad range of purposes. The current Section 9 program was not really a block grant, because of the specified division between capital and operating funds within the program. For a time, the general experience with the Section 9 program and the formula used was that there was too much capital available for smaller transit properties. In the late 1980s, the capital portion was cut back more sharply than was operating aid. In some states at least, transit properties became worried that there might be a shortage of capital.[8] This has been since mitigated by the trading of funds within states—and even between states that share interstate urbanized areas. Trading between states that are not closely related to one another has been done but has aroused the ire of UMTA.

Under the current law in 1989, the discretionary money for capital purposes is found under Section 3. This discretionary capital money is almost totally earmarked by Congress and is therefore hardly discretionary in the usual sense of that word. The reason is simple: Congress wants to target money to new rail starts and the completion of rail projects and is not happy about the administration, working through the U.S. Department of Transportation and the Urban Mass Transportation Administration, calling the shots on what may prove to be very large local investments. This practice became particularly strong during the Reagan years and was a reaction to the administration's efforts to stop rail starts and to generally cut rail transit investment.

There are obvious pork-barrel implications in this process. And there is serious concern that congressional pressure might cause totally unwarranted projects to be funded. Giving thought to the relatively primitive state of analysis and prediction of what is going to happen with a rail project in the near term and in the long term, it will probably be difficult for many years to determine whether the money has been wisely spent. The Miami system, although really underway before earmarking became so prevalent, is often pointed to as an unwarranted rapid transit system, largely because it is only carrying about thirty percent of the ridership predicted when the system was planned. Given ten to twenty-five years, development around the stations, and perhaps a dramatic increase in the price of gasoline, the investment would probably be praised as being incredibly intelligent and prescient. There is no doubt, however, that investment in rail projects will usually be controversial. This is as it should be, because the sums involved are large, and the investments should not be made lightly.

The operating aid program for urbanized areas began in fiscal year 1975 under Section 5 of the Urban Mass Transportation Act of 1964, as amended. This program was phased out in fiscal 1984 and replaced by the Section 9 program. Operating grants under the Section 5 program from FY 1975 to 1986 totaled $7,166,469,427. From fiscal 1984 through fiscal 1987 $3,203,496,117 was devoted to the Section 9 program. Over the years, the total transit operating aid has been $10,369,965,544 through fiscal 1987. The high in operating aid was $1,129,510,600 in fiscal 1981. Since then the trend has been downward; $820,410,674 was allocated for operating aid in fiscal 1987.

Operating aid is generally more important for smaller cities than it is for large ones. Large cities generally recover a fair amount of their costs through the farebox, because fares are usually relatively high. Regardless of city size, operating aid has been controversial almost from the start. Critics usually view it as a bottomless pit. The cutbacks in operating aid under the Reagan administration have been met by fare increases and by an increase in state and local support.

If Congress is willing to give continued support to the federal mass transportation program (even if at a lower level because of the enormous federal deficit), it will probably not promote terribly innovative approaches. In a certain context, Congress was burned in the past, as was the Urban Mass Transportation Adminis- tration, on some novel initiatives. The technological innovations of the 1960s and 1970s, the Morgantown peoplemover, and the Transbus come to mind as examples. Innovations in funding or the delivery of transit service will probably be the result of the effort of the transit industry and its many members, rather than the spirit of new ideas arising in the national legislative body.

The federal programs have not done a very good job of supporting transit research in the 1980s. The lack of backing is a result of the cutbacks in transit funding that were experienced under the Reagan administration. Even though research is vital, it doesn't bleed in the same way as a transit system that has had to cut back service and experience the outrage of discommoded transit users. If something had to be cut, research was the natural victim rather than operating aid. Funds for research were at a high of $96,250,000 in 1973; then $56,840,000 in 1981; the money available was only $12,217,000 in 1988.[9]

It is also fair to say that the transit industry has not been notably supportive of research partly because it needed operating money desperately, and the payoff from most of the federally sponsored research appears to be remote or focused too much on a given situation. Also, the industry was not really a part of the research program. There was very little transit industry input over the years on what UMTA would support with its research dollars.

However, concern over the diminishing level of research being supported by UMTA arose within the transit community in 1985, in large part as a reaction to the magnitude of the program cuts experienced under the Reagan administration. With the support of UMTA and under the aegis of the Transportation Research Board (TRB), the situation was reviewed. Later, the program, called Strategic Transit Research, was picked up by the American Public Transit Association. This author was a member of both the TRB and APTA research committee and was a first-hand participant in the discussion and the decisions made. The gist of the idea that emanated from this process was that a portion of the formula funds under Section 9 of the Urban Mass Transportation Act of 1964, as amended, should be placed in a pot of money for research. The sum involved would be in the range of $12-15 million. This program would not replace the UMTA research program. The idea had a certain amount of appeal to the large transit systems, which typically rely less heavily on the formula program than do the smaller systems and have a larger stake in potential innovation. Progress was slow in expediting the Strategic Transit Research program due to other problems facing the transit industry. The insistence on the part of the American Public Transit Association that it have complete control of the program might also scuttle the effort if UMTA gets nervous about this role for APTA. The idea of supporting research in this fashion is a good one. The important thing is that the transit industry should have as much input as possible in seeing that things are investigated that are important to it and to the traveling public. At this writing, there has yet to be legislation introduced to permit this change in the way research in transit is supported.

Perhaps the transit community's greatest criticism of the Reagan administration's cutbacks in research money was not that the amount had tumbled from about $70 million in 1980 to about $12 million in 1988 but that the administration was primarily supporting only research in which it was interested. It is not a totally fair assessment, but a number of people in the transit industry who are interested in research said that they would gag if they saw yet another research study on the wonders of the privatization of transit.

Why can't the industry fund research itself without the need for any federal funding, however derived? Individual operating properties are really not very well set up for research in any formal sense. Nevertheless, many transit systems do try out ideas and, in many ways, are conducting unsophisticated and often unreported research efforts. Some of the larger transit systems get involved in more complex and sophisticated investigative efforts. By and large, however, the transit industry is not research oriented. The same holds true for the supply industry. Most of the firms that supply buses and other transit components are too small, or the transit element is too small a portion of a large firm's total business, to devote much money to support innovative or basic research. For manufacturers, there is the typical upgrading of process or quality that is a result of at least a modest in-house research or testing program.

Turning to managerial training in mass transit, one may argue that management training is one of the better ideas in the federal spectrum of transit programs. It is a very reasonable activity for the federal government to support in that relatively small sums of money can, over time, help upgrade the skills and knowledge of people in the transit business. This program has been cut back and focused mainly on large transit properties.[10]

The university research and training portion of the Urban Mass Transportation Act comes under Section 11 and was added in 1966. This particular program started off with about $2 million a year, which is not much money. It is fair to say that the Section 11 program has been starved for funds over the years; it received no increase in appropriations and has had its appropriations cut significantly to less than $1 million a year in the 1980s. While suffering from financial malnutrition, this program is potentially a rich source of ideas and new personnel for the transit industry. More money devoted to research is needed and much more of the funds should be devoted to the education and training area. Internship programs and cooperative programs, with some federal support, could be a boon for attracting young people into the transit industry and developing a strong cadre of skilled and professional managers, planners, and other specialists.

There is at least some small concern in the transit community over the way the Section 11 research money has been distributed. The use of UMTA money has not always produced research that is perceived as highly useful to the transit industry and its customers. More input from the transit industry, and more interaction between academia, students, and transit professionals, could generate better and more useful research. For example, research publications are one way for an assistant professor to get promoted to the position of associate professor in the "publish-or-perish" world of academia. If there was sufficient money available, academics should also be encouraged to conduct transit-related basic research.

This comment should not be construed to mean that the investigative work carried out under Section 11 has been of low quality or irrelevant. Much of the work done is of high quality and value. Indeed, the research on performance indicators carried out at the University of California at Irvine is among the most useful research done on transit since the start of the program.[11]

Due to an understandable wish to spread limited funds as broadly as possible, too often the Section 11 funds appear to be awarded on too small and too much of a short-term basis. Funding has been available to given schools only in fits and starts. Good research and development of a good transit program for students as well as faculty need time to bear fruit. Ideally, a strong program with a decent level of funding would continue support to university programs that had proved their merit while constantly bringing in new people and new schools to the game.

A different approach was tried in 1982 with the creation of the Centers for Transit Research and Management Development. As originally proposed, the program was to start with two or three universities of proven record and competence in the study of mass transportation. They would divide up $1 million a year for a period of five to seven years. Each year that the program moved on, additional schools were to be added to the number of centers. The end product was to be a program of research and training that would be largely self-supporting. Unfortunately, the program was consistently underfunded; in the first year there were eight schools instead of two or three, and the total amount of money was cut steadily over a three-year period and finally eliminated. A program that might have produced very substantial results faded away. The reason was a change in UMTA administrators from Arthur Teele, who was a strong sponsor, to Ralph Stanley, who did not give support and killed the program.

The 1987 federal transit legislation earmarked funds for ten university research centers, one in each of the federal administrative areas. At the time of this writing the program is just getting underway and has produced few results as yet. The competition for the funds was extremely strong, and whether the amount of money is enough and whether anything that really amounts to solid research will be produced is unknown.

One obviously cannot discuss the federal mass transit program without touching on funding and the funding process. A dedicated source of money is very attractive for any kind of government program. The highway program has had its success and has gained its strength because of the funding earmarked for highways. There are many legitimate arguments for and against trust funds or other ways of reserving monies for a given purpose. Regardless of the merit of these arguments on both sides, any industry so blessed is in a better position to manage what it does and to develop a solid momentum than is an industry faced by the hazards and vagaries of the annual appropriations process by Congress.

In the case of the federal mass transit program, there was some discussion and debate about providing a regular source of funding through a trust fund, beginning with the efforts of DOT Secretary John Volpe in the late 1960s. In the mid–1980s, there was also a debate about taking the program off-budget. The consolidated budget practice of the United States includes such elements as the Social Security receipts and expenditures and the Highway Trust Fund. This practice amounts to a certain degree of deception. The money coming into these funds can be used only for the purposes of Social Security or highways and transit. The Social Security fund, which was developing large surpluses in the middle and latter 1980s, is especially attractive because the income surpasses the output by a significant amount and makes the federal budget deficit appear to be smaller. It would probably be wise, and it would remove a certain amount of deception from the picture, if the highway and mass transit program—and the other trust funds—were taken off-budget.

From the viewpoint of management it is a sound idea to support transit entirely by a trust fund because of the relatively high degree of certainty of funds available. The gas tax is an attractive way to support a trust fund. It is easy to collect and it generates, on a cents-per-gallon basis, a large stream of money each year. Moreover, most regular motorists don't have the faintest idea what the federal gas tax is (ask your friends; 90 percent of them won't know it is 9 cents), and, given the usual swings in gas prices over the course of the years, they wouldn't even know that the tax had been changed by a modest amount if they didn't read about it in the newspaper. Even so, the politicians of the 1980s recoil in fear from proposing any tax increases, remembering what happened to the 1984 Democratic presidential candidate Walter Mondale, who frankly stated that he would raise taxes if elected in order to tame the federal deficit. Political wisdom of the 1980s does not advise falling on one's sword to advocate the tax increases that most politicians agree are necessary to bring the federal deficit under control. Suicide is not less unpleasant because it is political in nature.[12]

By the late 1980s, however, opinion was beginning to form saying that additions to the gas tax might be a feasible way of supporting transit as well as some other useful activities. Assuming a continued large federal presence, two or three additional cents on the federal gas tax for transit, and the same amount added for highways, would not be out of line when considering the need. A penny on the gas tax in 1988 would generate about $1.4 to $1.5 billion each year. For transit a total of four cents would yield about $6 billion a year; six cents would yield about $8 billion a year. Assuming stable prices, that amount of federal funding joined with state and local funding could produce enough money for significant capital replenishment and stabilization and some expansion of services.

For the highways, the money could certainly be well spent on repairs to bridges—which are the Achilles' heel of the highway systems—and for massive rehabilitation of existing roads. Considering the need just to maintain what we now have in the way of transit and highway resources, it would probably not be a bad bargain to make such an innovative move. The additional step of not including trust funds in the federal budget would make deficit accounting more honest, and would cut down on the game of political ping-pong with trust funds in the federal budget process.

THE URBAN MASS TRANSPORTATION ADMINISTRATION

During the Reagan years, when the federal role in mass transportation was constantly threatened, the UMTA staff kept things going. The work often was carried out under threatening and soul-crushing conditions. It is hard to do a job that you very much believe in when the program is being derided and damned by the president and his appointees in the Department of Transportation. The transit industry and the transit community owe these people a tremendous debt. Whatever else one may think of bureaucrats and bureaucracy, one of bureaucracy's major aims is continuity and the imperative to treat everybody alike. To the best of their ability, and despite many interventions from above, the UMTA staff managed to keep the money flowing, even if not always in a timely fashion.

The Urban Mass Transportation Administration has a small, dedicated staff. Most of them, it is fair to say, believe sincerely in their work and its importance. UMTA plodded on despite reductions in force (RIFs) at the beginning of the Reagan administration that were to prove to be preparatory to the downsizing, not to say virtual dismantlement, of the program. At one point, the RIFs seemed to be aimed at discouragement of the UMTA staff as much as anything else. But, the bureaucracy knows how to fight back. In the first Reagan administration many people were cut from the staff and then cleverly recycled to come back into the agency in a different position. Nevertheless, morale suffered badly, and many fine staff members left for other positions in government or moved out of the federal government completely.

The professional staff on all levels tried to mitigate the worst efforts of the administration to make the UMTA program as unworkable as possible. Even so, an adversarial relationship developed between UMTA and its clients. In part, this was due to the attitude of some of the administrators. Ralph Stanley, who served as UMTA administrator from 1984-1987, was extremely hostile to the program and spoke out against it on many occasions, even gleefully accepting one of Senator William Proxmire's Golden Fleece Awards for useless federal expenditures. The suspicious attitude toward the program held by presidential appointees did not endear UMTA to the transit industry. Foot dragging was not uncommon during the Stanley years.

Nevertheless, when finally convinced that the program should be administered in as professional a manner as possible, Stanley was responsible for streamlining and speeding up the process of fund distribution and deserved high marks for the effort. UMTA applicants who followed the procedure and adhered to the timetable received their federal money promptly. Under Stanley's successor, Alfred DelliBovi, UMTA undertakings, while not all blue skies and sunshine, continued in a professional fashion. Mr. DelliBovi, who necessarily espoused the Reagan administration's party line in loyal fashion, seemed sincere in trying to have the program conducted in as efficient, effective and professional a fashion as was possible under the circumstances. Much of the routine of the UMTA program is administered by the regional offices.

In the final analysis, the UMTA bureaucracy kept the program moving as well as it did and did as much as was possible under trying conditions to help keep the transit industry alive and the federal role intact despite the wily and parsimonious efforts of the administration. Even so, the federal transit program was cut almost in half between 1981 and 1988.

DIFFICULTIES, ROADBLOCKS, PROBLEMS, AND EMBARRASSMENTS

Transit performs a difficult job. In large cities, with significant peaking of demand, large amounts of equipment are used for only a few hours a day, five days a week. For this reason, operating staff to handle the brief peaks can only be used effectively for a few hours per day. Most transit operations take place on the public streets, exposed to all the problems, hazards, and potential delays of traffic. In short, transit has a hard job to do and it must do it under circumstances that lend themselves to neither efficiency nor effectiveness. Transit operations are visited by other problems as well.

The federal urban mass transportation program helped to preserve jobs and stimulate employment in the transit industry. Just providing funds to support the industry and help it to grow would have achieved this. But, in addition to the funding, there was the labor protection clause under Section 13c of the Urban Mass Transportation Act of 1964; this was labor's *quid pro quo* for legislative support. Labor was not bashful about using it. In point of fact, because of 13c, labor has transit management over a barrel in the form of a threat to needed capital and operating grants. Whether or not the threat is carried out, transit managers chafe at the potential mischief they see arising out of 13c. When grants are received under Section 3 or Section 9 of the Urban Mass Transportation Act, labor must give its approval. The aim of Section 13c is that no member of labor will be worse off because the transit improvement is fostered by the federal grant process. At first blush, it would appear that automated transit systems or other efficient uses of labor are therefore prohibited by law. On the other hand, because of the growth of transit and the growth of jobs, the installation of potentially less labor-intense rail systems has not really become a major issue, because bus service is typically expanded to feed the rail line. In addition, bus operators are usually given the opportunity to take rail transit jobs when a rail system is initiated or expanded.

Labor expense is a very high proportion of total costs, usually somewhere in the range of 65 to 90 percent. There is much criticism that operating employees are paid too much; indeed, the reader will recall that opposition to federal operating aid arose in the Nixon and Reagan administrations because there was fear that labor demands would swallow up all the money and that there would be no really great improvement or expansion of service. On the other hand, and it is often forgotten by critics of the program, the money paid to transit workers is spent in the community—not somewhere else, as is the case with most capital equipment procurements. The good wages paid to bus drivers and other transit employees benefit the community when that money is spent. This does not mean, of course, that transit management is delighted at high labor costs or that it has not worked to use labor more productively.

There's another upside to the good wages paid in the transit industry: large transit properties are often an avenue for considerable numbers of minority people to enter the promised land of the good side of American life. Many blacks and Hispanics have hired on as bus drivers, service workers, or mechanics. Due to the good wages paid, they have made their way into the middle class. Because of federal anti-discrimination laws, women have also been accepted into the transit industry in large numbers, and many have excellent paying jobs as operators. Women have also made their way into the transit work force on staff levels and a few are in upper levels of management. It appears that maintenance and maintenance management are about the only areas of transit in which large numbers of women are not yet employed.

Another problem with labor has to do with the issue of bargaining. Most unionized employees in transit belong to the Amalgamated Transit Union. Employees of some of the large properties—New York, Philadelphia, and Miami—are represented by the Transport Workers Union. Other properties are organized by the United Transportation Union, which is typically identified as the principal union of railroad operating employees; these are often systems that had a rail operation at one time that was organized by a predecessor of the United Transportation Union. In any event, as a major advantage to organized labor, these large international unions typically supplied the key negotiators at bargaining sessions discussing new contracts. These people are professional bargainers; such work is their sole occupation. As a result, the union negotiators are often much more skilled at the process of hammering out a new contract than is local transit management. On the other side of the coin, some transit properties will hire their own labor relations experts to help in the negotiation procedures.

The use of organized labor in providing transit means that the cost of service is probably higher than it would be otherwise. Because of this, plus the substantial increase in transit pay during the period of federal transit support, controlling labor costs has become a key to increasing transit efficiency. However, efficiency gains are most likely to be found in the work rules involved in transit labor rather than in the hourly wage. The wage rates in transit are really not all that different from good industrial wages in the same community. It is the work rules that are often the most difficult labor elements for management to deal with. Examples are the prohibition of the use of part-time employees and the job classifications, which typically prohibit bus drivers from also working as mechanics or office staff in off-peak times. The result is that transit employees are guaranteed eight hours of pay per day but may actually work only four or five hours during the morning and evening peak hours.

On the issue of high wages for bus drivers, many people focus on $12 to $15 an hour plus fringe benefits as being exorbitant. Driving a bus may not be in the same league as brain surgery, but operating a transit vehicle in the big city is not easy. People should be paid for the problems they face, and a bus operator in particular often confronts very difficult tasks in driving through neighborhoods in which even the police may fear to go except in pairs. The sad fact of the criminalization of much of the urban areas of America is one that is experienced every day by bus operators. In addition, operating a bus or any other transit vehicle in heavy traffic at rush hour, and trying to stay on schedule, is not one of the truly fun things a person may do for a living.[13]

The threat or the promise of privatization that was fostered by the Reagan administration was primarily inspired by the hope of cutting labor costs. The idea behind privatization is that there should be competitiveness in carrying out certain transit jobs. In some cases Section 13c has prevented this; in other instances, non-union operators working at lower wages are providing certain kinds of services.

Contracting with the private sector is actually a very old practice in transit. Transit systems have for years, under public ownership and prior to it, contracted out certain parts of their operation. For instance, one of the more common facets of transit to be handled by the private sector is the demand-responsive service for the elderly and handicapped. Different kinds of equipment and a completely different kind of service than the standard, fixed route service is involved, and transit systems have long felt that it was a lot easier to deal with people who specialized in that sort of work rather than to try to do it by themselves. In addition, transit systems have contracted out such things as cleaning stations and vehicles, counting money, or other such practices. In some cities, as long as there was no cut in the union work force, except by attrition, the transit properties have used private, temporary-help agencies to supply drivers for peak hours as well as on weekends and at undesirable times (there are often hours and times of the week that regular union drivers with seniority would as lief not work).

There is some question regarding the long-run economics of contracting out. The Toronto Transit Commission (TTC) has had extensive experience with contracting out demand-responsive service for the elderly and handicapped; over time TTC and the contractors found that, in order to keep good drivers working, the wages paid by the private contractors had to increase. Eventually the wage rates for the contract drivers in the private system serving the mass transit agency tended to rise to about the same level as the union drivers operating regular fixed-route service. By 1988, the TTC was in the process of taking over direct operations for the special service for the elderly and handicapped.

The move to privatization is commonly misunderstood and often controversial. The Reagan administration pushed it as a solution to the cut in transit funding and often chided the transit industry that all it needed was a dash of private enterprise to break even or even to be profitable. This strikes one as an illogical position; if the private sector could really make it in the transit industry, it would be an active participant without any inspiration by the federal government.

Any transit property contemplating privatization and contracting out operation of service for the public should pay careful attention to the fact that it is not costless. The service may be privately operated, but it is still subsidized. The transit authority still has the responsibility for seeing that service is delivered, that service standards are maintained, and that the public interest is protected. Very careful supervision of the contracted service is absolutely necessary. Furthermore, auditing the private operation may be a costly and time-consuming business, involving many management hours devoted to both the financial and performance aspects of the contract. This is to make sure that the contract is met and that the public monies are being used for the purposes intended.

In retrospect, it is fair to say that the success of privatization has been genuine, although relatively limited, but it is certainly not a solution to the problems of urban mass transportation or a means of taking transit completely out of the public sector.[14]

A frequent question is whether or not the federal mass transportation program has stimulated investments that should not have been made. The pork-barrel syndrome is not unknown in any kind of public venture, and the temptation to overdo is certainly there. Large sums of federal money for transit capital projects are spent locally; this can be a boon to the local economy and can also be proof of the clout wielded by the local members of the House of Representatives or U.S. senators in bringing home the federal bacon. Indeed, it is not outside the scope of human understanding to assume that some projects may be selected for funding because of the power of a senator or congressman, rather than for the real benefit of the project. However, UMTA funding of a totally worthless undertaking is probably extremely rare. A more likely scenario would be that a worthwhile project, or at least a reasonable one, would get moved up on the agenda for funding because of the power of a key politician. There is certainly nothing new or anything necessarily evil about this, although it puts great pressure on the bureaucracy as it is caught between the limitations of federal funds and the influence and pressure of powerful members of Congress. Even under pressure, UMTA still requires satisfactory justification.

The worth of a mass transportation project is often a function of who is examining it. Economists and others will argue that cost-benefit analysis, or its UMTA equivalent of alternatives analysis, should be used in making sure that only the most worthwhile projects are undertaken. The use of cost-benefit analysis is a good idea if carefully carried out. Indeed, in a book written in the mid–1960s, this author devoted a fair amount of space on the virtues of cost-benefit analysis on decision making in transit and related projects.[15] One will always hope that the best projects were chosen; the difficulty is that cost-benefit analysis, like the words of the Holy Bible, can be used to prove just about anything.

Those familiar with cost-benefit analysis will realize that, because so much is dependent upon the assumptions made, the whole business is often shaky to begin with. Moreover, many of the numbers relating to social costs and benefits are educated guesses not available on any sort of reasonable and objective basis, but much of the analysis may depend perforce upon them. How does one measure the aesthetic impact—negative or positive—of a proposed project? How much traffic will a proposed project generate and what benefits in reduced operating cost will really accrue? In many cases it comes down to the application of political calculus in assuming that the benefits will exceed the costs. Due to the elusiveness of some data and to the weaknesses and highly subjective nature of some elements in what may appear to be an objective process of cost-benefit analysis, there is no guarantee that a good project (or a bad one) will be selected for funding or that the correct priority for project implementation will be chosen. The cost-benefit process can however be most useful in weeding out hopeless losers.

Cost-benefit analysis is most effective when the true economic costs and benefits are well-known and understood. Another important factor is the clarity of the purpose of the capital investment. Many times there is a mix of goals or benefits to be realized as a result of the particular undertaking, including: congestion relief, increasing corridor capacity, improved service for users, environmental improvement, economic development, time savings, and increasing economic opportunities for affected residents. Not all of these goals can be reached at the same time, and they would understandably have different payoff periods, all subject to a variety of forces outside the control of anyone on the local level. For instance, the goal of local economic development stimulated by a transit improvement may be thwarted by an unexpected downturn on the national economic scene.

A real problem with any kind of major capital project is that it is so difficult to predict what will happen over the long term in the process of planning, engineering, and construction that a great deal may change before anything actually operates. Indeed, long-range projects have extreme difficulty in dealing with changes that have occurred while the project is underway. For example, to refresh the reader's recollection, the Miami rapid transit project is one in which it is fair to say there are many negatives. That rapid transit system was planned in the 1970s in the belief that, when it was opened to serve the public, transit fares would be fifty cents; gas prices would be high (in the $2 per gallon range); there would be an extensive 1000-bus feeder service and no major addition to public parking spaces in downtown Miami; and that no significant highway improvements would be made parallel to the rapid transit line. In reality, gas prices went down; transit fares doubled; the bus fleet was only 60 percent of the size needed to provide the feeder function; many thousands of parking spaces were added in downtown Miami; and there were major highway improvements.

Any project that is very costly is rightly subject to concern and scrutiny. In the Washington, D.C. region the positive factors supporting the construction of a rapid transit system were generally favorable, although many doubted that the Washington Metrorail rapid transit system would really have much payoff, especially when considering the expected $9 billion price tag of the completed system. As the system began to open in stages, desired development did cluster around some of the stations and the traffic congestion in the outer regions of the Washington area meant that, as extensions of the rail system pushed farther out into the suburbs, the trains were soon crowded with many riders. Indeed, the uptake of the service was so strong that parking at the suburban stations became in very short supply. By 1988 the Metrorail trains were carrying over half a million riders each weekday on the 70 route miles of the system that were open.

Washington's rapid transit system appears to be a success, although some critics maintain that buses could do the job equally well and cheaper.

Another question is whether an entire rail system should be built as one large project or if its construction should be an incremental process. The older transit systems were, indeed, built on a piece-by-piece basis. This is understandable because the systems in Philadelphia, Chicago, and much of New York City were built by private enterprise or by private enterprise in close conjunction with city government. In the age before the automobile became potent competition, many of these segments were pushed into highly congested areas and enjoyed heavy ridership from the very start. Some of the newer systems have shown that the greatest benefit and value to the community may not actually occur until much of the construction is in place and many places are linked together. In other words, for a long time the system might not appear to be paying off. Moreover, because in the long haul the central city is one of the markets for which transit is most competitive when joining suburbs to downtown and other suburbs, many miles of line must be built before the potential value of a fixed facility can be realized. Each mile of a fixed facility does not have the same passenger-generating capability. For example, the payoff from the highly expensive downtown portion of the Los Angeles rapid transit system may not be justifiable until extensions have penetrated long distances into the outlying territory.

Criticism of a transit investment must be appropriate to the purpose of the investment. Those who have serious doubts about systems such as the one in Miami or about the first stages of the light rapid transit line in San Jose must be careful in contradicting an investment that is supposed to lead and guide development over many years rather than just serve what is already in place. The shaping function and the development of growth along a line means that in many cases the line will be built where there isn't much traffic to serve and where it may not exist for many years. In the railroad world, the Union Pacific and Central Pacific were built to knit the country together in the 1860s when there really was not all that much traffic in the great West, because there were so few people in the area served and thus only a small number of farms, ranches, and factories with freight to be hauled to a market. The transcontinental railroad did succeed in pulling the U.S. together in 1869. Nevertheless, within a few years the Union Pacific was bankrupt. From a political viewpoint the railroad was a great success, even though it was a commercial failure.

The developmental impacts of transit may take a long time to realize. One of the most touted development schemes related to rapid transit is in Canada. Flying into Toronto, one can tell exactly where the stations on the 1950s vintage Yonge Street rapid transit line are located because they are surrounded by high-rise office buildings and apartments. The same is true of many places along the Bloor-Danforth subway that was built in the 1960s and 1970s. However, the key intersection of Yonge and Bloor streets, where the two major subway lines cross, has seen really major development only recently, in 1987-88, even though it has been a major rapid transit intersection for twenty years. Moreover, the key station at Yonge and Queen Streets has, until 1987, seen new development at only one quadrant in the construction some years ago of the Eaton Centre.

The Washington (D.C.) Metrorail system, which has had a major developmental impact in many parts of its community, still had to wait a number of years before there was a really major outbreak of development at the key intersection of lines at the Metro Center Station in the heart of downtown Washington. The Bay Area Rapid Transit (BART) District in San Francisco also claims responsibility for many tens of thousands of square feet of new office space located along its lines and close to its stations in downtown San Francisco. The San Francisco development has also been criticized on the grounds that the development would have taken place anyway and that the presence of BART simply moved it into downtown San Francisco. There is no question that it was better for the development to take place along the rapid transit system, where there was good mobility and access provided by the railway line, rather than somewhere else in the region accessible only by automobile, where that development might have caused severe traffic congestion. One thing is clear. Construction of a rail line or other fixed facility can only really be effective in helping to shape growth if zoning is such as to allow the growth to take place in a reasonable fashion and if parking and feeder service are available at stations in order to provide ready access from outlying places to the new development.

A more reasonable criticism is that building a fixed facility service, such as a rail line, will merely switch people from using buses to the rail system and that a new rapid transit line will not really attract many auto riders. There is certainly some validity to this criticism. Which riders a rail system gathers are largely functions of where it goes and the quality of the service in relation to other alternatives. If a rail system provides a better alternative for bus riders but not for the current group of automobile users, then it will probably be largely diversionary in nature rather than creating new transit riders from auto drivers. Certainly the majority of motorists are rational enough to use transit if it is a better deal for them than driving their cars. In the long run, despite the negative image that transit has in the U.S., its quality of service relative to alternatives, the places a rail or busway system serves, and access to it are probably more important to transit's impact on patronage and the shaping and stimulation of growth than the fact that it is public transit.

Another factor in evaluating rail, bus, carpool, vanpool, and automobile alternatives is the cross-elasticity of demand, or the "substitutability" of one for another. There is a difference in the package of service provided by transit and the private automobile that is much more than a ride between two places. The automobile offers privacy and flexibility to a degree unmatched by any kind of a transit or pooled journey. The driver may smoke, play the radio or tape deck, sing, or talk to himself while taking a variety of routes to his destination. The vehicle itself may vary widely in its comfort and appointments from a bare compact car to an ultra-luxurious road locomotive that connotes the economic status of the owner and driver. The feeling of a motorist for his car may be subjective, but it is no less real. In many ways there is no way that transit can offer a real substitute to the value the motorist places on his or her private automobile. Subjectively a trip in a Mercedes may be better than a ride in a Ford, and both may be better than a bus ride, even if the money, effort, and time costs are objectively equal.

Moreover, there is a very real difference in the perceived cost of a trip by transit and automobile. Most motorists consider only the out-of-pocket cost of operating a car, which is dominated by expenses for fuel, oil, perhaps tires, and certainly parking charges. The original purchase cost, insurance, and taxes are generally forgotten in the consideration of any particular trip. A transit trip is usually paid for each time it is taken and the passenger must overtly part with money. If paying is painful, it is a pain that is repeated each time a transit ride is taken; this pain may be somewhat assuaged if monthly passes are used. The pecuniary cost of a transit ride, therefore, cannot be higher than the perceived pecuniary cost of driving a car. This puts a significant limit on how high fares can be and still be seen as competitive with the automobile, and is a major reason that transit fares have been kept low relative to transit costs. The fact that the automobile, and often parking, are subsidized, and the perception that auto costs are limited to out-of-pocket expenses are the primary reasons that transit is subsidized.

Picking up the ideas of cross-elasticity and substitutability once again, it is obvious that there is a difference between a ride on a bus or rail vehicle; they are not substitutes for one another. The quality of ride is different and there is generally more room in a rail vehicle. Some passengers dislike the diesel smell of a bus. The air conditioning may be more reliable or more effective on a rail vehicle than on a bus. There are subjective factors, too, such as the perception that the rail vehicle may be more substantial and more permanent than a bus. Some persons who would not consider the option of taking a bus to work may be quite happy to ride a rail vehicle. If the rail service is a commuter railroad, rapid transit, or light rail rapid transit, the ride may be faster and less time-consuming. On the other hand, bus service may be much more accessible and may offer a direct ride with no transfers necessary between origin and destination.

Vanpools and carpools are not substitutes for one another or for a rail, bus, or automobile trip. A certain degree of compatibility is necessary among the passengers in any pooled vehicle. There is more circuitry needed in a vanpool than in a carpool, because more riders must be accommodated than in an auto trip taken by fewer passengers. This is more time consuming and may be perceived as considerably less convenient than driving alone, even if it is notably less costly. As opposed to transit, pooling is less convenient because there is only one departure time per trip time.

The point of all this is that in cost-benefit analysis the means of travel and the costs involved are not comparisons of likes. It is a comparison of apples to pears, bananas, oranges, and lemons. Given the relative comfort of the automobile, the fact that the driver does not charge for the service, the perception of costs limited to out-of-pocket expenses, pride of ownership, and the fact that, even with jammed highways, the auto trip may still take less time than a transit or pooled journey, the auto is the travel means of choice for a large proportion of urban journeys. It will probably remain so for a long time to come, even if analysis shows it to be the most costly choice among a spectrum of possibilities.

A reasonable question to ask is whether or not rail construction is an anachronism in these times of suburban sprawl. Rail transit is not flexible enough to serve a large number of thinly developed areas directly and is really not intended to do so. Rail and other fixed facility systems are at their best when providing capacity and shaping growth in high demand corridors—or in potential corridors—while using less space than a highway of similar capacity. Carefully planned and supported, a rail line need not be an expensive, feckless venture. The local public and their elected officials often badly want a rail system; it has status. Despite their flexibility and many commendable points, buses conjure up little magic. Moreover, for those who are interested in the use of buses on busways, there was no evidence by the mid–1980s that busways have developmental impact; in part this is because busway systems are few in number and most haven't been around long enough to cause any measurable alteration. For example, the heavily used busways in Pittsburgh were constructed in old, well-populated areas, where little new development might be expected. It may also be related to the seeming lack of permanence of bus service, even when operating upon a dedicated highway. With respect to rail, for systems rooted in the central city, good access, parking areas, or other adjuncts to the rail system seem to be the key to making them worthwhile investments, assuming that they link together the proper places. Blanket condemnation of rail projects is just as unwise as blanket support of rail projects.

Perhaps the best incentives for careful investment are the recent rules of UMTA that funding recipients must prove they can support the project over time. The Miami system, for example, has as one of its major weaknesses its inability to support bus service that can effectively provide the necessary access to the rail system.

A major problem is the unclear long-range purpose of the federal mass transit policy. Is transit supposed to be a standby in most communities and a backup for the automobile system, as something to be used when the car breaks down? Is transit supposed to be a replacement or alternative for the car in some cities, or should it have some other purpose? Is transit supposed to be a shaper of growth? Is transit just for captive riders? Is transit supposed to be a substitute for expensive or highly controversial highway expansion? What about the goals for transit of reducing fuel use and air pollution and providing mobility for the elderly and handicapped? All of these things have been touted as reasons for the federal program or for any program encouraging mass transit. Yet the precise purpose of the transit program is foggy. Just providing transit service is clearly no guarantee that any of the purposes mentioned above will be met.

To achieve some of the proclaimed purposes would require substantial amounts of funds, plus other determined and well-targeted actions, to make sure the transit investment really does produce a desired result. A singular investment in transit is not likely to have much impact unless joined by a series of complementary actions, and such actions may demand too much change to sell to the public. If transit is supposed to be a shaper of growth, then local laws, rules, regulations, and zoning should make sure that growth does indeed take place along the transit line. If transit is to be a replacement for highways, then federal, state, and local policy must assure that no highways will be built in competition with the transit service that will be provided. Without full support, the various plans for transit are not practical goals but only wistful dreams.

Another difficulty in effectively carrying out a clearly focused transit program on a national basis is the significant problem of dealing with the wide variety of local situations and authorities. The federal transit program deals primarily with individual cities and transit systems, not with states. The variety of local situations is so great that it takes a fair amount of time to get all transit properties even in rough congruence with federal aims. The acceptability of federal goals and the magnitude of problems on the local level widely differ, as do the local needs. The diversified geographic fabric of urban places affects the interest in, importance, and potency of a transit effort. Major bodies of water, for instance, affect the travel and growth patterns of New York, Chicago, Seattle, and San Francisco, whereas Indianapolis and Columbus have no major geographical feature to hem in their expansion or to compress their development. As a generalization, densely developed places are well suited to transit; thinly occupied places resist transit's blandishments.

One reason we don't do better with urban-related policies involves the typically fragmented approach to problems that is common in U.S. government. In forging a program for transit that possesses reasonable and national goals, those desirable ends should be integrated with and congruent to a well-considered environmental policy, energy policy, economic development policy, etc. Transit policy should not—and cannot—exist in a vacuum. The lack of consideration and integration of policies on the federal level is at least partially understandable, because different committees of the Congress consider these many issues, which assures either chaos or weakness in carrying out an interrelated program. Congress has been a staunch supporter of transit but, so far, because of the way that it is organized, is really unable to develop an all-encompassing, realistic policy. John Kennedy's presidential message on transportation in 1962 contained recommendations concerning transit that were almost impudent under the prevailing highways-only urban transportation programs. No administration since then has made any bold recommendations or created any potentially useful and do-able programs.

The fuzzy goals for the transit program have produced fuzzy results. Being definite is difficult. Congress is reluctant to be very precise about many of the things its tries to do because of the fear that the public may keep score. It is politically wiser to keep things vague. Therefore it is in Congress's interest to shovel money at transit—and at a variety of other things—in the hopes that some general benefit will accrue to the public as a whole and to their own constituents in particular. And so, in a given corridor we build both a rail transit line and provide massive support for parallel highways and then bemoan the fact that, despite the money spent, more people don't ride the trains.

If the success of the federal transit programs is measured by the help it has offered in providing hardware and fixed facilities, in stimulating the preservation of urban mass transportation, and raising the public consciousness about mass transportation, it is fair to gauge it a winner. If success is measured by an increasing proportion of urban travel made by transit, by a major impact on shaping cities in a more rational or efficient fashion, or in significantly mitigating the burden of congestion on a nationwide basis, the federal transit program has been a failure.

IS ENCOURAGEMENT OF TRANSIT IRRELEVANT?

Whether or not it makes sense to push transit as a rational and reasonable means of transportation in the United States at the end of the twentieth century is a fair question. The pattern of scattered population distribution in this country and the forces pushing ever more broadcast development continue, and the pace of the scattering appears to have been mounting since the mid–1970s. Transit cannot serve scattered development very well. Suburbs, exurbs, the megaburb, the technoburb, or whatever name is given the development pattern, are mainly the products and the province of the automobile. As noted elsewhere in this volume, the trends at work to pull and push people away from the traditional central cities seem likely to continue well into the future. More people can afford to own and operate cars than ever before in American history. The suburban ideal shows no signs of weakening. Central cities still have huge problems of mediocre education, poor people, and a mix of people of different economic levels and vastly different demographic conditions. The population mix alone flies in the face of the popular wish, so successfully carried out in suburbia, for the segmentation of different groups into relatively homogeneous enclosures the like of which is new to both the suburban and the American experience. Despite the dismay with which some social critics, such as Lewis Mumford, view American urban life, there appears to be no popular pressure to change it; after all, the patterns of urban development now manifest in metropolitan areas are all most Americans know. America is a commercial society, and most of what happens is thrust forward because of the hope of making a profit, not in advancing beauty, the good life, or the benefit of society. There is no current sign that Americans want to dive into the diversity and problems of central cities.[16]

The restructuring of cities from past high density and tight development is not without cost. The current pattern of population distribution suffers from very obvious negative factors such as massive and widespread traffic congestion. The notion that travel feeds upon itself and that the availability of more transportation demands still more transportation is not a new idea; nor is the notion that automobiles, as useful as they are, are responsible for many problems that are politically tough to solve and economically difficult. The widespread use of automobiles is a generator of massive pollution of the environment. The 1980s saw increasingly serious warnings regarding the devastating impact the modern industrial world has had on the earth's environment. The dependence of this auto-based transportation service for the suburbs requires a massive use of fuel; unfortunately, the whole system is very fragile in times of rising fuel imports and the threat that outside forces (e.g., OPEC) can shut off the petroleum tap. The ease of mobility is highly sensitive to fuel availability and prices, and a prolonged shortage could be devastating, just as a sharp increase in fuel prices could seriously affect many family and corporate budgets.[17]

If the population distribution situation persists, and there is no reason that it will not in the short run, the role of transit in urbanized areas may be limited to certain markets and functions and not be useful for others. There appear to be certain niches, even given the prevailing situation, where transit may do a commendable and useful job. Transit can certainly continue to serve relatively dense central cities, some of the inner suburbs, and some of those classic suburbs that developed along commuter rail lines in the nineteenth and early twentieth century. Transit will continue to serve radial trips to and from the central city to the suburbs. The market for downtown distribution services may increase where downtowns remain strong or have been revivified. With careful planning, transit may find other niches, such as orbital services tying together outlying activity centers. Transit may also provide a valuable reverse commute service to link inner-city residents with the growth of jobs in the outer area. This new yet growing passenger traffic market could be served by means of express bus service and suburban rail service; reverse commuting has the potential benefits to transit of better personnel and equipment utilization. There is also a major role for carpooling and vanpooling and other forms of paratransit in metropolitan areas. It will take careful rethinking of its role for transit to go much beyond the above possibilities.

From the vantage point of the late 1980s, highway traffic congestion in outlying areas of all major urbanized areas will continue and will probably grow much worse. In some places, mass transportation may provide additional corridor capacity. Given current urban and transportation policy, however, and given the present situation and current trends of population and economic development, there is probably no place in which transit will solve the congestion problem, reduce poverty, greatly stimulate the national economy, make major savings in fuel possible, or reduce pollution.[18]

CAN THE SITUATION BE CHANGED?

Any real attempt to change the transportation situation that now prevails in American metropolitan areas would challenge the housing decisions of millions of people who like low density, segmented, and segregated suburban or exurban living. It would also challenge the locational decisions of millions of businesses. The success of such a challenge is not apt to be very great. The change demanded is too substantial, and only some truly stirring event will alter the situation in the near future. Of course a historical counterargument may be that the whole change in population distribution and in mode of travel that has occurred since 1920 was a major shift from past practice and that, in truth, other major shifts may take place. Put another way, American society and American urban areas have been faced with a restructuring of urban life since the early twentieth century. Restructuring changes relationships and priorities and shifts the importance of various factors in life. The importance of transit and the automobile have shifted radically since World War I, as has the locus of economic activity between central city and suburb. Restructuring is uncomfortable, as borne witness by the breakdown of the traditional family in the U.S.

The current situation in metropolitan areas is apt to prevail, for the common-sense reason that politicians are sensitive to voters. Voters have cars and want to use them. Voters want to live in places they can afford, and they appear to enjoy the segmented living style of the suburbs. Those who may rightfully believe in the joys of the great mix of cities clearly do not understand the American middle class of the late twentieth century.[19]

From an urban transport standpoint, is there some way of relieving congestion that doesn't cost much and is relatively effective? As mentioned earlier, carpools and vanpools are commonly cited as low-cost methods of providing a good means of relieving congestion. And it's true; pooling is potentially a highly useful tool. Unfortunately, pooling is not attractive enough to provide a long-term solution. Pooling success depends on a friendly group of travelers and concordance of schedules. Carpools and vanpools are also highly inflexible. In effect, pooling is a transit service that makes but one round trip per day, and this lack of flexibility and convenience is the reason for its limited appeal, despite its economy and potential effectiveness. The use of pooling as a positive force in the reduction of congestion depends primarily upon the cost of driving a car (especially fuel prices) and the encouragement of employers.

The so-called commuter buses have proven attractive in some areas, particularly in the Los Angeles metropolitan region where they are sometimes encouraged and supported by employers. In providing commuter bus service, an older vehicle is usually used, and the driver is not a full-time bus operator but someone employed in the destination area. The bus circulates in a city or suburban area, picking up passengers, then runs express to its destination and drops them off. The bus is then stored for the workday while the driver goes on to his or her employment. At the end of the day, the process is reversed. It is a relatively inexpensive means of providing transportation, while at the same time it is merely a big carpool and suffers from the same lack of flexibility.

At the other end of the spectrum are relatively large-scale efforts. One of the strange effects of suburban traffic development is that in many cases the demand pattern does not really provide sufficient density of traffic in a given corridor such that major works to relieve the malaise can be justified either economically or politically. In many cases politicians may not feel it is worth spending the economic and political capital to undertake some heroic measure, especially if it is hard to defend even one corridor for significant upgrading that safely justifies the expense.[20]

One of the hopes in some outlying areas is that there may be rail or power line rights-of-way that would tie together places that should be linked. Of course, just because there is a right-of-way available does not necessarily mean that it will be truly useful. And in all of this, the spirit of "NIMBY" (not in my backyard) is fully at play. In Los Angeles, to give one example, there is general agreement that there should be a light rail line built in the San Fernando Valley to tie in with the heavy rapid transit subway system running into downtown Los Angeles. One of the options would involve a lightly used rail right-of-way that appears to be ideally sited. In a classic dilemma, no one wants the line built close to his place because of perceived disruptions, but most everyone would like the service to be convenient for personal use. Transit development in the San Fernando Valley in 1988 was very clearly shifted into "park."[21]

Thwarting any efforts at really improving the highway traffic situation is the subsidy for autos that use the road. There is broad agreement that automobile use is generally subsidized and highly subsidized in urban areas. Some estimates hold that total subsidies amounted to $300 billion in 1987 alone, and another estimate puts the subsidy at $2400 per passenger car for that year. The subsidy, when added to the other positive factors of automobile use, makes cars an enormously attractive travel option; one is almost surprised that auto use is not even greater than it is. Probably the greatest incentive to use an automobile in metropolitan areas is the parking subsidy. The "free" parking at shopping centers is subtly reflected in the cost of the merchandise. The majority of employers provide parking at low cost or at no cost to their employees. Cutting or eliminating the subsidy, or trying to enact some sort of strong disincentive to automobile use, would most likely generate strong opposition from the auto-highway coalition and from the industries they represent. This is a very reasonable attitude for businessmen, but it is not really helpful in this situation. Because of the limited appreciation of transit alternatives by the public, it is difficult for other than automobile options to be considered, and those options will not include the motorist paying full cost for highway use or parking space. Comfort is the key; any actions that make the middle class uncomfortable in any way will have little chance of becoming policy. Increasing taxes and forcing diminished use of automobiles are good examples of such discomfort.[22]

One of the facts of American life is that the middle class wants benefits for its taxes as soon as possible. The improvement of a road, whether cheerfully accepted or not by adjacent property owners and residents, should mean that the taxpayers can drive their automobiles upon it as soon as the road opens. It is a palpable effect, a noticeable addition to the transportation stock. A transit project that will have at least some short-run benefit for the taxpayers will probably be popular, but one that can't get rolling quickly will face increasing hostility, because its eventual value will probably be obscure to most of the public—and nothing will be seen to be happening, despite the dollars spent. Taxpayers are unhappy when something keeps being put off. For example, the Dallas Area Rapid Transit Authority moved at a glacial pace after the voters approved taxes to support it, and after having been in place for five years not one mile of the light rapid transit rail system had been built. In a 1988 referendum vote on issuing bonds to get money up front to build the rail system quickly, the matter failed miserably. The benefits had just taken too long to deliver, although taxpayers had been paying the transit tax for five years.[23]

As a polar opposite, the Northern Indiana Commuter Transportation District (NICTD) managed to get its benefits in place rather quickly for the public to see. The major benefit was the complete replacement of cars used by the Chicago South Shore & South Bend railroad in providing commuter service between northwest Indiana and downtown Chicago. Thanks to federal and state programs, there was virtually no local money involved in the project, so the taxpaying pain was muted. Best of all, the riders and taxpayers could see the new cars within four years. Other improvements, such as station parking lots, are important but are really only visible to the immediately surrounding citizens and the patrons who use the lot. Anyone in the vicinity of the railroad could see the new cars in regular daily operation. Despite great visible improvement, and a sharp increase in ridership, local politicians refused to support local funding, and NICTD's efforts to gain taxing powers from the Indiana General Assembly were thwarted by a lack of local support.[24]

Another factor making transit a less attractive option than it might otherwise be is that on the local system basis, transit management has not always done a very good job of selling its product. Transit systems frequently do a poor job of market research and understanding the market they serve. Reflecting this, they often do not shape the service to meet the needs of the customers they are trying to attract. There is no doubt that transit marketing plays a very secondary role to operations at most transit properties. Marketing people, who should have a strong input on pricing decisions, are often left out of those decisions completely. Public information is often poor; the bus-stop sign informs the passenger of where buses stop, but all too commonly not which bus, where it goes, when it comes, how much it costs, or any other important information for the new traveler. The general level of promotion of transit is rather paltry and community relations is often a step-child function. In looking toward solutions for urban circulation problems, mass transportation does not necessarily spring to the minds of most people as a real option that would warrant strong political and financial support.

Perhaps transit managers cannot be blamed too much. They are usually caught between pressure from organized labor and local politicians. Some board members are troublesome and unhelpful because of ignorance, political ambition, or sheer orneriness. Federal cutbacks in funding caused great difficulty in the 1980s in finding money to provide capital improvements or to cover operating costs. Add to this the problems of operating in the goldfish bowl of the public sector and low pay relative to the private sector for the responsibility involved, and it is no surprise that numerous managers suffer from burnout. Many managers seek jobs elsewhere in the public sector or move into the private sector where the exposure is less and the rewards greater. It is not the sort of atmosphere to stimulate innovation but rather a setting that guarantees following the rubrics of the past.

This points up the lack of institutionalization on the part of transit. This is a fancy way of saying that transit should be carefully built into the value structure of the community so that it has a strong claim on that community for support. Institutionalization is usually not a goal in most places and even when it is it's not easy to pull off. It means that their transit system has to work very closely with the people and the community to help provide the things that they want and to help stimulate the development of things that are considered valuable and necessary to them. With the transit system as a full participant in many activities, it will have a strong claim for support and continuation by its community. It is not easy to develop the practice of responsive interaction necessary for successful institutionalization, and this is best accomplished if it is an explicit goal of the transit property.[25]

MASS TRANSPORTATION AND THE AMERICAN CITY IN THE 1990S

The job of mass transportation is to help provide urban mobility and thereby help give people access to the economic, social, and cultural benefits of an urban place. Given the lack of mobility suffered by some urban residents, the great social and economic cost of providing transportation, and the plague of traffic congestion, does transit offer any option that presents a real solution to urban mobility problems? In truth, America is now fully committed to the automobile; to imagine anything else flies in the face of sense and conventional wisdom. It is equally true that America was once fully committed to the horse and buggy; the present situation could change. The full bloom of the automobile age required major changes in society and government to foster its growth. The world of cities had to expand to make possible the automobile age, with all its promise, all its advantages, and all its problems. The cities of America evolved into their current situation over many decades, and to change or reverse the current situation would take a long time.

Change in the current urban transportation situation is most likely to come as the result of a crisis, such as a shortage of or a sharp increase in the price of fuel. There's also a possibility that the sheer weight of congestion in suburban areas may animate the public to demand strong solutions. It is hard to imagine bold actions or major changes in human and political behavior, but it is still possible. It will not happen without careful thought, public understanding, and bold action, all of which are difficult in our popular democracy. In a word, making America's cities better demands leadership.

Transit thrives on density. Will there be a shift of population and economic activity back to central cities when that density already exists? Can mass transportation play a constructive role in fostering an increase in central city population and an associated revivification of older parts of the urbanized area? There has been a very limited return of people to the older parts of American cities. Gentrification of some neighborhoods has taken place, often inspired by quaintness, variety, or sheer Victorian impudence (and one might even say the fun) of the architecture of the neighborhoods. People who can afford such things usually have put quite a big stake in the renaissance of their neighborhoods and in living in a place that may be very close to their work location. The gentrification process is usually very expensive and is certainly not for low-income people. The positive factors of attracting more middle-class residents to older parts of central cities is weakened by a potential worsening of housing for the poor.

An intriguing factor that may cause some shifts back to central cities is the potential re-use of the all too common, heavily vandalized and figuratively bombed out areas close to many central business districts that are linked to the CBD by transit. These places may be attractive for redevelopment, perhaps even on a massive scale, in some large cities. To give one example, the view from the Lake Street elevated line in Chicago is an alarming and sickening one in the 1980s. Once the area abutting the elevated railway was a relatively densely populated residential area of modest homes and streets full of the flats typical to Chicago. Close to Lake Street there were many small factories and other work places. Since the end of World War II, the area around the Lake Street El fell victim to some of the worst slum conditions in Chicago, resulting from a decline in the industries and an influx of poverty-stricken inhabitants who were scourged by hopelessness, street gangs, and rampant vandalism. Industry moved to outlying areas and all who could afford to do so moved away. What was left was an urban jungle that fed upon itself. Much of the area was abandoned and physically destroyed or is in the process of being destroyed. The El rider on the way out to pleasant suburban Oak Park looks down upon a scene of destruction not unlike that left by the saturation bombing of many German cities after World War II, when most of the rubble had been cleared but nothing new had been built. Much of this devastated area is within a ten or fifteen minute ride on the Lake Street El into the very heart of the Chicago Loop, and much of the land is already cleared and possesses all the essential items of infrastructure. There is room; a whole city of fair size could arise within Chicago geared not only to the automobile but to the elevated rapid transit lifeline into the economic heart of Chicago. An existing transit line could be an important factor in rebuilding a part of Chicago.

The South Bronx of New York is another area that may be ripe for revivification. Close to the heart of Manhattan and well served by rapid transit and bus lines, its location may make it enormously attractive sometime in the future. Again, the revivification of such places from their present dark age will take adventurous thought, physical courage on the part of the initial residents, boldness of vision and strong cooperation between the public and private sectors. It can happen, as is given witness by the resurrection of Boston's Quincy Market and Baltimore's Inner Harbor area. Perhaps the best example of the link between transit and urban renaissance is in London's Dockland area. Ancient and decrepit dock areas have been turned into a massive office complex that is linked to the heart of London by the new Docklands Light Railway.[26]

Given the present situation in the U.S., and assuming there is no current leader with bold vision and leadership to direct urban America into more humane directions, the role that transit may play in large parts of the metropolitan area of America is limited. This is because the densities are all wrong and the scattering of houses, work sites, shopping, and social and cultural activities cannot be served very well by anything resembling conventional transit services. In the foreseeable future, it is plain that the process of development in the United States for much of the twentieth century is not going to be changed to meet the needs of transit. The role of mass transportation is apt to be minimal in many settings but, in given situations, transit may be useful in fitting into the interstices where other means of transport cause more problems than they solve or where a transit niche is present.

WHAT ABOUT THE CITY?

Given the urban and metropolitan situation of the 1990s and beyond, is there any federal action that can help improve urban life and in which mass transportation may play a useful role? Are there any actions that may be taken by all levels of government and by the private sector that can improve the quality of urban life, strengthen cities, and mitigate transportation problems?

Transportation of any kind is, obviously, not an end in itself. Urban transit and transportation exist for the sake of urban life and the economic vitality and social quality of that life. Transportation, as we have seen, is intertwined with other aspects of life, and elements of federal and other governmental policy all interplay in setting the tone of the urban world of America. In seeking to help improve the urban situation that demands even more transportation, ever more driving and overcrowded highways, there are some factors to consider in shaping governmental policy toward cities, federal transit, and overall urban transportation policy.

The current malaise of cities is in part due to the inability of central cities to annex outlying areas. Annexation was the principal means of urban growth during the nineteenth and early twentieth centuries. Today, annexation ranges from difficult to impossible in most metropolitan areas. Foreclosing annexation means that almost all of the vital growth potential will tend to locate away from the heart of the city. Really good living places for the middle class are often sparse within the limits of the central city. And, as long as people with money run away from national problems, the leadership and the rich sources of tax revenue from the middle class will continue to move to the suburban areas.

Federal housing policy has played a very large role in enabling people to depart from central cities and rid themselves of the negative aspects of life in older parts of urban areas. Federal mortgage guarantees are primarily available for homes meeting the suburban dream and the suburban ideal. Such guarantees are usually not available for housing in the central city, which means that the new housing development attractive to the middle class will continue to take place well outside the core area. Public housing has been largely confined to the central cities and usually has resulted in the creation of slums—some of them high-rise, vertical slums, such as in Chicago. Public housing and the consistent concentration of the poor in central cities are two of the reasons why more affluent people move out of the cities in their search for Arcadia on the freeway.

Federal highway policy has had an enormous impact on making the present

American city and its metropolitan area what it is. Federal policy, in conjunction with state policy, has been to provide large sums of money for highways that tend to spread development. The money is there to build the highways, and the highways will be built whether or not it is the right option for a rational and humane urban future. Most states are very strongly highway oriented and that situation is not likely to change in the near future.

Given all these factors, what impact can the federal government policies have on the future of the American city? Answer: a limited one, if past experience and practical expectations are any guide.

Annexation is a highly delicate matter and one for state and local government to tackle. The federal government really has no current role to play in annexation, and to attempt to do anything concerning the matter would be viewed at best as over-intrusive, if not actually stretching the U.S. Constitution. On the local level, changing annexation laws or making annexation easier will not be a popular idea and will not get much public support. Americans like their segmented living patterns and annexation would be seen as a threat. In all likelihood, suburban governments will continue to resist annexation strongly. The suburbs base their opposition on the concern that, if annexation takes place, they will inherit the center-city problems of minorities and ethnic strife, crime and drugs, political corruption in some places, the cost of repairing obviously decayed central cities, and paying for services that will really be used primarily by central-city residents. Center-city taxpayers may continue to resent the fact that persons living beyond the civil city limits use city facilities and services—such as the city streets—and don't appear to pay for them. Other than some way of taxing suburban residents who work in the central city to pay for infrastructure use, there is not much a city can do. Worse, such a tax may encourage more suburban development as a way for central-city workers to avoid the tax.

Annexation made easier is unlikely to happen unless, for whatever reason, it is mandated by state general assemblies. Mandated annexation may take place under special conditions, or as a result of strong pressure from a city or cities. The unified government of Indianapolis and Marion County in Indiana is an example. Pushed through by skillful work on the part of the city and some county officials, Indiana's General Assembly created Unigov; it never went to a vote of the local residents. Even though Unigov has operated successfully for many years and is an excellent example of the benefits of city-county coordination, if a vote were taken today the people living under this system would probably reject it. But Indianapolis is a growing, vigorous city, a place to visit and enjoy, and a good place to live because the great bulk of the suburbs are part of the city. The tax take from Unigov is great enough to make and keep Indianapolis financially healthy.

It is more likely that special organizations, institutions, and authorities (such as transit authorities) will continue to be the means of cooperation and integration of services between central cities and their outlying areas. This can provide, in a sense, a kind of limited annexation and has already resulted in a profusion of metropolitan special-purpose agencies. There is little room here, it would seem, for direct federal policy or action other than to encourage such bodies. Federal mass transportation policy has encouraged the formation of metropolitan-wide transit agencies.

Federal housing policy is another situation altogether, and here federal policy may have a beneficial impact locally. Mortgage guarantees are limited mainly to suburban housing and have been a major factor in stimulating suburban, low-density development. Federal mortgage guarantee policy could be rethought to make central-city housing eligible for more of the guarantees. This would encourage more people to use existing housing stock now subject to only conventional mortgages—a policy that might help to preserve and strengthen central-city neighborhoods by inviting more home ownership. It might also encourage new housing development in central cities and the rebuilding of some of the devastated zones noted earlier. It might also be possible though housing policy to encourage well-planned, higher density housing and associated commercial, retail, and employment developments in the suburbs and outlying areas. Tightly built, multi-purpose developments might reduce the need to travel. Housing policy might also be shaped to be more favorably disposed not only to higher density patterns but also to housing that was along public transportation routes of a fixed facility or otherwise permanent nature. Such a change in policy would certainly not stop suburban sprawl, but it might slow it and create incentives for the formation of a decent nucleus of people who would not have to travel as far to meet their needs. Public transportation would then find a real niche in more densely populated suburbs and perhaps could offer attractive convenience and time and money savings in compact outlying areas.

Public housing is a difficult problem. High-rise slums have been and are a failure, but enormous amounts of federal money have gone into such housing. Low-rise, scattered housing would probably be a better and more effective solution to the need for shelter for low-income people. However, the American wish for segmentation and segregation will probably make it virtually impossible to change the present situation and provide some public housing in areas outside central cities. The option to take public housing is a local decision and the necessity of gaining permission of local suburban governments virtually rules out any scattered site public housing in most suburban areas. One may conclude that federal housing policy may have some value in controlling land use in a fashion that could reduce the need to travel long distances.

What about changes in federal highway policy? The Interstate Highway System is almost finished; its major impact has already been made. In the short run, it is difficult to undo any deleterious impact the Interstates have had. Tighter federal planning requirements could be imposed and higher standards of proof might be necessary before certain kinds of highway projects could get underway. A highway policy aimed at not making things worse would be hard to impose and hard to administer, but not impossible. Federal and state highway officials are understandably not terribly sensitive to anything but highways and highway solutions. These people are dedicated professionals, and an understanding of the fact that past highway policies are part of the problem as well as part of the solution may lead highway people to support policies that they would come to see are in the overall best interests of the public.[27]

One potential federal policy change might be to prohibit the use of federal funds for the construction of new major highways in urban and suburban areas. To an extent, this is already happening, because the bulk of the federal Interstate System is in place, as are other urban sections of the U.S. highway system. This does not mean that certain types of projects to improve safety or to remove bottlenecks would not be undertaken. General maintenance and repair work on highway bridges is very much needed. Indeed, much of the Interstate Highway System has now reached the end of its economic life and needs major maintenance and repair, work that will absorb much federal, state, and local highway funds in the foreseeable future.

Joint federal, state, and local efforts might possibly seek joint transportation solutions, including consideration of the role of transit and other transportation-related projects in helping to solve transportation problems. Along this line the so-called 20/20 program of 1987-88 addressed the question of what to do after the completion of the Interstate Highway System. The aim of this project, carried out under the aegis of the Transportation Research Board, the American Association of State Highway and Transportation Officials, and many other groups, was to review a host of options. Unfortunately, in many cases the state highway departments and highway solutions tended to dominate the proceedings and hearings that were held in each state. There were serious concerns, voiced by such groups as the National Association of Railroad Passengers, that the limited viewpoint would be the only one that would prevail. At the time of this writing it is still unclear what will happen.[28]

REDEFINING THE CITY

There are so many factors that have affected mobility in cities and metropolitan areas in current urban life that it is easy to lose sight of the notion that mass transportation may be highly useful in providing mobility in the future. The policies adopted will have to face the reality of the present situation and look to the future in the most useful and constructive fashion. Moreover, mass transportation policy must be forged as a part of a broader urban policy if it is to be useful.

The American city is constantly being redefined. Unless it can be defined satisfactorily, it cannot be understood, and its problems may not be dealt with effectively. Because the city is a moving target, the very word has a fugitive presence. The once clearly defined locational functions are no longer so. For example, retailing is not concentrated downtown. In most U.S. cities, a short walk will probably not place an urban person in the presence of a loaf of bread for sale. Many of the good office jobs are in the suburbs, as are factory jobs, hamburger emporiums, and department stores. The vast, dark downtown movie palaces that once dominated popular entertainment are rubble now or have been renovated into art centers or performance halls for legitimate attractions.

The traditional city in the U.S. that mass transportation helped to build and serve, with its strong downtown focus of commerce, office work, retailing, entertainment, government, and culture is probably gone forever. The central civil city is only a part of the metropolitan area, and in many cases it is a small part. Gone with what many think of as the conventional city is the classic, traditional suburb that was closely articulated to the central city and was primarily a place of residence, a quiet dormitory for workers from the hustle and bustle of downtown. The scale of today's urban place is mammoth in comparison with what it was in the past. As an urban dweller in the U.S. of today, what one needs is probably not blocks away, but miles away; transportation has the task of serving the living pattern of this new, far-flung urban setting.

Nevertheless, and however strained it may be, there is a connection and at least some integration, some thread, that binds the new metropolitan areas together into what amounts to a cluster of boroughs, some of them homogeneous in nature, some varied in their make-up but often sharing the service of a single electric utility and water company, the same group of local chain stores, often the same telephone area code, the same general taxes, and perhaps a generally similar view of the world. The tissue that binds a metropolitan area is less dense in the areas far from the traditional central business district; but even so, the binding agent may be the name of that traditional city. A barometer of how a central city is viewed can be seen in where people tell you they are from. For example, someone from the metropolitan area in northeastern Illinois may simply say he or she is from Chicago; if the politics of the old city are in a particularly corrupt state at the time, however, the person may say Arlington Heights instead.

To deal rationally with urban transportation, the policies and programs of today and tomorrow will have to deal with the less focused urban place of the late twentieth century. The one typically consistent element is that we have an urban transportation problem in our society primarily because of land use patterns and practices and unbridled use of the automobile for mobility. Experience tells us that doing more to support the automobile through more highways and more parking only results in the demand for still more highways and parking. The conventional wisdom offers no long-range cure for the plague of traffic congestion. There is no simple technical solution to most of the problem; that is, there is unlikely to be some technological breakthrough that will take care of the difficulties. As an example, we enjoy technically excellent communications systems, but this has not really lessened in any significant way for most of the American population the need to get together to work or to go to a store to shop. Automobiles and transit vehicles may become more efficient or more comfortable than present-day modes, but any changes in the foreseeable future will probably be marginal.

A real barrier to definitive action in the modern urban world is the fact that there are so many political jurisdictions involved. Metropolitan fragmentation is not new in the U.S., but the degree of fragmentation is greater than ever before, and promises to get no better. The virtual impossibility of metropolitan unification through annexation is a given. Even so, a concordance of action is possible through special governmental units, such as transit districts, which act as threads in the binding mechanism that offers at least a tenuous metropolitan fabric.

The transportation tools to accomplish mobility improvements include the private automobile, various modes of public transportation, and all the in-between types of transportation, such as the use of cabs and pooling. A closely related set of tools are the incentives and disincentives to use or not use the various transportation means; these are the means by which to control transportation demand. Policies involving land use and development include housing policy, as evidenced in mortgage guarantees and policies related to commercial, office, and industrial development and the various incentives and disincentives that affect and control land use. Controlling the demand for either transportation or land use is not likely to be popular.

A NEW FEDERAL URBAN TRANSPORTATION POLICY

The real chore of the federal policy makers and program managers, working with other levels of government, is to find a transportation and land use policy that works. In the main, that means working hard to craft policy that doesn't make things worse. It also means continuing to help provide mobility to those who need it, because not every American has ready access to an automobile or to public transportation that is useful. The development of land cannot be stifled, because there are genuine needs to be met, and economic development cannot be brought to a halt.

Mass transportation all by itself cannot do much; it must be used as part of a broader effort to improve mobility and enhance access.[29] The essential elements of current federal mass transportation programs and policy should remain in place. If the policy and programs are to be useful in helping to enhance urban mobility and access, transit policy must work in conjunction with other policies, especially housing and economic development. A variety of tools and approaches must be used to solve a common problem of impeded mobility and access. Furthermore, because of the importance of infrastructure investment in urban development—gas, water, sewers, etc.—policymakers must take infrastructure policy into account. Finally, any urban policy has to take into its embrace a close working and cooperative relationship with the private sector.

Mass transportation policy and transit itself can only play an important role if allowed to work in the context of political reality on all levels of government. The mass transportation policy and the programs must have broad benefits that affect all parts of the nation and all elements of the population. The policies adopted cannot upset the expectations of individuals or of other levels of government. In political reality, it means that a mass transportation policy cannot be carried out at the expense of the federal highway program. Whatever is done must be largely a modification of what has gone before, and it must work reasonably well. Finally, the policy must not harm the private sector, which is one good reason that the private sector must be one of the partners in whatever is done.

Every effort must be made to forge a policy that is effective, reasonably efficient, and that produces palpable results relatively quickly.

A realistic federal urban mass transportation policy along with a broader urban transportation policy must offer incentives to encourage the necessary behavior and action. Incentives to various actions can be either positive or negative, carrot or stick, but in practice, positive incentives would be more politically palatable. For example, an incentive to encourage greater use of public transportation by giving a federal tax break to regular transit users could be useful. One way to do this would be to allow those purchasing monthly transit passes to count the annual costs as a deduction on federal income tax. For many commuters of modest means this could be a pleasant windfall, and it might tip the balance toward leaving the car at home and taking the bus to work. In situations where employers pay all or a portion of the monthly transit pass cost, they would be allowed to use the entire expenditure on their employees as a deduction, something they are now permitted to do only for parking expenses. One could argue that this incentive would give a significant break to purchasers of costly monthly passes on commuter railroads, who tend to be more affluent than the typical transit rider. That should not be offputting on equity grounds, because one could hold that the more affluent suburban rail commuter pays higher federal taxes that are used to help provide the money for the federal transit program. The program might also appear to work against people of limited income who could not afford to put out the money all at one time for a monthly pass. There is no reason that weekly passes could not be used, as long as there is some sort of auditable record for tax-break purposes.[30]

Another incentive could be a tax break for developers who accommodate transit into their projects or develop property in conjunction with existing transit facilities. Many urban and suburban housing developments are extremely difficult to service with transit, many subdivisions are not well articulated into the highway network and, with their usual complement of cul-de-sacs and curvilinear streets, are hopeless from a transit viewpoint. A housing development planned and executed so that buses could easily provide service would be worthy of tax incentives and perhaps even federal mortgage guarantee breaks.

Strong land-use planning and strict enforcement of the plan is an obvious possibility. Americans have never been fond of planning, however, and businesses have worked hard to overcome tight controls in the political sphere, hence this recommendation of incentives through the tax code, which could share with the developer the benefits of better land use in the community. In effect, tax incentives would help create a partnership between various levels of government and the private sector. Idealistic? Perhaps, but it might be more successful and lead to wiser development than the current practice, which does little or nothing to encourage really wise development. Thwarting the best of plans in the fragmented metropolitan areas of the nation would be those jurisdictions that did not go along with a regional plan designed to rationalize development and the transportation tools that serve it. A community that wished to allow total developmental freedom in order to attract the maximum tax dollars could cause other adjacent communities to suffer. Regional agreements would be necessary for such a plan to be beneficial, and such agreements smack of unified government arrangements to which the public has historically been opposed. It would not be an easy policy to implement; it might only work in places where congestion difficulties are of a magnitude that the public and their political leadership are willing to accept politically tough solutions.

Another possibility in the category of incentives is to provide more operating aid for transit, with the federal government working in close partnership with state and local governments to lower transit fares dramatically. This might be helpful in luring more riders to transit and would assuredly be a boon to low-income people who would probably enjoy greater mobility. There is the question of whether or not it would woo anyone out of an auto; the automobile is so attractive that fare cuts might only be expensive and not terribly effective. Moreover, the determining factor in attracting riders is more often the quality of the service rather than its direct cost to the passenger, so that fare cuts alone might not really achieve large enough increases in patronage to relieve congestion. Selected, well-focused service improvements might boost transit ridership substantially enough to increase the proportion of urban trips taken by transit. The positive track record could encourage the use of other incentive programs and provide support for other innovative efforts.

Turning to the stick, disincentives to auto use may be a way of controlling the demand for use of the highways. Some studies show that the subsidy for downtown parking that reduces or eliminates parking cost to the individual motorist is a powerful incentive for automobile use. A tax on subsidized parking might be a very effective means of making the automobile less attractive. It is certainly feasible where employers provide their employees the perk of free parking in commercial structures. In another version of the disincentives, auto users might still get their parking costs covered by their employer but would have to show the commercial value of that space as income on their tax returns. Another way to handle it could be to change the tax laws so that employers could not take off expenses for employee parking on their corporate tax returns, thus removing the incentive to offer free parking.

Taxing parking could become complex in the cases of factories and office complexes where the employer owns the parking facilities. The commercial value of the space would have to be estimated, which could be difficult without the market helping to set a price. Even so, removing the parking subsidy might dramatically alter driver behavior, making the use of ride sharing or transit more attractive.

Raising auto user charges to more closely reflect the real cost of auto use is another possible disincentive to driving a car. The funds thus raised would certainly be helpful in making necessary repairs to the highway infrastructure and in other useful purposes to make highways safer. On the assumption that motorists only pay about half of the actual cost of driving, a full user charge, or something approximating it, would appear to be a powerful disincentive to driving. The difficulty of imposing such an increase, and the results thereof, would be sure to spark vigorous debate.

Given the current tenor of the time, politicians might have great difficulty in even thinking about the possibility of alienating large numbers of voters by such an increase in user charges, which is viewed as a tax. Interestingly enough, if the federal tax was imposed gradually, say a few pennies at a time, motorists might not even notice it. Under such circumstances the impact on auto use might be light. Just as the driving public became accustomed to much higher fuel costs in the 1970s, so they might simply accept the higher charges over time and not change their driving habits. The advantage would be more funds for highway and other infrastructure purposes, but the desired impact on auto use might not be at all visible. The price of gasoline might be more of a factor if state and local governments were also given the incentive to raise their user charges. If nothing else, an increase in auto user charges to reflect the real cost of driving an automobile would make the market competition between auto use, pooling, and transit more realistic. In so many cases today the market competition between auto and transit is so imperfect as to render it a useless test of the worth of either automobiles or transit.

A more complex and probably more controversial matter would be user charges that reflect costs of certain expensive highways and the congestion costs of using certain highways at the peak times of day. With the various electronic devices now available, it should not be difficult to impose such a charge and present motorists with a computerized bill each month. There is certainly nothing new about such ideas; similar suggestions have been made for at least thirty years. And nothing has been done for thirty years.

The political acceptability of any one of a spectrum of disincentives is problematic. As mentioned earlier, a condition that would make adoption of incentive and disincentive policies possible would be an overcrowding of the transport system to such a great degree that the public demanded action, even if it had to pay the price. To remain politically viable, there would have to be some clear evidence, given quickly, that the various remedies were working. There is an understandable perception problem here. New highways appear to be free; no specific charge is levied with a close tie-in to the construction costs. After a gestation period of building the road—or the rapid transit system, for that matter—it is open and usually travel is easier for a while. Disincentives—or incentives—to control transportation demand would have to show that they worked for at least a reasonable period of time.

THROUGH THE HAZE DARKLY

No work on urban transportation can ignore environmental considerations, and one of the arguments for a federal role in urban mass transportation is based on the potential of transit to help fight pollution. Transportation vehicles are major causes of environmental pollution and are major contributors to acid rain, health-threatening smog, and prime donors to elements in the atmosphere that promise to change the earth's climate.[31] Because of the nature of the environment, the federal government has a strong responsibility to enforce compliance with the standards already established. There is growing public concern about pollution in general. It tends to peak when some dramatic occurrence thrusts itself into the headlines, such as a smog attack in a city that causes death or serious debilitation. Citizens in parts of the U.S. and in Canada and other countries affected by the ruination caused by acid rain are demanding action. The reports on the greenhouse effect and the general warming of the earth's climate began to attract national attention and worry during the heat wave of 1988 throughout the U.S. The average citizen driving to work is doing a routine thing; it doesn't seem possible that such an innocent and ordinary activity could have lethal impacts, not just now but for years to come. Alfred Hitchcock frightened us with his great films by making the ordinary terrifying, and so it is with the journey to work by car. Its implications, repeated millions of times each day, are frightening.[32]

The standards for industrial and automotive vehicle pollution should not be adjusted downward for the convenience of vehicle manufacturers but upward to meet the demands of reality, and they need to be enforced. Many cities are not in compliance with the standards, and withholding of highway money or other federal support should be carried out strictly according to the law. Delaying the implementation of penalties is not doing any favors to anyone in the long run. Encouraging all means to cut vehicle use is a practical way of achieving the end of better air and less noise. Incentives and disincentives have to be used because, otherwise, there is no reason for people to change their habits for the good of all citizens.[33]

A federal Environmental Protection Agency that really means business and enforces the law strictly will likely encourage state and local governments to greater strictures. The battle will be a long one, but the price of lackluster enforcement is too high to be allowed to continue. Strong opposition to enforcement is to be expected; again, real leadership in Washington and in America's state houses will take the pollution issue seriously and really do something about it.

Either encouragement or pressure will undoubtedly lead U.S. and foreign automobile manufacturers to produce better, more fuel efficient and less polluting vehicles. Federal laws should encourage the pooling of ideas, if that is what it takes, or the rewards of patents and licensing for an entrepreneurial effort that builds a car that meets or betters the standards.

The federal carrot as well as the stick is needed. Metropolitan areas that are really serious about environmental improvement should have available increased transit aid and aid to promote various types of pooling, or land use that decreases the vehicle miles of travel. It should be taken into account that the potential consequences of any really determined effort of a city to improve by shifting more motorists to transit would probably overwhelm the transit system. Most transit properties are today geared to their current patronage levels and to absorb more peak hour riders would strain the resources to the utmost.

GETTING A HANDLE ON DEVELOPMENT POLICY

Land-use policy is a major element in the transportation picture because of its impact on mobility, the need to travel, and congestion, along with the price tag accompanying these items.

One way to optimize land-use planning would be to encourage the redevelopment of inner cities and already established suburbs and outlying areas. As mentioned previously, there are large areas in central cities that are conveniently located in relation to the established central business districts, which, with mortgage guarantees and other incentives, could be attractive to developers and to citizens who wished to reduce the time and effort of travel. This should likewise be attractive to cities because currently dormant property would produce more tax revenue. Centrally located enterprises would have an advantage in that workers living closer to the workplace would find such redevelopment as yet another means of making employment with these enterprises attractive.

Because these places are within the already developed part of the city or established outlying community, the infrastructure of roads, sewers, water, gas, and transit are already in place. Police and fire protection, libraries, churches, theaters, museums, parks, retailing, sanitation services, and all the other things that make up an established city or community are already there and would not have to be developed anew. It is possible that much of the pressure to supply new infrastructure and supporting services would be relieved.

Land use policy for new areas should promote greater densities and provision of needed local services close by. Stronger support could be offered for transit tie-ins, because with sufficient developmental density, transit service would be more viable. Careful planning, with enforcement of planning and incentives, could assure more local support of development of such a nature as to reduce travel needs. Development should be strongly encouraged along existing transit corridors, in order to make more intensive use of what already exists. Even so, many persons will not be able to use transit, given the overall living patterns, but concentration along transit lines should have a long-run impact on encouraging less use of automobiles and greater use of public transportation and pooling.

Another approach would be to provide strong support for the development of a transit corridor, such as a commuter rail line and well-planned adjacent development. These corridors need not be aimed at the central city, but could as well link together outlying centers of development and economic activity. If a busway or rail line is to encourage denser corridor development, planning and zoning of land use must support the desired type of activity. Transit networks in outlying areas, utilizing the timed-transfer methodology, would be another realistic approach to transit service outside the central city.

In sum, all levels of government need to encourage planning and development that discourage auto use by making it less necessary. This will not be easy, because it flies in the face of conventional wisdom developed in the years since 1945.

TRAVEL DEMAND POLICY

Transportation problems in urban areas will continue in the absence of policies that reduce travel demand. The development policy suggested above will help. Pooling will help, as will greater use of public transit. Staggering work hours may help reduce peak demand on roads and on transit service.

Innovation in transit service should be encouraged. This might take the form of shuttle buses or van services, linking together various developments in the outer portions of metropolitan areas. If the transit agency can provide such service, fine; if not, private firms should compete to deliver what is needed. The aim should be to offer mobility in a way that does not demand auto use and that does not protect the monopoly of the local transit agency.

Controlling travel demand is easier to talk about than it is to achieve. Education will help. The best means of achieving the goal of lessened travel demand is to combine efforts of the public and private sectors and all levels of government. It has to be made clear that it is in everybody's best interest to work together.

One way of achieving the desired ends is by encouraging more useful institutional structures. Transportation Management Associations, or TMAs, have proven successful in some places. These are combinations of the private sector and governmental agencies dealing with transportation. Working together, they develop goals for auto and transit use and then combine efforts to achieve these goals. Employers may reduce or eliminate parking subsidies and encourage pooling or transit use by providing choice parking spots for employees participating in vanpools or carpools, or employers may establish their own vanpools. The transit agency may offer subscription bus service for major employers, and employers might subsidize all or a portion of an employee's transit use.

Neither land-use controls nor transportation-demand control will work without public participation. Gaining public support will not be easy, but neither is living with the situation of the present. Local pride and concern in the quality of life, and real leadership by government, should make the job manageable.[34]

THE NEED FOR EDUCATION AND INFORMATION

Ignorance is never bliss; it is always an enemy. The American public is poorly informed about urban transportation and the importance of land use in their lives and their futures. Real leadership, spurred on by a few concerned and informed citizens, can push for better information and can insist that educational programs on all levels offer people the information that is needed.

It is clear that much more information about transportation options and impacts is needed by the American public. People can only consider or demand what they know about and, things being what they have been in the U.S. since the end of the Second World War, widening the road or building a new one and using a car is about the only option many people consider. It has become a self-fulfilling prophecy. Education is needed so that, in a popular democracy, the people will have a much better idea of what various kinds of transportation investments, transportation options, incentives, and disincentives will do to keep metropolitan areas truly fluid. People are rightfully concerned about the economic prosperity of the place in which they live; transportation obviously has a major impact on the economy of an area. The mobility and access offered by transportation can help the potential of a place become positive. A metropolitan area with a reputation for congestion and difficult access will become increasingly unattractive as the congestion and the reputation grow; such a place will not attract enterprise or residents. Despite the many blandishments of Los Angeles and Houston, their reputation for intolerable traffic congestion has undoubtedly led many businesses to seek more mobile pastures in which to operate. The public needs to know the consequences of various transportation actions. Public officials, too, need to have a broader view, otherwise only the conventional wisdom will hold sway. Planners, despite their education and the many frustrations of seeing their plans and knowledge ignored, also need to have their ideas broadened, especially in the area of land use. Education should aim at encouraging the public, public officials, and planners to stress less use of the single occupant automobile and greater use of pooling and the use of transit.

Education encouraging greater densities and the design of new developments to afford the use of transit or various types of pooling for as many trips as possible is needed. Multiple land use, anathema to many planners, makes good sense. Development in outlying areas and redevelopment of places both inside and outside the central city should consider not just a singular development of offices, industry, retailing, or residences, but a combination of land use with the aim of cutting down the need to use automobiles. Employees in suburban offices are often marooned at their workplace unless they climb into their cars to find a place to eat lunch, buy a greeting card or a necktie, or meet a friend. The beauty of campus-like office parks often obscures the fact that the complex is really an island, separated, save by an auto trip, from all other activities.

This much-needed information and education process is sadly wanting. Most reporters who cover transportation are poorly informed, often because transport issues are only a portion of their journalistic beat. Only a few of the largest metropolitan dailies assign a reporter to transportation and allow them the time to build up their knowledge and come to understand what is really going on. Radio and television news generally trivializes much of what is happening and transportation reports by such media usually lack depth. Public information programs on the broadcast media are relatively scarce, and transportation is just one of many topics to be covered in the limited time available. Probably the greatest contributions from radio are the reports from a helicopter on how bad the traffic is on certain highways during rush hours.

Except for the training of transportation professionals in colleges and universities, students are rarely exposed to anything about transportation other than their high school driver-education class. Broader study of transportation and its role in urban development should be offered.

A MODEST PRESCRIPTION

It is old hat to talk of setting realistic goals for federal mass transit policy and programs, but the fuzzy goals of the current policies and the lack of integration with other urban policies and programs are major reasons the program has not had more success. It is not that the governmental programs have made great changes, but that the transit industry has remained so much the same. The mass transportation community has to become a participant in a host of activities that work together to enhance urban mobility and the quality of urban life.

Barring a disaster or a sharp increase in the quality of political leadership, only modest efforts are realistic. We will, as a nation, remain innocent of the ideal urban places pictured so eloquently by social critics such as Lewis Mumford. The prescription is modest, but given the context, realistic.

Federal policy should encourage transit use through cooperative ventures between the public and private sectors, working together in such devices as transportation management associations. This policy would lead to a restructuring of the approach to the provision of urban transportation to meet the restructuring of urban areas that has been taking place. As a part of the program, transit properties must be encouraged to be as flexible as possible in the service they provide. Innovation is a key factor. More of the same is not going to work well in the future, because it has not been terribly successful in the past.

Through careful planning and control and a variety of incentives and disincentives, urban development that does not increase the transportation burden should be encouraged. If a development worsens the mobility problem, the developers should be obliged to pay for solutions.

Working with the communities they service, and the planners of those communities, transit properties should be strongly encouraged to carry out far better market research than has been the case. Transit managers should be encouraged to understand their markets as well as possible and to take the maximum advantage of the markets they can serve well. Where transit cannot serve, the transportation management associations can step in with various programs to alleviate transportation problems.

Congress should set some reasonable goals for transit and provide money to support the effort. The goals and effort should be carefully focused to gain maximum benefits from the money spent. Two high-priority targets would be programs aimed at providing transportation that meets the needs of low-income groups or others without access to an automobile. A major attack on congestion problems should be undertaken in tandem with transportation management associations. Another focus should be a combined attack on pollution, embracing the private sector and state and local governments. Maximum flexibility should be encouraged on the part of all concerned parties.

None of this will be easy, and real leadership must be shown by Congress and the current administration. Otherwise, a valuable resource will be squandered, and America's urban areas will be sentenced to ever worsening problems of mobility.

Notes

2. URBAN MASS TRANSIT IN THE MID–1980S

1. Tom Wicker, "Stockman's Tantrum Aside, Amtrak Is Needed," *Louisville Courier-Journal*, May 4, 1985.

2. Nineteen hundred eighty-five was not a great year for the Miami Metro. In addition to being subjected to presidential vituperation, it also suffered a wreck in June. See Dan Christenson and Denice L. Stinson, "Metrorail Collision: Cost $2 Million; U.S. Joining Dade's Investigation," *Miami News*, June 27, 1985; and Marc Fisher and Luis Feldstein Soto, "Driver in Metrorail Crash Has a Spotty Job Record," *Miami Herald*, June 28, 1985.

3. See "Pittsburgh's First Subway: A Midsummer's Dream Come True," *Passenger Transport*, Vol. 43, No. 22, June 3, 1985, p. 8; Ken Fisher, "Subway Gives City New Look," *Pittsburgh Post-Gazette*, July 4, 1985; and "Downtown Pittsburgh Gets 1.1 Mile Subway," *New York Times*, July 4, 1985.

4. See Judy McCusker, "Miami Builds for Growth," *Railway Age*, Vol. 187, No. 7, July 1986, pp. 79-83; and "Miami's Metro Dade Moves Ahead," *Passenger Transport*, Vol. 44, No. 40, October 6, 1986, p. 48. A more complete local view of what happened may be found in the rather subjective article by John Dorschner, "Metrofail?" *Tropic* (the Sunday magazine of the *Miami Herald*), September 15, 1985, pp. 10-12 and 18-25.

5. See News Releases from Massachusetts Bay Transportation Authority: "MBTA Begins Red Line Track Reconstruction," 85-05-53, May 4, 1985; "MBTA Receives Five Construction Awards for Red Line Extension," 85-05-62, May 29, 1985; "MBTA Begins Phase Two of Green Line Track Reconstruction," 85-06-65, June 11, 1985; and "Jubilant Day on Red Line," *Rider*, Vol. 2, No. 1, Jan.-Feb. 1985. Boston has always had much to cheer about in relation to the amount of money it has received from the federal mass transit program. A big part of this is due to effective political support in Congress (two Speakers of the House—John McCormick and Thomas P. "Tip" O'Neill—didn't hurt) and to strong political and financial support from the State of Massachusetts. One very good reason for the support was the sheer need for rehabilitation and capital refurbishment of a very old rail system. See William D. Middleton, "Boston Builds for Growth," *Railway Age*, Vol. 189, No. 3, March 1988, pp. 67-72; and *New Orange Line Opening*, May 4, 1987, published by the Massachusetts Bay Transportation Authority, 12 pages.

6. See "Philadelphia Opens Airport High Speedline," *Passenger Transport*, Vol. 42, No. 19, May 13, 1985, p. 21; "Reclamation Projects Prove Present, Future Values," *Passenger Transport*, Vol. 43, No. 26, July 1, 1985, p. 14; "SEPTA's New Way to Fly—An Unqualified Success," *Passenger Transport*, Vol. 44, No. 22, June 2, 1986, p. 8.

7. See Luther S. Miller, "Buffalo: A Cautionary Tale," *Railway Age*, Vol. 187, No. 9, September 1986, pp. 69-71; Michael Desmond, "Trying to Make Buffalo's Ends Meet," *Mass Transit*, Vol. 13, No. 10, October 1986, pp. 26 and 28; Elizabeth Kolbert, "New Projects Help Buffalo Lift Downbeat Image," *New York Times*, December 1, 1986; "Buffalo Holds Festivities for Metro Rail Opening," *Passenger Transport*, Vol. 44, No. 49, December 8, 1986, pp. 1, 8-9, and 13, and Luther S. Miller, "LRRT Confounds the Skeptics," *Railway Age*, Vol. 189, No. 5, May 1988, pp. 35-36.

8. See "CTA Forges Rail-Air Link," *Railway Age*, Vol. 185, No. 10, October 1984, p.

71; "Chicago's Test-Tube Line," *Railway Age,* Vol. 186, No. 9, September 1985, pp. 87-88; and David M. Young, *The Influence of Politics on Mass Transportation in Chicago,* Metropolitan Conference on Public Transportation Research, University of Chicago, June 19, 1986.

9. The interesting story of how the Portland light rail system came to be is found in Sheldon M. Edner, "Urban Intergovernmental Transportation Decision-Making: Portland's Investment in Light Rail Transit," in *Techniques for Making Key Transportation Decisions,* Transportation Research Record 980, Transportation Research Board, Washington, D.C., 1984, pp. 1-8. See also "San Diego's Euclid Line Speeds Along," *Passenger Transport,* Vol. 43, No. 22, June 3, 1985, p. 28; "San Diego Approves East Urban Trolley Link," *Passenger Transport,* Vol. 43, No. 25, June 24, 1985, p. 5; and Frank Sweeney, "Light Rail Ceremonies Were Dynamite," *San Jose Mercury News,* March 24, 1984.

10. See Joe Grata, "PAT Plans Closure, Scraps Cuts in Service," *Pittsburgh Press,* March 8, 1985; Kent Fisher, "PAT Board Adopts 14-Month Budget Plan," *Pittsburgh Post-Gazette,* April 27, 1985; and "Pittsburgh Confronts Funding Crisis," *Passenger Transport,* Vol. 43, No. 12, March 25, 1985, p. 8.

11. See Sally Smith, "People Mover Stirs Dust, Hopes," *Detroit Free Press,* September 23, 1984; Damon Daclin, "The People Mover May Run Someday, Has Overrun Already," *Wall Street Journal,* April 30, 1985; Roger Martin, "Mover's Backers Seek State Money," *Detroit News,* April 24, 1985; and David Kushma, "SEMTA, Mover Builder Reach Tentative Agreement to Fix Cost," *Detroit Free Press,* June 5, 1985.

12. Christopher Conte, "The Explosive Growth of Suburbia Leads to Bumper-to-Bumper Blues," *Wall Street Journal,* April 16, 1985. See also Kenneth C. Orski, "Suburban Mobility: The Coming Transportation Crisis?" *Transportation Quarterly,* Vol. 39, No. 2, April 1985, pp. 283-296.

13. See "L.A. Is Ready for Rail," *Passenger Transport,* Vol. 43, No. 22, June 3, 1985, p. 23; *The Rail Way,* Los Angeles County Transportation Commission, No. 6, September 1984; and William D. Middleton, "Los Angeles Metro Gets a Slow Order," *Railway Age,* Vol. 185, No. 8, August 1984, pp. 72-75.

14. See "It's Time," a supplement to the *Dallas Times Herald,* February 20, 1983; Allen R. Myerson, "DART Board Approves Final Transit Plans," *Dallas Morning News,* April 15, 1983; Peter Appleborne, "Mass Transit Is Suddenly Big in Texas," *New York Times,* August 21, 1983; Bill Fahrenwald, "Texas-Size Rail Transit," *Railway Age,* Vol. 185, No. 5, May 1984, pp. 69-70; and David Firestone, "DART Picks 4 Downtown Subway Plans," *Dallas Times Herald,* June 8, 1985.

15. Without doubt a major factor discouraging the continuation of private, subsidized transit is the large and inevitable role of politics and public scrutiny in tax-supported transit. The private role in transit and transportation has a strong case made for it in the following: Charles A. Lave, ed., *Urban Transit: The Private Challenge to Public Transportation,* San Francisco: Pacific Institute for Public Policy Research, 1985; Charles Lave, "The Yeast That Makes Transit Quality Rise," *Wall Street Journal,* April 22, 1985; John Semmons, "Public Transit: A Bad Deal Getting Worse," *Wall Street Journal,* June 6, 1985; and George M. Smerk, "Urban Mass Transportation: From Private to Public to Privatization," *Transportation Journal,* Vol. 26, No. 1, Fall 1986, pp. 83-91.

16. See "The New War between the States Will Be Fought over Taxes," *Business Week,* No. 2899, June 17, 1985, pp. 132-133.

17. The process of widespread population decentralization and the challenges and possibilities this phenomenon presents is the theme of a book that is both interesting and disturbing. Anyone curious about non-traditional locations of people and urban activities should read John Herbers, *The New Heartland: America's Flight Beyond the Suburbs and How It Is Changing Our Future* (New York: Times Books, 1986). The subject is also discussed in authoritative fashion in Robert Fishman, *Bourgeois Utopias: The Rise and Fall of Suburbia* (New York: Basic Books, 1987), Chapter 7. The social and political consequences of dispersion are well-handled in two informative works: Jon C. Teaford, *The*

Twentieth Century American City: Problem, Promise, and Reality (Baltimore: The Johns Hopkins University Press, 1986), especially Chapter 7; and Herbert J. Gans, *Middle American Individualism: The Future of Liberal Democracy* (New York: The Free Press, 1988).

18. Mr. Reagan was not the first president to take a dim view of the federal transit program; Jimmy Carter felt much the same—for practical rather than doctrinaire reasons—until the fuel crisis of 1979 made a born-again transit supporter of him.

3. THE ENVIRONMENT OF TRANSIT POLICY

1. Good examples of policy proposals that once were the stuff of drama, passion, and politics are the issues of U.S. tariff policy and the free coinage of silver in the 1890s. Whereas once these were topics to stir the mind, demand emotional support, and spur the long-winded to oratory, both issues now provide only a yawn.

2. As an example of a solution that became a problem, the use of coal as a source of heat and power developed in the eighteenth and nineteenth centuries; it provided an alternative to denuding the countryside of trees to supply cities with heat for houses and steam for the factories. Unfortunately, coal also helped produce the Dickensian smog under which cities such as London suffered for so long.

This section is not intended to be by any means a detailed history of urban development throughout history. It is derivative of many years of reviewing the situation. The books listed here are instructive and useful and are a good place to begin a study of urban history.

Leonardo Benevolo, *The History of the City* (Cambridge, Mass.: The MIT Press, 1980); K. H. Schaeffer and Elliott Sclar, *Access for All* (New York: Columbia University Press, 1980); Lewis Mumford, *The City in History: Its Origins, Its Transformations, and Its Prospects* (New York: Harcourt, Brace, 1961); Kenneth T. Jackson, *Crabgrass Frontier: The Suburbanization of the United States* (New York: Oxford University Press, 1985); Wilfred Owen, *The Metropolitan Transportation Problem*, Revised Ed. (Washington, D.C.: The Brookings Institution, 1966); Donald J. Olsen, *The City as a Work of Art* (New Haven: Yale University Press, 1986); and Robert Gray, *A History of London* (New York: Dorset Press, 1978).

3. Oxen were used because a relatively simple yoke could be fashioned, permitting their formidable strength to be fully utilized. Horses were faster but could not be pressed into service until a horsecollar was devised (not until around the eleventh century) that did not close off the horse's windpipe when it pressed forward to pull a loaded cart or a plow. Small, two-wheeled carts were used until steerable front wheels on a four-wheeled cart were invented. The original four-wheeled wagon, with its wheels rigidly attached as in a baby carriage, had substantially greater carrying capacity but was virtually unusable until it could be steered.

4. For a discussion of urban growth and development, see Lewis Mumford, "The Baroque City," in *The Lewis Mumford Reader,* Donald L. Miller, ed. (New York: Pantheon Books, 1986), pp. 127-147; Gray, *A History of London,* especially Chapters 4-5; Patrick Geddes, *Cities in Evolution: An Introduction to the Town Planning Movement and to the Study of Civics* (New York: Harper & Row, 1971; originally published in 1915 by Ernest Benn Limited, London); Harlan W. Gilmore, *Transportation and the Growth of Cities* (Glencoe, Ill.: The Free Press, 1953); and Kevin Lynch, *A Theory of Good City Form* (Cambridge, Mass.: The MIT Press, 1981).

5. See Robert Harris, *Canals and Their Architecture* (London: Hugh Evelyn, 1969); J. Douglas Porteous, *Canal Ports: The Urban Achievement of the Canal Age* (New York: Academic Press, 1977); Paul Fatout, *Indiana Canals* (West Lafayette, Ind.: Purdue University Press, 1972); David Jacobs and Anthony E. Neville, *Bridges, Canals, and Tunnels: The Engineering Conquest of America* (New York: American Heritage Publishing Company, 1968); Christopher I. Savage, *An Economic History of Transport* (London: Hutchinson University Library, 1959); Eric Pawson, *Transport and Economy: The Turnpike Roads of Eigh-*

teenth Century Britain (New York: Academic Press, 1977); W. T. Jackman, *The Development of Transportation in Modern England,* Revised Ed. (London: Frank Cass and Co., 1962; originally published in 1916 by the Cambridge University Press).

6. For the history of urban mass transit and the development of cities see John Anderson Miller, *Fares, Please!* (New York: Dover Publications, 1960; originally published in 1941 by D. Appleton-Century Co. Inc.); George M. Smerk, "The Development of Public Transportation and the City," in George E. Gray and Lester A. Hoel, *Public Transportation: Planning, Operations, and Management* (Englewood Cliffs, N.J.: Prentice-Hall, Inc., 1979), Chapter 1; Emerson P. Schmidt, *Industrial Relations in Urban Transportation* (Minneapolis: The University of Minnesota Press, 1937), Chapter 1; David W. Jones, *Urban Transit Policy: An Economic and Political History* (Englewood Cliffs, N.J.: Prentice-Hall, Inc., 1985), Chapter 3; Charles S. Dunbar, *Buses, Trolleys and Trams* (London: Paul Hamlyn, 1967); Stan Fischler, *Uptown, Downtown: A Trip through Time on New York's Subways* (New York: Hawthorn Books), pp. 3-33; Vukan R. Vuchic, *Urban Public Transportation: Systems and Technology* (Englewood Cliffs, N.J.: Prentice-Hall, Inc., 1981), Chapter 1; Kenneth T. Jackson, *Crabgrass Frontier,* Chapter 2; Frank Rowsome, *Trolley Car Treasury* (New York: McGraw-Hill Book Co., 1956); and William D. Middleton, *The Time of the Trolley* (Milwaukee: Kalmbach Publishing Co., 1967).

7. An interesting and varied literature has developed concerning the many aspects of urban development and the rise of the suburbs. On the evolving idea of home and comfort, for which the suburban ideal is so fitting, see Witold Rybcynski, *Home: A Short History of an Idea* (New York: The Viking Press, 1986). An enormously useful work, really a classic in the field, is Kenneth T. Jackson, *Crabgrass Frontier.* While all of this book is extremely interesting, the section on federal policy toward housing is especially so; see Chapters 11 and 12. A good book on federal policy toward cities and their development from the Roosevelt administration to the Johnson administration is by Mark I. Gelfand, *A Nation of Cities: The Federal Government and Urban America, 1933-1965* (New York: Oxford University Press, 1975).

For the shift beyond suburbia to what he calls the "technoburb," see the thought-provoking work by Robert Fishman, *Bourgeois Utopias: The Rise and Fall of Suburbia* (New York: Basic Books, 1987). It is perhaps the best work on defining the suburban ideal. The notion of the suburban type of setting as an ideal is also dealt with in an earlier work by Robert Fishman, *Urban Utopias in the Twentieth Century: Ebenezer Howard, Frank Lloyd Wright, and Le Corbusier* (Cambridge, Mass.: The MIT Press, 1982).

On the subject of architecture as well as urban development, see the beautifully illustrated book by Robert A. M. Stern, *Pride of Place: Building the American Dream* (Boston: Houghton Mifflin Co., 1986), which was issued in connection with an excellent television series of the same name on the Public Broadcasting System. There are two very interesting books on houses themselves and how they fit the American dream and the suburban ideal; see Alan Gowans, *The Comfortable House: North American Suburban Architecture, 1890-1930* (Cambridge, Mass.: The MIT Press, 1986); and Katherine Cole Stevenson and H. Ward Jandl, *Houses by Mail: A Guide to Homes from Sears, Roebuck and Company* (Washington, D.C.: The Preservation Press, 1986).

Additional works that provide interesting insight toward cities and their development for better or for worse are Michael Middleton, *Man Made the Town* (New York: St. Martin's Press, 1987); and again, Donald J. Olsen, *The City as a Work of Art.* The city as a place of elevation and aesthetic enrichment may appear to be an alien idea to those familiar only with American metropolitan areas. Olsen gives lessons on the possibilities of cities largely based on nineteenth-century artists' enhancement of cities preceding the American City Beautiful Movement of the turn of the century. A picture of the inability of the American city to meet the needs of the people may be found in Jon C. Teaford, *The Twentieth Century American City: Problems, Promise, and Reality* (Baltimore: The Johns Hopkins University Press, 1986).

The performance of mass transit under current conditions is the subject of a biannual report required by Congress: see U.S. Department of Transportation, Urban Mass Transportation Administration, *The Status of the Nation's Local Mass Transportation: Performance and Conditions—Report to Congress* (Washington, D.C.: U.S. Government Printing Office, June 1987), 181-763/40221.

Looking toward the future of transit was the mission of Transit 2000; this is the moniker given the Task Force on Public Transit for the 21st Century, which was created in 1987 by the American Public Transit Association, the trade organization for the U.S. transit industry. Some thought-provoking and information-filled background papers were written for the task force. They are: Alan E. Pisarski, *The External Environment for Public Transit to the Year 2020: A Speculative Assessment*; Harvey Schultz, Mira Barer, Chuck Smith, Terry Agriss, Robert Grassi, and Helena Barthell, *Energy and Environment* (prepared by the New York City Department of Environmental Protection in cooperation with the Mayor's Office of Energy and Telecommunications); Gregory Spencer, *Demographic Factors and Future Demand for Public Transit*; and Elizabeth Deakin, *Issues and Opportunities for Transit: An Exploration of Changes in the External Environment and Land Use and Development Trends*. All of the position papers are dated January 1988 and were the subject of intense discussion by the task force and members of the transit industry as they sought to develop the industry's strategy to meet a changing world. This is noteworthy because it was the first time the transit industry had undertaken such a venture. The task force was established, it should be noted, because of the debate over the future of the transit high-way program with the expected completion of the Interstate Highway program in 1991. The APTA work is being carried out in conjunction with an ongoing project of the American Association of State Highway and Transportation Officials, the Transportation Research Board, and other groups pondering the future of highway and transportation policy and programs.

For works on the automobile, John B. Rae, *The Road and the Car in American Life* (Cambridge, Mass.: The MIT Press, 1971); David L. Lewis and Laurence Goldstein, eds., *The Automobile and American Culture* (Ann Arbor: The University of Michigan Press, 1980); Ronald A. Buel, *Dead End: The Automobile in Mass Transportation* (Baltimore: Penguin Books, 1972). On the subject of highways, see Mark H. Rose, *Interstate: Express Highway Politics, 1941-1956* (Lawrence: The Regents Press of Kansas, 1979); Lawrence Halprin, *Freeways* (New York: Reinhold Publishing Corp., 1966); an interesting insight into roadside America is to be found in Chester H. Liebs, *Main Street to Miracle Mile: American Roadside Architecture* (Boston: Little, Brown and Company, 1985). Perhaps the best work on the early introduction and glad reception given the automobile is found in James J. Flink, *America Adopts the Automobile, 1895-1910* (Cambridge, Mass.: The MIT Press, 1970); Chapter 3 gives the motives for adoption. The belief that the automobile would solve many urban problems—particularly the waste products of the house—appears strange in retrospect.

8. For many years this author has been a member of the Board of Trustees of the Northern Indiana Commuter Transportation District (NICTD), a public body that supports the commuter service of the Chicago South Shore and South Bend Railroad. A continuing frustration has been the lack of local taxing authority for NICTD. Thanks to federal and state funds, the service kept on operating. As long as the trains continued to run, the local public and local politicians saw no reason to support NICTD in its efforts to gain taxing authority from the Indiana General Assembly. Cutting back on service or dramatically illustrating the problem by halting the trains would possibly have precipitated the crisis that would have created the sought after support, but the notion was always resisted.

9. For a succinct summation, see Jackson, *Crabgrass Frontier*, pp. 270-271. One of the best and most thoughtful analyses of urban transportation and the real world of policy making may be found in Alan Altshuler, James Womash, and John R. Pucher, *The Urban Transportation System: Politics and Policy Innovation* (Cambridge, Mass.: The MIT Press, 1979). The whole work is recommended reading, but the germ of practical politics and policy-making may be found at the bottom of p. 11.

4. THE RISE AND FALL OF MASS TRANSIT

1. Frank J. Sprague often gets the credit for inventing the electric streetcar, but he was only one of many. The pioneers include: Werner Von Siemens in Germany, Magnus Volk in England, and in the U.S. Edward M. Bentley, Walter H. Knight, Charles J. Van Depoele, Leo Daft, Thomas Edison, and Sprague; all built operating lines using power from a dynamo. Earlier pioneers such as Thomas Davenport, Moses G. Farmer, and Charles Grafton Page used batteries to operate models. Page used wet-cell batteries in 1851 to power a car and passengers along the Baltimore & Ohio Railroad between Washington, D.C., and Bladensburg, Maryland. There are a number of general histories of public transportation that shed much light on this interesting subject. The list that follows is incomplete, but is one worth the time of the curious reader. See Charles S. Dunbar, *Buses, Trolleys & Trams* (London: Paul Hamlyn, 1967); Frank Rowsome, Jr., *Trolley Car Treasury* (New York: McGraw-Hill, 1956); William D. Middleton, *The Time of the Trolley* (Milwaukee: Kalmbach Publishing Co., 1967); John Anderson Miller, *Fares, Please!* (New York: D. Appleton-Century, 1941); Frederick W. Speirs, *The Street Railway System of Philadelphia: Its History and Present Condition,* The Johns Hopkins University Studies in Historical and Political Science, Vol. VX, No. 3 (Baltimore: The Johns Hopkins Press, 1897).

Much insight into urban transportation is provided in Emerson P. Schmidt, *Industrial Relations in Urban Transportation* (Minneapolis: The University of Minnesota Press, 1937). The cable car is an interesting vehicle; its technology and impact on urban areas may be found in Edgar M. Kahn, *Cable Car Days in San Francisco* (Stanford, Calif.: Stanford University Press, 1940); a more general history is found in George W. Hilton, *The Cable Car in America* (Berkeley, Calif.: Howell-North Books, 1971).

The electric railway has attracted a substantial following of enthusiasts who have generated a large literature, usually focusing on one city or one system. These are instructive of the process of the development, rise, and fall of transit service and, in some cases, of its revivification. For example, see LeRoy O. King, Jr., *100 Years of Capital Traction: The Story of Streetcars in the Nation's Capital* (Dallas: Taylor Publishing Co., 1972); Michael R. Farrell, *Who Made All Our Streetcars Go? The Story of Rail Transit in Baltimore* (Baltimore: National Railway Historical Society Publications, 1973); George K. Bradley, *Fort Wayne and Wabash Valley Trolleys* (Chicago: Bulletin 122, Central Electric Railfans' Association, 1983); Carlton Norris McKenney, *Rails in Richmond* (Glendale, Interurban Press, Interurbans Special 102, 1986); Jack E. Schramm and William H. Henning, *Detroit's Street Railways,* Volume 1, *1863-1922* (Chicago: Bulletin 117, Central Electric Railfans' Association, 1978); and Jack E. Schramm, William H. Henning, and Thomas J. Dworman, *Detroit's Street Railways,* Volume 2, *1922-1956* (Chicago: Bulletin 120, Central Electric Railfans' Association, 1980).

Interesting vignettes of early omnibus service in London, where modern public transportation service has its beginnings, may be found in Jacob Korg, ed., *London in Dickens' Day* (Englewood Cliffs, N.J.: Prentice-Hall, 1960), pp. 16-18, 109-115, and 132-133.

2. A good description and analysis of the movement toward consolidation can be found in Schmidt, *Industrial Relations,* Chapter 2. See also Glenn Yago, *The Decline of Transit: Urban Transportation in German and U.S. Cities, 1900-1970* (New York: Cambridge University Press, 1984), pp. 52-56. The role of electric utilities as intertwined with transit operations is revealed in such works as Joseph M. Canfield, *TM: The Milwaukee Electric Railway & Light Company* (Chicago: Bulletin 112, Central Electric Railfans' Association, 1972). See James C. G. Conniff and Richard Conniff, *The Energy People: A History of PSE & G* (Newark: Public Service Electric and Gas Company, 1978). See also Bradley, *Fort Wayne and Wabash Valley Trolleys,* Chapters 5 and 7, for discussion of the work of the syndicates in promoting electric traction and the role of the electric utilities in the business. Another interesting source of information is Edward Hungerford, *The Story of Public Utilities* (New York: G. P. Putnam's Sons, 1926), especially Chapters 6, 7, and 19.

For the work of the promotion of street railways, see Harry James Carman, *The Street Surface Railway Franchises of New York City* (New York: Columbia University Press Studies in History, Economics and Public Law, Volume 88, No. 1, 1919). Carman documents the bribery and corruption that went hand in glove with expansion of the street railway system: see pp. 46-49, 66-67, and 97. In many instances, the franchises were granted to those paying the largest bribe to the alderman; the public was not considered and the city government received no financial benefit. The process of overcapitalization is also documented. See Chapter 10 for Carman's conclusions on the unpalatable business. Also see Mark D. Hirsch, *William C. Whitney: Modern Warwick* (New York: Dodd, Mead, 1948), Chapters 15 and 17; and Middleton, *The Time of the Trolley,* pp. 78 and 224-227. An excellent, concise history of the industry may be found in David W. Jones, *Urban Transit Policy: An Economic and Political History* (Englewood Cliffs, N.J.: Prentice-Hall, 1985), especially Chapter 3.

Some works that provide insight into the development and growth of the transit industry are: Russell L. Olson, *The Electric Railways of Minnesota* (Hopkins, Minn.: Minnesota Transportation Museum, 1976); Goodrich Lowry, *Streetcar Man: Tom Lowry and the Twin City Rapid Transit Company* (Minneapolis: Lerner Publication Company, 1978); Charles W. Cheape, *Moving the Masses: Urban Public Transit in New York, Boston, and Philadelphia, 1880-1912* (Cambridge, Mass.: Harvard University Press, 1980); Charles Seims, *Trolley Days in Pasadena* (San Marino, California: Golden West Books, 1982); John T. Labbe, *Fares, Please! Those Portland Trolley Years* (Coldwell, Idaho: The Coxton Printer, 1980); Lawrence J. Fleming, *Ride a Mile and Smile the While: A History of the Phoenix Street Railway* (Phoenix: Swaine Publications, 1977); O. E. Carson, *The Trolley Titans: A Mobile History of Atlanta* (Glendale, Calif.: Interurban Press, Interurban Special 76, 1981); and Charles V. Mutschler, Clyde L. Parent, and Wilmer H. Siegert, *Spokane's Street Railways: An Illustrated History* (Spokane: Inland Empire Railway Historical Society, 1987). An interesting little volume offering insight into the role transit played in its heyday is Raymond F. Crapo, *The Environment of the Traction Era* (Short Beach, Conn.: Branford Electric Railway Historical Publications, 1978).

3. The role of public transit in everyday life was nationally strongest during the heyday of the streetcar; by the time the motor bus became an important actor on the urban scene it was upstaged by the private automobile. For interesting and informative coverage of this period, see McKenney, *Rails in Richmond,* Chapters 11 to 16; Middleton, *The Time of the Trolley,* pp. 84-103; and Ransome, *Trolley Car Treasury,* Chapter 7. George Bradley, *Fort Wayne and Wabash Valley Trolleys,* does an excellent job of relating the advent and glory of "Splendid Robinson Park," in Chapter 3. Robinson Park was a fine example of the classic trolley park.

4. For an especially good description and analysis of political tie-ins with transit, see Paul Barrett, *The Automobile and Urban Transit: The Formation of Public Policy in Chicago, 1900-1930* (Philadelphia: Temple University Press, 1983). The most detailed treatment of the problems of the transit industry is to be found in the *Proceedings of the Federal Electric Railways Commission* (Washington, D.C.: U.S. Government Printing Office, 1920). This massive three-volume collection of information is indexed on pp. 2291-2349 of Volume 3. This study was systematically reviewed by one of the outstanding transit authorities of the day; see Delos F. Wilcox, *Analysis of the Electric Railway Problem* (New York: author, 1921). An interesting point: Wilcox held that public ownership was the only solution because private ownership tended to be corruptive, due to the value of the franchises, the potential of financial chicanery used to gain a franchise, and the profits emerging from a necessary service to the public. Moreover, even in that early day, Wilcox points out the intense competition between unregulated jitney buses and the private automobile—see Chapters 20, 24, and 54. In the Commission Hearings, see the testimony of Stiles P. Jones, pp. 1841-1877 and 2012-2014.

5. This is based on personal observation and conversations with Theodore N. Weigle, executive director of the Northeastern Illinois Regional Transportation Authority, and with

other public officials. It was also the theme of an excellent speech given by Frank Herringer, former administrator of the Urban Mass Transportation Administration at the 1985 Annual Meeting of the American Public Transit Association (October 6-10, the Bonaventure Hotel, Los Angeles, California).

6. The commission noted that the electric railway industry had no financial credit and that it faced serious impediments in carrying out its important function. It blamed the problem on financial mismanagement in the industry's early days, the high costs of the wartime and post-war period, and the insufficient revenue produced by the almost universal five-cent fare. It noted that the plight of the industry prevented it from expanding to meet the needs of growing cities already pushing out to the civil city limits and to the suburbs. It called for relief from franchise obligations, such as street sprinkling and the paving of streets and construction and maintenance of bridges used by the public. The commission recognized that the transit industry was subsidizing its competition. Concerning that competition, the commission recommended that competitive public transportation should be regulated in a fashion similar to the electric railways. The commission was cool toward the idea of public ownership, viewing it as a last resort. Rather, better and more scientific regulation was required. At the same time, the commission did call for recognition of the right of the public to own and operate transit and other utilities. In its reluctance to embrace public ownership, the commission disagreed markedly with the advice of its consultant, Delos F. Wilcox. See *Proceedings of the Federal Electric Railways Commission,* pp. 2264-2266. See also Wilcox, *Analysis of the Electric Railway Problem,* pp. xv-xx, Chapters 24 and 50-54.

7. See, for example, the discussion and analysis of the five-cent fare in Barrett, *The Automobile and Urban Transit,* pp. 122-126. The nickel fare was considered a major impediment to improving the quality and quantity of transit service and constructing new lines as the first decade of the twentieth century ended. See Conniff and Conniff, *The Energy People,* pp. 210-212.

8. Former President William Howard Taft set the anti-public ownership tone in the *Proceedings of the Federal Electric Railways Commission* when he gave the opening testimony, citing that public ownership reduced efficiency and increased costs of an essential public service to the detriment of that public. See pp. 4-5; also see Wilcox, *Analysis of the Electric Railway Problem,* Chapter 24. See also Schmidt, *Industrial Relations,* Chapter 4.

9. See John B. Rae, *The Road and the Car in American Life* (Cambridge, Mass.: The MIT Press, 1971), especially Chapters 3-4. For a more negative view, see Alvin L. Spivak, *The Immoral Machine* (San Jose, Calif.: Milieu Information Service, 1972).

10. The lightweight electric streetcar, a four-wheeled, one-man car, was introduced in the fall of 1916. It was developed by Charles O. Birney, an engineer for Stone and Webster, a utilities company that was one of the major streetcar operators. The Birney Safety Car was outfitted with a deadman controller and door interlocks and featured a stressed skin steel construction that gave strength despite weighing only 13,000 pounds in comparison with the 30,000 to 40,000 pounds of standard streetcar. See Rowsome, *Trolley Car Treasury,* pp. 171-172. For more information on the Birney car as well as other ventures in innovative lightweight cars, see Middleton, *The Times of the Trolley,* pp. 122-135. The development of the Street Railway Presidents Conference Committee (the PCC car) was another technological effort to build an economic and attractive streetcar with superior performance capabilities.

For the move to economical operation see Rowsome, *Trolley Car Treasury,* Chapter 10; and Middleton, *The Times of the Trolley,* pp. 122-127. For the development of the motor bus see Miller, *Fares, Please,* Chapters 10-11. For a comprehensive and more technical discussion of the various modes of urban mass transportation, see Vukan R. Vuchic, *Urban Public Transportation: Systems and Technology* (Englewood Cliffs, N.J.: Prentice-Hall, 1981), Chapters 2-5. The trolleybus, while enormously popular in other countries, has been in relative limbo in the U.S. There remain small operations in Boston and Philadelphia; until recently, at least, the backbone of the Dayton, Ohio system is the trolleybuses serving busy routes; there are large and expanding systems in hilly San Francisco and Seattle. See Mac Sebree and Paul Ward, *Transit's Stepchild, the Trolleybus* (Cerritos, Calif.: Interurban Special 58, 1973); and Mac Sebree and Paul Ward, *The Trolleybus in North America* (Cerritos, Calif.: Interurban Special 59, 1974).

11. The transit industry embarked on some really ingenious schemes to boost ridership and cut costs in the 1920s. The transit systems vied with each other for awards from the Charles A. Coffin Foundation that were given for innovation in electric railway transportation. See Henry H. Norris, ed., *Making Transportation Pay* (New York: American Electric Railway Association, 1927); and Henry H. Norris, ed., *Popularizing Public Transportation* (New York: American Electric Railway Association, 1928).

12. A considerable literature has developed on the PCC car. Possibly the most complete story of the criteria for the car and the industrial research and engineering program that created it is to be found in Stephen P. Carlson and Fred W. Schneider III, *PCC: The Car That Fought Back* (Glendale, Calif.: Interurban Press, 1980). Also see, by the same authors, *PCC from Coast to Coast* (Glendale, Calif.: Interurban Press, Interurban Special 86, 1983).

13. See Jones, *Urban Transit Policy,* pp. 50-58, 98-99, and 110.

14. See Schmidt, *Industrial Relations,* pp. 7-50 for a discussion on receiverships and abandonments of street railways. See Yago, *The Decline of Transit,* pp. 72-73, on the Holding Company Act. Public transit properties were typically several tiers down in the structure of a holding company; the transit system was usually a subsidiary of a power company (for example, Indianapolis Railways was a subsidiary of Indianapolis Power & Light Company) that was a subsidiary of another power company that was controlled by a holding company. In essence, the transit properties were usually at the base of a large pyramid up to five layers deep of ownership. The federal regulation reduced this to three layers. The holding companies were free to devise their own plans for reorganization and divestiture and submit them to the Securities and Exchange Commission for approval. Voluntary disintegration plans were submitted first in 1940 and about 85 percent of the work was done by 1952. Most holding companies chose to spin off the transit subsidiaries because of their marginal profitability and the downward trend in transit ridership that was uninterrupted from 1923 to 1972, save for the explosion of ridership during the Second World War. Nevertheless, some of the big power companies retained transit subsidiaries for many years; examples are New Orleans Public Service and Public Service of New Jersey. At this writing, Duke Power and Carolina Gas and Electric still operate transit properties. See Clair Wilcox, *Public Policies toward Business* (Homewood, Ill.: Richard D. Irwin, 1960), pp. 629-636; and Martin T. Farris and Roy J. Sampson, *Public Utilities: Regulation Management and Ownership* (Boston: Houghton Mifflin Company, 1973), pp. 145-151. See also Conniff and Conniff, *The Energy People,* pp. 336 and 341. The reputed master of the holding company device was Samuel Insull, who created the modern electric utility industry and did as much from the perspective of organization to create the modern world with his business genius as did Thomas Edison with his inventive genius. See Forrest McDonald, *Insull* (Chicago: University of Chicago Press, 1962). On the Wheeler-Rayburn bill, which became the Holding Company Act of 1935, see pp. 336-337.

15. The figures are from American Public Transit Association, *1987 Transit Fact Book* (Washington, D.C.: 1987), Table 9, p. 32. The figures do not include commuter rail, cable cars, inclined planes, automated guideways, or urban ferry boats prior to 1975.

16. See Jackson, *Crabgrass Frontier,* Chapter 11. The chapter tells of the importance of the federal housing program in stimulating suburban growth through subsidies.

17. The pattern of precipitous decline of the transit industry is nicely summarized in Jones, *Urban Transit Policy,* pp. 74-80; Rowsome, *Trolley Car Treasury,* tells the story from the side of the streetcars in Chapters 10 and 11; see also Middleton, *The Time of the Trolley,* pp. 380-397; Yago, *The Decline of Transit,* pp. 162-213; John Burby, *The Great American Motion Sickness: Or, Why You Can't Get There from Here* (Boston: Little, Brown & Co., 1971), Chapter 5; A. Q. Mowbray, *Road to Ruin* (Philadelphia: J. B. Lippincott Com-

pany, 1969), Chapter 13; and Lyle C. Fitch and Associates, *Urban Transportation and Public Policy* (San Francisco: Chandler Publishing Company, 1964), Chapter 2.

The role of General Motors and the support that it—and other firms—gave to National City Lines and its alleged process of doing away with streetcars and generally moving to subvert transit is a story familiar to urban transport observers. See, for example, Yago, *The Decline of Transit,* pp. 56-69; Jones, *Urban Transit Policy,* pp. 62-64; Bradford C. Snell, *American Ground Transportation* (Washington, D.C.: Subcommittee on Antitrust and Monopoly of the Judiciary Committee, U.S. Senate, 1974); Jonathan Kwitny, "The Great Transportation Conspiracy," *Harper's Magazine,* Vol. 262, No. 1569, February 1981, pp. 14-21; and Richard J. Solomon and Arthur Saltzman, *History of Transit and Innovative Systems* (Cambridge, Mass.: MIT Urban Systems Laboratory, USL TR-70-20, March 1971). It should be noted in more than a passing fashion that, given private, unsubsidized mass transit as the norm, sound business practice demanded that there be a shift to a technology that was less costly under conditions of modest passenger demand. Moreover, buses shared the use of the public highways and did not demand massive injections of capital to resuscitate overworn and overworked facilities and equipment that had soldiered on in a state of deferred maintenance through the tough years of the Depression and the Second World War.

A valuable source of information about many aspects of urban transportation is George E. Gray and Lester A. Hoel, eds., *Public Transportation: Planning, Operations and Management* (Englewood Cliffs, N.J.: Prentice-Hall, 1979). See Chapters 1-3 for historical development. Chapter 2 gives the story of the decline of transit.

18. See, for example, Robert Cervero, *Suburban Gridlock* (New Brunswick, N.J.: Rutgers, The State University, Center for Urban Policy Research, 1986), Chapters 1-2; Fishman, *Bourgeois Utopias,* Chapter 6; and Jackson, *Crabgrass Frontier,* Chapters 9, 10, 11, 13, and 14. A different, disturbing, and thought-provoking view of what has been happening in America's urbanization is to be found in John Henbens, *The New Heartland: America's Flight Beyond the Suburbs and How It Is Changing Our Future* (New York: Times Books, 1986), especially Chapters 1 to 3.

19. For the thinking behind the process of highway policy-making, see Rose, *Interstate,* Chapter 2; A critical view of the nation's highway policies may be found in Helen Leavitt, *Superhighway—Superhoax* (Garden City, N.Y.: Doubleday & Company, 1970). For a thoughtful discussion of the negative side of highway decision-making, see Richard Hebert, *Highways to Nowhere: The Politics of City Transportation* (Indianapolis: The Bobbs-Merrill Company, 1972). On the importance of the role played by Robert Moses in national highway policy as well as the highway and transportation policy of his own city of New York, see Robert A. Caro, *The Power Broker: Robert Moses and the Fall of New York* (New York: Vintage Books, 1974), Chapters 36, 40, 48 and 49. *The Power Broker* is a masterful work and reveals how much one brilliant man can do to shape and bend policy to fit his view of what is proper. For an apocalyptic view of the suburbs see Lewis Mumford, *The City in History: Its Origins, Its Transformations, and Its Prospects* (New York: Harcourt Brace Jovanovich, 1961), especially Chapters 16-17.

5. THE ADVENT OF FEDERAL TRANSIT POLICY

1. David Jones points out that the push for federal help did not come from what was then a largely comatose transit industry or from cities in general; the effort was launched by the work of the mayors of a few large cities. Moreover, Jones points out that the actions and initiatives of the federal government preceded in many cases those of local officials. See David Jones, *Urban Transit Policy: An Economic and Political History* (Englewood Cliffs, N.J.: Prentice-Hall, 1985), pp. 81-83.

2. Politicians are often pictured in mental shorthand as people of action, while academics are seen as people of thought; no thoughtful observer will fail to note that there is often little action or thought on the part of either group. Politicians are victims of a short

term of office and they can be forgiven for not looking too far beyond the next election. If the public is not demanding of serious consideration of problems, debate over issues and alternatives—and decisive action—the politician will act but little. The academic interested in getting promoted and enjoying pay increases must publish the fruits of research in refereed journals, many of which are remote and esoteric. What is acceptable in some academic fields is determined by a small and often relatively narrow group. If urban problems and urban transportation are not in fashion at the time, academics pursue them at their peril. Very simply, what they research and write will not be published in the "important" journals. After a while, the situation corrects itself when some stalwarts pass from the scene, and everyone notes how silly it is (or the politicians have grant money for research).

3. A valuable source of information on the events leading up to the beginning of federal participation in urban mass transportation programs is found in Michael Danielson, *Federal-Metropolitan Politics and the Commuter Crisis* (New York: Columbia University Press, 1965). The reader will also be instructed and entertained by John Burby, *The Great American Motion Sickness: Or Why You Can't Get There from Here* (Boston: Little Brown & Co., 1971), particularly Chapter 5. An excellent treatment is given in Jones, *Urban Transit Policy,* Chapter 6.

4. City of Philadelphia, Urban Traffic and Transportation Board, *Plan and Program 1955* (Conclusions and Recommendations of the Board—Report of Staff to the Board), April 1956; and Danielson, *Federal-Metropolitan Politics,* pp. 95-96.

5. See *The Composite Report, Bay Area Rapid Transit, May 1962* (San Francisco: Bay Area Rapid Transit District, 1962).

6. For discussion of the situation see, for example, Jameson W. Doig, *Metropolitan Transportation Politics and the New York Region* (New York: Columbia University Press, 1966); Michael N. Danielson, *Federal-Metropolitan Politics;* Lyle Fitch and Associates, *Urban Transportation and Public Policy* (San Francisco: Chandler Publishing Co. 1964); George M. Smerk, *Urban Transportation: The Federal Role* (Bloomington: Indiana University Press, 1965); Paul Barrett, *The Automobile and Urban Transit: The Formation of Public Policy in Chicago, 1900-1930* (Philadelphia: Temple University Press, 1983); Glenn Yago, *The Decline of Transit: Urban Transportation in German and U.S. Cities, 1900-1970* (New York: Cambridge University Press, 1984); and Mark S. Foster, *From Streetcar to Superhighway: American City Planners and Urban Transportation, 1900-1940* (Philadelphia: Temple University Press, 1981). A somewhat prophetic view of the urban transportation future can be found in Edward Hungerford, *The Story of Public Utilities* (New York: G. P. Putnam's Sons, 1926), especially the final chapter entitled "The Future of the American City."

7. See Fitch, *Urban Transportation and Public Policy,* pp. 52-54, for several examples. A notable case of outright opposition to improving the quality of mass transit can be found in New York City, where Robert Moses, the czar of highway construction and much of the built environment, was hostile to transit. No real transit progress, such as needed extension of rapid transit lines at a time when such work would have been possible at modest cost, was made during his lengthy tenure in the highest levels of power. Robert A. Caro, *The Power Broker: Robert Moses and the Fall of New York* (New York: Vintage Books, 1974), especially Chapters 35 and 39.

8. The exact losses from passenger operations are a somewhat debatable issue. The $723.7 million figure represents the result of the ICC's method of fully apportioned costs. On the basis of solely related costs, the deficit for 1957 was in the neighborhood of $114 million. In either case the losses involved were hardly a sum which would delight the railroads. See 306 ICC 419-425, 486 (ICC Docket No. 31954, May 18, 1959, Railroad Passenger Train Deficit); Association of American Railroads, Bureau of Railway Economics, *Statistics of Railroad Passenger Service* (Washington, D.C.: October 1966), p. 9; and *Avoidable Costs of Passenger Train Service* (Cambridge, Mass.: Aeronautical Research Foundation, September 1957). The story is well told in Donald M. Itzkoff, *Off The Track: The Decline of*

the Intercity Passenger Train in the United States (Westport, Conn.: Greenwood Press, 1985), especially pp. 14-15 and Chapters 2-3. In the years since 1936 and up to 1970, a period when the Interstate Commerce Commission separated passenger and freight net earnings, the only profitable years for passenger trains were 1942 through 1945. At no time was the passenger deficit as a percentage of freight net revenues less than 18.4 percent; in 1957 it was 44 percent. For subsidies to other modes of transportation see pp. 31, 49, and 127. See also John Burby, *The Great American Motion Sickness,* especially Chapter 6.

9. Public Law 85-625, 85th Congress. For a brief recapitulation of the contents of this act, see D. Philip Locklin, *Economics of Transportation,* 6th ed. (Homewood, Ill.: Irwin, 1966), pp. 254-258. For a more complete discussion, see George Hilton, *The Transportation Act of 1958* (Bloomington: Indiana University Press, 1969). Also see Itzkoff, *Off The Track,* pp. 56, 58, 81, and 125.

10. *75th Annual Report of the Interstate Commerce Commission for Fiscal Year Ended June 1961* (Washington, D.C.: U.S. Government Printing Office), p. 72.

11. See, for example, Finance Docket No. 20443, *Lehigh Valley Railroad Company Discontinuance of Service, All Passenger Operations,* 307 ICC 239, 307 ICC 257, 312 ICC 299; Finance Docket No. 20606, *Pennsylvania Railroad Company Discontinuance of Passenger Service between Trenton and Red Bank, N.J.,* 317 ICC 5; Finance Docket No. 20671, New Jersey & New York Railroad Company (Horace Banta Trustee) *Discontinuance of Service from Hoboken, N.J. to Spring Valley, N.Y.* 307 ICC 532; Finance Docket No. 20524, *New York Central Railroad Company Discontinuance of Service, St. Lawrence Division,* 312 ICC 4; and Finance Docket No. 20731, *Pennsylvania Railroad Co. Discontinuance of Service between Camden and Trenton, N. J.,* 312 ICC 167. For a variety of reasons the Southern Railway, The Chicago Rock Island & Pacific, and the Denver & Rio Grande Western continued to operate their own passenger trains outside the Amtrak system.

12. See Danielson, *Federal-Metroplitan Politics,* pp. 47-52. See also Doig, *Metropolitan Transportation Politics,* especially Chapter 9, and Alan Altshuler, "The Politics of Urban Mass Transportation," a mimeographed paper delivered at the annual meeting of the American Political Science Association, Sept. 4-7, 1963, pp. 16-21.

13. For more information on the Passenger Service Improvement Corporation of Philadelphia see *IRT News Letter,* Vol. 3, No. 3 (March 30, 1962), published by the Institute for Rapid Transit. Concerning activities in the New Jersey and New York areas, see Doig, *Metropolitan Transportation Politics,* Chapters 8 and 9; and John E. Debout and Ronald J. Grele, *Where Cities Meet: The Urbanization of New Jersey* (Princeton, N.J.: Van Nostrand, 1964), pp. 73-74.

14. For a detailed coverage of the advent of the Interstate System, see Mark H. Rose, *Interstate: Express Highway Politics, 1941-1956* (Lawrence: The Regents Press of Kansas, 1979), especially Chapter 6.

15. U.S. Department of Commerce, *Federal Transportation Policy and Program* (Washington, D.C.: U.S. Government Printing Office, March 14, 1960).

16. The text of Williams's letter of transmittal, dated April 14, 1960, and addressed to the Secretary of Commerce, is of interest:

> Transmitted herewith is a report, "Rationale of Federal Transportation Policy," which is supplemental to the report you recently released on "Federal Transportation Policy and Program."
>
> The attached report reflects the considered views of your Study Staff, arrived at after careful attention to the underlying reports of consultants and contractors as well as such other information as was available. Of course, it should be clearly understood that this report is the sole responsibility of the authors, and should in no way be construed as being attributable to you or the Department of Commerce.
>
> However, I feel that it may be helpful to have publicly available a some-

what simplified statement of the staff thinking on such conclusions as your report, necessarily very brief, has adopted.

From Ernest W. Williams, Jr., and David W. Bluestone, *Rationale of Federal Transportation Policy* (Washington, D.C.: U.S. Department of Commerce, U.S. Government Printing Office, 1969), p. 111.

17. Ibid., pp. 52-54. Allowing this expression of staff opinion was a remarkably civilized aspect of the Eisenhower administration, in stark contrast to the usual slavish acceptance of the party line of an administration, no matter how idiotic or counterproductive to the public good—or even the administration's welfare—the policy might be.

18. Edward Weiner, *Urban Transportation Planning in the United States: An Historical Overview* (U.S. Department of Transportation, Office of the Assistant Secretary for Policy and International Affairs: DOT-1-83-43, April 1983), p. 15.

19. News Release HHFA-OA-No. 60-649, "Joint Policy and Procedural Statements on Improved Coordination of Highway and General Urban Planning."

20. See "Joint Policy Statement," p. 1.

21. See Danielson, *Federal-Metropolitan Politics,* pp. 25-27. Also see Jones, *Urban Transit Policy,* p. 81, who notes that local indifference to transit was the norm, not the exception. The great power of thoughtlessness is well noted in Vukan R. Vuchic, "The Auto versus Transit Controversy: Toward a Rational Synthesis for Urban Transportation Policy," *Transportation Research,* Vol. 18-A, No. 2, pp. 125-133, esp. pp. 126-127.

22. See George M. Smerk, *Urban Transportation: The Federal Role,* pp. 99-113.

23. For a more detailed discussion, see Danielson, Chapter 10, especially pp. 183-189.

24. See Danielson, pp. 101-103.

25. *The Collapse of Commuter Service* (Washington, D.C.: American Municipal Association, 1959), p. 2.

26. Ibid., p. 3.

27. Danielson, *Federal-Metroplitan Politics,* pp. 104-105.

28. For example, Dilworth moderated a panel discussion on transport problems in large cities that kept straying from the rail issue. See "Better Urban Transportation," *Proceedings of the American Municipal Congress 1959* (Washington, D.C.: American Municipal Association).

29. See Altshuler, pp. 27-28.

30. See Danielson, *Federal-Metroplitan Politics,* pp. 111-113.

31. Danielson, ibid., notes that Williams had not happened on the commuter issue by chance; he saw the commuter issue as one of potential importance for his career. For that reason he had secured himself a place on the housing subcommittee of the Senate Banking and Currency Committee, see pp. 129-133. The bill that Williams introduced was U.S. Senate, *A Bill to Amend Section 701 of the Housing Act of 1954 and Title II of the Housing Amendment of 1955,* 86th Congress, 2d session, S.3278 (1960).

32. *Proceedings of the American Municipal Congress 1959,* p. 24. In retrospect, one might have expected the New Deal of Franklin Roosevelt to have focused much more attention on urban issues than it did. Certainly, the New Deal programs did not ignore urban matters but the focus would probably have been sharper had President Roosevelt cared for cities. In his 1985 biography of Roosevelt, Ted Morgan notes that F.D.R. had a genuine dislike for cities, seeing in them all that was inimical to the best values of American life. In this attitude he was not unlike Thomas Jefferson. The attitude of a president toward certain matters determines not only if he will address it, but also whether he will call on the most innovative minds to work on the issue. See Ted Morgan, *FDR: A Biography* (New York: Simon and Shuster, 1985), p. 37.

33. For an excellent summary of the work behind the various highway measures prior to 1970, especially the 1956 Act, see Vera Hirschberg, "CPR Report/Forces Gather for

Stormy Debate over Highways with Trust Fund as Lightning Rod," *National Journal,* June 6, 1970, pp. 1193-1207, especially pp. 1194-1199.

34. For an interesting appraisal and analysis of the initial entrance of the federal government onto the urban scene, see Charles Abrams, *The City Is the Frontier* (New York: Harper & Row, 1965), pp. 238-249. The American approach to public policy is admirably discussed in Joseph R. Hartley, "The American Way of Public Policy," in *Business Horizons,* Vol. 31, No. 3, May-June 1988, pp. 2-6.

35. Indeed, the criticism has been leveled that federal programs have often been far more beneficial to private business than to the general public. American history is full of scandals of government projects that lined the pockets of sharp businessmen, ranging from the Credit Mobilier fiasco of the Grant administration through the Teapot Dome infamy of the Harding administration to the Iran-contra and Pentagon scandals of the Reagan administration.

36. See Kenneth T. Jackson, *Crabgrass Frontier: The Suburbanization of the United States* (New York, Oxford University Press, 1985), Chapters 11, 12 and 14.

37. In a highly perceptive passage, Alan Altshuler noted that "the political system as a whole seems to strive for inclusiveness and broad support rather than theoretical consistency or elegance. That is, it seeks to accommodate new demands as they emerge by means, insofar as possible, that leave previous settlements (programs and administrative arrangements) undisturbed, that involve the least possible disruption for private enterprise, and that involve the least possible inconvenience and annoyance for individuals who have built their life styles around the expectation of system stability." Alan Altshuler, with James P. Womack and John R. Pucher, *The Urban Transportation System: Politics and Policy Innovation* (Cambridge, Mass.: The MIT Press, 1979), p. 11.

38. *The Transportation System of Our Nation.* Message from the President of the United States, 87th Congress, 2d session, House of Representatives Document No. 384, 1962, pp. 9-10.

39. See Rose, *Interstate,* p. 5; and Barrett, *The Automobile and Urban Transit,* pp. 132-133.

40. James M. Landis, *Report on Regulatory Agencies to the President-Elect,* submitted by the chairman of the subcommittee on administrative practice and procedure to the Committee on the Judiciary of the United States Senate, 86th Congress, 2d session (Washington, D.C.: U.S. Government Printing Office, 1980).

41. U.S. Senate Committee on Interstate and Foreign Commerce, *National Transportation Policy, Preliminary Draft of a Report Prepared by the Special Study Group on Transportation Policy for the United States,* 87th Congress, 1st session, January 3, 1961, pp. 552-635.

42. For a discussion of the ill-fated Bay of Pigs venture, see Theodore C. Sorenson, *Kennedy* (New York: Harper & Row, 1965), pp. 294-309.

43. The detailed and excellent coverage of this vital time in the genesis of federal transit policy and programs is found in Danielson, *Federal-Metropolitan Politics,* Chapter 9.

44. Robert C. Weaver, "The Federal Interest in Urban Mass Transportation," *Traffic Quarterly 17,* January 1963, pp. 25 and 29. Mr. Weaver was the administrator of the Housing and Home Finance Agency, within which the federal transit programs were initially lodged.

45. See *Urban Mass Transportation Act of 1962: Hearings before Subcommittee No. 3 of the Committee on Banking and Currency,* House of Representatives, 87th Congress, 2d session on H.R. 11158 (Washington, D.C.: U.S. Government Printing Office, 1962), pp. 517-522.

46. See Smerk, *Urban Mass Transportation,* pp. 170-171; and ArDee Ames, "An End to Highway Aid," in *A Look at Urban Transportation* (Washington, D.C.: National League of Cities, 1966), pp. 1-4.

47. As might have been expected, many cities had trouble finding planners to do the job before the planning deadline; the Bureau of Public Roads was equally hard pressed. Many planners who had trouble finding good planning jobs at good pay suddenly found

themselves to be in high demand. Some wags have dubbed the Highway Act of 1962 the "Urban Planners Relief and Rehabilitation Act."

48. T. J. Kent, Jr., *The Urban General Plan* (San Francisco: Chandler, 1964), p. 33.

49. Ibid., pp. 40-43.

50. Glenn Yago, *The Decline of Transit* (New York: Cambridge University Press, 1984), pp. 167-168; and Paul Barrett, *The Automobile and Urban Transit,* especially Chapter 6 and pp. 214-217.

51. For a thoughtful discussion of these issues, see Mark S. Foster, *From Streetcar to Superhighway,* especially Chapter 7. Also see Abrams, *The City Is the Frontier,* pp. 215-218.

52. See Caro, *The Power Broker,* especially Chapters 39 and 40. Caro sees Moses as totally uninterested in people with low income who did not possess the symbol of affluence, the automobile. Moses's works were for the well-off. Unthriftily, no space was left in the medians of New York's superhighways for the eventual inclusion of rapid transit.

6. A PROGRAM DEVELOPS

1. See Section 103(b) of the Housing Act of 1949 as amended by Section 303 of the Housing Act of 1961.

2. John C. Kohl, "The Federal Urban Transportation Demonstration Program," *Traffic Quarterly,* Vol. 18, No. 3, July 1964, p. 303.

3. See Michael N. Danielson, *Federal-Metropolitan Politics and the Commuter Crisis* (New York: Columbia University Press, 1965), p. 176.

4. *The Transportation System of Our Nation,* p. 10. The president's recommendations were based on a program of action advocated by Secretary of Commerce Hodges and HHFA Administrator Weaver as a result of a study prepared for them by the Institute of Public Administration. See Lyle C. Fitch and Associates, *Urban Transportation and Public Policy* (San Francisco: Chandler Publishing Co., 1964), Chapters 6-7; and Danielson, *Federal-Metropolitan Politics,* pp. 174-175.

5. See Alan Altshuler, "The Politics of Urban Mass Transportation," a paper delivered at the annual meeting of the American Political Science Association, Sept. 4-7, 1963, pp. 38-39.

6. David Jones, *Urban Transit Policy: An Economic and Political History* (Englewood Cliffs, N.J.: Prentice-Hall, 1985), especially pp. 81-82.

7. See *Urban Mass Transportation—1962, Hearings before a Subcommittee of the Committee on Banking and Currency,* U.S. Senate, 87th Congress, 2d session, on *Bills to Authorize the Housing and Home Finance Agency to Provide Additional Assistance for the Development of Mass Transportation Systems, and for Other Purposes,* April 24-27, 1962, especially pp. 273-281, 308-319, 397-403. See also *Urban Mass Transportation Act of 1962;* Altshuler, "The Politics of Urban Mass Transportation," pp. 39-40; and Danielson, *Federal-Metropolitan Politics,* p. 177.

8. See *Hearings before the Committee on Commerce,* U.S. Senate, 87th Congress, 2d session on S. 3615, Sept. 17-20, 1962. Senator Lausche was particularly intrigued by the testimony of Dr. Leon Moses of Northwestern University (see pp. 37-51), who made the point that urban travelers might have to be paid to use transit. Also see Altshuler, "The Politics of Urban Mass Transportation," p. 41.

9. Altshuler, "The Politics of Urban Mass Transportation," p. 41.

10. Altshuler, "The Politics of Urban Mass Transportation," pp. 43-51.

11. Victor Gruen, "Needed: A Prompt End to the Old Luxury of Limited Thinking," *Architectural Forum,* October 1963, p. 94. In the perspective of the 1980s, the lobbying effort for the transit legislation appears to be relatively crude and unorganized. Furthermore, considering the enormous growth of cities in the South since the 1960s, opposing urban programs appears to be the apex of short-sightedness. It also reveals that the members were reflecting the attitudes of a rural past that was then in the process of rapidly dissolving.

12. The tale of events leading up to the 1964 act, including division in the ranks of the transit and commuter rail industries and the role of the Urban Passenger Transportation Association, is found in Lewis M. Schneider, "Urban Mass Transportation: A Survey of the Decision-Making Process," in *The Study of Policy Formation,* ed. R. A. Bauer and Kenneth J. Green (New York: Free Press, 1968), pp. 254-266.

13. Mel Brdlik, "A Legislative Miracle," *Metropolitan Management, Transportation, and Planning,* Vol. 60, No. 5, September 1964, pp. 26 and 50; and Vincent J. Burke, "The Tangled Path of a Transit Bill," *The Reporter,* July 16, 1964. S.6 was the bill finally passed—the House bill was H.R. 3881. In passing the bill, 39 Republican congressmen joined 173 Democrats; the Republicans were from California, Connecticut, Massachusetts, Nebraska, New Jersey, New York, Ohio, Pennsylvania, and Washington. The House bill had originally authorized $500 million; this was cut to $375 million to conform with the Senate bill. See "Mass Transit Aid," *Congressional Quarterly Weekly Report,* week ending June 26, 1964, p. 1269.

14. On the subject of a more rational approach to urban policy, see Daniel R. Moynihan, ed., *Toward a National Urban Policy* (New York: Basic Books, 1970).

15. See, for example, "Congress Clears $375 Million Mass Transportation Bill," *Congressional Quarterly Weekly Report,* week ending July 3, 1984, pp. 1338-1341, especially p. 1339.

16. Congressman Albert Rains of Alabama was responsible for the pro-private amendments; he also sought to protect the rights of labor in the transit industry that might have been threatened by public takeover. Ibid., p. 1341.

17. "Urban Mass Transportation Act of 1964," *United States Code: Congressional and Administrative News,* 88th Congress, 2d session, Vol. 2, 1964, pp. 2569-2597. The justification embraces pp. 2569-2580; a description of the bill may be found on pp. 2580-2589; and the minority views are on pp. 2589-2597.

18. "The Administrator, on the basis of engineering studies, studies of economic feasibility, and data showing the nature and extent of expected utilization of the facilities and equipment, shall estimate what portion of the cost of a project to be assisted under Section 3 cannot be reasonably financed from revenues—which portion shall hereinafter be called 'net project cost.' " From Section 4(a) of the Urban Mass Transportation Act of 1964.

19. The Urban Mass Transportation Administration ended the "emergency" program on June 30, 1972, and subsequently provided up to 80 percent, or 75 percent of the net project cost depending on whether Section 3 or Section 9 money was used as the fund source.

20. Public Law 88-365, 88th Congress, 2d session, especially Appendix D; also see "At Last: Congress Approves Transit Aid," *Railway Age,* Vol. 157, No. 1, July 6, 1964, pp. 28-29; "Analysis of the New Federal Urban Transportation Act" (Chicago: Institute for Rapid Transit, July 1964); and George M. Smerk, "The Urban Mass Transportation Act of 1964: New Hope for American Cities," *Transportation Journal,* Vol. 5, No. 2, Winter 1965, pp. 37-38.

21. *Government Expenditures for Construction, Operation, and Maintenance of Transport Facilities by Air, Highway, and Waterway and Private Expenditures for Construction, Maintenance of Way, and Taxes of Railroad Facilities* (Washington, D.C.: Association of American Railroads, Bureau of Railway Economics, March 1965), p. 4.

22. In the mid–1960s railway commuter service on a large-scale basis was offered in Boston, Chicago, New York, and Philadelphia. San Francisco, which had once enjoyed a large commuter rail operation in the East Bay, had seen that abandoned, despite direct entrance into downtown San Francisco via the Bay Bridge; only the service of the Southern Pacific Railroad between San Francisco and San Jose remained. Cleveland, Detroit, Pittsburgh, and the Baltimore-Washington area had relatively small-scale operations in the 1960s. At the time of this writing, Pittsburgh, Detroit, and Cleveland had lost their service, while commuter service between Baltimore and Washington and from Washington to

Brunswick, Maryland, had been expanded substantially by the state of Maryland. A rail commuter service from Miami to West Palm Beach began in late 1988, and service was expected to begin between Manassas and Fredericksburg in Northern Virginia and Washington by 1991. Other cities, such as Atlanta and Seattle, were giving serious consideration to commuter rail service in order to provide fast service to their far-flung metropolitan areas. The eight Amtrak trains a day each way between Los Angeles and San Diego were in 1988 considered by some to be a commuter line offering service for commuters to both terminal cities.

23. See George M. Smerk, "The 'Hardware Gap' in Urban Transport," *Business Horizons,* Vol. 9, No. 1, Spring 1966, pp. 5-16. Also see the excellent monograph by Vukan R. Vuchic, *Light Rail Transit Systems: A Definition of Evaluation* (Springfield, Va.: National Technical Information Service, October 1972), PB 213 447. Immediately after World War II, the relatively cash-rich transit properties had spent heavily for new rail cars and diesel and trolleybuses. The rapid decline of patronage and the private ownership of most transit systems caused the demand for new equipment to fall drastically. Many of the smaller systems were using equipment that was close to two decades old by the mid–1960s. As for bus garage and maintenance facilities, most were originally streetcar barns and were not particularly well-adapted to buses. There was little money available prior to the federal programs for such facilities.

24. For some estimates of the amount of money needed during the time period under discussion, see Fitch, "Mass Transport: A $10 Billion Market," *Railway Age,* Vol. 154, No. 6, February 18, 1963, pp. 55-57; *IRT News Letter,* Vol. 7, No. 7, December 1966, p. 125, contains a most interesting review of transit developments in the preceding year; for some prognostication of the cities where rapid transit was expected to be a distinct possibility, see "Mapping Transit's Future: All Eyes Focus on Pittsburgh," *Railway Age,* Vol. 160, No. 3, January 24, 1966, pp. 18-19.

25. Syracuse, New York, for example, was unable to match an approved federal grant of demonstration funds. On June 30, 1964, $185,353 was approved for use by that city, provided a matching sum of $92,657 was forthcoming. Syracuse could not find the money, and the demonstration was canceled in January 1965.

In another case, in 1971, the Chicago South Shore & South Bend Railroad—a commuter railroad linking northwest Indiana with Chicago—gained approval of a capital grant for new passenger rolling stock to replace cars built in the 1920s. The railroad, a private company controlled at the time by the Chesapeake & Ohio Railroad, was willing to pay the local match required of the federal capital grant, so no local public funds were needed. Unfortunately, the railroad could find no local government unit to act as the recipient of the federal funds, and the grant was eventually canceled. It was not until 1977 that a public body with the relevant jurisdiction was finally established, and it was not until 1982 that new commuter cars began to ply the South Shore Line.

26. For an excellent survey of the city problems of the times see Jon C. Teaford, *The Twentieth-Century American City* (Baltimore: The Johns Hopkins University Press, 1986), especially Chapter 7, "The Fragmentation of the Metropolis."

27. See Evan Herbert, "Transporting People," *International Science and Technology,* October 1965, pp. 30-42.

28. *S.2599, a Bill to Amend the Urban Mass Transportation Act of 1964 to Provide for Additional Technological Research,* 89th Congress, 1st session, October 5, 1965. This bill was introduced again in the next session of Congress.

29. Senate Report No. 1436, Committee on Banking and Currency, 89th Congress, 2d session, August 8, 1966.

30. See House Report No. 1487 accompanying H.R. 14810, Committee on Banking and Currency, 89th Congress, 2d session, May 9, 1966.

31. Ibid., p. 10.

32. Ibid., p. 5.

33. Ibid., pp. 15-16.

34. *Congressional Record* 112, 89th Congress, 2d session, August 15, 1966, pp. 18576-18577.

35. Ibid., p. 18582.

36. Ibid., p. 18585.

37. Ibid., August 16, 1966, pp. 18712-18740.

38. Ibid.

39. David G. Lawrence, *The Politics of Innovation in Urban Mass Transportation Policymaking: The New Systems Example* (Washington, D.C.: Urban Transportation Center, Consortium of Universities, Spring 1970), pp. 3-4.

40. Ibid., pp. 7-8 and 10-11.

41. Ibid., p. 12 and 14-16.

42. Ibid., p. 21.

43. Ibid., pp. 22-25.

44. Ibid., pp. 24-34.

45. The findings from the studies were summarized in *Tomorrow's Transportation: New Systems for the Urban Future* (Washington, D.C.: U.S. Department of Housing and Urban Development, Office of Metropolitan Development, 1968).

46. An example of the adverse criticism may be found in the paper by Senator Gordon Allott, "Urban Transit: Paper or Progress," delivered at the Third International Conference on Urban Transportation, Pittsburgh, 1968 (reprinted by the WABCO Mass Transit Center, Westinghouse Air Brake Co., Pittsburgh).

47. Lawrence, *The Politics of Innovation,* pp. 42-44.

48. As the reader will recall, the Bureau of the Budget eventually was reorganized and its name changed to the Office of Management and Budget. Under the Reagan administration, this agency became the nemesis of the mass transit program, particularly when under the direction of David Stockman. In the 1960s the BOB had apparently recognized that highway policy or an almost singular transportation policy was wrong-headed and that continuation of the highways-only policy would be counterproductive. But BOB or OMB is an arm of the White House and thus must reflect the political attitudes of the president. There is, thus, no necessary consistency in the BOB/OMB position.

49. *Reorganization Plan No. 2, 1968, for Transportation,* 90th Congress, 2d session, House Document No. 262 (Washington, D.C.: U.S. Government Printing Office, February 26, 1968).

50. *Report to the President on Urban Transportation Organization by the Department of Housing and Urban Development and the Department of Transportation,* 90th Congress, 2d session, House Document No. 281 (Washington, D.C.: U.S. Government Printing Office, March 13, 1968), p. 4.

51. *Hearing before a Subcommittee of the Committee on Government Operations: Reorganization Plan No. 2 of 1968 (Urban Mass Transportation),* 90th Congress, 2d session (Washington, D.C.: U.S. Government Printing Office, April 22, 1968), especially pp. 14-17.

52. "Agreement between the Secretary of the Department of Housing and Urban Development and the Secretary of Transportation" (mimeographed document signed by the Secretary of Housing and Urban Development, Robert Weaver, on September 9, 1968, and by Transportation Secretary Alan Boyd on September 10, 1968). For commentary on the agreement, see "On the Washington Scene," *Metropolitan,* Vol. 24, No. 6, November-December 1968, pp. 28 and 30.

7. MAJOR GROWTH IN THE MASS TRANSIT PROGRAM

1. Senator Williams's bill was S. 1032, which, as an amended version, eventually became the Mass Transportation Act of 1970. See *Passenger Transport,* Vol. 27, No. 8, February 21, 1969; and *Passenger Transport,* Vol. 27, No. 12, March 21, 1969, for comments on the introduction of the legislation.

2. See *Passenger Transport,* Vol. 27, No. 33, August 15, 1969, p. 1; and for almost unalloyed gloom, *Metropolitan,* Vol. 65, No. 5, September-October, 1969, p. 36.

3. Fred Burke was from Michigan, where after graduating from the University of Michigan he became a legislative assistant to Senator Hart. His knowledge of the lobbying process and ways to put together the words and the coalition to sell an idea were formidable. Alan Boyd, the first secretary of transportation, utilized Burke's skill as his legislative liaison on Capitol Hill for the new DOT. With the coming of the Nixon administration, Fred Burke was axed from DOT. He sought consulting work, which was how he ended up lobbying for the USCM/NLC. Later he went on to handle the transit lobbying chores for a number of cities as well as being the principal strategy formulator, tactician, and lobbying agent for the American Public Transit Association. Until his untimely death in 1984, Fred Burke's mark was on every piece of transit legislation from 1969.

4. See "On the Washington Scene," *Metropolitan,* Vol. 65, No. 5, September-October, 1969, p. 36.

5. See "Villareal Answers Questions About Nixon's Public Transportation Bill," *Passenger Transport,* Vol. 27, No. 37, September 12, 1969, p. 1.

6. See "Williams Named Man of the Year," *Passenger Transport,* Vol. 27, No. 37, September 12, 1969, p. 1.

7. As originally introduced, the Williams amendment read as follows:

To finance the programs and activities, including administrative costs, under this act, the Secretary is authorized to incur obligations in the form of grant agreements or otherwise in amounts aggregating not to exceed $3,100,000,000.

This amount shall become available for obligation upon the effective date of this subsection and shall remain available until obligated.

There are authorized to be appropriated for liquidation of the obligations incurred under this subsection not to exceed $80,000,000 prior to July 1, 1971, which amount may be increased not to exceed an aggregate of $310,000,000 prior to July 1, 1972; not to exceed an aggregate of $710,000,000 prior to July 1, 1973; not to exceed an aggregate of $1,260,000,000 prior to July 1, 1974; not to exceed an aggregate of $3,100,000,000 thereafter.

This language was changed in the final bill (H.R. 18185, 91st Congress, 2d session) in Section 4c, to read as follows: ". . . not to exceed $80,000,000 prior to July 1, 1971, which amount may be increased not to exceed an aggregate of $310,000,000 prior to July 1, 1972, not to exceed an aggregate of $710,000,000 prior to July 1, 1973, not to exceed an aggregate of $1,260,000,000 prior to July 1, 1974, not to exceed an aggregate of $1,860,000,000 prior to July 1, 1975, and not to exceed an aggregate of $3,100,000,000, thereafter."

See "On the Washington Scene," *Metropolitan,* Vol. 66, No. 1, January-February, 1970, p. 29.

8. See "On the Washington Scene," *Metropolitan,* Vol. 65, No. 6, November-December, 1969, p. 44; and "House Adds a Transit Panel," *Passenger Transport,* Vol. 31, No. 11, March 16, 1973, pp. 1, 6.

9. See John Burby, *The Great American Motion Sickness* (Boston: Little, Brown, 1971), pp. 234-235. Also, William Lilley III, "Urban Report: Urban Interests Win Transit Bill with 'Letter-Perfect' Lobbying," *National Journal,* September 19, 1970, pp. 2021-2029, for a penetrating analysis of what it takes to get legislation through Congress.

10. See " 'Damnedest Coalition' Fights for Transit Aid Bill Passage," *Passenger Transport,* Vol. 28, No. 27, July 3, 1970, pp. 4-5.

11. See "Senate Passes Transit Aid Bill," *Passenger Transport,* Vol. 28, No. 6, February 6, 1970, pp. 1, 6; "Bill Passes!" *Passenger Transport,* Vol. 27, No. 39, October 2, 1970, pp.

1-7, 10-12; and "President Nixon Signs Transit Aid Bill," *Passenger Transport*, Vol. 27, No. 41, October 16, 1970, p. 1.

12. *Congressional Record*, 91st Congress, 2d session, September 29, 1970, p. H 9349.

13. Ibid., pp. H 9350-9351.

14. Ibid., p. H 9359.

15. For accounts of the activity, see "Cochran Leads Industry Support for Senate Bill 870," *Passenger Transport*, Vol. 29, No. 15, April 9, 1971, pp. 1, 7; "ATA Asks Senate to Raise Transit's '72 Funding Level," *Passenger Transport*, Vol. 29, No. 29, July 16, 1971, pp. 1, 3; ". . . A Harder Look at Transit'—Blatnick" and "Congress Okays $900 Million for Transit," *Passenger Transport*, Vol. 29, No. 32, August 6, 1971, pp. 1, 4-5; "Industry Calls for Operating Aid at Senate Hearings," *Passenger Transport*, Vol. 30, No. 5, February 4, 1972, pp. 1, 4-5; "Senate Okays Operating Aid," *Passenger Transport*, Vol. 30, No. 9, March 3, 1972, pp. 1, 7; "Volpe Urges Transit Aid from Highway Trust Fund," *Passenger Transport*, Vol. 30, No. 11, March 17, 1972, p. 1; "Administration Fails to Back Operating Aid," *Passenger Transport*, Vol. 30, No. 24, June 16, 1972, p. 1; "Transit and the Trust Fund: Senate Panel Reports Bill," *Passenger Transport*, Vol. 30, No. 30, July 28, 1972, pp. 1, 4; and "Lack of Quorum Kills Transit Aid," *Passenger Transport*, Vol. 30, No. 43, October 27, 1972, pp. 1, 5. Also see *IRT Digest*, Special Issue, Annual Conference 1972, pp. 4-10, 15-19; and "92d Congress Kills Federal Aid Bill," *IRT Digest*, No. 14, November-December 1972, pp. 2-6; "Nixon: Transit Is High Priority," *Passenger Transport*, Vol. 31, No. 8, February 23, 1973, p. 1; and "Nixon Urges Rail Use of Trust Fund," *Passenger Transport*, Vol. 31, No. 11, March 16, 1973, p. 6.

16. See "Anderson Re-Introduces Trust Fund Bill," *Passenger Transport*, Vol. 31, No. 2, January 12, 1973, pp. 1, 5; "Williams Introduces Transit Bill," *Passenger Transport*, Vol. 31, No. 3, January 19, 1973, p. 3; "St. Germain Offers Transit Aid Bill" and "Muskie Bill Would Open Trust Fund," *Passenger Transport*, Vol. 31, No. 4, January 26, 1973, pp. 1, 4; "Senate Holds Hearings on S. 386: DOT Head Fails to Back Operating Aid; Industry Says Williams Bill Is Essential," *Passenger Transport*, Vol. 31, No. 6, February 9, 1973, pp. 1, 4, 6; and the following bills introduced in the Senate and House in the first session of the 93rd Congress: S.386, S.502, S.885, H.R.576, H.R.991, and H.R.2734. The Senate hearings on the Highway Act of 1973 (which is essentially S.502, as amended) are most informative. The dedicated reader might be particularly interested in the following portions: testimony and discussion by Secretary of Transportation Claude Brinegar, pp. 95-123; testimony and discussion by William D. Ruckelshaus, director, Environmental Protection Agency, pp. 565-620; testimony of pro-highway advocates, pp. 135-181, 351-371, and 520-535; and testimony of U.S. Conference of Mayors/National League of Cities, pp. 671-701.

17. "Senate Passes Landmark Transit Aid Legislation," *Passenger Transport*, Vol. 31, No. 11, March 16, 1973, pp. 1, 8; "Where Does Transit Stand?" *Passenger Transport*, Vol. 31, No. 14, April 6, 1973, pp. 1, 2; and "House Says 'No' to Anderson, 'Yes' to Three Other Proposals," *Passenger Transport*, Vol. 31, No. 16, April 20, 1973, p. 3.

18. "Conferees Agree to Expand Use of Highway Trust Fund to Transit," *Passenger Transport*, Vol. 31, No. 30, July 27, 1973, pp. 1, 5.

19. "What the Highway Act Will Do for Mass Transit," *Railway Age*, Vol. 174, No. 19, October 8, 1973, p. 34.

20. The Highway Act of 1973 is a long and complex piece of legislation. The major portion of the final Highway Act, which is Public Law 93-87, is derived from S.502, 93rd Congress, 1st session, as amended. Important sections of the Act are as follows: Urban Planning funds, Section 112; Urban System Flexibility, Section 121; Bicycle Transportation, Section 124; Interstate Transfer, Section 137; Earmarking of Urban and System Funds, Section 157; UMTA Amendments, Section 301; Provisions for the Elderly and Handicapped, Sections 165b, 140, and 301g. Also see *Highways, Safety and Transit: An Analysis of the Federal-Aid Highway Act of 1973* (Washington, D.C.: Highway Users Federation for Safety and Mobility, 1973); "Federal Action: S. 502 Becomes a Law," *IRT Digest*,

No. 18, September-October 1973, pp. 1-10; "What the Highway Act Will Do for Mass Transit," pp. 34, 35; "Highway Act of 1973: What's in It for Mass Transit," *Passenger Transport,* Vol. 31, No. 32, August 10, 1973, pp. 4-5; and "Major Mass Transportation Related Provisions of the Federal Aid Highway Act of 1973," Department of Transportation News Release, UMTA 73-90.

21. *IRT Digest,* No. 18, September-October 1973, p. 8.

22. Ibid., p. 9.

23. "Administration Plan Would Allow Operating Aid," *Passenger Transport,* Vol. 32, No. 4, January 25, 1974, p. 1; "UTAP: Administration Plan Set," *Passenger Transport,* Vol. 32, No. 6, February 8, 1974, pp. 1, 3; and "UTAP: 'One Hand Giveth, and One Hand Taketh Away,'" *Railway Age,* Vol. 175, No. 21, March 11, 1974, p. 24. Also see George M. Smerk, "How Now, Highway Trust Fund?" *Business Horizons,* Vol. 17, No. 2, April 1974, pp. 29-38; *IRT Digest,* No. 18, September-October, 1973, pp. 1-10; "What the Highway Act Will Do for Mass Transit," *Railway Age,* Vol. 174, No. 19, October 8, 1973, pp. 34- 35; and "What's in It for Mass Transit," *Passenger Transit,* Vol. 31, No. 32, August 10, 1973, pp. 4-5.

8. THE NATIONAL MASS TRANSPORTATION ASSISTANCE ACT OF 1974

1. What is small and what is large in terms of federal expenditures is a subjective judgment, and another viewpoint on small or large reflects the need involved. The federal transit appropriations of the 1960s were never more than several hundred million dollars; when compared to the billions of dollars of deferred maintenance needed just for the rail transit systems of the time, these early sums were minuscule. Even though the federal transit program expenditure had risen to the billions by the 1980s, the amount was still but a tiny portion of the federal budget—less than half of one percent in 1986—and there were still unmet capital needs of large proportions. As an example, one estimate held that just to bring all of the existing rail transit and commuter services up to a reasonably good standard would cost over $17 billion in 1985 dollars.

2. The creation of APTA reflected the necessity of the transit industry to become much more of a lobbying organization than a traditional trade association. Bill Stokes, the former general manager of the Bay Area Rapid Transit District, became the first executive vice president of APTA. Stokes increased the number of professionals by adding to the staff inherited from the Institute for Rapid Transit and the American Transit Association. APTA meetings and conferences became much more business oriented, with strong emphasis on solving practical transit problems and helping members in their relations with government at all levels. The basic lobbying strategy for APTA remained in the hands of Fred Burke, who had played such a major role in the passage of the 1970 legislation. Burke headed a consulting firm that specialized in transit and other urban issues, and he was retained to work closely with APTA and its members.

3. For some perspective on transit and issues of the 1960s and 1970s, see David Jones, *Urban Transit Policy: An Economic and Political History* (Englewood Cliffs, N.J.: Prentice-Hall, 1985), pp. 83-84. Jones notes that transit in this time period was turned from a failing industry into a vital public service in the public mind. See also John R. Meyer and Jose A. Gomez-Ibanez, *Autos, Transit, and Cities* (Cambridge, Mass.: Harvard University Press, 1981), especially Chapter 1.

4. S.386, 93rd Congress, 1st session as introduced January 16, 1973, pp. 3-5.

5. Transit patronage flickered upward on a national basis in the fall of 1973 and continued to rise through 1974 at an annual rate of just under 8 percent. The shortage of gasoline during the winter of 1973-74 was partially responsible; in other instances, improvements in transit service—and some fare cuts—and marketing efforts were the culprits in the first upswing in patronage since transit ridership had begun its postwar decline in 1947. See "Nation Registers Ridership Rise for a Full Year," *Passenger Transport,* Vol. 32, No. 44, November 1, 1974, p. 1.

6. Senate Report 93-361.

7. See "Long Trip to Operating Subsidies," *National Journal Reports*, Vol. 6, No. 16, April 20, 1974, p. 573.

8. See, for example, "Pollock Spreads Transit's Message," *Passenger Transport*, Vol. 31, No. 44, November 2, 1973, pp. 1 and 3; "Energy Crisis: Nixon Urges Transit Empha-sis," *Passenger Transport*, Vol. 31, No. 45, November 9, 1973, pp. 1 and 7; and "Brinegar Urges Greater Transit Use," *Passenger Transport*, Vol. 31, No. 46, November 16, 1973, pp. 1 and 4. The transit industry, in the scurrying about that went on in the early stages of the gasoline shortage of the fall and early winter of 1973, calculated that a 20 percent increase in transit patronage would mean 700 million less automobile trips a year. Assuming that the average passenger car of the time got 13.5 miles per gallon, and the average trip was three miles in length, a 20 percent increase in transit use would save 210 million gallons of gasoline. See "Transit—Energy Saver," *Passenger Transport*, Vol. 31, No. 46, November 16, 1973, p. 1.

9. "Administration Is Considering Operating Aid," *Passenger Transport*, Vol. 31, No. 49, December 7, 1973, p. 1.

10. "Long Trip to Operating Subsidies," *Passenger Transport*, Vol. 31, No. 49, Decem-ber 7, 1973. See also "Nixon Prepares New Aid to Railroads, Mass Transit," *Congressional Quarterly*, February 11, 1974, p. 14.

11. "UTAP: Administration Plan Set," *Passenger Transport*, Vol. 32, No. 6, February 8, 1974, pp. 1 and 3. See also R.M.M. McConnell, "Watching Washington," *Railway Age*, Vol. 175, No. 3, February 11, 1974; and "Administration Proposes Transportation Aid Plan," *IRT Digest*, No. 21, March-April 1974, pp. 1-6.

12. Michael J. Malbin, "Mass Transit Bills Slowed by Jurisdictional Disputes," *Na-tional Journal Reports*, Vol. 6, No. 16, April 20, 1974, p. 572.

13. House Report 93-813, filed with the House on February 26, 1974, and with the Senate on February 27, 1974.

14. Malbin, "Mass Transit Bills Slowed," p. 572.

15. See "Conferences Agree on Operating Aid," *Passenger Transport*, Vol. 32, No. 9, March 1, 1974, p. 1; Malbin, "Mass Transit Bills Slowed," pp. 572 and 574; "Ronan Suggests UTAP Changes," *IRT Digest*, No. 22, May-June 1974, pp. 1-6; and "$800 Million Transit Aid Bill Killed by House Vote," *Urban Transport News*, Vol. 2, No. 16, p. 122.

16. "Transit Aid Bill Blocked in House," *Passenger Transport*, Vol. 32, No. 10, March 8, 1974, p. 1.

17. See Malbin, "Mass Transit Bills Slowed," pp. 574-575. Secretary Brinegar did not give up easily in his voicing of the administration's opposition to S.386. In a letter dated July 26, 1974, to House Minority Leader John Rhodes, Brinegar discussed his attitude toward what he called the "critical weaknesses" of S.386, such as: "(1) it effectively eliminates participation by state governments in planning and executing public transpor-tation programs; (2) the formula for distributing funds in S.386 is unsound; and (3) the funding authorizations in S.386 are out of line with the need to fight inflation." See *Urban Mass Transportation Assistance Act of 1974: Conference Report*, House of Representatives, 93rd Congress, 2d session, Report No. 93-1427, October 3, 1974, pp. 13-14.

18. The path to success in obtaining an UMTA grant at the time was outlined in a veritable treasure chest of red tape entitled *Urban Mass Transportation Administration External Operating Manual*. This two-inch thick, loose-leaf book is issued by the Depart-ment of Transportation and changed and supplemented as the situation demands. The whole point of all such impedimenta is to see that all parties are treated fairly and equally. Sadly, years passed before supplements were released, to the confusion and worry of applicants.

19. The moratorium and deletion made up one of several blows to the rail mode suffered while Congress was deliberating on transit legislation. There was suspicion on the part of rail interests that DOT and UMTA had a definite anti-rail bias. This was evidenced by a report issued by the Department of Transportation that apparently claimed that

express bus service was always less costly than rail rapid transit; it was, in effect, a benefit-cost study minus the benefit part. Other slings and arrows were hurled at rail transit by a *Business Week* article; rail advocates answered back, fearful that the ghost of the Meyer, Kain, and Wohl book of the 1960s, which came out strongly for rubber-tired transportation—private automobiles as well as buses—had not been laid to rest. See J. Haydon Boyd, Norman J. Asher, and Elliot S. Wetzler, *Evaluation of Rail Transit and Express Bus Service in the Urban Commuter Market* (Arlington, Va.: Institute for Defense Analysis, Program Analysis Division, prepared for the U.S. Department of Transportation, Assistant Secretary for Policy, Plans and International Affairs, Office of Transportation Planning Analysis, October, 1973); Vukan R. Vuchic, *A Critique of the Study "Evaluation of Rail Rapid Transit and Express Bus Service in the Urban Commuter Market,"* sponsored by the Office of Transportation Planning Analysis, U.S. DOT, submitted to the Urban Mass Transportation Administration under Contract with the Institute of Public Administration (mimeographed), February 1974; *Rail Transit: The Operators' View,* prepared by the Chicago Transit Authority, Development Planning Department (undated); "Making Mass Transit Work," *Business Week,* No. 2318, February 16, 1974, pp. 74-80; Joe Asher, "Viewpoint: Et tu, *Business Week,"* *Railway Age,* Vol. 175. No. 11, June 10, 1974, pp. 21 and 24-25; and Tom Kizzia, "Los Angeles: Will Tracks Be Back?" ibid., pp. 30-37 and 40-41.

20. Malbin, "Mass Transit Bills Slowed," pp. 574-576.

21. On the issue of the impact of capital subsidies, see William Tye, "Economics of Urban Transit Capital Grants," in *Price-Subsidy Issues in Urban Transportation* (Washington, D.C.: Highway Research Board, Highway Research Record Number 476, 1973), pp. 30-35; and Malbin, "Mass Transit Bills Slowed," p. 576.

22. See "Congress Seeks $21-25 Billion in Transit Funds," *Passenger Transport,* Vol. 32, No. 21, May 24, 1974, pp. 1 and 4; and "Details of Transit Bill Revealed," *Passenger Transport,* Vol. 32, No. 23, June 7, 1974, pp. 1 and 4.

23. "Bentsen Measure Calls for $17.5 Billion over Five Years," *Passenger Transport,* Vol. 32, No. 24, June 14, 1974, p. 1.

24. "Williams Measure Is Introduced," *Passenger Transport,* Vol. 32, No. 27, July 5, 1974, pp. 1 and 3.

25. See "$18 Billion Transit Bill Proposed," *Passenger Transport,* Vol. 32, No. 32, August 9, 1974, p. 1.

26. For some notion of the trials and tribulations along the way, see "Proposed House Transit Subsidy Bill Held 'More Acceptable' by White House," *Urban Transport News,* Vol. 2, No. 11, May 27, 1974, p. 82. For the revised bill—essentially a stripping of H.R. 12859—see H.R. 12859, Report No. 93-1256, 93rd Congress, 2d session, August 1, 1974.

27. See "Committee Reports $20 Billion Bill," *Passenger Transport,* Vol. 32, No. 31, August 2, 1974, p. 1.

28. See Michael J. Malbin, "Transportation Report/Defeat of Transit Bill Clears Way for Long-Range Measure," *National Journal Reports,* Vol. 6, No. 32, August 10, 1974, pp. 1205-1206; and "$800 Million Transit Aid Bill Killed by House Vote," *Urban Transport News,* Vol. 2, No. 16, August 5, 1974, p. 122.

29. See "House Deliberates Transit Bill," *Passenger Transport,* Vol. 32, No. 33, August 16, 1974, p. 1; "President Ford's Views on Mass Transit Held Worrisome," *Urban Transport News,* Vol. 2, No. 17, August 19, 1974, p. 132; and "House Rules Committee Reviews Minish-Williams Subsidy Bill," *Urban Transport News,* Vol. 2, No. 16, August 5, 1974, p. 124.

30. See "Ford Pledges Operating Support for Transit," *Passenger Transport,* Vol. 32, No. 37, September 13, 1974, p. 1; and "President Ford Calls for Realistic Restraint on Transit Aid," *Urban Transport News,* Vol. 2, No. 19, September 16, 1974, p. 146.

31. "House Voice Votes Changes FMTA Subsidy Formula to 67% Local, 33% U.S.," *Urban Transport News,* Vol. 2, No. 17, August 19, 1974, p. 132.

32. See "Compromise Bill Passes House," *Passenger Transport,* Vol. 32, No. 43, August 23, 1974, p. 1.

33. See "Enactment of the Transit Aid Legislation This Session Growing Remote," *Urban Transport News,* Vol. 2, No. 15, July 22, 1974, p. 117.

34. See Harrison Williams, "An Editorial: Enact S. 386 Quickly," *Passenger Transport,* Vol. 32, No. 45, November 8, 1974, p. 2.

35. See "Operating Aid Bill Resurfaces," *Passenger Transport,* Vol. 32, No. 38, September 20, 1974, pp. 1 and 3; and "Ford Is Urging Long-Term Bill," *Passenger Transport,* Vol. 32, No. 40, October 4, 1974, pp. 1 and 4.

36. See "Operating Aid Urged," *Passenger Transport,* Vol. 32, No. 39, September 27, 1974, pp. 1 and 4.

37. See "Editorial: The Answer," *Passenger Transport,* Vol. 32, No. 44, November 1, 1974, p. 1; "Editorial: Damnedest Coalition Is Back," *Passenger Transport,* Vol. 32, No. 46, November 15, 1974, p. 1; and "Ford, APTA, Mayors Boost S. 386," *Passenger Transport,* Vol. 32, No. 46, November 15, 1974.

38. See "Bipartisan Pressure Used to Get Congressional Approval of Transit Bill," *Urban Transport News,* Vol. 2, No. 25, December 9, 1974, p. 195.

39. James M. Naughton, "Senate Approves Transit-Aid Measure," New York Times News Service, appearing in the *Louisville Courier-Journal,* November 20, 1974; "Transit Bill Passed," from United Press International, appearing in the *Bloomington* (Ind.) *Herald-Telephone,* November 22, 1974; "Congress Passes Bill to Aid Mass Transit with Subsidies," from the Associated Press, appearing in the *Louisville Courier-Journal,* November 22, 1974; "Congress Passes S. 386," and "Editorial: Our Hats Are Off!" *Passenger Transport,* Vol. 32, No. 47, November 22, 1974, p. 1; "Ford Signs Transit Aid 48," November 29, 1974, p. 1; and "Needed: A People's Lobby for Railroads," *Railway Age,* Vol. 175, No. 24, December 30, 1974, p. 42.

40. *Urban Mass Transportation Assistance Act of 1974: Conference Report, Railway Age,* Vol. 175, No. 24, December 30, 1974, p. 42. p. 2.

41. Ibid., p. 15. The formula section of the Act reads as follows:

The Secretary shall apportion for expenditure in fiscal years 1975 through 1980 the sums authorized by subsection (c). Such sums shall be made available for expenditure in urbanized areas or parts thereof on the basis of a formula under which urbanized areas or parts thereof will be entitled to receive an amount equal to the sum of—
(A) one-half of the total amount so apportioned multiplied by the ratio which the population of such urbanized area or part thereof, as designated by the Bureau of the Census, bears to the total population of all the urbanized areas in all the States as shown by the latest available Federal census; and
(B) one-half of the total amount so apportioned multiplied by a ratio for that urbanized area determined on the basis of population weighted by a factor of density, as determined by the Secretary.

(As used in the preceding sentence, the term "density" means the number of inhabitants per square mile. Ibid., p. 3.)

42. Ibid., p. 15; also see p. 4, paragraph (e).

43. See Section 101 (b) of the Urban Transportation Assistance Act of 1974; also Ibid., p. 2.

44. Ibid., pp. 15-16.

45. Ibid., pp. 9 and 16.

46. Ibid., pp. 8 and 17.

47. This is found in Sections 201 through 207 of the Act. Ibid., pp. 10-11.

48. F.A.R.E. stands for Financial Accounting Reporting Elements. The development of F.A.R.E. was carried out by Arthur Andersen and Co. for UMTA. The final report is contained in five volumes obtainable from the National Technical Information Service in

Springfield, Virginia: Volume I, *Task and Project Summary* (PB-226 354); Volume II, *Reporting System Instructions* (PB-226 355); Volume III, *Reporting System Forms* (PB-226 356); Volume IV, *Commuter Rail Reporting System Instructions* (PB-226 357); and Volume V, *Commuter Rail Reporting System Forms* (PB-226 358).

9. THE SURFACE TRANSPORTATION ACT OF 1978

1. For more details, see the previous chapter.

2. Arthur E. Wiese, "Politics in Transit," *Mass Transit*, Vol. 4, No. 3, March 1977, pp. 8-9.

3. There were many forces at work within the industry affecting the total number of riders. Transit in New York was losing patrons due to the general economic decline and loss of employment in that city. Many other cities were claiming significant increases in transit use; the dominance of New York in the statistical totals tended to diminish the impact of patronage increases elsewhere. Total transit patronage in 1972 was 6,567,000,000 and an estimated 7,081,000,000 in 1976. Revenue passengers in 1972 added up to 5,253,300,000 and rose to an estimated 5,673,100,000 in 1976, with 5,723,000,000 predicted for 1977. See *Transit Fact Book: '77-'78 Edition* (Washington, D.C.: American Public Transit Association, 1978), p. 24.

4. Charles N. Conconi, "Going after the Money," *Mass Transit*, Vol. 4, No. 3, March 1977, pp. 16-18.

5. Ibid., p. 18.

6. Section 3 Capital Grants for the fiscal years 1978-1982 were set at the following rates: 1978—$1.9 billion; 1979—$2 billion; 1980—$2.2 billion; 1981—$2.5 billion; and 1982—$2.8 billion. "Key Features of the Bill," *Passenger Transport*, Vol. 35, No. 2, January 14, 1977, pp. 1-3.

7. Most management personnel receiving aid under Section 10 of the Act took advantage of the programs offered by Northeastern University and Carnegie-Mellon University. The original Section 10 legislation had assumed that those using the fellowships would enter degree programs for a year to complete an undergraduate degree or obtain a masters degree. What really happened was that most transit properties could not afford to have staff gone for as long as a year. Short courses were the means usually chosen to help train transit personnel, and they were not very expensive on a per capita basis. Because of the limitations on the number of fellowships, the Section 10 appropriations over the years were never spent. Later, the limitations on the number of fellowships were lifted by an amendment to the Urban Mass Transportation Act of 1964, and more people were trained by more providers of training. In the latter part of the Reagan administration, the program was adjusted several more times and came to emphasize training for large transit properties and to push in-house and on-site training rather than on a campus or place other than a transit property.

8. S.208, National Mass Transportation Assistance Act, 1977, 95th Congress, 1st session, introduced January 12, 1977; Tom Ichniowski, "Senator Williams: $11.4 Billion for Transit," *Railway Age*, Vol. 178, No. 3, February 14, 1977, pp. 25-26.

9. "APTA Resolution on S.208: Adopted February 20, 1977," *Passenger Transport*, Vol. 35, No. 8, February 25, 1977, p. 4. See also: "APTA Backs Williams' $11.4 Billion Transit Bill," *Passenger Transport*, Vol. 35, No. 8, February 25, 1977, p. 3.

10. "Bills Introduced: Conference Set," *Passenger Transport*, Vol. 35, No. 11, March 18, 1977, pp. 1-8.

11. National Mass Transportation Assistance Act of 1977. Hearings before the Subcommittee on Housing and Urban Affairs of the Committee on Banking, Housing and Urban Affairs. U.S. Senate, 95th Congress, 1st session on S.208, to amend the UMTA Act of 1964 to extend the authorization for assistance under such act and for such purposes. February 23-25, 1977, p. 398. Hereinafter called Mass Transportation Act of 1977.

12. Ibid., pp. 398-400.

13. News release, office of the secretary of transportation, DOT 46-77, April 6, 1977.

14. APTA Editorial, "We're Disappointed," *Passenger Transport,* Vol. 35, No. 10, March 11, 1977, p. 2.

15. Jack Burke, "Watching Washington," *Railway Age,* Vol. 178, No. 5, March 14, 1977, p. 15. One part of government appeared intent on preaching the virtues of competition for funds, while another part eschewed competition and advocated the good sense of designated funds and the ability to plan and manage more efficiently and effectively. Once funds have been earmarked for some purpose, it is extraordinarily difficult to make the funds competitive, if for no other reason than that constituencies have grown up supported by the dedicated money.

16. C. Carroll Carter, "An Investment We Must Make," *Mass Transit,* Vol. 4, No. 5, May 1977, pp. 48-49. President Carter was one of the most intelligent men to inhabit the White House and one of the best informed. His naive pronouncements are not so much embarrassing as evidence that even bright and usually well-informed persons have only the barest of knowledge about mass transportation—ignorance is the norm. It is a real problem when a leader grew up, as President Carter did, in a setting innocent of public transportation. One can speculate that progress was made in the federal mass transportation programs under the administrations of Presidents Kennedy and Nixon because both men were products of highly urbanized environments.

17. "How Adams Interprets Carter's Transit Memo," *Railway Age,* Vol. 178, No. 7, April 11, 1977, pp. 10, 12-13.

18. APTA Editorial, "Substantive Support," *Passenger Transport,* Vol. 35, No. 17, April 29, 1977, p. 2.

19. "APTA Issues Energy Policy Statement," *Passenger Transport,* Vol. 35, No. 15, April 15, 1977, pp. 1-2, 4-5, and 16. The National League of Cities Board of Directors adopted a national municipal policy on energy. This called for energy taxes which would be collected and utilized to provide additional capital, operating subsidies, and research and development funds for mass transportation. See "League of Cities Issues National Municipal Policy on Energy," *Passenger Transport,* Vol. 35, No. 35, September 2, 1977, p. 3.

20. For details of the Carter Energy Proposals, see the National Energy Plan, Executive Office of the President, Energy Policy and Planning, U.S. Government Printing Office, stock number 040-000-00380-1. For expected impacts on the home front, see Avery Camarow, "How the Energy Plan Would Hit Home," *Money,* Vol. 6, No. 6, June, 1977, pp. 48-50. Also see National Association of Railway Passengers *News,* "Energy and Transportation," Vol. 11, No. 5, May 1977, pp. 1-2. See also John R. Meyer and Jose A. Gomez-Ibanez, *Autos, Transit, and Cities* (Cambridge, Mass.: Harvard University Press, 1981), Chapter 8.

21. *An Evaluation of the National Energy Plan,* Report to Congress by the Comptroller General of the United States, the General Accounting Office (EMD-77-48), July 25, 1977.

22. For example, see *Transportation Energy Bulletin,* May 17, 1977, Transportation Association of America, Washington, D.C.; Jim Castelli, "Energy Plan: Pro and Con," *The Criterion,* Indianapolis, May 20, 1977, p. 5; and Robert Adams, "Mass Transit: Carter's Missing Link," *St. Louis Post-Dispatch,* May 15, 1977. Substantial doubt exists as to whether or not transit is a very effective means of saving energy. Critics contend that the transit service improvements have little impact on saving fuel and that the cost is high. Fare reductions are also expensive. See Alan Altshuler, with James P. Womack and John R. Pucher, *The Urban Transportation System: Politics and Policy Innovation* (Cambridge, Mass.: MIT Press, 1979), Chapter 5.

23. "Pay as You Park," *Washington Post,* April 26, 1977. In Ottawa, the capital of Canada, parking fees imposed on federal government employees appear to have reduced the number of federal employees driving to work by 23 percent. See Anthony Frayne, "The Difficulties of Energy Conservation in Urban Transportation," *RTAC Forum* (Roads and Transportation Association of Canada), April 1977, p. 12. See also John E. Hirten, "Subsidized Parking," *Mass Transit,* Vol. 5, Nos. 7-8, July-August 1978, p. 82.

24. "Gas Tax Proposed for Transit Use," *Passenger Transport,* Vol. 35, No. 20, May 20, 1977, p. 10; and "Transit Funding: Adams' Solo Stand," *Railway Age,* Vol. 178, No. 11, June 13, 1977, p. 10; see also Harry L. Tennant, "A Long Look at the Adams Saga," *Modern Railroads,* Vol. 32, No. 9, September 1977, p. 67.

25. See "A Hotbed of Anti-Transit Sentiments," a guest editorial by Robert W. Edgar, member of Congress, *Passenger Transport,* Vol. 35, No. 21, May 27, 1977, p. 2.

26. See "Mass Transit's Priority Isn't High in Carter Administration," by Ann Cooper, *Congressional Quarterly,* appearing in the *Bloomington* (Ind.) *Herald-Telephone,* July 21, 1977.

27. "Mavericks in the Carter Cabinet," *Business Week,* No. 2487, May 9, 1977, p. 135.

28. "Senate Passes Aid Bill," *Passenger Transport,* Vol. 35, No. 26, July 1, 1977, p. 135.

29. Amendment proposed by Mr. Hayakawa to S.208, 95th Congress, 1st session, Congressional Record, Senate, June 23, 1977, pp. S10556-S10574.

30. "Adams Proposing Single Fund," *Passenger Transport,* Vol. 35, No. 48, December 2, 1977, pp. 1 and 8.

31. For an excellent summary of transit in the first year of the Carter administration, see Arthur E. Wiese, "Money for Mass Transit: Much Talk, Little Action," *Mass Transit,* Vol. 4, No. 11, December 1977, p. 16.

32. See Altshuler, *The Urban Transportation System,* p. 48.

33. See "Transit Community Responds to 504 Regulations," *Passenger Transport,* Vol. 36, No. 24, June 16, 1978, pp. 1 and 4.

34. Congressman James Howard (D-New Jersey), chairman of the house surface transportation subcommittee, commented: "This package will provide the nation with its first unfragmented policy on surface transportation. With this approach, we can bury once and for all the urban-versus-rural, us-against-them battles that have threatened the passage of every mass transit bill in recent years. . . . My Subcommittee is trying, for the first time in history, to combine all authorizing legislation for mass transit, highway, bridges and safety programs into one package." *Metropolitan,* Vol. 74, No. 1, January-February 1978, p. 17.

35. Ibid., p. 18. See also "Adams Pushes Transportation Package," *Passenger Transport,* Vol. 36, No. 5, February 3, 1978, pp. 1 and 8; and U.S. Department of Transportation *News,* February 1, 1978 (DOT 13-78). The proposal also contained provisions to accelerate the completion of the Interstate System, as well as include more funds for resurfacing and rehabilitation of highways. Up to 50 percent of urban highway funds could be used for transit capital-improvement projects, and vice versa. A bridge replacement program was also included, as well as a new highway safety program that would pull together all existing programs.

36. David Young, "Transit Executives Blast Budget for Transportation," *Chicago Tribune,* February 5, 1978.

37. Section 6 covers research, development and demonstration programs; Section 10 is the Management Training Program, and Section 11 is the University Research and Training Program. Some of the other section numbers have changed over time, and any reader trying to piece things together should see *Urban Mass Transportation Act of 1964, as Amended through February 1988, and Related Laws* (Washington, D.C.: Urban Mass Transportation Administration, U.S. Department of Transportation, 1988). This book is well documented and the reader can determine the legislative change over time.

38. "Howard Introduces Transit Legislation," *Passenger Transport,* Vol. 36, No. 23, March 24, 1978, pp. 1, 9-10, and March 10, 1978, pp. 1 and 10; and "UMTA Asks Congress for Transit Money," *Passenger Transport,* Vol. 36, No. 14, April 7, 1978, pp. 1 and 3. See also Arthur E. Wiese, "Congress Takes on Carter," *Mass Transit,* Vol. 5, No. 5, May 1978, pp. 40-41, 44, 45, 47-48; and Robert Roberts, "UMTA's New Dollar Stretcher," *Modern Railroads,* Vol. 33, No. 4, April 1978, pp. 42-45.

39. See "APTA Calls for $4.4 billion in Fiscal 1979," *Passenger Transport,* Vol. 36, No. 15, April 14, 1978, pp. 1 and 3.

40. "Congress Acting on Transit Bills," *Passenger Transport,* Vol. 36, No. 17, April 28, 1978, pp. 1 and 10.

41. See for example "Transit Bills Move Forward," *Passenger Transport,* Vol. 36, No. 18, May 5, 1978, pp. 1 and 5.

42. Rochelle L. Stanfield, "Highway Aid Is Shifting from Construction to Reconstruction," *National Journal,* Vol. 10, No. 33, August 19, 1978, p. 1318. A factor not heavily considered earlier was the need to begin mending the Interstate System, even though it was not completed. Construction of the Interstate Highways had taken much longer than expected, and the early sections were old enough to be in need of major repair. What would later be called the infrastructure problem was just beginning to be understood, and it spread far beyond transit or highways.

43. Ibid., pp. 1316-19, especially p. 1319.

44. "Senate Nears Final Vote; House OKs Bills," *Passenger Transport,* Vol. 36, No. 39, September 29, 1978, pp. 1 and 12.

45. There were major differences between the House and Senate bills; the main difference at the time of the passage of S.2441 was in the level of funding. See "Senate Backs Transit Bill," *Passenger Transport,* Vol. 36, No. 40, October 6, 1978, pp. 1 and 7.

46. Arthur E. Wiese, "Doing Battle with the White House," *Mass Transit,* Vol. 5, No. 12, December 1978, pp. 6-7. This article contains a superb summary of the events leading up to passage of the bill as well as the content of the bill: see pp. 7, 48-49. See also "Carter Says He Will Sign Transit Bill," *Passenger Transport,* Vol. 36, No. 42, October 20, 1978, pp. 1 and 8.

47. The $1.58 billion in capital funds for fiscal 1983 was added by Senator Williams. Ibid., p. 49.

48. Ibid., p. 49.

49. This discussion of the Surface Transportation Act of 1978 is based on the following: "Conference Report on H.R. 11733, Surface Transportation Assistance Act of 1978," *Congressional Record-House,* October 14, 1978, pp. 12912-12951 (the portion dealing with mass transportation is on pages 12925-31): American Public Transit Association, "Passage of Transit Legislation," *APTA Bulletin,* October 18, 1978; Arthur E. Wiese, "Doing Battle with the White House," *Mass Transit,* Vol. 5, No. 12, December 1978, pp. 6-7, 48, and especially 49; "Carter Says He Will Sign Transit Bill," *Passenger Transport,* Vol. 36, No. 42, October 20, 1978, pp. 1 and 8; and "Briefing It" (an analysis of the new act by the Indiana Mass Transportation Improvement Project), Institute for Urban Transportation, Bloomington, Indiana, November 1978.

50. From a briefing derived from the Act presented to the office of the governor of Indiana by the Indiana Mass Transportation Improvement Project, Institute for Urban Transportation, Bloomington, Indiana, November 1978.

51. See *A Proposal: Surface Transportation Administration,* U.S. Department of Transportation, Office of the Secretary/Federal Highway Administration/Urban Mass Transportation Administration Policy Group, November 1978.

52. See Luther S. Miller, "The UMTA-FHWA Merger: The Minnow and the Whale?" *Railway Age,* Vol. 179, No. 23, December 11, 1978, pp. 29-31, 38; and Douglas B. Feaver, "Brock Adams Urges Consolidating Transit, Highway Programs," *Washington Post,* November 10, 1978, p. B-7.

53. Reacting to the proposal, B. R. Stokes of APTA was quoted as saying: "How can an agency whose primary goals have to do with social good and social purposes square those goals with those of an organization which, up to the very recent past and perhaps to the present, has had as a major employment consideration the fact that you're a civil engineer?" The head of a big eastern transit system puts it even more bluntly: "Are we going to have sensitive urban transportation decisions made by people whose principal talent is building cloverleafs?" Ibid., p. 29.

54. "APTA Meets with DOT on UMTA/FHWA Merger," *Passenger Transport*, Vol. 36, No. 46, November 16, 1979, pp. 1 and 8. Many higher level UMTA staff members began to seek positions in other agencies or outside government service when the STA proposal was made; they did not want to play second or third fiddle to what they perceived to be ignorant former FHWA staff, should the STA plan reach fruition.

10. A TROUBLED COALITION

1. There were publicly owned transit systems in the United States prior to the 1960s (most notably in Chicago, New York, and San Francisco), but the real trend toward public ownership came with the widespread financial distress of private transit firms in the 1960s and the availability of federal capital funds to pay part of the cost of public acquisition.

Estimates for 1978 showed that 90 percent of the operating revenue, 87 percent of bus ownership, and 91 percent of linked passenger trips were attributable to the 463 out of 1,003 transit systems that were publicly owned. See *Transit Fact Book, 1978-1979* (Washington, D.C.: American Public Transit Association, 1979), pp. 38-39. By 1983, 58 percent of the transit properties were publicly owned; most of the privately owned systems were relatively small and most were subsidized. Of the 68,562 transit vehicles in 1983, 93 percent were publicly owned; 95 percent of the 2,005,000,000 vehicle miles and 95 percent of the 7,530,000,000 unlinked (revenue) passenger trips were provided by the public sector. See *Transit Fact Book, 1985* (Washington, D.C.: American Public Transit Association, 1985), p. 17.

2. Ibid., p. 19. Often overlooked, state and local operating aid has always been a much higher proportion of operating aid than the federal government; for example, in 1975, 32.1 percent of operating assistance was from state and local sources, in 1983 this rose to 49.2 percent.

3. See "Memphis Plans to Cope with a Fuel Crisis," *Passenger Transport*, Vol. 37, No. 16, April 20, 1979, pp. 1, 8-9, and 12; Russell Baker, "Who Turned Americans into Gas Hogs?" *Louisville Courier-Journal*, May 16, 1979; "California Commuters Try Mass Transit to Avoid Lines, High Prices for Gasoline," *Wall Street Journal*, May 22, 1979; C. Carroll Carter, "Time for a Change," *Mass Transit*, Vol. 6, No. 6, June 1979, p. 90; "Transit Guaranteed Bus Fuel," *Passenger Transport*, Vol. 37, No. 26, June 29, 1979, pp. 1, 6; C. Carroll Carter, "What Does It Take?" *Mass Transit*, Vol. 6, No. 7, July 1979, p. 64; Arthur E. Wiese, "Mobility Crisis—Major Issue of the 80's," *Mass Transit*, Vol. 6, No. 8, August 1979; Anthony Lewis, "The Real U.S. Energy Policy Is to Import More Oil," *Louisville Courier-Journal*, October 27, 1979; and Douglas Feaver, "Transit Affects Urban Growth, Saves Energy," *Passenger Transport*, Vol. 38, No. 1, January 4, 1980, pp. 1, 4.

4. See "An Analysis: Transit Community Responds to 504 Regulation," *Passenger Transport*, Vol. 36, No. 24, June 16, 1978; for some of the earlier reactions, see pp. 1, 4. The final regulations are discussed in "Final 504 Regulation Promulgated," *Passenger Transport*, Vol. 37, No. 22, June 1, 1979, pp. 1, 5.

5. See David C. Hackney, "Elderly, Disabled See Transbus as Last Hope," *Mass Transit*, Vol. 6, Nos. 1-2, January-February 1979, pp. 16-19, 106; David Young, "The Transbus Compromise," *Mass Transit*, Vol. 6, Nos. 1-2, January-February 1979, pp. 12-15; Rochelle L. Stanfield, "An 8-Inch Step for Transbus. A Giant Step Backward for Bidders," *National Journal*, Vol. 11, No. 13, March 31, 1979, pp. 522-24; "Transbus Program Troubled: Flxible Pulls Out," *Passenger Transport*, Vol. 37, No. 11, March 16, 1979, pp. 1, 10; "No-Bids-Transbus: An Agonizing Reappraisal," *Passenger Transport*, Vol. 37, No. 18, May 4, 1979; and David Young, "Transbus: Left in Limbo," *Mass Transit*, Vol. 6, No. 8, August 1979, pp. 12-14. Problems with the components revolved in part around the extremely low ground clearance of the Transbus. There were no mass-produced, commercially available tires, batteries, or air tanks that would fit in the space available. These components

had been hand-fabricated for the Transbus prototypes that were built as part of the Transbus Project.

6. "Panel Hears APTA Views on Transbus," *Passenger Transport,* Vol. 37, No. 20, May 18, 1979, pp. 1, 3; "504 Regulations: DOT's Response—Disturbing," *Passenger Transport,* Vol. 37, No. 23, June 8, 1979, pp. 1, 10; and "Congressional Report: 504 Costs Too Much," *Passenger Transport,* Vol. 37, No. 46, Nov. 16, 1979, pp. 1, 9.

7. See the following articles which appeared in *Passenger Transport*: "APTA Sues Federal Government Over Accessibility Regulation," Vol. 37, No. 27, July 6, 1979, pp. 1, 10; "Hearing Held on 504 Suit," Vol. 37, No. 31, August 3, 1979, pp. 1, 10; "Court Denies Preliminary Injunction," Vol. 37, No. 32, August 10, 1979, pp. 1, 5; "Transbus Mandate Delayed," Vol. 37, No. 32, August 10, 1979, pp. 1, 3; John T. Mauro, "Section 504: Problems, Concerns, and What Could Be Done Differently," Vol. 37, No. 45, November 9, 1979, p. 6,; "Judge Calls: Lawyers Back on 504 Suit," Vol. 38, No. 3, January 18, 1980, pp. 1, 7; "504 Suit Judge Asks about Costs," Vol. 38, No. 4, January 25, 1980, pp. 1, 7; "APTA Suggests 504 Waiver Guidelines," Vol. 38, No. 7, February 15, 1980, pp. 1, 9; "APTA Pushes 504 Waiver Review," Vol. 38, No. 9, February 29, 1980, pp. 1, 9; and "Court Won't Review 504 Waivers," Vol. 38, No. 13, March 28, 1980, pp. 1, 9.

8. "UMTA Pushes Carter's Transit Budget," *Passenger Transport,* Vol. 37, No. 18, May 4, 1979, pp. 1, 9.

9. "Carter: Cut Driving, Take Transit," *Passenger Transport,* Vol. 37, No. 7, February 16, 1979, pp. 1, 6; C. Carroll Carter, "A First for Mass Transit," *Mass Transit,* Vol. 6, No. 5, May 1979, pp. 1, 9; "White House Announces Transit Plan," *Passenger Transport,* Vol. 37, No. 34, August 24, 1979, pp. 1, 9; "DOT Legislation Would Expand Mass Transit, Boost Auto Efficiency," U.S. *DOT News,* DOT 100-79, September 14, 1979; "Carter Says Transit Is Key Issue," *Passenger Transport,* Vol. 37, No. 39, September 28, 1979, pp. 1, 9; "President's Speech: Carter Supports Transit," *Passenger Transport,* Vol. 37, No. 40, October 5, 1979, pp. 1, 5-7; "Carter a Quantum Jump in Transit Outlays," *Railway Age,* Vol. 180, No. 19, October 8, 1979, p. 10; Arthur E. Wiese, "A New Love Affair with Transit," *Mass Transit,* Vol. 6, No. 10, October 1979, pp. 8-9, 70-72, 76, 82, 90; "U.S. DOT Sets Policy Objectives," *Passenger Transport,* Vol. 37, No. 45, November 8, 1979, pp. 1, 6; "A Presidential First . . . " *Mass Transit,* Vol. 7, No. 1, January 1980, pp. 6-7, 44; "$3.9 Billion in Budget Set for Transit," *Passenger Transport,* Vol. 38, No. 5, February 1, 1980, pp. 1-7; and "Budget Cuts Detailed," *Passenger Transport,* Vol. 38, No. 14, April 3, 1980, pp. 1, 6.

10. See "Budget Cuts Detailed." Louis Rukeyser wrote in his syndicated column: "Mass transit has become a significant pawn in a continual administration battle between the trimmers on one side and the expansionists in the Department of Transportation on the other." ("Mass Transit May Get Derailed," *Marion* (Ind.) *Chronicle-Tribune,* June 4, 1980.)

11. See for example, "Senate Budget Panel Slashes Transit Aid," *Passenger Transport,* Vol. 38, No. 17, April 25, 1980, pp. 1, 9; "Conferees Struggle on 1981 Budget" and "Budget Is Key Topic at APTA Eastern," *Passenger Transport,* Vol. 38, No. 20, May 16, 1980, pp. 1, 10.

12. Jack Burke, "Watching Washington: Yes, We Still Have No Policy," *Railway Age,* Vol. 179, No. 1, January 16, 1978, p. 14. Also, in the years that followed, nothing changed for the better; recommendations for "the play of market forces" and privatization obfuscated more than clarified the pursuit of national policy by mistaking means for ends.

13. "APTA Terms Surface Transportation Administration Plan 'Premature,' " *Passenger Transport,* Vol. 37, No. 2, January 12, 1979, pp. 1, 3; Edward T. Myers, "Will Transit Be Submerged?" *Modern Railroads,* Vol. 34, No. 1, January 1979, p. 29; Michael F. Conlan, "Adams Pushes for Highway-Transit Merger," *Mass Transit,* Vol. 6, Nos. 1-2, January-February 1979, pp. 92-94; "Transit Agency Merger Stalled at White House," *Wall Street Journal,* March 5, 1979; "Carter Ends Cabinet Reshuffle, Naming Heads to Housing,

Transportation Units," *Wall Street Journal,* July 30, 1979; and "Goldschmidt Nomination Is Well Received," *Passenger Transport,* Vol. 37, No. 31, August 3, 1979, pp. 1, 10.

14. Arthur E. Wiese, "Public Opinion—A Mixed Bag for Transit," *Mass Transit,* Vol. 5, No. 9, September 1978, pp. 24, 29-34; and Fern Schumer, "Mass Transit—Which Is the Right Way to Go?" *Forbes,* Vol. 125, No. 4, February 18, 1980, pp. 108, 112. Transit appeared to gain popularity in the 1970s, not only because it appeared to be an alternative to the automobile if petroleum fuel became truly scarce or dreadfully expensive. It also seemed to be one of the proper things that a city should have, an essential social and public service. Moreover, the expansion of transit formula grant programs to embrace small cities and rural areas expanded the base of transit support into the constituencies of many members of Congress whose districts did not include any large urban area.

15. Charles A. Lave, "The Mass Transit Panacea and Other Fallacies about Energy," *Atlantic,* Vol. 244, No. 4, October 1979, pp. 39-43; and John F. Kain, Gary R. Faulth, and Jeffrey Zax, *Forecasting Auto Ownership and Mode Choice for U.S. Metropolitan Areas,* Report No. DOT/RSPA/DPB-50/78-21 (Washington, D.C., U.S. Department of Transportation, Research and Special Programs Administration, Office of University Research, December 1978). See also, Alan Altshuler, *The Urban Transportation System: Policies and Policy Innovation* (Cambridge, Mass.: MIT Press, 1979); and John R. Meyer and Jose A. Gomez-Ibanez, *Autos, Transit, and Cities* (Cambridge, Mass.: Harvard University Press, 1981).

16. Stanley Sandler, "Can David Gunn Keep SEPTA Rolling?" *Today: The Inquirer Magazine,* Philadelphia, August 17, 1980, p. 10.

17. Rochelle L. Stanfield, "A New Plan to Target Transit Aid—But Will It Get You from Here to There?" *National Journal,* Vol. 12, No. 31, August 2, 1980, pp. 1277-81.

18. One result of the FHWA policy was to spread the influence of the transit program more widely than would have been the case had the aid been directed only to transit systems in cities of less than 50,000 people. By aiding truly rural transit services, the FHWA stewardship made the mass transit program much more of a grassroots program than would otherwise have been the case. The more rural constituency of transit that arose in the late 1970s was to prove vitally important in the survival of the program under the attacks of the Reagan administration.

19. See *Memorandum: Draft Notice of Proposed Rule-Making,* "Public Transportation for Nonurbanized Areas" (Washington, D.C.: Federal Highway Administration, March 17, 1980).

20. David C. Hackney, "The Bids Come In and Boeing Goes Out," *Mass Transit,* Vol. 6, No. 3, March 1979, p. 6. Budd, with a name change for its carbuilding subsidiary to Transit American in the 1980s, went out of the carbuilding business in 1987. The U.S. is the only major industrialized nation that has no railway carbuilding firms, much to the joy of carbuilders in Canada, France, Germany, Italy, and Japan.

21. "An Energy Boost for Builders of City Buses," *Business Week,* August 6, 1979, p. 60; and David C. Hackney, "Needed: More Buses—Fast," *Mass Transit,* Vol. 6, No. 12, December 1979, pp. 8-9, 42, 46.

22. "Flxible Will Reinforce Its 870 Buses," *Passenger Transport,* Vol. 38, No. 51, December 19, 1980, pp. 1, 9. See also *New York City's Action in Permanently Retiring Grumman-Flxible Model "870" Transit Buses,* Hearings before the Subcommittee on Investigations and Oversight of the Committee on Public Works and Transportation, House of Representatives, 98th Congress, 2d session, April 27, 1984 (New York), and May 31 and June 7, 1984 (Washington, D.C.).

23. Kenneth T. Berents, "GAO Questions UMTA's Red Tape," *Mass Transit,* Vol. 6, No. 11, November 1979, pp. 26, 28-29; and "Congress Works on Transit Oversight," *Passenger Transport,* Vol. 37, No. 12, March 23, 1979, pp. 1, 8.

24. See "Appropriations Hearings Held," *Passenger Transport,* Vol. 37, No. 15, April 13, 1979, pp. 1, 4.

25. "House Panel Approves UMTA Funding," *Passenger Transport,* Vol. 37, No. 24, June 15, 1979, pp. 1, 5.

26. "Howard Calls Hearing on Transit Trust Fund," *Passenger Transport*, Vol. 37, No. 28, July 13, 1979, pp. 1, 9.

27. See H.R. 5375, "Transportation Systems Efficiency Act of 1979," 96th Congress, 1st session.

28. See *Committee Correspondence* to the members of the AASHTO Standing Committee on Public Transportation, American Association of State Highway and Transportation Officials (hereinafter AASHTO), November 2, 1979. This includes an excerpt from the Senate Appropriations Committee's report on H.R. 4440. The figures on the level of fiscal year 1980 funding is found in AASHTO, November 9, 1979.

29. *AASHTO Committee Correspondence*, February 1, 1980. That the secretary of transportation was the former mayor of Portland, Oregon was, of course, the same sort of coincidence that had encouraged President Ford a few years earlier to see that Detroit was earmarked to receive $600 million in federal transit funds. It should be noted that at about this time Congress became much more involved in the large capital grants for rail systems, new starts, or expansion. The amount of money and the validity of the projects was such as to spark political interest and ribbon-cutting fever.

30. The *AASHTO Committee Correspondence* of February 1, 1980, includes the complete text of the proposed legislation along with a summary of salient points.

31. *AASHTO Committee Correspondence,* February 19, 1980.

32. "House Panel Hears Carter Transit Request," *Passenger Transport*, Vol. 38, No. 13, March 28, 1980, pp. 1, 9.

33. For coverage of the ups and downs of the windfall profits tax see Douglas B. Feaver, "Carter Weighs Oil Tax to Fund Transportation Needs," *Washington Post,* March 23, 1979; "Oil Concerns' Gains from Price Decontrol Would Be Taxed Heavily in Carter Plan," *Wall Street Journal*, April 4, 1979; "Windfall Tax to Transit," *Passenger Transport,* Vol. 37, No. 14, April 6, 1979, pp. 1, 7; "Mondale Details Plan to Assist Mass Transit," *Louisville Courier-Journal*, August 23, 1979; Anita Altenbern Pesses, "APTA Joins Windfall Tax Coalition," *Passenger Transport,* Vol. 37, No. 40, October 5, 1979, pp. 1, 9; "APTA Attends White House Meeting to Push Oil Tax," *Passenger Transport,* Vol. 37, No. 41, October 12, 1979, pp. 1, 9; "Windfall Tax Clears Senate Panel," *Passenger Transport,* Vol. 37, No. 43, October 26, 1979, pp. 1, 3; *AASHTO Committee Correspondence,* November 15, 1979; "Senate Adds, Subtracts on Oil Tax Bill," *Passenger Transport,* Vol. 37, No. 44, November 23, 1979, pp. 1, 4; "Senate Goes Ahead on Oil Profits Tax," *Passenger Transport,* Vol. 37, No. 49, December 7, 1979, p. 1; "Watching Washington; Windfall Profits and Rail Transit," *Railway Age,* Vol. 180, No. 23, December 10, 1979, p. 12; "Senate Votes $178 Billion Oil Tax Bill," *Passenger Transport,* Vol. 37, No. 51, December 21, 1979, pp. 1, 7; "Windfall Compromise Reached," *Passenger Transport,* Vol. 37, No. 52, December 28, 1979, p. 3; and " 'Easy Parts' Left on Oil Tax Bill," *Passenger Transport,* Vol. 38, No. 4, January 25, 1980, pp. 1, 6.

34. *AASHTO Committee Correspondence,* April 7, 1980: "The [Senate Budget] Committee also rejected any transit energy initiative funding for fiscal year 1980. The FY 81 level would also not have any funding for transit energy initiative funding and would further propose cuts of $600 million from the current budget authority level." Also, "Highway Construction, Mass Transit Aid May Be Delayed by Slashes in Spending," *Congressional Quarterly*, April 12, 1980, pp. 951-52; "Senate Budget Panel Slashes Transit Aid," *Passenger Transport*, Vol. 38, No. 17, April 25, 1980; and *APTA Bulletin*, May 12, 1980.

35. *AASHTO Committee Correspondence,* May 8, 1980; "Formula Plan Revised by Senate Panel," *Passenger Transport*, Vol. 38, No. 19, May 9, 1980, pp. 1, 13; and "UMTA Answers Questions about Accessibility Rules," *Passenger Transport*, Vol. 38, No. 20, May 16, 1980, pp. 1, 9.

36. *AASHTO Committee Correspondence,* May 15, 1980.

37. *AASHTO Committee Correspondence,* May 19, 1980.

38. *AASHTO Committee Correspondence,* May 20, 1980.

39. "Conferees OK 1980 Transit Supplemental," *Passenger Transport,* Vol. 38, No. 21, May 23, 1980, pp. 1, 9.

40. "Opposition Mounts on 1981 Budget," *Passenger Transport,* Vol. 38, No. 22, May 30, 1980, p. 1.

41. One tier strictly used population and population density; another tier had 85 percent of its money apportioned to cities with population over 700,000, with the remainder of the money distributed to all other urbanized areas, both on the basis of population-population density. The bus tier apportioned its funds for bus replacement only, again on the basis of population-population density; the rail tier apportioned its funds on the basis of transit and commuter rail miles in an urbanized area.

42. *APTA Bulletin,* June 3, 1980.

43. *APTA Update,* June 1980.

44. "Conferees Add to Transit Aid," *Passenger Transport,* Vol. 38, No. 24, June 13, 1980, p. 3.

45. *AASHTO Committee Correspondence,* June 13, 1980; "House Panel Sets UMTA 1981 Budget," *Passenger Transport,* Vol. 38, No. 25, June 20, 1980, p. 1. Under the prevailing law, Tier 1 money went to all urbanized areas on the formula basis of 50 percent population and 50 percent population density. Tier 2 money was apportioned 85 percent to cities of 700,000 people and larger; the remaining 15 percent was divided amongst the remaining urbanized areas. Once the initial division of Tier 2 money was made, the allocation between urban areas was made on the population-population density basis. Tier 3 money was for routine bus replacements and at the time was divided on the population-population density formula. Tier 4 money was for rail operations and depended on a formula based on fixed route mileage and certain operating factors.

On the matter of cutting back on Section 18 appropriations, there is some evidence that Washington did not fully understand how long it took to get a grant proposal together in small city and rural areas where the level of expertise in grantsmanship was typically small.

46. *AASHTO Committee Correspondence,* June 26, 1980; "Senate Approves Transit Aid Bill by 79-15," *Passenger Transport,* Vol. 38, No. 26, June 27, 1980, pp. 1, 9. In looking at a complex formula, it is obvious that particular interests, perhaps even a singular one, are being addressed.

47. "UMTA Gets $330 Million Compromise," *Passenger Transport,* Vol. 38, No. 30, July 25, 1980, pp. 1, 9.

48. Arthur E. Wiese, "Transit: Riding Out the Election," *Mass Transit,* Vol. 7, No. 11, November 1980, pp. 12-13.

49. Ibid., p. 13; See also "GOP Would Stop Subway Says Rhoades," *Passenger Transport,* Vol. 38, No. 43, October 24, 1980, p. 1. In retrospect, Reagan gave a fair indication of the policies his administration would follow in rolling as much responsibility as possible back on to state and local government.

50. Wiese, "Riding Out the Election," pp. 13, 26.

51. Ibid., p. 26; see also similar sentiments expressed in *A Republican Position Statement of a Transit Policy for the Future,* prepared by the transportation subcommittee of the Republican National Committee's Advisory Council on Human Concerns, February 1980. The transportation subcommittee was chaired by Robert Patricelli, UMTA administrator during the Ford administration.

52. Wiese, "Riding Out the Election," pp. 26-27.

53. See a letter from Herbert Scheuer, Acting Executive Vice President of APTA, dated July 30, 1980. This was a time of transition at APTA; Bill Stokes had resigned to take a senior position with the ATE Management and Service Company, and a permanent executive vice president had not yet been chosen. Other senior APTA staff filled in, and this transitional period did not appear to have a negative effect on the lobbying effort. Fred Burke was still at work developing the strategy for APTA and handling some tactical matters as well.

54. *AASHTO Committee Correspondence,* July 25, 1980; Rochelle L. Stanfield, "A New Plan to Target Transit Aid," *National Journal,* August 2, 1980, pp. 1277-1281; and "Lutz: Section 5 Will Change This Year," *Passenger Transport,* Vol. 38, No. 29, July 18, 1980, p. 1.

55. "1981 UMTA Budget Is $4.6 Billion," *Passenger Transport,* Vol. 38, No. 39, September 26, 1980, pp. 1, 6.

56. "New York Won't File 504 Transition Plan," *Passenger Transport,* Vol. 38, No. 39, September 26, 1980, pp. 1, 9; "New York's MTA Rejects Handicapped Rules," *National Journal,* September 27, 1980, p. 1627; and "APTA Backs New York on 504 Rule," *Passenger Transport,* Vol. 38, No. 42, October 17, 1980, pp. 1, 10.

57. "Senator Lugar to Chair Subcommittee on Housing and Urban Affairs," *Action Lines* (monthly newsletter of the Indiana Association of Cities and Towns), December 1980, pp. 1, 6.

58. "House Begins Work on 1980 Transit Bill," *Passenger Transport,* Vol. 38, No. 48, November 28, 1980, pp. 1, 9; and "House OKs Transit Bill," *Passenger Transport,* Vol. 38, No. 40, October 3, 1980, p. 1; also see *Congressional Record,* House, December 4, 1980, pp. H11959-H11965.

59. Reggie Todd, "Senate Filibuster by Lugar Kills Mass Transportation Bill," *Nation's Cities Weekly,* Vol. 3, No. 50, December 22, 1980, p. 8; "Bill Cutting Transit Funds to State Blocked by Lugar," *Indianapolis Star,* December 16, 1980; and "Bill Dies as Congress Adjourns," *Passenger Transport,* Vol. 38, No. 51, December 19, 1980, pp. 1, 9. The reader will remember that Indianapolis, Senator Lugar's hometown, would have had its federal funding cut under the new formula. There was no political mileage in the legislation for Senator Lugar.

60. Dan Balz, "Panel Urges New Urban Policy for '80s" (from the *Washington Post),* *Louisville Courier-Journal,* December 26, 1980; and Dan Balz, "Leaders in Older Cities Protest Urban Policy Proposed in U.S. Study" (from the *Washington Post), Louisville Courier-Journal,* December 27, 1980.

61. This point is belabored in George Smerk, *Urban Mass Transportation: A Dozen Years of Federal Policy* (Bloomington: Indiana University Press, 1974), Chapters 6-8.

62. Senator Lugar resigned his place as chairman of the subcommittee on housing and urban affairs on January 28, 1981. Lugar wanted one of his trusted staffers to head the subcommittee staff, but Senator Garn, the chairman of the parent committee, wanted to name all staff members. Garn refused Lugar's resignation and a compromise was struck; Lugar retained the subcommittee chairmanship and was to name two staff members.

11. FEDERAL MASS TRANSIT POLICY IN THE AGE OF REAGAN, 1981-1982

1. *Business Week* noted the defeat of the transit measure with some regret in an editorial entitled "Helping Mass Transit Before It Collapses." The editor noted: "The problem . . . is that mass transit is dying—of insufficient resources and excessive regulation—just at a time when it is essential to energy conservation and urban rehabilitation. By increasing federal help and putting it on a five-year basis, the proposed bill would have put a solid base under the shaky transit financing of the cities. At the same time, it would have given the three remaining manufacturers of mass transit equipment reason to stay in the business. . . . With gasoline costs rising and the cities close to collapse, a federal investment in mass transit is bound to be a high-pay proposition." *Business Week,* No. 2669, December 29, 1980, p. 172. Later on in the high summer of the Reagan administration, *Business Week* would not be so supportive of mass transportation.

2. Even before that inauguration, there was disquietude over what the Reagan administration was saying it would do. As a sample of reporting and concern see: "Editorial: Mischievous Ideas about 'Realism' on Cities," *Louisville Courier-Journal,* December 30, 1980; Albert R. Karr, "Slashed Transportation Aid, Regulation Are Proposed by Policy Team to Reagan," *Wall Street Journal,* December 15, 1980; Dan Balz, "Panel Urges New

Urban Policy for '80s," *Louisville Courier-Journal,* December 26, 1980 (from the *Washington Post*); and Dan Balz, "Leaders in Older Cities Protest Urban Policy Proposed in U.S. Study," *Louisville Courier-Journal,* December 27, 1980 (from the *Washington Post*).

3. This push to turn over to private enterprise as much as possible of what had traditionally been public enterprise was to become a major policy of the Reagan administration. What was intended, apparently, was to inject competition into government and thereby lower costs. For example, city trash collection could be put up for bid among private firms; if the lowest bid was cheaper than using city employees and equipment, then the task would be carried out privately. Some Reaganist zealots ("Reaganites") took privatization—as it came to be called—as an end in itself rather than as a means to the end of less costly government.

4. What became the guideline for the development of the administration's position on transportation was found in a report on transportation, delivered to the new president between his election and inauguration by the task force chaired by Claude Brinegar, former secretary of transportation under President Richard M. Nixon. The report said that "mass transit spending should be cut and that new subway projects probably shouldn't be funded. It also said that transit subsidies to cover day-to-day expenses, which then currently totaled about $1 billion a year, should be discouraged, or at least be based more on ridership and less on a city's population. Demonstration grants for urban mass transit pilot projects . . . should be eliminated because they are often worthless or politically motivated. . . . It also urged that provisions of existing law giving labor unions considerable influence over transit activities should be curtailed and that 'jitney' service, special company commuter runs and other private forms of transit services should be encouraged." Albert R. Karr, "Slashed Transportation Aid, Regulation Are Proposed by Policy Team to Reagan," *Wall Street Journal,* December 15, 1980. See also Douglas B. Feaver, "Reagan Advisory Group Averse to Mass Transit Aid," Washington Post Service, published in the *Philadelphia Inquirer,* December 28, 1980; and "Transit Aid Reviewed by Reagan Panel," *Passenger Transport,* Vol. 39, No. 1, January 2, 1981.

The position of the Brinegar task force report varied considerably from the position taken in *A Republican Position Statement on a Transit Policy for the Future,* prepared for the Transportation Subcommittee of the Republican National Committee's Advisory Council on Human Concerns, Washington, D.C., Republican National Committee, February 1980. A major thrust of this policy statement was a twenty-year investment program. A sampling: "Our objectives should be no less than to equip every major urban area in the country with effective transit and ridesharing systems. . . . The important thing is to set transit investment objectives and to work toward them with a stable financing base until they are met." To implement this program the position paper called for ". . . the creation of a trust fund of at least twenty years' duration to provide a stable source of federal funds for mass transit and ridesharing capital investment" (pp. 7-12). The last testament of the Carter administration toward transportation policy in general is to be found in *Transportation Agenda for the 1980s: Issues and Policy Directions,* U.S. Department of Transportation, August 1980.

5. Office of Management and Budget, *America's New Beginning: A Program for Economic Recovery,* pp. 5-3; reproduced in American Association of State Highway and Transportation Officials, Standing Committee on Public Transportation, February 19, 1981 (hereinafter *AASHTO Committee Correspondence*). David Stockman's black book and its somber message was both a source of wonder and fear because he was a legend as a wizard of the budget. As the only person in Washington who understood what all the numbers meant—a thought daunting to members of Congress and the bureaucracy, who regarded the budget with some awe. As the magician who prepared and understood the budget, Stockman won grudging admiration from even his critics and the many he rubbed the wrong way. Alas, Wizard Stockman admitted that his work was but a soda straw, in a series of interviews with reporter William Greider revealing Stockman's concern about the Reagan administration's flawed tax and budget program. See William Greider, *The Educa-*

tion of David Stockman and Other Americans (New York: E. P. Dutton, Inc., 1982). In his behavior and his testimony, Stockman drew considerable attention to himself; the strongly negative reaction to his statements and proposals took the spotlight and the opprobrium away from Ronald Reagan, leaving the president unsullied by the program devastation and general nastiness proposed by Stockman. Also see David Stockman, *The Triumph of Politics* (New York: Avon Books, 1987), pp. 149-151, 160-161, 171-178, 215, 227-228, 296-297, 344, 363-364, and 420-423.

On the issue of deliberate deficits to force the cessation of federal programs, see Daniel Patrick Moynihan, *Came the Revolution: Argument in the Reagan Era* (New York: Harcourt Brace Jovanovich, 1988), pp. 279-288.

6. Stockman, *Triumph of Politics,* pp. 4-28; see also "New Administration Studies Changes in Transit Program," *Passenger Transport,* Vol. 39, No. 7, February 13, 1981, pp. 1 and 9. There was legitimate concern about the way transit was organized and delivered well back into the 1970s. In the private as well as the public ownership eras of transit, it was considered a natural monopoly and almost always operated as such. This may have made sense at one time, but critics of the status quo called for a restructuring of transit delivery to meet the reality of the times. The aims of the changes would have been to improve the quality of service and its responsiveness to public need while at the same time restraining cost increases. For a particularly good discussion of this viewpoint, see David Jones, *Urban Transit Policy: An Economic and Political History* (Englewood Cliffs, N.J.: Prentice-Hall, Inc., 1985), especially Chapter 10. Serious concerns were raised about the falling productivity of the transit industry in several studies, as in John R. Meyer and Jose Gomez-Ibanez, *Autos, Transit and Cities* (Cambridge, Mass.: Harvard University Press, 1981), Chapter 4. See also *Improving Transit Productivity and Cost-Effectiveness: A Review of Promising Strategies,* prepared by Charles River Associates Inc., for the Office of Budget and Policy, Urban Mass Transportation Administration, U.S. Department of Transportation, Washington, D.C. (CRA Report No. 784.30), November 1987.

7. Not everyone agreed with the Reagan position on the federal role in transit, as seen in the editorial in the March 18, 1981, *Louisville Courier-Journal* entitled "Because It Meets National Needs, Public Transit Deserves U.S. Aid." The editorial ended with the statement: "The worst that can be said of federal transit aid is that it comes with too many strings attached. The answer is judicious pruning of unneeded regulations—not the Reagan meat-ax approach." One could take heart in understanding that the Reagan position was one consistent with certain dogma; it had nothing to do with the reasons that shaped the original nature of federal involvement in mass transit or the plainly visible urban transportation problems in which transit might play a salutary part.

8. For reactions to the budget cuts proposed for transit see: "Letter to APTA Members," February 23, 1981, Washington, D.C., American Public Transit Association; APTA Policy, Sixth Annual Legislative Conference, March 1981, Summary Statement, Washington, D.C., American Public Transit Association; Albert R. Karr, "Transit Systems Try to Derail Cutbacks in U.S. Aid by Pushing Development Role," *Wall Street Journal,* March 10, 1981; "Budget Cuts, Transit Plans Topics at APTA Legislative," *Passenger Transport,* Vol. 39, No. 11, March 13, 1981, pp. 1 and 8; Arthur E. Wiese, "Transit Advocates Resent Biting the Budget Bullet," *Mass Transit,* Vol. 8, No. 5, May 1981, p. 20; "Budget Cuts Topic at Rapid," *Passenger Transport,* Vol. 39, No. 24, June 12, 1981.

9. The $36.9 billion spending cuts were sliced from the Carter budget proposals— and they were not easy to swallow for some members of either party. See Helen Dewar and Richard L. Lyons, "Senate Unit Rebuffs Reagan in Rejecting his '82 Budget," *Louisville Courier-Journal,* April 10, 1981 (from the *Washington Post*). As the year moved on, various budget numbers were tried out as the Congress sought to pass a budget reconciliation bill. As of July 1, the Reagan-endorsed budget resolution for transit was $3.880 billion and the House appropriations subcommittee approved $3.938 billion, which included a $231 million carry-over from 1981. See *Public Transit Report,* Vol. 9, No. 12, July 1, 1981, pp. 97-98.

10. Reagan's proposal for transit in September was $3.5265 billion; the conference committee agreed on $3.8611 billion.

11. "Conferees OK 1982 Fund Ceiling," *Passenger Transport,* Vol. 39, No. 46, November 13, 1981, pp. 1 and 9.

12. See Helen Dewar, "The Time Has Finally Come for Congress to Pay Its Bills," *Louisville Courier-Journal,* Nov. 11, 1981 (from the *Washington Post*); "U.S. Spending Bill Goes to the Wire," *Passenger Transport,* Vol. 39, No. 47, November 20, 1981, pp. 1 and 9.

13. Editorial: "Mischievous Ideas Abound in New 'Realism' on Cities," *Louisville Courier-Journal,* December 30, 1980. The clouds also show in "Big Cuts in Federal Spending?" *Railway Age,* Vol. 182, No. 1, January 12, 1981, pp. 15-17.

14. Interest payments for the $1 trillion debt for fiscal year 1981 were calculated to be $96 billion. See Brian Horrigan and Aris Protopapadakis, "Federal Deficits: A Faulty Gauge of Government's Impact on Financial Markets," *Business Review,* Federal Reserve Bank of Philadelphia, March-April 1982, p. 8. No one could have dreamed how much the federal budget and the national debt would grow in the next years of the Reagan administration. David Stockman, however, saw his worst fears realized. Stockman, *Triumph of Politics,* Chapter 10.

15. "Administration's Budget 'Hit List' Bites Sharply into Transportation," *Traffic World,* Vol. 185, No. 7, February 16, 1981, p. 18; and, for even more of the flavor, see "The Stockman Report," *Railway Age,* Vol. 182, No. 4, February 23, 1981, p. 5.

16. Digging into the history of U.S. public transportation has convinced the author that, because of increasing public expenditures on highways by all levels of government in the 1920s, public ownership of transit would have been a wise move at that time. Ridership was high and the subsidies necessarily small in most places. Really top-notch transit (as exemplified in Toronto, Canada), would have made demands for highway improvements more modest. It may have also helped to orient suburban development to public transportation to a larger degree. Public investment at critical times could have avoided the serious problems of deferred maintenance that still plagues the transit industry. This is an example of the "what if" school of history.

17. The subject of institutionalization was covered in two doctoral dissertations at the Indiana University School of Business; they are: Harry S. Ross, "The Developing of Community Support for Public Transit Systems," School of Business, Indiana University, 1977; and Ellen Foster Curtis, "Institution Building in European Mass Transit," School of Business, Indiana University, 1979. Both of these dissertations are bound together in a volume entitled *Essentials for Success in Transit,* Division of Research, School of Business, Indiana University, Bloomington/Indianapolis, 1979. See also Harry S. Ross and George M. Smerk, "Institutionalization of Mass Transportation in the Community," *Traffic Quarterly,* Vol. 33, No. 4, October 1979, pp. 511-524.

18. To be realistic, transit occupies an extraordinary position as a public service. Transit charges its users a fee each time it is used, unlike police or fire protection or the use of a public library. Also, unlike other public services, it does not have a monopoly position; this is often a source of discomfort for those in government or transit management who have a background in public administration because transit demands careful marketing, something that would be ludicrous for other public services.

Subsidies are a strange and often emotional issue in American society. Virtually everything and everyone is subsidized in one way or another, and I believe most people fool themselves that such is not the case. Or, as I tell my students, many persons take the position that "A subsidy for me helps economic growth, guards the nation against Communism, strengthens constitutional democracy, strengthens the Chicago Cubs' batting averages, guarantees the prosperity of private enterprise, and assumes a bumper crop of wheat; a subsidy for you rots your moral fiber." There is a lot of rotten moral fiber about.

19. The point APTA was making was that transit is important to business in helping to maintain and improve property values as well as to transport customers and employees to places of business. See Albert R. Karr, "Transit Systems Try to Derail Cutbacks in U.S.

Aid by Pushing Development Role," *Wall Street Journal,* March 10, 1981; "APTA Tells House Transit Means Business," *Passenger Transport,* Vol. 39, No. 29, July 17, 1981, pp. 1 and 8; and "Transit Means Business," *Mass Transit,* Vol. 8, No. 10, October 1981, pp. 10-11, and 42.

20. For an excellent discussion of the need to refocus transit, see Jerry B. Schneider, *Transit and the Polycentric City* (Seattle: Urban Transportation Program, Department of Civil Engineering and Urban Planning, University of Washington) September 1981 (DOT-1-81-33).

21. This point is discussed in detail in Smerk, *Urban Mass Transportation,* pp. 250-256.

22. See *Transit Fact Book,* 1981 Edition (Washington, D.C.: American Public Transit Association, 1981), pp. 53-54, 58, and 60.

23. For a detailed and lucid discussion and analysis, see Alan Altshuler, *Urban Transportation Systems* (Cambridge, Mass.: MIT Press, 1979); and John R. Meyer and Jose A. Gomez-Ibanez, *Autos, Transit, and Cities* (Cambridge, Mass.: Harvard University Press, 1981).

24. See Altshuler, *Urban Transportation Systems.*

25. Interesting information on transit use and population trends can be found in William O'Hare and Milton Morris, *Demographic Change and Recent Worktrip Travel Trends,* Volume 1, *Final Report;* Volume II, *Statistical Tables;* prepared by the Joint Center for Political Studies for the UMTA Technical Assistance Program, U.S. Department of Transportation, Washington, D.C., February 1985 (Report No. UMTA-DC-09-7009-85).

26. A good recapitulation of the Reagan-inspired transit woes from early 1981 can be found in Arthur E. Wiese, "Reagan Administration: A Time of Not-So-Great Expectations for Transit," *Mass Transit,* Vol. 8, No. 3, March 1981, pp. 6, 8, 11 and 18. See also Luther S. Miller, "Reagan Pro and Reagan Con," *Railway Age,* Vol. 182, No. 6 [incorrectly given as No. 4], March 9, 1981, p. 5. A placid and friendly man, the president may have been bemused by the realization that, if he did not get ulcers, he certainly gave them to other people.

27. See *Soaring Transit Subsidies Must Be Controlled,* Comptroller General of the United States, U.S. General Accounting Office, Washington, D.C. (CED-81-28), February 26, 1981. The main points of the report are presented in the Digest, pp. i-vi. Discussion of the level of the deficit is on pp. 26-27. The thrust of the Reagan Urban Mass Transportation Administration toward greater use of competitive private sector involvement was stimulated by concern over the steadily mounting transit deficits and subsidies.

28. Neal R. Peirce and Carol Steinbach, "Cuts in Transit Aid May Hurt but Could Have a Silver Lining," *National Journal,* April 4, 1981, pp. 568-572; the Stockman quote is on p. 571.

29. See Albert R. Karr, "Mass Transit Riders Are Facing Prospect of Higher Fares to Keep Systems Running," *Wall Street Journal,* March 17, 1981; "New York Commuters Face 20% to 50% Rise in Rail and Bus Fares," *Wall Street Journal,* March 18, 1981; Richard J. Meislin, "Higher Fare Looms at the End of the Transit Tunnel," *New York Times,* March 22, 1981; Harlan S. Byrne, "Mass Transit Is Facing a Financial Crisis; Service Cutbacks and Higher Fares Loom," *Wall Street Journal,* April 2, 1981; "Transit Fares Climb Again, 45 cents Average," *Passenger Transport,* Vol. 39, No. 17, April 24, 1981, pp. 1 and 10. Information on total vehicle miles of transit are in *Transit Fact Book 1981* (Washington, D.C.: American Public Transit Association, May 1981), p. 34.

30. See "Can't Get There from Here," *Newsweek,* Vol. 91, No. 22, June 1, 1981, pp. 44-45; "Local Transit Lines Search for New Funds," *Business Week,* No. 2691, June 8, 1981, p. 64; John Curley, "Looming Shutdown of Chicago's Transit Heats Up Rivalry between City, Downstate," *Wall Street Journal,* June 16, 1981; Peter Derrick, "The NYC Mess: Legacy of the 5¢ Fare," *Mass Transit,* Vol. 8, No. 7, July 1981, pp. 12-13, and 26; David Young, "Transit's Fiscal Fiasco," *Mass Transit,* Vol. 8, No. 7, July 1981, pp. 6-8, 11, 20, and 24; and "Sick and Inglorious Transit," *Time,* Vol. 118, No. 3, July 20, 1981.

31. *The Financial and Productivity Problems of Urban Public Transportation,* Hearings before the Subcommittee on Investigation and Oversight of the Committee on Public Works and Transportation, House of Representatives, 97th Congress, 1st session, June 23-25 and October 21, 1981, Washington, D.C., U.S. Government Printing Office, 1981. Hereinafter referred to as *Oversight Hearings,* 1981.

32. *Oversight Hearings,* 1981, p. 2.

33. The opening testimony by Louis J. Gambaccini and Alan Altshuler covers most of the points made throughout the hearings; see *Oversight Hearings,* 1981, pp. 6-112. Testimony on labor issues may be found on pp. 460-520; the impact on public policy of the move to the Sunbelt is found on pp. 236-254; and the cost of providing transit is covered on pp. 316-329. The position of the administration is found in the testimony of UMTA Administrator Arthur H. Teele; his statement and subsequent discussion are on pp. 343-421. This author's testimony is on pp. 421-460.

34. The U.S. is not alone in providing subsidies to help urban mass transportation. A study initiated by the European Conference of Ministers of Transport, using the expertise of the Transport and Road Research Laboratory of Great Britain, investigated the policies of 18 countries. The aims of the subsidy programs, embracing both capital and operating assistance, although not very explicitly stated in most countries, could be boiled down to the following categories:

1. To create a better urban environment (less congestion, pollution, visual intrusion and improved traffic safety) by means of higher modal share to public transport
2. To create a more efficient, less costly, less energy-dependent solution to urban transport
3. To preserve the existing forms of towns
4. To maximize the use of existing public transport infrastructure and services
5. To maintain a "viable" public transport service as insurance against the future
6. To satisfy specific transport "needs" (e.g. of the old, the young, the handicapped, people without an available car, and people in remote areas)
7. To help "captive" users who, through no fault of their own, may be paying more and more for less and less service.

See P. H. Bly, F. V. Webster, and Susan Pounds, "Effects of Subsidies on Urban Public Transport," *Transportation,* Vol. 9, No. 4, December 1980. For some additional thoughts on transit subsidies see: Ata M. Kahn, "Urban Public Transit Subsidy Policy in a Resource Constrained Future," *Journal of Advanced Transportation,* Vol. 15, No. 3, Winter 1981, p. 195.

35. See, for example, "New Administration Studies Changes in Transit Programs," *Passenger Transport,* Vol. 39, No. 7, February 13, 1981, pp. 1 and 9; *AASHTO Committee Correspondence,* February 19, 1981. The Department of Transportation submitted draft legislation in early March of 1981; the proposal called for the elimination of operating aid by 1985, use of 1970 census data for apportionment of operating assistance, repeal of the half-fare requirements for elderly and handicapped, softening the requirement for accessibility of transit equipment, and phase-out of operating aid to cities of population under 50,000 in 1983. See *AASHTO Committee Correspondence,* March 4, 1981, and March 5, 1981. See also "Reagan Finishes Transit Proposals," *Passenger Transport,* Vol. 39, No. 12, March 20, 1981, p. 1. The DOT revised its original legislative submission by calling for local option in the matter of providing transit service for the handicapped; see *AASHTO Committee Correspondence,* May 12, 1981. See also Douglas B. Feaver, "Reagan Policies Could Throttle Mass Transit," *Washington Post,* May 28, 1981. Senator Lugar sought to find a compromise to soften the blow of the removal of operating subsidies by stretching out at least some of the subsidies until 1984; see Joseph P. Shapiro, "Demos Protest Lugar's Transit Bill," *Evansville Press,* June 10, 1981; *AASHTO Committee Correspondence,* May 18, 1981; and "Senate Hears Transit Spending Proposals," *Passenger Transport,* Vol.

39, No. 21, May 21, 1981, pp. 1 and 9. Representative Robert W. Edgar of Pennsylvania pushed for a program to continue aid for maintenance proposals; he explained his position in "Mass Transit Systems Must Be Maintained," an editorial in the *Philadelphia Inquirer,* June 10, 1981; see also "Maintenance Aid Proposed in House," *Passenger Transport,* Vol. 39, No. 16, April 17, 1981, pp. 1 and 9. See also Barbara Harsha, "NLC Policy Group Hears Latest Transit Proposals," *Nation's Cities Weekly,* Vol. 4, No. 24, June 15, 1981, pp. 1 and 11. For Congressman Howard's position see "Washington Outlook: Transportation," *Business Week,* No. 2695, July 6, 1981.

36. See J. Richard Munro, "Business Executives Find Burden on the Poor Harmful to the Nation," *Louisville Courier-Journal,* March 28, 1981; William B. Franklin, "Business Outlook: Hopes for Upturn Could Soon Be Dashed," *Business Week,* No. 2732, March 29, 1982, p. 27; "*Business Week*/Harris Poll: 'No Confidence' for Reaganomics," *Business Week,* No. 2732, March 29, 1982, p. 40; "Reagan's Polarized America," *Newsweek,* Vol. 99, No. 14, April 5, 1982, pp. 17-29; Roger Ricklefs, "Bosses' Confidence in Reaganomics, Though Still Strong, Has Dropped," *Wall Street Journal,* April 14, 1982; William Wolman, "Commentary: Why the Recovery Keeps Backing Away," *Business Week,* No. 2735, April 19, 1982; Robert Furlow, "Recession Worsened, New Figures Confirm," *Louisville Courier-Journal,* April 22, 1981; "What Keeps Interest Rates Up," *Business Week,* No. 2737, May 3, 1982; Adam Clymer, "Reagan's Economic Policies, GOP Losing Public Support, Poll Shows," *Louisville Courier-Journal,* May 29, 1982 (from the *New York Times*).

37. The Congressional Budget Office prepared an extensive study on the economy, the federal budget and the means that might be used to reduce the federal deficit. See *A Report to the Senate and House Committees on the Budget—Part I: The Prospects for Economic Recovery; Part II: Baseline Budget Projections for Fiscal Years 1983-1987; Part III.: Reducing the Federal Deficit: Strategies and Options,* Washington, D.C., Congressional Budget Office, February 1982. The strategies suggested in Part III of the study are: increasing user fees, shifting responsibilities to state and local governments, targeting funds to the neediest areas and populations, and reducing subsidies for private sector activities. See Part III, pp. 108-119.

38. See "The Decaying of America," *Newsweek,* Vol. 100, No. 5, August 2, 1982, pp. 12-18.

39. See Charles Bonser, "A Parachute for the Reagan Intergovernmental Reform," *Business Horizons,* Vol. 24, No. 4, July-August 1981, pp. 2-9; "Howard: Feds' Aid Cuts Give Ball to States," *Passenger Transport,* Vol. 39, No. 34, August 21, 1981, pp. 1 and 9; "State and Local Government in Trouble," *Business Week,* No. 2711, October 26, 1981, pp. 135-181; *Federalism Initiative,* The White House, Office of the Press Secretary, January 27, 1982 (mimeographed fact sheet, 32 pages); Arthur E. Wiese, "New Federalism: Transit on Its Own," *Mass Transit,* Vol. 9, No. 3, March 1982; "States of the Nation," *Time,* Vol. 119, No. 6, February 8, 1982, pp. 16-20; David Broder, "Federalism: Challenge in Redistricting," *Louisville Courier-Journal,* February 17, 1982 (from the *Washington Post*); "States Could Stall a Rebound," *Business Week,* No. 2732, March 29, 1982, pp. 30-31; "National Governors' Association Federalism Proposal for Transportation," *AASHTO Committee Correspondence,* April 5, 1982; "Reagan Suggests Cities, States Boost Aid to Mass Transit," *Wall Street Journal,* April 19, 1982; Robert Roberts, "Billions for Defense, but Only One Cent for Transit," *Modern Railroads/Rail Transit,* Vol. 37, No. 5, May 1982, pp. 40-43; Rochelle L. Stanfield, "The New Federalism Is Reagan's Answer to Decaying Highways, Transit Systems," *National Journal,* June 12, 1982, pp. 1040-1044; James Gerstenzang, Associated Press, "Reagan Trims New Federalism, Switching Fewer Programs to States," *Louisville Courier-Journal,* July 14, 1982; "Reagan Plan: Transit May Go to States," *Passenger Transport,* Vol. 40, No. 29, July 16, 1982, pp. 1 and 9.

40. See "FY 1983 Transit Budget Topic at Senate Hearing," *Passenger Transport,* Vol. 40, No. 19, May 7, 1982, pp. 1 and 29. For discussion of the budget, authorizing legislation, safe harbor leasing, and the Lewis proposal, see the "Washington Watch" section on p. 3. For discussion of Secretary Lewis's gas tax proposal see Arthur W. Wiese, "Drew

Lewis: Putting the Monkey on Backs of State and Local Government," *Mass Transit,* Vol. 8, No. 10, October 1981, p. 14; "A High Powered Drive to Raise the Gas Tax," *Business Week,* No. 2715, November 23, 1981; Lee Walczak, "Streamrolling a Gasoline Tax," *Business Week,* No. 2724, February 1, 1982, p. 91; "Lewis: Gas Tax Issue 'Still Open,' " *Passenger Transport,* Vol. 40, No. 9, February 26, 1982, pp. 1 and 9; "User Fee Support Grows," *Passenger Transport,* Vol. 40, No. 13, March 26, 1982, p. 1; "User Fee Increases Rejected," *Passenger Transport,* Vol. 40, No. 21, May 21, 1982, pp. 1 and 9.

41. See a letter of transmission from Frank B. Francois, executive director of the American Association of State Highway and Transportation Officials to the chief administrative officers of AASHTO and to the members of the Standing Committee on Public Transportation, dated April 14, 1982; this included the letter of transmission by Secretary Lewis and a copy of the draft legislation. Also see "Two Transit Legislative Proposals Introduced: Administration," *Passenger Transport,* Vol. 40, No. 16, April 16, 1982, pp. 1 and 10.

42. Report from the Committee on Public Works and Transportation, U.S. House of Representatives, No. 2, April 1982, p. 3. Section 9 was the section of the Act covering technical studies (planning) until the 1978 Amendments to the Urban Mass Transportation Act of 1964, when technical studies was moved to Section 8. What the proposed Section 9 did was provide some room for operating aid. Paradoxically, as 1982 went by, when UMTA officials made speeches calling for no more operating aid under the formula grant program through Section 5, many noted that the statement was, indeed, true; something that looked very much like operating aid would be available under Section 9. The mills of the gods grind extremely fine.

43. During the time of the legislation discussion in 1982, many Republican supporters of the Reagan administration's wish to do away with as much of the federal transit programs as possible agreed that the administration would be successful because there were only nine states, usually not specified, in which transit was really important. As a result, there would be support for transit from only 18 senators. Apparently this logic neglected the fact that many senators, both Republicans and Democrats, from states not highly urbanized were still supporters of the transit legislation. The reason behind this was that the Section 18 program of the 1978 transit legislation had made federal money available to non-urbanized areas and to rural places. Transit, or at least public transportation and support for it, was more ubiquitous than many encamped within the Washington Beltway were aware of or were willing to admit.

44. See *Congressional Record-Senate,* April 15, 1982, pp. S.3599-83601; *AASHTO Committee Correspondence,* April 19, 1982; and "Two Transit Legislation Proposals Introduced by D'Amato," *Passenger Transport,* Vol. 40, No. 16, April 16, 1982, pp. 1 and 9.

45. *AASHTO Committee Correspondence,* April 26, 1982, side-by-side comparison.

46. See "Transit Bills Topic on Capitol Hill," *Passenger Transport,* Vol. 40, No. 18, April 30, 1982, pp. 1 and 9. In the House subcommittee hearings, Administrator Teele requested an appropriation of $3.15 billion for transit, down 15 percent from 1982 and a 33 percent cut from the 1982 level. Ibid., pp. 1 and 8. Additional information on the hearings may be found in *AASHTO Committee Correspondence,* May 3, 1981; and "FY 1983 Transit Budget Topic at Senate Hearing," *Passenger Transport,* Vol. 40, No. 19, May 7, 1982, pp. 1 and 29.

47. See *Congressional Record-Senate,* May 6, 1982, pp. S.4680-S 4683; and *AASHTO Committee Correspondence,* May 7, 1982.

48. See American Public Transit Association, *A Newsletter for APTA Associate Members,* Washington, D.C., May 4, 1982; also see *News From: Committee on Public Works and Transportation,* May 11, 1982.

49. See *Surface Transportation Assistance Act of 1982; Report Together with Additional Views to Accompany H.R. 6211,* House of Representatives, 97th Congress, 2d session, Report No. 97-555, May 17, 1982, pp. 2, 4, 41-42. The committee approved the authorization of $71.1 billion for highways and transit over a four-year period. See *News From:*

Committee on Public Works and Transportation, May 13, 1982. See also AASHTO Committee Correspondence, May 14, 1982; and "Congress Sets Transit Bills," *Passenger Transport,* Vol. 40, No. 20, May 14, 1982, pp. 1 and 6.

50. See "Teele Hints of Legislative Compromise," *Passenger Transport,* Vol. 40, No. 20, May 14, 1982, pp. 1 and 6. As additional evidence of the Reagan administration's willingness to compromise when that was the only way to move matters along, at the annual meeting of the Indiana Transportation Association, David Gogol, a key staff member of Senator Richard Lugar's subcommittee on housing and urban affairs, reiterated the point that, given some slight reduction or phasing down, operating aid would be continued. Moreover, capital would be generously defined to include what many would consider operating costs.

51. *AASHTO Committee Correspondence,* May 14, 1982. The Urban Mass Transportation Administration prepared a *Comparative Analysis of Three Senate Legislative Proposals,* showing the capital assistance levels of the three bills; it is dated May 17, 1982.

52. See "Washington Watch," *Passenger Transport,* Vol. 40, No. 22, May 28, 1982, p. 3.

53. See letter to all APTA members from Executive Vice President Jack R. Gilstrap, dated May 20, 1982.

54. See "Capital Need, Funds Viewed," *Passenger Transport,* Vol. 40, No. 22, May 28, 1982, pp. 1 and 5. The reason this is important is that capital expenditures mean buying and building things, projects that create jobs; elected officials are always sensitive to job creation. Jobs were an important matter during the time of the lamentably high level of unemployment in mid-1982.

55. *AASHTO Committee Correspondence,* June 11, 1982; "Transit Bills, Budget Plans Affect Industry," *Passenger Transport,* Vol. 40, No. 25, June 18, 1982, pp. 1 and 9; and *AASHTO Committee Correspondence,* June 25, 1982.

56. See American Public Transit Association, Letter to all Members from Jack R. Gilstrap, Executive Vice President, July 2, 1982. In the markup of the DOT appropriation by the subcommittee on transportation of the House Appropriations Committee, in contravention of the administration's feeling about new rail transit starts, $230 million was earmarked as follows: $30 million, Baltimore; $19.5 million, Buffalo; $59.5 million, Miami; $50.5 million, Detroit; $25 million, Santa Clara; $35 million, Los Angeles; $500,000, Denver; and $20 million, Atlanta. *Committee Correspondence,* July 28, 1982; and "House Sets Spending Level," *Passenger Transport,* Vol. 40, No. 31, July 30, 1982, pp. 1 and 9. The *AASHTO Committee Correspondence* of August 20, 1982, includes a Full Committee Print, dated August 19, 1982, of the Department of Transportation and Related Agencies Appropriation Bill, 1983; AASHTO notes that the bill directs Section 5 and Section 18 formula funding to be based on both the 1970 and 1980 census data unless a new formula was provided in the authorization bill.

57. See *News From: Committee on Public Works and Transportation,* August 10, 1982; "House Panel Calls for One-Year Bill," *Passenger Transport,* Vol. 40, No. 33, October 1, 1982, p. 1; and *AASHTO Committee Correspondence,* August 13, 1982. APTA continued to push for H.R. 6211 in a *Legislative Update* of August 13, 1982, even though the situation appeared virtually hopeless because of the congressional recess from August 10 until after Labor Day—this document contains an excellent review of the features of H.R. 6211.

58. See "Transit Funds Detailed as House Vote Looms," *Passenger Transport,* Vol. 40, No. 34, August 20, 1982, pp. 1 and 8; "Washington Watch," *Passenger Transport,* Vol. 40, No. 37, September 10, 1982, p. 3; "Congressman Benjamin Dead at 47," *Passenger Transport,* Vol. 40, No. 37, September 10, 1982, p. 1; and "Congress Tackles Key Rail Issues," *Railway Age,* Vol. 183, No. 17, September 13, 1982, pp. 10 and 12. On the safe harbor issue, see also Bill Paul, "Washington," *Modern Railroads,* Vol. 37, No. 10, October 1982, p. 25.

59. See "Appropriations Panel Acts on Transit Bill," *Passenger Transport,* Vol. 40, No. 38, September 17, 1982, pp. 1 and 9; and "House Moves Bill Along," and "Washington Watch," *Passenger Transport,* Vol. 40, No. 39, September 24, 1982, pp. 1 and 4; and

AASHTO Committee Correspondence, October 1, 1982. Under a continuing resolution, the money provided is available in proportion of the time period of the resolution relative to a year; this continuing resolution was for a period of about 21 percent of 365 days.

60. "Congress Zeroes in on Jobs," *Business Week,* No. 2767, November 29, 1982; "President Backs 5¢ User Fee," *Passenger Transport,* Vol. 40, No. 48, November 26, 1982, pp. 1 and 9; and "User Fee Would Spur Economy," *Passenger Transport,* Vol. 40, No. 47, November 19, 1982, pp. 1 and 8. While this was going on, the *Washington Post* was running a series on the need for capital replenishment of transit facilities, detailing the decrepitude in New York. See Douglas B. Feaver, "Patching Together Public Transit," *Washington Post,* November 23, 1982.

61. See "Washington Watch," *Passenger Transport,* Vol. 40, No. 48, November 26, 1982, p. 4.

62. See S.3072, Federal Public Transportation Act of 1982, 97th Congress, 2d session; "Congress Acting on Legislative Proposals," *Passenger Transport,* Vol. 40, No. 49, December 3, 1982, pp. 1 and 8; and *AASHTO Committee Correspondence,* December 3, 1982.

63. See "Transportation Bill Passed: Funds for Fiscal 1983 Approved," *Passenger Transport,* Vol. 40, No. 52, December 24, 1982, pp. 1 and 9.

64. See "House Backs User Fee," *Passenger Transport,* Vol. 40, No. 50, December 10, 1982, p. 1; "Senate Filibuster Threatens User Fee Bill," ibid.; and "Transportation Bill Passed; Authorizing Legislation Enacted," *Passenger Transport,* Vol. 40, No. 52, December 24, 1982, pp. 1 and 5. See also *AASHTO Committee Correspondence,* December 27, 1982; Making Appropriation for the Department of Transportation and Related Agencies for the Fiscal Year Ending September 30, 1983, and for Other Purposes, Conference Report to accompany H.R. 7019, 97th Congress, 2d session, House of Representatives, Report No. 97-960, pp. 16-18; and Conference Report on H.R. 6211, *Congressional Record-House,* December 21, 1982, pp. H 10793-H 10798, and H 10821-H 10825.

65. See letter and fact sheet from Arthur E. Teele, Jr., administrator, Urban Mass Transportation Administration, dated December 23, 1982.

66. *AASHTO Committee Correspondence,* December 28, 1982. The best guesstimates for the revenue arising from the penny on the gas tax devoted to transit was $1.1 billion per year. In actuality the take proved to be higher—probably about $1.4 to $1.5 billion by 1986. Because the authorization was set at $1.1 billion, there were hundreds of millions of dollars in the Mass Transit Account that could not be spent. This was just fine with the Reagan Administration because it made the deficit seem to be less.

67. At the end of 1982 there was a loss of the government leadership that could have potentially forged such goals. Congressman Adam Benjamin, Jr., departed through his sudden death; Senator Richard Lugar, chairman of the Senate subcommittee on housing and urban affairs, left the scene by his resignation from the parent Committee on Banking, Housing and Urban Affairs, in order to conform with Republican rules in the Senate that no senator should serve on more than two committees at any one time; and Secretary of Transportation Drew Lewis, who convinced the president to support the gas tax, resigned to take a position in private industry.

68. A major challenge to the transit industry was a substantial reduction in the budget for transit to a point well below the amount authorized. For example, the initial apportionment of federal transit money for fiscal year 1983 was only 65 percent of the total budgeted. Originally this was to be added to later on; however, there were fears at the time that the Office of Management and Budget would not permit any more money to be apportioned. Moreover, the budget authority for fiscal year 1983 called for UMTA to receive $4.345 billion; President Reagan's budget proposals for fiscal year 1984 called for $3.915 billion. See *AASHTO Committee Correspondence,* February 1, 1983; "DOT Releases 1983 Mass Transit Apportionments," *U.S. Department of Transportation News,* February 1, 1983; "Howard Opposes Transit Funding Cutbacks," *News From: Committee on Public Works and Transportation,* February 1983; *AASHTO Committee Correspondence,* February 3,

1983; and "Transit Budget Slashed," *Passenger Transport,* Vol. 41, No. 5, February 4, 1983, pp. 1-2.

12. THE URBAN MASS TRANSPORTATION ACT AT 20

1. Letter to the President of the Northern Indiana Commuter Transportation District (NICTD) from Ralph Stanley, Administrator, Urban Mass Transportation Administration, Washington, D.C., September 7, 1984.

2. See, for example, K. H. Schaeffer and Elliott Sclar, *Access for All: Transportation and Urban Growth* (New York: Columbia University Press, 1980), especially Chapters 4 and 6; and Kenneth T. Jackson, *Crabgrass Frontier: The Suburbanization of the United States* (New York: Oxford University Press, 1985), Chapter 14. Also see James A. Dunn, Jr., *Miles to Go: European and American Transportation Policies* (Cambridge, Mass.: The MIT Press, 1981), Chapters 5, 7 and the introduction to Part 4.

3. "Federal Transit Assistance Program Turns Twenty," *Passenger Transport,* Vol. 42, No. 28, July 9, 1984, pp. 1 and 8.

4. There is some question as to whether the support for President Reagan in his election in 1980 was positive for his programs or mostly negative toward Jimmy Carter. President Carter was seen as being ineffective, and his lack of trenchant policy and performance did not appeal to the American public. It was widely held that Reagan had put into words in his campaign and later in his presidential pronouncements what many people felt or what they perceived and were unable to voice as effectively themselves. Much the same was probably behind Reagan's overwhelming re-election success in 1984. In any event, the conservative position toward government, which had reposed in dogmatic slumber since the Coolidge and Hoover administrations, awoke and found strong support in the national leadership. A major help to President Reagan in his first administration was a Senate that was dominated by his fellow Republicans for the first time since the 1950s.

5. John L. Palmer and Elizabeth V. Sawhill, eds., *The Reagan Experiment: An Examination of Economic and Social Policies under the Reagan Administration* (Washington, D.C.: The Urban Institute Press, 1982), p. 5.

6. Ibid., p. 6. See also David Stockman, *The Triumph of Politics* (New York: Avon Books, 1987), especially Chapter 10, the Epilogue, the Appendix, and the Postscript.

7. Ibid., p. 10.

8. "Reagan's Major Budget Proposals for Fiscal 1984," *Wall Street Journal,* January 31, 1983; Walter Pincus and Ward Sinclair, "Recession's Tab Is Picked Up by Uncle Sugar," *Louisville Courier-Journal,* February 2, 1983 (from the Washington Post Service); Jonathan Fuerbringer, "Recession Sets Record for Length—Inflation Aims for Ten-Year Low," the *Louisville Courier-Journal,* December 22, 1982 (from the New York Times News Service); Victor F. Zonana, "Is the U.S. Middle Class Shrinking Alarmingly? Economists Are Split," *Wall Street Journal,* June 20, 1984; Ashok Chandrasekhar, "Gauging Living Standards in '84," *Wall Street Journal,* July 24, 1984; James J. Kilpatrick, "Republicans Should Forget Landslide Victory Talk," *Louisville Courier-Journal,* June 14, 1984; Tom Wicker, "Reagan's Ax Is a Dull and Stupid Blade," *Tallahassee Democrat,* December 11, 1984; and George Will, "Thatcher Felt the Budgetary Anger of the Middle Class; Reagan Will Too," *Louisville Courier-Journal,* December 10, 1984. David Broder, a distinguished columnist of the *Washington Post,* contributed a number of thoughtful articles about the situation; these were published in the *Louisville Courier-Journal* on the dates shown. "The Trillion Dollar Tax Cut Loss," February 2, 1983; "Elements Seem to be Conspiring to Insure a Big Reagan Victory," November 14, 1983; "Democrats May Face Plan to Make Reagan's Revolution Permanent," February 1, 1984; "Similarities to 1972 Election Aside, This Year's Winner Isn't Preordained," April 18, 1984; "Democratic Party Is in Danger of Losing Its Franchise on Hope," May 30, 1984; "Historically, Presidential Challengers Have the Right to Say 'I Told You So,' " June 13, 1984; and "Britain's 19th Century View of America Is Still a Clear One," July 2, 1984.

9. Edward Weiner, "Devolution of the Federal Role in Urban Transportation," *Journal of Advanced Transportation*, Volume 18, No. 2, Summer 1984, pp. 114-115. Clearly, much of the emphasis in this approach is on costs that are justified by benefits. Lamentably, it is often far more difficult for analysis to derive or discover benefits than costs. In such cases it is all too common to let the costs call the tune, making it easy to justify discarding an unwanted activity. Moreover, some analysts would hold that, apart from cost-benefit analysis being a structure of cobweb erected on a bubble, varying assumptions can make or break almost anything. Two points: reasonable persons would agree that careful economic analysis, such as cost-benefit analysis, is highly desirable. Reasonable persons would also agree that carrying out such analysis objectively can be extraordinarily difficult; in clumsy hands cost-benefit analysis may be little more than a neat ordering of prejudices. How one views cost-benefit analysis, of course, is subject to the principle of ox-goring.

10. Ibid., pp. 116 and 118.

11. Adapted from tables in ibid., pp. 116 and 118.

12. See, for example, those concerns for the need to continue the federal-state-local partnership noted in *A Study on Future Direction of Public Transportation in the United States,* Standing Committee on Public Transportation, American Association of State Highway and Transportation Officials, Draft Report, November 1984, especially Chapter 4; hereinafter called *AASHTO Future Directions.*

13. The U.S. Bureau of Labor Statistics showed, for example, a 7.1 percent revised national rate of unemployment in June 1984 and a preliminary rate of 7.5 percent for July 1984 (both rates seasonally adjusted). Figures published August 30, 1984, in *Labor Force Estimates* by Indiana Employment Security Division, Labor Market Information and Statistical Services, Indianapolis.

14. Allan Parachini, "Employment: Boom Time in the 90s," *Louisville Courier-Journal,* September 12, 1982 (from the Los Angeles Times Service); "The Revival of Productivity," *Business Week,* No. 2828, February 13, 1984; Robert Roberts, "Washington: RPI Starts Transit Campaign," *Modern Railroads,* Volume 37, No. 12, December 1982, page 23; Edward F. Patrick, "U.S. Transit: Opportunity Ahead for Better Times," *Mass Transit,* Vol. 11, No. 5, May 1984, p. 8 and supra; "Toward the Year 2000: Thoughts about Transit," *Mass Transit,* Vol. 11, No. 5, May 1984, pp. 12-14. The *AASHTO Future Directions* report postulated a shortfall in operating funds for transit of $4.61 billion by 1989; of the approximately $14 billion in operating cost, $4.34 billion would be generated by operating revenue, $4.0 billion would be captured by state and local government, and $87 million would be contributed by the federal government. APTA projected capital needs of $7.292 billion per year between 1984 and 1989, with federal money plus local share equaling only $4.274 billion per year for a shortfall of $3.018 billion each year. See pp. 3-1 to 3-8.

15. The Urban Mass Transportation Administration, through the Transportation Research Board, sponsored a thought-provoking conference at Woods Hole, Massachusetts, in late September 1982, which explored some of the principal issues in transit. See *Future Directions of Urban Public Transportation,* Special Report 199, Washington, D.C., Transportation Research Board, 1983. The report contains many interesting thoughts and ideas, including the notion of well-planned, intentional cities, rather than the accidental cities we have had in the past. See Richard V. Knight, "Changes in the Economic Base of Urban Areas: Implications for Urban Public Transportation," pp. 46-53. On the always captivating subject of the future of the city, see Gail Garfield Schwartz, *Where's Main Street, U.S.A.?* (Westport, Conn.: Eno Foundation for Transportation, Inc., 1984).

16. George Will, "Future May Seem Daunting, but Everyday Is a Miracle," *Louisville Courier-Journal,* December 31, 1982; "How Strong a Recovery?" *Business Week,* No. 2775, January 31, 1983; Roger Lowenstein, "Energy Outlook," *Wall Street Journal,* February 24, 1983; "Fielding a Recovery," *Wall Street Journal,* February 25, 1983; and Robert L. Simison, "Car Trouble," *Wall Street Journal,* November 1, 1983. On the issue of controlling labor costs, see "Business Will Keep Labor in Line," *Business Week,* No. 2822, December 26, 1983.

17. An unseemly flap developed between UMTA and the New York City Transit Authority over the permanent withdrawal from service of 851 Grumman-Flxible Advance Design Buses without notice to Congress, New York State, or UMTA, which were the sources of the money to buy the buses. No one really won the conflict; it was quite grotesque. See "Federal Official Calls NYCTA Bus Action Fiscally Irresponsible," *News Release,* U.S. DOT, Office of Public Affairs, Washington, D.C., April 27, 1984, UMTA 09-84. The situation was of sufficient interest to stimulate a congressional hearing. See *New York City's Action in Permanently Retiring Grumman-Flxible Model "870" Transit Buses,* Hearings before the Subcommittee on Investigations and Oversight of the Committee on Public Works and Transportation, House of Representatives, 98th Congress, 2d session, April 27, 1984 (New York, N.Y.); May 31, June 7, 1984 (Washington, D.C.: U.S. Government Printing Office, 1985). The buses were eventually taken back by Flxible (after Grumman sold out its interest) and rebuilt for service at places other than New York.

18. See, for example, David Young, "RTA, Other Transit Units Getting Tough with Unions," *Chicago Tribune,* November 7, 1982; David Young, "Chicago-Downstate Division of Transportation Aid Outlined," *Chicago Tribune,* December 15, 1982; Pat Wingert, "Transit Running into a Mass of Problems," *Chicago Sun-Times,* December 21, 1982; Gary Washburn, "RTA Ridership on Commuter Lines Slid Again in '83," *Chicago Tribune,* March 25, 1984; "RTA Takes Big Step toward Fiscal Health with Major Loan Repayment," *Indianapolis Star,* April 8, 1984; Pat Wingert, "Bill to Hit RTA Plan Labor Curbs," *Chicago Sun-Times,* April 13, 1984, and "RTA Finally in Black," *Chicago Sun-Times,* April 2, 1984; and Harlan S. Byrne, "Chicago's Troubled Transit System Takes Unorthodox Steps to Attract Commuters," *Wall Street Journal,* January 17, 1984.

19. "Philadelphia Travelers Face Transit Shut Down," *Louisville Courier-Journal,* December 27, 1982; Robert Roberts, "A Better Break for Amtrak," *Modern Railroads,* Volume 37, No. 12, December 1982, pp. 55-56; and Michael Roddy, "Philadelphia Transit System Tunnels Out of 'PITS' toward a Brighter Day," *Louisville Courier-Journal,* January 1, 1984. For a view of the serious transit problem in Pittsburgh, see Joe Grata, "PAT Addresses Budget Woes by Hinting Huge Service Cuts," *Pittsburgh Press,* December 22, 1984. A good example of the deterioration of transit facilities came to light immediately after SEPTA opened a new downtown commuter rail tunnel that linked the rail lines of the former Pennsylvania Railroad and the former Reading Company. Shortly after the trains began to use the tunnel, running through from one side of the city to the other, a bridge on the former Reading Line was found to be in such seriously decomposed condition that service had to be halted. See Amy Linn, "Bridge Breaks Commuter Link," *Philadelphia Inquirer,* November 18, 1984; and Amy Linn and Robin Clark, "SEPTA Bridges Neglected; Condition of Many Called Deplorable," *Philadelphia Inquirer,* November 19, 1984. Reporters found that SEPTA was so financially strapped that it had no money in its budget for bridge work.

20. Washington's Metro Rail System had its knuckles rapped in the U.S. General Accounting Office Study entitled *Metro Needs to Better Manage Its Railcar Procurement* (GAO/NSIAD—83-26, August 10, 1983). For information on New York, see "NYCTA: A Big Plan Gets Bigger," *Railway Age,* Vol. 184, No. 6, June 1983, pp. 67-69; Tom Shedd, "Five-Year MTA Program Moves Ahead in New York," *Modern Railroads,* Vol. 38, No. 10, November 1983, pp. 26-32; Ari L. Goldman, "The City's Subway Chief Decides to Take a Walk," *New York Times,* August 21, 1983; "Federal Official Calls NYCTA Bus Action Fiscally Irresponsible," *News Release,* Office of Public Affairs, U.S. Dept. of Transportation, UMTA 09-84; "Industry News: UMTA Blasts NYCTA, MTA Sues Grumman," *Metropolitan,* Vol. 80, No. 3, May-June 1984; and M. A. Farber wrote a three-part series on the decline of the New York subway in the *New York Times,* July 30, July 31, and August 1, 1984. See also George M. Smerk, "Advice for the Chairman," *Bus Ride,* Vol. 19, No. 8, January, 1984, p. 88. The brighter side was revealed in Fox Butterfield, "On New York Walls, the Fading of Graffiti," *New York Times,* May 6, 1988, and "Subways' Next Frontier: Quality of Life," *New York Times,* June 5, 1988.

21. Jill Bettner, "The Boys on the Bus," *Forbes,* Vol. 133, No. 6, March 12, 1984, p. 94; Joe B. McKnight and *Enquirer* staff, "Flxible Buses Still in Demand, Despite Past," *Cincinnati Enquirer,* May 6, 1984; "Industry News: Neoplan to Build Another U.S. Facility," *Metropolitan,* Vol. 80, No. 1, January-February 1984, p. 5; and David Young, "GM Revives Older Model in Drive for New Life in Bus Market," *Chicago Tribune,* August 6, 1983. On the more negative side, see "A Rescue That Will Not Succeed," *Maclean's,* Vol. 97, No. 48, November 26, 1984, p. 58. On the issue of average age of equipment, the American Public Transit Association provided interesting information based on a survey of its membership in *Transit Passenger Fleet Inventory, 1984 Edition* as of January 1, 1984, Washington, D.C.: American Public Transit Association, 1984. The APTA survey showed that there was a total of 53,752 buses owned and leased reported by United States transit systems that were APTA members (most of the large transit properties and many of the smaller ones were members, so the APTA figures show a fairly good picture of the transit industry); of these, 50,562 were in active service. Reviewing the figures, there were more 1980-built buses in active service—4,947 or 9.8 percent of the fleet—than any other single year models. Two hundred forty-four 1960 model buses were still in active service (0.5 percent of the total fleet), and there were still over 1,000 buses of 1966 vintage in service as of January 1, 1984. UMTA considered twelve years to be the economic life of a standard transit bus; 79.8 percent of the buses in the U.S. fleet were 12 years of age or less. The average age of the total number of buses was 8.3 years; the average of the buses in active service was 7.8 years. See Table 4, pp. A-08, A-09, A-10.

22. Bill Paul, "Publisher's Perspective: All That Glitters Is Not Gold," an editorial in *Metropolitan,* Vol. 80, No. 5, September-October 1984, p. 168.

23. Frank E. Shaffer, "News Front: Transit Looks for Bonanza," *Modern Railroads,* Vol. 37, No. 12, December, 1982, p. 11; Robert Reinhold, "Jammed Freeways Lead Sunbelt to Mass Transit," *New York Times,* October 24, 1982; John Schnapp, "America Breaks Off Its Romance with the Car," *Wall Street Journal,* February 28, 1983; Bill Paul, "Many New Train Systems Being Planned as States and Cities Grapple with Traffic," *Wall Street Journal,* March 4, 1983; Albert R. Karr, "Mass Transit Systems Are Being Aided by Downtown Firms as Two-Way Street," *Wall Street Journal,* November 26, 1982; and Christopher Waddell, "Transit Operators on Twisting Route to Better Revenues and More Riders," *Financial Post,* January 7, 1984.

24. The well-publicized openings of the first phases of the Miami and Baltimore rapid transit systems promised to lure even more cities to consider rail transit as a serious alternative. The Baltimore system opened in November of 1983; its first piece of line totaled eight miles. Another six miles was completed in 1986. The first part of the all-elevated Miami system opened in May of 1984 and included only about half of its 20-mile length; it did not yet include the absolutely essential people mover system that linked the rapid transit line with the actual business center of Miami. The people mover opened in 1986.

For more information, see Jim Pettigrew, Jr., "Directions in Mass Transit," *Sky,* Vol. 12, No. 11, November 1983, pp. 36-43; Douglas B. Feaver, "Rail Transit Booming," *Washington Post,* April 17, 1984; "The Californian Rail Transit Conversion," *Metropolitan,* Vol. 80, No. 3, May-June, 1984, pp. 80-91; Dan Morris, "Pre-Marketing for Today and Tomorrow," *Metropolitan,* Vol. 80, No. 3, May-June, 1984, pp. 72, 74, 77-78 and 80; and in the same number of *Metropolitan,* Bill Paul, "Rapid Transit in Miami—Finally," pp. 82, 85, 88, and 92; "Miami Opens Metrorail on May 20," *Passenger Transport,* Vol. 42, No. 20, May 14, 1984, pp. 1 and 12; "Rail Starts and Extensions Plan Unveiled," *Transactions,* December 1983-January 1984, Metropolitan Transportation Commission, Berkeley, California; Bill Fahrenwald, "Watching Washington: Jobs Bill Will Juice Up Amtrak and Transit Budgets," *Railway Age,* Vol. 184, No. 5, April 1983, p. 17; Frank Gilman, "New Life for Light Rail," ibid., p. 65; Tom Shedd and Karen Beamer, "User Fee Creates Dedicated Source of Transit Funds," *Modern Railroads.,* Vol. 38, No. 5, May 1983, pp. 41-52; and "Three Billion Dollars for Light Rail?" *Railway Age,* Vol. 184, No. 6, June 1983, p. 71.

The information on the 53 new-start projects is from the Urban Mass Transportation Administration and was published in *Urban Transport News,* Vol. 12, No. 12, June 11, 1984, pp. 93-95.

25. "Reagan Signs Funding Bill," and "Washington Watch," *Passenger Transport,* Vol. 41, No. 33, August 22, 1983, pp. 1 and 4.

26. See "Transit Budget Slashed," *Passenger Transport,* Vol. 41, No. 5, February 4, 1983, pp. 1-2; "Howard Opposes Transit Funding Cutbacks," *News From: Committee on Public Works and Transportation,* February 1, 1983; Judy Sarasohn, "Mass Transit Budget Prompts Complaints," *Congressional Quarterly,* February 5, 1983, p. 310; "APTA Attacks Administration Proposals," and "Dole Defends Transit Cuts," *Passenger Transport,* Vol. 41, No. 8, February 25, 1983, pp. 1 and 8.

27. See "Transit Budget Slashed." For subsidies that are considered blessed, see Eugene H. Methvin, "Power Play on the Potomac," *Reader's Digest,* September 1984, Vol. 125, No. 749, pp. 125-128. The article reviews a situation in which very unneedy and not very rural Americans benefit by subsidies through the Rural Electrification Administration and enjoy cheaper electricity than would otherwise be the case. For an interesting approach to the reasons for the decline of urban public transportation and governmental support for transit, see Glenn Yago, *The Decline of Transit: Urban Transportation in German and U.S. Cities, 1900-1970* (New York: Cambridge University Press, 1984), in particular Chapters 4 and 7. For a slightly different view see David Jones, *Urban Transit Policy: An Economic and Political History,* Chapter 3 and especially pp. 63 and 64.

28. It is very difficult to get a hammerlock on philosophy, but the following may help: Arthur E. Wiese, "OMB: Urban Transit's Nagging Nemesis," *Mass Transit,* Vol. 10, No. 1, January 1983, p. 16. The lack of a love affair between OMB and transit was not new and certainly could not be blamed on the Reagan administration. The article points out that transit has been the site of a constant battleground between the Department of Transportation and the Office of Management and Budget. A good reason for this was that there was no overall political consensus in the country for the role of transit, a truth which was also made obvious by the fact that there were no workable goals and objectives for urban mass transportation policy. As the reader will recall, this was a different attitude at OMB than had prevailed in the early 1960s.

29. "Lugar: 'Act Provisions Will be Realized,'" *Passenger Transport,* Vol. 41, No. 5, February 4, 1983, pp. 1 and 5; "Administration's Budget Unconscionable Says Transit Industry," *American Public Transit Association News,* February 23, 1983; and "Anderson: Budget Cuts Are Inconsistent," *Passenger Transport,* Vol. 41, No. 6, February 11, 1983, pp. 1 and 9. The position of the American Public Transit Association was to be expected; for example, Jack Gilstrap, executive vice president of APTA, knew that he was "getting tired of hearing from federal officials about how much money has been poured into transit over the years. Overall, maybe there's been $22 billion [a more accurate figure is $30 billion] used in this program over the 18 or so years," he said. "I like to remind people that based on this year's defense budget alone, that's about 5 to 6 weeks of what the Pentagon gets." Cited in Arthur E. Wiese, "OMB: Urban Transit's Nagging Nemesis," p. 19.

30. See "APTA Seeks Resolution," *Passenger Transport,* Volume 41, No. 9, March 4, 1983, p. 1; Carl Nolte, "A Plan to Cut Transit Aid," *San Francisco Chronicle,* March 15, 1983; "Reagan's Fast Shuffle on Gas Tax for Transit," editorial in the *Philadelphia Inquirer,* February 24, 1983, p. 20A; "The New UMTA Budget: Did Reagan Renege?" *Railway Age,* Vol. 184, No. 3, March 1983, p. 24; "Transit Cuts Will Cancel Gas Tax Gain, Expert Says," *Seattle Post-Intelligencer,* April 12, 1983; and "Transit Funding: Triumph . . . Then Tribulation," *Mass Transit,* Vol. 10, No. 4, April 1983, p. 14.

31. "APTA Delegates Urged to Push Full Federal Transit Funding," *Passenger Transport,* Vol. 41, No. 15, April 15, 1983, pp. 1 and 9. On the ability of the states to pick up the slack, note the Michigan DOT *Uptran Update,* Vol. 7, No. 7, October 1982 and the headline section "Public Transportation Program Drastically Reduced for Fiscal Year 1983."

32. *An Analysis of the President's Budgetary Proposals for Fiscal Year 1984,* prepared at the request of the Senate Committee on Appropriations, Congress of the United States, Congressional Budget Office, February 1983, pp. 123, 124, and 126. An interesting view of what the federal government considered to be operating aid and not operating aid is presented in an editorial in *Metro* Magazine. The editor noted that it was virtually impossible to find out anything about the operating assistance to the Federal Highway Administration or the Federal Aviation Administration. The point is that the operating budgets of these agencies don't have a section defined as "Operating Assistance." For example, vehicle maintenance is considered as operating assistance in the UMTA budget but maintenance is "capital" assistance in the Federal Highway Administration budget. It is impossible to pull operating assistance out of the budgets of most agencies at DOT. What brings it to notice is that it is very clearly defined in transit. The writer notes, "If the wise men of the Potomac judge operating assistance to be poor public policy for transit, why isn't it for other modes?" See Bill Paul, "The Kumquat School of Accounting," *Metro,* Vol. 80, No. 3, May-June, 1984, p. 104.

33. Bill Fahrenwald, "Watching Washington: The House Giveth, the Senate Taketh Away," *Railway Age,* Vol. 184, No. 9, September 1983, p. 20. The 1984 budget for UMTA was as follows: Administrative expense, $29.2 million; research and development, $54.8 million; formula grants, $2.388 billion; discretionary grants, $1.225 billion; interstate transfer grants, $295.4 million; and Washington Metro, $250 million, for a total of $4,242,590,000. Places earmarked for capital aid were as follows: Baltimore, $3.5 million; Miami, $35 million; Detroit, $45 million; Santa Clara County, $40 million; Los Angeles, $117.2 million; Jacksonville, $15.5 million; Atlanta, $91.25 million; San Diego, $8.3 million; Portland, $44.25 million; St. Louis, $2 million; Buffalo, $2 million. See "House Approves Spending Bill," *Passenger Transport,* Vol. 41, No. 25, June 27, 1983, pp. 1 and 15; and "Transportation Funds Cleared by House Panel," *Wall Street Journal,* June 17, 1983.

34. "Reagan Slashes Operating Assistance in Fiscal Year '85 Budget," *Metro,* Vol. 80, No. 2, March-April 1984, pp. 5-6; Cliff Henke, "Rapid Transit under Siege," *Metro,* Vol. 80, No. 1, January-February 1984, p. 16; Christopher Conte, "Cities Push for Costly Rail Systems, but Federal Aid Is Severely Limited," *Wall Street Journal,* February 16, 1984; and "States and Cities Are an Easy Target for More Cuts," *Business Week,* No. 2835, March 26, 1984, p. 90. Gratuitous violence was done to transit's cause in the editorial entitled "Mass Transit Rides the Gravy Train," *Business Week,* No. 2857, August 27, 1984, p. 102.

35. *An Analysis of the President's Budgetary Proposals for Fiscal Year 1985,* prepared at the request of the Senate Committee on Appropriations, Congress of the United States, Congressional Budget Office, February 1984, p. 98. See also *Department of Transportation and Related Agencies Appropriation Bill 1985,* House of Representatives, 98th Congress, 2d session, Report 98-833, June 11, 1984, Report to Accompany H.R. 5813; the Urban Mass Transportation Administration discussion is found on pages 75 to 89. Also see *Department of Transportation and Related Agencies Appropriation Bill, 1985,* United States Senate Committee on Appropriations, Calendar No. 1057, 98th Congress, 2d session, Report 98-561, July 17, 1984, Report to Accompany S.2852; pp. 57 to 69.

36. Serious commentary or discussion on the need for some means of making the tough decisions on new starts predates by more than a year the formal issuance of the new starts policy on May 18 of 1984. For example, see "Opening Statement of Arthur E. Teele, Jr., Urban Mass Transportation Administration, Department of Transportation, before the Senate Appropriations Committee, Subcommittee on Transportation, April 14, 1983." On page 9 of his testimony Mr. Teele states:

> We take note that the Congress in the Conference Report accompanying the Surface Transportation Assistance Act of 1982 has specifically stated that "a fair share of the funds to be set aside for mass transit be allocated to rapidly growing cities to fund cost-effective new rail construction." I also note Secre-

tary Dole's commitment in Congressional Testimony that she will support full consideration of funding new starts for the recently established transit trust fund.

In considering potential projects, we will pay particular attention to the following factors:

Results of alternative analysis;
Cost effectiveness; and
The degree of local financial commitment, including evidence of stable and dependable funding sources to operate the system.

Other factors that may be considered include:

Degree of local government support;
Degree of private sector support;
Degree of community support; and
Participation of minority business

However, in no case will UMTA support any new start project that is not cost-effective. This Administration firmly believes that prior to the commencement of new starts, existing commitments, rail modernization and both extraordinary and ordinary bus demands must be fully addressed. APTA has estimated that approximately $3 billion of projects in these categories are currently ready to proceed.

Another commentary on new starts, similar in many ways to Mr. Teele's testimony, is found in the report of the Senate Appropriations Committee on the fiscal year 1984 appropriations; the key part reads:

The Committee is concerned that the allocation of contract authority pro-vided by Public Law 97-424 for new transit systems be undertaken as part of a balanced national policy. Such projects, therefore, should be funded within the framework of the following new start policy:

(1) In evaluating potential new start projects, the Department will pay particular attention to the following factors: the results of alternatives analysis; the degree of cost-effectiveness; and the degree of local financial commitment, including evidence of stable and dependable funding sources to maintain and operate the system. Other factors that may be considered include degree of community support, and participation of minority business.

(2) The Department may work toward establishing a funding goal of 50 percent of the total cost of a new start proposal that should be met from funding sources other than Section 3. The Committee recognizes that some urbanized areas may need a transitional period to identify additional sources of funds. Consequently, this goal may not be initially met in all instances. The 50 percent goal could be met through the sum of the local match for the Federal project plus those proposal costs that are funded totally from sources other than Section 3, such as Section 9 and interstate transfer funds which are appropri-ately used for this purpose.

See *Department of Transportation and Related Agencies Appropriation Bill, 1984,* 98th Con-gress, 1st session, Senate Report No. 98-179, Calendar No. 284, Committee on Appropri-ations, July 14 (legislative day, July 11), 1983, pp. 73-74.

The subject of new starts came up once more in testimony of UMTA Administrator Ralph Stanley (who replaced Arthur Teele in the fall of 1983) before the House Committee on Public Works and Transportation:

During the last year, UMTA has been reviewing its policy with respect to new start rail projects. We have considered a number of factors to develop a policy to allocate the scarce Section 3 funds for new starts including factors specified by the Appropriations Committees. UMTA will fund new start projects that are cost-effective, in addition to paying particular attention to factors such as the results of alternatives analysis and the degree of local financial commitment, which would include evidence of stable and dependable funding sources to operate the system. Other factors we may consider include the degree of local government support, the degree of private sector support, the degree of community support, and the participation of disadvantaged business enterprises.

The degree and reliability of local financial commitment and cost-effectiveness are the two primary criteria in this quantifiable measure of relative merit. We place a great deal of emphasis on the degree of local financial commitment for a new start project. This factor not only rewards those communities that make the greatest local fiscal effort, but also obviously maximizes the return on the Federal investment. We strongly encourage localities to take a fresh look at methods of generating new funding resources for major rail investments. UMTA will work towards a goal of financing 50 percent of total project costs from sources other than discretionary grants. Taxes, local bonds, and other financing concepts should be considered to develop reliable sources of funding that do more than simply meet a twenty-five percent local share level. The measure of cost-effectiveness we will rely on is marginal cost, that is, added cost per added passenger, also taking into account travel time savings for existing riders as a desired benefit. The lower the marginal cost, the more cost-effective the project and the better return of the federal dollars invested.

See "Statement of Ralph L. Stanley, Administrator, Urban Mass Transportation Administration, Before the Subcommittee on Surface Transportation of the Committee on Public Works and Transportation, House of Representatives on Tuesday, February 7, 1984."

Stanley continued in a similar vein in his testimony before the Appropriations Committee in the House; see "Opening Statement of Ralph L. Stanley, Urban Mass Transportation Administrator, Department of Transportation, before the House Appropriations Committee, Subcommittee on Transportation, March 21, 1984," pp. 6-7 in *American Association of State Highway and Transportation Officials, Standing Committee on Public Transportation, April 27, 1984*. From hereafter the items from AASHTO sources will be dubbed *AASHTO Committee Correspondence* with the date.

37. *A Detailed Description of UMTA's System for Raising Proposed Major Transit Investments*, U.S. Department of Transportation, Urban Mass Transportation Administration, May 1984, pp. 2-3.

38. Ibid., p. 4. One should note that these may be called objectives but they hardly fit the definition. Objectives were supposed to be extremely specific and measurable in nature and include a time line for completion and the responsibility for action. Clearly, these so-called "objectives" were neither very specific nor really capable of measurement. They were neither useful operational objectives nor operational goals, so it is fair to say that from a policy or management viewpoint, they were useless.

39. Ibid., pp. 4-5.

40. A good example of a TSM possibility would be an increase in street capacity at rush hour by imposing limited parking hours; the capital cost involved in such a project would be the preparation and installation of signs directing motorists not to park in the street during certain hours. A traffic lane is thus gained at a tiny fraction of the capital cost of widening the street. In transit it could be a simple matter of reserving a lane for buses-only during rush hours, thus permitting more throughput by speeding up the service, which is clearly a cheaper option than building a totally separate bus lane.

41. Ibid., p. 5. On the question of whether these measures really include everything,

UMTA argued that the recognition of most of the secondary benefits of the transit project were a consequence of the service and patronage impacts of that project. UMTA took the position that these measures were good surrogates for a wide range of benefits. The example was given of a service that would attract a substantial number of new riders; this gain would provide the associated benefits of less highway congestion, lower energy consumption, and lower pollution emissions. Moreover, improvement in service to existing riders was thought to be a good indicator of improved mobility for the transit dependent and increased accessibility to employment locations. Ibid., p. 6.

42. Ibid., p. 7.

43. Ibid., p. 8. For other information and comments about the announcement of the proposed new starts policy, see "Urban Mass Transportation Major Capital Investment Policy; Notice," *Federal Register*, Vol. 49, No. 98, Department of Transportation, Urban Mass Transportation Administration, Friday, May 18, 1984, pp. 21284-21287; "Stanley Announces Policy for New Fixed Guideway Systems," *U.S. Department of Transportation News: UMTA 16-84*, Friday, May 18, 1984; and "UMTA Announces New Start Criteria," *Passenger Transport*, Vol. 42, No. 22, May 28, 1984, pp. 1 and 5.

44. Robert D. Hershey, Jr., "New Rules on Federal Mass-Transit Aid Favor Sun Belt Cities," *New York Times*, April 1, 1984; Christopher Conte, "Cities' Battle for U.S. Mass-Transit Funds Enters New Phase with Rating of Projects," *Wall Street Journal*, May 21, 1984; "APTA Takes Issue with UMTA's New Start Criteria," *Passenger Transport*, Vol. 42, No. 30, July 23, 1984, pp. 1 and 4; also see the editorial entitled "Let's Work Together," *Passenger Transport*, Vol. 42, No. 30, July 23, 1984, p. 2; and "Industry News: New Start Policy Announced," *Metro*, Vol. 80, No. 4, July-August 1984, pp. 6, 8. Also on the unhappy side of the coin, see "Is UMTA Anti-Rail?" *National Association of Railroad Passengers News*, Vol. 18, No. 7, July 1984, pp. 1-3.

45. "UMTA Pinpoints 53 New Start Projects Which Might Cost $19 Billion," *Urban Transportation News*, June 11, 1984, pp. 93-95.

46. See Cliff Henke, "Rail Starts Criteria and Other Misnomers," *Metro*, Vol. 80, No. 4, July-August 1984, p. 12.

47. See *Department of Transportation and Related Agencies Appropriation Bill, 1985*, the U.S. Senate, Committee on Appropriations, Calendar No. 1057, 98th Congress, 2d session, Report 98-561, July 17, 1984, Report to Accompany S.2852, pp. 58-59. The zest with which the cities sought federal funding for major mass transit expenditures may be found in "Mass Transit: The Expensive Dream," *Business Week*, No. 2857, August 27, 1984, pp. 62-69.

48. As was usual in this era, the standard for the transit cause was carried by the American Public Transit Association, APTA. For interesting insight into APTA, see Arthur E. Wiese, "Fighting for Transit: 100 Years of Practice to Be Put to the Test," *Mass Transit*, Vol. 9, No. 10, October 1982, p. 8; and "A Dialogue with Jack Gilstrap," *Metro*, Vol. 80, No. 2, March-April 1984, p. 66. APTA knew it was in for a fight; see "Budget Slashes Operating Assistance," *Passenger Transport*, Vol. 42, No. 6, February 6, 1984, p. 1; and "APTA Informs Capitol Hill of Transit's Capital Needs," *Passenger Transport*, Vol. 42, No. 8, February 20, 1984, pp. 1 and 13.

49. *AASHTO Committee Correspondence*, February 10, 1984. Mr. Stanley also gave the UMTA budget proposal for the use of the expected $1.1 billion in Section 3 discretionary money arising from the Mass Transit Account. It was put forward to be:

Rail modernization	$520 million
New systems	400 million
Bus and bus facilities	100 million
Planning	50 million
Elderly and Handicapped	25 million
Innovative techniques	5 million
	$1.1 billion

Ibid., p.2. There had been an earlier hearing, mainly on the subject of crime and transit held by Senator Alfonse D'Amato of New York as he chaired the senate subcommittee on transportation appropriations. See "Fighting Transit Crime Is Subject of Hearing," *Passenger Transport*, Vol. 42, No. 5, January 30, 1984.

50. The estimates of capital needs for the five-year period, up to 1989, were: $7.7 billion for buses and bus facilities; $15.1 billion for rail modernization; rail extensions at $3.8 billion; and a total of $9.9 billion for new starts. See *AASHTO Committee Correspondence*, February 10, 1984, page 3. Also see "Transit's Penny Could Generate $1.5 Billion," *Passenger Transport*, Vol. 42, No. 7, February 13, 1984, pp. 1 and 9; and in the same number of *Passenger Transport*, "Editorial: Capital Needs," p. 2.

At about the same time, a staff proposal from the Heritage Foundation recommended ways to cut the federal deficit by phasing out the federal transit program entirely. For the complete text of this latter item, see John Palffy (editor), "How to Slash $119 Billion from the Deficit," a proposal by the staff of the Heritage Foundation for the budget of the U.S. government fiscal year 1985, the Heritage Foundation, 214 Massachusetts Avenue, N.E., Washington, D.C. 20002.

51. *AASHTO Committee Correspondence*, March 16, 1984; "House Acts on Highway Funds," *Passenger Transport*, Vol. 42, No. 10, March 5, 1984; "Transit Takes to the Hill," *Passenger Transport*, Vol. 42, No. 11, March 12, 1984, pp. 1 and 5; and "Transit Takes Its Case to Capitol Hill," *Passenger Transport*, Vol. 42, No. 12, March 19, 1984, pp. 1 and 4. See also Richard E. Cohen, "Congressional Focus: Budget Shares," *National Journal*, April 7, 1984, p. 670.

52. "APTA Adopts Resolution," *Passenger Transport*, Vol. 42, No. 12, March 19, 1984, pp. 1 and 8. Anyone thinking that the Section 3 money would not be used mainly for rail purposes would have been disabused of the notion by this resolution.

53. *AASHTO Committee Correspondence*, April 13, 1984. D'Amato's bill is reproduced in full. See also "Senate Bill Is Coming," *Passenger Transport*, Vol. 42, No. 12, March 19, 1984, pp. 1 and 8; and "House Panel Seeks Funds for Section 9," *Passenger Transport*, Vol. 42, No. 13, March 30, 1984, pp. 1 and 9.

54. Memo entitled *The D'Amato Public Transit Improvement Act of 1984* from Senator D'Amato to his colleagues, dated March 13, 1984, and found in *AASHTO Committee Correspondence* for March 16, 1984. The bill also proposed to expand the definition of associated capital maintenance costs by lowering the eligible threshold costs from 1 percent to .5 percent of the value of the asset or assets in question. Included in the D'Amato bill were eligible expenses for such things as the cost of leasing equipment, such as computers and heavy construction equipment. The bill also earmarked a portion of the Section 3 discretionary capital money for crime prevention grants and provided for multi-year contracting authority so that local transit systems could better plan construction projects and financing arrangements. It also attempted to clarify congressional intent regarding operating assistance for newly urbanized areas by indicating that 40 percent of the "authorized" Section 9 funds for such areas might be used for operating assistance.

55. See "House Panel Hears APTA Testimony," *Passenger Transport*, Vol. 42, No. 18, April 30, 1984, pp. 1 and 8.

56. The breakdown of the use of the funds was proposed as follows: bus, $140 million; rail modernization, $562 million; new starts, $562 million; general, $141 million; planning, $50 million; Sections 16 (b) and 4 (i), $40 million; and university transportation centers, $5 million from the Mass Transit Account (another $5 million was to come from the Highway Trust Fund). Detailed coverage of this proposed legislation is found in the *AASHTO Committee Correspondence*, April 27, 1984, pp. 1-2.

57. See *AASHTO Committee Correspondence*, May 3, 1984.

58. As a decision reserved only for the executive branch of government, the discretionary Section 3 money was alluring; it would be possible for the president, working through his appointee, the secretary of transportation, to provide large sums of expensive transit projects in any city it wished, thus courting votes and strong support from, or rewards to, local political leaders. Discretionary money is a powerful political tool. Pro-

jects so blessed were not usually bad in any sense but were moved up significantly on the priority ladder. This was especially important as it became clear that the number of eligible projects was well beyond government funding capability at any given time. Even money for the Section 11 University Research and Training may have been subject to political influence. At one time a particular school, which had never been involved in transit activities before, received four times as much money as any other, apparently by congressional direction. This favored institution had not even told UMTA what the money was to be used for at the time the federal largesse was ordained. See the document in the *AASHTO Committee Correspondence* for May 3, 1984, which was circulated at the Democratic caucus meeting by a member of the House Appropriations transportation subcommittee.

59. *Congressional Record—House,* June 7, 1984, p. H.5382. Mr. Lehman felt that, under H.R. 5504, Congress would be abdicating its powers to the executive branch.

60. See the "Dear Colleague" letter from Senator Symms, dated June 8, 1984, and reprinted in *AASHTO Committee Correspondence,* June 13, 1984; and a letter dated April 26, 1984, from Jack Gilstrap, Executive Vice-President of APTA, to all U.S. members of APTA, entitled "Urgent Congressional Matters." See also S.2718 (to authorize appropriations for the construction of highway projects, to increase taxes to finance such authorizations, and other purposes), 98th Congress, 2d session, May 24 (legislative day, May 21), 1984.

61. Wisconsin offered a particularly thoughtful approach to greater equity in the distribution of the Section 3 money by proposing that each state be guaranteed a given percentage of its contribution to Section 3 through the Mass Transit Account. See the letter of May 4, 1984, to Senator Proxmire from Lowell B. Jackson, the Wisconsin secretary of transportation, as reprinted in *AASHTO Committee Correspondence,* June 15, 1984. See also "Editorial: Moves Afoot," *Passenger Transport,* Vol. 42, No. 19, May 7, 1984, p. 2.

62. APTA Legislative Report, May 16, 1984; and "House Panel Approves Transit Bill," *Passenger Transport,* Vol. 42, No. 21, May 21, 1984, pp. 1 and 4.

63. See *News From: Committee on Public Works and Transportation,* "House Approves Surface Transportation Act of 1984," June 8, 1984; and "House Approves Transit Authorizing Legislation," *Passenger Transport,* Vol. 42, No. 25, June 18, 1984, pp. 1 and 8.

At about the same time, the Advisory Commission on Intergovernmental Relations, working as a presidential advisory commission, issued a report that was joyless for the transit industry. APTA's position was that the report, entitled *Metropolitan Transit in the '80s: An Intergovernmental Challenge,* contained assumptions biased by the views of the Reagan administration in that it relied heavily on private providers, transference of transit responsibility to state and local levels, and called for major cuts in federal support for transit. See "APTA Critiques Transit Study," *Passenger Transport,* Vol. 42, No. 24, June 11, 1984. The battle for federal programs in transit that had seemed to be won in the heady days of the 1970s appeared to the transit industry to need fighting for once again, and the administration's position against public-sector activities was apparently immutable. It was a clash in philosophy, a matter far deeper and more threatening to the viewpoint of the transit industry than a mere quibbling over funding levels.

See also Francis B. Francois, *Statement for Submittal to the Advisory Commission on Intergovernmental Relations Relating to Draft ACIR Recommendations on Metropolitan Transit Issues,* American Association of State Highway and Transportation Officials, June 6, 1984, reproduced, along with key portions of the draft ACIR statement, in *AASHTO Committee Correspondence,* June 8, 1984.

64. See *Congressional Record—Extension of Remarks,* June 26, 1984, p. E-2995. This is reproduced in *AASHTO Committee Correspondence,* July 3, 1984.

65. See the letter to Senator Symms from James J. Marquez, general counsel of the U.S. Department of Transportation, dated June 26, 1984, and the letter from Jack Gilstrap of APTA to Senator D'Amato, dated July 30, 1984, both reproduced in *AASHTO Committee Correspondence,* August 3, 1984. See also "Administration Opposes Symms Amendment,"

Passenger Transport, Vol. 42, No. 29, July 20, 1984, p. 1; and *APTA Legislative Report,* "Symms Amendment," July 19, 1984.

66. See the "Dear Colleague" letter from Congressman Howard, dated July 26, 1984; and a letter to all U.S. APTA members from Jack Gilstrap, APTA Executive Vice President, on the subject of appropriations and the likelihood of a continuing resolution, dated July 27, 1984.

67. See *AASHTO Committee Correspondence,* October 18, 1984.

68. "Appropriations Battles in Full Tilt," *Metro,* Vol. 80, No. 5, September-October 1984, p. 5; "Symms Amendment Threatens Transit Funding," Ibid., p. 6; *APTA Legislative Report,* "Countdown on Transit Legislation," September 7, 1984; "House Action on Continuing Resolution Is Imminent," *Passenger Transport,* Vol. 42, No. 39, September 24, 1984; *Report from Committee on Public Works and Transportation,* U.S. House of Representatives, 98th Congress, No. 5, October 1984; *APTA Legislative Report,* "Transit Legislation in the 98th Congress," October 17, 1984; "Tentative Agreement Is Reached on Transit Funding," *Passenger Transport,* Vol. 42, No. 42, October 15, 1984, pp. 1 and 6; and "Congress Approves Transit Budget for FY 1985," *Passenger Transport,* Vol. 42, No. 43, October 22, 1984, pp. 1 and 8.

69. As the reader will recall, the innovative Surface Transportation Assistance Act of 1982 was forged in the crisis of the lack of authorizing legislation for either the highway or the transit program. Congressman Howard put the two programs in one package and deferred action until the last year of the authorization to help create the crisis atmosphere.

70. There is much to be said for feeling good, even though critics could rightfully hold that important issues—such as those Candidate Mondale tried fruitlessly to parlay into voter support—were brushed under the carpet while the voting public merely played the role of audience at the pleasant performance. But "Send in the Clowns" is not the national anthem and the public could not be blamed for taking heart at an administration that had been reasonably successful after a run of disastrous presidencies. For an interesting view of the election as a trumpet call to inaction ("Our public life has been disabled and paralyzed by an expression of the public will"), see "The Talk of the Town: Notes and Comments," *The New Yorker,* Vol. 60, No. 43, December 10, 1984, pp. 43-44. Candidate Mondale was not a master of television, as was Ronald Reagan. Humorist Garrison Keillor, a fellow Minnesotan, on his "Prairie Home Companion" radio show, remarked that Mondale's charisma was somewhere between that of a Presbyterian Elder and an oak tree.

71. Proposals for transit ranged from total elimination of the program to raising the user charge on motor fuel by three or four more cents in order to pay for the transit program completely from that source, with no reliance on the general fund of the U.S. Treasury. Other proposals called for elimination of all parts of the federal transit program funded by the general fund, leaving only the Mass Transit Account of the Highway Trust Fund to supply the money for discretionary capital programs. Congress had blocked all of the efforts of the first Reagan administration to dismantle any part of the federal transit program; because the makeup of the key congressional committees had been changed but little by the 1984 election, the correct expectation was that the second Reagan administration would be a playback of the first on the transit issue. Such was to prove the case; indeed, when the Democrats took control of the Senate once again in the 1986 election, the administration had even less luck in getting its way. See, for example, Arthur E. Wiese, "After the Election: What Lies Ahead for U.S. Transit?" *Mass Transit,* Vol. 11, No. 10, October 1984, p. 9; "Election Brings Little Change to Transit Committees," *Passenger Transport,* Vol. 42, No. 46, November 12, 1984, pp. 1 and 5; and *AASHTO Committee Correspondence,* December 21, 1984.

72. For a flavor of the problem facing the second Reagan administration, see "Reagan's Deficit Dilemma," *Business Week,* No. 2871, December 3, 1984, pp. 26-27. Several reports were issued toward the end of 1984 that offered some thoughtful appraisal of the transit situation and gave suggestions and recommendations to Congress and other deliberative and planning bodies. Their substance was that the trends of the past 30 years in

the U.S. would be sustained and that cities would continue to suburbanize and population densities would, nationally, remain low. Public transportation was expected to carry a lower proportion of total urban travel but was likely to carry larger absolute numbers of passengers. The speculation was that there would probably be more private enterprise involved in public transportation and more reliance on various kinds of vehicle pooling.

Few have provided prescriptions of what urban areas and urban life ought to be and whether there is some better, more humane, more profitable, lower-cost (in all dimensions) way of associating in the groups we call urban. Prescriptive pronouncements were in their heyday in the 1960s and early 1970s. The trend among most thoughtful persons was, apparently, not to give thought to urban places. See Urban Mass Transportation Administration, *The Status of the Nation's Local Public Transportation: Conditions and Performance—Report to Congress*, U.S. Department of Transportation, September 1984; and the draft of *A Study of Future Directions of Public Transportation in the United States*, prepared by the Task Force on Future Directions of Public Transportation of the Standing Committee on Public Transportation, American Association of State Highway and Transportation Officials, Washington, D.C., December 3, 1984.

The efforts to cut the deficit were reflected in the Reagan administration's budget proposals. The 1986 budget passback for the Urban Mass Transportation Administration called for a 67 percent budget reduction from the 1985 fiscal year, a drop from $4.1 billion to $1.4 billion. The Section 3 discretionary grant would be terminated and the Mass Transit Account of the Highway Trust Fund was to be the only support of the Section 9 program. All general fund support was to be dropped, which would include the Interstate transfer grant program. See Urban Mass Transportation Administration, Department of Transportation 1986 Budget Passback, in *AASHTO Committee Correspondence*, January 10, 1985.

13. THE FEDERAL MASS TRANSIT PROGRAMS, 1984-1987

1. Even though the transit program continued, there were casualties along the way. The extreme negativism of the Reagan administration and its appointees to the leadership of the Urban Mass Transportation Administration was a major blow to the morale of UMTA staff. Some were caught in a reduction in force in the early 1980s; others sought greener pastures in other parts of federal service or went to the private sector. Among transit managers, burnout was a serious problem. To the ordinary difficulties of running a transit system was added the chore of scurrying to find state and local funds to make up for the loss (or threatened loss) of federal money. The threat was almost as bad as the actual cut because any good manager had to assume the worst in order to act responsibly. Add the usual fights with labor unions in many places, governing board intrusion into managerial prerogatives, the problems of managing in a goldfish bowl, political pressure, and the need to play an often unfamiliar and trying political role, and it was more than enough. Then add the common attacks or innuendo in the press for being paid too much (it appears to be an American truth: public officials or public employees are always paid too much, regardless of the difficulty of the job or the degree of managerial responsibility), and many managers threw in the towel and opted for the quiet life of the private sector.

2. If there were funds to continue operations and capital improvements, there were severe cuts in money for research and training. These were not the sort of things generally supported by state and local funding. In retrospect, the cut in research may have been the most negative legacy of the Reagan administration.

3. Representative coverage of the various states and openings, which often included plans for the future, may be found in the following references which are not intended in any way to be complete. "Pittsburgh LRT: America's Most Livable City Gets a Subway," *Notes* (published by Parsons Brinckerhoff), Spring 1986, pp. 4-7; "A Year of Milestones for Allegheny County," *Passenger Transport*, Vol. 44, No. 40, October 6, 1986, p. 58; "Pittsburgh Hits Paydirt," *Railway Age*, Vol. 186, No. 8, August 1985, pp. 71 and 73; "Metro

Seattle Plans Transit Tunnel to Relieve Congestion in Downtown," *Passenger Transport,* Vol. 44, No. 40, October 6, 1986, pp. 20-21; Dan Beyers, "Here Comes Metro's Orange Line," *Arlington Journal,* June 5, 1986, pp. 1 and 11; Ray Hebert, "Portland Opens the MAX," *Mass Transit,* Vol. 13, No. 10, October 1986, p. 10; "Buffalo Holds Festivities for Metro Rail Opening," *Passenger Transport,* Vol. 44, No. 49, December 8, 1986, pp. 1 and 13; "San Diego Breaks Ground for Third Light Rail Line," *Passenger Transport,* Vol. 44, No. 47, November 24, 1986, pp. 1 and 8; "SCRTD Holds Groundbreaking for Los Angeles Metro Rail," *Passenger Transport,* Vol. 44, No. 42, October 20, 1986, p. 5; "Los Angeles Ready for Metro Rail Start," *Railway Age,* Vol. 187, No. 9, September 1986, p. 65; and Robert Lindsey, "Sacramento Finds Trolley Is a Symbol of the Future," *New York Times,* April 5, 1987.

4. The reader of previous chapters will recall that the Carter White House was cool to federal transit programs until the Iranian revolution disturbed the flow of crude oil in the world and the prices for petroleum skyrocketed. See Albert R. Karr, "Mass Transit Gets Short Shrift," *Wall Street Journal,* December 30, 1977.

5. Future historians may wonder what Gramm-Rudman-Hollings was all about. Essentially, the legislation took away from Congress decisionmaking on what to cut in trimming the budget to fit within certain targets of deficit reduction specified in the legislation. If the targets were not attained, across-the-board cuts—usually dubbed a meat-ax approach by critics—would automatically lower federal spending. Much ink was devoted to GRH; some examples are noted here: David Rogers, "Budget Compromise Clears Path for Passage of Debt-Ceiling Bill," *Wall Street Journal,* December 9, 1985; George Lardner, Jr., "Budget-Balancing Bill Likely to Face a Challenge in Court," *Louisville Courier-Journal,* December 12, 1985 (from the *Washington Post*); "Gramm-Rudman-Hollings Bill Explained," *Passenger Transport,* Vol. 43, No. 50, December 16, 1985, p. 1; Essell Thomas, "New Gramm-Rudman Law Could Cost Transport Agencies $500 Million," *Traffic World,* Vol. 204, No. 14, December 30, 1985, pp. 47-48; Paul Blustein and David Rogers, "Budget Struggle Gets Major Changes Due to Gramm-Rudman," *Wall Street Journal,* January 17, 1986; "Showdown Time for Gramm-Rudman," *Business Week,* No. 2929, January 20, 1986, pp. 22-24; "It's Time to Kill Gramm-Rudman" (editorial), *Business Week,* No. 2929, January 20, 1986, p. 100; Joann S. Lublin, "Bureaucracy's Budget Officers Are Beleaguered by Spending Curbs in the Gramm-Rudman Law," *Wall Street Journal,* January 23, 1986; "GAO Issues Sequestering Report," *AASHTO Public Transportation Bulletin,* Vol. 86, No. 3, January 24, 1986; "Gramm-Rudman Is Bringing Congress to a Standstill," *Business Week,* No. 2930, January 27, 1986, p. 40; David Rogers and Alan Murray, "Reagan Gains an Edge from Ruling Hobbling Gramm-Rudman Law," *Wall Street Journal,* February 10, 1986; "Gramm-Rudman's Weak Hand Leaves Reagan Holding Aces," *Business Week,* No. 2934, February 24, 1986, p. 33; Desar V. Conda and William P. Orzechowski, "Putting Teeth Back in Gramm-Rudman," *Wall Street Journal,* February 24, 1986; "Gramm-Rudman-Hollings Cuts Take Effect," *AASHTO Public Transportation Bulletin,* Vol. 86, No. 6, March 5, 1986; Ann Reilly, "Gramm-Rudman Is Starting to Work," *Fortune,* Vol. 113, No. 8, April 14, 1986, p. 89; "A Gramm-Rudman Deadline Passes—And Congress Yawns," *Business Week,* No. 2944, April 28, 1986, p. 35; "Transit Conference Confronts Gramm-Rudman," *Metro,* Vol. 82, No. 3, May-June 1986, pp. 44-50; Allen Schick, "Explanation of the Balanced Budget and Emergency Deficit Control Act of 1985—Public Law 99-177," 85-1130 GOV, Congressional Research Service, Library of Congress, HJ 2005 U.S. D2, December 1985, revised February 1986; Sally J. Cooper, "Brother Can You Spare a Dime? or Gramm-Rudman-Hollings, the States & Public Transit," at the 1986 APTA Eastern Education and Training Conference, Cincinnati, Ohio, May 20, 1986; "G-R-H Was No Way to Cure Deficit" (editorial), *Louisville Courier-Journal,* July 8, 1986; "And You Thought the Budget Mess Couldn't Get Any Worse," *Business Week,* No. 2957, July 28, 1986, p. 37; Lindley H. Clark, Jr., "Someone Will Have to Learn to Play This Game," *Wall Street Journal,* September 23, 1986; and David Rogers, "Senate Sends Spending Bill to Conferees; Debate to Pose Test for Gramm-Rudman," *Wall Street*

Journal, October 6, 1986. As can be seen, the furor over GRH died down over time. The budget itself was given detailed coverage in the *Wall Street Journal* on February 6, 1986.

6. The tax reform legislation was a major story in 1985 and 1986; it is summarized fairly well in the following: "Nobody Said It Would Be Easy," *Business Week,* No. 2897, June 3, 1985, pp. 33 and 37; "What Tax Reform Really Means," *Business Week,* No. 2899, June 17, 1985, pp. 128-139; "The Making of a Miracle," *Time,* Vol. 128, No. 8, August 25, 1986, pp. 12-21; and "Tax Reform—At Last," *Business Week,* No. 2962, September 1, 1986, pp. 54-65.

7. See "Election Brings New Leaders to Senate Transit Panel," *Passenger Transport,* Vol. 44, No. 45, November 10, 1986, pp. 1 and 4.

8. See, for example, "Who Was Betrayed?" *Time,* Vol. 128, No. 23, December 8, 1986, pp. 16-43; "Crisis at the White House," *Business Week,* No. 2976, December 8, 1986, pp. 30 and 31; Walter S. Moosberg, "White House's Overtures toward Iran over Six Years Entangled Administration in Web of Covert Dealings," *Wall Street Journal,* December 12, 1986; "Reagan Still Hasn't Stopped the Bleeding," *Business Week,* No. 2977, December 15, 1986, p. 28; and "What the Democrats Will Push While Reagan Is Hamstrung," *Business Week,* No. 2978, December 22, 1986, p. 31. Congress held joint hearings on the Iran-contra scandal in mid–1987.

9. The increase in support by state and local government was considered good because it raised the commitment of state and local government to transit, a commitment that tended to be larger the more money one had involved. The American Public Transit Association put it well in its discussions of funding in drawing attention to the partnership between the various levels of government and the transit agencies that served the public. See Kumares C. Sinha, Michael J. Doherty, Richard Muncey, and John D. N. Riverson, *Evaluation of State Transit Subsidy Policies in Response to Reduction in Federal Assistance* (West Lafayette, Indiana: Purdue University School of Civil Engineering, September 30, 1986, revised January 28, 1987).

10. The interested reader can find much to worry about by perusing the following potpourri of news reports, studies, and general information. Basic information on changing patterns of commuting may be found in Dwight Briggs, Alan Pisarski, and James McDonnel, *Journey-to-Work Trends Based on 1960, 1970, and 1980 Decennial Census* (Washington, D.C.: U.S. Department of Transportation, Federal Highway Administration, Office of Highway Information Management, July 1986). The study points to a drop in the proportion of commuting by transit, largely as a result of increased ownership of automobiles by households.

Other studies of interest are: Dick Netzer, James O'Donoghue, and Marion Vandersteel, *Developing an Approach for the Analysis of the Long-Range Future of Public Transportation in Large Cities* (Washington, D.C.: U.S. Department of Transportation, Urban Mass Transportation Administration, Office of Technical Assistance, University Research and Training Program, 1984. The report is available from the National Technical Information Service, Springfield, Virginia 22161; the accession number is PB84-229129); and *The Status of the Nation's Local Public Transportation: Conditions and Performance,* Report of the Secretary of Transportation to the United States Congress Pursuant to Section 310, Surface Transportation Act of 1982 (Public Law 97-424) (Washington, D.C.: U.S. Department of Transportation, Urban Mass Transportation Administration, September 1984). More specifically relating to the pain and the problems of traffic, transit, and an infrastructure in trouble are the following: "Mass Transit: The Expensive Dream," *Business Week,* No. 857, August 27, 1984, pp. 62-69; Daniel Machalaba, "Lower Manhattan Streets, Subways Face Rising Traffic and Congestion," *Wall Street Journal,* October 15, 1984; Margot Hornblower, "Big Apple's Riders Are Responding to Its Revolting Subways in Kind," *Louisville Courier-Journal,* November 24, 1984 (from the *Washington Post*); "An Average Commute Put at 22.4 Miles a Day," *Washington Post,* November 26, 1984; Christopher Conte, "The Explosive Growth of Suburbia Leads to Bumper-to-Bumper Blues," *Wall Street Journal,* April 16, 1985; Daniel Machalaba, "Like Other Cities, Hartford Has Gridlock; Unlike

Others, It Is Not Building Roads," *Wall Street Journal,* April 29, 1985; Luther S. Miller, "Transit's Trauma: Back to the Bad Old Days?" *Railway Age,* Vol. 186, No. 5, May 1985, pp. 58-61; Pat Wingert, "Suburb-to-City Run Out with Commuters," *Chicago Tribune,* June 19, 1985; C. Kenneth Orski, "Suburban Mobility: The Coming Transportation Crisis?" *Transportation Quarterly,* Vol. 39, No. 2, April 1985, pp. 283-296; John Semmens, "Public Transit: A Bad Deal Getting Worse," *Wall Street Journal,* June 6, 1985; C. Kenneth Orski, *Toward a Policy for Suburban Mobility,* Washington, D.C. (prepared for the National Conference on Site Development and Transportation Impacts, held March 23-26, 1986, in Orlando, Florida); Michael Arndt, "Traffic Rush Has Commuted to the Suburbs," *Chicago Tribune,* September 15, 1986; Daniel Machalaba, "Debate Grows over Whether Employers Should Give Incentives to Car Commuters," *Wall Street Journal,* November 12, 1986; "Los Angeles Traffic Snarls Spur Growls and Gunfire," *Louisville Courier-Journal,* November 29, 1986 (from the Associated Press); "The Crumbling of America: A New Crisis in Public Works," *Business Week,* No. 2975, December 1, 1986; Shaun Assael, "Detour from Danger: Treacherous Bridge Closed; 'Giant U-turn' Rattles Commuters," *Gannett Westchester Newspapers,* December 24, 1986; Gurney Breckenfield, "Where to Live—and Prosper," *Fortune,* Vol. 115, No. 3, February 2, 1987.

Many newspapers carried vivid stories of local traffic congestion and gridlock problems in 1986. Some particularly interesting difficulties were covered in a series in the *Gannett Westchester Newspapers,* by Tony Brown: "Transportation: I-287 Decisions Have Just Begun," November 24, 1986; "Transportation: Traffic Control; It Simply Needs a New Approach," December 11, 1986; "Deciding The Fate of I-287," November 19, 1986; "Why Our Parkways Always Flood," December 4, 1986. *Newsday* ran a number of feature articles on traffic problems in its issue of September 19, 1986; the principle article was William Bunch, "Poll: Driving Time and Frustration Are Up." The apparent hopelessness of efforts to counter the traffic jam is perhaps best illustrated in several articles from America's quintessential home of congestion, Los Angeles. See Kevin Roderick, "Rx Freeways: From Bad to Worse," *Los Angeles Times,* April 19, 1987; and Kevin Roderick, "Can't Build Traffic Solution, Experts Say," *Los Angeles Times,* April 21, 1987. For whatever cheer it offers, the problems of traffic are international; see John Fraser, "European Cities Suffering Clogged Traffic Arteries," *Toronto Globe & Mail,* November 3, 1986.

One of the funniest and most insightful commentaries on congestion and transportation policy is found in the May 11, 1988, essay of *New York Times* columnist Russell Baker entitled "One of Our States Is Missing." It contains the trenchant observation: "The American traffic solution is to widen the road."

11. Senator Lautenberg's proposal in S.1359 would have provided $2.35 billion in funding from general revenues and would have raised the sum from the Highway Trust Fund Mass Transit Account from $1.1 billion to $1.5 billion for the years from 1986 to 1989. The senator proposed to support the Section 3 capital program from general revenues rather than the Mass Transit Account; the Section 9 and Section 18 formula grant programs would have been funded from the Mass Transit Account along with general funds. See American Association of State Highways and Transportation Officials, Standing Committee on Public Transportation, July 2, 1985 (Hereinafter *AASHTO Newsletter*). For Senator Lautenberg's comments upon introducing the legislation, see *Congressional Record—Senate,* June 25, 1985, pp. S8747-S8750.

There had been earlier thoughts on what action should be taken; see Robert Pear, "Reagan Reportedly Will Propose Combining Mass Transit, Road Aid," *Detroit Free Press,* January 4, 1985 (from the *New York Times*); "Transit Leaders Ponder Industry's Future," *Passenger Transport,* Vol. 43, No. 4, January 28, 1985, pp. 1 and 9; "APTA Weighing Transit Ideas," *AASHTO Newsletter,* January 28, 1985; "Congressional Update," *AASHTO Newsletter,* March 28, 1985. Concern over the deleterious impact of the Reagan administration's proposed cuts in federal transit funding are found in "Editorial: Food for Thought," *Passenger Transport,* Vol. 43, No. 10, March 12, 1985, p. 2; "Dodd Pledges Vigorous Opposition to Budget," ibid., p. 4; "What Happens If . . . ," *Mass Transit,* Vol.

12, No. 4, April 1985, pp. 11 and 33; and Edward F. Patrick, "U.S. Transit Rallies to Take on Reagan Budget Cuts," ibid., pp. 10, 30-32.

12. See *News From: Committee on Public Works and Transportation,* July 31, 1985; and H.R. 3129, *The Surface Transportation and Uniform Relocation Assistance Act of 1985,* 99th Congress, 1st session, July 31, 1985.

13. *News From: Committee on Public Works and Transportation,* September 10, 1985. The *APTA Legislative Report* of September 19, 1985 provides more detail and spells out some of the other issues that were delaying movement of the reauthorizing legislation. The APTA material also contains a comparison of the current and proposed federal transit funds. The actual funding level for fiscal 1985 was $4.151 billion; the president's budget request for fiscal 1986 was $1.401 billion, the first congressional budget resolution for fiscal 1986 was $3.677 billion. The House-passed DOT appropriations bill called for $3.778 billion. The respective percentage cuts from the 1985 level were 66.2 percent, 11.4 percent, and 9.0 percent. For additional information on appropriations and other matters of interest to transit, including copies of testimony on the transit industry's concerns over liability insurance, see *APTA Legislative Report,* November 22, 1985.

14. *News From: Committee on Public Works and Transportation,* December 3, 1985. For later discussion on the infrastructure problem, see George Melloan, "Infrastructure Repair Needs More Than Money," *Wall Street Journal,* March 29, 1988; Jean V. Murphy, "Infrastructure Policy Decisions Will Challenge Next President," *Traffic World,* Vol. 215, No. 2, July 11, 1988, pp. 9-15; and Gary S. Becker, "Why Potholes and Police Get Such Short Shrift," *Business Week,* No. 3062, July 25, 1988, p. 12.

15. Christopher Conte, "Merger of Road, Mass Transit Aid to Cities Proposed," *Wall Street Journal,* December 12, 1985. A more detailed description of the proposed merger of the transit and highway programs is to be found in the *APTA Legislative Report,* December 20, 1985. In the "his bark is worse than his bite" department, the president signed a continuing resolution (there was no regular DOT appropriations bill passed) for $3.702.81 billion for transit; this was a 10.8 percent reduction from the actual fiscal 1985 numbers and a far cry from the 66 percent that the administration had originally called for. The APTA report noted that the funding level was for the full year although changes might occur as a result of the Gramm-Rudman-Hollings Act.

16. See *APTA Legislative Report,* January 24, 1986. The report contains an informative item from the January 10, 1986 *Washington Post* with the arresting title "(Almost) Everything You Ever Wanted to Know About Gramm-Rudman." Also see "D'Amato, Dixon, Stanley to Discuss Transit Funding Reauthorization," *Passenger Transport,* Vol. 44, No. 5, February 3, 1986, p. 1. The issue of privatization, dear to the heart of the Reagan administration, was being pushed by UMTA very strongly at this time. See "Privatization Implementation Guidelines Expanded," ibid., pp. 1 and 4; also see George M. Smerk, "From Private to Public to Privatization," *Transportation Journal,* Vol. 26, No. 1, Fall 1986, pp. 83-91.

17. See *AASHTO Public Transportation Bulletin,* Vol. 86, No. 5, February 6, 1986. Secretary of Transportation Dole noted that it was the intent of the administration's proposal to "give state and local decisionmakers the tools and flexibility to meet their own unique transportation needs." See "Administration Unveils Surface Transportation Legislative Proposals," *Traffic World,* Vol. 205, No. 11, March 17, 1986, p. 125; *APTA Legislative Bulletin,* March 25, 1986; and "Administration Proposes Revamped Highway and Transit Programs," *ITE Journal,* Vol. 56, No. 3, March 1986, p. 7. In order to push private sector initiatives, UMTA regional administrators were to have their pay increases partially based on the degree of privatization achieved within their jurisdictions.

18. *AASHTO Public Transportation Bulletin,* Vol. 86, No. 10, April 17, 1986.

19. "D'Amato Proposes Oversight Bill," *Passenger Transport,* Vol. 44, No. 16, April 21, 1986, pp. 1 and 4.

20. "Senate Defeats Program Cuts," *Passenger Transport,* Vol. 44, No. 18, May 5, 1986, p. 1. See also *APTA Legislative Update,* May 16, 1986; it includes a copy of a "Dear

Colleague" letter from Senator D'Amato, dated May 6, 1986, that gives an excellent outline of his legislative proposal.

21. See *AASHTO Public Transportation Bulletin,* Vol. 86, No. 16, June 16, 1986; and Douglas B. Feaver, "Federal Highways Bill Passes Hill Intersection," *Washington Post,* June 20, 1986. See also *News From: Committee on Public Works and Transportation,* June 25, 1986.

22. See *News From: Committee on Public Works and Transportation,* July 22, 1986; *AASHTO Public Transportation Bulletin,* Vol. 86, No. 17, June 30, 1986; "Bipartisan Support Carries Transit Act through Subcommittee," *Passenger Transport,* Vol. 44, No. 26, June 30, 1986, pp. 1 and 9; and Laurie McGinley, "Transport Bill of $92 Billion Clears House," *Wall Street Journal,* August 18, 1986.

23. See Laurie McGinley, "Transport Bill of $92 Billion Clears House," *Wall Street Journal,* August 18, 1986; *APTA Legislative Report,* August 18, 1986; "House to Act on H.R. 3129," *Passenger Transport,* Vol. 44, No. 33, August 18, 1986, pp. 1 and 9; and "House Passes Mass Transit Reauthorization," *Passenger Transport,* Vol. 44, No. 34, August 25, 1986, pp. 1 and 9. The bill passed by a large margin, 345-34.

While the reauthorization legislation was being passed by the House, appropriations bills were also being approved or recommended. The fiscal year 1986 funds, including the Gramm-Rudman-Hollings reduction of 4.3 percent, was $3,530.29 billion. In contrast, the president's fiscal 1987 budget proposal was for $1,220.00 billion; the House-passed transportation appropriation for fiscal 1987, H.R. 5205, was $3.480 billion, and the Senate Appropriations Committee recommendation for fiscal 1987, under H.R. 5205, was $3.423.40 billion. See "What's Being Proposed for FY 1987," *Passenger Transport,* Vol. 44, No. 33, August 18, 1986, p. 4.

24. See *AASHTO Public Transportation Bulletin,* Vol. 86, No. 21, September 8, 1986; also, "Congress Faces Deficit Ceiling: Balanced Budget Law Could Impact on Transit," *Passenger Transport,* Vol. 44, No. 35, September 1, 1986, pp. 1 and 8.

25. See Laurie McGinley, "Special Highway Project Funding in House Bill Stirs Pork-Barrel Charges, Could Block Measure," *Wall Street Journal,* September 16, 1986; David M. Cawthorne and Leo Abruzzese, "Highway Funding Bill Unlikely to Pass in '86," *Journal of Commerce,* September 25, 1986; *APTA Bulletin,* September 26, 1986; "Highway Bills Await Conferees' Action," *Traffic World,* Vol. 207, No. 13, September 29, 1986, pp. 8-9; "Senate OKs Road Bill; States May Now Set 65-MPH Speed Limit," ibid., p. 63; and David M. Cawthorne, "Speed Limit Issue Tied to Highway Funding," *Journal of Commerce,* September 29, 1986. Congressman Howard was strong in his opposition to any increase in the speed limit, but he did seek to find grounds for a compromise with the Senate's desire to raise the speed limit in non-urban areas. Howard proposed the following conditions before the negotiations between the House and Senate began: (1) States had to achieve and maintain a 65 percent statewide use of seatbelts before raising the speed limit; (2) After the first year of the higher limit, to maintain that level the states would have to have a minimum of 85 percent compliance on roads with higher than the 55 mph limit; (3) If there is an increase in the fatality rate on highways with the higher speed limit, states must reduce the speed limit to 55 mph. "Restrictions Proposed on 65-mph Speed Limit," *Louisville Courier-Journal,* September 28, 1986; and "Speed Limit Compromise Offered," *Journal of Commerce,* September 30, 1986.

26. See "Highway Bill Logjam Is Broken, but Howard Still Opposes 65 mph," *Traffic World,* Vol. 208, No. 1, October 6, 1986, p. 7; "Howard Says Highway Bill Is 'Dead' for This Year," *Traffic World,* Vol. 208, No. 2, October 13, 1986, p. 7; "Congress: Funding Compromise Progress Reported," *Passenger Transport,* Vol. 44, No. 41, October 13, 1986, pp. 1 and 8; "Transportation Measures Unresolved at Press Time," *Traffic World,* Vol. 208, No. 3, October 20, 1986, pp. 7-8; *APTA Bulletin,* October 21, 1986; "House, Senate Deadlock on Reauthorization Bill: President Signs Funding Bill," *Passenger Transport,* Vol. 44, No. 43, October 27, 1986, pp. 1 and 9; *APTA Legislative Report,* October 27, 1986; Lee Coney, "Major Transportation Legislation Was Passed by the 99th Congress," *Traffic*

World, Vol. 208, No. 5 [incorrectly given as No. 3], November 3, 1986, pp. 82-85; "Highway System Dead-End Threatened by Congress' Failure to Pass Program," *Traffic World*, Vol. 208, No. 3, November 3, 1986, p. 127; and Bill Paul, "Publisher's Perspective: No Time for Rest," *Metro*, Vol. 82, No. 7, November-December 1986, p. 88. For congressional plans to reintroduce the legislation, see *AASHTO Newsletter*, December 12, 1987, pp. 1-2.

27. See "Highway Bills Introduced as Congress Begins Task of Authorizing Funds," *Traffic World*, Vol. 210, No. 20, January 12, 1987, p. 45; and APTA *Legislative Report*, January 12, 1987, pp. 3-4. There were several approaches to the transit reauthorization that had to be reconciled by banking subcommittee chairman Alan Cranston of California. Senator D'Amato had introduced S.224, almost identical to his S.2543 of the 99th Congress. In the early days of the 100th Congress it was thought that Senator Dixon of Illinois might also introduce a bill. Also see "House Sets Reauthorization Vote," *Passenger Transport*, Vol. 45, No. 3, January 19, 1987, pp. 1 and 8.

28. See Allen R. Wastler, "Reagan's FY 1987 Budget Requests More Air Money and End to Amtrak," *Traffic World*, Vol. 210, No. 2, January 12, 1987, pp. 11-13; "Administration Proposes Drastic Cuts in Transit Funding," *Passenger Transport*, Vol. 45, No. 2, January 12, 1987, pp. 1 and 13; and "Lautenberg, Coalition Blast Transit Cuts," *Passenger Transport*, Vol. 45, No. 6, February 9, 1987, pp. 1 and 8.

29. How historians will view the Iran-contra business is a matter of conjecture; it did garner much ink and broadcast time, and it did change the relationship between the Reagan administration and the Congress, because the psychology surrounding the normal tension between the White House and Capitol Hill put the president on the defensive in a way that had not been experienced since he had taken office. Legislation would definitely be affected for a while; how much would be determined only after time provided some perspective. Here is a sample of pertinent news and commentary on the situation: Anthony Lewis, "The Deeper Flaw," *Louisville Courier-Journal*, February 6, 1987; Anthony Lewis, "The Man Responsible," *Louisville Courier-Journal*, February 25, 1987; David Shribman, "Out of Control: As Reagan's Problems Grow, Many Now Say Damage Is Irreparable," *Wall Street Journal*, February 25, 1987; Steven V. Roberts, "Report Blasts Reagan, Top Aides for Handling of Iran Arms Dealings," *Louisville Courier-Journal*, February 27, 1987; George de Lama, "Panel Rips Reagan and Regan," *Chicago Tribune*, February 27, 1987; George F. Will, "The President's Grave Flaw: Sloth," *Louisville Courier-Journal*, February 28, 1987; William Greider, "The Lonesome Drifter," *Louisville Courier-Journal*, March 1, 1987; Ellen Hume and David Shribman, "Taking Over: New Staff Chief Baker to Wield Great Power in a Conciliatory Way," *Wall Street Journal*, March 2, 1987; Jane Mayer, "Nancy Reagan's Behind-the-Scenes Maneuvering Stands Out in Circumstances of Regan's Ouster," *Wall Street Journal*, March 2, 1987; Colman McCarthy, "The Undermining Truth of the Reagan Presidency," *Washington Post*, March 8, 1987; David Broder, "Repaired White House Reopens For Business," (Bloomington/Bedford, Ind.) *Sunday Herald-Times*, March 22, 1987; Christopher Layne, "The Overreaching Reagan Doctrine," *Wall Street Journal*, April 15, 1987; and David S. Broder, "Behind the Front Page: Control of News Worked—for a While," *Louisville Courier-Journal*, April 19, 1987. Norman Ornstein, a prominent political analyst, noted the many things that occupied the attention of the Congress and the White House in early 1987. These included the Iran-contra scandal; foreign policy, especially arms control; the budget; the deficit, and the general disarray and infighting accompanying an open presidential election (no incumbent running) in 1988. All of these matters were a critical part of the environment in which the transit legislation was reauthorized as well as the immediate future of the legislation and policy making. Mr. Ornstein gave this information in a speech at the Legislative Conference of the American Public Transit Association in Washington, D.C. on March 8, 1987.

30. The following is a sample of contemporary accounts of the process of arriving at a bill acceptable to both houses of the Congress: "House Overwhelmingly Approves Mass Transit Reauthorization Bill," *Passenger Transport*, Vol. 45, No. 4, January 26, 1987, pp. 1

and 8; "House Passes Measure Authorizing Road Funds," *Traffic World*, Vol. 210, No. 4, January 26, 1987, pp. 5-6; "Senate Votes to Allow States to Raise Speed Limit to 65 in Rural Areas," *Louisville Courier-Journal*, February 2, 1987; Laurie McGinley, "Senate Votes to Let States Lift Speed Limit to 65 MPH on Interstates' Rural Sections," *Wall Street Journal*, February 4, 1987; Allen R. Wastler, "Speed Limit Increase in Road Bill Raises Concern over Final Version," *Traffic World*, Vol. 210, No. 6, February 9, 1987, pp. 1 and 62, "Transit Reauthorization Bills Go to Congressional Conference," *Passenger Transport*, Vol. 45, No. 7, February 16, 1987, pp. 1 and 9; Allen R. Wastler, "House, Senate Conferees Commence Negotiations for Highway Legislation," *Traffic World*, Vol. 209, No. 9, March 2, 1987, pp. 4-5; Robert M. Butler, "Governors Approve 65 MPH Option, Get Assurance on Highway Transit Bill Scheduled for Floor Vote," *Passenger Transport*, Vol. 45, No. 11, March 16, 1987, pp. 1 and 8; Helen Dewar, "Highway Bill Passes after Veto Threat," *Washington Post*, March 20, 1987; Allen R. Wastler, "House Votes to Raise Speed Limit to 65 MPH on Rural Interstates," *Traffic World*, Vol. 209, No. 12, March 23, 1987, pp. 4-5; Dale Russakoff, "Pork Barrel and the Public Good," *Washington Post*, March 27, 1987; *AASHTO Public Transportation Bulletin*, Vol. 87, No. 1, January 16, 1987; *Congressional Record-Senate*, January 6, 1987, S.459–S.463; and *Congressional Record-House*, January 6, 1987, H.42–H.47.

31. See *AASHTO Public Transportation Bulletin*, Vol. 87, No. 5, March 19, 1987; "Reagan Vetos Highway Bill; State, Local Officials Critical," *Bloomington* (Ind.) *Herald-Telephone*, March 27, 1987 (Associated Press Wire Service); "Reagan to Face Tough Battle over Highway Legislation Veto," *Bloomington* (Ind.) *Herald-Telephone*, March 28, 1987; "DOT Secretary Predicts Senate Will Sustain Veto of Highway Legislation," *Traffic World*, Vol. 209, No. 13, March 30, 1987, p. 49; Laurie McGinley, "Democrats Face Crucial Vote in Senate in Bid to Override Veto of Highway Bill," *Wall Street Journal*, March 30, 1987; Jeffrey H. Birnbaum, "House Approves Overriding Veto of Highway Bill," *Wall Street Journal*, April 1, 1987; Helen Dewar, "Senate Backs Reagan's Veto of Highway Bill, but New Vote Scheduled," *Louisville Courier-Journal*, April 2, 1987 (from the *Washington Post*); Hodding Carter III, "Democrats Decry Potholes in Reagan's Policies," *Wall Street Journal*, April 2, 1987; Laurie McGinley and Jeffrey H. Birnbaum, "Senate Fails to Override Reagan Veto of Highway Bill, but May Vote Again," *Wall Street Journal*, April 2, 1987; "Second Override Attempt Today," *Bloomington* (Ind.) *Herald-Telephone*, April 3, 1987; Donald P. Rothberg, "Reagan Proved Vulnerable on Highway Bill," *Bloomington* (Ind.) *Herald-Telephone*, April 3, 1987 (from the Associated Press); Jeffrey J. Birnbaum and Ellen Hume, "Senate, Ignoring President's Personal Plea, Overrides Veto of $87.5 Billion Highway Bill by Vote of 67-33," *Wall Street Journal*, April 3, 1987; Helen Dewar and Edward Walsh, "GOP Senators Reject Reagan's Plea, Vote Highway Bill into Law," *Louisville Courier-Journal*, April 3, 1987 (from the *Washington Post*); R. W. Apple, Jr., "Risky Effort Shows Reagan Is 'His Own Man,'" *Louisville Courier-Journal*, April 3, 1987 (from the *New York Times*); "Congress Enacts Highway Bill Despite Presidential Plea," *Washington Post*, April 3, 1987 (from the New York Times News Service); "Several States Hurry to Raise Speed Limits, Others Apply Brakes," *Louisville Courier-Journal*, April 4, 1987; *AASHTO Public Transportation Bulletin*, Vol. 87, No. 6, April 6, 1987; and "Congress Overrides Veto of Highway, Transit Bill," *Passenger Transport*, Vol. 45, No. 14, April 6, 1987, p. 1. The speed limit issue attracted attention but, despite many arguments over the potential increase in costs to life and property, there was general public approval of the change. The *Louisville Courier-Journal* opposed the legislation in an editorial: "Better Road Bill Is Possible," March 31, 1987. The Insurance Institute for Highway Safety also opposed raising the speed limit; see "55 MPH: 'It Still Makes a Difference,'" *IIHS Status Report*, Vol. 22, No. 4, April 11, 1987, p. 3. Many states wasted no time in adjusting their laws to fit with the change in the federal laws. Truckers were generally delighted, claiming that the higher speeds would enable more trips to be made per month. Some held that it would keep many truckers from going broke and were reported to feel that another 10 mph would not kill anybody. At the same time, there was concern over the increase in fatalities; this was

borne out by a study conducted by the Injury Prevention Center of the Johns Hopkins School of Hygiene and Public Health and published in the *New England Journal of Medicine*. According to the research, the highest level of road deaths per 100,000 people took place in the rural west; on the same basis, Manhattan was the safest to drive. See "The New 65 MPH Limit," and "Speed Could Go Up on Three-fourths of Interstates," *Bloomington* (Ind.) *Herald-Telephone*, April 5, 1987 (both from the Associated Press); Mary Dieter, "Legislature Passes 65 MPH Bill," *Bloomington* (Ind.) *Herald-Telephone*, April 25, 1987; "Truckers Laud 65-MPH Limit, Others Warn of Hazards," *Bloomington* (Ind.) *Herald-Telephone*, April 26, 1987 (from the Associated Press); and "Rural West Has Highest Rates of Road Deaths," *Louisville Courier-Journal*, May 28, 1987 (from the Associated Press). The bill was, as one observer put it, as covered with goodies and gifts as a Christmas tree. There was some commentary on the goodies: James J. Kilpatrick, "No Speed Limit on Pork?" *Louisville Courier-Journal*, April 10, 1987 (Universal Press Syndicate); and William F. Buckley, "Highway Bill Gooey, Fat-Filled, Pork Barrel Starch," *Bloomington* (Ind.) *Herald-Telephone*, April 11, 1987 (Universal Press Syndicate).

32. The key points of the new law are to be found in "Highlights of Mass Transit Law," *Passenger Transport*, Vol. 45, No. 18, April 20, 1987, pp. 1 and 9. Another valuable source of information and interpretation is *An Explanation of the Federal Mass Transportation Act of 1987, Public-Law 100-17*, prepared by the American Public Transit Association, Washington, D.C., April 1987.

33. *Explanation*, pp. 1-2; P.L. 100-17 sections 305, 314, and 328.

34. *Explanation*, p. 1; P.L. 100-17, section 328. The Interstate Transfer provision allows urban areas that don't wish to complete a section of the Interstate System, usually because of the disruption it would cause and the public pressure against it, to put the dollars back in the interstate fund and to receive a like amount from the general fund of the U.S. Treasury. The money may be used for transit or highway capital purposes.

35. *Explanation*, p. 3; P.L. 100-17, Sections 309 and 312. The two-thirds proportion for new urbanized areas put them on the same footing as existing properties in the 50,000-200,000 population range, which had traditionally expended about two-thirds of formula money to cover operating costs.

36. *Explanation*, p. 6; P.L. 100-17, Sections 303 and 310.

37. *Explanation*, pp. 6, 7, and 9; P.L. 100-17, Sections 337, 338, 329, 335 and 336. There were many other provisions and the ones selected are for illustration only. The truly interested reader will refer to a copy of the law itself. The publication is *Urban Mass Transportation Act of 1964, as Amended through February 1988, and Related Laws* (Washington, D.C.: Urban Mass Transportation Administration, U.S. Department of Transportation, U.S. Government Printing Office, 1988-516-018/80284). Interested persons should contact the U.S. Department of Transportation, Urban Mass Transportation Administration, UCC-10, 400 Seventh Street S.W., Washington, D.C. 20590.

38. *Explanation*, p. 8; P.L. 100-17, Section 317. See also Bill Paul, "Publisher's Perspective: The Tar Baby Theory of Government," *Metro*, Vol. 83, No. 3, May-June 1987. Assuming that the diesel-powered standard transit bus is a mature product, the bus testing rule may preserve the present technology like a fly trapped in amber.

14. THE ONCE AND FUTURE PROGRAM OF FEDERAL MASS TRANSIT POLICY

1. One would expect the states with large metropolitan areas, in which transit plays a very large role, to have the most advanced programs, but even some of the least likely states have developed aid programs of substance. Indiana is a case in point. A careful lobbying effort, a few far-sighted legislators, and a willing governor gave Indiana a matching grant program that is supported by a percentage of the gross sales and usage tax money called the Public Mass Transit Fund (PMTF). One could argue that the sum is not enough and that the percentage of the tax receipts dedicated to transit should be raised,

but the principle of a guaranteed source of funding works well. Transit managers are happy because the state money received through the PMTF is relatively predictable. Because it is based on the sales tax, the PMTF goes up with inflation, and because it is earmarked, there is no need to fight the appropriations battle each year. The program has worked well—so well that state Department of Transportation officials are proposing to add to the funding through the use of general fund money to stimulate improved performance, by means of a program intended to penalize no one and to offer the incentive carrot to all transit service providers. In addition, Indiana created the special Commuter Rail Service Fund and the Electric Rail Service Fund to help support the improvement and operation of the Northern Indiana Commuter Transportation District's service on the Chicago South Shore and South Bend Railroad. One of the reasons the program is attractive to state and local officials is that Indiana, usually a donor state when it comes to federal taxes, gets to see some of that tax money come back through the use of the Hoosier matching program. The program was enacted during the administration of Governor Otis R. Bowen, M.D., from 1973 to 1980. "Doc" Bowen was usually viewed as a conservative Republican, but he was a true progressive in many ways. Whereas Indiana politicians had once taken the official position of eschewing all federal money, Bowen wanted Indiana to get back every possible cent to which it was legally entitled. The Institute for Urban Transportation at Indiana University was under contract to Governor Bowen's office from 1975 to 1981 to provide local technical assistance to transit properties throughout the state—especially the small city and rural systems—so as to make every transit property in Indiana eligible for federal money, to administer the state program, and to help improve the quality of management of the Hoosier transit systems.

2. Thirty states provided some sort of transit aid by 1987. See *An Overview of State Mass Transit Programs: Financing and Distribution Mechanisms,* prepared by the Division of Planning and Budget of the Wisconsin Department of Transportation, Staff Report #6, November 1987. This is available from Technology Sharing, U.S. Department of Transportation, Office of the Secretary, as its publication DOT-T-88-07.

3. The high in transit employment before the federal transit program was in 1945, when 242,000 persons were reported in the ranks of transit employees. The low was 138,040 in 1970. The preliminary estimate for 1985 was 261,933. See *1987 Transit Fact Book* (Washington, D.C.: American Public Transit Association, 1987), Table 13 on p. 36. The trends in transit ridership may be found in *The Status of the Nation's Local Mass Transportation: Performance and Conditions,* Report of the Secretary of Transportation to the United States Congress (Washington, D.C.: U.S. Department of Transportation, June 1988), pp. 34-36. See also *Summary of Travel Trends: 1983-1984 Nationwide Personnel Transportation Study* (Washington, D.C.: U.S. Department of Transportation, November 1985), p. 18.

4. As of this writing in the spring of 1990, with the exception of San Francisco's cable cars, the oldest equipment in use in regular transit revenue service is in Philadelphia. These ancients—some former Reading Company multiple-unit electric commuter cars and third-rail, electric high-speed cars (including the Bullet Cars) of the old Philadelphia and Western—are sets of equipment now operated by the Southeastern Pennsylvania Transportation Authority. Most of these cars were built in the early 1930s—a few date from the mid–1920s—and have been refurbished to some extent. It is not expected that they will see much more service, as SEPTA is in the process of replacing its railcar fleet. Pittsburgh, Philadelphia, and Boston are operating some 40-year old PCC (Street Railway Presidents Conference Committee) cars, most of which have been extensively rebuilt. In San Francisco, some PCCs of similar vintage are to be rebuilt for what will essentially be a tourist service along Market Street and the Embarcadero to Fisherman's Wharf. This is no small part of transit demand in the City by the Bay.

In terms of age, the U.S. bus fleet is in relatively good shape, but simple observation will reveal that not all buses are well cared for. Some properties have completely refurbished many of their late 1960s vehicles (now relatively rare) and 1970s models for more years of useful life. Some properties don't appear to know how to keep buses in good repair, regardless of age, and many managers complain that the equipment they purchase is less than it should be. For information on the expenditures see Jo Tucci, *1987 Statistical Summaries: Grants Assistance Programs* (Washington, D.C.: Urban Mass Transportation Administration, August 31, 1988); Table 13 gives a listing of fixed facilities projects.

5. Total vehicle miles operated, according to the American Public Transit Association, were 3,007,600,000 in 1950. This figures fell to 1,883,100,000 in 1970. The estimate for 1985 was 2,452,700,000, or about the same total miles as in 1955. See *1987 Transit Fact Book*, Table 11 on p. 34.

The federal program has expended, through 1987, about $53 billion in capital, which has been used to purchase 66,928 buses (mostly the 35-foot and 40-foot long standard vehicles), 6,896 railcars and 26 ferry boats. See "Presidential Candidates Address Transit," *Passenger Transport*, Vol. 46, No. 43, October 24, 1988, p. 4. See also Tucci, *1987 Statistical Summaries*.

6. The unhappiness with highways in Boston has been well covered. See Alan Lupo, Frank Colcord, and Edmund P. Fowler, *Rites of Way: The Politics of Transportation in Boston and the U.S. City* (Boston: Little, Brown and Company, 1971); Allan K. Sloan, *Citizen Participation in Transportation Planning: The Boston Experience* (Cambridge, Mass.: Ballinger, 1974); and Ralph Gakenheimer, *Transportation Planning as Response to Controversy: The Boston Case* (Cambridge, Mass.: The MIT Press, 1976). The figures on the numbers of transit systems are found in the *1978 Transit Fact Book* (Washington, D.C.: American Public Transit Association, 1978), p. 15; and the *1987 Transit Fact Book* (Washington, D.C.: American Public Transit Association, 1987), p. 10.

7. See David Jones, *Urban Transit Policy: An Economic and Political History* (Englewood Cliffs, N.J.: Prentice-Hall, 1985), Chapter 7. Author's comments on participation are based on personal observation over many years, including time spent as a member of a transit governing board, as one of the planners of the local transit service in Bloomington, Indiana, and as an active member of a state transit trade organization.

8. See *Legislative Report*, American Public Transit Association, October 11, 1988. The capital grants for 1989 were down by about 14 percent from the previous year. See also *Congressional Record House*, September 23, 1988, p. H8369. Capital funds in Section 3 money fell from $2,095,000,000 in 1981 to a low of $915,000,000 in 1987; $1,050,500,000 was earmarked for 1988. Some Section 5, 9, and 18 money was for capital purposes. Before it was phased out in favor of Section 9, Section 5 peaked at $1,455,000 in 1981; Section 9 reached a high of $2,377,729,650 in 1985, falling to $1,667,064,000 in 1988. Section 18 reached a high at $91,325,000 in 1983, with a low of $60,286,215 in 1986; it was $69,389,000 in 1988. See *1987 Statistical Summaries*, Table 8. The American Public Transit Association estimated that the 1989 formula apportionments were $1,595,578,418, with $798,043,753 as the operating fund limit and $797,534,665 for capital. This was a total reduction in funding from 1988 of $144,201,561, with operating funds down $5,260,784 and capital down $130,940,777. See *Legislative Report*, October 26, 1988, American Public Transit Association, Washington, D.C.

9. See *1987 Statistical Summaries*, Table B.

10. The author is not a disinterested party. The Indiana University Institute for Urban Transportation (IUT) has one of the largest training programs in transit management. When the IUT programs began in 1982, the attendees came from transit properties of all sizes. With the concentration of Section 10 aid on the larger properties, most of those in attendance after 1988 were almost exclusively from large and medium-sized transit properties. This is a real loss to people from smaller transit properties, because they miss not only the formal training but also the informal relationships and networking springing from attendance at training programs.

11. For a distillation of this research work, see Gordon J. Fielding, *Managing Public Transit Strategically* (San Francisco: Jossey-Bass Publishers, 1987), especially Chapter 4.

12. A colleague of mine on the board of trustees of the Northern Indiana Commuter Transportation District (NICTD) was a victim of this feverish anti-tax attitude rampant in the U.S. in the 1980s. Walter Liebig had been a county councilman in LaPorte County, Indiana, for 20 years. In response to citizen demands for improvements in roads and bridges and other county services, he pushed for and got a tax increase. Shortly thereafter, in the Democratic primary, Liebig was defeated by a candidate who branded him a big spender. With Liebig off the council, the tax was repealed. The citizens of LaPorte County still complain about the need for repairs to roads and bridges and the need for improved county services, apparently without understanding the irony of the situation. The fate of Walter Liebig was a lesson not lost on other politicians in northern Indiana when NICTD sought local tax funding in 1986 and 1987; the effort failed dismally, despite the agreement of virtually all politicians in the area that the service provided by NICTD was invaluable to the four Hoosier counties it served.

13. See Gordon J. Fielding, *Managing Public Transit Strategically*, Chapter 6; Darold T. Barnum, *From Private to Public: Labor Relations in Urban Mass Transit* (Lubbock, Texas: College of Business Administration, Texas Tech University, 1977); Kenneth M. Jennings, Jr., Jay A. Smith, Jr., and Earle C. Traynham, Jr., *Labor Relations in a Public Service Industry: Unions, Management, and the Public Interest in Mass Transit* (New York: Praeger Publishers, 1978).

14. There has been a great deal written about the notion of privatization (horrible word!) in recent years, and here are some recent items at the time of this writing: Charles A. Lave, ed., *Urban Transit: The Private Challenge to Public Transportation* (Cambridge, Mass.: Ballinger Publishing Company, 1985); Wendell Cox, *The Potential for Optimizing Public Transit Service through Competitive Contracting* (Washington, D.C.: American Bus Association, March 1987), prepared for the U.S. Department of Transportation under Contract #DC-06-0514; ATE Management and Service Co., *Private Sector Contracting for Transit Services; Operator Handbook* (Washington, D.C.: International Taxicab Association, October 1987), prepared for the Urban Mass Transportation Administration; Carter Goble Associates, *Strategies for Expanding the Use of Private Sector Transit and Paratransit Operators and Reducing UMTA Subsidy in Rural, Small Urban and Suburban Areas* (Washington, D.C.: Urban Mass Transportation Administration, October 1987), UMTA-PA-06-0102-87-1; Jose A. Gomez-Ibanez and John R. Meyer, with Paul Kerin and Leslie Meyer, *Deregulating Urban Bus Service: Britain's Early Experience and the Lessons for the United States* (Cambridge, Mass.: Graduate School of Design and John F. Kennedy School of Government, Harvard University, November 1987), prepared for the Office of Private Sector Initiatives, Urban Mass Transportation Administration, U.S. Department of Transportation; Roger F. Teal, Genevieve Guiliano, Jacqueline M. Golob, Terry Alexander, Edward K. Morlok, Donald R. Ellerman, and Frederick A. Moseley, *Estimating the Cost Impacts of Transit Service Contracting* (Institute for Transportation Studies and School of Engineering, University of California, Irvine, and School of Engineering and Applied Science, University of Pennsylvania: Philadelphia, Penn., December 1987), prepared for the Office of Budget and Policy of the Urban Mass Transportation Administration, U.S. Department of Transportation. Also see George M. Smerk, "Urban Mass Transportation: From Private to Public to Privatization," *Transportation Journal*, Vol. 26, No. 1, Fall 1986, pp. 83–91.

15. George M. Smerk, *Urban Transportation: The Federal Role* (Bloomington, Ind.: Indiana University Press, 1965), Chapter 10.

16. See, for example, Kenneth T. Jackson, *Crabgrass Frontier: The Suburbanization of the United States* (New York: Oxford University Press, 1985), especially Chapters 13 through 16; and John Herbers, *The New Heartland: America's Flight Beyond the Suburbs and How It Is Changing Our Future* (New York: Times Books, 1986). For vintage Mumford, see Lewis Mumford, *The City in History: Its Origin, Its Transformation and Its Prospects* (New York: Harcourt Brace Jovanovich, 1961), especially Chapters 16 through 18.

17. A fact-filled and thoughtful work on the automobile and all its associated baggage

is to be found in Michael Renner, *Rethinking the Role of the Automobile* (Washington, D.C.: Worldwatch Institute, June 1988), Worldwatch Paper 84.

18. For a largely negative view of the sense of the federal transit program, see Congressional Budget Office, *New Directions for the Nation's Public Works,* September 1988, especially the Summary and Chapter 2.

19. Remarkable insight into the American character of the 1980s may be found in Herbert J. Gans, *Middle American Individualism: The Future of Liberal Democracy* (New York: The Free Press, 1988). The middle Americans of whom Gans writes are the bulk of the U.S. citizenry, with moderate or middle incomes and average schooling. One major point of the book is that these people are not full participants in much of American life, preferring the narrow microsociety of family and close associations rather than the broader community.

20. For an interesting description and analysis of the problem see Theodore G. Weigle, Jr., "Causes of Change: Internal and External Pressure," in *New Organizational Responses to the Changing Transit Environment,* Proceedings of a Conference, Norfolk, Virginia, December 2-4, 1987 (Washington, D.C.: Transportation Research Board, 1988), pp. 37-55. An interesting approach to offering transit service as a network connecting key urban and suburban points, rather than as the familiar radial configuration of the conventional transit system, is found in Jerry B. Schneider, Stephen P. Smith, Paul D. Thompson, James L. Heid, and Irene W. Ng, *Planning and Designing a Transit Center Based Transit System: Guidelines and Examples from Case Studies in Twenty-Two Cities* (Seattle: Urban Transportation Program, Departments of Civil Engineering and Urban Planning, University of Washington, September 1980), Report No. UMTA-WA-0007-RR80-2. This work was supported by the University Research and Training Program under Section 11 of the Urban Mass Transportation Act of 1964, as amended.

21. The heavy rapid transit line from downtown Los Angeles was to penetrate into the southeastern portion of the San Fernando Valley; service to the west was proposed to be carried out by means of a light rapid transit line that would connect with the subway at a station in the vicinity of the intersection of the Hollywood Freeway and the Ventura Freeway. See Rick Orlov, "Council OKs Valley Subway Line," *Van Nuys* (Calif.) *Daily News,* July 14, 1988; James Quinn, "4 Main Options: Panel Votes Tonight for Rail Route," *Los Angeles Times,* July 21, 1988; May Ann Milbourn, "Rail Fund Decision Delayed," *Van Nuys* (Calif.) *Daily News,* July 22, 1988; James Quinn, "Trolley Panel Passes Buck; Backs 2 Routes," *Los Angeles Times,* July 22, 1988; and James Quinn, "Late Backing for Double-Deck Plan Splits Trolley Panel," *Los Angeles Times,* July 23, 1988. The final decision was dumped back in the lap of the Los Angeles City Council. On the issues of using existing rights-of-way, see George M. Smerk, "Looking at the Commuter Railroad Option," *Passenger Transport,* Vol. 46, No. 47, November 21, 1988, pp. 1-9.

22. See Michael Renner, *Rethinking the Role of the Automobile,* p. 48. Also see K. H. Schaeffer and Elliott Sclar, *Access for All: Transportation and Urban Growth* (New York: Columbia University Press, 1980), Chapters 4, 6, and 8; Kenneth T. Jackson, *Crabgrass Frontier,* Chapters 9, 10, 11, and 15; Robert Fishman, *Bourgeois Utopia: The Rise and Fall of Suburbia* (New York: Basic Books, 1987), Chapters 4-6; James A. Dunn, Jr., *Miles to Go: European and American Transportation Policies* (Cambridge, Mass., The MIT Press, 1981), Chapters 5-8, especially p. 134; Robert Cervero, *Suburban Gridlock* (New Brunswick, New Jersey: Center for Urban Policy Research, Rutgers, The State University, 1986), Chapter 7; Lyle C. Fitch and Associates, *Urban Transportation and Public Policy* (San Francisco: Chandler Publishing Co., 1964), especially Chapter 1 and pp. 122-156; and Wilfred Owen, *The Metropolitan Transportation Problem,* Revised ed. (Washington, D.C.: The Brookings Institution, 1966), pp. 144-150.

On the issue of free parking recognized as causing difficulties, see Donald C. Sharp and Don H. Pickrell, *Free Parking Is a Transportation Problem* (School of Architecture and Urban Planning, University of California at Los Angeles, October 1980). The project was supported by the Office of University Research, Research and Special Programs Administration, U.S. Department of Transportation. Also see *The Coordination of Parking with Public Transportation and Ridesharing,* prepared by Public Technology, Inc., for the Urban Consortium for Technology Initiatives, June 1982.

23. See Robert V. Camuto, "Why Voters Rejected DART Bonds," *Dallas Times Herald,* June 27, 1988. Not helping was what was seen by the public as a large bureaucracy, loads of empty buses wandering about in the outlying parts of the metropolitan area, a governing board that fought amongst itself and took expensive trips at taxpayers' expense, and the sore point of a board room with a price tag of $1 million located in a building that DART did not even own.

24. This author has been the representative of the governor of Indiana on the board of trustees of the Northern Indiana Commuter Transportation District since the District got under way in 1977. The rolling stock then in use by the South Shore Line had been built in the 1920s. We moved as quickly as possible to make substantive, visible improvements. The new commuter rail cars were delivered starting in January 1982 with the arrival of the prototype car; 43 more cars were delivered starting in August 1982; by Thanksgiving of 1983, all South Shore service was being provided by the new cars. Invisible to the public, but as important to the project as the cars, were the new electrical substations and power distribution system (it is an electric railroad) and an expanded and remodeled maintenance facility. Station improvements came more slowly due to the Reagan administration's cutbacks in capital. Mindful of the need to keep positive things happening, the District opened a new station (Dune Park) in Chesterton, Indiana, in 1986, new platforms at Randolph Street Station in Chicago in 1988, a new parking lot in East Chicago, Indiana in 1988, and expanded parking in Hammond, Indiana in 1988-1989. The NICTD management and board felt that it had done a good job in building good will in the region, but it was not good enough for NICTD to gain taxing power.

25. The subject of institutionalization as applied to transit has not drawn a great deal of attention, sadly enough. See Harry Ross and Ellen Foster Curtis, *Essentials for Success in Transit* (Bloomington, Ind.: Indiana University School of Business, Division of Research, 1979).

26. See *Traveling Light* (London: Docklands Light Railway Limited, 1987).

27. Probably the best treatment of policies that have led to the major changes in the fortune of cities may be found in Jackson, *Crabgrass Frontier.* See also Schaeffer and Sclar, *Access for All,* pp. ix–x.

28. See "NARP Presses Rail's Importance in AASHTO's 20/20 Process," National Association of Railroad Passengers *News,* Vol. 22, No. 7, July 1988, pp. 1 and 4.

29. Trying to work in a vacuum is one reason behind much of the criticism of federal transit policy. A good example of criticism rooted in the falling proportion of trips made on transit is found in the Congressional Budget Office's *New Directions for the Nation's Public Works,* Chapter 2. The lack of sufficient bang for the buck is the complaint; more reliance on state and local government is the solution. In the absence of a combined effort, with transit as a part of a coordinated effort to a clear goal, there really can't be as much to show for the money spent as would otherwise be the case.

30. One important study reveals that higher income groups are more highly subsidized by federal operating aid than are low-income groups. It also shows that poorer persons are not the great majority of transit users. The study does not deal with the issue of how the taxes used to raise the subsidy funds are collected. One might assume that higher income persons pay a greater proportion of the total tax take than do lower income persons. See Charles River Associates Incorporated, *Allocation of Federal Transit Operating Subsidies to Riders by Income Group,* CRA Report No. 784.15, March 1986, prepared for the Urban Mass Transportation Administration, U.S. Department of Transportation, Washington, D.C.

31. See Renner, *Rethinking the Role of the Automobile,* pp. 35-45, for discussion of the polluting effects of automobile use. See also Jeremy Main, "Here Comes the New Cleanup," *Fortune,* Vol. 118, No. 12, November 21, 1988, pp. 102-118.

32. For some contemporary comments on pollution problems in general and the greenhouse effect in particular, see Robert Engelman, "Hotter Times? Greenhouse Effect Gains Credence" (Scripps Howard News Service), (Bloomington/Bedford, Ind.) *Sunday Herald-Times,* June 26, 1988; Baily Thompson, "It'll Take Mass Transit to Cure Ills Cars Have Wrought," *Orlando Sentinel,* July 3, 1988; Tim Smart, "The Earth's Alarm Bells Are Ringing," *Business Week,* No. 3060, July 11, 1988; Georgie Anne Geyer, "Our Wanton Exhaustion of the Earth" (Universal Press Syndicate), *Louisville Courier-Journal,* August 29, 1988; "Greenhouse Effect Looms under Several Scenarios" (Associated Press), *Bloomington* (Ind.) *Herald-Telephone,* August 30, 1988; S. Fred Singer, "Fact and Fancy on Greenhouse Earth," *Wall Street Journal,* August 30, 1988; and Jerry E. Bishop, "Global Threat—New Culprit Is Indicted in Greenhouse Effect: Rising Methane Level," *Wall Street Journal,* October 24, 1988.

33. "Energy-Saving Drive Stalled, Agency Says" (Associated Press), *Louisville Courier-Journal,* July 19, 1988.

34. The classic work on innovative approaches to help solve congestion problems is Robert Cervero's *Suburban Gridlock* (New Brunswick, N.J.: Rutgers, The State University of New Jersey, Center for Urban Policy Research, 1986), especially Chapters 4-7.

Index

GEORGE M. SMERK is Professor of Transportation
at the Indiana University School of Business. He is
author of *Urban Transportation: The Federal Role,*
Readings in Urban Transportation, and *Urban Mass*
Transportation: A Dozen Years of Federal Policy.